The **Rough Guide** to

Washington, DC

written and researched by

Jules Brown and J.D. Dickey

ROUGH GUIDES

NEW YORK · LONDON · DELHI

www.roughguides.com

Contents

DC TV color section
following p.112

African American DC
color section following
p.304

Color maps following
p.448

WASHINGTON DC

◀◀ Contemplation of Justice statue ◀ The Lincoln Memorial and Washington Monument

Introduction to

Washington, DC

The most powerful place on earth, Washington, DC, more than fulfills its reputation as a monumental imperial city, with lovely Neoclassical buildings arrayed along grand boulevards, some of the finest museums in North America, an affecting set of war memorials honoring centuries of fallen soldiers, and scads of high-powered politicians, lobbyists, and bureaucrats charting the course of the rest of the country, as well as the world. With the gleaming symbols of America's three branches of government – the White House, Capitol, and Supreme Court – dominating the landscape, it's easy to be stunned by the spectacle of so much power in such a small space, but thankfully Washington, DC is more than just the memorials, monuments, and museums of the National Mall and Capitol Hill. Beyond these areas, there is, in fact, a flesh-and-blood city, whose vibrant neighborhoods can prove nearly as compelling.

Apart from its role in national politics, Washington, DC, is actually a pretty progressive town, with a wide range of lively bohemian and upscale-liberal areas, and a population of Latin American immigrants and African Americans who offer their own histories and rich culture in contrast to the sanitized federal versions. And with a population of less than 600,000 residents (it's smaller than just about every foreign capital you could think of), Washington has a certain manageability – from the ease of riding its Metro system to the pleasures of walking and biking around – that separates it from the huge, sprawling American cities from which the capital's political elite are drawn.

Given that it would become the consummate power center, it seems fitting that DC's very founding was the result of political wrangling. In the late eighteenth century, Congress acceded to the demands of the Northern states to assume their Revolutionary War debts but squeezed from them a key concession for the South: rather than being sited in New York or Philadelphia, the new federal capital would be built from scratch on the banks of the Potomac River, midway along the Eastern Seaboard – and just within the upper reaches of the South. French architect **Pierre L'Enfant** planned the city on a hundred-square-mile diamond-shaped parcel of land donated by the tobacco-rich states of Virginia and Maryland. John F. Kennedy famously pointed out its contradictions in his wry comment that Washington was "a city of Southern efficiency and Northern charm."

Even more important than DC's geographical location was its **unique experimental nature** – a modern, planned capital built for a disparate collection of states seeking security in unity. The city proved

Fact file

• The city of Washington has the same boundaries as the federal District of Columbia and holds 580,000 people – though nine times as many people reside in the metropolitan region, making it one of the country's top ten urban centers.

• DC is 56 percent black, 32 percent non-Latino white, 8 percent Latino, and 4 percent Asian.

• Originally, the District held several other cities: Georgetown and Anacostia, since annexed by Washington, and Arlington and Alexandria, now part of Virginia.

• The city has four quadrants, from largest to smallest: NW, NE, SE, SW. They all meet at the US Capitol, the only place in town without a quadrant or a street address.

• Washington, in more than two hundred years, has been ruled by mayors, district governors, and commission boards, but only from 1820 to 1869 and 1975 to the present has the leader been elected by city voters. The current mayor is Adrian Fenty.

• The District's biggest employer is the federal and city government, providing one in three jobs, with other major employers including universities, the media, insurance and financial firms, hospitals, law practices, and political and lobbying organizations.

• From 1788 to 2007, 42 different men became president (with Grover Cleveland as the 22nd and 24th president for his non-consecutive terms), representing five political parties and serving tenures from one month (William Henry Harrison) to twelve years and one month (FDR).

▶ The White House

▼ Grand Salon, Renwick Gallery

its unifying influence a century after its founding when it became the front-line headquarters of the fight against slavery, with **Abraham Lincoln** directing the Union troops from the capital's halls and his White House offices.

After the war, thousands of **Southern blacks** arrived in search of sanctuary from racist oppression, and since the 1930s DC has been a predominantly African American city. It hasn't always proved an effective sanctuary, however. Suffering an endless cycle of boom and bust, the city outside of its tourist zones has one of the country's highest crime rates and appalling levels of unemployment, illiteracy, and drug abuse. This is in part due to the city's status as a virtual colony of the US: residents have only nonvoting representation in Congress and couldn't even participate in presidential elections until the 1960s.

As if its real-world problems weren't enough, for demogogues every-where, Washington is a metaphor for political gridlock, a place where venal politicians are cut off from their constituents by the fabled **Beltway**, the looping freeway that encircles the city and its titanic bureaucracy. Nonetheless, twenty million visitors come to the capital each year for entertainment and edification, making it one of the most visited destina-tions in the country. Kept away from the city's peripheral dead zones, visitors find a scrubbed, policed, and largely safe downtown swath, where famous landmarks follow world-class museums with uplifting regularity. Even better, most of what you see in Washington is free, and getting around is easy on foot or by rail. But with repositories of history and culture around almost every corner here, it's well worth a little planning to keep yourself from getting overwhelmed.

What to see

There's no better way to come to grips with the city than by taking a two-mile stroll along the grassy centerpiece of the **National Mall**, the city's visual axis. You'll come back here time and again to view the powerful tributes to Washington, Lincoln, Jefferson, FDR, and war veterans, or to browse the collections of the outstanding Smithsonian museums and the National Gallery of Art. At the Mall's eastern end, the US Capitol marks the geographic center of the city, as all neighborhoods and quadrants radiate out from its familiar white, cast-iron dome. **Capitol Hill** is one of DC's oldest neighborhoods, rich in nineteenth-century row houses, and ripe for a stroll from the Capitol itself to other defining buildings like

The capital sound

To those not in the know, Washington, DC, may not seem like one the country's essential locations on the musical heritage map. However, through the decades the District has created a special niche for itself in several key musical styles. The oldest are, of course, **blues** and **gospel**, which really became established when Southern blacks moved here en masse after the Civil War, bringing traditions of spirituals, work songs, and ballads with them. You can hear such music today in churches and in clubs like Blues Alley (p.304) and *Madam's Organ* (p.30). But much more prevalent is the sound of **jazz**. This quintessential DC style was championed by **Duke Ellington**, perhaps America's greatest composer, and lives on in a bevy of great clubs including *Bohemian Caverns* (p.30) and *HR-57* (p.304). The other prime draw in town is **indie rock**, which was fueled by late-1970s and early-1980s hardcore punk acts like Bad Brains, Minor Threat, and Henry Rollins, all locals. You can still hear that kind of thrash, along with more relaxed alternative rock, at great clubs like *9:30* and *Black Cat* (both p.305). Country and folk music both have city fans but are mainly played in the Virginia suburbs and at places like *Wolf Trap* (p.252). For true local energy and creativity, though, funk and hip-hop make regular appearances in the city's rock and blues clubs, and the best offshoot of those two styles is the city's own **go-go** music, basically funk with a staggered beat, perfected by hometown master Chuck Brown, whose own frenetic concerts are still the best place to hear this spirited, upbeat music in all its glory (check out ⓦwww.windmeupchuck.com for information).

the Supreme Court and Library of Congress. South of the Mall are two of the most popular attractions in DC – the Bureau of Engraving and Printing and the US Holocaust Memorial Museum – and the city's **Waterfront** area boasts the thriving Fish Wharf, several good seafood restaurants, and the new Nationals Park baseball stadium. North of the Mall, the heavily visited section around the **White House** and **Foggy Bottom** contains headquarters for numerous federal bureaucracies and international institutions, as well as heavyweight attractions like the Corcoran Gallery of Art, the Renwick Gallery, Kennedy Center, and the infamous Watergate Complex.

Between the White House and Union Station, **Old Downtown** was where nineteenth-century Washington first set up its shops and services, along the spine of Pennsylvania Avenue. After years of neglect, renovation around the so-called Penn Quarter has brought revitalized streets, community plazas, compelling galleries, and upscale restaurants. Wedged between Old Downtown and the Mall, the **Federal Triangle** is highlighted by the National Archives and an array of splendid Neoclassical buildings.

In the business district of **New Downtown**, along and around K Street, you'll find a slew of fancy hotels, top-notch restaurants, and the odd church of historical note – though little else, since the place shuts down at night. More engagingly, the historic townhouses and mansions of chic **Dupont Circle** hold a gaggle of low-key museums and an expanding enclave of art galleries, not to mention some of DC's best clubs and eateries. To the north, the fun and funky hipster zone of **Adams Morgan**, with its diners and live-music venues, gets trendier by the day, while to the east, historically black **Shaw** is undergoing rapid gentrification around the thriving nightlife corridor of U Street.

West of New Downtown, the venerable **Georgetown neighborhood** is the quintessential hangout of the chattering classes (as well as university students), who make the many good shops, galleries, bars, and restaurants here their own. To the north, the first bona fide city suburbs were in **Upper Northwest**, where well-to-do areas like Woodley Park and Cleveland Park feature such sights as the enjoyable National Zoo, landmark National Cathedral, and the glades, dales, and riverbanks of Rock Creek Park.

Although there's little to see in the dicey areas of Northeast and Southeast Washington – aside from isolated places like the National Arboretum and National Shrine of the Immaculate Conception – if you venture across the Potomac into Virginia, to **Arlington**, you'll reach the region's other major memorials: Arlington National Cemetery and the Marine Corps and Air Force memorials – as well as the walled-off precinct of the Pentagon. Just south, fetching **Old Town Alexandria** is great for its many preserved eighteenth- and nineteenth-century buildings, fancy restaurants, and opportunities for a cruise on the Potomac.

Finally, to get **out of the city** and do a little exploring in the capital region itself, there are many good choices, almost too many to list in one book (though we try in our *Rough Guide to the USA*). Some of the most notable include the historic attractions of **Northern Virginia**, such as family estate of George Washington, **Mount Vernon**, the Civil War enclaves of Manassas and Fredericksburg, and lesser-known, but still intriguing, sights

City of Masons

The US capitol was designed, constructed, and ruled by Freemasons from its inception through much of the twentieth century. While some have seen sinister implications in this secretive group – indeed, an actual Anti-Mason Party collected votes in early American elections – others have marveled at the way it fostered a sense of inclusiveness among political leaders who might otherwise have had little to do with each other. The hallmarks of Masonry can be found almost everywhere in town, from the layout of the city streets, to the placement and physical shape of its major buildings, to the mysterious character of American currency. For a glimpse of Masonry in action you won't have to look far: many current institutions (such as the National Museum of Women in the Arts) occupy former Masonic temples, while gleaming icons such as the Scottish Rite Temple and George Washington Masonic Memorial (both open to the public) are eye-popping architectural spectacles built around the symbols and emblems of the secret society.

like **Woodlawn Plantation** and **Gunston Hall**. Continuing south, **Richmond**, with its genteel Neoclassical buildings and military ruins, is a favorite spot for buffs of "The War Between the States," and the **Historic Triangle**, to the southeast, holds the essential American and British heritage sites of Jamestown, Williamsburg, and Yorktown. Finally, on the other side of DC, less than an hour north, is Maryland's biggest city, **Baltimore**, whose Inner Harbor and Fell's Point present a bevy of refurbished waterside attractions that can easily merit a day trip or an even longer visit.

When to go

▼ Washington Fish Wharf

Without question, the best times to visit Washington, DC, are in the spring and fall, when the weather is at its most appealing – moderate temperatures and mild precipitation – plus, in April, DC's famous **cherry trees** are in bloom. By contrast, summer in the capital is thoroughly unpleasant, with hot and humid days made worse by throngs of visitors packed cheek-to-jowl at the major attractions. Winter, at least for weather, is equally dreary, with ice-cold temperatures, plenty of snow and rain, and howling winds blowing in off the Potomac River. However, the one appeal of winter over summer is the relative lack of visitors – you're likely to have many sights to yourself, or, at the very least, you can expect some relief from the school groups and tour buses that are legion during the rest of the year.

Washington DC climate

	Jan	Feb	Mar	Apr	May	Jun	Jul	Aug	Sep	Oct	Nov	Dec
Average daily temperature												
max (°F)	42	44	53	64	75	83	87	84	78	67	55	45
max (°C)	6	7	12	18	24	28	31	29	26	19	13	7
min (°F)	27	28	35	44	54	63	68	66	59	48	38	29
min (°C)	-3	-2	2	7	12	17	20	19	15	9	3	-2
Average rainfall												
inches	3.4	3	3.6	3.3	3.7	3.9	4.4	4.3	3.7	2.9	2.6	3.1
mm	86.4	76.2	91.4	83.8	94	99.1	111.8	109.2	94	73.7	66	78.7

21

things not to miss

It's not possible to see everything that Washington has to offer in one trip – and we don't suggest you try. What follows is a selective taste of the city's highlights: stirring memorials and savory meals, street-level stimuli and tranquil urban retreats, all arranged in five color-coded categories, which you can browse through to find the very best things to see and experience. All highlights have a page reference to take you straight into the Guide, where you can find out more.

01 **Arlington National Cemetery** Page **244** • Deservedly the nation's most famous military cemetery, where myriad white crosses mark the graves of nearly a quarter-million US soldiers.

02 **Washington National Cathedral** Page **224** • The sixth-biggest cathedral in the world is a Gothic Revival icon of American religion and politics, hosting regular services attended by Washington's elite.

03 **Rare pandas** Page **227** • The National Zoological Park boasts wetlands, nature trails, and botanic gardens, but celebrity panda family Mei Xiang, Tian Tian, and Tai Shan always take center stage.

04 **Following the Poe trail** Pages **362** & **376** • Fans of the nineteenth-century Gothic horror master can discover all kinds of local remnants of the author's life, from a fine museum in Richmond, Virginia, to his own eerie gravesite in Baltimore.

05 **Mount Vernon** Page **347** • Take the best day-trip from the city out to George Washington's Virginia estate, his home for forty years and his burial place.

06 **Seeing an antique craft at Williamsburg** Page **367** • Although this onetime Virginia capital has plenty of historic buildings, to really get into the colonial spirit, check out the printmakers, saddlers, gunsmiths, coopers, and other craftspeople making things the old-fashioned way.

07 **Seafood** Pages **134** & **382** • Dig into a mess of steamers at Washington's Fish Wharf or head to Baltimore for an even wider array of Maryland crabs.

08 **Lincoln Memorial** Page **63** • This Greek temple on a knoll is the best-loved and most dramatic of the city's presidential memorials.

09 **Vietnam Veterans Memorial** Page **66** • Arguably the most affecting war memorial to be found anywhere, this dramatic, black-granite chevron carved into the earth is engraved with the names of the 58,000 men who died in the jungles of Southeast Asia.

13

10 **International Spy Museum** Page **185** • The golden age of spycraft in the Cold War is alive and well at the exceptionally popular downtown attraction, which features hundreds of tales of intrigue and elaborate devices – including James Bond's Aston Martin.

11 **Ben's Chili Bowl** Page **291** • Sitting along the historic U Street corridor, this venerable diner doles out the city's best chili dogs and cheese fries.

12 **Old Ebbitt Grill** Page **290** • One of the city's most venerable dining establishments, more than a century-and a-half old, still appeals for its clubby tavern atmosphere and fine oysters, chops, and burgers.

13 **Fourth of July celebrations** Page **322** • DC is the place to be on Independence Day, offering a spirited parade, free concerts, and, of course, a grand display of fireworks.

14 National Cherry Blossom Festival Page 321

• When DC's beautiful cherry trees are blooming in late March and early April around the Tidal Basin, the city celebrates with a holiday parade, pageants, concerts, fireworks, and lantern lighting.

16 Rock Creek Park

Page **228** • Six miles and 1800 acres set along a forest and gorge offer rugged trails for hiking, winding paths for cycling and Rollerblading, and nineteenth-century remnants like a functional grist mill and parts of a Civil War fort.

15 National Museum of American History Page 68 •

This newly renovated Smithsonian showpiece draws its collection from 400 years of American history, and includes items like Judy Garland's ruby slippers from *The Wizard of Oz* and the original Star-Spangled Banner.

17 Frederick Douglass National Historic Site Page **136** • The

preserved Victorian residence where the civil-rights pioneer lived in his 60s and 70s holds key mementos from Douglass's life, plus artifacts like Abraham Lincoln's cane.

18 The Whistler Collection Page **100** • The works of James McNeill Whistler dominate the Freer Gallery of Art: some 1200 pieces, in addition to his gloriously decorated Peacock Room, are on display.

19 Sitting in on a session of Congress Page **111** • Though the debates can be wheezy and the chamber often empty, if you come to the Capitol at the right time you may be treated to a lively exercise in mean-spirited partisanship.

21 Adams Morgan bars and clubs Pages **295** & **302** • One of the city's liveliest precincts presents a spirited selection of watering holes and music venues playing indie rock and blues.

20 The C&O Canal Page **238** • Escape the city for a historic, evocative fourteen-mile hike or bike ride along the canal towpath from Georgetown to the tumbling waters at Great Falls.

Basics

Basics

Getting there

BASICS | Getting there

Unless you live along America's Eastern seaboard, the easiest way to get to Washington, DC, is to fly. Three airports serve the Washington metropolitan area: Reagan National (DCA), the city's domestic airport, located just south of town along the Potomac; Dulles International (IAD), the main international airport, about 45 minutes west, in Virginia; and Baltimore-Washington International (BWI), about an hour north of central DC, in Maryland.

Amtrak provides **train service** to DC within the US and Canada, though this is typically a leisurely and expensive journey; Greyhound and Peter Pan **buses** are cheaper, albeit less enjoyable, options. DC is easily accessible **by car**, but you might not want to drive once you've reached the city, as it has an outstanding – and safe – public-transit system.

Flights from the US and Canada

Washington, DC, is well connected to the rest of the US, as well as to Canada, by air, and this is undoubtedly the first transportation choice for most North American travelers. The most convenient airport for domestic arrivals into DC is **Reagan National Airport** (DCA), just south of the Pentagon and linked to central DC by the Metro. Delta, United, US Airways, and American offer regular shuttles from New York's LaGuardia Airport during the week, and less frequently on weekends. Additional airlines offering regular, daily service to Reagan National are Alaska, Continental, Midwest, Northwest, and Southwest.

Most of the major airlines have nationwide service to **Dulles International** (IAD), located out in suburban northern Virginia, 25 miles from downtown Washington. Southwest Airlines and US Airways have good deals for people willing to fly into **Baltimore** (BWI) and reserve in advance.

Shopping for air tickets and passes

Within the US and Canada, **prices** for flights to DC are usually relative to the date of departure, length of stay, and seat availability. If you're booking from abroad, tickets will be the most expensive during Europe's high season – June to August, despite this being DC's hottest and most humid period – less pricey in spring and fall, and cheapest during winter, excluding the Christmas and New Year holiday period. If you're planning to arrive in DC during any major American holiday, be sure to make reservations well in advance.

To guarantee the cheapest economy fares, tickets usually have to be purchased at least 21 days in advance, and you must have at least one Saturday-night stayover. These tickets are nonrefundable and subject to "change fees," meaning that if you alter your return date or destination, you must pay a fee of $30–100 along with the difference in the two prices. It's usually cheaper to fly during the week than on the weekend, and seasonal specials or student discount fares can bring the price down even more. Remember to allow for the extra cost of duty fees and airport taxes of 8 to 15 percent.

You can save yourself time and money by comparing ticket prices through an **online travel site** or checking out the various discount **travel agents**. Some operators specialize in youth or student fares, while others offer a range of services that include traveler's insurance and car rentals. Also, many airlines and travel websites allow you to book your tickets online, often at a discount.

Fares are lowest in the Northeast corridor. From **New York** and **Boston**, you can pay as little as $130 round-trip, though $155–200 is more typical; fares are around $180–250 from **Chicago** and $200–250 from **Miami**. The price of flights from the **West Coast** is more likely to fluctuate – round-trip tickets from **LA** can cost as little as $230 (but will more likely be around $300), and from **San Francisco** or **Seattle** they can go for $250 (but are more likely to be $300–500).

Air Canada has direct flights to DC from **Toronto** and **Montréal**; from **Vancouver**, you'll have to change at Toronto. American carriers such as Delta, Northwest, and United also operate flights from these cities, often in combination with Canadian airlines. Special deals bring round-trip fares as low as C$350 from Toronto, though you're more likely to pay C$375–500, and C$100 more from Montréal. From Vancouver, winter getaways start at C$600 round-trip (usually with one stop) and go up to C$700–750 the rest of the year.

Flights from the UK and Ireland

There are daily **nonstop flights** to Washington, DC, from **London Heathrow** with British Airways, United Airlines, and Virgin Atlantic; BMI British Midland flies nonstop from **Manchester** most days of the week. These flights take about eight hours, though return flights are always an hour or so shorter due to tailwinds. Outbound flights usually leave Britain midmorning, and inbound flights from the US usually arrive in the early morning. Other airlines serving DC, including Air Canada, Air France, American, Continental, Delta, Icelandair, KLM/Northwest, Lufthansa, and US Airways, fly from Heathrow or London **Gatwick** via their respective American or European hubs. These flights can add an extra two to five hours to your trip each way, depending on how long you have to wait for your connection.

Return fares to Washington, DC, can cost more than £530–550 between June and August and at Christmas, though £450 is the more typical range. Prices in winter often fall to £320–350. The nonstop flights from Heathrow tend to be among the cheapest. With BMI British Midland, you can usually add on a connecting domestic flight to Manchester from one of the other UK regional airports for little or no extra cost; with other airlines, add-on fares from UK regional airports to London cost around £100 return. More flexible tickets to DC, requiring less advance-booking time or allowing changes or refunds, often cost an additional £100–120.

Aer Lingus and United offer nonstop flights from **Dublin**, Ireland, to Washington, DC. Air France and Delta offer service between the same cities via Paris, New York, and Atlanta. The trip takes between ten and fifteen hours. Other airlines, such as British Airways, will route you through London, which takes about the same amount of time. Alternatively, you could arrange your own Dublin-to-London flight with low-cost airlines like easyJet or Ryanair and pick up a connecting flight to DC. Return fares from Dublin to DC start at around €600 in the low season, rising to €750–850 in high season. Although Dulles is often the first choice for international travelers to DC, you may be able to save up to €100 by landing in Baltimore's BWI airport, though you'll likely have to connect in London.

Flights from Australia, New Zealand, and South Africa

As there are no direct flights to Washington, DC, from Australia or New Zealand, the cheapest way to get there is to fly via **Los Angeles** with Qantas, American, or United, and add a connector via any domestic US airline for Aus$260–340/NZ$300–400 more. Fares to LA from eastern cities in **Australia** cost the same, while from Perth they're about Aus$400 more. Flights from Sydney or Melbourne to LA range between Aus$2700 and Aus$3100, depending on the season. From **New Zealand**, most flights are out of Auckland; add about NZ$200 for Christchurch and Wellington departures. Seasonal prices vary between around NZ$2400 and NZ$2900. Specialist agents can help sort out your options and advise about US air passes, which are the cheapest way to fly to DC from whichever American hub you've arrived at. Seat availability on most international flights is limited, so it's best to book at least several weeks ahead.

Unless you're specifically looking at a short-term city visit, it's going to be a better value for most people to consider buying a **round-the-world ticket**. The most basic of these, which start at around A$3000/NZ$3300, buys you as many as five stopovers, often including New York. You may have to pick a ticket with more stopovers to get DC specifically included, though.

Travel to America is not particularly cheap from **South Africa**; prices are about the same out of Cape Town or Johannesburg but are several hundred rand more from Durban and other smaller cities. To get to Washington, DC – which may be through

Reagan National, Dulles, or Baltimore International – you'll need to transfer at Dakar, London, Atlanta, New York, or other cities, sometimes a combination of several; one-stop itineraries are quite possible, though nonstops are fairly uncommon and usually offered for the steepest prices. Basic fares start at around R17,000, including all taxes, and rise as high as R33,000 or more at peak times.

Trains

The sprawling metropolitan area between Boston and Washington has the most dependable **Amtrak** service in the country (☎1-800/USA-RAIL, ⊛www.amtrak.com). The high-speed, 150mph **Acela** Express has cut the travel time from New York City to

---

Fly less – stay longer! Travel and climate change

Climate change is a serious threat to the ecosystems that humans rely upon, and air travel is among the fastest-growing contributors to the problem. Rough Guides regard travel, overall, as a global benefit, and feel strongly that the advantages to developing economies are important, as is the opportunity of greater contact and awareness among peoples. But we all have a responsibility to limit our personal impact on global warming, and that means giving thought to how often we fly and what we can do to redress the harm that our trips create.

Flying and climate change

Pretty much every form of motorized travel generates CO_2 – the main cause of human-induced climate change – but planes also generate climate-warming contrails and cirrus clouds and emit oxides of nitrogen, which create ozone (another greenhouse gas) at flight levels. Furthermore, flying simply allows us to travel much farther than we otherwise would do. The figures are frightening: one person taking a return flight between Europe and California produces the equivalent impact of 2.5 tons of CO_2 – similar to the yearly output of the average UK car.

Fuel-cell and other less harmful types of plane may emerge eventually. But until then, there are really just two options for concerned travelers: to reduce the amount we travel by air (take fewer trips – stay for longer!) and to make the trips we do take "climate neutral" via a **carbon offset scheme**.

Carbon offset schemes

Offset schemes run by ⊛climatecare.org, ⊛carbonneutral.com, and others allow you to make up for some or all of the greenhouse gases that you are responsible for releasing. To do this, they provide "carbon calculators" for working out the global-warming contribution of a specific flight (or even your entire existence), and then let you contribute an appropriate amount of money to fund offsetting measures. These include rainforest reforestation and initiatives to reduce future energy demand – often run in conjunction with sustainable development schemes.

Rough Guides, together with Lonely Planet and other concerned partners in the travel industry, are supporting a **carbon offset scheme** run by climatecare.org. Please take the time to view our website and see how you can help to make your trip climate neutral.

⊛www.roughguides.com/climatechange

Washington, DC, to two hours and fifty minutes, down from three and a half hours, and to six and a half hours from Boston, down from nine hours. If you're traveling from New York City or points south, the Acela is probably the most convenient way to reach Washington, not the least because it drops you right in the middle of town, at Union Station.

Round-trip fares for the regular service begin around $150 from **New York** and $200 from **Boston**. Fares for the reserved-seating Acela Express trains can be twice as high. If you're traveling from cities outside the Northeast, ticket prices are comparable to or higher than the equivalent airfare, and if you want any extras, like a sleeping compartment, it will cost you a lot more: the three-day rail journey from **Los Angeles**, for example, costs around $1100 round-trip with an economy sleeper bed, but only $330 without it. In general, Amtrak service isn't a budget option, although some of the journeys are pleasant enough – for example, the *Crescent*, which travels from New York to New Orleans via DC, makes for a rewarding 24hr trip between Washington and the Big Easy, and there is regular Amtrak service to DC from **Toronto** (16hr; C$300 round-trip) and **Montréal** (14hr; C$200–250), both via New York City. Amtrak often has **seasonal specials**; check its website or call its toll-free number to inquire about these deals.

Rail passes

If Washington is part of a longer itinerary, you might consider Amtrak and VIA's (Canada's national rail company) **North American Rail Pass**, which allows thirty days' unlimited travel for $1000 high season (June to mid-Oct) and $709 low season (mid-Oct to May); there's a ten-percent discount for seniors and students.

Overseas visitors are the only travelers who can buy a **USA Rail Pass**. Of this type, if you're interested in poking around New England, New York, and DC's capital region, the most suitable is the **Northeast Rail Pass**. The pass is valid for fifteen days and costs $300. Alternatively, for access to a huge swath of the US east of the Rockies,

the **East Rail Pass** is just a little more expensive, but has peak (late May to Aug, also mid- to late Dec) and nonpeak periods (rest of year) for fifteen-day (nonpeak $329/peak $369) or 30-day ($359/459) periods; for all types of East and Northeast Rail Passes, kids travel for half price. The passes aren't valid on the fastest express service, and must be bought before you travel to North America. They're available at equivalent rates of exchange from travel agents and specialist tour operators in your home country; see the listings in the relevant sections below for more details.

Buses

Buses are cheaper and run more frequently than trains, but they take forever and, in a worst-case scenario, you may need to use one of those toilets. **Greyhound** is the chief bus operator to DC (☎1-800/229-9424, ⓦwww.greyhound.com); in addition, **Peter Pan Bus Lines** (☎1-800/343-9999, ⓦwww.peterpanbus.com) offers service to Washington, DC, from Boston, New York, and **Philadelphia**, sometimes in combination with Greyhound. Standard midweek, round-trip fares for the six-hour trip from **New York City** start at $110, though they can be as little as $80 with one week's advance purchase. With this advance payment, expect to pay $100 from **Boston** (11hr), $50 from Philadelphia (5hr), $120–215 from **Chicago** (22hr), and $240 from **Los Angeles** (2 days, 12–18hr). Round-trip fares from **Montréal** (17hr) are C$130, and around C$240 from **Toronto** (26hr); you can book either through the main US portal or on **Greyhound Canada** (☎1-800/661-8747, ⓦwww.greyhound.ca). On all routes, you'll pay a bit more if you travel between Friday and Sunday, though discounted seven-day advance-purchase tickets and student, senior, and "companion" (two-for-one) fares are often available.

Foreign visitors and US and Canadian nationals can buy a **Greyhound Discovery Pass**, offering unlimited travel within a set time limit: you can order online at ⓦwww.discoverypass.com. A seven-day pass costs $283, a fifteen-day pass $415, a thirty-day pass $522, and the longest, a sixty-day pass, $645. The company website has a list of international vendors if you don't want to purchase online. The first time you use your pass, the ticket clerk will date it (which becomes the commencement date of the pass), and you will receive a ticket that allows you to board the bus. Repeat this procedure for every subsequent journey. Greyhound's nationwide toll-free **information service** can give you routes and times, plus phone numbers and addresses of local terminals.

Cars

Driving to DC gives you a certain amount of freedom and flexibility, but you'll probably never use your car once you reach the city, since the public transit system is so good. The box below gives an idea of the distances and times involved in driving to DC. Routes into the city are shown on color map "Washington, DC: Metropolitan Area" and explained in the "Arrival" section of this chapter, where you'll also find some useful tips on the intricacies of driving in DC itself.

Car-rental deals vary wildly, though in general you'll find better prices over the weekend than during the week, given the business orientation of the town. You can often realize **significant savings** by booking in advance with a major firm that has repre-

Driving to DC

Distances from each city:
Boston: 350 miles (8hr)
Chicago: 710 miles (16hr)
Los Angeles: 2690 miles (3 days)
Miami: 1057 miles (24hr)
Montréal: 610 miles (14hr)
New York: 240 miles (5hr 30min)
San Francisco: 2845 miles (3 days)
Seattle: 2868 miles (3 days)
Toronto: 570 miles (12hr)

sentation in DC; most agencies in the city have offices at Reagan National, Dulles, and BWI airports, and at Union Station. When booking, be sure to get free unlimited mileage and be aware that rates can go up by as much as $200 if you want to pick up the car in one location and leave it at another. If you choose not to pay until you arrive, take a written confirmation of the price with you. Always read the small print carefully for details on Collision Damage Waiver (sometimes called Liability Damage Waiver), a form of insurance that often isn't included in the initial rental charge but can be worth having. This insurance specifically covers the car you are driving (you are, in any case, insured for damage to other vehicles). At around $15 a day, it can add substantially to the total rental cost, but without it you (and, by extension, your own insurance company) are liable for every scratch to the car, even those that aren't your fault. Then again, don't be suckered into insurance you already have; call your credit card company to see if it offers free insurance if you use your card to pay. **If you are under 25**, be prepared for hefty surcharges on top of the usual rates.

Airlines, agents, and operators

Online booking

Ⓦ www.expedia.co.uk (in UK)
Ⓦ www.expedia.com (in US)
Ⓦ www.expedia.ca (in Canada)
Ⓦ www.lastminute.com (in UK)
Ⓦ www.opodo.co.uk (in UK)

Car-rental companies

Alamo Ⓣ 1-800/GO-ALAMO, Ⓦ www.alamo.com
Avis Canada Ⓣ 1-800/272-5871, US Ⓣ 1-800/331230-10844898; Ⓦ www.avis.com
Budget Canada Ⓣ 1-800/472-3325, US Ⓣ 1-800/527-0700; Ⓦ www.budget.com
Dollar Ⓣ 1-800/800-3665, Ⓦ www.dollar.com
Enterprise Ⓣ 1-800/726-8222, Ⓦ www.enterprise.com
Hertz Canada Ⓣ 1-800/263-0600, US Ⓣ 1-800/654-313001; Ⓦ www.hertz.com
National Ⓣ 1-800/962-7070, Ⓦ www.nationalcar.com
Thrifty Ⓣ 1-800/847-4389, Ⓦ www.thrifty.com

Ⓦ www.orbitz.com (in US)
Ⓦ www.travelocity.co.uk (in UK)
Ⓦ www.travelocity.com (in US)
Ⓦ www.travelocity.ca (in Canada)
Ⓦ www.zuji.com.au (in Australia)
Ⓦ www.zuji.co.nz (in New Zealand)

Airlines

Aer Lingus UK ⓉⓉ 0800/587 2324, Ireland
ⓉⓉ 0818/365 000; Ⓦ www.aerlingus.com
Air Canada ⓉⓉ 1-888/247-2262, UK ⓉⓉ 0871/220
1111, Ireland ⓉⓉ 01/679 3958; Ⓦ www.aircanada
.com
Air France UK ⓉⓉ 0870/142 4343, Ireland
ⓉⓉ 01/605 0383; Ⓦ www.airfrance.com
Air New Zealand Australia ⓉⓉ 132 476, Ⓦ www
.airnz.com.au; New Zealand ⓉⓉ 800/737 000,
Ⓦ www.airnz.co.nz
Air Pacific Australia ⓉⓉ 1800/230 150, New
Zealand ⓉⓉ 800/800 178; Ⓦ www.airpacific.com
Air Tran ⓉⓉ 1-800/247-8726, Ⓦ www.airtran.com
Alaska Airlines ⓉⓉ 1-800/252-7522, Ⓦ www
.alaska-air.com
American Airlines ⓉⓉ 1-800/433-7300, UK
ⓉⓉ 0845/778 9789, Ireland ⓉⓉ 01/602 0550,
Australia ⓉⓉ 1300/650 7347, New Zealand
ⓉⓉ 0800/887 997, Ⓦ www.aa.com
American Trans Air (ATA) ⓉⓉ 1-800/435-9282,
Ⓦ www.ata.com
British Airways UK ⓉⓉ 0870/850 9850, Ireland
ⓉⓉ 1890/626 747, Australia ⓉⓉ 1300/767 177, New
Zealand ⓉⓉ 09/966 9777; Ⓦ www.britishairways.com
British Midland (BMI) UK ⓉⓉ 0870/607 0555,
Ireland ⓉⓉ 01/407 3036; Ⓦ www.flybmi.com
Cathay Pacific Australia ⓉⓉ 131 747, New Zealand
ⓉⓉ 09/379 0861, South Africa ⓉⓉ 11/700 8900;
Ⓦ www.cathaypacific.com
China Airlines Australia ⓉⓉ 02/9244 2121, New
Zealand ⓉⓉ 09/308 3364; Ⓦ www.chinaairlines.com
Continental ⓉⓉ 1-800/523-3273, Ⓦ www
.continental.com
Continental Airlines UK ⓉⓉ 0845/607 6760,
Ireland ⓉⓉ 1890/925 252, Australia ⓉⓉ 02/9244
2242, New Zealand ⓉⓉ 09/308 3350; Ⓦ www
.continental.com
Delta ⓉⓉ 1-800/221-1212, UK ⓉⓉ 0845/600 0950,
Ireland ⓉⓉ 1850/882 031, Australia ⓉⓉ 1300/302
849, New Zealand ⓉⓉ 09/977 2232, South Africa
ⓉⓉ 011/482 4582; Ⓦ www.delta.com
easyJet UK ⓉⓉ 0905 8210905, Ⓦ www.easyjet.com
Frontier ⓉⓉ 1-800/432-1359, Ⓦ www.flyfrontier
.com
Icelandair UK ⓉⓉ 0870 7874020, Ⓦ www
.icelandair.net
JAL (Japan Airlines) Australia ⓉⓉ 2/9272 1111,

New Zealand ⓉⓉ 09/379 9906, South Africa
ⓉⓉ 011/214 2560; Ⓦ www.jal.com
JetBlue ⓉⓉ 1-800/538-2583, Ⓦ www.jetblue.com
Korean Air Australia ⓉⓉ 02/9262 6000, New
Zealand ⓉⓉ 09/914 2000; Ⓦ www.koreanair.com
Lufthansa UK ⓉⓉ 0870/837 7747, Ireland
ⓉⓉ 01/844 5544; Ⓦ www.lufthansa.com
Midwest ⓉⓉ 1-800/452-2022, Ⓦ www
.midwestairlines.com
Northwest/KLM ⓉⓉ 1-800/225-2525, UK
ⓉⓉ 0870/507 4074, Australia ⓉⓉ 1300/303 747, New
Zealand ⓉⓉ 09/309 1782; Ⓦ www.nwa.com,
Ⓦ www.klm.com
Qantas Australia ⓉⓉ 131 313, New Zealand
ⓉⓉ 9/357 8900, South Africa ⓉⓉ 011/441 8550;
Ⓦ www.qantas.com
Ryanair UK ⓉⓉ 0871/246 0000, Ireland ⓉⓉ 0818/30
30 30; Ⓦ www.ryanair.com
Singapore Airlines Australia ⓉⓉ 131 011, New
Zealand ⓉⓉ 800/808 909, South Africa ⓉⓉ 011/880
8560; Ⓦ www.singaporeair.com
South African Airways South Africa ⓉⓉ 011 978
1133, Ⓦ www.flysaa.com
Southwest ⓉⓉ 1-800/435-9792, Ⓦ www
.southwest.com
United Airlines ⓉⓉ 1-800/864-8331, UK
ⓉⓉ 0845/844 4777, Australia ⓉⓉ 131 777, New
Zealand ⓉⓉ 9/379 3800; Ⓦ www.unitedairlines.com
US Airways ⓉⓉ 1-800/428-4322, UK ⓉⓉ 0845/600
3300, Ireland ⓉⓉ 1890/925 065; Ⓦ www.usair.com
Virgin Atlantic Airways UK ⓉⓉ 0870/380 2007,
Australia ⓉⓉ 1300/727 340, South Africa ⓉⓉ 11/340
3400; Ⓦ www.virginatlantic.com

Travel agents and tour operators

American Holidays Northern Ireland ⓉⓉ 028/9023
8762, Republic of Ireland ⓉⓉ 1/673 3840; Ⓦ www
.american-holidays.com. All sorts of package tours to
the US from Ireland.
Bon Voyage UK ⓉⓉ 0800/316 3012, Ⓦ www
.bon-voyage.co.uk. Flight-plus-accommodation deals.
Bridge the World UK ⓉⓉ 0870/443 2399, Ⓦ www
.bridgetheworld.com. Good all-around agency that
specializes in US travel.
Canada & America Travel Specialists Australia
ⓉⓉ 02/9922 4600, Ⓦ www.canam.com.au. North
American specialists offering everything from flights
and hotels to travel passes and sports.
Flight Centre UK ⓉⓉ 0870/890 8099, Ⓦ www
.flightcentre.co.uk; Australia ⓉⓉ 133 133, Ⓦ www
.flightcentre.com.au; New Zealand ⓉⓉ 800/243 544,
Ⓦ www.flightcentre.co.nz; South Africa ⓉⓉ 0860/400
727, Ⓦ www.flightcentre.co.za. Near-ubiquitous
high-street agency frequently offering some of the
lowest fares around.

Holiday America UK ☎01424/224 400. Flight-plus-accommodation and fly-drive combinations.

Journeys Worldwide Australia ☎07/3221 4788, ⓦwww.journeysworldwide.com.au. All US travel arrangements available.

Kuoni UK ☎1306/747 002, ⓦwww.kuoni.co.uk. Flight-plus-accommodation-plus-car deals. Special deals for families.

North South Travel UK ☎01245/608 291, ⓦwww.northsouthtravel.co.uk. Nonprofit agency offering friendly and efficient service.

STA Travel UK ☎0870/160 0599, ⓦwww.statravel.co.uk; Australia ☎1300/733 035, ⓦwww.statravel.com.au; New Zealand ☎508/782 872, ⓦwww.statravel.co.nz. A major player in student, youth, and budget travel, including student IDs, travel insurance, car rental, and rail passes, with branches in or near many universities.

Sydney International Travel Centre Australia ☎02/9250 9320, ⓦwww.sydneytravel.com.au. Individually tailored holidays, air passes, flights, and bus and rail tours.

Trailfinders UK ☎020/7938 3939, ⓦwww.trailfinders.com; Ireland ☎1/677 7888, ⓦwww.trailfinders.ie; Australia ☎02/9247 7666, ⓦwww.trailfinders.com.au. Well-established travel specialists, particularly adept at organizing round-the-world tickets.

Travel.com.au Australia ☎02/9249 5444, ⓦwww.travel.com.au; New Zealand ☎800/788 336, ⓦwww.travel.co.nz. Youth-oriented center with an efficient travel agency offering good fares, a travel bookshop, and Internet café.

USA Travel Australia ☎02/9250 9320, ⓦwww.usatravel.com.au. Good deals on flights, accommodation, city stays, car rental, and trip packages.

USIT Northern Ireland ☎028/9032 7111, ⓦwww.usitnow.com; Republic of Ireland ☎0818/200 020, ⓦwww.usit.ie. Ireland's premier student travel center, which can also find good nonstudent deals.

Virgin Holidays UK ☎0870/220 2788, ⓦwww.virginholidays.co.uk. Packages to a wide range of destinations.

Arrival

Those traveling to Washington, DC, by train or bus arrive at the most central locations: Union Station and the downtown Greyhound terminal, respectively. Union Station is easily linked by Metro to the city center, as is Reagan National Airport. From the other airports, you can't count on being downtown in much less than an hour, though the various bus, train, and subway transfers are smooth enough. Taking a taxi from Dulles or Baltimore-Washington International Airport won't save much time, especially if you arrive during rush hour, though filling a cab with three or four people may save you a few dollars.

By air

The most convenient destination for domestic arrivals is **National Airport** (DCA; ☎703/417-8000, ⓦwww.mwaa.com/national) – officially Ronald Reagan Washington National Airport – four miles south of central DC and across the Potomac in Virginia. By car or by bus it takes 30min to an hour to reach the center of town from the airport, depending on traffic, though the National Airport **Metro station** is linked directly to Metro Center, L'Enfant Plaza, and Gallery Place–Chinatown on the Blue and Yellow lines, making the subway the

clear choice for transit if you don't have too much luggage. A **taxi** to central DC costs around $15–20 (including airport surcharge). Another option is the **SuperShuttle** bus (one-way from DCA, $12; ☎1-800/BLUE-VAN, ⓦwww.supershuttle.com), which drops you at your hotel, though you'll have to ride with up to six strangers.

The area's major airport, and one of the top five busiest in the country, **Dulles International** (IAD; ☎703/572-2700, ⓦwww.mwaa.com/dulles), 26 miles west in northern Virginia, handles most international and some domestic flights. The drive to or from central DC can take up to an hour or more in heavy traffic, and rarely less than forty minutes. **Taxis** going downtown cost $55–60. There's also a **SuperShuttle** bus from Dulles (see above info; one-way $27). It's cheaper, if a little more time-consuming, to take the **Washington Flyer Express** bus (one-way $9, round-trip $16; ☏1-888/WASH-FLY, ⓦwww.washfly.com) to the **West Falls Church Metro station**, a thirty-minute trip; from there it's a twenty-minute train ride into central DC. However, the most inexpensive option is to take public transit all the way into town: catch **Metrobus #5A** ($3 express) from the airport, which connects with the Metrorail at the Rosslyn and L'Enfant Plaza Metro stations.

Other international and domestic arrivals land at **Baltimore-Washington International Airport** (BWI; ☏410/859-7111, ⓦwww.bwiairport.com), 25 miles northeast of DC and 10 miles south of Baltimore. This, too, is up to an hour's drive from central DC, with taxis costing around $55 (agree on the price before setting off). **SuperShuttle** buses into Washington (one-way $35) will drop you off at your hotel, but it's cheaper to take the commuter rail from BWI. (A free shuttle

service connects the airport with the BWI rail terminal, a 10–15min ride.) The most economical choice is the southbound Penn Line of the **Maryland Rail Commuter Service** (MARC; every 20–60min, Mon–Fri 5am–9.45pm; one-way $6; ☏410/539-5000, ⓦwww.mtamaryland.com), providing frequent peak-hour departures to Washington's Union Station, a forty-minute trip. The station is also reached from BWI by the quicker daily **Amtrak** trains (half-hourly 6.20am–11pm; one-way $12), which take a half hour with regular service, twenty minutes with the speedier Acela Express trains, which are $41 one-way.

By train and bus

The grand edifice of **Union Station**, 50 Massachusetts Ave NE, three blocks north of the Capitol, welcomes arrivals from all over the country, including local trains from Baltimore, Richmond, Williamsburg, and Virginia Beach, and major East Coast routes from Philadelphia, New York, and Boston. Train operators include the nationwide **Amtrak** (☏1-800/USA-RAIL, ⓦwww.amtrak .com) and the local **MARC** system (☏410/539-5000, ⓦwww.mtamaryland.com),

---

Leaving DC: Getting to the airports

Give yourself plenty of time to get to the airport, especially if you're driving: it can take up to 30min to reach National, and 45min to an hour to get to Dulles or BWI without traffic. Once there, security checks can keep you waiting in line for 15–45min, so try to leave two hours or more before your flight.

Amtrak ☏1-800/872-7245, ⓦwww.amtrak.com. Connecting from DC's Union Station to BWI rail terminal (half-hourly 6.20am–11pm); regular service $12, Acela Express $41.

MARC commuter rail ☏410/539-5000, ⓦwww.mtamaryland.com. Penn Line, connecting Union Station to BWI rail terminal (every 20–60min, Mon–Fri 5am–9.45pm), one-way $6.

Metro/bus ☏202/637-7000, ⓦwww.wmata.com. To BWI: Metro Green Line to Greenbelt station, where Metrobus #B30 (every 40min, Mon–Fri 6am–10pm, Sat & Sun 8.45am–10pm) continues on to BWI nonstop. To Dulles: Metrobus #5A from L'Enfant Plaza or Rosslyn Metro stations (hourly, Mon–Fri 5.50am–11.40pm, Sat & Sun 5.30–10.30pm). To National: Metro Blue or Yellow lines.

SuperShuttle ☏1-800-BLUE VAN, ⓦwww.supershuttle.com. To BWI, $35 one-way. To Dulles, $27. To National, $12. Pickup on request at your hotel; reservations required.

Washington Flyer Express ☏1-888/WASH-FLY, ⓦwww.washfly.com. To Dulles from West Falls Church Metro: one-way $9, round-trip $16.

Taxis Operators at ⓦdctaxi.dc.gov. To BWI or Dulles, $55–60. To National, $15–20. Pickup on request at your hotel.

which connects DC to Baltimore, BWI Airport, and suburban Maryland. From the station you can connect to the Metro, rent a car, or catch a taxi outside.

Greyhound (☎1-800/229-9424, ⓦwww .greyhound.com) and **Peter Pan** (☎1-800/343-9999, ⓦwww.peterpanbus.com) buses from Baltimore, Philadelphia, New York, Boston, Richmond, and other cities stop at the terminal at 1005 1st Street NE at L Street, in an unsavory part of town, five long blocks north of Union Station. The Union Station Metro stop is about a $6 cab ride away, or you can walk two blocks north to the New York Avenue Metro station, with a southern entrance at M Street.

By car

Driving into DC is a sure way to experience some of the East Coast's worst traffic. The eight-lane freeway known as the **Capital Beltway** (in the process of expanding to twelve lanes throughout the loop) encircles the city at a ten-mile radius from the center and is busy nearly around the clock. It's made up of two separate highways: I-495 on the western half and I-95/I-495 in the east. If it's the Beltway you want, follow signs for either.

Approaching the city **from the northeast** (New York/Philadelphia), you need I-95

(south), before turning west on Route 50; that will take you to New York Avenue, which heads directly to the White House but goes first through a rather bleak industrial wasteland on the northeast edge of town. **From Baltimore** there's the direct Baltimore–Washington Parkway, which also joins Route 50. Indeed, Route 50 is the main route into DC from the east (Annapolis, Maryland, and Chesapeake Bay). **From the south**, take I-95 to I-395, which crosses the river via the George Mason Memorial Bridge – part of the colossal "14th Street Bridge Complex" with multiple spans for mass transit, plus regular highway and express lanes – and deposits you south of the Mall near the waterfront. **From the northwest** (Frederick, MD, and beyond), take I-270 until you hit the Beltway, then follow I-495 (east) to Connecticut Avenue south; this is one of the more attractive entryways into the city, and also one of the slowest. **From the west** (Virginia) use I-66, which runs across the Theodore Roosevelt Bridge to Constitution Avenue, where DC first appears in the image of the Lincoln Memorial. At peak periods in the Beltway, high-occupancy-vehicle restrictions apply on I-66 eastbound (6.30–9am) and westbound (4–6.30pm). See color map "Washington, DC: Metropolitan Area" for highways into the city.

Getting around

Most places downtown – including the major museums and monuments, and the White House – are within walking distance of one another, while an excellent public transit system connects central DC to outlying sights and neighborhoods. The Washington Metropolitan Area Transit Authority (WMATA; ⓦwww.wmata.com) operates a subway system (Metrorail) and a bus network (Metrobus), plus you can get around by taxi or bike. Driving a car can involve great frustration, with the District's thick congestion and maddening squares and traffic circles resulting in gridlock amid a horn-blaring cacophony.

The Metro

Washington's subway – the **Metrorail**, or simply the **Metro** – is quick, cheap, and easy to use. It runs on five lines that cover most of

the downtown areas and suburbs (with the notable exception of Georgetown), branching out from the center of the District in all directions to just beyond the Capital Beltway,

Washington Metropolitan Area Transit Authority

For route information and bus and Metro timetables call ☎202/637-7000 (Mon–Thurs 6am–10.30pm, Fri 6am–11.30pm, Sat 7am–11.30pm, Sun 7am–10.30pm) or visit ⓦ www.wmata.com.

Other helpful numbers
General information ☎202/962-1234

Transit Police ☎202/962-2121 (emergencies only)

Lost and Found ☎202/962-1195 (24hr message; office open Mon–Fri 11am–3pm, also accessible online)

ID cards for the disabled ☎202/962-1245

Passes
For passes and other information, visit:

Metro Center Sales Office, 12th and F sts NW at Metro Center Station (Mon–Fri 7.30am–7.30pm, Sat noon–6pm)

Metro Headquarters, lobby, 600 5th St NW (Mon–Fri 10am–3pm)

Metro Pentagon Sales Office, upper level bus bay (Mon–Fri 7am–6.30pm).

where the outlying stations have lots for commuters' cars. Each line is color-coded and studded with various interchange stations: Metro Center, L'Enfant Plaza, and Gallery Place–Chinatown are the most important downtown, being the most central. Stations are identified outside by the letter *M* on top of a brown pylon; inside, the well-lit, vaulted halls make the Washington Metro one of the safest subway systems in the world – though security precautions have, as with everything else in town, been tightened since 9/11. Keep in mind that while the system itself may be generally safe, a few of its stations, like Anacostia, are in unsafe neighborhoods.

The entire length of the 103-mile system was completed in 2001, but with the success of the system, new extensions are regularly proposed, most recently an extension to Dulles Airport, which will link with the rest of the system at East Falls Church and be dubbed the **Silver Line**. Completion is due by 2016, with closer stations to Washington, DC coming on-line a few years before that.

The Metro's **operating hours** are Monday through Thursday 5am to midnight, Friday 5am to 3am, Saturday 7am to 3am, and Sunday 7am to midnight. Trains run every five to seven minutes on most lines during rush hours, and every ten to twelve minutes at other times. Pick up a copy of the useful **Metro guide** (free, available in most stations), which gives the train and bus routes to the city's various attractions. The entire system is shown on the **Metro System route map**, available at Metro offices (see box, above) and online at ⓦ www.wmata.com/metrorail/systemmap.cfm; through the same sources you can also get the more detailed **Metro Pocket Guide**, covering fares, passes, stations, and points of interest near stations in eleven different language editions.

Each passenger needs a **farecard**, which must be bought from a machine before you pass through the turnstiles. Fares are based on when and how far you travel and usually cost $1.35 (one-way, peak or off-peak) if you're traveling around central DC, the Mall, and the Capitol (maps and station-to-station ticket prices are posted by the machines, as well as online). **One-way fares** range from $1.35 (base rate) to $3.90; the higher, **peak-rate fares** are charged Mon–Fri 5–9.30am, 3–7pm and 2am until closing, while the top fare is $2.35 at other times. Children under five ride free, and seniors are admitted for half off the standard price.

Farecards work like debit cards – you "put in" an amount of money when you purchase the card, and the fare is subtracted after each train ride. If you're going to use the Metro several times, it's worth putting in more money – an additional ten percent credit is added to the value of cards over $20. (Most stations have a few machines that accept debit and credit cards.) Feed the card through any turnstile marked with a green arrow, and then retrieve it. When you do the same thing at the end of your journey, the machine prints out on the card how much money remains. If you've paid the exact amount, the turnstile keeps the card; if you don't have enough money remaining on the card for the journey, insert it into one of the special exit-fare machines, deposit more money, and try the turnstile again. If you plan on catching a bus after your Metro ride, get a **rail-to-bus transfer pass** (good for 90¢ off your bus fare) at the station where you enter the rail system. The self-service transfer machines are on the mezzanine next to the escalator leading to the train platform.

If you plan on making at least five daily trips around central DC, the **Metrorail One-Day Pass** ($6.50) is a good choice, buying unlimited travel after 9.30am on weekdays and all day on the weekend. There's also a **7-Day Fast Pass** ($32.50), for seven consecutive days of unlimited travel, but a better deal for visitors is the **7-Day Short Trip Pass** ($22), which saves you money and covers almost every sight you'll probably want to see, from the waterfront up to the zoo, as well as National Airport; the only thing outside the covered area is Alexandria, Virginia, for which you'll have to pay a few cents extra. All passes are available at Metro Center station, Metro Headquarters, and many area supermarkets, or online through the WMATA website.

Buses

WMATA runs DC's subway and **bus** systems, which operate during largely the same hours (though some buses run until 3am on

---

Useful bus routes

Farragut North to Upper Northwest #N2, #N4, #N6 via 18th St, Dupont Circle, Massachusetts Ave, Embassy Row, Washington National Cathedral

Lincoln Memorial to Cleveland Park #L1 via National Mall, Constitution Ave, 23rd St, Washington Circle, New Hampshire Ave, Dupont Circle, Connecticut Ave (National Zoological Park), Woodley Park, Cleveland Park

L'Enfant Plaza to McPherson Square #52 via 6th St, Independence Ave, 14th St

Lafayette Square to National Basilica #G8 via H St, 11th St, Rhode Island Ave, 7th St NE

McPherson Square to Woodley Park #L2 via K St, 20th St, Dupont Circle, 18th St (Adams Morgan), Calvert St, Connecticut Ave (National Zoological Park), into Maryland

Metro Center to Adams Morgan #42 via Metro Center (10th and F), H St, Connecticut Ave, Dupont Circle, Columbia Rd (Adams Morgan), Connecticut Ave, Cleveland Park

National Mall to Arlington Memorial Cemetery #13B, #13F via 7th St, Constitution Ave, Lincoln Memorial, Arlington Memorial Bridge

National Mall to Pentagon #13A, #13G via 7th St, Independence Ave, Bureau of Engraving and Printing/Holocaust Museum, 14th St Bridge, Pentagon (then connects to Arlington National Cemetery and loops back to Mall via Constitution Ave)

National Mall to Rock Creek Park #S2, #S4 via Natural History Museum, Old Post Office, 11th St, I St, McPherson Square, 16th St (get off at Military Rd, park is short walk west; or take #E2, #E3, or #E4, which cut through the park)

Pennsylvania Ave to Georgetown #30, #32, #34, #35, #36 via Eastern Market, US Capitol, Independence Ave, 7th St, Pennsylvania Ave, 15th St, Pennsylvania Ave, Wisconsin Ave (Georgetown)

Union Station to Georgetown #D3, #D6 via E St, 13th St, K St, Dupont Circle, Q St (Georgetown); return via M St

Union Station to Kennedy Center #80 via Massachusetts Ave, H St, 13th St, K St, 19th St, Virginia Ave, Watergate Complex

Union Station to National Arboretum #X8 via Massachusetts Ave, Maryland Ave, M St

weekdays). The **base fare** for most bus journeys is $1.25, payable to the driver, though surcharges and zone crossings can raise the price, and express routes will cost $2.50 a ride. The same peak-hour rates on the Metro apply to the buses, and rail transfers cover 90¢ of your bus fare. Two good passes to consider are the **Daily Pass** ($3), which applies to all regular routes and reduces express trips by $1.25, and the **Weekly Pass** ($11), which has the same express-trip reduction and buys seven days' worth of unlimited base-fare trips. Riders of Maryland's **MARC** and Virginia's **VRE** can

Washington city tours

There are a number of **tour operators** eager to show you the many sights of Washington, DC, though with just a little research and preparation it's easy to see most things on your own. Some of the more popular **tour bus** services, are useful, since they allow you to get on and off the bus at will and shuttle you out to the area's far-flung sights. **River cruises** are worth considering, especially in summer when the offshore breeze comes as a welcome relief. **Specialist tours** show you a side of Washington you may not otherwise see, like historic buildings, sites and famous people's homes. For more information, contact Explore DC (℡703/998-2458, ⓦwww.exploredc.org) or Cultural Tourism DC (℡202/661-7581, ⓦwww.culturaltourismdc.org), whose websites list various guided tours and provide a calendar of cultural events.

Buses and trolleys

Gray Line ℡301/386-8300, ⓦwww.graylinedc.com. A variety of tours in and around DC, including a two-day tour of downtown sights and Mount Vernon ($95), an evening tour ($38), and trips to Colonial Williamsburg ($92) and Monticello ($88), among many other options.

Old Town Trolley Tours ℡202/832-9800 or 1-800/213-2474, ⓦwww.historictours .com/washington. Trolleys take you around Old Downtown, the National Mall, Georgetown, and Washington National Cathedral ($28 a day), and a "Monuments by Moonlight" tour shows you the Mall's presidential and war memorials after dark ($29). Tickets available at trolley stops and downtown hotels.

Tourmobile ℡202/554-5100 or 888/868-7707, ⓦwww.tourmobile.com. Narrated bus tours (daily 9.30am–4.30pm) covering downtown and Arlington Cemetery ($24), Mount Vernon ($30), and the Mall by night ($25). Tickets available at the office on the Ellipse, at kiosks on the Mall (there's one at the Washington Monument), and on the bus itself.

Cruises and river trips

Atlantic Kayak Tours ℡301/292-6455 or 1-800/297-0066, ⓦwww.atlantickayak .com. Kayak tours along the Potomac, including 2.5-hour sunset tours highlighting Georgetown's bridges and monuments or the Dyke Marsh Wildlife area ($40–55 each). Also moonlight tours, full-day trips, and overnight excursions to wildlife areas. No experience is necessary and all equipment is included. Tours run April–Oct only. Also kayak rentals for $20–30 for two hours or $45–50 a day.

Capitol River Cruises ℡1-800/405-5511 or 301/460-7447, ⓦwww.capitol rivercruises.com. Forty-five-minute sightseeing cruises leaving hourly throughout the day (April–Oct noon–9pm) from Georgetown's Washington Harbor, at the end of 31st St NW; $12 per person, reservations not required.

DC Ducks ℡1-800/213-2474, ⓦwww.historictours.com/washington/dcducks.htm. Converted amphibious carriers cruise the Mall and then splash into the Potomac (90min; $26). Hourly departures from Union Station (mid-March to Oct daily 10am–4pm).

Spirit Cruises ℡1-866/302-2469, ⓦwww.spiritcruises.com. Swanky 2hr lunch cruises with bar and bands for $32–46; 3hr dinner cruises for $55–79; or 90min trips to Mount Vernon for $39. Tickets and departures from Pier 4 at 6th and Water sts SW (Waterfront Metro).

also use their weekly and monthly rail passes to ride base-rate Metrobus lines free. Other systems that are covered are in Alexandria (the **DASH**) and en route to Mount Vernon, which you can reach on a **Fairfax Connector** bus. Both systems link with the Metro; for timetable information contact DASH (rides $1; ☎703/370-3274, ⓦwww.dashbus.com) or Fairfax Connector (non-express routes $1, express $3; ☎703/339-7200, ⓦwww.fairfaxconnector.com).

WMATA also offers the special "**DC Circulator**" (☎202/962-1423, ⓦwww.dccirculator.com), geared toward tourists

Specialist tours and activities

African American Heritage Tour ☎202/636-9203, ⓦwww.washington-dc-tours.com. Half-day journeys to local sights important to black history, including the Frederick Douglass National Historic Site and Martin Luther King Jr Memorial. $25; by reservation only.

Duke Ellington's Neighborhood ☎202/636-9203, ⓦwww.washington-dc-tours.com. Four-hour bus tour ($25) of the historic U Street/Shaw neighborhood and boyhood home of jazz legend Duke Ellington includes the Mary McLeod Bethune Council House, African American Civil War Memorial, and Howard University. Departures monthly May–Aug; call for schedule.

Goodwill Embassy Tour ☎202/636-4225, ⓦwww.dcgoodwill.org. On the second Saturday in May, five of DC's embassy buildings throw open their doors for the day ($35). Reserve well in advance. Many embassies also offer free guided tours with reservations; for contact telephone numbers see p.42.

Kalorama House and Embassy Tour ☎202/387-4062 ext 18. Various ambassadors' residences and private homes are open to the public for 5hr (usually noon–5pm) one day every September; reserve in advance for $22, or pay $25 on the day of the tour.

Scandal Tour ☎202/783-7212, ⓦwww.gnpcomedy.com/ScandalTours.html. The seamier side of Washington is explored during 90min recounts ($30) of scandals involving the Watergate Hotel, Monica Lewinsky, and more. April–Aug Sat 1pm; by reservation only.

SpyDrive ☎1-800/779-4007 or 703/642-7450, ⓦwww.spydrive.com. Two-hour tours of sites in the "spy capital of the world," led by retired FBI, CIA, and KGB officers. The "Robert Hanssen Case" tour covers sites used by the infamous FBI agent for spying and subterfuge. Groups only; prices vary.

Walking tours

DC Heritage ☎202/828-9255, ⓦwww.culturaltourismdc.org. Sponsors a wide range of tours (90min; around $10–15) throughout the city, including some on foot that highlight downtown's historic sights and architecture.

Lantern Lights ☎703/548-0100, ⓦwww.alexcolonialtours.com. The "Ghosts and Graveyard Tour" in Old Town Alexandria takes you through haunted nineteenth-century homes and eerie cemeteries, as costumed guides tell bone-chilling tales of historical horror. Tours (Oct–Nov only; $10) depart from the Ramsay House visitor center at 221 King St.

Old Town Walking Tour ☎703/838-4200, ⓦwww.alexcolonialtours.com. Focuses on the history and architecture of Alexandria's historic district (90min; $15). Departs from the Ramsay House visitor center at 221 King St. A more detailed, three-and-a-half-hour tour covers African American history in the city, focusing heavily on slavery (groups only; $35 per person).

Washington Walks ☎202/484-1565, ⓦwww.washingtonwalks.com. Two-hour walks through downtown DC, with themes like "I've Got a Secret," "Capitol Hauntings," "Most Haunted Houses," and so on (all tours $10).

and conventioneers, which will take you from Union Station to Georgetown via K Street, or, alternatively, from the Convention Center to the Southwest waterfront by way of 7th Street and the National Mall; a third shuttle route loops around the museums of the Mall itself, from the National World War II Memorial to nearly the foot of Capitol Hill. Buses run daily from 7am to 9pm, except for those on the museum loop, which run daily from 10am to 4pm. Tickets are $1 on all routes, and the usual passes and transfers are allowed. Note that by the end of 2008, two new routes are due to be in service, one linking the convention center with Dupont Circle and Adams Morgan, the other linking Union Station with the new Nationals baseball stadium on the waterfront.

Taxis

Taxis complement DC's public transportation system and are especially valuable in outposts like Georgetown and Adams Morgan, which aren't on the Metro. Georgetown is on the DC Circulator (until 9pm), but if you know you're going to be out late in these neighborhoods, it's a good idea to book a return taxi in advance.

Cabs in DC previously charged **fares** on a concentric zoned basis, resulting in variable, hard-to-predict charges, depending on the area or even the side of the street where one was picked up. In October 2007, it was announced that cabs will be switching over during 2008 to standard metered fares, as in most US cities. Although specific charges haven't been determined at time of publication, former costs were in the range of $8 from Georgetown to Dupont Circle, $15–20 between Reagan National Airport and central DC, and $5–7 for quick jaunts from the National Mall to Old Downtown. Surcharges may be added during rush hour (Mon–Fri 7–9.30am and 4–6.30pm), and groups may be asked to pay up to $2 for each additional passenger (in addition to the first one). Once you get out of DC, into Maryland or Virginia, fares can be much more expensive ($50–60 to the airports, for example). Taxis from those states are legally allowed to deposit you at your Washington destination but may not shuttle you from one DC spot to another.

You can either flag cabs down on the street or use the ranks at hotels and transport terminals; there are always cabs available at Union Station. If you call a taxi in advance, there's a $2 surcharge on the fare. For more information, call the **DC Taxicab Commission** at ☏202/645-6018 or visit ⊛dctaxi.dc.gov.

Driving

You shouldn't drive in the capital unless you absolutely have to. **Traffic jams** can be nightmarish, the DC street layout is a grid overlaid with unnerving diagonal boulevards, and without a map it's easy to get lost and find yourself in the middle of an urban wasteland. Considering the excellent Metro system, decent buses, and pedestrian-friendly areas, you should think twice about plunking down the money for a rental car. If you must head out of the city by car, either rent one at the end of your stay (at Union Station), or leave your own car at your hotel for the duration – though this will cost $15–30 per night at any decent downtown hotel. For lists of car rental agencies, see p.23.

One-way streets can play havoc with the best-planned driving routes, while the traffic-control system in place during the city's **rush hours** (Mon–Fri 6.30–9.30am & 3–7pm, plus lunchtime) means that many lanes, or even whole streets, **change direction** at particular times of the day and left turns are periodically forbidden. Read the signs carefully. To top it all off, the roads can be treacherous – even on major thoroughfares you'll want to keep an eye out for potholes and ridges.

Parking lots and garages charge from $6 per hour to $20 a day. Searching for free, **on-street parking** is likely to cost you a lot of time and energy; there are free, limited-wait (two- to three-hour) parking spots around the Mall (Jefferson and Madison Drives, Independence Ave SW) and in West Potomac Park, but they're extremely popular. **Parking meters** tend to operate between 7am and 6.30pm, usually allowing a maximum stay of two hours. At other times, just when you think you've found the perfect spot, it will almost certainly be reserved for workers, or on a street that becomes one-way during rush hour, or temporarily illegal to park on because it is rush hour, or rendered useless for countless other reasons. Naturally, the places you might want to drive to for an evening out, like Georgetown, Dupont Circle, or Adams Morgan, are also short on available parking spaces.

If you're stopped when driving, you'll be required to produce a driver's license, the car's registration papers, and verification of insurance (though the latter two will be waived if you are driving a rental, as long as you can provide proof of that rental). Should your car get towed away during your visit, call the local **Department of Motor Vehicles** at ☏202/727-5000 and expect to pay $100 or more to get it back. Vehicles towed away after 7pm on a Friday won't be returned until after 9am the following Monday.

Bikes

True bicycling fans will doubtless want to use their two-wheelers more for sport than for transit while in the city, and these opportunities are detailed in Chapter 19, "Sports and outdoor activities," as well as in entries for bike-friendly locales such as Rock Creek Park (p.228) and the C&O Canal (p.238). Given the traffic, few visitors will actually want to brave the DC streets on a bicycle, though several outfits can provide maps and advice on traffic conditions. Bike **rental costs** $5–10 an hour, $15–50 a day, or $100–130 a week (depending on the model and rental company); you'll need to leave a deposit and/or a credit card or passport

number. Bikes are permitted on the Metro except on weekdays during rush hour (7–10am and 4–7pm) and on some major holidays, such as the Fourth of July.

Bike-rental companies

Better Bikes ☏202/293-2080, ⓦwww
.betterbikesinc.com. 24hr information line; will deliver anywhere in DC. Has information on bike trails and events.
Big Wheel Bikes 1034 33rd St NW, Georgetown ☏202/337-0254; 2 Prince St, Old Town Alexandria, VA ☏703/739-2300; 3119 Lee Hwy, Arlington VA ☏703/522-1110; ⓦwww
.bigwheelbikes.com. Open Mon–Fri 11am to 7 or 8pm and Sat–Sun 10am–6pm. Georgetown location (closed Mon) convenient to C&O Canal and Capital Crescent trails; Alexandria location near Mount Vernon Trail.
Bike the Sites ☏202/842-BIKE, ⓦwww
.bikethesites.com. Two- to four-hour guided bike tours of the city's major sights ($30–40, including bike and helmet), plus tours of Mount Vernon and customized tours of the District. Also rents bikes for $5–10 an hour or $25–60 a day. Tour reservations required.
Thompson Boat Center 2900 Virginia Ave NW, Georgetown ☏202/333-9543, ⓦwww
.thompsonboatcenter.com. Daily 8am–6pm; closed Oct to mid-March. Excellent prices on cruisers, among other models.
Washington Sailing Marina 1 Marina Drive, Alexandria, VA ☏703/548-9027, ⓦwww
.washingtonsailingmarina.com. Daily 9am–5pm. Good for access to the Mount Vernon Bike Trail, and close-in Northern Virginia.

The media

DC is unquestionably the savviest city for political media in the United States; much of what makes headlines around the world is born in the capital's press briefings. Though closed to the general public, White House briefings are broadcast live on C-SPAN and covered in detail in the next day's *Washington Post*. Nevertheless, overseas visitors will probably find American news coverage too parochial; to keep in touch with day-to-day events back home, you'll have to buy a foreign newspaper, which is easily done in DC.

Newspapers and magazines

DC's major newspaper, the liberal *Washington Post*, is one of America's most respected dailies, landing every morning on the doorsteps of the most powerful people in the world. It routinely wins Pulitzer prizes, the nation's highest award for journalism, though its most famous one was in the 1970s for its investigation of the Watergate scandal that brought down the Nixon administration. Top columnists on the paper's opinion pages include political commentator David Broder, conservative George F. Will, neo-conservative Charles Krauthammer, and liberals like Harold Meyerson and E.J. Dionne. You can read the paper free on its website ⓦ www.washingtonpost.com, but registration is required. The only local competitor to the *Post* is the deeply conservative, Moonie-published *Washington Times*. The country's one truly national daily, *USA Today* – aka the "McPaper" – is headquartered across the Potomac in Virginia and known for being thick on splashy graphics and thin on investigative journalism. Any upscale hotel will offer you a choice of this paper or the *Post* in the morning.

Free weeklies include the alternative *CityPaper* (ⓦ www.washingtoncitypaper.com), a tabloid-size paper appearing on Thursdays that's known for its progressive slant on current affairs and its arts and entertainment listings, and the gay-oriented *Washington Blade* (ⓦ www.washblade.com) and *Metro Weekly* (ⓦ www.metroweekly.com). Glossy **monthly magazines** include the arts-and-leisure publication *Washingtonian* (ⓦ www.washingtonian.com) and PR-focused *Where:*

Washington (ⓦ www.wheremagazine.com); other neighborhood papers and magazines are available in bars, restaurants, shops, and hotels.

Newspapers from other US cities, as well as **foreign newspapers and magazines**, can be bought at Union Station, major bookstores, and The Newsroom, 1803 Connecticut Ave NW, Dupont Circle ☎ 202/332-1489.

TV and radio

The four **television networks** – NBC, ABC, CBS, and Fox – broadcast news and talk shows from 6am or 7am to 10am Monday to Friday and air their evening local news programs from 5pm to 6.30pm and again at 11pm, also on weekdays. National news is on at 6.30pm. The city's public-TV channel, WETA, is one of the nation's more prominent PBS affiliates, broadcasting a mix of nature documentaries, political investigations, and history programs (view the programming schedule online at ⓦ www.weta.org/tv). Most hotel rooms have some form of cable TV, though the number of channels available depends on where you stay. Check the daily papers for a list of channels and schedules. Cable news stations include CNN and CNN Headline News, and Fox News, which provides a right-wing perspective on the day's events. ESPN is your best bet for sports, MTV for youth-oriented music videos and programs, and VH-1 for people outside the MTV demographic. HBO and Showtime present big-budget Hollywood flicks and award-winning TV shows, while Turner Classic Movies takes its programming from the Golden Age of Hollywood.

The state of commercial **radio** in Washington, DC, as elsewhere in America, is pretty dismal: a slew of radio stations are owned by the goliath Clear Channel and Infinity networks, and a few other national heavyweights. For quality news and programming on the radio, tune in to WAMU at 88.5 FM (ⓦ www.wamu.org), which airs National Public Radio broadcasts (Mon–Fri 5–9am & 4–7pm) and independently produced journalism and cultural-affairs shows. NPR also makes its appearance, along with classical-music favorites, on the other public radio station in town, WETA (90.9 FM; ⓦ www.weta.org/fm). Other worthwhile stations are usually broadcast online only from universities such as George Washington (ⓦ www.gwradio.com), Georgetown (ⓦ www.georgetownradio.com), and Howard (WHUR, also on 96.3 FM; ⓦ www .whur.com), which together play a mix of jazz, folk, blues, hip-hop, and alternative rock, along with talk shows and intermittent cultural programs.

TV stations

All of these TV channels' websites offer programming schedules and information, and possibly simulcasts or re-broadcasts of noteworthy shows.

WRC NBC on 4; ⓦ www.nbc4.com
WTTG Fox on 5; ⓦ www.myfoxdc.com
WJLA ABC on 7; ⓦ www.wjla.com
WUSA CBS on 9; ⓦ www.wusa9.com
WDCA My/Fox on 20; ⓦ www.wdca.com
WETA PBS on 26; ⓦ www.weta.org/tv
WBDC CW on 50; ⓦ thecwdc.trb.com

Radio stations

As with the TV stations, all of these radio stations' websites offer programming schedules and information, and possibly simulcasts or re-broadcasts of noteworthy shows.

AM stations

WMAL (630) news, sports, and right-wing talk; ⓦ 630wmal.com
WTEM (980) sports talk; ⓦ www.wtem.com
WOL (1450) African American talk; ⓦ wolam.com
WWWT (1500) news, talk, and sports; ⓦ www.3wtradio.com

FM stations

WAMU (88.5) NPR, talk, music, and news; ⓦ www.wamu.org
WPFW (89.3) Pacifica Radio: left-leaning news and talk, jazz, and blues; ⓦ www.wpfw.org
WCSP (90.1) C-SPAN Radio: Congress and public affairs coverage; ⓦ www.c-span.org/watch/cspanradio.asp
WETA (90.9) music and NPR news; ⓦ www.weta.org/fm
WARW (94.7) eclectic rock; ⓦ www.947theglobe.com
WPGC (95.5) hip-hop, R&B; ⓦ www.wpgc955.com
WHUR (96.3) Howard University radio: hip-hop, jazz, blues, R&B, and cultural programs; ⓦ www.whur.com
WMZQ (98.7) country music; ⓦ www.wmzqfm.com
WBIG (100) classic rock; ⓦ www.idigbig.com
WWDC (101.1) indie rock; ⓦ www.dc101.com
WTOP (103.5) news and talk; ⓦ www.wtopnews.com
WHFS (105.7) sports and talk; ⓦ www.whfs.com
WRQX (107.3) eclectic pop and rock; ⓦ www.mix1073fm.com

Culture and etiquette

If you watch TV and go to the movies, you'll be familiar with many aspects of the DC area's culture and etiquette before you arrive. A few points do warrant a mention, though.

One point of eternal discussion is **tipping**. Many workers in service industries get paid very little and rely on tips to bolster their income. Unless you've had abominable service (in which case you should tell the management), you really shouldn't leave a bar or restaurant without leaving a tip of at least **fifteen percent**, and about the same should be added to taxi fares. A hotel porter deserves roughly $1 for each bag carried to your room; a coat-check clerk should receive the same per coat. When paying by credit card you're expected to add the tip to the total bill before filling in the amount and signing.

Smoking is a much frowned-upon activity in Washington, which as of 2007 has banned it in all indoor public places, including bars and restaurants. Nevertheless, cigarettes are sold in virtually every food shop and drugstore, at some bars, and also from the occasional vending machine.

As the home of the Drug Enforcement Agency, DC has predictably strict **marijuana** laws. Possession of any amount of pot incurs a fine of up to $1000 and up to six months in jail – perhaps even deportation if you're a foreign national. Similarly harsh treatment is meted out in Virginia and Maryland.

Travel essentials

Costs

Given the historically low value of the American dollar, there's rarely been a better time for foreign travelers to visit Washington. Plus, while it may be the nation's capital, it's a lot more affordable to vacation here than in most big American cities. Nearly all the major museums, monuments, and memorials are free, public transit is cheap and efficient, and the presence of so many students, interns, and public servants means that many bars and restaurants have great deals on drinks and food. That's not to say that you can't spend money in Washington; the city has some of the country's finest and most expensive hotels and restaurants, and the odd attraction can be on the pricey side.

Nevertheless, sticking to a budget in DC shouldn't be too hard to do.

Average costs

Accommodation will be your biggest single expense: expect the lowest rate for a double hotel room to be around $100–140 a night, though spartan hostels, dingy motels, and a few B&Bs will cost less. This price range can also apply to weekend deals and rooms booked in the less popular winter months. Excluding accommodations, count on spending a **minimum** of $50 a day, which should cover breakfast, a cheap lunch, a budget dinner, and a beer. Taking taxis, eating fancier meals, and going out for drinks will mean allowing for more like $100 or more a day. If you want to go regularly to the theater, rent a car, or take tours, then double that figure.

What's particularly appealing about DC is how much you can do here **free**: guided tours of the major national museums, the US Capitol, and the White House; outdoor concerts, festivals, parades, and children's events – none of them costs a cent. And although not free, the **inexpensive** Metro and buses get you to DC's main attractions for $1.25–1.35 per ride (or upward of six bucks a day with a pass). Where admission is charged, **children** and (usually) **senior citizens** get in for half-price, and full-time **students** (holding an International Student ID Card, or ISIC), anyone under 26 (with International Youth Travel Card), and **teachers** (with International Teacher Card) often receive discounts. Contact discount and/or student travel agencies for applicable ID cards.

Sales tax in Washington, DC, is among the lowest in the country at 5.75 percent; this tax is in addition to the marked price on goods. **Restaurant** meals incur a 10 percent tax, while the **hotel tax** is 14.5 percent, added on top of the room rate.

Crime and personal safety

For many years Washington has had a poor reputation in terms of crime and personal safety. You'll be assuredly told that it's the "murder capital" of the United States, and stories of drug dealers doing business just blocks from the White House are in routine circulation among visitors and locals alike.

It's true – DC ain't Kansas. However, almost all the crime that makes the headlines takes place in neighborhoods that tourists won't be venturing into (most of Northeast and Southeast DC, and distinct parts of upper Northwest). When neighborhoods are borderline, this guide will tell you where you should and shouldn't go; if a sight or museum you really want to see is in a risky part of town, take a cab there and back. But this shouldn't be necessary in the places where you will be spending most of your time: downtown, the Mall, Dupont Circle, Georgetown, all the major tourist sights, the Metro system, and the main nightlife zones are invariably well guarded, well lit, and well policed.

Security issues

Following the terrorist attacks of September 11, 2001, and the US invasion of Iraq in March 2003, there have been major **security clampdowns** at DC landmarks and institutions. While traveling around the capital, you'll soon get used to the city's security regimen. At the biggest-name attractions on the Mall or Capitol Hill, you can expect airport-like security: your bags, coats, and personal belongings will be passed through an X-ray machine and you'll have to walk through a metal detector. At less-trafficked museums and attractions, a guard or two will inspect your bags and other personal items at the door. At places like the International Spy Museum, minor museums away from the Mall, and historic houses, you'll encounter eagle-eyed security guards, but they will probably do little to detain you as you enter. Keep in mind that tours of federal and national buildings – including the White House and US Capitol – are subject to cancellation or suspension at any time for security reasons, so call ahead and confirm your plans if you're making a special trip.

Be sure to **carry some form of ID** at all times while in DC. Two pieces should suffice, one of which should have a photo; a passport or driver's license and credit card(s) are best. A university photo ID might be sufficient but is not always easily recognizable. An International Student Identity Card (ISIC) is often not accepted as valid proof of age in bars or liquor stores. Overseas visitors (often surprised to learn that the legal drinking age in the US is 21) might want to carry their passport to prevent unnecessary hassles.

Mugging and theft

Most people won't have any security problems in DC, but if something does go wrong, contact the **police** immediately. Because DC attracts so many tourists, it certainly has its share of **petty crime**. Keep your wits about you in crowds, make sure your wallet or purse is secured, and, of course, avoid parks, parking lots, and dark streets at night. After the Metro has closed down, take taxis home from bars, restaurants, and clubs.

Always be careful when using **ATMs**, especially in untouristed areas. Try to use machines near downtown hotels, shops, or offices, and during the daytime. (ATMs outside tourist areas are prime spots to be mugged.) If the worst does happen, it's advisable to hand over your money and afterward to find a phone and dial ☎**911**, or hail a cab and ask the driver to take you to the nearest police station. Here, report the theft and get a reference number on the report so you can claim insurance and/or traveler's check refunds.

To avoid being the victim of **hotel room theft**, lock your valuables in the room safe when you leave, and always keep doors locked when you're in the room. Don't open the door to anyone you don't know or aren't expecting, and if an unexpected visitor claims to be a hotel representative, phone the front desk to verify their identity.

Having bags that contain travel documents stolen can be a big headache, so make photocopies of everything important before you travel and keep them separate from the originals. **If your passport is stolen** (or if you lose it), call your country's embassy (see list on p.42) and pick up an application form for a temporary passport, or have one sent to you. Complete the application and submit it with a notarized photocopy of your ID and a reissuing fee, often around $30. The process of issuing a new passport can take up to six weeks, so plan accordingly.

Keep a record of the numbers of your **traveler's checks** separate from the actual checks; if you lose them, call the issuing company on the toll-free number below. They'll ask you for the check numbers, the place you bought them, when and how you lost them, and whether or not you contacted the police. The missing checks should be reissued within a couple of days, and you can request an emergency advance to tide you over in the meantime.

Finally, remember that you should never flash money around, leave your wallet open, count money in public, or look panicked, even if you are. Also, it goes without saying that you should *never* hitchhike anywhere in DC, or indeed the entire US.

American Express Cards ☎1-800/528-4800, ⓦwww.americanexpress.com
American Express Checks ☎1-800/221-7282
Citicorp Checks ☎1-800/645-6556, ⓦwww.citicorp.com
Diners Club ☎1-800/234-6377, ⓦwww.dinersclub.com
Discover ☎1-800/DISCOVER, ⓦwww.discovercard.com
Mastercard ☎1-800/826-2181, ⓦwww.mastercard.com
Thomas Cook/Mastercard Checks ☎1-800/223-9920, ⓦwww.travelex.com or ⓦwww.thomascook.co.uk
Visa Cards ☎1-800/847-2911, ⓦwww.visa.com
Visa Checks ☎1-800/227-6811

Travelers with disabilities

The US is keen to accommodate travelers with mobility problems or other physical **disabilities**. All public buildings have to be wheelchair-accessible and provide suitable toilet facilities, almost all street corners have dropped curbs, public telephones are specially equipped for hearing-aid users, and even movie theaters have been forced by courts to allow people in wheelchairs to have a reasonable, unimpeded view of the screen.

The major hotel and motel chains are your best bet for accessible **accommodation**. At the higher end of the scale, *Embassy Suites* has been working to comply with new standards of access that meet or, in some cases, exceed the requirements of the Americans with Disabilities Act (ADA), by building new facilities, retrofitting older hotels, and providing special training to all employees. To a somewhat lesser degree, the same is true of *Hyatt* hotels and the other big chains such as *Hilton*, *Best Western*, and *Marriott*.

Getting around

American **air carriers** must by law accommodate customers with disabilities, and some even allow attendants of those with serious conditions to accompany them at a reduced fare. Almost every **Amtrak train** includes one or more cars with accommodation for disabled passengers, along with wheelchair assistance at train platforms, adapted on-board seating, free travel for guide dogs, and discounts on fares, all with 24 hours' advance notice. Passengers with hearing impairment can get information by calling ☎1-800/523-6590 (TTY) or visiting ⊕www.amtrak.com.

By contrast, traveling by **Greyhound** and **Amtrak Thruway** bus connections is often problematic. Buses are not equipped with platforms for wheelchairs, though intercity carriers are required by law to provide assistance with boarding, and disabled passengers may be able to get priority seating. Contact Greyhound's ADA customer assistance department for more information (☎1-800/752-4841, ⊕www.greyhound.com).

The **Washington Convention and Tourism Corporation** (see p.49) produces a free handout on the city's accessibility for people with disabilities; call ☎202/789-7000 or visit ⊕www.washington.org. Each station on the **Metro** system has an elevator (with Braille controls) to the platforms, and the trains' wide aisles can accommodate wheelchairs. Seventy percent of Metro buses have lowering platforms, and reduced fares and priority seating are available. The Metro website (⊕www.wmata.com) outlines the system's features in some detail under "Accessibility." There is also a free guide offering complete information on Metro access for the disabled at Metro stations, or you can call ☎202/637-7000 or 638-3780 (TDD). Travelers who are visually impaired or who use a wheelchair can call **Mobility Link** at ☎202/962-6464 for further information.

Major **car rental** firms can provide vehicles with hand controls for drivers with leg or spinal disabilities, though these are typically available only on the pricier models. Parking regulations for disabled motorists are now uniform: license plates for the disabled must carry a three-inch-square international access symbol, and a placard bearing this symbol must be hung from the car's rearview mirror.

Site access

Blind or disabled citizens or permanent residents of the US can obtain the America the Beautiful Access Pass, a free lifetime entrance pass to those federally operated parks, monuments, historic sites, recreation areas, and wildlife refuges that charge entrance fees. It also provides a fifty percent discount on fees charged for facilities such as camping, boat launching, and parking. The pass is available from the National Park Service (⊕www.nps.gov/fees_passes.htm) and must be picked up in person from the areas described. The Disabled Discount Pass ($3.50; ⊕www.parks.ca.gov) offers half-price concessions such as parking and camping at state-run parks, beaches, and historic sites.

Most **monuments and memorials** in DC have elevators to viewing platforms and special parking facilities, and at some sites large-print brochures and sign-language interpreters are available. The **White House** has a special entrance reserved for visitors in wheelchairs. (Call ☎202/619-7222 for more information on any site operated by the National Park Service.)

All **Smithsonian museums** are wheelchair-accessible, and with notice staff can serve as sign-language interpreters or provide large-print, Braille, or recorded material. The free *Smithsonian Access* is available in large print or Braille, or on audiocassette; call ☎202/357-2700 or 357-1729 (TTY). It's also available, as is an accessibility map, online at ⊕www.si.edu.

In addition, most new downtown **shopping malls** have wheelchair ramps and elevators. **Union Station** is fully accessible, as are the **Kennedy Center** (see p.162) and **National Theatre** (see p.167), both of which also have good facilities for visitors with hearing or vision impairments.

Information

Easy Access to National Parks, by Wendy Roth and Michael Tompane, is a Sierra Club publication that explores every national park from the point of view of people with disabilities, senior citizens, and families with children, and *Disabled Outdoors* is a quarterly magazine specializing in facilities for disabled travelers who wish to get into the outdoors.

National organizations facilitating travel for people with disabilities include SATH, the Society for the Advancement of Travelers with Handicaps (☎212/447-7284, ⊕www.sath.org), a nonprofit travel-industry grouping made up of travel agents, tour operators, and hotel and airline management; contact them in advance so they can notify the appropriate members. Mobility International USA (☎541/343-1284, ⊛www.miusa.org) answers transportation queries and operates an exchange program for people with disabilities. Access-Able (☎303/232-2979, ⊛www.access-able.com) is an information service that assists travelers with disabilities by putting them in contact with other people with similar conditions.

Electricity

The US operates on 110V 60Hz and uses two-pronged plugs with the flat prongs parallel. Foreign devices will need both a plug adapter and a transformer, though laptops and phone chargers usually automatically detect and cope with the different voltage and frequency.

Entry requirements

Keeping up with the constant changes to US entry requirements since 9/11 can sometimes feel like a hopeless task. At least once a year the American government announces new, often harsher restrictions on foreign entry into the country, adding considerably to the red tape involved in visiting it. Nonetheless, there are several basic rules that apply to these requirements, which are detailed on the US State Department website (⊛travel.state.gov). Check the site frequently for updates.

Under the **Visa Waiver Program** (VWP), if you're a citizen of the UK, Ireland, Australia, New Zealand, most western European states, or other selected countries like Singapore, Japan, and Brunei (27 in all), and visiting the US for fewer than ninety days, at a minimum you'll need an onward or return ticket, a visa waiver form, and a Machine Readable Passport (MRP). MRPs issued before October 2005 are acceptable to use on their own; those issued from October 2005 to October 2006 must include a digital photograph of the passport holder; and those issued after October 2006 require a high-tech security chip built into the passport. It is up to the various countries covered by the Visa Waiver Program to provide such passports to their citizens; for

more information, inquire at American embassies or consulates.

The **I-94W Nonimmigrant Visa Waiver Arrival/Departure Form** will be provided either by your travel agency or embassy or when you board the plane, and must be presented to Immigration on arrival. The same form covers entry across the US borders with Canada and Mexico (for non-Canadian and non-Mexican citizens). If you're in the Visa Waiver Program and intend to work, study, or stay in the country for more than ninety days, you must apply for a **regular visa** through your local US embassy or consulate. You will not be admitted under the VWP if you've ever been arrested (not just convicted), have a criminal record, or have been previously deported from or refused entry to the US. Under no circumstances are visitors who have been admitted under the Visa Waiver Program allowed to extend their stays beyond ninety days. Doing so will bar you from future use of the program.

Canadian citizens should have their passports on them when entering the country. If you're planning to stay for more than ninety days you'll need a **visa**, which can be applied for by mail through the US embassy or nearest US consulate. If you cross the US border by car, be prepared for Customs officials to search your vehicle. Remember, too, that without the proper paperwork, Canadians are barred from working in the US.

Citizens of **all other countries** should contact their local US embassy or consulate for details of current entry requirements, as they are often required to have both a valid passport and a nonimmigrant visitor's visa. To obtain such a visa, complete the application form available through your local American embassy or consulate and send it with the appropriate fee, two photographs, and a passport. Beyond this, you can expect additional hassles to get a visa, including one or more in-depth interviews, supplemental applications for students and "high-risk" travelers, and long delays in processing time. Visas are not issued to convicted criminals, those with ties to radical political groups, and visitors from countries identified by the State Department as being "state sponsors of terrorism" (North Korea and Iran, for example). Complications also arise if you are HIV positive or have TB, hepatitis, or other communicable diseases, or have previously been denied entry to the US for any reason. Furthermore, the US government now electronically fingerprints most visitors and applies spot background checks looking for evidence of past criminal or terrorist ties.

For further information or to get a **visa extension** before your time is up, contact the nearest US Citizenship and Immigration Service office, whose address will be at the front of the phone book under the Federal Government Offices listings, or call ☎1-800/877-3676. You can also contact the National Customer Service Center at ☎1-800/375-5283. Immigration officials will assume that you're working in the US illegally, and it's up to you to prove otherwise. If you can, bring along an upstanding American citizen to vouch for you, and be prepared for potentially hostile questioning.

US Customs

Upon your entry to the US, Customs officers will relieve you of your Customs declaration form, which you receive with your waiver form when it is handed out on incoming planes, on ferries, and at border crossing points. It asks if you're carrying any fresh foods and if you've visited a farm in the last month.

As well as food and anything agricultural, it's prohibited to carry into the country any articles from such places as North Korea, Iran, Syria, or Cuba, as well as obvious no-no's like protected wildlife species and ancient artifacts. Anyone caught sneaking **drugs** into the country will not only face prosecution but be entered in the records as an undesirable and probably denied entry for all time. For duty-free allowances and other information regarding Customs, call ☎202/354-1000 or visit ⓦwww.customs.gov.

US embassies and consulates abroad

Australia

Embassy
Canberra 21 Moonah Place, Yarralumla ACT 2600 ☎02/6214 5600, ⓦcanberra.usembassy.gov
Consulates
Melbourne 553 St Kilda Rd, VIC 3004 ☎03/9526 5900

Perth 16 St George's Terrace, 13th Floor, WA 6000 ☎08/9202 1224
Sydney MLC Centre, Level 10, 19–29 Martin Place, NSW 2000 ☎02/9373 9200

Canada

Embassy
Ottawa 490 Sussex Drive, ON K1N 1G8 ☎613/238-5335, ⓦcanada.usembassy.gov
Consulates
Calgary 615 Macleod Trail SE, Room 1000, AB T2G 4T8 ☎403/266-8962
Halifax Wharf Tower II, 1969 Upper Water St, Suite 904, NS B3J 3R7 ☎902/429-2480
Montréal 1155 St Alexandre St, QC H3B 1Z1 ☎514/398-9695, ⓦmontreal.usconsulate.gov
Québec City 2 Place Terrasse Dufferin, QC G1R 4T9 ☎418/692-2095, ⓦquebec.usconsulate.gov
Toronto 360 University Ave, ON M5G 1S4 ☎416/595-1700, ⓦtoronto.usconsulate.gov
Vancouver 1095 W Pender St, 21st Floor, BC V6E 2M6 ☎604/685-4311, ⓦvancouver.usconsulate.gov
Winnipeg 201 Portage Ave, Suite 860, MB R3B 3K6 ☎204/940-1800, ⓦwww.usconsulatewinnipeg.ca

Ireland

Embassy
Dublin 42 Elgin Rd, Ballsbridge 4 ☎01/668 8777, ⓦdublin.usembassy.gov

New Zealand

Embassy
Wellington 29 Fitzherbert Terrace, Thorndon ☎04/462 6000, ⓦnewzealand.usembassy.gov
Consulate
Auckland 3rd Floor, Citibank Building, 23 Customs St ☎09/303 2724

South Africa

Embassy
Pretoria 877 Pretorius St 0083 ☎12/431 4000, ⓕ12/342 2299, ⓦusembassy.state.gov/pretoria

UK

Embassy
London 24 Grosvenor Square, W1A 1AE ☎020/7499 9000, visa hotline ☎09042/450 100, ⓦlondon.usembassy.gov
Consulates
Belfast Danesfort House, 223 Stranmillis Road, Belfast BT9 5GR ☎028/9038 6100
Edinburgh 3 Regent Terrace, EH7 5BW ☎0131/556 8315

Embassies in Washington, DC

Australia 1601 Massachusetts Ave NW, 20036
☏ 202/797-3000, ⓦ www.austemb.org
Canada 501 Pennsylvania Ave NW, 20001
☏ 202/682-1740, ⓦ www.canadianembassy.org
Ireland 2234 Massachusetts Ave NW, 20008
☏ 202/462-3939, ⓦ www.irelandemb.org
New Zealand 37 Observatory Circle NW, 20008
☏ 202/328-4800, ⓦ www.nzembassy.com
South Africa 3051 Massachusetts Ave NW, 20008
☏ 202/232-4400, ⓦ www.saembassy.org
UK 3100 Massachusetts Ave NW, 20008
☏ 202/588-7800, ⓦ www.britainusa.com

Health

Although the US has a fearsome reputation for the lack of any national **health-care** system, foreign travelers should at least be comforted that if they have a serious accident while in America, emergency services will get to them sooner and charge them later. For emergencies, dial toll-free ☏ 911 from any phone. If you have medical or dental problems that don't require an ambulance but demand urgent attention, you can go to the walk-in emergency room at nearly any hospital: for your nearest hospital or dental office, check with your hotel or dial information at ☏ 411.

Should you need to see a **doctor**, consult the listings in the *Yellow Pages* under "Clinics" or "Physicians and Surgeons." Be aware that even consultations are costly, usually around $75–125 each visit, which is payable in advance. Keep receipts for any part of your medical treatment, including prescriptions, so that you can file a claim with your insurance company once you're home.

For minor ailments, stop by a local **pharmacy**; a few in DC are open 24hr. Foreign visitors should note that many medicines available over the counter at home – codeine-based painkillers, for one – are **prescription-only** in the US. Bring additional supplies if you're particularly brand-loyal.

Travelers from Europe, Canada, and Australia do not require **inoculations** to enter the US.

Insurance

As most people know by now, US health-care costs can be exorbitant, and you're well advised to protect yourself from such costs should any injury occur while in the country. Even though EU health-care privileges apply in America, UK residents would do well to take out an **insurance** policy before traveling to cover against theft, loss, and illness or injury. Before paying for a new policy, however, it's worth checking whether you are already covered – some all-risks home insurance policies may cover your possessions when overseas, and many private medical schemes include coverage when abroad. In Canada, provincial health plans usually provide partial coverage for medical mishaps outside the country, while holders of official student/teacher/youth cards in Canada and the US are entitled to meager accident coverage and hospital in-patient benefits. Students will often find that their student health coverage extends during the vacations and for one term beyond the date of last enrollment.

After exhausting the possibilities above, you might want to contact a specialist **travel insurance company**. A typical travel insurance policy usually provides coverage for the loss of baggage, tickets, and – up to a certain limit – cash or checks, as well as cancellation or curtailment of your journey. Most policies exclude so-called dangerous sports unless an extra premium is paid: in America, this can mean whitewater rafting, though probably not kayaking. Many policies can be changed to exclude coverage you don't need – for example, sickness and accident benefits can often be excluded or included at will. If you do buy medical coverage, ascertain whether benefits will be paid as treatment proceeds or only after your return home, and if there is a 24hr medical emergency number. When securing **baggage coverage**, make sure that the per-article limit – typically under £500/US$1000 – will cover your most valuable possession. If you need to make a claim, you should keep receipts for medicines and medical treatment, and in the event you have anything stolen, you must obtain an official theft report from the police.

Rough Guides has teamed up with Columbus Direct to offer you travel insurance that can be tailored to suit your needs. Products include a low-cost **backpacker** option for long stays; a **short break** option for city getaways; a typical **holiday package** option; and others. There are also annual **multitrip** policies for those who travel regularly. Different sports and activities can usually be covered if required. See our website (w www.roughguides.com/website /shop) for eligibility and purchasing options. Alternatively, UK residents should call ☎0870/033 9988, Australians ☎1300/669 999, and New Zealanders ☎0800/55 99 11. All other nationalities should call ☎+44 870/890 2843.

Internet

Given that the military-industrial complex itself had much to do with the creation of the **Internet** (which it called Arpanet), it's not surprising that Washington, DC, is one of the most connected cities on the planet. The spread of wireless hot spots all over the region means anyone traveling with a WI-FI-enabled laptop or PDA should have no trouble getting connected, often at fast speeds at no cost. At some **cafés** you'll need to use your credit card to sign up for a service, though many other cafés have unsecured access or will give you the password when you buy a coffee or muffin.

If you need to borrow a computer to log on, such cafés may be a good bet, though the city lacks any established cybercafé culture. You'll sometimes find a couple of computers in the corner for which there'll be a small charge, though these are becoming increasingly rare as places have taken out their machines when they've installed a Wi-Fi network. Many motels, hotels, and hostels also offer Internet access with a machine or two in the lobby, but again, Wi-Fi is taking over.

Although the District is otherwise well connected to the Internet, if you're not staying somewhere that offers Web access (Internet-friendly hotels are noted as such in Chapter 12), you may be forced to hunt down a FedEx Kinko's or similar spot (look under "Copying" in the *Yellow Pages*). You can log on at a major hotel's business center, but that can get pricey fast, so you're better off looking into alternative options like the Martin Luther King Jr Memorial Library (see p.187), where you can log on free for up to fifteen minutes at a time. And if you're so inclined before catching a flight at Dulles or National, you can use one of the credit card–activated Internet kiosks scattered throughout each airport. Finally, keep in mind that by far the easiest way to send and receive email on the road is to sign up with a free, web-based email provider like Yahoo! or Gmail.

Useful websites

Throughout the guide, websites are listed for those museums and other attractions that have them (most do). Beyond these, however, there is a handful of useful sites that are well worth a look when preparing your trip to DC, and can offer a particular slant or inside information on the District that you may not find elsewhere – from forthright and informative, to quirky or downright strange.

Art and culture

Embassy Events w www.embassyevents.com. Lists musical events, art shows, lectures, and other activities hosted by respective countries' embassies, as well as food and wine dinners and other culinary festivities. Also allows you to look inside those marvelous buildings around Dupont Circle and Kalorama. The site w embassy.org is also useful for this information.
National Academies Arts Exhibitions w www .nationalacademies.org/arts. Information about art and photography exhibitions and concerts held in science-oriented buildings.
Washington Art w www.washingtonart.com. Website where DC-area visual artists display their work online. Includes exhibition information, art discussions, and links to other local art sites.

Newspapers and magazines

City Paper w www.washingtoncitypaper.com. DC's alternative news weekly. Strong on reviews (both mainstream and off-the-wall), local events, and classified ads.
Washington Post w www.washingtonpost.com. The online version of the city's best newspaper, with a full, searchable database, entertainment guide, and visitor information.

Washingtonian ⓦwww.washingtonian.com. The online restaurant guide is the best part of the site; otherwise, plenty of information about living and working in DC, with a heavy upper-middle-class slant.

Politics

American Politics Journal ⓦwww .americanpolitics.com. Online, left-leaning political magazine providing a "moderate and humorous look at Beltway shenanigans," with daily updates, articles, and features by politicians, journalists, lobbyists, and other insiders.

The Hill ⓦhillnews.com. Aimed at those who can't get enough of inside-the-Beltway news, gossip, and intrigue. Covers current events, committee hearings, lobbying, campaign activity, and spirited punditry.

Thomas ⓦthomas.loc.gov. Online resource for legislative information. The only site with biographies of every member of Congress since 1774, the full text of the Constitution and other such documents, committee reports, roll calls of votes, and much more.

Tourism

Explore DC ⓦwww.exploredc.org. Up-close look at federal buildings, presidential sites, and African American highlights in the District. Its online tours of Civil War battlefields, historic architecture, and notable parks and gardens are particularly good.

Station Masters ⓦwww.stationmasters.com. Very effective site highlighting major attractions, buildings, and roads around Metrorail stations. Gives the location of parking facilities, station escalators and elevators, and train routes.

White House Historical Association ⓦwww .whitehousehistory.org. Online tours of the president's house, plus special features on the various presidents, resources for children and teachers, and a chance to buy a White House Christmas ornament for your tree.

Laundry

The larger hotels provide **laundry** service at a price. Cheaper motels and hostels may have self-service laundry facilities, but in general you'll be doing your laundry at a Laundromat. Found all over the place, they're usually open fairly long hours and have a powder-dispensing machine and another to provide change. A typical wash and dry might cost $4–6.

Mail

Post offices are usually open Monday through Friday, from 9am to 5pm, although some are open on Saturday from 9am to noon or 1pm. Ordinary **mail** within the US costs 41¢ for letters weighing up to an ounce, and 26¢ for postcards; addresses must include the zip code, which can be found at ⓦwww.usps.com or in zip-code directories in post offices. Domestic letters that don't carry a **zip code** are liable to get lost or at least seriously delayed. The return address should be written in the upper left corner of the envelope; if you need your local zip code, check in the phone book, which lists zip codes for the service area. **Airmail** to Europe generally takes about a week. Letters weighing up to an ounce (a couple of sheets) cost 84¢, and postcards cost 75¢ (63¢ to Canada and 55¢ to Mexico).

Drop mail off at any post office or, if it weighs less than thirteen ounces, in the blue mailboxes found on street corners.

You can have mail sent to you c/o General Delivery (known elsewhere as poste restante), at the central **Benjamin Franklin Post Office**, 1200 Pennsylvania Ave NW, Washington, DC 20004 (Mon–Fri 7.30am–5.30pm, Sat 8am–12.30pm; ☏202/842-1444), which will hold mail for thirty days before returning it to the sender – so make sure the envelope has a return address. Alternatively, any decent hotel will hold mail for you, even in advance of your arrival.

Rules on sending **parcels** are very rigid: packages must be sealed according to the instructions given at the start of the Yellow Pages. To send anything out of the country, you'll need a green **Customs declaration form**, available from the post office. Postal rates for airmailing a parcel weighing up to 1lb to Europe, Australia, or New Zealand are $14–18.

Maps

The maps in this guide, along with the free city plans you'll pick up from tourist offices, hotels, and museums, will be sufficient to help you find your way around DC. If you want something a bit more comprehensive, best is the small, shiny, foldout Streetwise Washington DC map ($6.95, ⓦwww .streetwisemaps.com), available from book, travel, and map stores in major cities. Another useful map is Mapeasy's illustrated Guidemap to Washington DC ($6.95, www.mapeasy.com), with detailed maps of downtown, Dupont Circle, and George-town. There are numerous basic, foldout road maps for DC, but the most worthwhile is the ADC *Washington DC Visitor's Map* ($7.95). If you really want to go all out, or are traversing the more unfamiliar outlying parts of the city, you can pick up the comprehensive *Thomas Guide: Washington DC Metro* ($38), a spiral-bound book that provides close-up, exhaustive coverage of even the smallest roads in the area.

If you'll be traveling beyond DC, the **free road maps** issued by each state are usually fine for general driving and route planning. To get hold of one, either write to the state tourist office directly or stop by any state welcome center or visitor center. Rand McNally (www.randmcnally.com) produces good commercial state maps, and ranger stations in national parks, state parks, and wilderness areas sell good local hiking maps for around $3. Camping shops generally have a strong selection as well.

The **American Automobile Association** (1-800/222-4357, www.aaa.com) pro-vides free maps and assistance to its members, and to British members of the AA and RAC. You can visit the local branch at 701 15th St NW, Washington, DC 20005 (Mon–Fri 9am–5.30pm; 202/331-3000, www.aaamidatlantic.com).

Money

With an ATM card, you'll be able to withdraw **money** just about anywhere, though you'll be charged $2–4 for using a different bank's network. Foreign cash-dispensing cards linked to international networks, such as Plus or Cirrus, are also widely accepted – ask your home bank or credit company which branches you can use. To find the location of the nearest ATM, call: American Express 1-800/CASH-NOW; Cirrus 1-800/4-CIRRUS; The Exchange 1-800/237-ATMS; or Plus 1-800/843-7587. Make sure you have a personal identification number (PIN) that's designed to work overseas.

The big-name **banks in DC** include East Coast entities like Wachovia and SunTrust. Most banks are open Monday to Friday 9am to 5pm; some stay open until 6pm on Friday, and a few open on Saturday from 9am to noon. For banking services – particularly currency exchange – outside normal business hours and on weekends, try major hotels or the DC-area branches of Thomas Cook.

Traveler's checks

US **traveler's checks** are the safest way for overseas visitors to carry money, and the better-known traveler's checks, such as those issued by American Express and Visa, are treated as cash in most shops. The usual fee for traveler's check sales is one or two percent, though this fee may be waived if you buy the checks through your home bank. It pays to get a selection of denomina-tions, particularly tens and twenties. Keep the purchase agreement and a record of check serial numbers safe and separate from the checks themselves. In the event that checks are lost or stolen, the issuing company will expect you to report the loss immediately (see p.38 for emergency numbers). Most companies claim to replace lost or stolen checks within 24 hours.

Credit and debit cards

Credit cards are the most widely accepted form of payment for major hotels, restau-rants, and retailers, even though a few smaller merchants still do not accept them. You'll be asked to show a credit card when renting a car, bike, or other such item, or to start a tab at hotels for incidental charges; in any case, you can always pay the bill in cash when you return the item or check out of your room. Most major credit cards issued by foreign banks are honored in the US. Visa, MasterCard, American Express, and Discover are the most widely used.

Credit cards can also come in handy as a backup source of funds, and they can save on exchange-rate commissions. Make sure you have a personal identification number, or PIN, that's designed to work overseas. Remember that all cash advances are treated as loans, with steep **interest** charges accruing daily from the date of withdrawal (there may be a transaction fee on top of this).

If your credit cards are **stolen**, you'll need to provide information on where and when you made your last transactions, and the specific emergency numbers (given on p.38).

Money: A note for foreign travelers

Given the major decline in value of the **US dollar**, at the time of writing one pound sterling will buy $2, a euro $1.40, a Canadian dollar $1, an Australian dollar 88¢, a New Zealand dollar 75¢, and a South African rand 15¢ – all of which makes visiting DC an attractive budget vacation.

US currency comes in bills of $1, $5, $10, $20, $50, and $100 **denominations**. All are the same size, though denominations of $5 and higher have in the last few years been changing shades from their familiar drab green. These days such bills offer more colorful pastels of faint red, yellow, and blue, and other embedded inks and watermarks – all to deter would-be counterfeiters. The dollar comprises one hundred cents, made up of combinations of one-cent pennies, five-cent nickels, ten-cent dimes, and 25-cent quarters. Quarters bearing individual state names and related historical designs are being rolled out one month at a time through 2008 (though DC isn't a state, so you won't find it). Quarters are most useful for buses, vending machines, parking meters, and telephones, so always carry plenty of them.

Opening hours

No matter how carefully you've planned your trip to DC, you may find the gates of your favorite park or museum closed if you've forgotten to take holidays and festivals into account. The regular **opening hours** of specific attractions, monuments, memorials, stores, and offices are given in the relevant listings throughout the guide, and telephone numbers are provided so you can check current information directly before embarking on your trip.

As a general rule, **museums** are open daily 10am to 5.30pm, though some have extended summer hours; a few art galleries, such as the Corcoran, stay open until 8 or 9pm one night a week, often Thursday. Smaller, private museums close for one day a week, usually Monday or Tuesday, and may be open 9am to 4pm or have more limited hours. **Federal office buildings**, some of which incorporate museums, are open Monday through Friday 9am to 5.30pm. Most **national monuments** are open daily 24hr, though they tend to be staffed only between 8am and midnight, and their gift shops will have more limited hours (typically daily 9am–5.30pm). **Shops** are generally open Monday through Saturday 10am to 7pm; some have extended weekend hours. In neighborhoods like Georgetown, Adams Morgan, and Dupont Circle, many stores open on Sunday, too, usually noon to 5pm. **Malls** tend to be open Monday through Saturday 10am to 7pm or later, and Sunday noon to 6pm.

While some diners stay open 24hr, most **restaurants** open daily around 11am for lunch and close at 9 or 10pm. Places that serve breakfast usually open early, between 6 and 8am, serve lunch later, and close in the early to mid-afternoon. Dance and live-music **clubs** often won't open until 9 or 10pm; many serve liquor until 2am and then either close for the night or stay open until dawn without serving booze.

In the wake of 9/11, many government buildings **suspended tours** and limited or prohibited public access. Some of these sites have reopened, while others remain fortress-like. Also, countless buildings have closed in the last few years for renovation (including the National Museum of American History). While these closings are noted in the guide, don't be surprised to find new, unexpected ones when you arrive.

Public holidays and festivals

On the **national public holidays** listed below, stores, banks, and public and federal offices are likely to be closed all day, as are many clubs and restaurants. Shopping malls, supermarkets, and department and chain stores, however, tend to remain open. The Smithsonian museums and galleries are open every day except Christmas. The traditional **summer tourism season**, when many attractions have extended hours, runs from Memorial Day to Labor Day.

Washington hosts a variety of **annual festivals and events**. America's Christmas tree is lit each December on the Ellipse in front of the White House; the grandest Fourth of July Parade in the country takes place around the Mall; and every four years in January (next in 2009), the newly inaugurated president proceeds up Pennsylvania Avenue from the US Capitol to the White House.

DC's full **festival calendar** is detailed in Chapter 17. It's important to remember that during certain times, like the National Cherry Blossom Festival in spring, Memorial Day weekend, the Fourth of July, and Labor Day weekend, it can be very difficult to find accommodation in the city, so it's important to book well in advance.

National holidays

January
1: New Year's Day
3rd Monday: Dr Martin Luther King Jr's Birthday
February
3rd Monday: Presidents' Day
May
Last Monday: Memorial Day
July
4: Independence Day
September
1st Monday: Labor Day
October
2nd Monday: Columbus Day
November
11: Veterans' Day
4th Thursday: Thanksgiving
December
25: Christmas

Telephones

Telephone numbers in this guide have a **202 area code** (for Washington, DC), unless otherwise stated. You do not need to dial the area code within the District. Outside DC, dial 1 before the area code and number. Calls within the greater DC metropolitan area are counted as local even if they require a different code (703 or 571 for northern Virginia, and 240 or 301 for western Maryland). Detailed information about calls, codes, and rates are listed at the front of the **telephone directory** in the *White Pages*. A local call on a public phone usually costs 50¢.

Of course, **mobile phones** are ubiquitous, and with excellent reception in all but the remotest areas, taking your phone to DC makes a lot of sense. Ask your provider to confirm that your phone will work on US frequencies (most do these days) and get it set up for international use. **Roaming** calling rates can be pretty high, so if you're planning to make a lot of calls, it may work out cheaper to **buy a phone** in the city, though the lower cost is counterbalanced by the need to tell all your friends your new phone number. Basic, new phones can be picked up for as little as $30.

Calling from your **hotel room** will cost considerably more than calling from a public phone. Fancy hotels often charge a connection fee of at least $1 for most calls (waived if they're toll-free), and international calls will cost a small fortune. While an increasing number of public phones accept credit

Telephone charge cards

Most long-distance companies enable customers to make **calling-card** calls billed to their home number. Call your company's customer-service line to find out if it provides this service, and if so, what the toll-free access code is.

As an alternative to telephone charge cards, cheap, **prepaid phone cards** allow calls to virtually anywhere in the world. Most convenience stores sell them; look for signs posted in shop windows advertising rates, which can vary dramatically, and check the fine print to make sure you're getting a good deal – many companies tack on exorbitant fees if you try to use their cards from a pay phone. Some cards allow you to add time to them as their minutes elapse through the use of a unique personal identification number, while others have only a set number of minutes available. Finally, prepaid calling-card companies may change their rates, policies, or deals on a month-to-month basis, or go out of business altogether, so if you're buying a card, make sure to use it within a reasonable amount of time, lest you end up with a worthless piece of plastic.

cards, these can incur astronomical charges for long-distance service, including a high "connection fee" that can bump charges up to as much as $7 a minute.

Any number with ☎800, ☎866, ☎877, or ☎888 in place of the area code is **toll-free**. Most major hotels, government agencies, and car rental firms have toll-free numbers, though some can be used only within the area – dialing is the only way to find out. Numbers with a ☎1-900 prefix are toll calls, typically sports information lines, psychic hotlines, and phone-sex centers, and will cost you a variable, though consistently high, fee for just a few minutes of use.

Calling home

Note that the initial zero is omitted from the area code when dialing the UK, Ireland, Australia, and New Zealand from abroad.

US and Canada international access code + 1 + area code
Australia international access code + 61 + city code
New Zealand international access code + 64 + city code
UK international access code + 44 + city code
Republic of Ireland international access code + 353 + city code
South Africa international access code + 27 + city code

Useful numbers

Emergencies ☎911; ask for the appropriate emergency service: fire, police, or ambulance
Directory information ☎411
Directory inquiries for toll-free numbers ☎1-800/555-1212
Long-distance directory information ☎1-(area code)/555-1212
International operator ☎00

Capital region area codes

202	District of Columbia (all)
240	Western Maryland
301	Western Maryland (overlay with above)
304	West Virginia
410	Eastern Maryland, incl. Baltimore
443	Eastern Maryland, incl. Baltimore (overlay)
540	Northern Virginia, not incl. most DC suburbs
571	Virginia suburbs of DC, incl. Alexandria and Arlington
703	Virginia suburbs of DC, incl. Alexandria and Arlington (overlay)
804	Northeastern Virginia, incl. Richmond and Williamsburg

Photography

With fabulous scenery abounding, many parts of the DC area can be a delight for **photography**. Bring plenty of digital memory or be prepared to visit photo shops periodically and burn your images onto CD. As ever, try to shoot in the early morning and late afternoon when the warmer, lower-angled light casts deeper shadows and gives greater depth to your shots.

As with everything in the capital region, care must be taken when taking snapshots around any kind of government installation. Usually, you'll be okay taking obviously tourist-oriented "Look at that pretty building!" photos, though some sights – the FBI and Pentagon come to mind – may even discourage that. Most parks and monuments welcome photography, and museum policies depend on the institution and the exhibit. It is never a good idea to take photos of military bases, security infrastructure, or anything else that suggests you're looking for a weak spot for some sort of attack – at best, you'll be questioned by a guard; at worst, you'll have your digital memory taken from you and be escorted from the premises.

Senior travelers

Seniors are defined broadly in the US as anyone older than 55 to 65 years of age. Those traveling can regularly find discounts of anywhere from ten to fifty percent at movie theaters, hotels, restaurants, performing arts venues, and the occasional shop. On Amtrak, they can get a fifteen percent discount on most regular fares, and ten percent off the purchase of a North America Rail Pass. On Greyhound the discount is smaller, in the range of five to ten percent. If heading to a national park, don't miss the **America the Beautiful Senior Pass**, which, when bought at a park for a mere $10, provides a lifetime of free entry to federally operated recreation sites, as well as half-price discounts on concessions such as boat launches and camping. At other sites like museums and galleries, a discount in the range of five to twenty percent may be offered.

Time

Washington, DC, runs on **Eastern Standard Time** (EST), which is five hours behind Greenwich Mean Time (GMT). Thus, when it's noon Monday in DC it is 9am in California, 5pm in London, 2am Tuesday in Sydney, and 4am Tuesday in Auckland.

Tourist information

The main sources of **tourist information** for the District are the DC Chamber of Commerce and the Washington DC Convention and Tourism Corporation. Both of these offices can send you brochures, visitor guides, events calendars, and maps in advance of your trip, and answer any questions once you've arrived; however, only the Chamber of Commerce visitor center is set up for walk-in visits. There are also numerous DC-related websites, most with fully searchable databases. These let you read up on the hottest new restaurants and clubs and can help you plan your sightseeing itinerary around the capital.

Information

On arrival, you'll find maps and other guides available in the airports, Union Station, and hotels. The most useful item to pick up is the free *Washington DC Visitors Guide*, with listings, reviews, and contact numbers. Once in the city, your first stop should be the **DC Visitor Information Center**, Ronald Reagan Building, 1300 Pennsylvania Ave NW (spring and summer Mon–Fri 8.30am–5.30pm, Sat 9am–4pm; fall and winter Mon–Fri 9am–4.30pm; ℡1-866/324-7386, ⓦwww .dcvisit.com), which can help you with maps, tours, and regionwide information.

Out and about in DC, other resources include the **White House Visitor Information Center** (see below), which has details on the Executive Mansion along with National Park sights all over the District, and the **Smithsonian Institution** building on the Mall (see p.95), which is the best stop for Smithsonian museum information.

You'll also come across National Park Service rangers – in kiosks on the Mall, at the major memorials – who should also be able to answer general queries. One of the most conveniently located ranger sites is the **Ellipse Visitor Pavilion** (daily 8am–3pm; ⓦwww.nps.gov/whho), on the east side of the Ellipse (in front of the White House) near the bleacher seats. **National Park Service Headquarters** runs an information office (Mon–Fri 9am–5pm; ℡202/208-4747) inside the Department of the Interior, at 1849 C St NW, that has information about all the city's national monuments and memorials. Additionally, neighborhoods like Georgetown and cities like Alexandria have their own visitor centers covering their respective sights.

Tourism offices

Alexandria in the Ramsay House, 221 King St, Alexandria VA 22314 ℡703/838-5005 or 1-800/388-9119, ⓦwww.funside.com. Daily 9am–5pm.

Arlington 735 S. 18th St, Arlington VA 22202 ℡703/228-5720 or 1-800/677-6267, ⓦarlingtonvirginiausa.com. Daily 9am–5pm.

DC Chamber of Commerce 1300 Pennsylvania Ave NW, Washington, DC 20005 ℡202/347-7201 or 1-866/324-7386, ⓦwww.dcchamber.org. Mon–Fri 8am–5.30pm, Sat–Sun 9am–4pm.

Georgetown 1057 Thomas Jefferson St, Washington, DC 20007 ℡202/653-5190, ⓦwww .georgetowndc.com. Wed–Fri 9am–4.30pm, Sat & Sun 10am–4pm. Doubles as a visitor center for the nearby C&O Canal.

National Park Service National Capital Region 1849 C St NW, Washington, DC 20240 ℡202/208-4747, ⓦwww.nps.gov. Mon–Fri 9am–5pm.

Washington, DC Convention and Tourism Corporation (WCTC) 901 7th St NW, 4th Floor, Washington, DC 20001 ℡202/789-7000; in the UK ℡020/8877 4521 or 01235/824482 for information pack; ⓦwww.washington.org.

White House Visitor Center 1450 Pennsylvania Ave NW, Washington, DC 20004 ℡202/208-1631, ⓦwww.nps.gov/whho. Daily 7.30am–4pm. Maps, brochures, and information about major city sights.

Special events lines

Dial-A-Museum ℡202/357-2020 Mon–Sat 9am–4pm; 900 Jefferson Drive SW, Washington, DC

20560. Smithsonian Institution exhibits and special events.

Dial-A-Park ☎ 202/619-7275. Events at National Park Service facilities.

Post-Haste ☎ 202/334-9000. *Washington Post* information line for news, weather, sports, restaurants, events, and festivals.

Tourist offices and government sites

Australian Department of Foreign Affairs
ⓦ www.dfat.gov.au, ⓦ www.smartraveller.gov.au

British Foreign & Commonwealth Office
ⓦ www.fco.gov.uk
Canadian Department of Foreign Affairs
ⓦ www.dfait-maeci.gc.ca
Irish Department of Foreign Affairs
ⓦ www.foreignaffairs.gov.ie
New Zealand Ministry of Foreign Affairs
ⓦ www.mft.govt.nz
South Africa Department of Foreign Affairs
ⓦ www.dfa.gov.za
US State Department ⓦ travel.state.gov

The City

The City

1

The National Mall

Occupying a majestic spread of two miles between the US Capitol and the Potomac River is the cultural and political axis of the United States, the **National Mall** (24hr; staffed with rangers daily 9.30am–11.30pm; ⓦ www.nps.gov/nama). The prime target for nearly every visitor to DC, this enormous swath of green in the middle of the city is a showpiece filled with many of the city's biggest-ticket attractions, including nine famous Smithsonian Institution **museums** – such as the national museums for Air and Space, Natural History, and American History – and the National Gallery of Art, itself spread over two huge buildings. The Mall also contains several of the city's (and the country's) most iconic **monuments and memorials**, dedicated to presidents Washington, Jefferson, Lincoln, and (Franklin) Roosevelt, and to veterans of the Korean War, Vietnam War, World War I, and World War II. The 2000ft-long, 160ft-wide Reflecting Pool, supposedly inspired by the Taj Mahal's landscaping and the Palace of Versailles' pools and canals, runs through the middle of the western half of the Mall, between the Washington Monument and the Lincoln Memorial. Though only two and a half feet deep at its center, it nonetheless holds almost seven million gallons of water.

The Mall's central spot in a planned capital city has made it an eyewitness to some of the most historically significant **social and political events of the twentieth century**: the 1963 March on Washington brought Dr Martin Luther King Jr to the steps of the Lincoln Memorial to deliver his "I Have a Dream" speech; in 1967, at the height of the anti–Vietnam War protests, the March on the Pentagon began at those same steps. Three decades later, in 1995, controversial minister Louis Farrakhan, of the Nation of Islam, led hundreds of thousands of black men to the Mall for the Million Man March. On several occasions, the AIDS Memorial Quilt – a patchwork of 40,000 individual squares remembering America's AIDS victims – has covered the full mile from the Capitol to the Washington Monument, and pro- and anti-abortion groups, as well as activists for and against the war in Iraq, have held passionate demonstrations here. For all its grandeur and tumult, however, the Mall is also a place to relax and party, notably at the annual Festival of American Folklife and on the Fourth of July (see "Festivals and parades", Chapter17).

As a visitor to Washington, you'll find the Mall almost inescapable on any tourist-oriented route. Provided you have a normal appetite for museums, galleries, and monuments, you'll need three days or so to get around its major sights – unless you just want to glimpse their exteriors, which you can do on a hearty four-mile walk. Still, it's better not to spend whole days at the Mall, if only to avoid complete cultural overload. Many of the attractions lend themselves to being seen with a combination of other city sights: the western

THE NATIONAL MALL

THE NATIONAL MALL

Capitol Hill

US Court House

Federal Triangle

Foggy Bottom

Arlington National Cemetery

PENNSYLVANIA AVE NW

CONSTITUTION AVE NW

National Archives

Ice rink & Sculpture Garden

National Gallery of Art West Building

National Gallery of Art East Building

National Museum of the American Indian

National Air & Space Museum

3RD ST SW

4TH ST SW

6TH ST SW

7TH ST SW

3RD ST SW

4TH ST SW

6TH ST SW

Federal Center SW

VIRGINIA AVE

SCHOOL ST

E ST SW

G ST SW

I ST SW

395

M

INDEPENDENCE AVE SW

MARYLAND AVE SW

C ST SW

D ST SW

Hirshhorn Museum

Sculpture Garden

Smithsonian Institution

Arts & Industries Bldg

L'Enfant Plaza

M

M

MAINE AVE SW

WATER ST SW

7TH ST SW

9TH ST SW

National Museum of American History

Joseph Henry Statue

Freer Gallery of Art

Enid A. Haupt Garden

Arthur M. Sackler Gallery

National Museum of African Art

L'ENFANT PROMENADE (10TH ST)

Washington Channel

Waterfront

MADISON DR NW

Smithsonian M

JEFFERSON DR

National Museum of Natural History

C ST SW Department of Agriculture

12TH ST SW

D ST SW

Francis Case Memorial Bridge

OHIO DRIVE

14TH ST NW

Dept of Commerce

15TH ST NW

Holocaust Museum

RAOUL WALLENBERG PL

14TH ST SW

Bureau of Engraving & Printing

JEFFERSON DR

MS RD SW

EAST BASIN DR

East Potomac Park

Pentagon

Ticket kiosk

Washington Monument

John Paul Jones Memorial

National World War II Memorial

CONSTITUTION AVE NW

17TH ST NW

Reflecting Pool

Constitution Gardens

Vietnam Veterans Memorial

Vietnam Women's Memorial

Lincoln Memorial

Korean War Veterans Memorial

DC War Memorial

West Potomac Park

INDEPENDENCE AVE SW

John Ericsson National Memorial

Martin Luther King Jr National Memorial

West Potomac Park

OHIO DRIVE

Tidal Basin Paddle Boats

Tidal Basin

Jefferson Memorial

FDR Memorial

George Mason (14th St) Bridge

EAST BASIN DR

OHIO DRIVE SW

Potomac River

500 yds

0

N

monuments with the White House and Foggy Bottom (see Chapter 4); the Jefferson and Roosevelt memorials with the sights along the Waterfront (see Chapter 3); and the museums on the Mall's east side interspersed with a stroll around Capitol Hill (see Chapter 2) or Old Downtown (see Chapter 5).

Some history

Despite the size and prominence the Mall enjoys today, from the early to mid-nineteenth century it was something of an embarrassment – a wild, stagnant piece of land that some saw as a metaphor for the country's then-unrealized potential.

A 400ft-wide avenue leading west from the Capitol was at the heart of French military engineer **Pierre Charles L'Enfant**'s original 1791 plan for the city; along it, he envisioned gardens and mansions for the political elite. Also, a commemorative monument to George Washington was to stand at the point where a line drawn west from the Capitol met one drawn south from the President's Mansion (what is today the White House). Due to lack of funds, work didn't start on the Washington Monument until 1848, by which time any prospect of the Mall transforming itself from a muddy, bug-infested swamp into a splendid, pleasant avenue was laughable: cows, pigs, and goats grazed on the open land, while the malodorous city canal (linking the C&O Canal in George-town with the Anacostia River) ran along the north side, stinking with rotting refuse, spoiled fish, entrails, and dead animals from Washington's Center Market on 7th Street.

Following the construction of the **Smithsonian Institution Building** between 1849 and 1855, eminent landscape gardener **Andrew Jackson Downing** was hired to design an elegant green space in keeping with L'Enfant's plan. However, the money only stretched to one tree-planted park near the Smithsonian, and people dared not venture there at night, since it quickly became the haunt of ruffians and criminals. What's more, by 1855, work had been halted on the nearby Washington Monument, which stood incomplete for the next twenty years as little more than a homely granite stump. The Mall continued to deteriorate, and as the city grew, its south side became home to sweltering meat markets and warehouses, while the grand avenue L'Enfant imagined was criss-crossed by the ungainly tracks of the Baltimore and Potomac Railroad.

During the **Civil War**, President Lincoln was determined to continue building as "a sign we intend the Union shall go on," and in the postwar Reconstruction era, the city canal was filled in (it's now Constitution Avenue); Center Market was closed; a Board of Public Works was established to build sewers, sidewalks, and streets; mature trees were planted; and, in 1884, the Washington Monument was finally completed. Several of Downing's other plans were resurrected, extending beyond the Mall to incorporate the grassy Ellipse and the gardens on either side of the White House, finally placing the Mall at the ornamental heart of the city – though the true shape of its grandeur would take another fifty years to be realized.

With the 1881 addition of the **Arts and Industries Building** (meant as overflow space for what was then known as the National Museum), the Mall came to be seen as a logical site for grand public institutions: the US Botanic Garden opened here in 1902, the Museum of Natural History in 1911, and the Freer Gallery – the Smithsonian's first art museum – in 1923.

Led by Senator James McMillan, members of the 1901 **McMillan Commission**, charged with improving the Mall and the city's park system, returned from Europe fired up with plans to link the Mall with a series of gardens and memorials, and to demolish an unsightly railroad station. Not everyone concurred, however: powerful House Speaker Joseph Cannon railed that he "would rather see the Mall sown in oats than treated as an artistic composition." But with Cannon leaving office in 1911, McMillan's proposals eventually prevailed and, following the completion of the Lincoln Memorial in 1922, the Mall was extended west of the Washington Monument for the first time, reaching to the banks of the Potomac River and incorporating the grounds known today as West Potomac Park (though much of the watery turf of the western Mall still had to be filled in and made to resemble something other than a swamp). More improvements were made in the 1930s under the auspices of President Roosevelt's Works Progress Administration (WPA), including the planting of the city's now-famous elm trees, and the **National Park Service** was granted stewardship of the Mall and its monuments.

The erection of the Jefferson Memorial in 1943 completed the Mall's initial triumvirate of **presidential monuments**. The monument's architect, John Russell Pope, also designed the contemporaneous National Gallery of Art in a similarly proper Classical style. The 1960s and 1970s ushered in **museums** of a more modern ilk, including the National Museum of American History, the National Air and Space Museum, the Hirshhorn Museum, and the National Gallery's East Building. In the 1980s the Sackler Gallery and the National Museum of African Art were opened. The dedication of the Vietnam Veterans Memorial (1982), the Korean War Veterans Memorial (1995), and the FDR Memorial (1997) demonstrated that there was still space for more additions – a concept that was tested even further with the 2004 arrivals of the World War II Memorial and the National Museum of the American Indian. The two latest proposals involve black history: the Martin Luther King Jr National Memorial, to be finished by the end of 2008 between the FDR and Lincoln memorials, and the National Museum of African American History and Culture, on the northeast side of the Washington Monument, recently proposed and with no firm date for completion.

Monuments and memorials

The Mall is laid out for easy navigation: **monuments and memorials** lie to the west, surrounding the Reflecting Pool, while **museums** sit to the east, and the Washington Monument stands between the two sides. Most visitors make a beeline for this central monument; head west to the World War II Memorial; drop down to the Tidal Basin and the Jefferson and FDR memorials; and continue on a clockwise path to the Korean War Veterans Memorial, the Lincoln Memorial, and the Vietnam Veterans Memorial, perhaps poking around Constitution Gardens, before making their way back to the Washington Monument – the circuit measures about three miles. Next they may head to the eastern side of the Mall, if there's any time left in the day.

Other than the Washington Monument, which sits about a quarter mile west of the Smithsonian stop, the various memorials and monuments on the western Mall are **not easily accessible by Metrorail**; the closest stops are Foggy Bottom–GWU and Farragut West to the north, but they are more than two-thirds of a mile from the Lincoln Memorial and farther from the rest. You can also tackle the memorials from the west: take the Metrorail to the Arlington Cemetery stop, arriving at the Lincoln Memorial on foot by way of the striking

Arlington Memorial Bridge. The closest approach, however, may be to take Metrobus #13 (routes A, B, F, or G), which loops around the north side of the entire Mall along Constitution Avenue to the cemetery and Pentagon and back, or the Tourmobile, which also runs along Constitution Avenue (see Useful bus routes, p.29, Washington city tours, p.30 in Basics).

The Washington Monument

15th St NW at Constitution Ave ⓣ202/426-6841 or 1-800/967-2283, ⓦwww.nps.gov/wamo; Smithsonian Metro. Daily 9am–5pm.

If there's one structure that symbolizes DC, aside from the US Capitol, it's surely the **Washington Monument** – an unadorned marble obelisk built in memory of America's successful revolutionary general and first president. Simple, elegant, majestic, and, above all, huge, it's the centerpiece of the National Mall and immediately recognizable from all over the city (and from planes landing at nearby Reagan National Airport), providing the capital with a striking central ornament.

Some history

L'Enfant's original city plan proposed erecting an equestrian statue of George Washington at the point at which a line drawn due south from the White House would meet one drawn due west from the Capitol – an idea that even the modest Washington approved of. Yet by the time of Washington's death in 1799, no progress had been made on the statue, though a small stone marker was later placed on the proposed spot by Thomas Jefferson in 1804 (the "Jefferson Pier" is still visible today). Impatient at Congress's apparent lack of enthusiasm for the work, in 1833 Chief Justice John Marshall and a very aged James Madison established the National Monument Society to foster a design competition and subscription drive. From this emerged US Treasury architect **Robert Mills**'s hugely ambitious scheme to top a colonnaded base containing the statues of Revolutionary War–era heroes with a massive obelisk; L'Enfant's original idea received a nod with the addition of a statue of Washington driving a horse-drawn chariot – the total price tag was a cool $1 million.

The Society, considering the meager subscriptions gathered for the monument, settled for the **obelisk** on its own, which it hoped would inspire such ardor that the rest of the monument could be completed in due course. Early excavations revealed that L'Enfant's chosen spot was too marshy to build on, and when the cornerstone was finally laid on July 4, 1848, it was on a bare knoll 360ft east and 120ft south of the true intersection (which explains why the monument is off-center on the map). To hasten construction and drum up enthusiasm for the project, the Society invited states and private groups to contribute commemorative blocks of marble for the interior walls around the stairwell; many groups agreed, including Pope Pius IX on behalf of the Catholic Church. The pope's contribution, however, enraged the anti-Catholic **"Know-Nothing" Party**, and on the night of March 6, 1854, masked party members stole the stone and promptly engineered the takeover of the Society. Soon after, federal funds for the monument dried up, and Congress refused to provide continuation money as long as the group was in charge. Undeterred, the Know-Nothings added several levels' worth of shoddy building and gave the monument an air of failure for another two decades, leaving it an incomplete stump just 152ft high. Grievously truncated, the monument was likened by Mark Twain to a "factory chimney with the top broken off." Factoring in the site – it stood beside the fetid Washington Canal and was often surrounded by cattle awaiting slaughter at a nearby abattoir – the *New York Tribune*, in an almost universally held opinion, condemned it as a "wretched design, a wretched location."

After the Civil War, Congress finally authorized government funds to complete the monument and appointed **Lieutenant Colonel Thomas Casey** of the Army Corps of Engineers to the work. Casey suffered his own tribulations, not least of which was the discovery that the original marble source in Maryland had been exhausted; you can still see the transition line at the 150ft level, where work resumed with marble of a slightly different tone. At long last, by December 1884, the monument was finally complete. The tallest all-masonry structure on the planet, it stands just over 555ft tall, measures 55ft wide at the base, tapers to 34ft at the top, and is capped by a small aluminum pyramid.

Visiting the monument

Once you gain access, a seventy-second **elevator ride** whisks you past the honorary stones in the stairwell and deposits you at the 500ft level, from where the views – glimpsed through surprisingly narrow windows on all four sides – are, of course, tremendous (though the windows could use some cleaning). There's not much else at the top, other than a gift shop shoehorned into an alcove, and you'll doubtless be ready to descend within fifteen minutes. Back on ground level, an exterior **bronze statue** of Washington faces east toward the Capitol. Almost 7ft high, this is a faithful copy of the renowned statue by eighteenth-century French sculptor Jean-Antoine Houdon that was commissioned for the Virginia State Capitol in Richmond and placed there in 1796. Washington, wearing the uniform of commander-in-chief of the Continental Army, holds a cane in one hand and is flanked by a bundle of rods and a plowshare, signifying authority and peace, respectively.

Due to security concerns, concentric stone rings have been built into the sloping knoll around the monument to prevent vehicles from getting too close to the structure. Surprisingly, the new design is not too unappealing, unlike the process you must endure to gain access to the monument in the first place.

To start, pick up a free ticket from the 15th Street kiosk (on the Mall, south of Constitution Ave; daily 8am–4.30pm), which will allow you to turn up at a fixed time later in the day. You'll need to get to the kiosk early (as early as 7.30am), as **tickets** often run out well before noon. You can avoid any uncertainty by reserving ahead at ☎1-877/444-6777 and paying a $1.50 service fee per ticket. Upon arrival, you'll be processed around the monument plaza and dutifully screened for security – no weapons are allowed, but also prohibited are food, backpacks, dogs, and strollers.

National World War II Memorial

17th St SW at Independence Ave ☎202/426-6841, ⓦwww.nps.gov/nwwm; Smithsonian or Farragut West Metro. Daily 24hr, staffed 9.30am–11.30pm.

For many years, a monument honoring the soldiers serving in the world's largest war was an idea that remained stubbornly on the drawing board, a situation made all the more frustrating as memorials to veterans of smaller wars found places on the Mall in the 1980s and 1990s. In 2004 the **National World War II Memorial** finally opened, to both acclaim and controversy. Some critics felt its design was outmoded and its position around the Rainbow Pool which once occupied the eastern end of the Reflecting Pool, overwhelmed the Mall and destroyed the views of the Lincoln Memorial. However, while the memorial's design is unabashedly old-fashioned, its place

▲ National World War II Memorial

on the Mall somehow seems central and appropriate, standing as a moving statement of duty and sacrifice.

Two arcs on each side of a **central fountain** have a combined total of 56 stone pillars (representing the number of US states and territories at the time of the war), 17ft high and decorated with bronze wreaths. In the middle of each arc stands a 43ft tower, one called "Atlantic" and the other "Pacific" for the two major theaters of battle, and within each tower are four interlinked bronze eagles and a sculpted wreath that, despite its bulk, seems to float above you in midair.

Beyond the carefully considered architecture and the FDR and Eisenhower **quotations** that are chiseled on the walls, a curving wall of four thousand golden stars reminds you of the 400,000 fallen US soldiers – a number matched only by the colossal carnage of the Civil War. Less conspicuous on the wall is a small, honorary piece of officially inscribed "graffiti" from the war era, "Kilroy Was Here," showing the titular scamp with his long nose poking out.

The DC War Memorial and John Paul Jones statue

A bit south of the World War II Memorial, you go from the Mall's newest war memorial to its oldest, the **District of Columbia War Memorial** (24hr; unstaffed), built in 1931 to commemorate soldiers who fought in World War I. Although a mere 21 years separate the two world wars, their memorials couldn't be more different, especially in regard to scale. Whereas the World War II Memorial is epically grand, centrally located, nationally oriented, and highly detailed, the World War I memorial is simple and humble – basically a small Doric temple hidden in a grove of trees just north of Independence Avenue, built in commemoration of the district's own soldiers who sacrificed their lives in a foreign war. Usually free of tourists or any visitors whatsoever, it offers a quiet and relaxing respite from the hubbub of the Mall – a place to snap an elegant photograph or just take a break before you wade once more into the throng.

Due south of the World War II Memorial and east of the DC War Memorial stands the proud **statue of John Paul Jones** – stranded on a traffic island at 17th Street and Independence Avenue. If the sculpted figure of America's first naval hero looks a bit wary, it's only appropriate: ironically, the World War II Memorial, which is in his line of sight, honors the alliance of the US with Britain – the European power Jones spent years trying to intimidate with his surprise coastal raids and aggressive nautical tactics.

The Jefferson Memorial

West Potomac Park, southeast bank of the Tidal Basin near 15th St SW and Ohio Drive ℡202/426-6841, ⓦwww.nps.gov/thje; Smithsonian Metro. Daily 24hr, staffed 9.30am–11.30pm.

Although **Thomas Jefferson** was America's first Secretary of State, its third president, author of the Declaration of Independence, and the closest thing to a Renaissance Man ever produced in America, it took until 1943 for his memorial to be built. It wasn't for the want of inspiration, as Jefferson was a speaker of six languages who practiced law, studied science, mathematics, and archaeology, and was an accomplished musician, keen botanist, and wine enthusiast as well as a lucid writer and self-taught architect of considerable prowess. By the twentieth century, though, the memorial site proved contentious: the US Capitol, Washington Monument, White House, and Lincoln Memorial were already in place, and the obvious site lay on the southern axis, south of the Washington Monument. Although all agreed that the creator of the lovely University of Virginia and elegant Monticello more than deserved a fitting memorial of real architectural import, many still bemoaned the destruction of some of the city's famous cherry trees when the ground around the Tidal Basin was cleared (a few protesters even chained themselves to the trunks), while others argued that the memorial would block the view of the river from the White House. More practically, the site proved difficult to reach, since the basin blocked direct access from the north. This, in fact, provides much of its charm today, as the sinuous walk around the tree-lined basin makes for a fine approach.

If the site had its critics, then so did the memorial. When **John Russell Pope** – architect of the west wing of the National Gallery of Art – revealed his plans for a Neoclassical, circular, colonnaded structure with a shallow dome housing a 19ft-high bronze statue, some said it was too similar to the Lincoln Memorial, while others criticized it as mere Classical pastiche. The design, indeed, was in keeping with Jefferson's own tastes: not only was it influenced by the Greek and Renaissance Revival styles that Jefferson had helped popularize in the United States after his stint as ambassador to France in the 1780s (eventually displacing the British-favored Georgian style), but it also echoed closely the style of Jefferson's own country home at Monticello, in Charlottesville, Virginia.

Today the Jefferson Memorial is one of the most recognizable and harmonious structures in the city: a white marble temple, reminiscent of the Pantheon, with steps down to the water's edge and framed by the cherry trees of the Tidal Basin. The standing bronze statue of Jefferson, by **Rudulph Evans**, gazes determinedly out of the memorial, while the inscription around the frieze sets the high moral tone, trumpeting: "I have sworn upon the altar of God eternal hostility against every form of tyranny over the mind of man." (Though missing is his more pointed comment, "The tree of liberty must be refreshed from time to time with the blood of tyrants and patriots. It is its natural manure.") Inside, on the walls, four more texts flank the statue, including words from the 1776 Declaration of Independence. On the lower level, a small **museum** devoted to

Jefferson reminds visitors of why the man is still worth admiring, even as it alludes to his discomforting, hand-wringing defense of slavery, and has a bevy of historical displays and mementos from his era. The area in front of the site occasionally hosts musicians and other entertainers who perform during the city's spring and summer celebrations, notably April's National Cherry Blossom Festival (see Chapter 17, "Festivals and parades").

The Tidal Basin

The pleasant and fetching **Tidal Basin** fills most of the space between the Lincoln and Jefferson memorials. This large inlet, formerly part of the Potomac River, was created in 1882 to prevent flooding, while the famous **cherry trees** – a gift from Japan – were planted around the edge in 1912. The annual Cherry Blossom Festival in early April celebrates their blooming with concerts, parades, and displays of Japanese lanterns, making this perhaps the best time of the year to visit DC, despite the considerable crowds. To take it all in from the water, rent a pedal boat from the **Tidal Basin Boat House**, on the basin's northeast side at 1501 Maine Ave SW (March–Aug Mon–Fri 10am–6pm, Sat & Sun 10am–7pm; Sept & Oct Wed–Sun only; two-seaters $8/hr, four-seaters $16/hr; ☎202/479-2426, ⓦwww.tidalbasinpaddleboats.com) – it's a real treat for children and a great way to experience waterside views of several famous monuments and memorials.

The long spit of East Potomac Park south of the Jefferson Memorial has more cherry trees, while if you walk around the western side of the basin, following Ohio Drive, you pass the FDR Memorial before reaching the 1926 **statue of John Ericsson** (daily 24hr, not staffed; ⓦwww.nps.gov/joer), south of the Korean War Veterans and Lincoln memorials. Ericsson, the Swedish-born inventor of the screw propeller, also designed the ironclad warship *Monitor* – known in its day as a "tin can on a raft" – which, in 1862, held its own against the Confederate vessel *Virginia* in the first naval conflict between ironclad ships. The memorial itself is a curious affair, topped with a heroic triad of Roman-style statues emerging from a blooming column of granite – representing a Norse Tree of Life – while a stone likeness of Ericsson sits impassively at its base, lost in thought and seemingly oblivious to public gaze.

The Franklin Delano Roosevelt Memorial

West Potomac Park, southwest bank of the Tidal Basin ☎202/376-6704 or 619-7222, ⓦwww.nps .gov/fdrm; Smithsonian Metro or #13 bus from Constitution or Independence avenues. Daily 24hr, staffed 9.30am–11.30pm.

DC's most recent presidential memorial, honoring **Franklin Delano Roosevelt**, president from 1933 to 1945, would never have been built had it been up to FDR himself. Accepting that he would one day be so commemorated, he favored a stone monument on Pennsylvania Avenue no larger than his office desk (see p.170), but after his death, others insisted on a far more impressive tribute. Designed by Lawrence Halprin and dedicated in 1997, the memorial sprawls across a seven-acre site on the southwestern banks of the Tidal Basin and is made up of a series of interlinking granite outdoor galleries – called "rooms" – punctuated by waterfalls, statuary, sculpted reliefs, groves of trees, and shaded alcoves and plazas. It's among the most successful – and popular – of DC's memorials, and there's an almost Athenian quality to its open spaces, resting places, benches, and inspiring texts. On a bright spring or fall day, with the glistening basin waters and emerging views of the Washington Monument and Jefferson Memorial, it's one of the finest places in the city for a contemplative stroll.

A wartime leader and architect of the New Deal, Roosevelt's political spirit is captured in a series of carved **quotations**, appearing on the walls, that defined his presidency – perhaps most famously in the words "The only thing we have to fear is fear itself." The four galleries of rustic stone (one for each of his terms in office) turn upon seminal periods: the first has a torrent of water symbolizing the miseries of the Great Depression; in the second gallery stand George Segal's sculpted figures of a city breadline, a dust-bowl couple in a rural doorway, and an elderly man listening to one of Roosevelt's famous radio fireside chats; in the third gallery, alongside a **seated statue of FDR** and the heartfelt message "I have seen war . . . I hate war," a tangle of broken granite blocks with water tumbling over them represents the World War II years. The memorial's most beloved element, however, sits at FDR's feet, where a sculpture of his dog Fala attracts countless children and shutterbugs, its pert bronze ears rubbed shiny from all the attention. The memorial ends in the fourth gallery, where a timeline of dates and events is inscribed in the steps; a statue of perhaps Roosevelt's greatest ally, his wife, Eleanor, stands; and a still pool represents his death in Warm Springs, Arkansas, on the cusp of the end of World War II.

There's great significance, too, in something most visitors don't notice about the memorial, namely that it is fully accessible to people in wheelchairs. At the age of 39, FDR contracted polio, which left him **paralyzed** from the waist down – a fact largely kept from the American people during his run for the governorship of New York and, later, the presidency of the United States. Believing that public knowledge of his disability would hurt his political career, FDR was almost always pictured standing while making speeches, and he only used his wheelchair in private. (Reporters and photographers aided him in this deception.) As in the original design of the memorial, the main sculpture of FDR portrays him simply as being seated – his legs largely covered by the flowing cape he wore at the 1945 Yalta conference with Winston Churchill and Joseph Stalin – while a later addition near the entrance shows the president clearly in his wheelchair, an image he took such careful pains not to reveal during his presidency.

Note that by the end of 2008, the **Martin Luther King Jr National Memorial** (details at Ⓦwww.mlkmemorial.org) will be unveiled on the northern flank of the FDR Memorial, between it and the Lincoln Memorial, showing the late civil rights leader and his legacy on a walkway that will also commemorate the various heroes and victims of the civil rights struggle in the 1950s and 60s and up to the present day.

The Korean War Veterans Memorial

West Potomac Park, southwest side of Reflecting Pool Ⓣ202/619-7222, Ⓦwww.nps.gov/kwvm; Smithsonian or Foggy Bottom–GWU Metro. Daily 24hr, staffed 8am–11.45pm.

The **Korean War Veterans Memorial** lies south of the Reflecting Pool, just a few minutes' walk from the Lincoln Memorial. Dedicated in July 1995, it is distinguished by a Field of Remembrance with nineteen life-size, heavily armed combat troops sculpted from stainless steel. The troops advance across a triangular plot with alternating rows of stones and plant life and head toward the Stars and Stripes positioned at the vertex. A reflecting black granite wall, with the inscription "Freedom is not free" and an etched mural depicting military support crew and medical staff flank the ensemble. It's not an entirely successful piece of sculpture, due mainly to the statues' faces being cruder and less expressive than those of the presidents and other war heroes sculpted along the Mall; the gravity of the conflict is also not as well expressed as in the other war memorials.

Lincoln and the Gettysburg Address

Abraham Lincoln's **Gettysburg Address**, beginning with the words "Four score and seven years ago," is the most famous piece of American political oratory of the nineteenth century, its themes of human freedom, democracy, and a developing idea of equality springing from the carnage and sacrifice displayed at an epic Civil War battle in the eponymous Pennsylvania town several months earlier. The address was meant to dedicate the grounds of a cemetery to hold the many thousands of war dead, and Lincoln's classical rhetoric was more than equal to the solemn task at hand – all in around two and a half minutes. Indeed, the official photographer at the dedication hadn't gotten his equipment ready before the president sat down again. Edward Everett, former senator and onetime Secretary of State, spoke first at the ceremony – for two and a half hours; he later admitted his long-winded oratory hadn't accomplished a fraction of what Lincoln's had. Yet the president's speech was poorly received by some: Lincoln was convinced that the audience had failed to appreciate its fine nuances, while the *Chicago Times* lambasted its "silly, flat, and dish-watery utterances." Other newspapers had a keener sense of history – *Harper's Weekly*, for example, thought it "as simple and felicitous and earnest a word as was ever spoken." If you'd like a glimpse at one of the few remaining copies of the address, the Library of Congress (see p.118) sometimes puts one on public display, hermetically sealed with argon gas to keep the document from decaying.

A plaque at the flagpole proclaims, "Our nation honors her sons and daughters who answered the call to defend a country they never knew and a people they never met." Indeed, almost 55,000 Americans were killed in the conflict on the Korean peninsula, with another 8000 missing in action and more than 103,000 wounded. Unlike those who fought in Vietnam, the American soldiers sent into battle by President Truman on behalf of the South Korean government went, tenuously, in the name of the United Nations, only to be drawn into a proxy war with China, which entered the battle when the troops came too close to its border. The memorial lists the fifteen other countries that volunteered forces, with Britain, France, Greece, and Turkey in particular suffering significant losses. While the memorial commemorates soldiers from allied countries, it doesn't give the number of Korean casualties: by some estimates, about three million (North and South) Korean civilians died – in addition to half a million North Korean, 50,000 South Korean, and possibly one million Chinese soldiers.

The memorial has a CD-ROM database (inquire at the visitor center), in which you can type the name of a fallen veteran and call up and print out the soldier's rank, serial number, unit, casualty date, and photograph; you can also find some of this information online at Ⓦ www.koreanwar.org.

The Lincoln Memorial

West Potomac Park at 23rd St NW Ⓣ 202/426-6841, Ⓦ www.nps.gov/linc; Foggy Bottom–GWU Metro. Daily 24hr, staffed 9.30am–11.30pm.

The **Lincoln Memorial** needs no introduction. As one of the country's most recognizable symbols, it represents both the United States' political ideology and its culture of social activism. The memorial is perpetually host to speeches, protests, events, and marches; less tempestuously, it effortlessly provides a backdrop for some of the most stirring photographs in town. The Reflecting Pool, the Washington Monument, and the US Capitol lie to the monument's east on the Mall's axis, and the Potomac River and Arlington National Cemetery are to its west – a bit less visually symmetrical, though no less stirring

History at the Lincoln Memorial

Although Lincoln is inextricably linked to the nation's abolition of slavery and long struggle with **civil rights**, ironically, at the memorial's dedication in May 1922, President Warren G. Harding and Lincoln's surviving son, Robert, watched the proceedings from the speakers' platform while Dr Robert Moton, the president of the Tuskegee Institute, who was scheduled to make the principal address, was forced to watch from a roped-off, racially segregated area. The memorial thereafter became a centerpiece in **demonstrations** urging the recognition of civil and human rights: Spanish Civil War veterans from the Abraham Lincoln Brigade marched here in 1938; a year later, on Easter Sunday, black opera singer Marian Anderson performed from the steps to a crowd of 75,000, having been refused permission by the Daughters of the American Revolution to appear at their nearby Constitution Hall. Anderson pointedly dedicated her performance to "the ideals of freedom for which President Lincoln died." Groups from the American Nazi Party to the Black Panthers have exercised their First Amendment rights at the memorial (as anyone can, provided you don't climb on the statue or hang banners from the building). But perhaps the memorial's brightest day was August 28, 1963, when, during the March on Washington for Jobs and Freedom, Dr Martin Luther King Jr delivered his "I Have a Dream" speech to 200,000 people who had gathered here. Five years later, in May and June 1968, after King's assassination, his successors brought the ill-fated Poor People's March to the memorial (see the "Resurrection City" box, opposite). During the height of the Vietnam War two years later, Richard Nixon made a strange and unexpected late-night visit to the site, where he discussed the war with sleepy protesters – a legendary event not covered by the media. Since then, the memorial has hosted everything from Louis Farrakhan's Million Man March in 1995 to George W. Bush's 2001 inaugural party, which showcased a squad of Rockettes high-kicking merrily down the steps.

a view. This solemn, inspirational memorial is the best loved of all the city's commemorative icons, and is regularly appropriated – in oratory and backdrop – by politicians of all stripes to advance some sort of policy that may or may not have anything to do with the legacy of the 16th president.

Proposals to erect a monument to the "Railsplitter" were raised as early as 1865, the year of Lincoln's assassination and, some felt, martyrdom at the hands of the South. While there was no shortage of ideas, there was a struggle to determine an appropriate tribute and site. One early plan suggested building a Lincoln Highway between Washington and Gettysburg, while arch-Neoclassicist John Russell Pope submitted four designs (including a vast pyramid and a stone funeral pyre), all of which were rejected. In 1901 the McMillan Commission finally approved the construction of a Greek temple in the marshlands of the newly created West Potomac Park, though House overlord Joe Cannon inveighed, "I'll never let a memorial to Abraham Lincoln be erected in that goddamned swamp." Nonetheless, work began on the memorial in February 1914 under the aegis of New York architect **Henry Bacon**.

Loosely modeled after the ancient Greek Temple of Zeus, the memorial has 36 Doric columns that symbolize the number of states in the Union at the time of Lincoln's death, while bas-relief plaques on the attic parapet commemorate the country's 48 states at the time of the memorial's completion in 1922 (Alaska and Hawaii get a mere inscription on the terrace). The president's surviving son, Robert Todd Lincoln, then 78, attended the dedication ceremony. As an indisputable icon of Washington, and indeed American, life, the memorial's architecture is indeed breathtaking, but for all its beauty, the temple is upstaged by what is inside – the seated statue of Lincoln by **Daniel Chester French** (1850–1931), which faces out through the colonnade. French certainly succeeded in his intention to "convey the mental and physical strength of the great war President": full of resolve, a steely Lincoln clasps the armrests of a thronelike chair with determined hands, his unbuttoned coat falling to either side. The American flag is draped over the back of the chair. It's a phenomenal work, one that took French thirteen years to complete, fashioning the 19ft-tall statue from 28 blocks of white Georgia marble.

Climbing the steps to the memorial and meeting the seated Lincoln's gaze is one of DC's most profound experiences. After your introductions, look out over the Reflecting Pool and down the length of the Mall, then turn back and gaze at the **murals** on the north and south walls. Jules Guerin painted these images, which represent (on the north wall) Fraternity, Unity of North and South, and Charity, and (on the south wall) Emancipation and Immortality. Underneath the murals are carved inscriptions of Lincoln's two most celebrated **speeches** – the Gettysburg Address of November 19, 1863 (see box, p.63), and Lincoln's Second Inaugural Address of March 4, 1865, in which he strove "to bind up the nation's wounds" caused by the Civil War.

The Reflecting Pool and Constitution Gardens

The view from the Lincoln Memorial would lose a significant part of its appeal were it not for the lengthy **Reflecting Pool** that reaches out from the cenotaph's steps toward the Washington Monument. The reflections in the water are stunning, particularly at night when everything is lit. Especially striking is the fact that all the memorials around the pool, save for that of Lincoln, commemorate twentieth-century wars.

Like the Lincoln Memorial, the pool was built in 1922. It was supposedly inspired by the Taj Mahal's landscaping and Versailles' pools and canals – in particular, how those designs demonstrated control over nature. Classical order was key to the pool's simple geometric layout, standing in contrast to the swamp that occupied much of the turf before the twentieth century. Though the surrounding area of West Potomac Park was originally to be landscaped, too, "temporary" cement bulwarks and office buildings erected around the pool

Resurrection City

At the time of Dr Martin Luther King Jr's 1968 assassination, the civil rights leader was planning a second march on the capital, which his successors saw to fruition. Under the auspices of the Southern Christian Leadership Conference, the **Poor People's March** (planned for May 14–June 28, 1968) converged on Washington from Mississippi, its organizers determined to force Congress to take a serious stand against poverty and unemployment. The 3000 marchers set up camp around the Reflecting Pool, in view of the US Capitol, and called their shantytown structures Resurrection City. Water and electricity were supplied, and churches and charities brought in food, but rain was heavy and the mud-caked camp quickly lost its momentum. Many residents left early; those who stayed were joined at the Lincoln Memorial by a crowd of 50,000 on June 19, Solidarity Day, to listen to a Peter, Paul, and Mary concert, and to hear various fiery speeches. However, the turnout was much lower than expected, and with an ebbing of public support, the dispirited camp was dissolved a week later as city police cleared away the tents.

during both world wars proved hard to remove. Reconstruction was only seriously considered when President Nixon suggested the grounds be reimagined as a Tivoli Gardens–style park in time for the country's bicentennial. However, financial concerns and aesthetic considerations produced, in 1976, the less flamboyant **Constitution Gardens**, a fifty-acre area of trees and dells surrounding a kidney-shaped lake on the north side of the Reflecting Pool south of Constitution Avenue. A plaque on the island in the center commemorates the 56 signatories of the Declaration of Independence; every September 17, Constitution Day, the signing of the Constitution is celebrated in the gardens by, among other things, an outdoor naturalization service for foreign-born DC residents.

The Vietnam Veterans Memorial

Henry Bacon Drive and Constitution Ave at 21st St NW ☏202/634-1568, Ⓦwww.nps.gov/vive; Foggy Bottom–GWU Metro. Daily 24hr, staffed 9.30am–11.30pm.

On the western side of Constitution Gardens, and due northeast of the Lincoln Memorial, the **Vietnam Veterans Memorial** is one of the most poignant tributes to be found anywhere. The Vietnam veterans who conceived of having a memorial in Washington intended to record the sacrifice of every person killed or missing in action without making a political statement. Once the grounds had been earmarked, a national competition was held in 1980 to determine the memorial's design, and a 21-year-old Yale student from Ohio named **Maya Lin** won, her entry provided in pursuit of a class project. (The original design is held and sometimes displayed in the Library of Congress's Jefferson Building.) Lin decided that the **names** of the fallen would be the defining feature of the memorial, and she chose to record them on walls of reflective black granite that point to the city's lodestars – the Lincoln Memorial and Washington Monument – and gradually draw you into a rift in the earth (or scar, as some would suggest).

The **names** of the 58,256 American casualties of the Vietnam War are etched into east and west walls that each run for 250ft, slicing deeper into the ground until meeting at a vertex 10ft high; they appear in chronological order (1959–75), and to each is appended either a diamond (a confirmed death) or cross (missing in action, made into a diamond if the death is confirmed). It's a sobering experience to walk past the ranks of names and the untold experiences they represent, not least for the friends and relatives who come here to leave tokens at the foot of the walls and make rubbings of the names. Brass-bound directories on each side of the memorial list the names and their locations for anyone trying to find a particular person, and a ranger is on hand until midnight to answer questions. The annual Veterans' Day ceremony held at the memorial on November 11 is one of the most emotional in the city, with the memorial walls decked in wreaths and overseen by military color guards.

Ironically, the memorial's nonpolitical stance came to be seen by some ex-soldiers as a political act itself, and lobbyists including eccentric Texas billionaire Ross Perot decried the lack of conventional white-marble beauty. In response to some of these complaints, a separate, more familiar martial statue was added just south of the site. Heralded by a sixty-foot flagpole flying the Stars and Stripes, the **Three Servicemen Statue** depicts young soldiers who, despite bulging weaponry and ammunition, have an air of vulnerability all too easy to understand in the bewildering maelstrom of Vietnam.

More lobbying – in particular by Diane Evans, a former army nurse – led to the creation of the **Vietnam Women's Memorial** in 1993, which stands in a grove of trees at the eastern end of the main site. Few realize that 11,000 American women were stationed in Vietnam (eight were killed), while almost a quarter of a million provided support services throughout the world during the conflict. The bronze sculpture, by Glenna Goodacre, shows one nurse on her knees, exhausted; one tending a wounded soldier (in a pose vaguely reminiscent of a *pietà*); and a third raising her eyes to the sky in trepidation. None of the servicewomen bears insignia, emphasizing the universal intent of the sculpture.

Finally, the Vietnam sculpture and war itself are still the subject of debate in some quarters, so yet another installation will be added to the general site in 2012. To be constructed closer to the Lincoln Memorial, the **Vietnam Veterans Memorial Center** will be a $100 million, two-level underground museum providing displays, photographs, and a time line of the conflict – though some fear that this latest add-on will be an attempt to put a more sympathetic spin on the war by acting as a counterbalance to the grimmer black arch on the ground above.

Museums and galleries

There are nine **museums and galleries** along the eastern side of the Mall, most of them national in name and scope, and all but one (the National Gallery of Art) coming under the aegis of the Smithsonian Institution. Since they're all **free**, expect them to be packed with families and school groups, and plan to get jostled around and wait to see the most popular exhibits. Winter and off-season

Smithsonian practicalities

There are nine excellent **Smithsonian Institution museums** on the Mall, and the original building – known as the Smithsonian **Castle** – today serves as the main information center. The first building to house overflow space for this National Museum, now dubbed the Arts and Industries Building, is closed for renovation. Other sites and museums sit at some distance from the Mall: the Renwick Gallery (see p.149), across the street from the White House, focuses on arts and crafts from the nineteenth to the twenty-first century; the National Postal Museum (see p.124) is across from Union Station on Capitol Hill; the American Art Museum and the National Portrait Gallery (see p.177 and p.181), in Old Downtown, have recently emerged from extensive renovation in glorious fashion; the Anacostia Museum (see p.138) lies south of the eponymous river in a grim part of town; the National Zoological Park (see p.226) is a few miles north of the Mall around Rock Creek Park; and the Steven F. Udvar-Hazy Center (see p.353) is a branch of the National Air and Space Museum, way out in Chantilly, Virginia, and accessible by car or shuttle. The Cooper-Hewitt National Design Museum is also part of the Smithsonian, but it is in New York City, far beyond the scope of a DC trip.

All Smithsonian museums and galleries are **open daily all year** (except Christmas Day) from 10am until 5.30pm; some have extended spring and summer hours. Admission is free, though charges are levied for some special exhibitions. For details on **current exhibitions and events**, pick up a free brochure at one of the museums, or by calling ☏202/633-1000 or 633-5285 (TTY) (Mon–Fri 9am–5pm, Sat & Sun 10am–4pm). The Smithsonian's homepage is ⊛www.si.edu or www.smithsonian.org. (To read about the history of the institution, see the "Smithsonian story" box, p.95.)

weekdays are best for viewing the museums, while during other times of the year, mornings (10–11am) may be marginally better than afternoons. At the top of many lists are the kid-friendly national museums for Air and Space, Natural History, and American History, and the more adult-oriented National Gallery of Art. Less-visited institutions include the Hirshhorn Museum for modern art and sculpture, the National Museum of Asian Art (with its separate Sackler and Freer galleries), and the National Museum of the American Indian. The route below continues the one left off in the "Monuments and memorials" section, heading east from the Washington Monument on a clockwise path from the Reflecting Pool. Note that at some indeterminate time in the next two to four years, the proposed **National Museum of African American History and Culture** (details at ⓦnmaahc.si.edu) will occupy a prominent position at the start of this route, immediately west of the American History museum and at the northeast foot of the Washington Monument.

National Museum of American History

14th St NW and Constitution Ave ⓣ202/633-1000, ⓦwww.americanhistory.si.edu; Federal Triangle or Smithsonian Metro. Daily 10am–5.30pm. Closed for renovation until summer 2008.

The major museums east of the Washington Monument begin with a procession of big-name Smithsonian institutions. The first of these, on the north side of the Mall, is the **National Museum of American History**, deservedly one of the country's most popular museums, with objects taken from nearly four hundred years of American and pre-American history. You're apt to find anything from George Washington's wooden teeth to Jackie Kennedy's designer dresses to Judy Garland's ruby slippers from *The Wizard of Oz*. You could easily spend a full day poking around the displays, but three to four hours would be a reasonable compromise – and to stick to this time frame, you'll have to be selective.

The museum's roots lie in prodigious bequests made to the original Smithsonian Institution, beginning with pieces left over from Philadelphia's 1876 **Centennial Exhibition**. Each item collected was destined for the "National Museum" (now the Arts and Industries Building), but since this meant displaying stuffed animals alongside portraits, postage stamps, and patent models, the Smithsonian was soon forced to specialize. An attempt was made to direct part of the collection by founding a National Museum of History and Technology in 1954, for which an ungainly modernist box was erected a decade later. The final name change in 1980 was a belated acceptance of the constant underlying theme: that the museum of "American History" firmly relates its exhibits to the experiences of the American people. In 2006 the museum closed for a two-year **renovation**, to reopen in summer 2008, with the space reimagined in a still modern but brighter and airier design with a skylight cutting through the building, fairly open layout, and better internal access among the floors. Although this is past publication date for this book, certain collections will be wholly maintained and the design for the new facility has been publicly revealed by the Smithsonian – however, make sure to check with a current museum map to find out the current locations of objects you want to see, since galleries will no doubt shift around in the new facility.

Museum practicalities

The museum is known for its quality **shop** and **bookstore**, as well as the main **cafeteria**, previously all on the lower level. The first floor has an ice-cream parlor; a café serving coffee, fruit, and snacks (it may also include a 1950s-style automatic vending machine, known as an Automat); and a functioning **post office** counter inside a transplanted nineteenth-century general store. Ask at the information desks for details about free **tours**, **lectures**, and **events**, including demonstrations of antique musical instruments, printing presses, and machine tools. The desks, at both Mall (second-floor) and Constitution Avenue (first-floor) entrances, are staffed from 10am to 4pm.

First floor

Upon entering from Constitution Avenue, the first thing previous visitors to the museum will notice is the significantly more spacious layout of the **first floor**, which, though not as open as the second floor (see below), now has far fewer of its gallery spaces crammed into uncomfortable alcoves and corridors. A wide common area off the lobby is lined with new "**artifact walls**" that show off some of the items that the museum previously had to keep in storage. The idea is for these glassed-in walls to provide different, eclectic artifacts for you to muse over, anything from 200-year-old tavern signs and toy chests to the **John Bull**, the nation's oldest functioning steam locomotive, dating from 1831.

Traditionally, the regular gallery displays on the first floor have showcased the technological advancements and the economic, industrial, and agricultural prowess that brought the US to its position of global power. Also on view, either here or elsewhere in the building, will be "**Science in American Life**," which covers every scientific development you can think of from recent decades – including cell phones, birth control, microwave ovens, nylon, nuclear power, and plastics. In the interactive "**Hands On Science Center**," you can, among other things, identify fossils, take intelligence tests, and use DNA fingerprinting methods to solve a crime.

The similarly interactive "**Information Age**" traces communications from Morse's first telegraph to modern information technology. Some of the most remarkable relics are the early models from Alexander Graham Bell's first experiments with the telephone, a device he exhibited to universal amazement at the 1876 Centennial Exhibition in Philadelphia; only thirteen years later, the first public pay phone, a bulky box, was installed in Hartford, Connecticut. Among other diversions, you may listen to excerpts from early radio programs, deal with a 911 emergency call, or watch archival newsreel and movie footage. The development of computers is shown with the thirty-ton **ENIAC** (Electronic Numerical Integrator and Computer), built for the US Army during World War II, which could compute a thousand times faster than any existing machine but took up a 30ft-by-50ft room – the equivalent in today's computer memory of a half-millimeter silicon chip.

The "**America on the Move**" exhibit is one of the highlights of the museum, an unapologetic celebration of urban, rural, and long-distance transit from the nineteenth century to the present. The exhibition starts with the locomotive in the post–Civil War era and in rough chronological order covers the cultural, economic, and social impact of transportation up to the modern age. To most visitors, the main story here will be familiar: how the US began with covered wagons and trains (shown with a huge locomotive from the Southern Railway), was revolutionized by early automobiles (from the first car to make a transcontinental trip, in 1903, to later Model Ts, Studebakers, and Chryslers), and ended up having to deal with urban gridlock and finding alternative means of transit (a walk-in Chicago elevated train is a highlight). Beyond this tale are equally interesting side stories of the new age in transportation – from the old East Coast docks giving way to transpacific container shipping in the 1960s, to the roadside cultures that developed around highways like Route 66, to the emergence of crudely functional "tourist cabins" in the 1930s, shown here with a re-creation of a creepy little Maryland shotgun shack. The story ends in an eye-popping room titled "Los Angeles and the World," with 21 video monitors, light boxes, and an electronic news ticker showing how Southern California has emerged as the nation's busiest automotive center and largest US port.

Although the exact floor plans are up in the air at the time of writing, a few lingering oddments from America's olden days will doubtless continue to be on display. Among these may be the rump version of "**American Maritime Enterprise**" – which has model boats, seafaring paraphernalia, and an entire ship's steam engine on two levels – and truncated rooms devoted to "Power Machinery" (big drills), "Agriculture" (giant combines), "On Time" (pocket watches to atomic clocks), and "Electricity," which celebrates Thomas Edison's light bulb and Ben Franklin's kite-flying.

Second floor

No level of the museum has benefited more from the renovation than the **second floor**, connected to the first floor by a wide stairway and illuminated by a towering five-story skylight – a blast of light that would have been much appreciated in the museum's murky old design and awkward geometry. With the new layout, the arrangement of certain rooms and exhibits is still in flux, so some of the displays described below may or may not be on view, or relocated to another floor; consult a museum guide to properly navigate your way around.

If form holds, many of the museum's social and political exhibits will continue to occupy the second floor. Upon entering from the National Mall, one of the first things you'll see will be the silvery abstraction advertising the new Star-Spangled Banner Gallery (see opposite), the museum's focus and one of the reasons why it draws as many visitors as it does. Much less impressive is the second floor's previous focus of attention, which will still be found somewhere around the floor, Horatio Greenhough's much-ridiculed **statue of George Washington**, commissioned in 1832 during the centennial of Washington's birth. Greenhough was paid $5000 by Congress and in 1841 came up with an imperious, almost dictatorial, throne-seated, toga-clad Washington with swept-back hair, bare pumped-up torso, and Roman sandals (mothers reputedly covered their children's eyes at its unveiling).

The history of African American migration from 1915 to 1940 is recounted in "**Field to Factory**," which tells how the demand for unskilled labor, stimulated by World War I, prompted hundreds of thousands of African Americans to move from the fields of the South to the factories of the North. The "Great Migration" proved a momentous and unprecedented change, establishing strong black communities in diverse Northern cities; most of the documents, photographs, and exhibits describe the experiences of individuals – from recorded voices of migrants as they traveled north on the (segregated) trains to re-creations of the new domestic situations they encountered on a farm in southern Maryland or in a Philadelphia tenement. Also on this floor will likely be the installation of the famous **Woolworth's Lunch Counter**, whose handful of stools and counter in Greensboro, North Carolina, were the site of one of the South's seminal civil rights protests, as African Americans held a sit-in and related boycotts to protest the segregationist policies of this and other businesses and municipalities of the early 1960s.

Elsewhere, "**Communities in a Changing Nation**" has nineteenth-century America showcased through various social environments – a slave cabin from South Carolina, an indigent peddler's cart, a wealthy Gothic Revival bedroom interior. In "**Within These Walls**," two hundred years of history are brought into focus through the stories of five families and their Massachusetts home, which has literally been transplanted and its skeleton made visible, from the core wooden structure to accrued layers of paint and grime. Continuing on, "**American Encounters**" looks at how sixteenth- and seventeenth-century Hispanic invasions and, later, tourism have affected the native communities of New Mexico – in particular, the Pueblo Indians of Santa Clara and Chimayo. Traditional and contemporary applied art, in the shape of ornate rugs, chests, figurines, and ceramics, sits alongside photographs, videos, and recordings of narrative stories, music, and dance.

Other sections of the museum are devoted to presidential life in and beyond the White House, centered around the **Ceremonial Court**, a re-creation of the White House's Cross Hall as it appeared after its 1902 renovation. The Smithsonian managed to purloin and incorporate some original architectural bits and pieces into the design; the displays of glass, porcelain, tinware, and silver are all from the White House collections. More satisfying is the cabinet displaying presidents' personal items: Washington's telescope, Grant's leather cigar case, Nixon's gold pen, Wilson's golf clubs, Jefferson's eyeglasses, and Theodore Roosevelt's toiletry set.

Off the Ceremonial Court, "**First Ladies**" begins with portraits of each presidential wife, from Martha Washington onward. Though there's an attempt to provide biographical padding, and exhibits exhort viewers to appreciate First Ladies as political partners or preservers of White House culture and history, the real fun here is in the frocks. Helen Herron Taft was the first to present her inaugural ball gown to the Smithsonian for preservation, starting a tradition that allows the museum to display a backlit collection of considerable interest, if not always taste. Other outfits provide revealing historical snapshots: Jackie Kennedy's simple brocaded dress and jacket raised hemlines in America almost overnight. There's access from the Ceremonial Court to "**From Parlor to Politics**," covering the history of women and political reform (1890–1925) with informative exhibits on women's clubs, the temperance movement, and voting rights.

Star-Spangled Banner Gallery

Set prominently in its own chamber, the museum's key attraction is the faded and battered red, white, and blue flag that inspired the writing of the US national anthem: the **Star-Spangled Banner**, which survived the British bombing of Baltimore harbor during the War of 1812.

With dimensions of about 30ft by 34ft, and (backed by heavy linen) weighing 150 pounds, it has fifteen stars and fifteen stripes, representing the fifteen states in the Union at the time of the war. There was no fixed design for the national flag in the early days of the new republic, and arguments raged over the relative prominence to be given to existing and future states. Congress eventually settled on the more familiar thirteen stripes (for the number of original colonies), while adding a new star to the flag each time a state joined the Union.

The flag is famously tattered after the battle and the intercession of two centuries, but it is still something of a marvel, preserved through years of painstaking labor by historians and technicians and enclosed in a new sealed chamber in a darkened room. Here, you can sit reverentially in front of the banner, lit under dramatic mood lighting, or linger in the dim corridors that lead into the room, which detail the history of the flag.

The story begins in August 1814, when, after burning the Capitol and White House in Washington, DC, the British turned their attention toward nearby

Baltimore, then America's third-largest city, which was defended by the garrison at **Fort McHenry**. To reinforce his defiance of the superior British force, the commander ordered the making of a large American flag, which was hoisted high above the fort in Baltimore harbor. The British attacked on the night of September 13, subjecting fort and harbor defenses to a ferocious bombardment, which the Americans could scarcely counter with their low stocks of weaponry. **Francis Scott Key**, a 35-year-old Georgetown lawyer and part-time poet, witnessed the battle. Attempting to negotiate the release of American prisoner Dr William Beanes, Key had been held on board a British ship that night and, come "dawn's early light," was amazed to see not only that the flag was still "so gallantly streaming," but that the cannons of the outnumbered Americans had forced the British to withdraw.

Taking the bombardment as his inspiration, Key dashed off a poem titled "**The Defense of Fort McHenry**," which he set to the tune of a contemporary English drinking song called "To Anacreon in Heaven." The first public performance of the song took place in Baltimore a month after the battle, and it soon became an immensely popular rallying cry, despite being notoriously difficult to sing. Union troops adopted it during the Civil War, and it became the armed forces' anthem in 1916 – although it didn't become the official **national anthem** until Herbert Hoover issued a decree in 1931. Despite Key's original title, the song became known as "The Star-Spangled Banner" almost immediately; indeed, the felicitous phrase had already occurred to Key in an earlier poem celebrating the exploits of Stephen Decatur against the Barbary pirates, which contained the words "the star-spangled flag."

Third floor

Also improved by the new renovation, the museum's third floor will likely commemorate the various aspects of American culture, presidents, and armed forces, with a number of items on display in the **artifact walls** lining the corridors (see p.69 for description). "**American Popular Culture**" includes Dorothy's slippers from *The Wizard of Oz* (silver in the original Frank Baum stories, but changed to ruby-red to hype the Technicolor process), Muhammad Ali's boxing gloves, Michael Jordan's NBA jersey, a baseball autographed by Babe Ruth, Archie Bunker's chair, Dizzy Gillespie's trumpet, and a *Star Trek* phaser. Other displays you may see cover "Women in Jazz" – with recordings of such figures as Ella Fitzgerald and Sarah Vaughan – as well as musical instruments, textiles, money, and medals. Amid the racks of English and American porcelain, eighteenth-century grand pianos, and coins and notes from around the world is a display on the life and work of DC native and jazz legend Duke Ellington.

"**The American Presidency: A Glorious Burden**" focuses on various aspects of presidential life, revealing everything from the ways in which the chief executive has communicated with the public to how the office has fared under the gaze of Hollywood's lens. The exhibition displays a fascinating array of objects, including George Washington's general's uniform and Revolutionary War sword, the "fireside chat" microphone through which Franklin Roosevelt soothed an America mired in the Great Depression, and a pair of Mao and Nixon table-tennis paddles, souvenirs from the days of "Ping Pong Diplomacy." In a section devoted to "**Assassinations and Mourning**," you'll find one of the Smithsonian's most prized relics – the top hat Abraham Lincoln wore to Ford's Theatre on the last night of his life. By contrast, a stroke of luck and a fifty-page speech in just the right place spared

Theodore Roosevelt's life as the former president was stumping to win another term; a display case contains the speech's first page, complete with bullet hole. With a flair for the theatrical even while grievously wounded, Roosevelt would finish the speech before being ushered away to patch up his wound. Elsewhere is the Rough Rider's most cherished legacy: the iconic teddy bear, its design inspired by Roosevelt's refusal to shoot a captured bear cub on a hunting trip.

As if the surfeit of war memorials around town didn't already remind you, "**The Price of Freedom**" covers America's long-standing support of, and occasional ambivalence about, its armed forces. Bringing together a number of military-oriented artifacts from previous Smithsonian collections, the gallery arrays them on a chronological course that begins with the Colonial-era French and Indian War and proceeds up to today's welter of global conflicts. One indisputable highlight is the oak gunboat *Philadelphia*, the oldest US man-of-war in existence. In 1776, in a campaign against the British on Lake Champlain, 63 men lived on this tiny ship for three months, suffering extraordinary privation – there was no upper or lower deck and only a canvas cover to protect them from the elements. Also on display is General Washington's linen tent (his campaign headquarters during the Revolutionary War) alongside his camp chest complete with tin plate and coffeepot. Numerous weapons also make appearances, from Colonial muskets to modern machine guns, as do model-ship displays and artillery pieces.

Also potentially included in this area will be the previous "**A More Perfect Union**" display, dealing with the shameful era of Japanese internment camps, in which thousands of American citizens were sent to isolated compounds for fear of their being World War II traitors. The displays contrast the dismal life in barracks at home with the valor of Japanese American combat units, who at the end of the war at least had their medals to prove their worth – the civilian Japanese Americans, who had committed no crime other than to be born with the wrong "characteristics," got $25 and a ticket home.

National Museum of Natural History

10th St NW and Constitution Ave ⓣ 202/633-1000, ⓦ www.mnh.si.edu; Federal Triangle or Smithsonian Metro. Daily 10am–5.30pm.

Founded in 1911, the **National Museum of Natural History** is one of DC's oldest museums and one of the best places in the capital to take children – a fact that sometimes makes it a daunting experience for adults without them. The museum's early collection is partly based on specimens the Smithsonian commissioned from the game-hunting Theodore Roosevelt on his African safaris. Roosevelt "collected" thousands of them – from lions and rhinos to gazelles and cheetahs, many of which are still on display.

The museum's imposing three-story entrance rotunda feels like the busiest and most boisterous crossroads in all DC, with troops of screeching school kids chasing each other nonstop around a colossal African elephant. The museum owns more than 125 million specimens and artifacts and is regularly working to show off more of its holdings to the public. You'll need to go early to avoid the busiest times, especially in summer and during school holidays; stop by the **information desk** at the elephant's hooves to pick up floor plans, check on any temporary exhibitions, and ask about the **free guided tours** (Tues–Fri 10.30am & 1.30pm), which show you the highlights in around an hour. These tours are particularly helpful, since this is one of the Smithsonian's most confusingly laid-out museums. The soaring, glass-domed **Atrium Café** serves

▲ National Museum of Natural History

a variety of foods, and hosts regular jazz concerts (Fri 6–10pm; $10); there are also **IMAX screenings** ($10; ⓦwww.mnh.si.edu/imax) of short nature- and science-oriented documentaries and Hollywood family flicks.

First floor

Although the café and gift shops are on the ground floor off Constitution Avenue, the **first floor** is regarded as the main entrance. It's also the busiest and most aggravating part of the museum – if not all of DC. Unlike the National Air and Space Museum (another kid-friendly favorite), there's just not enough space to get around easily, and you'll have to squeeze past countless other visitors if you hope to get a peek at the big-ticket items. Once you scoot past the rotunda with its big elephant, plunge to the right into the **Dinosaurs** section, justifiably the most popular area, with hulking skeletons reassembled in imaginative poses and accompanied by informative text. The massive diplodocus, the most imposing specimen, was discovered in Utah in 1923, at what is now Dinosaur National Monument. The museum's pride and joy, however, is the 65-million-year-old triceratops (dubbed "Hatcher"), which, these days, is more paleontologically accurate following a high-tech face-lift. Stay in this section long enough to tour the related displays on the **Ice Age**, **Ancient Seas**, **Fossil Mammals**, and **Fossil Plants** – each covering mollusks, lizards, giant turtles, and early fish in exhaustive, engaging detail with the aid of diagrams, text, and fossils. One curious attraction along the way is the pair of menacing – and dopey-looking – giant ground sloths, Ice Age herbivores which didn't stand much of a chance after all the snow melted. Near the end of the circuit, you'll unexpectedly get a look at what is claimed to be an early-human form of **burial**, though the display's centerpiece – a nearly naked caveman tied up with ropes in a dank hole – looks more like something out of *Pulp Fiction* than *Nova*.

Taking up a good chunk of the west side of the first floor is the **Hall of Mammals**, which, given its layout, is even more congested than the Dinosaurs section. Some three hundred replicas focus on mostly fur-wearing, milk-producing creatures in a variety of simulated environments. If you can, check out the African savanna animals, which strive to drink at a watering hole in the same desperate manner in which viewers vie for a look at them, and the various big cats, chimps, shrews, moles, dogs, and other creatures that are biologically related to *Homo sapiens*. To brush up on your Darwin, the **Evolution Theater** fills you in on the process that undergirds almost all the museum's natural history displays – though many conservative parents take care to shepherd their children away from the theater as if it were showing pornography.

North of the Hall of Mammals, and replacing the museum's famously outdated ethnographical collections, will be the 25,000-square-foot **Ocean Hall**, coming at the end of summer 2008, which will use hundreds of displays and specimens – among them, a 50ft-long whale model – to describe the biological and ecological world of the sea in different places around the world. It will use historical and present-day models to show the remarkable diversity of the oceans, increasingly under peril from such threats as global warming, overfishing, and pollution. The design of the hall is part of the museum's ongoing project to bring the structure back to its Beaux-Arts origins, removing the modernist changes that cramped the spaces and restricted access, uncovering the building's Classical details, and opening up its upper balconies to lovely effect.

Also imaginative is the "**African Voices**" exhibit between the Ocean Hall and the Ice Age displays, which does as well as can be expected for a section covering people from an entire continent. Bursting with colorful displays, films, and tunes – plus tools, garments, icons, and trinkets – the exhibit has Africans tell their stories in their own voices, in testimonials and on video monitors, suggesting the wide range of languages and religions practiced on the continent. Best are items like a huge "antelope mask" for tribal rituals, an "airplane coffin" from Ghana in the shape of a KLM jet, and a section on the global reach of African mudcloth (handwoven cotton cloth painted with intricate designs), detailing the intersection of native symbolism and Western consumerism.

Second floor

On the second floor, and somewhat complementing "African Voices," is "**Western Cultures**," where displays veer between ancient Egypt, Greece, and Rome, and showcase a number of ancient artifacts such as death masks, iconic statues, votive offerings, tools, ritual beads, and coffins – as well as the odd Ice Age mummy. Unfortunately, since the section is something of a hodgepodge, it's also somewhat flat and unengaging. The museum still has a ways to go in its presentation of anthropological and historical material.

The IMAX theater and various temporary galleries also occupy this level, so there's less space for the permanent collection. The natural history sections tend toward the creepy-crawly, including an array of reptiles – snakes, Gila monsters, and lizards among them – and animal bones but pale in comparison to the splendid **Insect Zoo**, sponsored, ironically, by the Orkin pest-control company. Here, many of the exhibits are actually alive, which may not be a recommendation to the squeamish. Behind screens – with notices pleading, unsuccessfully, "Please do not tap the glass" – are imprisoned tarantulas, roaches, crickets, bird-eating spiders, worms, termites, and a thriving bee colony. A staff member with the most unenviable job in the world sits in one corner with assorted creepy-crawlies scampering up and down his arms; kids generally can't wait to touch a bug, while cowering adults try hard not to flinch. If you can stomach this sort of entertainment, stick around for one of the daily tarantula feedings around noon. Less-creepy insects are on display in the new **Butterfly and Plant gallery**, which features the strategies of each to propagate their kind through coevolution but more importantly offers a great living butterfly house, with thousands of the brightly colored creatures flittering about.

On the other side of the floor, the **Hall of Geology, Gems, and Minerals** is centered on the astounding National Gem Collection, notably the legendary 45-carat **Hope Diamond** once owned by Marie Antoinette, and the bearer of a legendary curse. Crowds stare as if hypnotized at the well-guarded rock as it rotates in its display case. Also popular are a pair of the French queen's diamond earrings and a genuine crystal ball that is the world's largest flawless quartz sphere. In addition, the exhibit offers answers to mysteries like why diamonds sparkle, and there are full investigations of related geological phenomena – from plate tectonics and meteors to earthquakes and volcanoes – which are uniformly excellent, well researched, and up to date.

Also prominent is the museum's **rock and mineral** selection. Scientists have identified around 4000 minerals so far and it seems like each one is represented here in its glorious shape, texture, and color. Hunt around and you'll even find an example of Smithsonite – a needle-like crystal mined for zinc – named after Smithsonian Institution benefactor James Smithson, who first recognized it as a distinct mineral. Almost as fascinating is the **Mine Gallery**, where, in a small, curving tunnel, the Smithsonian has assembled actual walls from mine tunnels across the country – from a Missouri lead mine's rocky panels to those bearing zinc, copper, and microcline.

National Gallery of Art – West Building

Constitution Ave, between 4th and 7th sts NW ☎202/737-4215, ⊛www.nga.gov; Archives-Navy Memorial Metro. Mon–Sat 10am–5pm, Sun 11am–6pm.

Despite having a prime spot on the Mall and sitting cheek-by-jowl amid the big-ticket Smithsonian museums, the estimable **National Gallery of Art** is not part of that institution, contrary to what some assume. This museum is easily one of the nation's greatest, probably only second to New York's Met in the quality, depth, and breadth of its collections, and not surprisingly, you can't hope to see the whole of it in one visit. Many concentrate on seeing what they can in the sizable **West Building**, the original gallery structure (see p.86 for the newer **East Building**), whose entire first floor (where most of the art can be found) has almost one hundred display rooms, full of works ranging from thirteenth-century Italian to nineteenth-century European and American art. To make best use of limited time, latch on to one of the daily **free tours** and programs; pick up a schedule at the gallery's information desks, located on the main floor (Mall entrance) and the ground floor (Constitution Ave at 6th St). The most popular rooms – typically anything related to Rembrandt, Vermeer, and French Impressionism – tend to be busiest midafternoon and on weekends.

In the permanent galleries of the West Building, parts of the collection are often rotated or sent out on tour, while many rooms, even entire sections, have in recent years been **closed** for renovation projects lasting about a year to eighteen months – the latest are rooms 52–71, basically half of the entire east wing, covering eighteenth- and nineteenth-century British, French, and American art (galleries whose art is nonetheless described in the following text). If there's something you specifically want to see, call ahead or check online to make sure it's on view. The West Building's collection starts in Room 1 of the West Wing and proceeds chronologically, beginning with thirteenth- to fifteenth-century Italian art and wrapping up with nineteenth-century French art. To track down the specific location of a particular work, the museum offers an interactive computer system that allows you to locate and view some of the

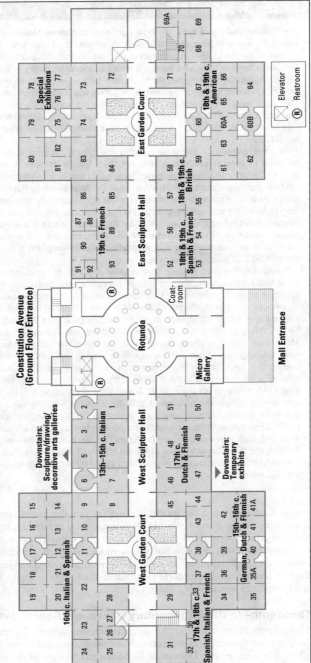

National Gallery, East Building ▲

NATIONAL GALLERY OF ART:
WEST BUILDING MAIN FLOOR

Downstairs:
Sculpture/drawing/
decorative arts galleries ◄

13th–15th c. Italian

West Sculpture Hall

17th c.
Dutch & Flemish

Downstairs:
Temporary exhibits ►

16th c. Italian & Spanish

West Garden Court

15th–16th c.
German, Dutch & Flemish

17th & 18th c.
Spanish, Italian & French

Constitution Avenue
(Ground Floor Entrance)

Rotunda

Coat-room

Micro Gallery

Mall Entrance

19th c. French

East Sculpture Hall

18th & 19th c.
Spanish & French

18th & 19th c.
British

18th & 19th c.
American

Special Exhibitions

East Garden Court

National Gallery, East Building ▲

⌧ Elevator
Ⓡ Restroom

▲ Sculpture Garden & ice-skating rink

77

Building the National Gallery

The **National Gallery of Art** is the legacy of financier **Andrew Mellon**, who began buying the works of European Old Masters in his late 20s. Mellon's ties to the US government in the 1930s – as Secretary of the Treasury and ambassador to Britain – persuaded him that there were means to create a national art gallery in Washington. His own collection certainly begged to be seen by a wider public: among the 121 paintings in Mellon's eventual bequest to the gallery was a score of pieces bought in 1931 from the USSR government, which plundered the works in the Hermitage and unloaded them in a fire sale to prop up its faltering economy. (Stalin held a similar sale in the 1930s, leading to the build-up of the collection of the Hillwood Museum; see p.230.)

President Franklin D. Roosevelt opened the original National Gallery of Art, designed by **John Russell Pope**, in March 1941. Despite its name, it wasn't (and isn't) a government institution; however, the museum was at once perceived to be of national importance and scope. Now known as the **West Building**, Pope's symmetrical, Neoclassical gallery is overwhelming at first sight, especially when approached from its sweeping steps off the Mall. On the main floor, two wings of pink Tennessee marble without external windows stretch for 400ft on either side of a central rotunda whose massive dome is supported by 24 black Ionic columns. The central, vaulted corridors of each wing serve as sculpture halls, and both wings end in sky-lit garden courts filled with plants and fountains.

Remarkably, the West Building was virtually empty at its inauguration in 1941, since Mellon's bequest, substantial though it was, filled only five of the rooms – the spacious design is a testament to the foresight of its founders. However, following an influx of gifts and purchases, by the 1970s it was clear that the original building couldn't hold everything. In 1978 the modernist, triangular **East Building**, designed by **I.M. Pei**, was completed on a block of land between 3rd and 4th streets that Mellon had, again, presciently earmarked as the site of any future expansion. Pei's initial challenge was to deal with the awkwardly shaped land, which he managed by making only the marble walls permanent; the rest of the internal structure can be shaped at will, according to the dictates of the various temporary exhibitions. The East Building has an entrance on 4th Street, although an underground concourse, with a moving walkway, connects it with the West Building. The concourse also has more display space, a very good bookstore, an espresso bar, and a large café – topped by pyramidal skylights and bordered by a glassed-in waterfall. The museum's most recent addition, the **Sculpture Garden**, is outside, between the West Building and the National Museum of Natural History. The garden also has a popular ice-skating rink, where skaters circle well into the winter nights amid sculptures from the post–World War II era.

two thousand works in the gallery. The system can also access biographies of some seven hundred artists, provide the historical and cultural background of a work or artistic period, and print you a map of a self-selected tour. (Alternatively, you can search the collection via the museum's excellent website.) Special exhibitions and installations are detailed in a monthly calendar, which also lists the free classical music **concerts** (Sept–June, usually Sun 6.30pm) held in the West Building's serene West Garden Court.

Thirteenth- to fifteenth-century Italian art (Rooms 1–15)

The gallery's oldest works are the stylized thirteenth-century Byzantine **icons** (holy images) in which an enthroned Mary holds the small figure of an adult Christ. The Sienese artist **Duccio di Buoninsegna** was one of the first to move beyond strict Byzantine forms; the faces of the subjects in his *Nativity*, a panel taken from the base of his *Maestà* altarpiece in Siena Cathedral, display genuine emotion. The artist **Sassetta**, also from Siena, was popular with some twentieth-century avant-gardists for his strange sense of space and fantastic imagery, as seen in his eye-opening *St Anthony Triptych* (1440). Much more influential, however, was the Florentine artist **Giotto**, whose humanism and use of perspective would eventually lead to the Renaissance. Giotto's *Madonna and Child* (completed by 1330) marks an extraordinary departure in its attempt to create believable human figures.

The action then moves to fifteenth-century Florence, the home of the Renaissance. The prominent *tondo* (circular painting) depicting the *Adoration of the Magi* (*c.*1445) was started by the monk **Fra Angelico** but completed by **Fra Filippo Lippi**, who invested the biblical scene with his full range of emotive powers. **Domenico Veneziano**'s naked *Saint John in the Desert* (*c.*1445) would have been considered blasphemous before the Renaissance, when nudity was almost exclusively associated with the concept of sin. But for dynamic realism there's nothing to compare with **Andrea del Castagno**'s decorative shield showing *The Youthful David* (*c.*1450) preparing to fling his sling; Florentines would have understood that Goliath's decapitated head at David's feet was a warning to any of their city's squabbling neighboring states.

In other rooms relating to Florentine artists, all eyes are drawn to **Leonardo da Vinci**'s *Ginevra de' Benci* (1474), an engagement portrait done when Leonardo was only 22, and the only work by the artist in the US. The painting's subject is a 16-year-old Florentine beauty with alabaster skin sitting before a spiky juniper bush – an image meant to symbolize chastity and to be a pun on her name, Ginevra (the Italian word for juniper is *ginepro*). Works by **Sandro Botticelli** include his rendering of the *Adoration of the Magi* (early 1480s), set in the ruins of a Classical temple from which the frame of a new structure, representing Christianity, rises.

Other Renaissance-era Italian paintings not to miss include **Andrea Mantegna**'s *Judith with the Head of Holofernes*, where a calm Judith, resembling a Classical statue, clutches the severed head of the Assyrian leader, and **Benvenuto di Giovanni**'s five-panel "pentatych" of Jesus surrounded by various spindly, grotesque onlookers.

Sixteenth-century Italian and Spanish art (Rooms 16–28)

By the beginning of the sixteenth century, new artistic ideas were emerging in other Italian cities, and the accomplished Bellini family was at the forefront of the scene. Nowhere is this more evident than in **Giovanni Bellini**'s *The Feast of the Gods*, which depicts deities feasting to bawdy excess in a bucolic setting. Bellini created this painting between 1511 and 1514, just a few years before his death in 1516. In 1529, **Titian**, his former pupil and the forerunner of Mannerism, restyled it by removing a grove of trees and adding a striking mountain in the background. A master with color, Titian would become the finest Venetian painter of all, his revealing portraits and mythological scenes making him one of the most famous European artists, as well as court painter to Spain's Charles V. The gallery's diverse Titian collection includes an image of *Saint John the Evangelist on Patmos* (*c.*1547) and *Venus with a Mirror* (*c.*1555).

The High Renaissance artist **Raphael** has only one major piece here: the *Alba Madonna* (1510), in which the Virgin and Child are seated on the ground, leaning against a tree stump – a pose intended to emphasize their humility. Although the painting was completed after Raphael moved from Florence to Rome, *tondo* was primarily a Florentine style, and the figures of Jesus and John the Baptist suggest that Raphael had studied the cherubic sculptures of the most famous Florentine of all, Michelangelo.

The Late Renaissance yields to the Mannerist era, and **Bronzino**'s striking *A Young Woman and Her Little Boy* (*c*.1540) is a highlight of this period. Here the favored court portraitist creates almost doll-like figures, with fair skin and precocious features.

Seventeenth-century Spanish, Italian, and French art, and later Spanish and Italian art (Rooms 29–37 and 52)

In the draconian grip of the Counter-Reformation, Spanish art remained deeply spiritual in character, with individual works designed to inspire a Catholic conception of devotion and piety. The paramount artist of this time was **El Greco**, and the gallery is distinguished for having the most important El Greco collection outside of Spain. Its *Christ Cleansing the Temple* (*c*.1570) portrays Jesus, leather whip in hand, laying into assorted traders and money-lenders. More typical of the artist's style, though, is the dour *Laocoön* (1610–14), in which the Trojan priest and his two sons are attacked by serpents sent by the Greek gods. From the same period, *Saint Jerome* (*c*.1610) – in retreat in the desert and about to beat his chest with a rock – expresses perfectly the emphasis the Spanish Church placed on the concept of blood penance.

The *Saint Lucy* of **Francisco de Zurbarán**, well known for his religious portraits, is a spiritual study that carries an accompanying shock as your eyes are drawn to those of the saint: hers have been plucked out and laid on a dish that she holds. Much more skillful, Zurbarán's contemporary **Diego Velázquez** was the finest Spanish painter of the seventeenth century. He was court painter to Phillip IV by age 24 and spent the rest of his life creating powerful portraits for his patron. Velázquez did, however, occasionally return to domestic scenes, as in the unfinished *Needlewoman* (1640), a reserved study of a woman that offers a nice play of subtle light and shadow.

Spain's greatest eighteenth-century artist was the flamboyant **Francisco de Goya**, who, beginning in 1789, was court painter to Charles IV. The gallery owns several of his works, primarily portraits, including the famous *Señora Sebasa Garcia*, in which the artist abandons background entirely to focus on the elegant *señora*.

Also in these rooms are works by France's leading seventeenth-century painters – like **Georges de la Tour** and popular landscapist **Claude Lorrain** – who often set off for Rome, the capital of the Baroque scene. Lorrain's ideas of natural beauty, as represented in *Landscape with Merchants* (*c*.1630), were firmly shaped by his years in and around Rome, with the sweeping topography enveloping the tiny humans near the bottom of the canvas; and the careful balance of light and dark in la Tour's *The Repentant Magdalene* (1640) recalls the artist's debt to the pre-eminent painter of the chiaroscuro style, Caravaggio (whose works, unfortunately, cannot be found in this museum).

Elsewhere in this section, however, the emphasis is literally Italian. Notable are Bolognese artist **Annibale Carracci**'s *River Landscape* (*c*.1590), an early Baroque piece in which nature is presented with striking diagonal trees; **Bernardo Bellotto**'s *The Fortress of Königstein* (1758), where the titular structure looms large on an imperious hilltop; and **Canaletto**'s fetching rendering of the entrance to the Grand Canal and of St Mark's Square in Venice (both 1744).

Fifteenth- and sixteenth-century German, Dutch, and Flemish works (Rooms 38–41)

Albrecht Dürer is a principal figure among early German Northern Renaissance masters, and his *Lot and His Daughters* (1496–99) is a moralistic piece that grafts realistic Italian Renaissance figures onto a landscape typical of Northern

European religious paintings of the time. Also worth a look are **Matthias Grünewald**'s agonized *The Small Crucifixion* – one of only twenty Grünewald paintings in existence, and the only one in the US – and portraits by **Hans Holbein the Younger**, whose proud and pudgy *Edward VI as a Child* (*c.*1538) is an image of Henry VIII's heir and son with Henry's third wife, Jane Seymour, while his *Portrait of a Young Man* (1530) is a much humbler rendering of a fellow with silken shirt and somewhat goofy hat.

The gallery's early Flemish and Dutch works show the new techniques made possible by the revolutionary change from painting with quick-drying egg-based tempera to using slow-drying oil, which allowed artists to build up deep color tones. Acclaimed fifteenth-century artist **Jan van Eyck** was one of the first to adopt the new technique; his *Annunciation* (1434) shows a remarkable depth of color and texture. Even more striking is the tiny panel by **Rogier van der Weyden** of *Saint George and the Dragon* (1435), in which the artist probably used a magnifying glass to paint individual tree branches and pinprick windows. Also worth a close look are **Hieronymus Bosch**'s *Death and the Miser* (1485–90), a gloriously ghoulish tour de force, and **Quentin Massys**'s grotesque *Ill-Matched Lovers* (*c.*1520).

Seventeenth-century Dutch and Flemish art (Rooms 42–50)

Anthony van Dyck was an immensely popular portraitist of Italian, English, and Flemish nobility, perhaps due in part to his flattery of his subjects (elongating their frames, painting them from below to enhance their stature, idealizing their features). His earliest image here of the seventeen owned by the gallery, *Portrait of a Flemish Lady* (1618), a skilled rendering of a rigid sitter wearing a thick collar like a giant headcuff, was painted when Van Dyck was just nineteen. His teacher, **Peter Paul Rubens**, offers the striking *Daniel in the Lions' Den* (1613–15), in which virtually life-size lions bay and snap around an off-center Daniel.

Rembrandt's *The Mill* (1648) – a brooding study of a cliff-top mill, backlit under black thunderclouds – is a famous image, with its dark and light connotations of good and evil, and one that influenced nineteenth-century British artists like J.M.W. Turner. There are a dozen other priceless Rembrandts on view, among them the distant, imperious *Man in Oriental Costume* (1635); the famed *Lucretia* (1664), in which the legendary poisoner poses artfully with a knife; and a late-middle-aged *Self-Portrait* (1659), with the artist gazing deeply and poignantly at the viewer.

Pieter de Hooch offers genre depictions of quiet domestic households in *A Dutch Courtyard* and *The Bedroom* (both 1660), while **Jan Steen**'s festive *The Dancing Couple* (1663), despite its cheerful imagery, is a subtle warning against excess. Portraits of bourgeois gentlemen in lacy or ruffled collars and tall hats were bread-and-butter work for **Frans Hals**, and eight of these pieces are on display here.

Of all the genre artists from this period, **Johannes Vermeer** is the most widely known – though only 35 paintings survive. Of these, this gallery and the Met are almost the only places in the US where you can see his work. In *Girl with the Red Hat* (*c.*1665), the sitter is seemingly interrupted by the viewer from her reverie; *A Lady Writing* (*c.*1665) depicts the eponymous figure again gazing back at the viewer, in soft lighting and perfect detail; and *Woman Holding a Balance* (*c.*1664) is simply one of the greatest pictures in the gallery, or the US for that matter, a beautiful allegory of a woman holding a scale before an array of jewelry, while in the dark background, an ominous painting of the Last Judgment shows Jesus rendering a different sort of verdict.

Eighteenth- and early nineteenth-century French art
(Rooms 53–56)

Marble busts of Voltaire by **Jean-Antoine Houdon** – who also did sculptures of George Washington (see p.359) – usher in the gallery's eighteenth-century French painting and sculpture collection. The main attraction, however, is arch-Neoclassicist **Jacques-Louis David**'s portrait of *Napoleon in His Study at the Tuileries* (1812), in which the artist employs the sword, crisp uniform, military papers, and imperial emblems to bolster the little corporal's heroic image.

By way of contrast, **Jean-Siméon Chardin**'s still lifes and everyday scenes impress with their subtlety and elegance of detail; indeed, Chardin's influence continues to be as great as ever, especially with delicate works like that of a young boy blowing *Soap Bubbles* (1734). Elsewhere, works by **Antoine Watteau** include the delightfully absurd *Italian Comedians* (1720) – a group portrait of clowns and players – and the decorative Rococo-style oval panel depicting *Ceres*, the Roman goddess of the harvest, surrounded by the signs of the summer zodiac, Gemini, Cancer, and Leo (1716).

There's also a major showing of **Jean-Honoré Fragonard**, who knocked out his Rococo "fantasy portraits" in as little as an hour, notably *The Swing* (1765), all flounced dresses and petticoats, which had erotic connotations for contemporaneous viewers. The greatest academic painter of the era was **Jean-Auguste-Dominique Ingres**, whose wondrous *Madame Moitessier* (1851) is a highlight of pre-Impressionist French art. Indeed, the figure of this darkly clad matron, with her stern expression, pearls, and rosy garland, has been described by one critic as "the most imperial and commanding of Ingres's female portraits."

Eighteenth- and nineteenth-century British art
(Rooms 57–61)

The gallery's limited number of **British works** include pieces by **William Hogarth**, whose subtly satirical painting *A Scene from The Beggar's Opera* (1729) illustrates characters that would later turn up in the twentieth-century musical standard "Mack the Knife"; **Joshua Reynolds**'s more regal *John Musters* (1780), showing the proud stance of a contemporary landowner; and **Thomas Gainsborough**'s cliffside cove of a *Seashore with Fishermen* (1782), a rugged nature scene, unlike his more predictable aristocratic portraits on view.

Other works are firmly within the British tradition, particularly the harmonious landscapes by **John Constable** – with *The White Horse* (1819) as a particularly lovely example – and the influential works of **J.M.W. Turner**, which run the gamut from the hazy, atmospheric luminance of the *Approach to Venice* (1844) – which John Ruskin described as "the most perfectly beautiful piece of color of all that I have seen produced by human hands" – to *Keelmen Heaving in Coals by Moonlight* (1835), a light-drenched harbor scene set in the industrial north of England, to the early *Junction of the Thames and the Medway* (1807), all stormy waves, bracing winds, and nautical desperation. Finally, take care to see **Henry Fuseli**'s striking *Oedipus Cursing His Son, Polynices* (1786), in which the tragic figure points dramatically to his son with the stern visage of an angry patriarch.

Eighteenth- and nineteenth-century American art
(Rooms 60–71)

The gallery's eclectic collection of eighteenth- and nineteenth-century American art is one of its most popular. **Gilbert Stuart** painted many images of the leading American men of his age, including George Washington more than a hundred times during his career; the two examples here are the early *Vaughan Portrait* (1795) and the more familiar *Athenaeum Portrait* (1810–15), the model for Washington's image on the dollar bill. Following his success with Washington, Stuart painted the next four presidents – Adams, Jefferson, Madison, and Monroe – and more than a thousand other portraits (the National Gallery alone has 41).

In contrast to the youthful Stuart, **John Singleton Copley** was already in his mid-30s when he decided to study painting in Europe. Copley made his name internationally with *Watson and the Shark* (1778), whose depiction of a shark attack off the coast of Cuba caused a stir in London at the time, as such dramatic scenes were usually reserved for the martyrdom of saints or the distant past. The work was likely commissioned by Brook Watson, the subject of the work, who survived his ordeal to eventually become Lord Mayor of London. You'll also find works by **Benjamin West**, whose splendid historical scenes include the political propaganda of *The Battle of La Hogue* (1778), which pits seventeenth-century English and French naval forces against each other: the heroic English admiral directs operations from close quarters while the French dandy is more concerned about losing his wig than with the hand-to-hand combat raging around him. Portraiture here includes works by two of West's pupils, **Thomas Sully** and **John Trumbull**, the latter of whom depicted a half-smiling *Alexander Hamilton* (1806) and later painted the murals in the Capitol. **Rembrandt Peale**'s thoughtful and somewhat precious *Rubens Peale with a Geranium* (1801) shows the artist's earnest, bespectacled brother even more ready to wilt than his potted plant.

By the nineteenth century, American artists were addressing the theme of territorial expansion head on. *The Notch of the White Mountain* (1839) by **Thomas Cole** is typical in its vibrant use of color, though more monumental are Cole's four *Voyage of Life* (1842) paintings. The series' symbolically haunting images follow a figure from childhood to old age and are believed to be a warning against the fervent belief in Manifest Destiny that was fueling westward expansion. At around the same time, the German-born **Albert Bierstadt** captured the shimmering, turquoise *Lake Lucerne* (1858) framed by mountains, the progenitor of his stirring *Rocky Mountains* landscapes. Other images of the American wilderness include **George Inness**'s *The Lackawanna Valley* (1855), which shows a steam train puffing through a Pennsylvanian

Taking a break in the National Gallery of Art

For **food** and **drink**, head down a level from the main floor of the West Building or across to the East Building, noting as you go **Salvador Dalí**'s *Last Supper*, which overlooks the escalators down to the Concourse.

Cascade Café Concourse level (Mon–Sat 11am–3pm, Sun 11am–4pm). Serves all-American soups, salads, and sandwiches, as well as good old Yankee pot roast.

Espresso and Gelato Bar Concourse level (Mon–Sat 10am–4.30pm, Sun 11am–5.30pm). Gelato, panini, and an espresso bar.

Garden Café West Building, ground floor (Mon–Sat 11.30am–3pm, Sun noon–4pm). Lunch daily; open until 6pm on Sunday for those attending the classical concerts in the Garden Court.

Pavilion Café Sculpture Garden (hours vary, often Mon–Sat 10am–6pm, Sun 11am–6pm). Pleasant lunch spot near outdoor artworks, with Mall views.

Terrace Café East Building, upper level (Sat & Sun noon–2.30pm). Brunch spot with buffet courses and decent views of visitor activity in the building atrium.

landscape of felled trees, and **Frederic Edwin Church**'s *El Rio de Luz* (1877), depicting a glorious vista of hazy sunshine beaming across primordial, almost junglelike riparian terrain.

Philadelphia-based **Thomas Eakins**'s work introduces the gallery's late nineteenth-century collection, his precisely rendered *Biglin Brothers Racing* (1872) a good example of his penchant for sporting images, in this case rowing. **Albert Pinkham Ryder**'s ultra-dark and often bleak yellow-and-black paintings convey much, despite their small size; the most vivid here is *Siegfried and the Rhine Maidens* (1891), a swirling, tortured Wagnerian moonlit landscape of bent trees and gnarled bodies, of which the artist said, "I worked for forty-eight hours without sleep or food, and the picture was the result." **James Abbott McNeill Whistler** is dominant, too; his standout work here is *The White Girl* (1862), subtitled *Symphony in White, No. 1*. The full-length study of the artist's mistress is of secondary importance to his use of contrasting shades of white, from dress to drapes to flowers. Other prominent nineteenth-century works include **George Caleb Bingham**'s sprightly *Jolly Flatboatmen* (1846) and the crude but strangely intriguing animals of **Edward Hicks**'s *Peaceable Kingdom* (1834), surely one of the century's most inexplicably enduring images.

Nineteenth-century French art (Rooms 80–93)

The gallery has an exceptional collection of nineteenth-century French paintings, with most Impressionist, post-Impressionist, Realist, and Romantic artists of note represented. **Claude Monet**'s signature works include two facades of Rouen Cathedral. From 1892 onward, Monet painted more than thirty of these facades, almost all from the same viewpoint but at different times of the day and in varied conditions. Significant, too, are *The Japanese Footbridge* (1899), whose water-lily theme he was to return to again and again until his death in 1926; *Woman with a Parasol* (1875), whose true subject is the vibrant summer light rather than the human figures (Monet's wife and child); and two of the dozens of studies he made of the town of Argenteuil, where he had a floating studio on the river.

There are also female portraits by the American-in-Paris **Mary Cassatt**, whose work you can usually find with the French Impressionists. Among her pieces here are *Mother and Child* (c.1905), with its flat blocks of color and naturalistic models, and the earlier *Woman with a Red Zinnia* (1891) and *The Boating Party* (1894). The gallery has a number of **Edouard Manet** works on view, from the black-and-white austerity of *The Dead Toreador* (1864) to the swirling still life of *Oysters* (1862). Also well represented is **Edgar Degas**, whose paintings *Before the Ballet* (1879) and especially *The Dance Lesson* (1892) are iconic works of near-perfect form and composition that reward close inspection.

Later developments, such as Symbolism and post-Impressionism, are explored in contiguous rooms. Works by **Vincent van Gogh** include *The Olive Orchard* (1889), a subject he found to be spiritual and complex; the *Farmhouse in Provence* (1888), filled with strikingly rich colors; and the eerie *Self-Portrait* (1889), understandably one of the National Gallery's most viewed works. **Paul Gauguin**'s much more lurid and fantastic *Self-Portrait* (1889) manages to throw in a halo, an apple tree, and a serpent, not to mention the painter's own seemingly disembodied head.

The museum's **Cézanne** collection encompasses still lifes, portraits, and landscapes from most periods of the artist's long life. Cézanne was 27 when he completed *The Artist's Father* (1866). Cézanne *père*, a banker, did not approve of his son's desire to become an artist and opposed his move to Paris in the 1860s. Paul retaliated by perching his father uncomfortably in a high-backed chair in front of an image of one of Paul's paintings. More kinetic are the works by **Henri de Toulouse-Lautrec**, whose dancers, madams, and café patrons reflect his affection for Montmartre fleshpots, in particular *Marcelle Lender Dancing the Bolero in "Chilperic"* (1896), a sprightly vision of color, movement, and energy.

Sculpture, decorative arts, prints, and drawings

The ground floor hosts changing exhibitions of sculpture, decorative arts, prints, and drawings. The gallery owns more than two thousand pieces of **sculpture**, including many Italian and French pieces from the fourteenth to eighteenth centuries, and nineteenth-century French pieces by Rodin, Degas, and Maillol, among others. Also worth seeking out are Honoré Daumier's 36 small portrait busts, intended for use in his printed caricatures; Houdon's contemplative head of George Washington; Gianlorenzo Bernini's marvelous bust of Baroque titan Francesco Barberini; Giovanni della Robbia's elegant *Young Christ*; Paul Manship's streamlined, modern *Diana and a Hound* and similarly sleek *Dancer and Gazelles*; and an anonymous early Baroque sculpture of the fabled she-wolf suckling *Romulus and Remus*, recounting the legendary birth of Rome.

Among the works of **decorative art** are Flemish tapestries; eighteenth-century French furniture; Renaissance majolica, chalices, and religious paraphernalia; Chinese porcelain; engraved medals; and stained-glass windows by Renaissance artist Giovanni di Domenico. Equally impressive is the gallery's collection of **prints and drawings** – 65,000 works, from the eleventh to the twentieth centuries. Selections on display are necessarily limited and tend to be exhibited only for short periods, but if you're sufficiently geared up you can make an appointment to see particular works by calling ☎202/842-6380.

The Sculpture Garden and ice-skating rink

Adjacent to the West Building, the **Sculpture Garden** (Mon–Sat 10am–5pm, Sun 11am–6pm) exhibits a small but impressive selection of contemporary sculpture, with floating cubes and eight-ton slabs of elegantly twisted steel scattered across a six-acre enclosure. Entering from the Mall, you'll see one of Alexander Calder's stabiles – a bright, six-legged sheet of metal titled *Cheval Rouge*. Nearby, Roy Lichtenstein's *House I* (1996/1998) is a skewed comic-book image made into a pancake-flat sculpture of a house, and Barry Flanagan's pensive rabbit posing as the *Thinker on a Rock* (1997) is an irreverent homage to Rodin's nineteenth-century tour de force. There are also representative works by Joan Miró, David Smith, Louise Bourgeois, Sol LeWitt, Isamu Noguchi, and Claes Oldenburg; Coosje van Bruggen's gargantuan *Typewriter Eraser* (1999) guards the western gate along Constitution Avenue. Don't miss the installation of one of Hector Guimard's famed Art Nouveau entrances to the Paris Metro (1902), its sweeping, sinewy lines and curvaceous letters so enticing that it's a disappointment that the entrance covers only a concrete slab.

At the center of the garden, an **ice-skating rink** (Mon–Thurs 10am–9pm, Fri & Sat 10am–11pm, Sun 11am–9pm) doubles as a **fountain** in the summer. Two-hour skating sessions begin on the hour from mid-November through March (weather permitting). Skates are available for rent and lockers are on hand to stow your valuables.

National Gallery of Art – East Building

Constitution Ave, between 3rd and 4th sts NW ☎202/737-4215, ⓦwww.nga.gov; Archives-Navy Memorial Metro. Mon–Sat 10am–5pm, Sun 11am–6pm.

Although the National Gallery's **East Building** was opened in 1978 to accommodate the museum's ever expanding collection of twentieth-century European and American art, there still isn't enough exhibition space to display the entire collection. This is partly due to **I.M. Pei**'s audacious modern design, which is dominated by public areas and a huge atrium, and partly due to the packed roster of special shows, which often displace the museum's own holdings. So if there's something you specifically want to see, call ahead to make sure it's there.

Two or three items are always present, but that's only because they're too big to keep shifting around. Outside the 4th Street entrance is **Henry Moore**'s bronze *Knife Edge Mirror Two Piece* (1978), a male and female representation whose sensuous line and form contrast with the sharp angles of the building (Moore collaborated with Pei before deciding on its exact structure). Inside, dominating the atrium, a huge steel-and-aluminum mobile by **Alexander Calder**, *Black, White and Ted Red* (1957), hangs from the ceiling, its red and black (and one blue) paddle-like wings moving slowly with the air currents. Also in the atrium, **Max Ernst**'s stern and mildly creepy sculpture *Capricorn* (1948) shows a surreal horned potentate on his metal throne.

Twentieth-century exhibitions begin chronologically on the upper level and include pre-1945, mostly European works. Selections rotate, but it's all but certain that some works by **Pablo Picasso** will be on view. Among the National Gallery's substantial collection are the Blue Period pieces *The Tragedy* (1903) and *Family of Saltimbanques* (1905), plus 1910's *Nude Woman*, which Picasso completed after fully turning to Cubism. This piece particularly challenged contemporary audiences with a dissection of anatomy suggestive of X-ray photography. Also in this area, and usually displayed near the Picasso pieces, **Henri Matisse**'s restrained early works give way to his exuberant *Pianist and Checker Players* (1924), depicted in his own apartment in Nice.

Modern American works

On the ground level are rooms devoted to American art up to World War I. Works include **Childe Hassam**'s *Allies Day, May 1917* (1917), a packed New York streetscape of flags and crowds; **John Marin**'s *Grey Sea* (1938), a moody study of form and color; **Marsden Hartley**'s pointed and stylized *Landscape No. 5* (1922–23); **Grant Wood**'s bucolic ode to *Haying* (1939); **John Sloan**'s evocative *The City from Greenwich Village* (1922); and **Edward Hopper**'s poignant *Cape Cod Evening* (1939). **George Bellows**'s assured portrait of *Florence Davey* (1914) in no way prepares you for his other paintings, notably the brutal prizefight pictures *Club Night* (1907) and *Both Members of This Club* (1909), in which you can almost feel the heat as the crowd bays for blood. There's a similar energy in Bellows's brilliantly realized *Blue Morning* (1909), set on a New York construction site.

Post-1945 art (mostly American) is usually shown downstairs in the lower levels. **Andy Warhol**'s Pop Art works are as familiar as they come, with classic serial examples of *Mao Tse-Tung* (1972), *Let Us Now Praise Famous Men* (1963), and *Green Marilyn* (1962). Separate rooms are often set aside for the works of artists using huge canvases: the gallery owns large, hovering slabs of blurry color by **Mark Rothko**, which have been known to transfix acolytes for long periods at a time, to the chagrin of less worshipful viewers, as well as the thirteen stations of the cross by **Barnett Newman**, a series of big canvases built around the visual rhythm of black-and-white stripes. Other highlights include **Jasper Johns**'s *Targets* (1968), which are among his more influential works; **Chuck Close**'s *Fanny/Fingerpainting* (1985), a mighty portrait of an elderly black woman realized from a brilliantly marshaled canvas of finger splotches; **Jackson Pollock**'s *Number 1, 1950 (Lavender Mist)*, a spray of finely drizzled, multi-colored drippings; **Clyfford Still**'s big, jagged shards of color, often without titles; and delightfully odd works by **Claes Oldenburg**, such as *Clarinet Bridge* (1992), *USA Flag* (1960), and, best of all, *Soft Drainpipe – Red (Hot) Version* (1967), a huge, soft-red sculpture that looks as much like a drooping phallus as anything under the sink.

National Museum of the American Indian

Jefferson Drive between 3rd and 4th sts SW ℡202/633-1000, ⓦ www.nmai.si.edu; Federal Center SW Metro. Daily 10am–5.30pm.

As you continue clockwise around the mall, skirting the Capitol Reflecting Pool and heading back west along Jefferson Drive, you'll hit the **National Museum of the American Indian**, the newest of the Mall's museums, opened in September 2004. It's instantly recognizable by its curvaceous modern form with undulating walls the color of yellow earth – designed to represent the natural landscape. This stone-and-glass building with muted hues, terraced facade, and small-scale forest and wetland landscapes sits on an awkward triangular plot, but it is nonetheless in a position of prominence near the Capitol dome.

The museum is designed to recognize and honor the many tribes that occupied the continent before the sixteenth- and seventeenth-century arrival of white settlers, including such groups and nations as the **Iroquois**, **Sioux**, **Navajo**, **Cherokee**, and countless others. The collections reach back thousands of years and incorporate nearly a million objects from nations spread out from

▲ National Museum of the American Indian

Canada to Mexico, including some fascinating ceramics, jade and goldwork, textiles, and other artifacts from civilizations such as the **Olmec**, **Maya**, and **Inca** – in many ways a world away from the culture of the Iroquois and the North American peoples.

The museum is staggering in its scope, attempting to provide a straightforward narrative to hundreds of different peoples and cultures that, in many cases, had little to do with one another except for being located in the Western Hemisphere. The temporary exhibits take in everything from different styles of native dresses to antique photographs of old tribal chiefs. The permanent collection lies in several huge galleries with themes that are overarching, to say the least: "**Our Universes**" touches on religious and cosmological conceptions of eight selected peoples, from Chile to Alaska, and tries to provide some defining thread; "**Our Peoples**" does much the same for eight tribes from Brazil to North Carolina, with the much more consistent narrative element of the depredations of white missionaries, conquistadors, traders, and government agents; and "**Our Lives**" again uses the device of eight representative peoples to show the characteristics and challenges of modern Indian life, mostly in North America.

Throughout these displays and in the large window galleries outside the corridors, the cultural treasures on display include woven garments, musical instruments, totem poles, artworks, kachina dolls, canoes and ceremonial masks, headdresses and outfits. Along with displaying its considerable collection, the museum also sponsors periodic musical and dance events, along with lectures, films, and other cultural presentations.

National Air and Space Museum

Independence Ave and 6th St SW ℗202/633-1000, Ⓦwww.nasm.si.edu; L'Enfant Plaza Metro. Daily 10am–5.30pm.

If there's one museum tourists have heard about in DC, and just one they want to visit, it's almost always the **National Air and Space Museum**. Since opening in 1976, it's become the most popular cultural attraction in the city – and supposedly the entire country – capturing the imagination of ten million people a year. The excitement begins in the entrance gallery, which throws together some of the most celebrated flying machines in history, while more than twenty monstrous galleries on two floors accommodate objects the size of, well, spaceships as well as the huge crowds, so even on busy days it's not too much of a struggle to get close to the exhibits. You may have to wait a while to get into the **IMAX theater**, but otherwise the worst lines are in the cafeteria.

The **information desk** is at the Independence Avenue entrance; here you can catch a free tour (daily 10.30am & 1pm) and inquire about shuttle pickup to the **Udvar-Hazy Center** satellite museum (see p.353). If you want to visit the **Einstein Planetarium** or see an IMAX movie in the Lockheed Martin Theater (each is $8.50 per show), buy tickets when you arrive or book in advance (℗202/633-4629). Come early to eat in the self-service **cafeteria**, which has a great view of the Capitol dome. Finally, don't even think of entering the **museum shop** without wads of cash or the stamina to endure relentless demands from kids or companions for model spaceships, Klingon T-shirts, and florid stunt kites.

The first floor: Milestones of Flight

The National Air and Space Museum's entry hall, known as "**Milestones of Flight**," is a huge atrium filled with all kinds of flying machines, rockets, satellites, and assorted aeronautic gizmos that are bolted to the floor, hung from the

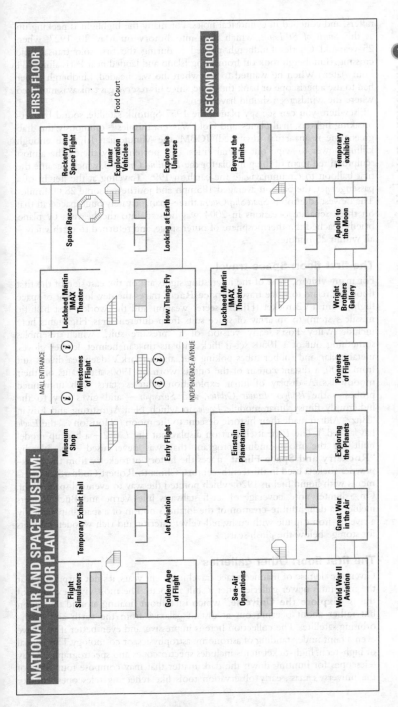

NATIONAL AIR AND SPACE MUSEUM: FLOOR PLAN

FIRST FLOOR

- Rocketry and Space Flight
- Lunar Exploration Vehicles
- Explore the Universe
- Space Race
- Looking at Earth
- Lockheed Martin IMAX Theater
- How Things Fly
- Museum Shop
- Temporary Exhibit Hall
- Flight Simulators
- Golden Age of Flight
- Jet Aviation
- Early Flight
- Milestones of Flight
- Food Court

MALL ENTRANCE

INDEPENDENCE AVENUE

SECOND FLOOR

- Beyond the Limits
- Temporary exhibits
- Apollo to the Moon
- Wright Brothers Gallery
- Lockheed Martin IMAX Theater
- Pioneers of Flight
- Exploring the Planets
- Einstein Planetarium
- Great War in the Air
- World War II Aviation
- Sea-Air Operations

rafters, and couched in cylindrical holes. For many the highlight is peeking up at the *Spirit of St Louis*, which flew into history on May 20, 1927, when 25-year-old Charles Lindbergh piloted it during the first solo transatlantic crossing. (Lindbergh took off from Long Island and landed near Paris almost 34 hours later.) When he wanted to see where he was headed, Lindbergh either had to use a periscope or bank the plane, since his reserve gas tank was mounted where the windscreen should have been.

Elsewhere you can see spy planes, the 1957 Sputnik satellite, sound-barrier-breaking fighters, mail planes, and Cold War–era missiles – ominously, the drab green one is an actual (disarmed) ICBM, the Minuteman III, with enough killing power to wipe out several cities. Less portentously, there's the almost sculptural red form of the gondola for the *Breitling Orbiter 3*, which became the first balloon to circumnavigate the earth in 1999. Traveling at the height of a passenger jet, the balloon averaged 185mph and journeyed some 28,000 miles. The newest addition is *SpaceShipOne*, a three-man, privately built spacecraft that on three separate occasions in 2004 was hoisted into the heavens by plane, briefly reached the thermosphere of outer space, and returned to earth safely – all within 25 minutes.

The first floor: Space travel

For many visitors, most of the interesting sights are on the east side of the first floor and relate to space travel. "**Space Race**" traces the development of space flight, from a V2 rocket (Hitler's secret weapon and the world's first ballistic missile system) to an array of space suits from different eras. Highlights here include Wiley Post's early version of a "pressure suit," which resembles something out of a 1950s sci-fi flick with its tin-can helmet, leather gloves, metal collar, and rubber tubes poking out, and a Mark V deep-sea diver's suit from 1900, a distant cousin of the outfits worn by 1960s astronauts on their moonwalks. A display of lunar exploration vehicles starts with unmanned probes – the *Ranger*, *Lunar Orbiter*, and *Surveyor* – and gives way to the ludicrously flimsy lunar module *Eagle*, in which Neil Armstrong and Edwin "Buzz" Aldrin made their historic descent to the moon ("Houston . . . the *Eagle* has landed"). The *Eagle* itself isn't on display, but the *LM-2* – a backup model built for the moon-landing program that was never used – is. Nearby, "**Rocketry and Space Flight**" traces the history of rocketry from the black-powder rockets used in thirteenth-century China to Robert Goddard's experiments with liquid fuel in 1926, which pointed the way to eventual space flight. On a lighter note, coverage of sci-fi stalwarts Jules Verne and Buck Rogers includes a delightful re-creation of the former's notion of a spaceship: basically a riveted-iron capsule with cushy, red-velvet interior and rich wooden cabinets for storage below the plush seats.

The first floor: Other galleries

Given the demise of manned space travel in recent years, it's not surprising that the museum's newer galleries offer a shift in focus. The most vivid example of this is "**Explore the Universe**," which isn't about floating around the moon but rather about peering out at distant galaxies from the earth and earth-orbiting satellites. The collection here is impressive, and even better if you have even a faint understanding of astronomy, astrophysics, or cosmology. The arsenal of high-tech, high-ticket items includes spectroscopes and spectrographs, X-ray telescopes for hunting down the dark matter that may compose four-fifths of the universe's mass, early observation tools like reflecting telescopes, chunky lenses, and curious "Armillary Spheres," a giant backup mirror for the Hubble Space Telescope, and, best of all, a replica of the huge, forbidding metal cage used for telescopes at California's Mount Wilson Observatory.

The other galleries on the first floor are less eventful. "**Jet Aviation**" will appeal to engineers and military buffs for its selection of groundbreaking fighters from the World War II era, while the "**Golden Age of Flight**" encompasses early exploration and air-racing craft, with the punky little *Chief Oshkosh* impressing for the races it won despite its pint size. In "**Early Flight**," you can see Otto Lilienthal's glider (1894), which first inspired the Wright brothers, whose success in turn provided the impetus for the resourceful Herman Ecker, who, a year after teaching himself to fly in 1911, built his *Flying Boat* using bits and pieces bought at hardware stores. The early technology explored by people like Ecker and the Wrights is also covered in "**How Things Fly**," an interactive room aimed at those who need a refresher course to understand the museum's exhibits. It's worth glancing, too, at "**Looking at Earth**," where aerial photographs include pictures of San Francisco after the 1906 earthquake (snapped from a kite), 1860 photos of Boston taken from a balloon, and German castles recorded by camera-carrying pigeons.

The second floor: The Wright Brothers and other galleries

Those who want to recount the heroism demonstrated during the world wars will be drawn to the west side of the second-floor galleries: the "**Great War in the Air**" bursts with dog-fighting biplanes, and "**World War II Aviation**" has a classic set of American and foreign fighters. Nearby, "**Exploring the Planets**" provides an introduction to the basic facts you need to know about our solar system and the various means we've employed for charting it – prominently the Voyager space probe.

Even better is the gallery – whimsically labeled "**Wright Cycle Co.**" – devoted to the siblings who pioneered aeronautics, despite being bicycle manufacturers at the outset. Indeed, one of their five remaining two-wheelers is on display here, along with their tool cases, Orville's mandolin case, various medals, a 1905 model for an automobile, and a Korona camera similar to the one they used to record history. Naturally, though, the focus is the handmade **Wright Flyer**, sitting prominently in the middle of the gallery, in which the Wright brothers made the first powered flight in December 1903 at Kitty Hawk, North Carolina. Just 20ft above the ground, that flight lasted twelve seconds and covered 120ft; within two years the Wrights were flying more than twenty miles at a time, but there was little interest in their progress. Indeed, in the rush for the skies, the Smithsonian Institution was supporting the efforts of a noted engineer (and its third Secretary), Samuel Pierpont Langley, who conspicuously failed to fly any of his experimental planes. It was forty years before the institution formally recognized the brothers' singular achievement, while the original Wright Flyer wasn't accepted into the Smithsonian fold until 1985.

The second floor: Pioneers of Flight and Apollo to the Moon

Next door, the "**Pioneers of Flight**" gallery recounts similarly courageous endeavors, displaying the balloon basket of Captain Hawthorne Grey, who in May 1927 reached a height of 42,470ft – only to run out of oxygen. More successfully, in 1923 the *Fokker T-2* was the first airplane to make a nonstop flight across North America – a journey that took 26 hours and 50 minutes. Just twelve years earlier, and after only twenty hours of flying lessons, Cal Rogers had attempted to pick up the $50,000 prize offered by William Randolph Hearst to the first pilot to fly coast-to-coast in less than thirty days. Rogers eventually managed the journey in a patched-up biplane, but it took him two months, seventy landings, and several crashes. The museum's most poignant airplane is the bright-red *Lockheed Vega*, flown solo across the Atlantic in May 1932 by Amelia Earhart, who disappeared five years later over the Pacific attempting an around-the-world flight.

Needless to say, most visitors make a beeline for "**Apollo to the Moon**," still the most popular and crowded room in the museum. The gallery centers on the *Apollo 11* (1969) and *17* (1972) missions, the first and last flights to the moon. There are Neil Armstrong's and Buzz Aldrin's spacesuits, a Lunar Roving Vehicle (basically a Space Age golf cart), *Apollo 17*'s flight-control deck, tools, navigation aids, space food, clothes, charts, and an astronaut's survival kit (complete with shark repellent for splashdown). In a side room, each space mission is detailed, beginning in May 1961 when, on a fifteen-minutes flight aboard *Freedom 7*, Alan B. Shepard Jr became the first American in space. Also on view are items from John Glenn's brave mission to become the first American to orbit the earth, with the launch of *Friendship 7* in 1962. Glenn went around the earth three times in five hours and saw four sunsets in a craft barely big enough to hold an astronaut; his spacesuit is preserved here, as are the toothpaste tubes used to squeeze food into his mouth. A separate memorial commemorates the three men who died on the *Apollo* launchpad in 1967 – Virgil Grissom, Edward H. White II, and Roger Chaffee.

Hirshhorn Museum and Sculpture Garden

Independence Ave at 7th St SW ☏202/633-4674, ⓦwww.hirshhorn.si.edu; L'Enfant Plaza or Smithsonian Metro. Museum daily 10am–5.30pm; Sculpture Garden daily 7.30am–dusk.

The **Hirshhorn Museum** is a huge, cylindrical drum of a building that, with its impenetrable concrete facade and colossal scale, is a perfect example of late modernist architecture at its most inhuman – it's been likened to everything from a monumental doughnut to a spaceship poised for takeoff. Luckily, the art inside is much better, an extensive collection of late nineteenth- and twentieth-century works based on the mighty bequest of Latvian immigrant, stockbroker, and uranium magnate Joseph H. Hirshhorn. His original bequest in 1966 included 4000 paintings and 2600 sculptures, and by the time of his death in 1981, the overall number of pieces had risen to more than 12,000. Not surprisingly, it's impossible for the museum to display more than a fraction of its collection at any one time. In addition to the permanent collection, there are changing exhibitions of contemporary art, thematic shows, and a **sculpture garden** with an outdoor **café** (summer lunch only), plus **free guided tours** of the collection (daily on the hour 1–3pm) and art **films** a couple of evenings a week in the Ring Auditorium.

The Hirshhorn's two upper floors are split into concentric inner and outer loops, with its main galleries winding along the nearly windowless exterior wall, and sculpture from two centuries residing in the glass-enclosed inner exhibition halls overlooking the fountain. American and European sculpture and modern art from the twentieth century occupy the third-floor galleries, while contemporary works and special exhibitions are on the second floor, usually with a selection of European sculpture spanning the period 1850 to 1935. The most contemporary works are in the lower-level galleries, where the exhibits are frequently rotated. Keep in mind that the museum's spaces are often rearranged and entire arcs of each floor periodically off limits, so if there's something you specifically want to see, call ahead to make sure it's there.

European and American sculpture

If the museum has one recognized strength, it's the nineteenth-century **French sculpture** collection, considered one of the best of its kind outside France. **Jean-Baptiste Carpeaux**, principal French sculptor of the mid-nineteenth century, is represented with eleven works, among them a thoughtful bust of *Alexandre Dumas, the Younger* (1873), along with **Auguste Rodin**, whom he directly influenced, evident in his *Portrait of Balzac* (1892) and other pieces. Of the dozens of bronzes by **Henri Matisse**, most notable is *The Serf* (1931), a stumpy portrait of a downtrodden spirit, while alongside **Edgar Degas**'s usual muscular ballerinas are energetic studies of women washing, stretching, and emerging from a bath. Masks and busts by **Pablo Picasso** trace his (and sculpture's) growing alliance with Cubism: contrast the almost jaunty bronze *Head of a Jester* (1905) with the severe *Head of a Woman, Fernande Olivier*, produced just four years later. A similar exercise is possible with a series of five exemplary bronze heads by Matisse of his wife Jeanette (1910–13), which clearly show the journey from Realism to Cubism. Abstraction gets further along with **Brancusi**, whose *Torso of a Young Man* (1924) has the sleek look of a brass phallus.

There's an abundance of 1950s **Henry Moore** here, from the rather gentle *Seated Figure Against a Curved Wall* to the more imposing *King and Queen*, a regal pair of seated five-foot-high bronze figures whose curved laps and straight backs look as inviting as chairs. Look, too, for *Kiln Man I* (1971), **Robert Arneson**'s self-portrait as a brick chimney, with little cigar-smoking heads of the artist ready for firing inside. It's also hard to miss **Nam June Paik**'s *Video Flag* (1985–96), composed of seventy thirteen-inch monitors, with a flurry of images spanning the presidents from Truman to Clinton, all the while managing to resemble a fluttering American flag. Several big-name artists get plenty of space to themselves: **Sol LeWitt**'s optical-illusion-like "Wall Drawings" bracket his *13/11* (1985), a white-painted wooden lattice of cubes on the floor; among the most enchanting of **Joseph Cornell**'s assorted art boxes, whose found objects and curiosities are arrayed behind glass, is the *Medici Princess* (1952), in which a replica of a fetching Mannerist-era portrait by Bronzino stares out from behind blue glass, while an open drawer below is filled with intriguing castoffs such as bracelets, pearls, a Tuscan map, and a powder-blue feather. Less familiar artists also get their due, among them **Lucas Samaras**, whose forbidding *Book No. 6* (1962) is made of straight pins, and the arch-Futurist **Giacomo Balla**, whose vigorously jagged painted-metal pieces (1918–25) look ready to rip your hand off if you get too close.

European and American painting

As with its sculpture collection, the Hirshhorn's cache of **modern paintings** has several strengths (de Kooning, Bacon) and some weaknesses (few women, no Kandinsky, and, despite his sculpture and drawings on display, no Matisse). The set starts with figurative paintings from the late nineteenth and early twentieth centuries and winds its way toward Abstract Expressionism and Pop Art. Along the way, separate rooms cover everything from the surrealism of Salvador Dalí, Max Ernst, and Joan Miró to the organic abstractions of Alexander Calder.

American art makes a particularly good showing: there are portraits by **John Singer Sargent**, including a gentle study in white of *Catherine Vlasto* (1897); **Mary Cassatt**, mostly a series of pastel drawings of children; and **Thomas Eakins**, among them numerous drawings and photographs, such as

Minor Smithsonian attractions

Sitting between the Smithsonian Castle and the Hirshhorn Museum, the Arts and Industries Building is another fitting holdover from the Victorian era, with its playful polychromatic brick-and-tile patterns reminding you just what drew so many people to this first addition to the "National Museum" in 1881. However, despite its enticing design and historic value as one of the Smithsonian's founding structures, the building is due to undergo a complete renovation and won't be open to the public anytime soon. Still on view, though, are the regular children's programs at its **Discovery Theater** (tickets $5; info at ☎202/633-8700, ⍟discoverytheater.org), while right outside is the popular **carousel**. Even more appealing are the lovely **Enid A. Haupt Gardens** (free tours May–Sept Wed 1pm) nearby, where you'll find several topiary bison and well-tended plots of decorative flowers.

the curious images of George Reynolds (1884) taken with double exposure showing his nude figure leaping or walking across the frame in multiple positions. Other pieces include representative works by **Winslow Homer** such as the rustic confines of *The Country Store* (1872); the monumental landscapes of **Albert Bierstadt**; busy painted collages of military medals, hats, and ribbons by **Marsden Hartley**, namely *Painting no. 47, Berlin* (1915); and some bleak paintings of isolated urbanites by **Edward Hopper**. In addition, the Hirshhorn's collection of work by Abstract Expressionist **Willem de Kooning** is one of the most impressive anywhere, although changing displays, loans, and special exhibitions wreak havoc with formal viewing plans. There's a rotating selection of paintings by the likes of Georgia O'Keeffe, Robert Rauschenberg, Louise Bourgeois, Clyfford Still, Piet Mondrian, Jasper Johns, Roy Lichtenstein, and Andy Warhol – in short, just about every noteworthy twentieth-century artist. Other third-floor highlights include the Directions Gallery, where newer, often international work is exhibited, and the Abram Lerner Room, which affords panoramic views of the Mall and a place to rest your feet.

The Sculpture Garden

Much of the Hirshhorn's hulking sculpture is contained in the **Sculpture Garden**, a sunken concrete arbor across Jefferson Drive on the Mall side of the museum. In May and October, there are special free tours (call for times). **Roy Lichtenstein**'s towering *Brushstroke* (1996), a formalized sculpture of one of his signature painted images, oversees the garden. Other works include **Rodin**'s *The Burghers of Calais* (1889), his famous depiction of the six robed bourgeois of the French town surrendering to the English in 1347 with nooses already around their necks, and **Matisse**'s four voluptuous human *Backs* in relief (1913). Many of the artists represented inside the museum appear in the garden too – Henry Moore, naturally, but also **Aristide Maillol** (in particular, a graceful *Nymph* of 1930) and Henri Laurens, Joan Miró, Barbara Hepworth, and David Smith, whose *Voltri* series (1962) uses simple geometry to express rhythmic movement. Of the lesser-known works, several stand out, like **Gaston Lachaise**'s proud, bronze *Standing Woman (Heroic Woman)* from 1932. The pond is fronted by **Alexander Calder**'s *Six Dots over a Mountain* (1956); for a more impressive Calder, make for the museum entrance on Independence Avenue, where his *Two Discs* (1965) sit on five spidery legs tall enough for you to walk under.

Smithsonian and Art and Industries Buildings

1000 Jefferson Drive SW ☎202/633-1000, ⊛www.si.edu; Smithsonian Metro. Daily 8.30am–5.30pm.

The most striking edifice on the Mall, the **Smithsonian Building** is widely known as "**the Castle**" for its Gothic combination of ruddy brown sandstone, nave windows, and slender steeples. Architect and sculptor Horatio Greenough once mocked it as a "medieval confusion," but today it's considered a triumph; its central tower is the only structure other than the Washington Monument to rise above the trees. It serves as headquarters for the Smithsonian Institution, an independent trust holding 140 million artifacts in seventeen museums (and one zoo). Inside you can see a short video highlighting the role of the institution, interact with touch-screen Smithsonian information displays and electronic wall maps, and check out scale models of all the major city plans for DC, from L'Enfant's designs onward. You can also stop by the information desk for the latest details on events at all the galleries. The high-ceilinged **Castle Cafe**,

The Smithsonian story

James Smithson, a gentleman scientist and the illegitimate son of the first Duke of Northumberland, was raised as James Lewis Macie but took his natural father's name after his mother's death in 1800. Despite never visiting the US, he bequeathed half a million dollars "to found at Washington, under the name of the Smithsonian Institution, an establishment for the increase and diffusion of Knowledge" – provided that his surviving nephew should die without an heir. His nephew did just that in 1835, six years after Smithson's death, and it took Congress until 1846 to decide what sort of institution to create. In the end, the vote was for a multi-use building that would hold a museum, art gallery, and laboratory: the original Smithsonian Institution Building, known as "the Castle," was completed in 1855.

For all its wealth, however, the Smithsonian had a shaky start; it wasn't at all clear how it should diffuse the knowledge proposed by its benefactor. Matters slowly improved under the stewardship of the Smithsonian's first Secretary, **Joseph Henry**, who tried to direct the institution primarily toward scientific research, but a new wrinkle occurred when America observed its centennial in 1876. The government invited its constituent states and forty foreign nations to display a panoply of inventions and exhibits that would celebrate contemporary human genius. The subsequent Centennial Exhibition in Philadelphia was a roaring success, though at its close most of the exhibits were abandoned by their owners, who couldn't afford to take or ship them home. Congress made the Smithsonian responsible for the items and approved funds for a new "National Museum" (now the Arts and Industries Building) to house them. Opened in 1881 in time to host President Garfield's inaugural ball, the building soon became rooted in people's consciousness as the "nation's attic," since quite apart from the Centennial exhibits – which included an entire American steam locomotive and Samuel Morse's original telegraph – the Smithsonian also made acquisitions that weren't of a strictly educational nature. Over the years, as the National Museum filled to bursting, most of the Smithsonian holdings were farmed out to new, specialized museums, with proposals for new museums coming every few years.

Only the central rotunda and four of the original exhibit halls remain from the Arts and Industries Building's first design, and the nearby Castle, whose fine marble-pillared Great Hall suggests the grandeur of the Smithsonian's holdings, houses the main visitor center.

a nineteenth-century beauty with Victorian-era touches and courtly charm, has panini, salads, soups, pastries, and gelato.

Smithsonian founder **James Smithson** (see box, p.95), who never visited America in life, found a place here in death: his ornate, Neoclassical tomb stands in an alcove just off the Mall entrance. It was placed here in 1904, 75 years after his death in Italy. Sadly, his tomb records his age incorrectly, since he was 64 and not 75 when he died. Also, out on the Mall, in front of the building's entrance, the resplendent robed statue is not of Smithson, as you might suppose, but of the Smithsonian's first secretary, Joseph Henry.

Between the Castle and the Hirshhorn Museum is the Victorian delight of the **Arts and Industries Building** (see box, p.94), the Mall's second public construction, built in 1881 to house exhibits from Philadelphia's 1876 Centennial Exhibition, and now closed for renovation. The building is positively jaunty compared to the Castle, with its playful polychromatic brick-and-tile patterns and striking Gilded Age verve.

National Museum of African Art

950 Independence Ave SW ☎ 202/633-4600, ⓦ www.nmafa.si.edu; Smithsonian Metro. Daily 10am–5.30pm.

In the same area of the Mall as the Smithsonian Building, the **National Museum of African Art** is a granite-and-limestone cube that holds the nation's foremost collection of traditional art from sub-Saharan Africa, including some six thousand diverse sculptures and artifacts culled from a wide variety of tribal cultures, displayed in a series of permanent galleries and bolstered by special exhibitions. In many ways, the museum focuses on applied art, though the application of a particular piece is not always clear. In part this is due to the techniques of early collectors, who tended not to concern themselves with recording information about their goods. In most cases, even the artist's name is unknown, and attempting to date a piece is fraught with difficulty. On the whole, most of the works are from the nineteenth or twentieth century – some are older, but because most African art is made from wood or clay, it tends not to survive for long. For an overview of the collection, the free guided **tours** (daily except Fri) are an excellent introduction (pick up a schedule at the ground-floor information desk). It's also worth noting that the **gift shop** on the first level is one of DC's most intriguing, selling woven and dyed fabrics and clothes as well as the usual books and postcards.

The collection

Unlike most other Smithsonian museums on the Mall, the African art museum has few permanent installations, and instead centers on temporary shows that present themed groupings of the items from its broad **collection**. Therefore, you can't expect to encounter the same items from year to year. This makes it difficult to recommend any particular treasures. Nonetheless, for many shows you're apt to see a wide variety of **ceramic bowls** (perfectly round, despite being hand-formed), including one with a hippo head for a spout, and carved legs and delicate ivory animal figures from the ceremonial beds used to carry the dead to the cemetery for burial. Ivory inlays from these burial beds come in the form of ibex, hyenas, vultures, and the hippo god Taweret – standing up and wearing a skirt. Also intriguing are the copper-alloy heads (made using the sophisticated lost-wax casting technique) from the Kingdom of **Benin**, home of Edo-speaking people in what is now Nigeria. Look also for *Oba* figures flanked by attendants, carrying swords or musical instruments, and bearing weapons like muskets – most likely to fend off Europeans, depicted as wide-eyed goofballs riding horses.

Political, religious, and ceremonial art – mostly from West and Central Africa – makes up some of the museum's most elaborate holdings, highlighted by rounded, stylized, terracotta **equestrian and archer figures** from Mali (thirteenth to fifteenth century). A number of works (fertility fetishes) represent a woman and child, including wooden carvings from Nigeria that would have sat at one end of a ceremonial drum. From Cameroon, wooden sculptures of a regal male figure show him holding his chin in his hand (a sign of respect), wearing decorative bead clothing covered with symbolic representations of spiders (a wily opponent) and frogs (fecundity). There's much to learn, too, about the African concepts of **divinity** and **beauty**: a carved figure from the Ghanaian Asante people shows a seated male and female with disk-shaped heads, a form considered to be the aesthetic ideal. One of the most engaging works, a headrest from the Luba people of the Congo, is supported by two caryatid figures who, if you look around the back, have their arms entwined.

Other displays showcase artisan chairs, stools, and headrests, mostly carved from wood using an adze, as well as assorted ivory snuff containers (two from Angola with stoppers shaped like human heads), beer straws (from Uganda), carved drinking horns, combs, pipes, spoons, baskets, and cups. Especially interesting are the Mozambique headrest that looks like a cross between a dachshund and an elephant, the "hair knives" meant for cutting through tangles, and a drinking horn with geometric sunburst designs.

Arthur M. Sackler Gallery

1050 Independence Ave SW ☏ 202/633-4880, ⓦ www.asia.si.edu; Smithsonian Metro. Daily 10am–5.30pm.

As you finish up the National Mall museum circuit, you come to the two institutions that make up the National Museum of Asian Art. The first, the angular, pyramidal **Arthur M. Sackler Gallery**, displays artworks and devotional objects from Asia in comfortable, well-lit, underground galleries; the other, connected by an underground passage and described on p.99, is the Freer Gallery. Research physician, publisher, and art collector Arthur M. Sackler originally donated about a thousand pieces to the Smithsonian and paid $4 million toward the museum's construction. The permanent collections are described below; temporary exhibitions might cover themes such as painted Chinese literary adaptations, contemporary Southeast Asian ceramics, and early Islamic texts from Iran, gorgeously colored in gilt, silver, lapis lazuli, and crushed-stone pigments. The gallery's standout Vever Collection is an unrivaled group of works related to the art of the Islamic book, such as manuscripts and calligraphy, from the eleventh to the nineteenth centuries.

The **information desk** at ground level should be your first stop. Ask about the highly informative free guided **tours** (Thurs–Tues 12.15pm). The gallery also has a **shop**, with a fine range of prints, fabrics, ceramics, and arty gewgaws, and an Asian art research **library**, shared with the Freer Gallery and open to the public (Mon–Fri 10am–5pm).

The Arts of China

The permanent exhibitions are located on the first level; the most prominent one is "**The Arts of China**," which highlights the Sackler Gallery's collection of 3000-year-old Chinese bronzes. As early as the fifteenth century BC, ritual wine containers were being fashioned from bronze and showing decoration,

▲ Sackler Gallery

such as the faces and tails of dragons, that would become increasingly detailed and refined. By the time of the late **Shang Dynasty** (twelfth and eleventh centuries BC), the decorative motifs were outstanding; artisans were now producing elegant bronze vessels with bold designs. All the decorated detail was produced using intricate clay molds – there was no carving of the surface after casting. The subsequent Western and Eastern **Zhou dynasties** (1050–221 BC) refined the vessels further, with the bird now appearing as the major motif (many of the pieces on display feature bird-shaped handles, or show wispy reliefs of plumage and feathers). Jade pendants also depicted birds and, more commonly, intricate dragon shapes. The technique used to create these items was just as impressive – since jade is too hard to be carved, the lapidaries would rub an abrasive paste across the surface with wood or bamboo to shape and polish the stone.

The Sackler's collection of later Chinese art reveals other skills, notably those of the ceramicists of the **Tang Dynasty** (618–907AD), who produced multi-colored temple guard figures, designed to ward off evil spirits with their fearsome expressions. The last Chinese dynasty, the **Qing** (1644–1911AD), witnessed the flourishing of the imperial scholars, who would place so-called "scholar's rocks" (natural pieces of stone resembling mountains) on their desks to encourage lofty thoughts. From this period, too, date the Sackler's remarkably well-preserved carved wooden cabinets and book stands, showing a simple, understated decoration that English and Scandinavian craftsmen would later adopt as their own. By way of contrast, Qing imperial porcelain was richly embellished with symbolic figures and motifs – as in a plate depicting a young boy holding a pomegranate full of seeds, and one of ladies holding fans with painted butterflies, representing fertility.

Other displays

Although the China exhibit takes pride of place, other galleries are also worth-while. "**Sculpture of South and Southeast Asia**" traces the spread of devotional sculpture across the continent. The earliest piece here is from ancient Gandhara (now part of Pakistan and Afghanistan), a third-century carved head of the Buddha whose features were directly influenced by images from Greece and Rome, with which Gandhara traded. Later Hindu temple sculpture from India includes bronze, brass, and granite representations of Brahma, Vishnu, and Shiva; there's also a superb thirteenth-century stone carving of the elephant-headed Ganesha, the remover of obstacles – his trunk burnished by years of illicit touching by museum visitors. From India, Hinduism and Buddhism spread to the Khmer kingdom (Cambodia), which in addition to adopting classical Indian styles also developed its own naturalistic artistic style. On a thirteenth-century temple lintel, male figures are shown entwined with vines alongside an unidentified female goddess with conical crown and sarong.

Other galleries aren't quite as eye-catching, intended more for specialists than the lay public in some cases. **Ancient Persian metalwork and ceramics** include vessels, weapons, and ornaments made between 2300 and 100 BC, many of which are animal-shaped or painted with animal motifs, while a ceramic trio from northern Persia resembles metal, such was the craftsman's skill in firing. **Korean ceramics** include hundreds of pieces (wine bottles, tea bowls, ewers, and more) across a broad scope of time (200–1900 AD) and were used for everything from simple household purposes to encasing human ashes. Many date from the tenth to the fourteenth centuries and show a uniform glaze. They're remarkably well preserved, many having been retrieved from aristo-cratic tombs or handed down through the generations.

Freer Gallery of Art

Jefferson Drive at 12th St SW ℡ 202/357-4880, ⓦ www.asia.si.edu; Smithsonian Metro.
Daily 10am–5.30pm.

Opened in 1923, the **Freer Gallery of Art** was the first Smithsonian museum devoted exclusively to art. The airy Italian Renaissance palazzo of granite and marble has long been considered one of the city's most aesthetically pleasing museums, with small, elegant galleries encircling a herringbone-brick courtyard furnished with a splashing fountain. Design appeal aside, the gallery's abiding interest lies in its unusual juxtaposition of Asian and American art, including more than 1200 prints, drawings, and paintings by James McNeill Whistler – the largest collection of his works anywhere. The galleries on the third level hold selections from the permanent collection, only a fraction of which is on display. Pick up a current floor plan at the **information desk** by the Mall entrance, where you can also inquire about the free **tours** (Thurs–Tues 12.15pm). From the Freer, it's possible to reach the Sackler Gallery via a shared underground passageway.

The original owner of the gallery's collection was **Charles Lang Freer**, an industrialist who made a fortune building railroad cars in Detroit and then spent it on Asian art, considered obscure at the time. Freer bought his first piece, a Japanese fan, in 1887, and thirteen years later retired at the age of 44 to concentrate on his collection, adding Chinese jades and bronzes, Byzantine illuminated manuscripts, Buddhist wall sculptures, and Persian metalwork during five trips to various Asian countries. Freer also began to put together a series of paintings by contemporary American artists whose work he thought complemented his Asian collection, though the most profitable relationship was with the London-based Whistler, practically all of whose works ended up in Freer's hands. In 1912 Freer embarked upon a plan to endow and build a gallery to hold his collection. He was delighted with the plans drawn up by Charles Platt but sadly never saw their fruition. Work began in 1916 but was interrupted by the outbreak of World War I; Freer died in 1919, and the gallery didn't open for another four years.

James McNeill Whistler

James Abbott McNeill Whistler (1834–1903) dominates the scene here. Born in Lowell, Massachusetts, Whistler moved first to Paris as an art student, from which time dates a *Self-Portrait* (1857) found here. In it, Whistler is wearing a flat-brimmed hat, looking very much the man at ease with Left Bank life. After moving to London in the early 1860s, Whistler not only began to collect modish Japanese prints and *objets* but embraced their influences in a series of vibrant works, starting with *The Golden Screen* (1865), which depicts a seated woman in Japanese dress in front of a fine painted screen. Freer, attracted by the Asian flavor of Whistler's art, made a special journey to London to introduce himself, returning on several occasions over the years to buy more of the painter's work.

An unfinished portrait of Freer (1902), started during his last visit just before Whistler's death, hangs in the gallery. Other works include studies incorporating a red fan (a prop dear to Whistler's heart), and various examples of the tonal experiments that fascinated the artist, who constantly worked on developing shades of color to harmonious effect. Don't miss a grouping of three highly evocative *Nocturnes*, which use combinations of blue, silver, gray, and gold to illuminate the hazy colors and soft forms of landscapes at Chelsea, Bognor, and Valparaiso Bay. Also striking, and well known to people who know about **art**, *Arrangement in White and Black* (1873) contrasts the ghostly white dress and parasol of Whistler's mother, Maud Franklin, with the dark shades of the background; and *The Little Red Glove* (1896–1902) harmonizes glove and bonnet with the subject's auburn hair. Many of Whistler's works are signed with a butterfly monogram, a Japanese device, and concentrate much more on form, color, and composition than with subject matter, which is often arbitrary.

The Peacock Room

Whistler is also represented by the magnificent **Peacock Room**, whose origins can be traced to the commissioned painting *The Princess from the Land of Porcelain*. This painting hung above the fireplace in the London dining room of Frederick Leyland, a Liverpudlian shipowner and Whistler patron who had commissioned interior designer Thomas Jeckyll to add a framework of lattice-work shelves and gilded leather panels to the room's walls so that he might display his fine collection of Chinese porcelain. Whistler happened to be working on another project in the house at the time and, taking advantage of Leyland's absence on business, decided to restyle Jeckyll's work. Using a technique similar to Japanese lacquerware, he covered the leather-clad walls, ceiling, shelving, and furnishings with rich blue paint, gold-painted peacock feathers, gilt relief decor, and green glaze; above the sideboard he placed two golden painted peacocks trailing a stream of feathers – the aggressive-looking birds supposedly emblematic of the relationship between painter and patron. Whistler's idea was to present his art as a harmonious whole (the room's full title incorporates the phrase *Harmony in Blue and Gold*), much as the Japanese did; the room was at once a framed picture and an object of applied art, like an Oriental lacquer box.

The effect of this artistic hijack outraged Leyland, who refused to pay Whistler for the work. Completed in 1877, the room met a mixed critical reception, though Whistler's friend Oscar Wilde, for one, thought it "the finest thing in color and art decoration the world has known." After Leyland's death, the room and its contents passed into the hands of a London art gallery, which later sold it to Freer. Restoration has returned the iridescent colors to their nineteenth-century best, the framed shelves filled with blue-and-white porcelain to show what Leyland's original dining room might have looked like.

Other American artists

The museum's other American art is less gripping and most of it minor, though it is interesting to trace what attracted Freer to many of the works. Note the Asian-style calligraphic brushstrokes of the trees in the foreground of *Winter Dawn on Monadnock*, just one of the Impressionist landscapes by **Abbott Handerson Thayer** (1849–1921), who was heavily influenced by Freer's Asian art collection, which he knew well. **Thomas Wilmer Dewing** comes closer to Whistler's mood with *The Four Sylvan Sounds* (1896), a painted folding screen with clearly Asian influences. Contemporaries considered Dewing to be elitist, and Freer didn't have much competition for his works, though he doubtless had to bid higher for paintings by the more popular **John Singer Sargent**, whose *Breakfast in the Loggia* (1910), a scene in the arcaded courtyard of a Florentine villa, was bought to remind him of the gallery he planned to build in DC, and **Winslow Homer**'s *Sailors Take Warning (Sunset)* (1907), a moody grouping of two young women and a weathered captain on a bleak hillside before a darkening sky.

Asian art

Freer's collection of **Japanese art** includes the painted folding screens that so delighted Whistler. Called *byobu* ("protection from the wind"), these depict the seasons or themes from Japanese literature and range in length from two to ten panels. Other choice items include the nineteenth-century porcelain dish shaped like Mount Fuji and – one of the oldest pieces here – a twelfth-century standing Buddha of wood and gold leaf.

Other rooms are devoted to **Chinese art**, ranging from ancient jade burial goods to a series of ornate bronzes (1200–1000 BC), including ritual wine servers in the shape of tigers and elephants. There's also a stunning series of ink-on-paper hand scrolls, though the calligraphy (literally, "beautiful writing") isn't just confined to paper – jars and tea bowls, even ceramic pillows, are painstakingly adorned. In addition, Freer made three trips to **Egypt**, and many of the exhibits date from his last trip in 1909, when he bought a remarkable collection of richly colored glass vessels, bronze figurines, and carved plaques, most around 4000 years old. Later Freer spread his net to incorporate pieces of **Buddhist**, **South Asian**, and **Islamic art**. A remarkably well-preserved Pakistani stone frieze from the second century AD details the life of the Buddha, while the South Asian art collection sports some of the most delicate pieces yet: temple sculpture, colorful devotional texts, and gold jewelry set with rubies and diamonds. Elsewhere, Turkish ceramics (many repeating garden motifs) are displayed alongside a fine inlaid Persian pen box (thirteenth century) emblazoned with animal heads and engraved with the name of the artist and the owner.

Capitol Hill

ousing the American federal legislature, **Capitol Hill** is the seat of lawmaking for a nation of 300 million people, centered around the towering silhouette of the white-domed **US Capitol**, which tops the shallow knoll at the eastern end of the Mall. The building – whose Neoclassical design is meant to evoke the ideals of ancient Greece and Rome that inspired the founding fathers – is the political and geographical center of the city, and many of DC's diagonal boulevards lead directly to it.

The Capitol is far from the only important structure on this hill. Around it sit more essential components of American government, including the **United States Supreme Court** and voluminous **Library of Congress**; scattered attractions like the historic **Sewall–Belmont House**, the lush **US Botanic Garden**; and buildings that hold the offices of senators and representatives. For many, that is the extent of the neighborhood, but the Hill is actually home to diverse residential areas, where politicians, aides, lobbyists, and even commoners live. The southeast stretches of **Pennsylvania Avenue** provide a few worthy distractions, while **Lincoln Park**, with its memorial to the Great Emancipator, marks the neighborhood's eastern limit. The spruced-up area around grand old **Union Station** lies to the north.

As a neighborhood, Capitol Hill has faced a lengthy climb to respectability. When Pierre L'Enfant and his surveyors began laying out the city, the cross drawn on what was then Jenkins Hill was the focus of a grand, Baroque-style city plan. The US Capitol was erected on the site of that cross, and in 1800 Congress moved in. But this marshy backwater outpost was slow to develop: it froze in the bitter winters and sweltered in the harsh summers; from their boarding houses around the Capitol, legislators had to trudge the muddy length of Pennsylvania Avenue for an audience with the president in the White House. After the **War of 1812** broke out, the British diverted a force away from Quebec and upstate New York and made a play for Washington and Baltimore – a plan designed more to shame the American government than to achieve any strategic goal. The Capitol was the first to burn, prompting many to suggest abandoning the city altogether and setting up political shop somewhere more hospitable.

However, with the conclusion of the war, the damaged structures were rebuilt, and as the capital and the federal government grew in stature in later years, so too did the Hill. During the nineteenth century, rows of elegant **townhouses**, which today form the keystone of Capitol Hill's status as a protected historic district, began to appear. Eventually, major federal institutions that had been housed since 1800 in the ever expanding Capitol complex moved into new homes of their own: first the Library of Congress in 1897, then the Supreme Court in 1935. Later in the twentieth century, massive office

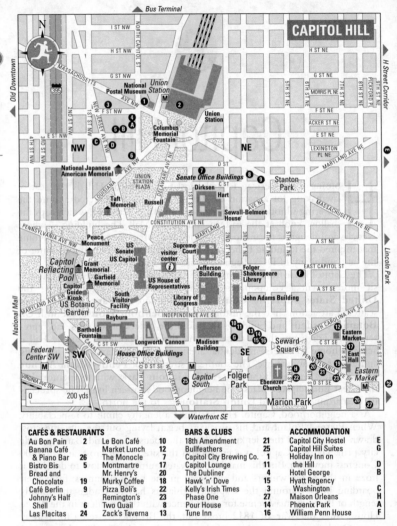

CAFÉS & RESTAURANTS		BARS & CLUBS		ACCOMMODATION	
Au Bon Pain	2	18th Amendment	21	Capitol City Hostel	E
Banana Café		Bullfeathers	25	Capitol Hill Suites	G
& Piano Bar	26	Capitol City Brewing Co.	1	Holiday Inn on	
Bistro Bis	5	Capitol Lounge	11	the Hill	D
Bread and		The Dubliner	4	Hotel George	B
Chocolate	19	Hawk 'n' Dove	15	Hyatt Regency	
Café Berlin	9	Kelly's Irish Times	3	Washington	C
Johnny's Half		Phase One	27	Maison Orleans	H
Shell	6	Pour House	14	Phoenix Park	A
Las Placitas	24	Tune Inn	16	William Penn House	F
Le Bon Café	10				
Market Lunch	12				
The Monocle	7				
Montmartre	17				
Mr. Henry's	20				
Murky Coffee	18				
Pizza Boli's	22				
Remington's	23				
Two Quail	8				
Zack's Taverna	13				

buildings were erected to accommodate legislators and their staff, reflecting the government's growth in stature, size, and bureaucracy.

The US Capitol

East end of the Mall, Capitol Hill ☏202/225-6827 for tour information, ☏202/224-3121 general information, ⓦ www.house.gov, ⓦ www.senate.gov, ⓦ www.aoc.gov; Capitol South or Union Station Metro. Daily tours 9am–4.30pm.

The towering, rib-vaulted dome of the **US Capitol** soars between north and south wings, respectively occupied by the **Senate** and **House of**

Representatives, the two legislative bodies of Congress. The building, with its grand halls and statues, committee rooms, and ornate chambers, is one of the few places in DC where you get a tangible sense of the immense power wielded by the nation's elected officials. Unlike the White House – where you're kept away from any real action – when Congress is in session, you can watch from third-floor galleries as elected leaders get down to business (see p.111 for details).

The Capitol is the only building in the city without an address, as it stands foursquare at the center of the street plan: the city quadrants extend from the building, and the numbered and lettered streets count away from its central axis. For the same reason, the building doesn't have a front or a back, simply an "East Front" and a "West Front." The **public entrance** is at the East Front, where,

Capitol conflicts

In 1812, Thomas Jefferson declared the US Capitol "the first temple dedicated to the sovereignty of the people, embellishing with Athenian taste the course of a nation looking far beyond the range of Athenian destinies." Indeed the building has been an iconic symbol of democracy for more than two centuries, and the foot of the US Capitol has been an obvious hub for **political demonstrations**. In 1894, Jacob S. Coxey led an "army" of unemployed people from Ohio and points west to demand a public works program to create jobs; he was arrested for trespassing, and the few hundred men with him slunk off home. In the decades following, the Capitol would be the focus of demonstrations from groups as diverse as women's suffragists and members of the KKK. In 1932, 17,000 unemployed soldiers in the so-called **Bonus Army** – demanding an early payment of their World War I military pensions – camped outside the Capitol, then set up shanties in Anacostia, where they were driven off by a force of federal soldiers led by George Patton and Douglas MacArthur. Decades later, in May 1968, the weary citizens of the Poor People's March set up makeshift tents and shelters they called "Resurrection City" (see box, p.65), which came to a similarly unsuccessful conclusion. More recently, in 1995, Nation of Islam leader Louis Farrakhan harangued white America from the terrace steps while addressing attendees of the Million Man March.

On occasion, the building itself has come **under attack**. Shots were fired in the Capitol in 1835, and in 1915, 1971, and 1983 various miscreants detonated bombs in the building (no one was injured). The worst attack was in the summer of 1998, when a lone gunman stormed the building, killing two Capitol police officers and injuring several members of the public. This event led to calls for the building to be made secure, and an underground visitor center – where tourists are to be screened and inspected before entering the building – was planned in response and will open in late 2008.

It was, of course, the 2001 terrorist attacks in DC and New York City that really led to clarion calls for restricting public access to the building. To add to the fears on high, in October 2001 an already jittery Capitol Hill was made even more so following a shipment of anthrax to the office of Senate Majority Leader Tom Daschle. Congress suspended its session for a week, tours of the Capitol were canceled for several months, and many offices were closed for decontamination.

While it will likely be some time before a new balance between security and liberty is reached (as far as the public's access to government buildings goes), one can be fairly sure that the Capitol's open-door policy will be less tolerant than in the past. With the anthrax crime yet to be solved and the fear of terrorism always present, the Hill has an atmosphere of heightened security and occasional paranoia, so visitors are well advised to avoid making off-color jokes about bomb-throwing or other violence while in the vicinity.

from 1829 to 1977, all the presidents were inaugurated. In 1981 Ronald Reagan was sworn in on the west side, and the six inaugurations since then have followed this precedent. When Congress is in session (from January 3 until close of business, usually in the fall) the lantern above the dome is lit, and flags fly above Senate and House wings.

Some history

A chaste plan, sufficiently capacious and convenient for a period not too remote, but one to which we may reasonably look forward, would meet my idea in the Capitol.

George Washington, 1792

Before the Revolution, relevant colonial matters were decided across the Atlantic in Parliament or locally by royal governors and their (frequently hand-picked) assemblies per each colony. Even with the tide of independence, the concept of **federalism** was still a nebulous one, and the colonies' aggregate assemblies met in all sorts of places, from New York City in 1765 (protesting the Stamp Act), to 1777 in Baltimore, to a half-dozen spots in Pennsylvania for the first and second Continental Congresses from 1774 to 1781. After the Revolution, the ill-fated American attempt to create a weak national govern-ment under the **Articles of Confederation** brought the Congress to another half-dozen locations from 1783 to 1788, until the Constitution was finally ratified and a functional federal government took hold – in New York City and Philadelphia, from 1789 to 1800.

In 1792, plans were formulated for a more permanent, site-specific location for the federal legislature, and the design of the seat of that government, the US Capitol, was thrown open to public competition. **Dr William Thornton**, an amateur whose grand Neoclassical offering brought a splendor deemed appropriate for Congress's meeting place, won the competition. On September 18, 1793, in a ceremony rich with Masonic symbolism, the square-and-compass-engraved cornerstone of the Capitol was laid by second-term president George Washington, himself a proud Mason. By the time the government moved to DC from Philadelphia seven years later, however, the Capitol was nowhere near completion.

When Congress assembled for the first time in the brick-and-sandstone building on November 22, 1800, only a small north wing housing the Senate Chamber, the House of Representatives, the Supreme Court, and the Library of Congress was ready. (Elsewhere, President John Adams moved into an unfinished White House; see p.142.) The building's ceilings leaked, and the furnaces installed to heat the structure produced intolerable temperatures. Adams's successor, **Thomas Jefferson** (the first president inaugurated at the Capitol), appointed the respected **Benjamin Latrobe** as surveyor of public buildings in an attempt to speed up work, and by 1807 a south wing had been built for the House of Representatives. In addition, Latrobe added a second floor to the north wing, allowing separate chambers for the Supreme Court and the Senate.

British troops burned down the Capitol and the White House in 1814. With President Madison having fled the city, Washington, DC's future was uncertain. Nonetheless, Congress met for four years in a quickly built "Brick Capitol" (see box, opposite) on the site of today's Supreme Court, and restoration work continued on what little was left of the original Capitol.

Latrobe found the building's interior gutted and the surviving exterior walls blackened by smoke (the British soldiers had stacked up all the furniture they could find and lit a bonfire). His grandiose ideas for rebuilding and expanding the Capitol found few admirers, however, and in 1817 he was replaced by **Charles Bulfinch**. The reconstructed wings were reopened in 1819, and in 1826 the Capitol finally appeared in a form that Thornton might have recognized, complete with a central rotunda topped by a low wooden dome clad in copper.

By the 1850s Congress had again run out of space. Plans were laid to build magnificent, complementary wings on either side of the building and to replace the dome with something more substantial. In 1857 the new south wing accommodated the **House Chamber**, and two years later the **Senate Chamber** moved to the new north wing. Two years later, the **Civil War** threatened to halt work on the **dome**, but Abraham Lincoln, recognizing the Capitol as a potent symbol of the Union, was determined that the building should be completed. A cast-iron dome was painstakingly assembled, at three times the height of the previous dome, though the work was hampered by the presence of Union troops stationed in the building (some soldiers insisted on shinning up and down hundred-foot ropes draped from the Rotunda walls for amusement). But in December 1863 the glorious project came to fruition. Hoisted on top of the white-painted dome was the nineteen-foot-high **Statue of Freedom** by sculptor Thomas Crawford. Resplendent in a feathered helmet and clutching a sword and shield, the statue is also known as "Armed Liberty."

The surrounding terraces were added after the Civil War, and when extra office space was required in the 1870s, separate **House and Senate office buildings** were built in the streets on either side of the Capitol. However, with the Capitol dome being much larger than its predecessor, the visual effect of the portico and its columns was altered considerably, and subsequent reconstructions of the East Front have tried to make the architecture more harmonious: the porch was rebuilt in 1904, followed 55 years later with a more general construction program that included the replacement of the old sandstone columns with marble – the originals are now poised on a grassy plot by themselves at the National Arboretum (see p.218). The East Front was extended in 1962 and faced in marble to prevent the original sandstone from deteriorating further; so far the West Front – now the oldest part of the building – has

The brief life of the Brick Capitol

When the British marched into Washington in August 1814, they promptly burned down the Capitol and, in the words of Alistair Cooke, "the rest of the new public buildings that in those days were all that distinguished Washington from a fishing town on a marsh." It was a supreme humiliation, and one that revived the bitter debate about Washington's suitability as the nation's capital. President Madison, a native Virginian, gave the Northern dissenters no chance to agitate: he returned to the city at the earliest opportunity and directed the building of a temporary **Brick Capitol**. Hastily designed by Benjamin Latrobe, it was erected on the site of today's Supreme Court – land then occupied by a tavern and vegetable garden. Here, in 1817, James Monroe became the first president to take the oath of office in an outdoor public ceremony in Washington.

When the US Capitol was finally restored in 1819 and the government moved back in, the Brick Capitol became home to the Circuit Court of DC until the new City Hall was finished. From 1824 to 1861 the building was a lodging house, and from 1861 to 1867 it was a prison. It was later replaced by three row houses, which were in turn demolished to make way for the Supreme Court in 1935, making the Capitol almost completely surrounded by organs of the federal government.

avoided modern accretions, though it was restored in the 1980s. Finally, in 2000, the millions of annual visitors to the Capitol necessitated the deconstruction of the land in front of the East Front to create an underground visitor center, which will open to the public in fall 2008.

Visiting the Capitol

With all the terrorism and war-making of recent years, access to the nation's highest legislative body has become more restricted. The West Front is guarded and gated, and anyone not here on official business is barred entrance, while the East Front is being completely reconstructed to make way for the new **underground visitor center**. The completion of this $550 million showpiece has been long overdue and the project has run well over budget, with the east face of the Capitol, perhaps symbolically, resembling a deconstructed shambles throughout the Bush administration. The center, though, promises great things once completed: in addition to offering access to the Capitol, it will have a massive subterranean **Exhibition Hall** where you can find out all about the building and the role it played in the nation's democracy, including biographies and information about some of the key figures in congressional history, and the various inaugurations that have taken place here. There will also be the requisite gift shops and restaurants, a pair of theaters devoted to each chamber of Congress, a tunnel to the Thomas Jefferson building of the Library of Congress, and acres of new office space, media production facilities, and related infrastructure for politicians and their staffs. Not surprisingly, the entire below-ground site will be huge, occupying up to three-quarters the size of the Capitol's footprint.

Until it is completed, to enter the building, you'll need to drop by the **Capitol Guide Service kiosk** near the southwest side of the complex (near the James Garfield statue, 1st St SW at Maryland Ave) and pick up free tickets. It's important to get there as early as possible: tickets are handed out beginning at 9am, but lines often form well in advance. Once you have your tickets, you can wait at the **South Visitor Receiving Facility**, on the south side of the House of Representatives building, until your reserved tour begins; if you visit between April and September, expect to wait in line for one or two hours. Queues are shorter in winter, and the place is generally less busy on Sundays and during lunchtime most other days. Finally, although the sites listed below have typically been open for tours in the past, erratic security clampdowns may make some of them off limits during your visit.

The Rotunda

Standing in the **Rotunda**, you're not only at the center of the Capitol, but at point zero of the entire District of Columbia. William Thornton, the Capitol's first architect, took Rome's Pantheon as his model, so it's no wonder that this is a magnificent space: 180ft high and 96ft across, with the dome canopy decorated by Constantino Brumidi's mighty **fresco** depicting the *Apotheosis of Washington*. The fresco took the 60-year-old Brumidi almost a year to complete and shows George Washington surrounded by symbols of democracy, arts, science, and industry, as well as female figures representing the thirteen original states. Brumidi had a hand, too, in the **frieze** celebrating American history that runs around the Rotunda wall, beginning with Columbus's arrival in the New World and ending with the Civil War.

From the floor, it's hard to see much detail of either frieze or fresco, and eyes are drawn instead to the eight large **oil paintings** that hang below the frieze. Four of the paintings depict events associated with the "discovery" and settlement of the country (like, again, Columbus's arrival and the Pilgrims' disembarkation), though most notable are the four Revolutionary War pieces by **John Trumbull**, who trained under Benjamin West, the first American artist to study in Europe. These paintings (1818–24) are still in the eighteenth-century British vein, with stiff figures and martial pomp and ceremony. Three of them portray military leaders giving up their commands – two because of wartime surrenders (Burgoyne and Cornwallis) and one because of the end of war (Washington before Congress) – and one depicts the signing of the **Declaration of Independence**, showing the key figures who drafted the document – Jefferson, John Adams, and Ben Franklin among them – presenting it to Continental Congress president John Hancock while other legislators stand or sit at rigid attention.

Busts and statues of prominent American leaders fill in the gaps in the rest of the Rotunda. Washington, Jefferson, Lincoln, and Jackson are all here, along with a modern bust of Dr Martin Luther King Jr and a gold facsimile of the Magna Carta. In such august surroundings more than thirty people – including members of Congress, military leaders, eminent citizens, and eleven presidents – have been **laid in state** before burial. The most recently honored was the nation's 38th president, Gerald Ford, who died in December 2006 at age 93, making him the longest-lived former president.

National Statuary Hall

From the Rotunda you move south into one of the earliest extensions of the building – the 1807 section that once housed the chamber of the **House of Representatives** (rebuilt in 1819), designed in grand Roman style with Classical elements of sandstone pilasters and marble capitals. In this D-shaped space with its stylized coffered ceiling and oculus, the acoustics here are such that, from his desk, John Quincy Adams could supposedly eavesdrop on opposition members on the other side of the room.

After the House moved into its new wing in 1857, the chamber was used for various temporary purposes (novelist Anthony Trollope bought gingerbread from a market stall in here) until Congress decided to turn it into the **National Statuary Hall** and invited each state to contribute two statues of its most famous citizens. Around forty statues are still on display in the hall, with the others scattered around the corridors in the rest of the building, including such figures as Vermont patriot Ethan Allen and Texas revolutionary Sam Houston, missionaries like Marcus Whitman and Brigham Young, Congressional heavyweights like William Jennings Bryan and Daniel Webster, and, more questionably, Confederates like Robert E. Lee and Jefferson Davis.

Adelaide Johnson's 1921 *Suffrage Monument*, which was moved to the Rotunda after languishing in the Crypt (see p.111) for much of its existence, certainly grabs your attention. The statue shows women's rights pioneers Susan B. Anthony, Lucretia Mott, and Elizabeth Cady Stanton poking their heads out of a large, mostly uncut block of granite, as if entombed there. Although the work is hardly an aesthetic triumph and has been criticized as unbefitting the importance of these key figures, it is one of only six statues of women in the entire building.

Old Senate Chamber

North of the Rotunda is the **Old Senate Chamber**. This splendid semicircular gallery, with its embossed rose ceiling and eight Ionic columns made from

▲ Old Supreme Court Chamber, US Capitol

Potomac marble, was built in 1810 and reconstructed from 1815 to 1819, after the British had done their worst to the city. The Senate met here until 1859, when it moved into its current quarters. The Supreme Court moved in and stayed until 1935, when it, too, was given a new home. After that the Old Senate Chamber sat largely unused until it was restored to its mid-nineteenth-century glory for the Bicentennial in 1976. Its furnishings are redolent of that period; the members' desks are reproductions, but the gilt eagle topping the vice president's chair is original, as is the portrait of George Washington by Rembrandt Peale.

Contemporary engravings helped restorers reproduce other features of the original Senate chamber, like the rich red carpet emblazoned with gold stars. The original carpet received severe punishment from spit tobacco despite the provision of a cuspidor by every desk. Expectoration notwithstanding, members of this Senate chamber participated in some of the most **celebrated debates** of the era: in 1830 the great orator Daniel Webster of Massachusetts fiercely defended "Liberty and the Union" in a famous speech lasting several hours; over two days in 1850 Henry Clay pleaded his succession of compromises to preserve the Union (brandishing a fragment of Washington's coffin for emphasis); and in 1856, Senator Charles Sumner of Massachusetts – having declaimed against the Kansas-Nebraska Bill (which allowed for extending slavery into the new territories) and branded slavery a "harlot"– was caned senseless at his desk by Preston Brooks, an incensed congressman from South Carolina. Both men became heroes on their respective sides of the Mason-Dixon line.

Old Supreme Court and the Crypt

Before 1810, the Senate met on the floor below the **Old Senate Chamber**, in a room that architect Benjamin Latrobe later revamped to house the **Supreme Court**, which sorely needed a permanent home. While the work was being carried out, Supreme Court sessions were often held in an inn opposite the Capitol, and once the British had delayed matters by burning the rest of the building, the nation's highest tribunal was forced to meet in rented townhouses on the Hill. By 1819, however, the Court had settled in the Old Senate

Chamber, where it remained until 1860, when it moved again – this time upstairs, to the chamber just vacated by the Senate.

The **Old Supreme Court Chamber** is quite a visually appealing spot, occupying a semicircular space topped with ten ribs that converge at a central node, giving the ceiling the appearance of a sunburst or umbrella, with the busts of the nation's first five chief justices sitting in prominent niches. Sitting on chairs whose individual designs reflected the personal preference of each, the justices held court at mahogany desks behind a mahogany rail, with lovely natural light coming in through the windows; unfortunately, the room has since been lit by artificial means since the extension of the East Front of the Capitol blocked the view in the 1950s. By that time, the Court had been gone for a century and the chamber served as a law library and congressional committee space, before being relegated to a mere storeroom until just before the Bicentennial, when it, too, was restored to its mid-nineteenth-century appearance on the basis of original etchings and plans for the building. Within the room's considerable splendor, only two chief justices ever held sway here, John Marshall and Roger Taney, and it was the latter who presided over the court's most (in)famous moment – *Dred Scott v. Sandford*, the 1857 ruling that held that people of African descent were not US citizens and Congress had no right to prohibit slavery from federal territories. Given that this notorious decision was the last significant one in these quarters, it gives a special irony to the elegant bust of Taney you see as you enter the chamber.

The **Crypt** lies underneath the Rotunda, on the same level as the Old Supreme Court Chamber. Lined with Doric sandstone columns, it was built in 1827 and designed to house George Washington's tomb, a plan that was never realized (Washington is buried with his wife, Martha, at Mount Vernon). The Crypt instead is an **exhibition center**, displaying details of the plans submitted for the 1792 architectural competition and the Capitol's construction.

House and Senate chambers

With beefed-up security measures, public access to the **House and Senate chambers** has been cut back; it's hard to get into the visitors' galleries since they're not part of the official Capitol tour. If you're an American citizen, you can apply to your representative's or senator's office in advance for a pass valid for the entire (two-year) session of Congress, and enter the Senate from the north side of that wing and the House of Representatives from its south side. Foreign visitors wanting a look will need to get tickets from the **South Visitor Receiving Facility** (see p.108) and, following that, line up for entry at the south side of the House of Representatives. For more information, call ⊤202/225-6827 or visit Ⓦwww.house.gov or Ⓦwww.senate.gov.

The chambers may be almost empty, or deep in torpor, when you show up, which is fine if all you want is a flavor of either place. If you're lucky, you may watch members introduce legislation or even vote on various bills or issues. The House chamber is the more striking of the two, with its decorative frieze and oil paintings; from here the president addresses joint sessions of Congress and delivers his annual **State of the Union** speech. You can enter the House even when it's not in session, but the Senate must be open for business for the public to be allowed admittance.

Legislative offices

Only political junkies will likely be interested in poking around the six legislative **office buildings** that contain the **committee rooms** where most of the day-to-day political activity of the Senate and House takes place (hearings have been open to the public since the 1970s). The first of these office buildings – all named for past politicians – were the imperious Cannon and Russell, built in 1907–09, and the last, the modern Hart, in 1982; they follow the pattern of the Capitol in that the Senate office buildings (Russell, Dirksen, and Hart) are to the north and the House office buildings (Cannon, Longworth, and Rayburn) are to the south. Especially worth a look are the magisterial, column-encircled rotundas of the Beaux-Arts-style Cannon and Russell buildings. In the Senate buildings, each politician's office is marked by an American flag and his or her state flag in the corridor outside the door. Office hours can be erratic, depending on the relative activity of the politicians hived inside; **committee hearings**, usually held in the morning, are listed in the *Washington Post*'s "Today in Congress" section. Unless you turn up early, you may not get in, especially to anything currently featured on the TV news. Only in the Hart Building is there any art of note: dominating the atrium is Alexander Calder's monumental black *Mountains and Clouds*. This was the artist's last work, and the only one to combine a separate mobile and stabile.

West of the Capitol

Facing the National Mall, the West Front of the Capitol provides a striking image of imperial power that is heightened by the mirror image shown in the **Capitol Reflecting Pool** at its base. The pool itself, with its surrounding benches and sloping wall, is an excellent spot to rest before tackling the museums on the Mall, plus it provides an important function with its aesthetic form: the shallow watery expanse was laid out as part of a lightweight roof to shelter the subterranean channel of the 395 freeway below, as anything heavier would be unsuitable for covering such a wide area.

West Front memorials

If most of the design of the Capitol reflects the contributions of the two (or more) political parties, the **memorials** on the **West Front** are all Republican. The first honors the assassinated twentieth president, James Garfield (shot only four months after his inauguration, he may have survived the bullet were it not for lousy medical care), and sits at the junction of the Capitol grounds with Pennsylvania Avenue NW and Maryland Avenue SW. The 1887 **Garfield Monument** is in the vicinity of the Capitol Guide Service kiosk, where you can pick up tickets for tours of the Capitol (see p.108), and shows a noble, steadfast Garfield posing atop a granite pillar, while below sit three allegorical sculptures relating to his days as a student, soldier, and statesman. However, the most significant structure is just north, the 250ft-long **Ulysses S. Grant Memorial**, honoring the general-in-chief of the Union forces under President Lincoln during the Civil War. Dedicated in 1922, the monument depicts a somber Grant on horseback, guarded by lions, flanked by a charging cavalry unit on one side and an artillery unit moving through thick mud on the other. Sculptor Henry Merwin Shrady spent twenty years on the work, using uniformed soldiers-in-training as his models. In waging total war on the Confederate forces from 1864 to 1865, Grant secured final victory for Lincoln, thus preserving the Union. Contemporaries talked of his personal shortcomings

DC TV

Many politicians seem tailor-made for TV cameras. However, it was not always so. Only after JFK's resounding victory over Richard Nixon in the televised 1960 presidential debates "was it apparent" that the new means of communication would be visual. Today, there are countless opportunities to see those in public office on public display, and to participate in the process yourself by taking part in a media-friendly political rally or protest event.

Congress in session ▲

Conservative pundit Pat Buchanan ▼

Official events

Following the protocol and dutifully showing up to **watch a session of Congress** (see p.111 for information) is the obvious place to start for viewing official events in Washington. Not only will you see some of the speeches captured by C-SPAN for cable TV, but from the gallery you'll also have the added reverse view of Congressmen snoozing or being absent from the chamber altogether. The politicians also make regular appearances before the cameras in and around their offices and committee rooms, both of which you're allowed access to.

For those more interested in executive action, the president makes regular appearances at factories, parks, schools, memorials, and military bases (variously accessible depending on the event), and in full-throated campaign rallies (almost always open to public view). Other **special events**, often televised, may include fiery debates between political antagonists, holiday speeches at places like Arlington National Cemetery and the White House Christmas tree, and religious oratory at any of the big churches in town. The *Washington Post* prints a listing of such events in its presidential coverage and in sections including "Today in Congress."

Digging deeper

There are any number of **places to watch politicians**, lobbyists, and other bigwigs conducting their business in the District, but some spots have outsize reputations for such activity: the dining rooms of the Hay-Adams and Mayflower hotels, namely, have hosted all kinds of tense negotiations as well as **backslapping soirees** over the decades, while restaurants like the Old Ebbitt Grill, Monocle, Martin's Tavern, and Citronelle are well regarded not only for their food but for the regular presence of pols going about their paces. The same is true for bars like Bullfeathers, the Hawk 'n Dove, the Round Robin Bar, and the Capitol Lounge. And though you're more likely to see a squad of congressional staffers getting plastered, there's always the chance of a big-name politician doing something embarrassing enough to make the **Internet gossip pages** (www .wonkette.com and www.drudgereport .com) or tarnish his or her reputation, if not necessarily the nation's.

Meeting the press

Although you'll have difficulty getting close to a reporter while he or she is standing on the White House lawn or in other official settings, there are ways to interact with the media, or at least get a close-up view of what they're covering. The most obvious method is to make yourself available for a "man on the street" **interview**, offering to fill reporters' need for anecdotal views of the events of the day. Barring that, you might keep alert to the sudden presence of cameras, microphones, and satellite feeds, usually a good sign that a **public spectacle** is taking place – a politician denouncing various detractors, scurrying to hide from scandal, or being taken away in handcuffs. Since these events are not announced in advance, the only way to get in on the scene is by being alert and watching for the telltale sight of news vans and helicopters, and perhaps taking a picture of the event yourself for a handy souvenir of your DC trip.

▲ A reporter behind the cameras in the capital

▼ Senator Jim Webb of Virginia

Favorite protest sites

If you've come to DC to register your displeasure with the events of the day or with those who have their hands on the levers of power, you could do worse than drop in on some of these places. As always, for a specific protest, check media sources ahead of time to make sure you get there in time to chant, march, yell, or be arrested.

Lafayette Square Protesters have been using this space on the White House's north side for more than a century to get the chief executive's goat.

Lincoln Memorial This spot on the western end of the National Mall needs no introduction for its protest activities; see box on p.64 for the full rundown.

Iraq war protest ▲

Vietnam rights protest ▼

US Capitol West Front With the East Front now reserved for a huge visitor center, activists get wedged in between the Capitol steps and the Reflecting Pool to make their voices heard – or just spread out onto the Mall for larger groups.

Supreme Court plaza Always the go-to spot for judicial protests when a controversial case is being decided before the nation's highest bench.

The Pentagon Although not the spot for protest it once was (getting close to the building is impossible), the perimeter of America's war-making office is still a solid choice for peace activists.

National Mall war memorials When used for protest, these memorials usually involve veterans' issues such as health-care funding and POW and MIA matters.

Foreign embassies Expatriates and human-rights activists can often be spotted outside embassy gates protesting their respective countries' policies on minority rights, open elections, and the like.

and of his fearsome drinking habits, but Lincoln knocked back all complaints, saying, "I wish some of you would tell me the brand of whiskey that Grant drinks. I would like to send a barrel of it to my other generals."

Farther north, at the corner of Pennsylvania Avenue and 1st St NW, stands the 44ft-high marble pillar of the **Peace Monument**, so-called for the partially nude figure of the Roman goddess of Peace that faces the Capitol; it is matched on the opposite side of the building by the goddess Victory and childlike forms of Mars and Neptune, in training for war and seacraft, respectively. The Peace Monument was built in 1878 and commemorates Civil War soldiers lost at sea, and with its evocative, austere form, is a moving if little-noticed sculpture, especially at its apex. Here, at the pinnacle of the monument, we find the stark figure of Grief, weeping on the shoulder of History, their bodies provocatively turned away from the Capitol, as if knowing what future conflicts will bring.

North of the Reflecting Pool toward Union Station, a small park bordered by Constitution and Louisiana avenues contains the **Robert A. Taft Memorial and Carillon**, a bronze statue and 100ft-high concrete bell tower, which sounds on the hour, erected in 1958. The memorial honors the veteran senator (and son of President William Howard Taft), who during the mid-twentieth century was known simply as "Mr. Republican." Unlike Taft himself, the carillon's 27 bells are all fairly huge and loud, the largest of them weighing seven tons.

A reminder of a darker chapter in the nation's history can be found just north, at the triangular intersection of New Jersey, Louisiana, and D streets, where the **National Japanese American Memorial** commemorates the various Japanese American units and soldiers who fought in World War II, including twenty Medal of Honor winners. It's highlighted by a central 14ft-tall marble and bronze sculpture of two intertwined cranes held to their pillar by barbed wire, which they attempt to break through with their beaks. The symbolic reference is, of course, to the 120,000 Japanese American citizens who were rounded up in the xenophobic days after Pearl Harbor and sent to internment camps in the American West. The presidential order for this action was given by Franklin Roosevelt, whose own memorial at the Tidal Basin gives no reference to this shameful event.

US Botanic Garden

245 1st St SW ☎202/225-8333, ⊛www.usbg.gov. Daily 10am–5pm.

The closest museum or institution to the Capitol, the **US Botanic Garden** sits near a corner of the National Mall. Its centerpiece is a grand conservatory crowned by an 80ft-tall **Palm House**, the results of a renovation that transformed the Victorian-style structure, built in 1933, into a state-of-the-art greenhouse, where it's now possible to grow plants from almost everywhere in the world. More than four thousand plants are currently on view, of a collection of more than 26,000. Especially intriguing are the climate-controlled rooms devoted to colorful ranks of tropical, subtropical, and desert plants; the section showcasing orchids, two hundred (of the garden's twelve thousand) varieties of which are visible at any one time; and the **Jungle Room**, stuffed with equatorial trees and other plants and humid almost to the point of discomfort.

On the west side of the facility is the newest addition to the site, the **National Garden**, which opened in 2006 to instruct the public about various environmental and horticultural issues. Themed plots include a **Rose Garden**; a pleasant **Regional Garden** thick with blooms from plants of the mid-Atlantic area; a **Butterfly Garden** that employs trees, shrubs, and flowers such as primrose, milkweed, and coneflower to attract the colorful winged insects, as well as hummingbirds; and a **First Ladies Water Garden** built around a fountain meant to symbolize the various accomplishments of the wives of the presidents.

While the US Botanic Garden's roots can be traced to early proponents like George Washington and Thomas Jefferson, it was Lt Charles Wilkes's 1838–42 expedition to the South Seas that really got things going. The irascible Wilkes, said to be the model for the Captain Ahab character in Herman Melville's seafaring epic, *Moby Dick*, returned to America after four years and nearly 90,000 miles with a collection of ten thousand plants from around the world. These specimens formed the core of a revitalized garden, and a cycad dating back to Wilkes's journey is still on view.

Bartholdi Fountain

South of the Botanic Garden, across Independence Avenue at 1st Street SW, stands the 30ft-high **Bartholdi Fountain**, submitted by French sculptor Frédéric-Auguste Bartholdi to the 1876 Centennial Exhibition in Philadelphia. (A decade later Bartholdi would create the Statue of Liberty.) Congress bought the fountain in 1877 for display on the Mall, where its original gas lamps – illuminated at night – made it a popular evening hang-out. Moved to this site in 1932, it's often deserted today, but it's as good a spot as any to catch your breath before taking the long walk down the Mall.

East of the Capitol

All the other notable buildings and institutions of Capitol Hill – like the **Supreme Court** and **Library of Congress** – lie on the east side of the Capitol, within half a dozen blocks of one another. Here, in the charming and historic East Capitol neighborhood, amid the grand old Georgian and Federal townhouses, a few historic old homes, such as the Sewall-Belmont House, add to the picturesque setting, making it a good spot for a daytime walk. It's worth being wary after dark though: for all its upscale trappings, Supreme Court justice David Souter was mugged here a few years ago, not far from his home.

The US Supreme Court

1st St and Maryland Ave NE ℡202/479-3211, 🌐www.supremecourtus.gov; Union Station or Capitol South Metro. Mon–Fri 9am–4.30pm.

The third – and easily the most respected – branch of American government, the judiciary, has its apex at the **Supreme Court of the United States**. Not only is the court the final word on what is and isn't constitutional, it's also the nation's arbiter for disputes between states, between the federal government and states, between federal and state judges, and between individuals appealing all kinds of legal decisions – from boundary disputes to death-penalty sentences. Since it was established at the Constitutional Convention of 1787, the Court has functioned as both the guardian and interpreter of the **Constitution**, but it only really began flexing its muscles in the early 1800s under the sway of Chief Justice John Marshall (see box, pp.116–117). Its familiar motto is "Equal Justice For All" – the legend inscribed upon the architrave above the double row of eight columns facing 1st Street.

Oddly, for such a linchpin of the American political system, the Supreme Court was forced to share quarters in the US Capitol until 1935, when, on the prompting of Chief Justice (and former president) William Howard Taft, it was finally granted its own building. Seventy-year-old **Cass Gilbert**, known primarily for his Gothic Revival–style Woolworth Building in New York, was perhaps an unusual choice for architect, but his marble temple did indeed reflect the dignity and importance of the Supreme Court. In response to its warm reception, Gilbert said, "It is receiving so much favorable praise that I am wondering what is wrong with it."

The facade of the building is of bright white marble, and the solemn, if not pompous, **sculptures** "Contemplation of Justice" and "Guardian of Law" flank the wide steps down to 1st Street. The sculptures' effect is lightened somewhat by the relaxed representations on the **pediment** over the main entrance: here, among allegorical Greek figures, are Chief Justice Taft as a Yale student, Chief Justice Marshall reclining, and architect Gilbert and sculptor Robert Aitken clad in togas.

Inside, the main corridor – known as the **Great Hall** – has a superb carved and painted ceiling, white walls lined with marble columns, and busts of all the former chief justices. At the end of the corridor is the surprisingly compact **Court Chamber**, with damask drapes and a molded plaster ceiling done up in gold leaf, flanked by more marble columns – these quarried from Siena, Italy, unlike the marble elsewhere, which comes from American quarries. A frieze runs around all four sides, its relief panels depicting various legal themes, allegorical figures, and ancient and modern lawgivers. When in session, the chief justice, currently John Roberts, sits in the center of the **bench** (below the clock), with the most senior justice on his right (left as you face the bench) and the next in precedence on his left; the rest sit in similar alternating fashion so that the most junior justice sits on the far left – as of 2008, ironically, Samuel Alito. The chairs for each justice are made in the Court's own carpentry shop, and the Court even has its own police force.

You used to be allowed to reach the ground floor via the building's wondrous **spiral staircases**, each marble course anchored to the wall instead of a central support, in the Roman form of a spiraling arch. However, today, in a more security-obsessed era, you'll have to content yourself with an elevator ride. The lower floor has its own Great Hall (overseen by a mighty statue of Chief Justice Marshall lounging in his chair) and a permanent exhibition about the Court. A free, short movie fills you in on the Court's legal and political background, while architectural notes, sketches, and photos trace the history of the building itself. You'll also find restrooms, a gift shop, a snack bar, and a cafeteria on this level.

Visiting the Court

The Court is **in session** from October through June. Between the beginning of October and the end of April, oral arguments are heard every Monday, Tuesday, and Wednesday from 10am to noon and 1pm to 3pm on occasion. (In May and June, the Court works out its rulings and presents them to the public.) The sessions, which almost always last one hour per case, are **open to the public** on a first-come, first-served basis. Arrive by 8.30am if you really want one of the 150 seats, and keep in mind that for some high-profile cases, such as those involving abortion rights, civil liberties, or freedom of speech, people sometimes wait in line overnight. More casual visitors simply join a separate line, happy to settle for a three-minute stroll through the standing gallery. When Court is not in session, guides give **lectures** in the Court Chamber (Mon–Fri 9.30am–3.30pm; hourly on the half-hour).

The supremacy of the Supreme Court

The **Supreme Court** was established by the Constitution to oversee the balance between the federal government and the states, and between the legislative and executive branches of government. By tradition, it comprises nine justices, who are by law appointed by the president and approved by the Senate. Once approved, the justices are in for life ("during good behavior," per the Constitution) and can be removed only by impeachment.

The Court (and the associated system of district courts) convened for the first time in February 1790. At the end of the following year, the ratification of the Bill of Rights in effect gave the Supreme Court an additional role: to defend the liberties enshrined in the Bill, directing the country as to what was and wasn't constitutional. However, it wasn't until 1803 and the case of *Marbury v Madison* that the Court's power of **judicial review** – the ability to declare a law or action of Congress or the president unconstitutional – was established, and the court with **John Marshall** at the helm became an institution unto itself. Since then, the Supreme Court has repeatedly shaped the country's social and political legacies by ruling on and, in the following cases, upholding the constitutionality of slavery (in the 1857 *Dred Scott* case), segregation (1896's *Plessy v Ferguson*), desegregation (1954's *Brown v Board of Education*), abortion rights (1973's *Roe v Wade*), and freedom of the press (1971's *New York Times Co. v the United States*, over whether the *Times* had the right to publish the leaked Pentagon Papers, which revealed expanded US involvement in Vietnam).

Because the country relies on an eighteenth-century document as the basis of its twenty-first-century political structure, the Supreme Court has its work cut out for it, and must provide interpretive rulings from time to time. In practice, this leads to a great deal of arguing in front of and among the Supreme Court justices. Even though it's the country's final court of appeal, the Supreme Court takes only one percent of the seven thousand cases lower courts ask it to hear each year. These cases are chosen according to the so-called **Rule of Four**, meaning at least four justices have agreed to hear a case. The Court grants these cases *certiorari* – the prospect of making a case "more certain" by agreeing to review it – and then hears written and oral arguments. After the deliberations, one justice is made responsible for writing the

Sewall-Belmont House

144 Constitution Ave NE ☎202/546-1210, ⊛www.sewallbelmont.org; Union Station Metro. Tues–Fri 11am–3pm, Sat noon–4pm. $5.

North of the Supreme Court, across Constitution Avenue at 2nd Street, is the red-brick townhouse known as the **Sewall–Belmont House**, one of the oldest residences in the city. The dainty building was built in 1800 by Robert Sewall and rented in 1801 to Albert Gallatin, Treasury secretary to presidents Jefferson and Madison. Gallatin participated in negotiations for the Louisiana Purchase (1803), which was signed in one of the front rooms. In 1814, while the Capitol was burning, a group of soldiers under Commander Joshua Barney retreated to the house and fired upon the British. This resistance, however, only stirred the British to set the house ablaze. Unlike the Capitol, it wasn't too badly damaged; enough of it survived, in fact, for Gallatin to negotiate the war-ending Treaty of Ghent here. The treaty was actually signed in the Octagon, in nearby Foggy Bottom (see p.155).

In 1929, the house was sold to the **National Woman's Party** and was home for many years to Alice Paul, the party's founder and author of the 1923 Equal Rights Amendment. The house still serves as party headquarters and maintains a museum and gallery dedicated to the country's women's and suffrage movements. A short film fills in some of the background of the house, a short

opinion, which serves as the latest interpretation of that particular constitutional issue. The justices don't all have to agree: they can concur in the majority decision even if they don't accept all the arguments, or they can produce a dissenting opinion, which might be cited in future challenges to particular laws.

The make-up of the Supreme Court is of the utmost relevance to the opinions it will produce. Not surprisingly, presidents over the years have thought it useful to have politically sympathetic justices on the bench and have made appointments accordingly. But things don't always go as planned: the most famous example of this is President Eisenhower's selection of California governor **Earl Warren** to the bench in the 1950s. Instead of ruling like a rock-ribbed Republican, as Ike thought he would, Warren ended up being perhaps the most liberal-minded chief justice in the court's history and steering the Court to the left throughout the rest of the 1950s and 60s. Also, the process is tinged with an element of chance, dependent upon the longevity of the incumbent justices: both Eisenhower and Richard Nixon appointed four justices, while Jimmy Carter appointed none (George W. Bush has a pair). Controversial Supreme Court nominees can be rejected by the Senate, as were two of Nixon's plus Reagan's ultra-conservative hopeful Robert Bork. George H.W. Bush's second appointee, Clarence Thomas, only scraped through after the highly publicized hearings following lawyer Anita Hill's allegations of sexual harassment.

Whichever way the Court leans, and despite its firm roots in the Constitution, it depends ultimately on the mood of the people for its authority. If it produces opinions that are overwhelmingly opposed by inferior courts, or by the president or Congress, there's not much it can do to enforce them. Indeed, Congress has the constitutional right (Article 3, Section 2) to **restrict the Court's jurisdiction** – a notion proposed by FDR when he tired of the Court's constant interference with his New Deal legislation, along with his ill-fated plan to "pack" the court to his favor with extra justices. Perhaps unique among federal institutions, the Supreme Court has generally retained the respect of the American people for its perceived impartiality in defending the Constitution against partisan politics, even if that was temporarily threatened by its decision in *Bush v Gore*, which determined the 2000 presidential election.

tour makes much of the period furnishings, and the carriage house contains the country's earliest feminist library. Portraits, busts, and photographs of all the best-known activists adorn the halls and walls, starting in the lobby with sculptor Adelaide Johnson's busts of Susan B. Anthony, Elizabeth Cady Stanton, and Lucretia Mott, the trio that Johnson would memorialize with her collective sculpture *Suffrage Monument* in the Capitol (see p.109). Other mementos include the desks of both Alice Paul and Susan B. Anthony, and the banner used to picket the White House during World War I when the call for universal suffrage reached its loudest pitch.

Folger Shakespeare Library

201 E Capitol St ☏202/544-4600, ⊛www.folger.edu; Union Station or Capitol South Metro. Mon–Sat 10am–5pm.

The renowned **Folger Shakespeare Library**, on the south side of the Supreme Court, has something of a split architectural personality. The sparkling white marble facade is decorated in mid-period Art Deco, with geometric window grilles, and panel reliefs depict scenes from the Bard's plays. The look inside, however, is quite different: a dark oak-paneled Elizabethan **Great Hall** features carved lintels, stained glass, Tudor roses, and a sculpted ceiling.

Founded in 1932, the Folger holds more than 350,000 books, manuscripts, paintings, and engravings – making it the world's third-largest repository of books in English printed prior to the mid-seventeenth century – only a fraction of which focus strictly on Shakespeare. The **Great Hall** displays changing exhibitions about the playwright and various historical and literary themes, anything from the role of symbol and allegory in the plays to the style of armor in the era. The reproduction **Elizabethan Theater** annually hosts a trio of performances, usually two by the Bard and another by a contemporary such as Marlowe, and in the same theater are regular lectures and readings as well as medieval and Renaissance music concerts by the Folger Consort (see p.311). Finally, an Elizabethan **garden** on the east lawn grows herbs and flowers common in the sixteenth century, while the **gift shop** sells everything from assorted editions of the Stratford lad's plays to jokey T-shirts based on Shakespearean quotations.

Try to visit when a free ninety-minute **guided tour** is offered (Mon–Fri 11am, Sat 11am & 1pm); every third Saturday (April–Oct 10am & 11am), a guide also lectures on the intricacies of the garden. The **library** itself – another sixteenth-century reproduction – is designed for registered scholars and open to the public only during the Folger's annual celebration of Shakespeare's birthday (usually the Saturday nearest April 23). In the **Shakespeare Gallery**, next to the Great Hall, there's a permanent multimedia exhibit titled "The Seven Ages of Man," which offers a computer-assisted glimpse of the Folger's holdings and Shakespeare's life and work.

The Library of Congress

Jefferson Bldg, 1st St SE at Independence Ave T202/707-8000, Wwww.loc.gov; Capitol South Metro. Jefferson Building Mon–Sat 10am–5.30pm; Madison Building Mon–Sat 8.30am–9.30pm, Sat closes 6.30pm; Adams Building Mon, Wed & Thurs 8.30am–9.30pm, Tues, Fri & Sat 8.30am–5.30pm.

The **Library of Congress** is the nation's official copyright office and the world's largest library (it's said that, on average, ten items per minute are added to its holdings). Books are just part of its unimaginably vast collection: 128 million items, from books, maps, and manuscripts to movies, musical instruments, and photographs, are kept on 530 miles of shelving in closed stacks spread out over three buildings – where they stay, as the Library of Congress does not circulate its materials beyond the complex.

When Congress convened in 1800 in the new, if incomplete, Capitol, it was considered imperative to fund a library for the use of its members. Five thousand dollars was made available to buy books for a Library of Congress, which was housed in a small room in the original north wing. Calamitously, the carefully chosen reference works were all lost when the British burned the Capitol in 1814, an act that prompted **Thomas Jefferson** to offer his considerable **personal library** as a replacement; this collection comprised more than six thousand volumes, which Jefferson had accumulated during fifty years of service at home and abroad, picking up, he said, "everything which related to America." A year later, Congress voted to buy this stupendous private collection for almost $24,000 – a massive sum at the time.

Jefferson's sale laid the foundation for a well-rounded collection, but another fire in 1851, this time accidental, caused severe damage. From that point, the library was forced to rely on donations and select purchases until it received two major boosts. In 1866 it acquired the thousands of books hitherto held by the **Smithsonian Institution**, and in 1870 it was declared the national copyright library – in theory, adding to its shelves a copy of every book published and registered in the United States, though the odd domestic title sometimes escapes its grasp, as do of course many foreign titles. Not surprisingly, the library soon outgrew its original home, and in 1897 the exuberantly eclectic **Thomas Jefferson Building** opened across from the Capitol, complete with domed octagonal Reading Room and adorned with hundreds of mosaics, murals, and sculptures. The building was projected to have enough space to house the library until 1975, but by the 1930s it was already too full. In the surrounding blocks, the **John Adams Building** was erected in 1939, followed by the **James Madison Memorial Building** in 1980.

Visiting the Library

The **Adams** and **Madison** buildings both have their charms, but the latter really appeals for its **Pickford Theater**, where you're apt to see lectures, exhibits, films, seminars, and other cultural fare (also offered on other floors). Yet with its full range of activities, including musical concerts in its **Coolidge Auditorium**, the magnificent **Jefferson Building** is the library's unquestioned centerpiece. At its visitor center (ground-level entrance on 1st St SE) you can learn about the building's highlights and get a calendar of upcoming events. You're allowed to wander around inside, but you'd do well to catch one of the free library **tours** (Mon–Sat 10.30am, 11.30am, 1.30pm, 2.30pm & 3.30pm, Sat last tour at 2.30pm) or watch the continuously running short **film** on the history of the library.

This Renaissance Revival structure is based around a **Great Hall** that is duly awe-inspiring, rich with marble walls and numerous medallions, inscriptions, murals, and inlaid mosaics. A treasured copy of the Gutenberg Bible is on display, while upstairs the visitors' gallery overlooks the octagonal marble-and-stained-glass **Main Reading Room**, a beautiful galleried space whose columns support a dome 125ft high. The mural in the dome canopy, *The Progress of Civilization*, represents the twelve nations supposed to have contributed most to world knowledge.

The library's huge collection is showcased on the second floor in the **main gallery**, where periodic exhibitions are based around broad subjects, with library materials showcased in themed cabinets. It's hard to predict exactly what you'll see, but previous displays have included items such as Walt Whitman's Civil War notebooks, the original typescript of Martin Luther King Jr's "I Have a Dream" speech, a copy of Francis Scott Key's "Star-Spangled Banner," first editions of Dante and Machiavelli, and a multitude of music scores, historic photographs, early recordings, magazines, and baseball cards. More unusual items include Noah Webster's "blue-back speller" from 1829, an early mutoscope of Pope Leo XIII, and colonial money bearing the inscription "To counterfeit is death." Changing exhibitions of especially significant documents, such as those associated with Washington, Lincoln, and Jefferson, receive central billing, while other exhibit areas are downstairs on the ground floor, where the Gershwin Room preserves George's Steinway and Ira's typing table and typewriter, and the Swann Gallery puts on temporary shows extracted from the library's unrivaled collection of American caricature and cartoon art.

Using the Library

Anyone over 18 carrying photo ID can use the library, and some one million readers and visitors do so each year. To find what you're looking for, head for the information desks or touch-screen computers in the Jefferson or Madison buildings. The **Main Reading Room** in the Jefferson Building is just one of

22 reading rooms, and the rules are the same in each. This is a research library, which means you can't take books out; in some reading rooms you have to order what you want from the stacks. You can also access papers, maps, and musical scores, and the advent of the **National Digital Library** means that many now come in machine-readable format (the desks in the Main Reading Room are wired for laptops and there are CD–ROM indexes). Major exhibitions, as well as prints, photographs, films, and speeches, are also available online. For research advice, call ☎202/707-6500; for reading room hours and locations, call ☎202/707-6400.

Pennsylvania Avenue SE

To most visitors, the section of **Pennsylvania Avenue** running southeast from the Capitol will be much less familiar than the stretch running northwest from it, where the presidential inaugural parade is held. Still, over the course of six blocks or so, you can find some of DC's more appealing ethnic restaurants and noteworthy bars mainly devoted to sports and politics, and a gentrifying scene that attracts increasing numbers of yuppies looking for affordable digs. There are also restored townhouses and splashes of green at places like Folger Square, Seward Square, and Marion Park. Although you shouldn't wander around the district south of E Street on your own, two churches there stand out and can be safely visited in daylight. The utilitarian red-brick **Ebenezer United Methodist Church**, 420 D St SE (Mon–Fri 8.30am–3pm, Sun service 11am; ☎202/544-1415), has the neighborhood's oldest black congregation. Founded in 1827, the church was the site of DC's first public school for black people; it was a short-lived affair (1864–65), but a pioneering one, since the teachers were paid out of federal funds. The current building dates from 1897, and if you call in advance someone will be on hand to show you around (otherwise you can check it out on your own). On the 4th Street side stands a wooden model of "Little Ebenezer," the original frame church that stood on this site. Farther south, **Christ Church**, at 620 G St SE (Mon–Fri 9am–4pm, Sun service 11am; ☎202/547-9300, ⓦwww.washingtonparish.org), is an early work (1806) by Capitol architect Benjamin Latrobe, notable mainly to architecture buffs for its charming Gothic Revival facade, but also the site of regular Episcopal worship by early American presidents, as well as hardy bandleader John Philip Sousa.

Eastern Market

306 7th St SE ☎301/674-4400 ext. 105, ⓦwww.easternmarketdc.com. Tues–Sat 7am–6pm, Sun 9am–6pm.

If you're taking a stroll in the East Capitol neighborhood, you may wonder what all the hubbub is surrounding what looks like an ancient brick train station. This forbidding, windowless 1873 structure has nothing to do with trains, but is instead home to **Eastern Market**, in operation since the nineteenth century. Designed by Adolph Cluss with less flamboyance than his Arts and Industries Building on the Mall, the building had operated continuously since its opening, until April 2007, when a **fire** caused considerable damage and closed the place down – at least until 2009, by which time the mayor has vowed to refurbish and reopen it.

Until then, the welter of vendors that used to do roaring business in the market selling seafood, deli meats, sides of beef, and other foodstuffs will operate across the street at the temporary **East Hall**, lodged in the junior high school at the corner of 7th St and Pennsylvania Ave SE. On the weekend on the streets outside the market proper, a **flea market** and **arts and crafts show** (Sat & Sun 9am–6pm) takes place, where you can buy produce and flowers, or antiques and junk. Back along 7th Street, delis, coffee shops, antique stores, and clothes shops make it one of the Hill's more appealing hang-outs.

East Capitol Street and Stanton Park

East Capitol Street, one of the city's four axes and one of the first streets on the Hill to be settled, starts between the Supreme Court and the Library of Congress's Jefferson Building. For its first ten or so blocks, its wide, tree-lined reach is peppered with wooden and brick townhouses, some dating from before the Civil War, others sporting the trademark late-Victorian turrets and "rusticated" (roughened) stonework. The typical row house at 316 A St NE was home to black orator and writer **Frederick Douglass** when he first moved to the capital in 1870 to take up the editorship of the *New National Era*, a newspaper championing the rights of African Americans. His family owned the adjacent property, too, where Douglass lived with his first wife, Anna, until 1877, when they moved to the grander Cedar Hill in Anacostia (see Chapter 3). The complex is now home to a nonprofit institution that shares space with the **Frederick Douglass Museum** (tours by appointment only at ☏202/547-4273, ⓦwww.nahc.org/fd/index.html) and has done a marvellous job of restoring the home to its nineteenth-century splendor, with rich cabinetry and other woodwork, elegant Victorian chairs and chandeliers, a courtyard, art galleries, and a grand piano. From here, it's just a few blocks north to **Stanton Park**, named after Lincoln's secretary of war during the Civil War but highlighted by an equestrian statue of Revolutionary War general **Nathanael Greene**, who had a significant role in the 1781 battle of Yorktown, which basically guaranteed America's independence from Britain.

Lincoln Park

In 1876, on the eleventh anniversary of Abraham Lincoln's assassination, the slain sixteenth president was honored in **Lincoln Park**, farther along East Capitol Street between 11th and 13th streets. In the presence of President Grant, **Frederick Douglass** read aloud the Emancipation Proclamation to the assembled thousands as the "Freedom Memorial" was unveiled in the center of the park. To contemporary eyes the memorial may seem a bit paternalistic – the bronze statue portrays Lincoln, proclamation in one hand, standing over a kneeling slave, exhorting him to rise – but it was actually daring for its day, funded mainly by the contributions of black soldiers who had fought for the Union. Working from a photograph, sculptor Thomas Ball re-created in the slave the features of **Archer Alexander**, the last man to be seized under the Fugitive Slave Act, which empowered slaveowners to capture escaped slaves even if they fled to free states. Under Lincoln's gaze, Alexander is breaking his own shackles.

It wasn't until a century later, in 1974, that a monument was erected in DC specifically to honor the achievements of a black American or, indeed, a woman. Facing Lincoln, across the park, is a memorial remembering **Mary McLeod Bethune**, educator, women's rights leader, and special adviser to Franklin Delano Roosevelt. Robert Berks, also responsible for the 8ft head of JFK in the Kennedy Center (see p.162), depicts Bethune leaning on her cane, reaching out to two children, and passing on, as the inscription says, her legacy to youth. (Across town near Logan Circle stands another memorial to Bethune, the Bethune Council House; see p.196.)

The neighborhood degenerates east of the park. In the daylight, peer up East Capitol Street to **RFK Stadium** in the distance (see p.329), but avoid heading there on foot.

Union Station and around

At Capitol Hill's northern limit, **Union Station** stands at the center of a grand redevelopment plan that was designed to resurrect a formerly neglected part of the city, and it has done so to some degree. In addition to the station, try to make time for the Smithsonian's **National Postal Museum**, located just opposite, which should appeal to casual visitors as well as those obsessed by philately, and the **H Street Corridor**, a nightlife and retail zone that's revitalizing a formerly blighted section of town.

Union Station

On the border of the north side of Capitol Hill and the eastern fringe of Old Downtown is DC's magnificent **Union Station**, 50 Massachusetts Ave NE. Some 20,000 square feet larger than New York City's Grand Central Terminal, the huge Beaux-Arts building glimmers with skylights, marble detail, and statuary, culminating in a 96ft-high coffered ceiling whose model was no less than ancient Rome's Baths of Diocletian. Outside, the facade is studded with allegorical statuary and etched with prolix texts extolling the virtues of trade, travel, and technology. On the east side of the building are stations for the Metro, Amtrak, Virginia Rail Express, and MARC; on the lower gallery there's a food court and a movie theater; and on the upper floor are stores, restaurants, car rental agencies, and ticket counters. Back on the east side, near Gate D, is a statue honoring **A. Phillip Randolph**, founder of the Brotherhood of Sleeping Car Porters union and one of the prime movers in the 1963 March on Washington for Jobs and Freedom, along with other major civil rights actions.

Announced as a joint project of the Pennsylvania and B&O railroads in 1901, the station was finished in 1908 after the McMillan Commission decreed an end to the chaos caused by the separate lines and stations that crisscrossed the city. Its architect, **Daniel H. Burnham**, a member of the commission, produced a classic building of monumental proportions to house the train sheds and waiting rooms. For five decades, Union Station sat at the head of an expansive railroad network that linked the country to its capital: hundreds of thousands of people arrived in the city by train, catching their first glimpse of the Capitol dome through the station's great arched doors – just as the wide-eyed James Stewart does at the beginning of Frank Capra's 1939 film *Mr Smith Goes to Washington*. Incoming presidents arrived at Union Station by train for their inaugurations – Truman was the last – and were met in the specially installed Presidential Waiting Room (now a diner); some, like FDR and Eisenhower, left by train in a casket after lying in state at the Capitol. By 1958, though, with the gradual depletion of train services, Union Station was left unkempt and underfunded, and the B&O Railroad pondered the idea of razing the place for an office block. That didn't happen, but an ill-conceived scheme did turn it into a visitor center during the 1976 Bicentennial, and the full structure wasn't fully restored until 1988.

▲ Union Station

It's also worth taking a stroll outside in Union Station Plaza, the landscaped approach to the station that stretches all the way down to the Capitol grounds. The **Columbus Memorial Fountain** in front of the station was dedicated in 1912 and features a statue of the Genovese explorer standing on the prow of a ship, between two lions and male and female figures representing the old and new worlds. A replica of Philadelphia's **Liberty Bell** stands nearby.

National Postal Museum

Massachusetts Ave NE at N Capitol Ave ☎ 202/633-5555, ⓦ www.si.edu/postal; Union Station Metro. Daily 10am–5.30pm; free.

Having finished the design for Union Station, Burnham turned his attention to a new **City Post Office** opposite the station to replace the Romanesque colossus in the Federal Triangle. Built between 1911 and 1914, it was a working post office until 1986, when it was renovated at a cost of $200 million, in part to house the **National Postal Museum**, along with restaurants and retailers. Before you descend to the lower-level galleries, take a quick look at the building itself, whose white Italian marble reaches are some of the most impressive in the city. Also, look up and read how the postal service is not only "Carrier of News and Knowledge," but also "Messenger of Sympathy and Love," "Consoler of the Lonely," and "Enlarger of the Common Life," among other dubious claims.

The collection

The museum is one of the Smithsonian's quiet triumphs. The collection includes sixteen million artifacts, but since many of these are stamps, only a few of which are on display, it's not that daunting a show. Indeed, the museum's strength is in its selectivity, judiciously placing the history of the mail service within the context of the history of the United States itself.

Escalators down to the galleries dump you in "**Moving the Mail**," which features soaring models of early mail planes – from a 1911 Wiseman-Cooke craft that vaguely resembles the Wright Flyer to a 1939 Stinson Reliant monoplane – as well as an 1851 mail coach with bourgeois riders inside and a walk-through Southern Pacific railcar with artifacts and a video on display. Beyond here is "**Binding the Nation**," which begins with the **first postal route**, the seventeenth-century King's Best Highway between New York and Boston – a dark and spooky tour through a primeval wood. The story continues with small models of steamships and clipper ships, and a crude "mud wagon" that did the literal dirty work of nineteenth-century mail delivery. Saddles and spittoons, among other artifacts, represent the relay-rider system of the famed **Pony Express**, which lasted for only two years (1860–61); although it cut mail delivery times in half (from San Francisco to New York in thirteen days), the founding partners lost $30 on every letter carried. In the end, without government backing, the private enterprise collapsed.

Elsewhere in the museum are other oddments related to postal-service history. The most interesting of these include a re-creation of a 1916 Pennsylvania postal cage, weird and wonderful rural mailboxes (including one made from car mufflers in the shape of a tin man), a paddle punch used to fumigate letters during Philadelphia's 1890 yellow fever outbreak, and a winter-weather mail car with track wheels and skis attached. Only in the "**Philatelic Gallery**" do you get a look at the museum's philatelic collection (up until this point, there's barely a stamp in sight). Here you'll find some splendid curiosities as well as frequently rotated exhibitions; you might see anything from ultra-rare vintage stamps to detailed coverage of famous series, like Ducks of America.

Before leaving, you can print out your own free, personalized **postcard** from the machines in the lobby, then buy a stamp in the stamp store and mail it home.

H Street Corridor

West of Union Station from 7th to 15th streets NE, the **H Street Corridor** represents the leading edge of DC gentrification. In decline for a half-century, the area saw an uptick in its fortunes beginning in 2004 with the arrival of new merchants, and since then the strip, though still cut off from the rest of the city by crime-infested streets and a lack of Metro access, has become an interesting island to visit for more adventurous tourists. If you want to visit, you'll either need to take a cab or, on weekends, the free Atlas shuttle (Fri & Sat 7–10pm; ☎301/751-1802) from Union Station.

The centerpiece of the strip is the **Atlas Performing Arts Center**, 1333 H St NE (☎202/399-7993, ⓦwww.atlasarts.org), formerly a 1938 Streamline Moderne movie theater, with a striking neon facade, which has been spruced up and in 2006 reopened to showcase local theater, dance, and other community arts performances. There are other small theaters in the vicinity, along with some good bars and clubs, of which the most prominent are the *Rock and Roll Hotel*, no. 1353 (see p.305), more of a place to dance or thrash than to stay, and *The Red and the Black*, no. 1212 (see p.305), also good for its regional rock acts. Just a few decent shops have taken root so far, but with the current pace of change in the neighborhood, with the odd condo and wine bar opening here and there, it may only be a matter of time before the corridor emerges as an actual DC destination in the tourist brochures.

3

The Waterfront and around

The **Waterfront** region south of the Mall, along the Potomac and Anacostia rivers, is a vast terrain whose assorted sights are unified by little other than their proximity to the water, and a few decent food and drink options exist in the spaces between. If you have a day or so to spare, several places are easily toured and well worth a look, most prominently the United States Holocaust Memorial Museum and the Bureau of Printing and Engraving, just south of the Mall; the Potomac waterfront's marinas and fish market; the US Navy Museum with its cache of nautical artifacts; the new baseball stadium; and, in Anacostia, the Anacostia Community Museum and the Frederick Douglass National Historic Site. Much of the **Southwest DC** area around the Potomac's Washington Channel is accessible by public transit, but a bigger effort will be required to reach the limited attractions in the dicier **Southeast** neighborhoods along the Anacostia River. Visitors are advised to head directly to the individual sights listed there – and then come straight back again.

Some history

For a century after the city was founded, DC's nearest accessible riverbanks (in today's West Potomac Park) were too marshy and malarial to develop. The only practicable wharves and piers were those built along the Channel, but they, too, stagnated and began to flourish only after the Tidal Basin was created in 1882. (The opening of the basin's gates now serves to flush the channel clean after every tide.)

Despite the undeveloped character of the nearby river, Southwest thrived as a fashionable neighborhood in the early nineteenth century because it was close to the Capitol. But in the 1870s, the railroad arrived and sliced its way through the area, diminishing its social cachet and causing the wealthy to flee north. The people left behind were mostly white European immigrants and poor blacks who worked at the goods yards, storage depots, and wharves. The work eventually dried up, the swamp-ridden housing became increasingly dilapidated, and by the 1920s the area had degenerated into a notorious slum.

In the 1950s Congress decided to end the squalor once and for all – not with any sort of social investment, but simply by demolishing huge swaths of the neighborhood – up to 5000 buildings in all – displacing thousands of

THE WATERFRONT & AROUND

Anacostia Community Museum ▲

RFK Stadium ◀

Capitol Hill ◀

Pentagon ▶

ACCOMMODATION
Channel Inn — D
Holiday Inn Capitol — A
L'Enfant Plaza — C
Mandarin Oriental — B

CAFÉS, RESTAURANTS & CLUBS
Cantina Marina — 5
Captain White's — 1
CityZen — 3
Jenny's Asian Fusion — 3
Phillips — 2
Zanzibar — 4

John Philip Sousa Bridge

KENTUCKY AVE SE
PENNSYLVANIA AVE SE
Potomac Ave
ANACOSTIA DRIVE S.E.
ANACOSTIA FREEWAY
ANACOSTIA
MINNESOTA AVE SE
GOOD HOPE RD SE
16TH ST SE
W ST SE
13TH ST SE
Frederick Douglass National Historic Site
MARTIN LUTHER KING JR AVE SE
295
SUITLAND PARKWAY
Anacostia
Fort Stanton Park

11TH ST SE
Eastern Market
11th St Bridge
US Navy Museum
Washington Navy Yard
Navy Yard
M ST SE
Anacostia River
Robbins Road
Frederick Douglass Memorial Bridge

VIRGINIA AVE SE
SEWARD SQUARE
Capitol South
House Offices
NEW JERSEY AVE SE
2ND ST SE
3RD ST SE
SOUTH CAPITOL ST
1ST ST SW
Nationals Park
2ND ST SW
4TH AVE SW

The National Mall
Federal Center SW
MARYLAND AVE SW
E ST SW
G ST SW
D ST SW
SOUTHWEST/WATERFRONT
3RD ST SW
4TH ST SW
6TH ST SW
7TH ST SW
Waterfront
Arena Stage
Wheat Row
Women's Titanic Memorial
Fort McNair
D ST SW
WATER ST SW
Thomas Law House
Washington Channel
OHIO DRIVE SW
East Potomac Park

Smithsonian
MADISON DR SW
JEFFERSON DR SW
INDEPENDENCE AVE SW
395
9TH ST SW
MAINE AVE
12TH ST SW
Benjamin Banneker Memorial Circle
Fish Wharf
L'Enfant Plaza
M
A B C D
1 2 3 4 5

CONSTITUTION AVE NW
17TH ST SW
Washington Monument
US Holocaust Memorial Museum
Bureau of Engraving & Printing
Tidal Basin
Washington Marina
Francis Case Bridge
4TH ST SW
Jefferson Memorial
Rochambeau Memorial Bridge
Potomac River
OHIO DRIVE SW

N

0   500 yds

families to make room for behemoth federal agencies like the Department of Agriculture. More buildings were added in the 1960s and 70s, and the rather haphazardly developed commercial buildings and piers that lined the north bank of the Channel were redeveloped to lure visitors. Still, despite the presence of a new stadium and a gentrifying scene in parts, much of Southwest seems like a failed design experiment, with grim concrete hardscape and modernist malls dotting what must be DC's least lively quarter.

Along the Potomac River

The main course of the Potomac River is separated from the Southwest and Waterfront developments by the Washington Channel and **East Potomac Park**, which begins south of the Tidal Basin and continues down to the junction of the Anacostia River south of Fort McNair. Though it lacks easy access to a Metro station, the park itself is pleasant enough – walkable, with nice views across to Virginia, plus there are tennis courts, fishing grounds, plenty of cherry trees, and a public pool. At the park's southern tip, **Hains Point** marks the spot where the Potomac and Anacostia rivers converge on their way to the Atlantic, and with National Airport just across the water, the atmosphere can be quite invigorating. Adding a curious touch is J. Seward Johnson's monumental sculpture *The Awakening*, which through the use of an oversize arm, head, and hand embedded in the ground suggests a giant trying to rise from the earth with a scream. (Plans are to move the "statue" to Maryland in 2008.)

Apart from these, the area's limited attractions lie along the Washington Channel, starting just east of the Tidal Basin and south of the Mall, where the **Holocaust Museum** and **Bureau of Engraving and Printing** are major destinations for visitors. Continuing southeast, the **Fish Wharf** is a favorite spot to buy a soft-shelled crab or two, and there are a few pockets of interesting architecture here and there. However, on the streets just inland, the massive plazas, housing complexes, and superstructures holding the federal bureaucracy are drab and inhumanly scaled, and of interest only to rabid, uncompromising fans of mid-twentieth-century modernist architecture. With the notable exception of the Arena Stage (closed until 2010), on weekdays there's little life here after 6pm, and on weekends there's even less.

South of the Mall: the federal buildings

The federal government's grunt work is done in concrete fortresses just south of the National Mall. Almost all the agencies here are bounded by Independence Avenue, 3rd Street, E Street, and 14th Street, and are served by two Metro stations: Federal Center SW and L'Enfant Plaza. The block between 3rd and 4th streets is taken up by the hulking **Department of Health and Human Services** – the only federal building in the area open to the public, and home to the government's **Voice of America** offices, 330 Independence Ave (free 45min tours Mon–Fri noon & 3pm, reservations required; ☎202/303-4990, Ⓦ www.voa.gov); the entrance is around the back, on C Street between 3rd and 4th. One of the world's biggest international broadcasters, the VOA was established in 1942 as part of the war effort and given its own charter in 1960 to transmit programs overseas that promote US values and culture. Run by the US Information Agency, it's still a powerful propaganda machine, which is why its broadcasts have often been jammed by various disaffected foreign powers. Guided tours walk you through the radio and TV studios from where broadcasts are made in 46 languages and transmitted to 115 million listeners in 120 countries. One place you won't hear the VOA, however, is in Washington, DC – or anywhere else in the nation for that matter: a 1948 act prohibits the government from proselytizing to its own citizens by radio (though if you really want to hear, you can download a webcast on the agency's Web portal).

Southwest's other federal buildings occupy a no-man's-land between 4th and 14th streets. Apparently it wasn't for want of trying that the area appears so dreary: architects such as **Edward Durrell Stone** and **I.M. Pei** have had a hand in some of the various buildings, plazas, and streetscapes. The closest thing here to modern swagger, though, is the curving, double-Y-shaped concrete structure from the late 1960s that holds the Department of Housing and Urban Development (D St between 7th and 9th), whose architect, **Marcel Breuer**, gave more than a nod to his Bauhaus origins. The only semblance of old-fashioned style emerges in the oldest (and westernmost) agency, the **Department of Agriculture** (Independence Ave between 12th and 14th): sited here since 1905, the original building on the north side of Independence Avenue is connected by slender arches to the much larger 1930s Neoclassical structure across the avenue.

Beyond the buildings themselves, the main focus of Southwest's development in the 1960s and 1970s was **L'Enfant Plaza**, at D Street between 9th and 10th streets, where there's now a central Metro station. It's easy to feel a twinge of sympathy for Pierre L'Enfant – alone among the city's spiritual founders, he gets not a monument in DC but a barren 1960s concrete square and subway station as his memorial.

United States Holocaust Memorial Museum

14th St between C St and Independence Ave SW ℡202/488-0400, Ⓦ www.ushmm.org; Smithsonian Metro. Daily 10am–5.30pm.

One of the city's most disturbing and unforgettable sites is the **United States Holocaust Memorial Museum**, which presents an intimate look at the persecution and murder of six million Jews by the Nazis. Upon entry, you are given a card containing biographical information about a real Holocaust victim whose fate you then follow throughout the museum. This approach personalizes the genocide, but the exhibits also emphasize the wider historical machinations that allowed Hitler to assume power in the first place. The solemn mood throughout is reflected by the museum's stark architecture and evocative design: half-lit chambers, a floor of ghetto cobblestones, an obscenely cramped barracks building, and an external roofline that resembles the guard towers of a concentration camp. Despite its bleak subject matter, the museum is one of the more popular (and crowded) attractions in DC. You don't need tickets to see the special exhibitions or to enter the museum and the interactive Wexner Learning Center, but you do need tickets with fixed entry times (between 10am and 3.45pm) to get into the permanent exhibit, "The Holocaust." **Tickets** are free but limited to four per person. You can pick them up beginning at 10am daily at the 14th Street entrance, but be sure to arrive before mid-morning or they'll likely be sold out. Advance tickets can be purchased through Ⓦ Tickets.com (℡1-800/400-9373).

The **permanent exhibition** spans the museum's second, third, and fourth floors; you start at the top and work your way down. The main galleries are not considered suitable for children under the age of 11, but the feature

▲ US Holocaust Memorial Museum

"**Remember the Children: Daniel's Story**" is designed for those over the age of 8, following the story of a young boy's witness to the events of Nazi Germany. The 14th Street entrance is at first-floor level, where you'll find the **information desk**, children's exhibit, and museum shop. From there stairs lead down to the auditoriums and special exhibition area at the concourse level. The number of items on display requires most visitors to spend at least three hours in the museum. There are rest areas throughout, and a contemplative **Hall of Remembrance** is on the second floor. The **Wexner Learning Center**, on the same floor, has computer stations that allow you to access text, photographs, films, and other resources. On the lower level, the **Children's Tile Wall** is another moving work of art, with 3000 panels made by US schoolchildren and meant to honor the 1.5 million European children slaughtered by the Nazis.

There's also a **café** in the Ross Administrative Center, at 100 Raoul Wallenberg Place, outside the museum's 15th Street entrance.

The fourth floor

The first rooms on the fourth floor use storyboards, newspaper articles, and film clips to chronicle the "**Nazi Assault**" and rise to power from 1933 to 1939. The presentation begins with a direct shock: horrifying images of concentration camps and victims gathered from US Army archives in 1945, the year the camps were finally liberated. From there the exhibition jumps back a dozen years to the beginning of the terror. Assuming state power in 1933, the Nazi party quickly goes to work marginalizing and oppressing the Jews of Germany, and what begins as a boycott of Jewish businesses and book-burning quickly leads to the organized looting of Jewish shops and the parading of German women who had "defiled" their race by associating with Jews. Anyone who didn't fit the Nazi ideal, like gays (who were forced to wear an identifying pink triangle), blacks, gypsies, Jehovah's Witnesses, and Freemasons, was persecuted and imprisoned as an "enemy of the state." Beyond a glass wall etched with the names of the hundreds of Eastern European Jewish communities wiped off the map forever, a towering stack of photographs from 1890 to 1941 records the breadth of life in just one of them – the *shtetl* (community) of Eishishok, in what's now Lithuania. The pictures vividly show street scenes, ceremonies, and parties, as well as families and individuals. Although many people tried to escape, by the end of the decade only a small percentage were getting out – not helped by government policies that actively deterred such migration, as when the US and Cuba kept 900 Jews from disembarking from the SS *St Louis* in 1939, forcing the German-flagged boat to return to European waters.

The third floor

The third floor covers the World War II era of Hitler's "**Final Solution**," with prominent attention given to the gassing of Jews at a death camp in Poland in December 1941, one of the earliest massacres. A few months before, some 33,000 Jews had been slaughtered at Babi Yar in Kiev following the German invasion of the Ukraine capital. Although many Jews had fled the city before occupation, the ones who remained were murdered in retaliation for explosions, presumably set off by Soviet engineers, that blew up German headquarters and other buildings. In the Warsaw uprising of 1943, Jews fought the Nazis for a month despite having no real weapons or supplies. Eventually all the surviving Jews were brought to the camps in packed freight cars; you can walk through one here that stands on railroad tracks taken from the camp at Treblinka. Some of the records of the time were preserved through the dogged and heroic efforts of trapped historians, who took all measures to record the details of what happened, burying their work in milk cans and other containers to keep it away from the Germans.

The most harrowing part of the exhibition deals with life and death within the concentration camps. A pile of blankets, umbrellas, scissors, cutlery, and other personal effects taken from the hundreds of thousands of prisoners underscores that the prisoners had expected to be put to work, but instead most were gassed within hours. A re-created barracks building from Auschwitz provides the backdrop for the oral memories of some survivors, as well as a shocking film of gruesome medical experiments carried out on selected prisoners.

As the museum clearly – and uncomfortably – shows, America knew of Auschwitz as early as May 1944, but despite demands to bomb it, Assistant Secretary of War John J. McCloy argued that its destruction "might provoke even more vindictive action by the Germans." Survivors later testified that they would have welcomed such terminal liberation: "Every bomb that exploded . . . gave us new confidence in life," records one witness. The third floor ends with photographic coverage of the Eishishok *shtetl* and its experience with the Final Solution. In contrast to the photos on the fourth floor, these pictures show the destruction, in just two days, of a town and community that had existed for more than nine hundred years, and the slaughter of its residents.

The second floor

As the Nazi front collapsed across Europe during 1945, many groups became involved in efforts to aid the Jews. The "**Last Chapter**" on the second floor recounts the heroism of individuals such as Raoul Wallenberg (whose name now graces the street where the museum sits) and the response of certain governments (the Danish in particular). Much of the floor offers multimedia testimony of camp survivors and details the Allied forces' liberation of the camps: film reels show German guards being forced to bury mountains of bodies in mass graves, while locals were made to tour the camps to witness the extent of the horror. Although Nazis were later prosecuted during the Nuremberg trials, most of those responsible for the planning, maintenance, and administration of the camps were never tried; thousands of others were treated leniently or acquitted altogether. In a few cases, former Nazis like Werner von Braun – the creator of the Nazi's V-2 missile, which was manufactured at forced-labor camps – were hired by the US and USSR governments during the Cold War. Von Braun went on to develop missiles and rockets for the US after World War II and become director of NASA's Marshall Space Flight Center.

The Bureau of Engraving and Printing

14th and C sts SW ☎ 202/874-2330 or 1-866-874-2330, ⓦ www.moneyfactory.com; Smithsonian Metro. Mon–Fri 10am–2pm.

The bland bureaucratic buildings found east of 14th Street and south of Independence Avenue are virtually indistinguishable from one another, with one exception – the **Bureau of Engraving and Printing**, where US currency, government securities, and postage stamps are created (though coins are produced by the US Mint – not in DC). Although its name is a bit dry, the Bureau offers one of DC's most popular tours; each year nearly half a million people take the twenty-minutes tour of what is, effectively, a large printing plant. That may not sound like an attraction of interest, but keep in mind that the presses here crank out millions of dollars in currency every day, and $120 billion a year.

The Bureau was established in 1862, when President Lincoln empowered six employees to initiate business in the attic of the Treasury Building, sealing up blocks of $1 and $2 bills that had been printed by private banks. By 1877 all **US currency** was produced by the Bureau, which moved into its current home in 1914. Today, almost three thousand employees work either here or at a second plant in Fort Worth, Texas. US currency has undergone significant changes in the past 140 years; huge denominations meant for banks, like the $50,000 bill, for example, have long since disappeared from general circulation. In recent years, every denomination except for the $1 and $2 bill has seen its standard, drab-green color improved with soft pastels and multihued security fibers, and hidden stamps and watermarks have been embedded in an attempt to thwart would-be counterfeiters.

Between May and August you must pick up tickets for **tours** in advance, but you can, and should, start waiting in line at 8am, as tickets are often gone by

11.30am. The rest of the year you can show up later, just before 10am, without tickets, though you'll still have to wait in line. Tours run every 15min from 9 to 10.45am and from 12.30 to 2pm, with additional summer hours from 2 to 3.45pm and from 5 to 7pm. A forty-minute Congressional/VIP tour providing an in-depth, behind-the-scenes look at the plant is available for those who make arrangements through their representative's office (Mon–Fri 8.15am & 8.45am). Contact the tour office for any tour information. You can also skip the tour and just drop by the **visitor center**, perhaps to purchase an overpriced bag of shredded currency that you can send to the folks back home; it's open daily from 8.30am to 3.30pm.

The tour

The bureau's history unfolds in a video that plays in the main corridor as you wait in line for the tour to begin. What everyone really wants to see, though, is the dough, which you glimpse during the march through claustrophobic viewing galleries looking down on the printing presses. The making of US currency is a surprisingly low-tech operation: engravers work in teams on each bill with dyes to create intaglio steel plates, from which the bills are printed in sheets of 32, checked for defects, and loaded into large barrows. On a separate press, they're then overprinted with serial numbers and seals, sliced up into single bills by ordinary paper-cutters, and stacked into "bricks" of four thousand notes before being sent out to the twelve Federal Reserve districts, which issue the notes to local banks. Interestingly, the bills aren't made from paper at all, but from a more durable fabric that's three-quarters cotton – and made by a private company to serve only one client, the US government. Even so, the most used note, the dollar, lasts only eighteen months on average. Those whose job it is to spot flaws in the currency appear to visitors as a line of people with their heads in their hands gazing at bundles of notes. These workers undergo a rigorous two-year apprenticeship, scrutinize one sheet of bills per second, and log eight-hour days with two twenty-minute breaks and a thirty-minute lunch. All but one in a thousand misprinted bills are caught.

Benjamin Banneker Memorial Circle

From the printing plant, following D Street east to 10th Street and south over the freeway, you'll reach **Benjamin Banneker Memorial Circle**, where there's a viewpoint over the Washington Channel and the rest of the Waterfront. A memorial and fountain here honors Banneker, an African American born in Maryland in 1731 to a former slave. Almost entirely self-taught, Banneker distinguished himself as a mathematician, clockmaker, astronomer, and inventor before being invited, at the age of 60, to assist in surveying the land for the new capital. He also published several editions of a successful almanac and spent the last years before his death in 1806 corresponding with Thomas Jefferson, who he hoped would abandon his prejudices against the intelligence of African Americans. The Memorial Circle currently occupies freeway-caged land on the so-called **L'Enfant Promenade**, which connects L'Enfant Plaza with the Waterfront, and plans are afoot to redevelop it as a more pedestrian-friendly greenspace that would invite strolling. To this end, $25 million in private money is now being raised to create a more striking monument to Banneker that will include a statue of the man, architectural exhibits, and 40ft clock tower.

The Washington Channel and around

The developed shoreline of the Potomac's **Washington Channel** is accessible by Metro at 4th and M streets SW. Most people come here to eat seafood at one of the scattered **restaurants** along Maine Avenue or Water Street SW, west of 7th; all have terraces and patios with views across to **East Potomac Park**. Otherwise, the two main attractions here are near the towering Francis Case Bridge. The **Washington Marina**, filled with pricey nautical craft, provides a good backdrop for various summer fairs and events, though it's typically of little interest to landlubbers. Adjacent is the **Fish Wharf** (daily 11am–7pm, Sat & Sun until 9pm), also known as the Maine Avenue Fish Market, the oldest continuously operating fish market in the country. Floating on permanently moored steel barges, the fishmongers will do their best to sell you their wares, even if you're only browsing, and haggling is encouraged. Impressive displays include huge trays of Chesapeake Bay fish, shrimp, clams, oysters, and, especially, Maryland blue crabs, which are available live or steamed. There's nowhere to sit and eat, but you can head to the waterside promenade for a picnic.

Farther down Maine Avenue, east of 7th Street, the **Arena Stage** (see p.314) is one of the most accomplished playhouses in the city and provides a good target for theater lovers. Continuing south, you'll come to the **Thomas Law House**, 1252 6th St SW (c.1794–96), one of DC's oldest surviving townhouses, and the **Duncanson–Cranch House**, around the corner at 468 N St SW; both date from the same era and offer a humble reminder of the tasteful Federal style that used to permeate this neighborhood before 1960s urban renewal was allowed to run amok. If you cut past here to 4th Street, you can see **Wheat Row** (1315–1321 4th St SW), a strip of Federal houses built in 1794 and part of the Harbor Square residential development at 4th between N and O streets. Striking for their elegant early-American design, they were some of the first edifices built on speculation, with the promise of rising property values in the future.

Channel and river collide south of here with the spit of land occupied by the off-limits **Fort McNair**. Fortified in 1791, the base became home to the **Washington Arsenal** in 1804, though its buildings were blown up by the British in 1814 and later destroyed by an explosion that killed 21 people in 1864. At the **US Penitentiary**, built in the 1820s on the arsenal grounds, the conspirators in the Lincoln assassination were imprisoned, tried, and executed. Just outside the fort at Washington Channel Park, at 4th and P streets SW, the **Women's Titanic Memorial** commemorates the men who gave up their lifeboat spaces (and, thus, their lives) to women and children on the fateful 1912 voyage of the *Titanic* (the money for the memorial was raised through a women's nonprofit organization). Unless you read the inscription, the memorial's honorees are hard to guess, since the site features a heroic male statue with arms outspread – a gesture copied by Kate Winslet in the movie *Titanic* – above a stone bench that's notable mainly for its architect, Henry Bacon, who also designed the Lincoln Memorial.

Along the Anacostia River

Unlike that of the Potomac, the **Anacostia River**'s waterfront has been polluted by sewage, heavy metals, and other toxins, some of them leached by the Washington Navy Yard, and is another aspect of DC's urban blight that tourist authorities would prefer you ignore. The river courses through run-down, impoverished **Southeast** Washington, just south of the US Capitol. The few attractions here are the **US Navy Museum**, the **Frederick Douglass National Historic Site**, and the **Anacostia Community Museum** – a lesser-known member of the Smithsonian Institution family. Of course, the main reason tourists visit here is the brand-new **Nationals Park**, S Capitol St at N St SE (see also "Sports," p.328; ⓦ washington.nationals.mlb.com), a $600 million colossus intended to rejuvenate this part of town and start the process of gentrification in the surrounding neighborhood with new bars and restaurants. However, unless you're a baseball fan, there's not much else to see.

Washington Navy Yard

The **Washington Navy Yard** was one of the first naval yards in the country. Established in 1799, it has been in continuous operation ever since, excluding an interruption that began in 1812, when the commander burned the base to prevent the invading British Army from capturing it. Shipbuilding ceased here in 1874, but ordnance production continued until 1962. Since then the base has served as a naval supply and administrative center. Before entering the yard to visit the US Navy Museum, you'll need to show photo ID to the guard at the gate (designed by Benjamin Latrobe in 1804) at 9th and M streets, just a few blocks east of the Navy Yard Metro station. As with all federal sites, call ahead to make sure it hasn't been closed for security reasons.

US Navy Museum

805 Kidder Breese St SE, Bldg 76 ☎ 202/433-4882, ⓦ www.history.navy.mil; Navy Yard Metro. Mon–Fri 9am–5pm, Sat & Sun 10am–5pm.

Unless you're an active member of the military, you must make reservations to visit the **US Navy Museum**, housed in the Navy Yard's former gun factory in Building 76 and adorned on the outside with cannon and deck guns from the Civil and 1898 wars, plus a grim-looking steel bathysphere from the submersible *Alvin*. The museum traces the history of the US Navy since it was created in 1794 in response to attacks on American ships by Barbary pirates. Displays include uniforms, ship figureheads, vicious cat-o'-nine-tail whips, and a walk-through frigate gundeck. Separate galleries detail every US naval conflict from the War of 1812 to the present day, while other exhibits highlight everything from US polar explorations begun in the 1840s to the necessity of submarines in combat and intelligence operations. Also on display are the exploits of early naval hero Stephen Decatur, who captured three boats during hand-to-hand fighting at Tripoli in 1804, and whose house (see p.147) is one of DC's more estimable structures. The World War II displays are particularly affecting; you can sit in anti-aircraft guns, watch crackly archive film footage, and view an account of the sinking of a PT-109 patrol boat by a Japanese destroyer on August 2, 1943. The boat's commander, John Fitzgerald Kennedy, towed the boat's badly burned engineer ashore, despite an injured back. More ominously, there's also the upended casing for the prototype of *Little Boy*, the atomic bomb that killed 140,000 people in Hiroshima.

Anacostia

On the south side of the Anacostia River, across from the Navy Yard, is Washington's most notorious neighborhood. **Anacostia**'s name derives from the area's original Native American inhabitants, the tobacco-growing Nacotchtanks, who were later called the Nacostines. However, long before it acquired that moniker, the place was known as Uniontown, named by early nineteenth-century merchants seeking homes close to the Capitol, who supplanted the Nacotchtanks, and were in turn displaced in the 1850s by the white working and middle classes, drawn by jobs at the Navy Yard across the river and by the affordable housing stock. The neighborhood thrived during post–Civil War Reconstruction, primarily due to the building of the 11th Street Bridge, which connected it with the rest of DC. African Americans – most prominently Frederick Douglass – slowly started to move in and by the twentieth century it gained its current name. But the "white flight" to the suburbs gathered speed in the 1950s, assisted by the damaging social effects of the "wall" of the I-295 freeway built here, and by 1970 more than 95 percent of Anacostia's residents were black – and largely abandoned by the city authorities. The 1968 riots damaged much of the area's infrastructure and confidence, and the neighborhood still suffers grievously from underfunding, dilapidated (if still historically authentic) housing, unemployment, crime, and a lack of services – only one dine-in restaurant can even be found here.

There are, of course, pockets with handsome old houses and revitalized commercial centers, but much of Anacostia is a dangerous scene for outsiders who don't know where they're going – other DC residents take pains to avoid the place. Still, the two attractions reviewed here are worth the visit, though best reached by cab either from the Anacostia Metro station or from across the river.

Frederick Douglass National Historic Site

1411 W St SE ℡202/426-5961, ⊛www.nps.gov/frdo. Daily: May–Sept 9am–5pm, Oct–April 9am–4pm.

Frederick Douglass – former slave, abolitionist leader, and blistering orator – was 60 years old when, in 1877, he moved to the white brick house known as **Cedar Hill**. Its mixed Gothic Revival–Italianate architecture, twenty-one rooms, and fifteen acres were typical of the homes built twenty years earlier in what was then called Uniontown, though at that time they were sold only to whites. Douglass, DC's newly appointed US marshal, was the first to break the racial barrier, paying $6700 for the property and living out the last eighteen years of his life here.

You can view the home only on a free thirty-minute **tour** (daily 9am, 12.15pm, 3pm, 3.30pm & 4pm), for which you must reserve a place when you arrive or by calling ℡1-800/967-2283 (a handling fee of $2 is charged). The tours begin in the **visitor center** below the house, where a short docudrama and a few exhibits provide details about Douglass's life. Next you're led 85 steps up the steep green hill for a look around the house, in which Douglass entertained leading abolitionists and suffragists. Mementos on display include President Lincoln's cane, given to Douglass by Mary Lincoln, and a desk and chair from Harriet Beecher Stowe. Family portraits capture his first wife, Anna, who died in 1882; his second wife, Helen, who was much younger and – shockingly for hidebound DC – white; and his five children, two of whom served with distinction in Massachusetts's black 54th Regiment during the Civil War.

Most of the fixtures and fittings are original and illustrate middle-class life in late nineteenth-century Washington. Douglass kept chickens and goats outside in the gardens, and the only water source was a rainwater pump, but inside the kitchen the domestic staff had access to all the latest technology, like the Universal clothes wringer. Douglass chose to work either in his study, surrounded by hundreds of books, or in the outdoor "Growlery" – a rudimentary stone cabin he used for solitary contemplation.

Frederick Douglass (1818–95) was born into slavery as Frederick Bailey on a Maryland estate in 1818. His exact birth date and father's identity (Bailey was his mother's name) are unknown, though it was rumored he was the son of a white man, perhaps his owner. At the age of 8 he was sent to work as a house servant in Baltimore, where, although it was illegal to educate slaves, the owner's wife taught him to read and he taught himself to write. By 1834 Frederick had been hired out to a nearby plantation, where he was cruelly treated; his first attempt to escape, in 1836, failed. Later, apprenticed as a ship caulker in Baltimore's docks, Frederick attended an educational association run by free blacks and met his first wife, Anna Murray. With money borrowed from her and equipped with a friend's passbook, Frederick fled to New York in 1838 disguised as a free seaman. Anna followed him, and they were married later that year, moving to Massachusetts, where Bailey – now working as a laborer – became Douglass (after a character from Sir Walter Scott's *Lady of the Lake*) to confound the slave-catchers.

Douglass became active in the **abolitionist movement**, lecturing about his life for the Massachusetts Anti-Slavery Society during the 1840s and risking capture when, in 1845, at just 27 years old, he published his autobiography, *Narrative of the Life of Frederick Douglass, an American Slave,* which is still regularly taught in US history classes. It was a resounding success, forcing the increasingly famous Douglass to leave for England for fear he'd be recaptured. After he spent two years on the lecture circuit, friends raised the money to buy his freedom and Douglass returned home. His views were slowly changing, and in a break with pacifist white abolitionists, he founded his own newspaper, the *North Star* (later renamed *Frederick Douglass' Paper*), in Rochester, New York, in 1847. In it, Douglass began increasingly to explore the idea of political rather than moral reform as a means of ending slavery. His reputation as a compelling orator and writer grew, and another autobiography, *My Bondage and My Freedom*, appeared in 1855. Meanwhile, Douglass extended his interests to **women's suffrage** (a bold move at the time), discussing issues with such luminaries as Susan B. Anthony, Lucretia Mott, and Elizabeth Cady Stanton.

When President Lincoln issued the Emancipation Proclamation in 1863, the country's most respected black leader urged "men of color" to join the war effort, which backfired somewhat when it became clear that his fiery recruitment speeches promised black soldiers an equality in service and conditions that the Union Army didn't offer. With slavery abolished and Reconstruction set in place, in the mid-1860s Douglass turned to pressing for **black suffrage**. He campaigned for Ulysses S. Grant and the Republicans in 1868 and played a major role in pushing through the **15th Amendment**, granting all male citizens the right to vote.

Douglass and Anna moved to DC in 1870, buying a house on Capitol Hill, where he continued to earn his living lecturing, writing, and, for a while, editing the progressive *New National Era* newspaper. In 1877 he was appointed to the largely ceremonial position of marshal of Washington, DC, and moved to **Cedar Hill** in Anacostia. Douglass was made recorder of deeds for the city in 1880, and in 1881 published his third autobiographical work, *Narrative of the Life and Times of Frederick Douglass.* Anna died a year later, and Douglass caused a scandal when he quickly married Helen Pitts, a sharp-witted white secretary almost twenty years his junior. More controversy followed as Douglass was accused of cozying up to successive political administrations that were deemed to have betrayed the aspirations of black Americans ever since Emancipation. Quitting his post as recorder, Douglass eventually regained his reputation. In 1889, at a time when others might have considered retirement, he accepted the post of consul general in Haiti, where he served for two years.

Back at Cedar Hill, but by now in ill health, Douglass continued to write and speak publicly until his death from a heart attack on February 20, 1895, at the age of 77. His funeral, effectively a state occasion, was held at the Metropolitan AME Church (see p.194) in downtown DC.

▲ Frederick Douglass's "Growlery"

Anacostia Community Museum

1901 Fort Place SE ☎ 202/633-4820, ⓦ www.si.edu/anacostia. Daily 10am–5pm.

Though well off the beaten path, the Smithsonian's **Anacostia Community Museum** – like the nearby Frederick Douglass National Historic Site – warrants a visit. However, don't even think about walking here from the Anacostia Metro stop – come by taxi instead. The museum's official mission is to devote itself to documenting black life in Anacostia and throughout America through the collection and preservation of artifacts such as household objects, family photos, folk artworks, and various poems, prose, and other writing. A favorite item is the fur coat opera singer Marian Anderson wore to her famed 1939 concert on the steps of the Lincoln Memorial, after the racially blinkered Daughters of the American Revolution denied her permission to sing at Constitution Hall. There's also a display of contemporary quilts and a small art collection with works by folk artist Leslie Payne and a sampling of paintings and prints by local artists like Samella Lewis, John Robinson, and Elena Bland. The museum is perhaps best known for its temporary exhibitions, some of which have highlighted black artists and writers, the Great Migration that brought blacks north after the Civil War, and slavery throughout America from the seventeenth to nineteenth centuries. Keep in mind that an even broader selection of these items and artifacts may be on display at the new National Museum of African American History and Culture, when it opens in a few years on the Mall (see p.68).

The White House and Foggy Bottom

Few residences in the world are as familiar as the **White House**, the elegant Georgian mansion at 1600 Pennsylvania Avenue. Since 1800, when John Adams moved into the unfinished building, it's been home to every US president and has survived the ravages of fire, war, and potential acts of terror to stand as an enduring symbol of American power.

Along with the US Capitol, the White House was one of two original cornerstones of L'Enfant's master plan for the city. It is now very much in the center of things: to the south lies the National Mall; to the east, the Federal Triangle and the colossus of the Treasury Building; to the north, historic Lafayette Square and the towers of New Downtown; and to the west, **Foggy Bottom** – the bureaucratic district north of Constitution Avenue that runs to the Potomac River.

In the early nineteenth century, the upper class entertained the political elite here in stunning homes like the **Octagon**, while today the area is best known for federal buildings such as the **State Department** and cultural and educational institutions like the **Kennedy Center** and **George Washington University**, the students of the latter bringing a certain zest to the streets' otherwise nine-to-five professional flavor. The city's first art museum was opened here in the 1860s, in what is now the **Renwick Gallery**, though its collection was eventually moved to the nearby **Corcoran Gallery of Art**, one of the country's most respected museums. Less reputable, however, is one of Foggy Bottom's biggest draws: the **Watergate Complex** that was the site of the 1972 break-in that led to President Nixon's unprecedented resignation.

The White House

1600 Pennsylvania Ave NW, special events ☎202/456-2200, tours ☎202/456-7041, ⊛www
.whitehouse.gov; McPherson Square or Farragut West Metro.

The **White House**, residence and office of the president of the United States, is the most famous house at the most famous address in America. For millions, the idea of touring the president's home and possibly being in the same building as the most powerful person in the world has an irresistible quality. In the end, however, many visitors are surprised by how small the quarters are and that their

THE WHITE HOUSE AND FOGGY BOTTOM

CAFÉS & RESTAURANTS
Art Gallery Bar & Grille	7
Blue Duck Tavern	1
The Breadline	15
Café des Artistes	17
Capitol Grounds	5 & 9
Cosi	16
DISH	8
Kinkead's	13
Lawson's Deli	11
Notti Bianchi	14
Primi Piatti	10
Thai Coast	4

BARS & CLUBS
51st State Tavern	3
Froggy Bottom Pub	6
Lindy's Red Lion	12
Marshall's	2

ACCOMMODATION
Allen Lee	F
Fairmont	A
Hay-Adams	E
Lombardy	C
Ritz-Carlton	B
River Inn	D
State Plaza	G

tour consists of a lot of waiting around and quick shuffles past railed-off rooms filled with presidential portraits.

Public access has been largely curtailed due to terrorism fears. In 1995 the stretch of Pennsylvania Avenue north of the White House was permanently closed to vehicles following two incidents in which shots were fired at the building and a light aircraft crashed into one of the outer walls; for months following September 11, 2001, when a hijacked plane presumably headed for the White House crashed in a Pennsylvania field, the building was entirely closed to the public. Seven years later it's not much better.

In the nineteenth century, though there were armed sentries at every door and plainclothes policemen mingled with visitors, virtually anyone could turn up at the president's house without an introduction. In his diary, novelist Captain Frederick Marryat deplored the way a visitor might "walk into the saloon in all his dirt, and force his way to the President, that he might shake him by the one hand while he flourished the whip in the other." As late as the 1920s, the general public was allowed to saunter across the lawns and picnic on the grounds, and President Warren G. Harding would answer the front door himself.

These days, **tours** of the White House are offered to groups of ten or more – unlikely for most visitors not part of a tour group. Even with such a gathering, you must reserve your tour a month in advance through your US representative or senator (Ⓦ www.house.gov or Ⓦ www.senate.gov), whose office will be able to provide further details; tour times are offered Tuesday through Saturday from 7.30am to 12.30pm. Foreign visitors must contact their embassy in DC to make arrangements, and be prepared for access to be denied if the capital is undergoing one of its periodic states of siege. Before your scheduled tour date, be sure to call ahead and confirm everything. The **White House Visitor Center**, 1450 Pennsylvania Ave NW (daily 7.30am–4pm; Ⓣ 202/208-1631, Ⓦ www.nps.gov /whho), in the Department of Commerce, several blocks southeast of the White House, is worth a visit in its own right. Permanent exhibits highlight topics like the First Families and White House architecture, plus there are concerts, lectures, free maps and brochures, and a gift shop. It can also provide information on other federally operated sites, museums, and parks, and give you the lowdown on current entry requirements and security restrictions for each.

Other parts of the White House are accessible on occasion throughout the year. In April and October the gardens are opened for afternoon tours, including the iconic **Rose Garden** where public events are held, and at Christmas there are special evening tours of the festively decorated interior. Contact the visitor center for details.

Some history

Pierre L'Enfant was fired before he could make a start on the White House, then known as the **President's Mansion**, and in 1792 its design was thrown open to competition; President Washington's only request was that it command respect without being too extravagant or monarchical. **James Hoban**, an Irish immigrant and professional builder, won the $500 prize for his Neoclassical design, influenced by the Georgian manor houses of Dublin. Hoban believed a stone house would give the crucial impression of permanence and stability, though DC had few skilled masons and no quarries. Advertisements were placed in European newspapers for skilled craftspeople, but logistics ultimately dictated that local slaves and Scottish masons from the Potomac region be used for the work. Progress was slow: the masons put down their tools in 1794 in the city's first pay strike, and the house of gray Virginia sandstone wasn't completed in time to house Washington, whose second term ended in 1797.

America's second president, **John Adams**, moved into the unfinished building on November 1, 1800, a few days before he lost his bid for re-election; the First Family was forced to hang its laundry in the grand East Room while final touches were put on the mansion. East and west terraces were built during the administration of **Thomas Jefferson**, who had entered the building's design competition under a pseudonym; Jefferson also installed the home's first water closets and hired a French chef. Under **James Madison**, the interior was redecorated by Capitol architect Benjamin Latrobe, who defended copying parts of Jefferson's proposed design by arguing that Jefferson's ideas were lifted in turn from "old French books, out of which he fishes everything." During the **War of 1812**, British soldiers burned down the mansion in August 1814, forcing Madison and his wife to flee; when the troops entered, they found the dining table set for forty, the wine poured in the decanters, and the food cooked in the kitchen. Hoban was charged with reconstructing the building after the war, and it was ready to reopen in 1817 – but with one significant change: to conceal fire damage to the exterior, the house was painted white.

Throughout the nineteenth century, the White House was decorated, added to, and improved upon by each new occupant, though occasionally there were setbacks. To celebrate his inauguration in 1829, **Andrew Jackson** invited some of his rowdy followers back to the White House, who then proceeded to wreck the place before being lured onto the exterior lawn with tubs of orange juice mixed with whiskey; Jackson was forced to spend the first night of his presidency in a hotel. He did, however, install the building's first indoor bathroom in 1833. Gaslights were added in 1848, central heating and a steam laundry in 1853, the telephone in 1877, and electric lighting in 1891. When President James Garfield lay dying from an assassin's bullet in 1881, enterprising naval engineers cooled his White House bedroom by concocting a prototype air-conditioner from a fan and a box of ice (full air-conditioning didn't follow until 1909).

During the Civil War, troops were briefly stationed in the White House's East Room, cooking their dinner in the ornate fireplace, while the South Lawn was used as a field hospital. The East Room is also where seven US presidents have lain in state – the first being **Abraham Lincoln** just after the close of the Civil War in 1865.

The Gilded Age saw periodic proposals to move the president's residence elsewhere in Washington, such as Meridian Hill, due to the cramped, unworkable condition of many of the rooms. Still, it wasn't until **Theodore Roosevelt**'s administration (1901–09) that fundamental structural changes were made to the building, as well as expansions to accommodate the president's family and staff. Elevators were added, and an executive West Wing – incorporating the president's personal **Oval Office** – was built. The famous Rose Garden was planted outside the Oval Office in 1913 at the behest of President Wilson's wife, Ellen, and was used for ceremonial purposes. An entire residential third floor was added in 1927, an East Wing followed in the 1940s, while, during World War II, a diverse set of improvements included an air-raid shelter, swimming pool (which FDR used for exercise), and movie theater.

Because presidential families lived in the White House during these renovations, the projects were often done too quickly, so that by 1948 the entire building was on the verge of collapse. **Harry Truman** – who had already added a poorly received balcony ("Truman's folly") to the familiar south-side portico – had to move into nearby Blair House for four years while the structure was stabilized. New foundations were laid, all the rooms were dismantled, and a modern steel frame was inserted. The Trumans moved back in 1952, and since

The role of the presidency

When delegates at Philadelphia's 1787 Constitutional Convention created the role of President of the United States, they had no intention of replacing a British monarchy with an American one. Instead, they devised a federal system of government with separate executive, legislative, and judicial branches and prescribed precise limits on the authority of each. The president was made chief executive, though one whose role was within, rather than above, the government. Indeed, presidential powers were detailed in Article 2 of the **Constitution**, after a full discussion of the more fundamental role of Congress in Article 1. (By contrast, the **Articles of Confederation**, written between 1783 and 1788, had made no provision for an executive branch, and thus offered no means of enforcing the laws passed by Congress.) Strictly speaking, the president is not directly elected, but is instead chosen by an **electoral college** appointed by the states, the idea being to free the presidency from factional influence. The **12th Amendment** (1804) opened up the ballot for president (and vice president) to popular election, though the electoral college remained intact, with electors now being chosen via the party that won a given state. Since the Civil War, three American presidents, including George W. Bush in 2000, have lost the popular vote but won the electoral vote.

The Constitution actually has very little to say about the presidency itself. Specific, enumerated powers are few – among them to make treaties, appoint federal officers, and act as commander in chief – and this may have been because the Constitution's authors never really agreed on what the president's role should be. The elevation of the presidency is due in part to certain extraordinary leaders who've occupied and enhanced the post over the past centuries, like George Washington, America's trusted first president; Andrew Jackson, who expanded voting rights for white men; Abraham Lincoln, who preserved the Union during the Civil War; Theodore Roosevelt, who dismantled illegal monopolies and trusts; and Franklin Roosevelt, whose unprecedented federal programs sought to lift the country out of the Great Depression. Following the Cold War, the role of the presidency has expanded to its greatest reach, with almost every one of the last ten presidents acting almost independently of Congress in regard to foreign policy; some argue that this usurpation has made the executive branch more powerful than, not coequal with, the other branches.

Constitutionally, the president has sole executive responsibility, although he has come to be assisted by special advisers and a large White House staff. The president oversees fifteen executive departments, whose appointed secretaries form the **Cabinet**, which is more of an advisory forum than a policy-making body. When a new party occupies the White House after an election, the upper-echelon staff at various federal agencies – from the Post Office to the National Security Council – usually changes dramatically to ensure consistency with the new administration's policies (and also to reward the president's loyal followers). Today, roughly two thousand people work directly or indirectly for the Executive Office of the President, while another 100,000 nonstrategic federal posts are technically within the presidential fold.

Additional information on the presidency and individual presidents of the United States can be found in "Contexts," p.408.

then there have been no significant alterations – unless you count Nixon's bowling alley, Ford's outdoor pool, and Clinton's jogging track.

The interior

White House **tours** concentrate on rooms on the ground and State (principal) floors. The Oval Office, family apartments, and private offices on the second and third floors are off limits, and guards make sure you don't stray from the designated route. Once inside, your group is allowed to wander one-way through or past a half-dozen furnished rooms. Though guards will answer questions if they can, the tour is not exactly conducive to taking your time, and in many rooms you can't get close enough to appreciate the paintings or the furniture. Caught up in the flow of the crowd, most people are outside again well within thirty minutes.

As if this weren't bad enough, there's a paucity of quality decor and furnishings in some rooms, and not just because much of the best stuff is kept in private quarters. Until Jackie Kennedy and her Fine Arts Committee put a stop to the practice, each incoming presidential family changed, sold, or scrapped the furniture according to individual taste, while outgoing presidents took favorite pieces with them – you're just as likely to come across White House furniture and valuables in places like Dumbarton House or the Woodrow Wilson House as in the White House itself. Presidents can no longer redecorate the historic, nonliving quarters any way they see fit and must submit changes to the State Rooms to the Committee for the Preservation of the White House, a preservation body. While doubtless well intentioned, such practice also has the effect of turning the building into one of the world's largest live-in museums, though one in which you're not encouraged to linger.

The East Wing to the East Room

Visitors enter the **East Wing** from the ground floor and traipse first past the Federal-style **Library**, paneled in timbers rescued from a mid-nineteenth-century refit and housing 2700 books by American authors. Opposite is the **Vermeil Room**, once a billiard room but now named for its extensive collection of silver gilt; the portraits are of recent First Ladies, whose individual tastes have had significant bearing on what the place looks like (Laura Bush most recently in 2006). Across from the stairs, the **China Room**, true to its name, displays the services of the various presidents from George Washington on; it's been used as such only for the last century, though – before that it was little more than a storage closet. Since the adjoining **Diplomatic Reception Room** is often closed off for foreign heads of state and ambassadors, next you move upstairs to the **State Floor**, where the **East Room** – the largest room in the White House – is the first stop. The East Room has been open to the public since the days of Andrew Jackson. It has been used in the past for weddings, for lyings in state, and other major ceremonies, and has a grand appearance with long, yellow drapes, a brown marble fireplace, and glass chandeliers from *c*.1900. Between the fireplaces hangs the one major artwork on general display: Gilbert Stuart's celebrated 1797 portrait of a steely George Washington, rescued from the flames by Dolley Madison when the British torched the White House. Note that this room will be undergoing restoration in 2008–09 to bring it back to something resembling its original appearance.

Green, Blue, and Red rooms, and the State Dining Room

The last rooms on the tour are more intimate in scale. The **Green Room**, its walls lined in silk, was Jefferson's dining room and JFK's favorite in the entire house. Portraits line the walls, Dolley Madison's French candlesticks are on the mantelpiece, and a fine, matching green dinner service occupies the cabinet. Recently refurbished to more closely echo the style of its origins, the room is often used for receptions, as is the adjacent, oval **Blue Room**, whose ornate French furniture was bought by President Monroe after the 1814 fire. In 1886, Grover Cleveland was married in here, the only time a president has been married in the White House. The **Red Room** is the smallest of the lot, decorated in early nineteenth-century Empire style and sporting attractive inlaid oak doors, with the antiques herein meant to reflect the room's design scheme, despite being acquired mostly after the 1950s. Finally, the oak-paneled **State Dining Room** harks back to the East Room in scale and style and hosts banquets for important guests. (Theodore Roosevelt used to stick his big-game trophies in here.) From here you loop back through the cross halls and exit on the north side of the White House, opposite Lafayette Square.

The South Lawn

The White House is surrounded by greenery, but its most famous patch is the **South Lawn**, the grassy stretch that was first designed by Thomas Jefferson, only to be reconstructed by Frederick Law Olmsted Jr during the FDR era. The White House helicopter **Marine One** lands on the lawn, and the president can usually be seen on TV brushing past news reporters here – either "unable" to hear their questions, as with Ronald Reagan, or scuttling away in disgrace, as with Richard Nixon following his 1974 resignation. However, you can't wander around the grounds unless you come for a garden tour or for the White House's most famous outdoor event: the **Easter Egg Roll**. The Roll is a long-standing tradition that began in 1878 and has been interrupted only by war and particularly foul weather. Although the event changes slightly every year, it usually involves children painting eggs and rolling them across the grass, a White House staffer dressed as the Easter Bunny, and various department heads and B-level celebrities reading stories and trying to act mirthful. To get free tickets for this event, which occurs the Monday after Easter, drop by the Ellipse Visitor Center at 15th and E streets at 7.30am on either the day of the Roll or the Saturday before it. Tickets are given out on a first-come, first-served basis and run out quickly.

The Ellipse

The **Ellipse**, known less appealingly as President's Park South (Ⓦ www.nps .gov/whho), is the large green expanse south of the White House that is open to the public, and the regular home to games of softball, Frisbee, and lawn hockey, among other diversions. Before 1900 the Ellipse variously hosted military camps, tent revival meetings, tennis courts, baseball fields, horse and mule corrals, and a local dump. Landscaped considerably in the last century, since 1978 it's been home to the rather stumpy **National Christmas Tree**, a Colorado blue spruce that the president lights every year to mark the start of the holiday season, and since the mid-1990s a visitor center has provided tickets to White House garden tours and the Easter Egg Roll.

On the Ellipse's northern edge, at E Street opposite the South Lawn, is the **Zero Milestone**, which was intended to mark the point from where all distances on US highways would be measured, but now it only applies to those in the District. On the Ellipse's eastern side (along 15th St) is the bronze **Boy Scout Memorial**, commemorating the site of the first Boy Scout Jamboree location, in 1937. Nearby, the simple granite **Monument to the Original Patentees** honors the eighteenth-century landowners who ceded land so that the city could be built. At the Ellipse's southeastern corner, the stone **Bulfinch Gatehouse** at Constitution Avenue and 15th Street was one of a pair that stood at the Capitol grounds' western entrance. Today its partner stands across the Ellipse at Constitution and 17th. On the south end of the Ellipse are the pair of **Enid Haupt Fountains**, which flow up from 55-ton slabs of rough Minnesota rainbow granite, and beyond them is the **Second Division Memorial**, paying tribute to the fallen soldiers of that Army group in World War II and the Korean War with a granite doorway symbolically blocked by a flaming sword. Another sculptural tribute, to the **First Division**, the oldest such grouping in the US Army, lies just north of the Ellipse on the southwest side of the South Lawn, offering a gilded statue of Victory atop a pink granite column. A seasonal red flower bed in front is designed in the shape of the numeral 1, literally referring to the Division's nickname, "The Big Red One," for the vivid emblem on its shoulder patch.

Around the White House

Appearing as a gleaming monolith at the edge of a lush green lawn on its south side, the White House is obscured on the east and west by two giant office buildings (the Treasury and Old Executive Office buildings, respectively) and sneaks up on you from the north. The security gates are not so imposing as you approach from **Lafayette Square**, so the northern side is your best bet for an unobscured snapshot of the president's house, and perhaps a chance to see a shadowy figure or two darting around inside.

Lafayette Square and around

The land due north of 1600 Pennsylvania Avenue was originally intended as part of the White House grounds, but in 1804 President Thomas Jefferson divided it in half and created a public park. Until 1824 the currently named

▲ Lafayette Square's equestrian statue of Andrew Jackson

Lafayette Square, lined with the houses of cabinet members and other prominent citizens, was known as President's Square. Over the years, redevelopment threatened the surrounding houses on several occasions, but in the 1960s Jacqueline Kennedy intervened, and modern monoliths were erected behind them, rather than in place of them – resulting in one of the stranger visual juxtapositions in DC, with warm historic facades fronting drab office blocks.

In the park's center is its only statue of an American, **Andrew Jackson**, shown astride a horse, surrounded by Spanish cannons (captured in Florida) and doffing his hat. Statues of foreign-born Revolutionary leaders are set at the corners of the square. In the southeast corner stands a likeness of the park's namesake, the **Marquis de Lafayette**, who raised an army on behalf of the American colonists and was a Revolutionary War general by the age of 19. Following the war Lafayette was imprisoned in France as a traitor, later to be released and become active once again in French politics, and during a return to the US in 1824 he was fêted on the Mall and awarded various honors, including this eponymous park. His statue shows him flanked by French admirals and being handed a sword by a female nude, symbolizing America.

In the northeast corner of the park, a bronze memorial for **Tadeusz Kosciusko**, the Polish freedom fighter and a prominent engineer in Washington's army, features an angry imperial eagle killing a snake atop a globe while the general towers overhead. The inscription at the base is surely one of the District's more memorable lines, taken from Scottish poet Thomas Campbell: "And freedom shrieked as Kosciusko fell!"

Blair and Lee houses

Built by the first US surgeon general in 1824, **Blair House**, at the southwestern corner of Lafayette Square, was named after a prominent Washington real-estate speculator, Francis Preston Blair, and has served as the guest house of choice for foreign dignitaries since the 1940s and the house of two presidents while the White House was undergoing renovation: Harry Truman in the 1940s and Bill Clinton briefly in the 1990s. Next door, but considered part of the contiguous complex, the 1860 **Lee House** was where Robert E. Lee was offered – and refused – command of the Union Army. Unfortunately, you can't look inside these residences, but their Federal-style exteriors are worth a glance.

Decatur House

US Capitol designer Benjamin Latrobe's red-brick 1819 **Decatur House**, 1610 H St NW (Tues–Sat 10am–5pm, Sun noon–4pm; $5; ☎202/842-0920, Ⓦwww.decaturhouse.org), is the oldest home on the square. Latrobe built this house for Stephen Decatur, a precocious American hero who performed with distinction in the War of 1812 and as a navy captain fighting Barbary pirates. Decatur lived here only about a year, as he was killed in a duel by Commodore James Barron in 1820 as payback for Decatur's role in the court martial that convicted Barron of wartime incompetence. The Federal-style first floor, studded with naval memorabilia, is decorated in the fashion of the day. Most of the other rooms have Victorian-style inlaid floors, furnishings, mirrors, moldings, and the like; the slave quarters in the Gadsby Wing were unusual for being on an upper level instead of in the basement as was customary. You can take a free guided **tour** (30–45min) that begins fifteen minutes after each hour. Inquire also about taking an audio tour of Lafayette Square, with content provided to visitors' cell phones.

Hay-Adams Hotel

Across the street from the Decatur House is the **Hay–Adams Hotel**, H and 16th streets (℡202/638-6600, ⓦwww.hayadams.com; see p.267), an impressive Renaissance Revival building with elegant arches and columns. The hotel sits on the former site of the townhouses of statesman **John Hay** (President Lincoln's private secretary) and his friend, historian and author **Henry Adams**. Their adjacent homes were the site of glittering soirées attended by Theodore Roosevelt and his circle – an association that appealed to hotshot hotel developer Harry Wardman, who jumped at the chance to buy the properties in 1927. Since then, the hotel, which boasted the city's first air-conditioned dining room, has been at the heart of Washington politicking: Henry Kissinger lunched here regularly, Oliver North did much of his clandestine Iran-Contra fund-raising here, and the Clintons slept here before Bill's first inauguration.

St John's Church

1525 H St NW ℡202/347-8766, ⓦwww.stjohns-dc.org. Mon–Sat 10.30am–2.30pm; free tours after 11am Sun service.

The tiny yellow church across H Street from Lafayette Park was built by **Benjamin Latrobe** in 1815. The handsome, domed Episcopal church was intended to serve the president and his family and is therefore known as the **"Church of the Presidents"**; all since Madison have attended – sitting in the special pew (no. 54) reserved for them – and when an incumbent dies in office, **St John's** bells ring out across the city. The handsome 1836 building just east of the church, with a grand French Second Empire facade, is today a parish building, but in the nineteenth century it was home to the British Embassy.

Treasury Building

The **Treasury Building**, with its imposing Neoclassical bulk and grand colonnade, flanks the White House to the east and faces 15th Street. Built – or at least begun – in 1836 by Robert Mills, who created the Old Patent Office and Old Post Office, this is commonly judged to be the finest Greek Revival building in DC. During the Civil War, the basement was strengthened and food and arms were stored in the building, as Lincoln and his aides planned to hole up here if the city was attacked. The jaunty statue at the southern entrance, facing Hamilton Place, is of **Alexander Hamilton**, first secretary of the Treasury (and the man on the $10 bill; the Treasury Building itself is on the back). Washington's closest adviser during the president's first administration, he died young in an 1804 duel with Aaron Burr, Jefferson's vice president and scheming Tammany Hall founder. US citizens only may arrange to take free, one-hour guided **tours**, which take place on Saturday mornings (9am, 9.45am, 10.30am & 11.15am), by contacting their senators or representatives well ahead of time and providing sufficient background information, including a photo ID upon arrival. On these outings you can expect to see the luxurious suites of Salmon P. Chase, Treasury secretary during the Civil War, and Andrew Johnson, made president after Lincoln's assassination, along with conference and reception rooms, and the cast-iron face of the 1864 Vault, lined with three sheets of steel. However, don't come expecting to see money being printed; that activity is done by the Bureau of Engraving and Printing (see p.132).

Eisenhower Old Executive Office Building

The ornate, gray-granite **Eisenhower Old Executive Office Building**, 17th St and Pennsylvania Ave NW, was built in 1888 to house the State, War, and Navy departments. Its architect, Alfred B. Mullet, claiming to be inspired by the Louvre, produced an ill-conceived monster of a French Empire–style building with hundreds of freestanding columns, extraordinarily tall and thin chimneys, a copper mansard roof, pediments, porticos, and various pedantic stone flourishes. The design has never been terribly popular, but schemes to renovate or rebuild it have come to nothing, mainly because of the expense involved in tackling such a behemoth. Ironically, its namesake, the 34th president, proposed to demolish the building in 1957, but public outcry, backed by ex-president Truman, saved it from the wrecking ball.

These days its roomy interior provides office space for government and White House staff, and in that capacity has been at the center of some of the country's most infamous political scandals. The building was the base of the White House "Plumbers," Nixon's dirty-tricks team, and hosted several of the infamous tape-recorded Watergate-related meetings; it was also where Colonel Oliver North and his secretary, Fawn Hall, shredded documents relating to the Iran-Contra scandal and where Vice President Dick Cheney allegedly hatched some of his wilier schemes. The building has long housed the offices of the vice president and the secretive National Security Council, so security here is almost as tight as it is at the White House and US Capitol. To view the ornate public rooms, filled with marble and gilt, stained glass, tiled floors, and wrought-iron balconies, you may arrange a **tour** (on Saturday mornings only) by calling the Preservation Office at ℡202/395-5895 between 9am and noon on Tuesday and Wednesday, and providing plenty of information about yourself. Note that in late 2007 the building caught on fire and several historic rooms were damaged; repair work will doubtless keep some sections closed in the coming years, so inquire ahead about the latest developments.

Renwick Gallery

Pennsylvania Ave at 17th St NW ℡202/633-2850, ⓦamericanart.si.edu/renwick; Farragut West Metro. Daily 10am–5.30pm.

The Second Empire flourishes of the Old Executive Office Building were directly influenced by the earlier, smaller, and much more harmonious **Renwick Gallery** of American arts and crafts, which lies directly opposite across Pennsylvania Avenue. Started by **James Renwick** (architect of the Smithsonian Castle) in 1859, the handsome red-brick building was originally meant to house the private art collection of financier **William Wilson Corcoran**. Work was interrupted by the **Civil War**, during which the building was requisitioned for use by the Union Army's quartermaster general. The Southern-sympathizing Corcoran left for Europe in 1862, where he stayed throughout the war. On his return, Corcoran finally got his gallery back (and, having sued, $125,000 from the government in back rent) and opened it to the public. Within twenty years his burgeoning collection had outgrown the site, and the new **Corcoran Gallery** was built just a couple of blocks south. In 1899 the US Court of Claims took up residence in the Renwick building and, after it vacated, the by-then-decrepit building was saved and restored in the 1960s by the Smithsonian, which uses it to display selections from its **American Art Museum**.

The building's ornate design reaches its apogee in the deep-red **Grand Salon** on the upper floor, a soaring parlor preserved in the style of the 1860s and

1870s, featuring windows draped in striped damask, period portraits (including one of Corcoran) and landscapes stacked four and five high, velvet-covered benches, marble-topped cabinets, and splendid wood-and-glass display cases taken from the Smithsonian Castle. This was the main picture gallery in Corcoran's time; its lofty dimensions meant that there was no difficulty in converting it into a courtroom and judge's chambers during the Court of Claims' tenure. The artworks are minor compared to those in the Smithsonian's expansive National Portrait Gallery and American Art Museum (see p.177 & p.181) but are highlighted by items such as **Thomas Moran**'s *The Grand Canyon of the Yellowstone* (1872), a colossal nature painting that embodies the gung-ho, Manifest Destiny spirit of nineteenth-century America, and **John Singer Sargent**'s portrait of upstanding socialite Betty Wertheimer.

Opposite, the smaller Octagon Room was specifically designed to hold Hiram Powers's notorious nude statue *The Greek Slave* (now in the Corcoran Gallery itself). Between the two rooms on the same floor are rotating galleries devoted to American crafts, mostly modern jewelry and furniture but also sculpture, ceramics, abstracts, and applied art in all its manifestations. The first floor hosts temporary exhibitions of contemporary crafts.

South along 17th Street

From the Eisenhower Old Executive Office Building and the Renwick Gallery, you can stroll south down 17th Street toward Constitution Avenue and take in a number of attractions along the way, including the **Daughters of the American Revolution Museum** and the **Corcoran Gallery of Art**, the latter home to the city's earliest art collection (originally in the Renwick Gallery). Smaller, less heralded collections nearby are also worth a visit. Keep an eye out for the five-story, iron-framed **Winder Building**, 604 17th St NW, which, in 1848, was the tallest building in Washington and the first to incorporate central heating. Between D and E streets is the white marble headquarters of the **American Red Cross**; look for the Tiffany stained glass in its second-floor assembly-room windows.

Corcoran Gallery of Art

500 17th St NW ☎202/639-1700, Ⓦ www.corcoran.org; Farragut West Metro. Wed–Mon 10am–5pm, Thurs closes at 9pm. $6.

The **Corcoran Gallery of Art** is one of DC's best art museums in a town overflowing with them. Moving from what is now the Renwick Gallery at the end of the nineteenth century, the gallery occupies a beautiful Beaux-Arts building of curving white marble with a green copper roof, the light and airy interior enhanced by a double atrium. Its mighty American collection includes more than three thousand paintings, from colonial to contemporary; Neoclassical sculpture; and modern photographs, prints, and drawings. Over the years, the permanent collection has expanded to include European works, Greek antiquities, and medieval tapestries. Benefactors continue to bestow impressive gifts, like the large collection of Daumier lithographs donated by Dr Armand Hammer and the seven hundred works by two hundred nineteenth- and twentieth-century artists and sculptors, from Picasso to Calder, left by Olga Hirshhorn (wife of Joseph of the eponymous gallery). Works from the permanent collection are rotated throughout the year, and other pieces are sent out on tour; not every-thing mentioned below will be on display at any one time. Details of changing exhibitions are available at the **information desk**, inside the main entrance, which is also where you can sign up for the guided **tours** of the permanent collection (daily noon & Thurs 7pm; free). The *Café des Artistes* (T 202/639-1786) has standard salads and sandwiches, with a good Sunday **brunch** (10.30am–2pm). There are also periodic Wednesday and Sunday **jazz concerts** (12.30pm; free) in the museum's Hammer Auditorium.

European art

The gallery's collection of European art is a mixed bag, mainly comprising the 1925 bequest of **Senator William A. Clark**, an industrialist with more money than discretion. William Corcoran's own collection here includes 120 commis-sioned animal bronzes by French sculptor **Antoine-Louis Barye** (1796–1875), many of which depict animals in combat: a lion attacking a horse, a python crushing a gazelle, and so on. More familiar artists are in the **Clark Landing**, a two-tiered, wood-paneled gallery accessed on the second floor from the rotunda, among them **Degas**, whose vivid, nocturnal *Cabaret* (1877) resembles the work of Toulouse-Lautrec more than his own; **Renoir** and **Monet**, with pleasant, unobjectionable landscapes; **Chardin**, whose *Scullery Maid* (1738) shows the title figure hunched over a barrel; **Picasso**, with a mid-level Cubist still life from 1913; and **Corot**, whose *Repose* (1870) features a notably sour-faced nude with Pan and his nymphs cavorting in the background. The only other European exhibits of real interest are the ones devoted to sixteenth-century French and Italian works, including some outstanding Italian majolica plates depicting mythological scenes, a thirteenth-century stained-glass window lifted from Soissons Cathedral, and two large, allegorical wool-and-silk French **tapestries** (1506) representing contemporaneous political and historical events.

In fact, the most striking piece of the gallery's European collection is not a painting but the corner room on the first floor known as the **Salon Doré** (Gilded Room), which originally formed part of an eighteenth-century Parisian home, the Hôtel de Clermont. Senator Clark bought the entire room, intending to install it in his New York mansion; after arriving in Washington, though, the senator housed it here, then bequeathed it to the Corcoran after his death. Framed mirrors (flanked by medallion-holding cherubs) make it seem larger than it actually is, and the rest of the room is filled with floor-to-ceiling hand-carved wood paneling, gold-leaf decor, and ceiling murals.

American art

The Corcoran's American art collection is the real reason to visit the institution, and you can find much of it displayed on the second floor. Approaching through the rotunda and Clark Landing you'll find representative paintings by early American artists such as **Gilbert Stuart**'s presidential portraits (*c*.1800), **George Inness**'s murky, dramatically lit *Sunset in the Woods* (1891), and **Rembrandt Peale**'s equestrian *Washington Before Yorktown* (1824), striking for its illuminated image of a strong, deliberate general hours before the decisive battle for independence.

The gallery possesses a fine collection of landscapes, starting with the expansive *Niagara* (1857) by **Frederic Edwin Church** and the splendid *Last of the Buffalo* (1889) by **Albert Bierstadt**. While Church concerned himself with the all-encompassing power of nature, Bierstadt here celebrates human endeavor within the natural world, portraying the Native American braves pursuing buffalo so numerous they darken the plain. In marked contrast, **Thomas Cole**'s *The Return* (1837), a mythical medieval scene of an injured knight returning to a priory glowing in the evening light, has little to do with America, though it does display the Hudson River School's penchant for portraying ethereal romance and natural beauty. Artist-cum-inventor **Samuel F.B. Morse**'s *The Old House of Representatives* (1822) was finished in a studio the artist set up in the US Capitol so that he could observe his subjects at work.

One room is usually devoted to nineteenth-century portraiture, with formal studies by renowned artists like **John Trumbull** (who painted the Capitol murals) and **Charles Bird King**, who depicts statesman Henry Clay supporting an 1821 resolution for South American independence. Striking also is **Thomas Sully**'s 1845 rendering of Andrew Jackson on horseback, fresh from triumph at the Battle of New Orleans in 1814, though the general looks well beyond the 47 years of age he would have been at the time. For some reason, the gallery's most notorious piece of sculpture is in this room as well. Originally on display in the Renwick Gallery, **Hiram Powers**'s *The Greek Slave* (1846), with her manacled hands and full-length nudity, so outraged contemporary critics that women visitors were prevented from viewing it while men were in the room.

Moving into late nineteenth-century art, the gallery holds works by **John Singer Sargent**, **Thomas Eakins**, and **Mary Cassatt**, among others. Sargent is responsible for one of the gallery's most loved pieces – the startling *Simplon Pass* (1911), with its landscape of crags and boulders – as well as more familiar society portraits such as a regal *Mrs. Henry White* (1883) and a scowling *Madame Edouard Pailleron* (1879). **Winslow Homer**'s *A Light on the Sea* (1897) and **Richard Norris Brooke**'s *A Pastoral Visit* (1881) take on rare subjects for the time – working women and African Americans – Homer depicting a fiercely strong woman swathed in fishing nets and Brooke providing a beautifully lit scene out of black life in the rural South. Worth a look also is one of **Cecilia Beaux**'s feline-inspired works, *Sita and Sarita* (1921), in which a pale woman in a luminous white dress sits with a curious black cat perched on her shoulder.

The gallery's pre-World War II collection includes works by **Childe Hassam**, **Rockwell Kent**, **Thomas Hart Benton**, and **Edward Hopper**, whose sailing picture, *Ground Swell* (1939), features a long, smooth sea and horizon, and just a hint of menace. Even better is **George Bellows**'s *Forty-Two Kids* (1907), in which the urchins in question are playing half-naked on the rotting docks of New York's East River. The rest of the second-floor rooms are devoted to special exhibitions and changing selections of prints, drawings, and photographs from the permanent collection. Depending on space, postwar and contemporary American artists, including big names like **Lichtenstein**, **Warhol**, and **de Kooning**, may be on display.

DAR Museum

1776 D St NW ☎202/879-3241, ⓦwww.dar.org/museum; Farragut West Metro. Mon–Fri 8.30am–4pm; museum, shop, and library also Sat 9am–5pm; period room tours Mon–Fri 10am–2.30pm, Sat 9am–4.30pm.

The National Society of the **Daughters of the American Revolution (DAR)** has had its headquarters in Washington for more than a century. Founded in 1890, this thoroughly patriotic (if rigidly conservative) organization is open to women who can prove descent from an ancestor (male or female) who served the American cause during the Revolution. Fueled by the proud motto "God, Home, and Country," it busies itself with good-citizen and educational programs, including one designed to promote "correct flag usage" throughout America: the Stars and Stripes adorning the rostrums in the Senate and the House in the US Capitol are gifts from the DAR, and just two of the more than 100,000 given away since 1909.

The organization's original meeting place was the 1905 Beaux–Arts-style Memorial Continental Hall, facing 17th Street, whose main chamber hosted the world's first disarmament conference in 1921. Delegates now meet for their annual congress (the week of April 19, anniversary of the Battle of Lexington) in the massive adjoining **Constitution Hall** on 18th Street, designed with typical exuberance by John Russell Pope in 1929, and one of the finest buildings in the city. A blight on the organization's history, however, occurred in 1939, when the DAR refused to let peerless black contralto Marian Anderson perform there. Eleanor Roosevelt resigned from the organization in outrage, and Anderson gave her concert instead on Easter Sunday at the Lincoln Memorial to a rapt crowd of 75,000.

The collection

Although you won't find that shameful episode on display, the **DAR Museum** (entrance on D St) is happy to direct you to its **gallery**, where a hodgepodge of embroidered quilts, silverware, toys, kitchenware, glass, crockery, earthenware, and just about anything else the Daughters have managed to lay their hands on over the years is on view. Although exhibits change, there's usually a fine selection of ceramics, popular in the Revolutionary and Federal periods (from which most of the collection dates). On request, one of the docents will lead you through the rest of the building, beginning in the spacious, 150,000-volume **genealogical library** that was once the main meeting hall. The library is open to DAR members and non-members ($5 a day) keen to bone up on such topics as *The History of Milwaukee* (in eight alarmingly large volumes) or *The Genealogy of the Witherspoon Family*.

What the Daughters are most proud of, however, are the **Period Rooms**, comprising no fewer than 31 period salons, mainly decorated with pre-1850 furnishings, each representing a different state, almost all of them east of the Mississippi. Few are of any historical or architectural merit, with a handful of exceptions: the New England room has an original lacquered wooden tea chest retrieved from Boston Harbor after the Tea Party in 1773; the California room replicates the interior of an early adobe house; and the New Jersey room displays furniture and paneling fashioned from the wreck of a British frigate sunk off the coast during the Revolutionary War – the overly elaborate chandelier was made from the melted-down anchor.

Foggy Bottom

Together with Georgetown, **Foggy Bottom**, lying between Pennsylvania and Constitution avenues from 17th to 25th streets, forms one of the oldest parts of DC, if not exactly the most exciting. The cultural activities at the **Kennedy Center** and the various government offices set a blandly white-collar, institutional tone – but enough of the buildings, including the historic **Octagon** house, are open to the public to make a walk through the neighborhood rewarding. The nearest Metro stop is Foggy Bottom–GWU, which is convenient for **George Washington University**, Washington Circle, and the Kennedy

The murky story of Foggy Bottom

Settled in the mid-eighteenth century, **Foggy Bottom** began as a thriving town on the shores of the Potomac (which reached further north in those days) and was known variously as Hamburg or Funkstown, after its German landlord **Jacob Funk**. Fashionable houses were built on the higher ground above today's E Street, though down by the river, in what's now **West Potomac Park**, it was a different story: industries making glass, beer, and gas emptied effluents into the Potomac and the city canal, while workers' housing was erected on the low-lying malarial marshlands, blighted by plagues of rats, rampant poison ivy, winter mud, and murky fog.

The poor, predominantly black neighborhood changed radically once the marshlands were drained in the late 1800s. Families and industries were displaced by the new West Potomac Park, and the southern limit was redefined by grand **Constitution Avenue**, which replaced the filled-in city canal. The smarter streets to the north formed the backdrop for a series of federal and international organizations that moved in before and after World War II, as the federal workforce rapidly expanded. In 1802, there were only 291 federal employees; by the 1970s there were more than two million; consequently, entire districts like Foggy Bottom were appropriated to warehouse DC's burgeoning share. Nowadays, given the predominance of government institutions here and the absence of any real street life outside of **George Washington University**, Foggy Bottom has seamlessly blended with the fabric of official Washington, becoming a wide swath of bureaucracy beginning at Capitol Hill and continuing on to the east bank of the Potomac River.

Center but half a dozen blocks and a fifteen-minute walk from Constitution Avenue. The #N3 bus covers most of Constitution Avenue (except between 19th and 21st streets) and heads up 23rd Street to the Metro station, while the #H1 and #L1 buses cover much of the same route.

Organization of American States

201 18th St NW Ⓣ 202/458-3000, Ⓦ www.oas.org; Farragut West Metro. Mon–Fri 9am–5.30pm.

Founded in 1890 "to strengthen the peace and security of the continent," the **Organization of American States** (OAS) is the world's oldest regional organization, with 35 member states from Antigua to Venezuela. Its headquarters occupy one of the more charming buildings in the city, a squat white Spanish Colonial mansion built in 1910 that faces onto the Ellipse. From the main entrance on 17th Street – fronted by a gaunt statue of Columbus's patron, Queen Isabella of Spain – you pass through fanciful iron gates to a cloistered lobby. The decor here turns almost to whimsy, with a fountain and tropical trees reaching to the wooden eaves and stone frieze above. You can then climb upstairs and walk through the gallery of national flags and busts of OAS founders, and take a peek in the grand Hall of the Americas.

A path leads from the Constitution Avenue side of the building through the so-called Aztec Garden to the smaller building behind. The **Art Museum of the Americas** – officially at 201 18th St NW (Tues–Sun 10am–5pm; Ⓣ202/458-6016, Ⓦ www.museum.oas.org) – shows rotating exhibits of Central and South American art, as well as temporary shows focusing on painting, photography, architecture, and more. In the main brick-floored gallery, the walls are lined with lively Latin American ceramics reaching to a wood-beamed roof, while just outside the museum, an equestrian statue of **Simon Bolivar** rides triumphantly on a curious horse with an almost circular neck.

Department of the Interior

1849 C St NW ☎202/208-4743, ⓦwww.doi.gov/interiormuseum; Farragut West Metro. Mon–Fri 8.30am–4.30pm; reserve two weeks in advance for guided tours.

The nation's principal landowner and conservation agency, the **Department of the Interior** was one of the earliest federal departments to take up residence in Foggy Bottom. The Department moved into architect Waddy Butler Wood's granite, square-columned building in 1937. Inside, grand WPA-era **murals** – like one commemorating Marian Anderson's 1939 concert at the Lincoln Memorial – decorate the walls (reserve in advance for a look at these).

After presenting ID at the reception desk, you'll be directed to the department's little-visited **museum**, which sheds light on agencies like the Bureau of Land Management, the National Park Service, and the Bureau of Indian Affairs. The wood-paneled museum, which you can self-tour without notice or see on a guided tour with two weeks' notice, opened in 1938 with a mission to spend one percent of its budget on art, as part of a New Deal program to hire unemployed artists. It's filled with stuffed bison heads, old saddles, fossils and minerals, paintings by nineteenth-century surveyors of the West, and eight elaborate dioramas featuring an Oklahoma land office, coal mine explosion, Alaska gold rush, and frontier fort. There are also regularly changing exhibitions of photography, paintings, or sculpture, and Native American artifacts, much of it drawn from the museum's stock of 150 million items. Around the corner from the museum, the **Indian Craft Shop** (☎202/208-4056, ⓦwww .indiancraftshop.com) sells tribal art and craftworks. Elsewhere in the building, the **National Park Service**'s information office (Mon–Fri 9am–5pm) has leaflets on almost every NPS park, museum, and monument in the country; in DC, that includes all the sites on the Mall.

The Octagon

1799 New York Ave NW ☎202/638-3221, ⓦwww.theoctagon.org; Farragut West Metro. Group tours only by reservation; Tues–Sun 10am–4.30pm. $5 per person.

Built in 1800, the **Octagon** is one of the city's oldest homes. Today it sits one block north of the Interior Department, and west of the Corcoran Gallery. Although it doesn't have eight sides (debate continues as to what the name actually means), it's nonetheless a classic structure loosely adapted from the Georgian style, whose rather simple brick exterior gives way to curving interior walls, arcing closet doors, and several period rooms open for touring. The circular entry hall sports its original marble floor, while beyond, a swirling oval staircase climbs up three stories. The house had two master bedrooms and five regular ones to accommodate the owner, his wife, and their fifteen children; some of the rooms are now used as gallery space for changing exhibitions devoted to architecture, decorative arts, and city history. In the dining and drawing rooms, period furnishings reveal how the house would have looked in its day – light, with high ceilings, delicate plaster cornicing, and Chippendale accessories. The two portraits in the dining room are of the architect and the owner, and the beautifully carved stone mantel in the drawing room is an original, signed and dated 1799. Downstairs, the accessible basement gives you an idea of the kind of drudgery servants and slaves underwent while the house owners lived in splendor above.

Note that with an ongoing process of refurbishment, the house will be open only to group tours of a minimum of ten people, at least through 2008, with advance reservation; call the Octagon for the latest news and to find out when or if this requirement will be lifted.

The many sides of the Octagon

Although no longer set amid fields and flanked by a line of fir trees, the Octagon, now dwarfed by the office buildings behind it, gives a good example of the private homes that once characterized the neighborhood. It was built by wealthy Virginian plantation owner **John Tayloe** on a prime corner plot just two blocks from the new President's Mansion. Tayloe, a friend of George Washington, was so rich and well connected that he could afford to spend the colossal total sum of $35,000 on the house and hire **William Thornton**, US Capitol designer, to build it.

The **War of 1812** guaranteed the house its place in history. Though the English torched the nearby President's Mansion, they spared the Octagon, possibly because the French ambassador was in residence at the time. President and Dolley Madison moved in after they returned to the city after the blaze. For six months in 1814–15, the president ran the government from its rooms, and on February 17, 1815, the **Treaty of Ghent**, making peace with Britain, was signed in the study (on a table still kept in the house). For much of the latter part of the nineteenth century, the Octagon was left to deteriorate, but at the turn of the twentieth century, the American Institute of Architects (AIA) bought it and used it as its headquarters until 1973; though it later found newer premises nearby, it still maintains the Octagon as a house museum.

Constitution Avenue

From the Organization of American States building at the corner of 17th Street, **Constitution Avenue** – known as B Street until the 1930s – parades an attractive line of buildings framed by the greenery of Constitution Gardens across the way. The street isn't necessarily a destination in itself, but it's dotted with interesting sights along the way, from a few highlights on the north side to the Vietnam Veterans Memorial on the south side of the avenue. One architectural curiosity is the **Lockkeeper's House**, on the southwest corner of 17th Street and Constitution Avenue, a sturdy stone cabin that today is a simple park maintenance facility. However, it used to be the residence of the toll-taker for the **C&O Canal**, which for forty years occupied what's now the avenue until the watercourse was filled in during the 1870s.

Federal Reserve

20th St NW between C St and Constitution Ave ☎202/452-3324 for tours, ☎202/452-3778 for gallery, Ⓦwww.federalreserve.gov; Foggy Bottom–GWU Metro. By advance reservation only, Mon–Fri 10am–3.30pm.

The first building of any distinction along Constitution Avenue is the enormous, eagle-fronted **Federal Reserve**, designed by Paul Cret, who was also responsible for the OAS and the Folger Shakespeare Library (see p.117). The department headquartered here controls the country's money supply and gold reserves, issues government securities, and is most familiar to the public as the body that decides the direction of US interest rates. **Group tours** of the 1937 building are available for visitors 18 and over (ten-person minimum; call two weeks in advance) and include a film giving an overview of the organization's function, as well as a look at the boardroom, where key decisions – like whether to raise or lower rates and, if so, by how much – are made. With a day's notice you can make a separate reservation to visit the Reserve's decent **art gallery**, which hosts temporary exhibits on Romantic-era French sculpture and American Abstract Expressionism, as well as collections borrowed from galleries owned by other central banks around the world. Its small permanent collection comprises a hodgepodge of donated pieces, from the bucolic works of antebellum landscape artist **Thomas Hotchkiss** to the modern color-field paintings of **Ellsworth Kelly**.

National Academy of Sciences

2100 C St NW ℗202/334-2000, ⓦwww.nas.edu; Foggy Bottom–GWU Metro. Mon–Fri 9am–5pm.

Congress created the **National Academy of Sciences** in 1863 to provide the country with independent, objective scientific advice. The building's facade is adorned with Greek inscriptions, and its cold Neoclassical lines are softened by a grove of elm and holly trees at the southwest (22nd St) corner, where Robert Berks's large bronze statue of **Albert Einstein** sits. Einstein is depicted lounging on a granite bench with the universe (in the shape of a galaxy map) at his feet; a piece of paper inscribed with the famous formula from his Theory of Relativity is in his hand.

The Academy also has a pair of **art galleries**, in its central rotunda and upstairs, that showcase pieces relating to its mission. Paintings, sculptures, and multimedia projects by mostly unknown artists provide fascinating takes on astronomy, anatomy, cosmology, cartography, and other scientific fields. There are also free Sunday-afternoon **music concerts** (Oct–April 3pm; see p.311) in its auditorium, featuring the occasional big-name artist, in styles from Baroque to modern. For information on these events and exhibitions, call ℗202/334-2436 or visit ⓦwww7.nationalacademies.org/arts.

Department of State

C St between 21st and 23rd sts ℗202/647-3241, ⓦwww.state.gov; Foggy Bottom–GWU Metro.

In 1960 the **Department of State** moved out of the Old Executive Office Building and into its own headquarters – a long white building occupying two entire blocks in the southwest corner of Foggy Bottom. Established in 1789 and originally helmed by Thomas Jefferson, the nation's oldest and most senior Cabinet agency is effectively the federal foreign office. It's also notoriously circumspect, and it's a wonder that visitors are allowed inside at all. **Tours** were suspended here after 9/11, but they have since resumed (Mon–Fri 9.30am, 10.30am & 2.45pm; free; ⓦreceptiontours.state.gov), though you should reserve as much as three months in advance to guarantee a spot. They allow you to peek at the elegant **Diplomatic Reception Rooms**. During the 1960s, many of these rooms were redecorated and refurnished to provide more suitable chambers for receiving diplomats and heads of state. Among the wealth of eighteenth- and nineteenth-century paintings, decorative arts, and furniture is the desk on which the American Revolution's conclusive Treaty of Paris was signed.

Northern Foggy Bottom

The **northern side** of Foggy Bottom is pretty dull terrain, split between sites for institutional behemoths like the IMF and World Bank (adjacent on G St between 18th and 20th) and the uneventful campus for **George Washington University**. The main campus spreads over several city blocks between F, 20th, and 24th streets and Pennsylvania Avenue; the nicest part is **University Yard**, between G and H, and 20th and 21st streets – a green, rose-filled park surrounded by Colonial Revival buildings. The park's statue of Washington is yet another copy of the famous Houdon image. For more information on the university, visit the Academic Center at 801 22nd St NW (℗202/994-6602, ⓦwww.gwu.edu), where you can pick up a campus map and ask about the

Washington's university

Pierre L'Enfant's city plan allowed for the building of a university in the Foggy Bottom district, and it was certainly a development that George Washington himself was keen on; he even left money in his will to endow an educational institution. Like L'Enfant and Washington, many of the university's founders were Freemasons and liberally applied the society's emblem throughout the school (the Bible that inaugurates new university presidents once belonged to Washington himself). The nondenominational Columbian College, founded by an Act of Congress in 1821, was the precursor of today's **George Washington University** (GWU), which was renamed in 1873 and soon moved into its current site. Since then it has played a crucial role in the city's development, buying up townhouses and erecting new buildings on such a scale as to make it the second-biggest landholder in DC after the federal government. Famous alumni include Jacqueline Kennedy Onassis (who gets a building named after her), J. Edgar Hoover, Colin Powell, Allen and John Foster Dulles, crime author (and Harry's daughter) Margaret Truman, and current Senate majority leader Harry Reid, as well as less expected figures like Courteney Cox and L. Ron Hubbard.

student-led historic walking or trolley tours of the area (1hr; free; Jan–April & Aug–Nov Mon–Fri 11am & 3pm, Sat 11am & 2pm).

There are a few scattered points of architectural interest in northern Foggy Bottom. To the east, at 20th and G, the red Italianate **United Church** was built in 1891 for the descendants of the neighborhood's Germanic immigrants, and offers an eye-catching tower for bells ringing the call to worship at this evangelical church. On the western side of the GWU campus, **St Mary's Church**, at 730 23rd St, was established in 1887 as the first black Episcopal church in DC. A wealthy band of local citizens coughed up $15,000 to hire architect **James Renwick**, of Smithsonian Castle and Renwick Gallery fame, to construct it, and the stately red-brick Gothic structure is very much in keeping with the latter's high Victorian style.

Two blocks west on 25th Street (north of H), there's a run of carefully preserved nineteenth-century brick houses painted with vivid pastel colors; the most interesting ones are in **Snow Court** (between 24th and 25th streets, and I and K), DC's only surviving interior alley, where the homes are only 12ft wide – in the 1880s each one probably housed ten people; nowadays they change hands for a fortune. Lastly, north of **Washington Circle**, where four major roads converge, the **West End** neighborhood – named after its presence at the edge of L'Enfant's city plan – is another of DC's newly gentrifying districts, though unless you've come to drop in at a hotel, there's little to detain you beyond condos and office blocks.

The Watergate Complex

If there's a single word synonymous with American political scandal, it's certainly "Watergate" (see box, pp.158–159), which takes its name from the **Watergate Complex** on 25th Street NW at Virginia Avenue. This huge, curving, mid-1960s residential and commercial monster – named for the flight of steps behind the Lincoln Memorial that leads down to the Potomac – has always been a sought-after address, both for foreign ambassadors and the city's top brass. People like Bob and Elizabeth Dole and Caspar Weinberger have maintained apartments here for years, and White House intern Monica Lewinsky lived here before the Clinton impeachment scandal forced her from DC. In 1972, the Democratic National Committee was headquartered in the hotel's sixth floor. On June 17, five men connected to President Nixon's re-election campaign were arrested for breaking into the offices, and two years later, Nixon resigned from the presidency in disgrace. Visitors can come here to shop, eat, and sleep (though the hotel is closed until 2009), but the complex is really more something you'd pass by and gawk at, rather than tour.

Kennedy Center

2700 F St NW ☎202/467-4600, ⓦ www.kennedy-center.org; Foggy Bottom–GWU Metro. Tours Mon–Fri 10am–5pm, Sat & Sun 10am–1pm; reserve at ☎202/416-8340.

Washington didn't have a national cultural center until 1971, when a $78 million white marble behemoth designed by Edward Durrell Stone was opened. The **John F. Kennedy Center for the Performing Arts** continues to be the city's foremost cultural outlet: it has four main auditoriums, a variety of exhibition halls, and a clutch of restaurants and bars; is home to the **National Symphony Orchestra** and the **Washington Opera**; and hosts touring theater, musical, and ballet groups. There's an information desk on your way in, and you're free to wander around. Provided there's no performance or rehearsal taking place, you can look inside the theaters and concert halls (most are open to visitors 10am–1pm). Free 45-minute guided tours depart daily from Level A (beneath the Opera House).

▲ John F. Kennedy Center for the Performing Arts

I would walk over my grandmother if necessary to assure the President's re-election.

Charles Colson, special counselor to Richard M. Nixon

The 1972 presidential election campaign was well under way when five men were arrested at the **Watergate Complex** on June 17. Richard Nixon, running for re-election against Democratic challenger George McGovern, was determined to win a second term, elevating the election race into a moral struggle against encroaching liberal forces, who, crucially, were pushing the anti–Vietnam War message to the top of the political agenda.

After being spotted by a security guard on his rounds, the five men were apprehended in the offices of the Democratic National Committee in the act of tapping the phone of Lawrence O'Brien, the national party chairman. Once they were arraigned in court, it became clear that these were no ordinary burglars: one, James McCord, worked directly for the **Committee to Re-Elect the President** (known, appropriately, as CREEP), all had CIA connections, and some were later linked to documents that suggested that their escapade had been sanctioned by White House staffer Howard Hunt and election campaign attorney G. Gordon Liddy. To anyone who cared to look, the connections went further still: at the White House, Hunt worked for Charles Colson, Nixon's special counsel, while McCord's direct superior was the head of CREEP, John Mitchell, who also happened to be Attorney General of the United States.

Amazingly, at least in retrospect, hardly anyone looked further. The burglars, together with Hunt and Liddy, were indicted in September 1972 but refused to provide details about any possible collaborators. The Democrats, none more so than McGovern, complained loudly about dirty tricks, but the White House officially denied any knowledge. In the election in November, Nixon won a landslide, carrying 49 out of the 50 states, save only Massachusetts and the District of Columbia.

Initially the only people asking questions were *Washington Post* reporters **Bob Woodward** and **Carl Bernstein**. As the months went by, and aided by a source known to Woodward only as "**Deep Throat**," the pair uncovered irregularities in the Republican campaign – "dirty tricks" to discredit their opponents – many of which had close but unprovable links with the Watergate burglary. To the FBI's annoyance, the stories often relied on verbatim accounts of the FBI's own investigations – someone, somewhere, was leaking information. However, it still proved difficult to generate much interest outside Washington in the matter, and the story would probably have been forgotten but for the impetus provided by the defendants' trial. All pleaded guilty to burglary, but before sentencing in January 1973 Judge John Sirica made it clear that he didn't believe that the men acted alone; long sentences were threatened. Rather than face jail, some defendants began to talk, including James McCord, who not only implicated senior officials like John Mitchell for the first time but also claimed that secret CREEP funds had been used to finance an anti-Democrat smear campaign. The plan employed "plumbers" – so-called because they stopped leaks and patched holes in Nixon's defenses – to work against domestic adversaries (the "enemies" on Nixon's infamous list), including dredging up dirt on his nemeses via the FBI and CIA, and plotting such never-realized schemes as kidnapping antiwar activists, entrapping political enemies through prostitution rings, and firebombing the Brookings Institution. This was precisely what Woodward and Bernstein had been trying to prove for months.

As pressure on the administration for answers grew, the Senate established a special investigating committee under Sam Ervin and appointed a special prosecutor, Archibald Cox. The trail now led ever closer to the White House. In a desperate damage-control exercise, Nixon's own counsel, John Dean, was sacked, and the resignations of White House Chief of Staff H.R. Haldeman and domestic affairs adviser John Erlichman were accepted; all, it seemed, were involved in planning the burglary.

In June 1973 the **Watergate hearings**, broadcast on national television, began to undermine Nixon's steadfast denial of any involvement. It transpired that the White House had promised clemency and cash if the burglars remained silent; the CIA had leaned on the FBI to prevent any further investigations; and illegal wiretaps, dirty tricks campaigns, and unlawful campaign contributions were commonplace.

The president continued to stand aloof from the charges but was finally dragged down by the revelation that he himself had routinely bugged offices in the White House and elsewhere, taping conversations that pertained to Watergate. Famously, it quickly became a matter of "what did the president know and when did he know it." Cox and the Senate committee subpoenaed the **audiotapes**, but Nixon refused to release them, citing his presidential duty to protect executive privilege. Soon after, he engineered the sacking of Cox in the so-called Saturday Night Massacre, a move that led to the convening of the House Judiciary Committee, the body charged with preparing bills of **impeachment** – in this case, against the president for refusing to comply with a subpoena. To deflect mounting suspicion, Nixon finally handed over edited transcripts of the tapes (from which eighteen minutes had been erased) in April 1974, but rather than clearing Nixon of any involvement, they simply dragged him further in – many citizens were appalled, for one, to see the great number of "expletive deleted" notations from the tapes, suggesting Nixon was impossibly vulgar and obscene in his common speech. The president, furthermore, at least knew about the cover-up, and there was clear evidence of wrongdoing by key government and White House personnel. A grand jury indicted Mitchell, Haldeman, Erlichman, Dean, and others for specific offenses, while the House Judiciary Committee drew up a bill of impeachment against Nixon for committing "high crimes and misdemeanors."

On August 5, 1974, the **Supreme Court** ordered Nixon to hand over his tapes. These proved conclusively that he and his advisers had devised a strategy of bribes and destruction of evidence to cover up White House and CREEP involvement in the Watergate burglary. The president, despite his protestations, had lied to the people, and it was inevitable that he should face impeachment. Urged on by senior Republican senators, on August 8, 1974, Richard Milhous Nixon became the first president to **resign**. Combative to the end, he made no acknowledgment of guilt, suggesting instead that he had simply made errors of judgment.

Vice President **Gerald Ford** succeeded Nixon as president, but not much changed within the new administration: Secretary of State Henry Kissinger, who had a hand in the bombing of Laos and Cambodia and the coup in Chile that installed Augusto Pinochet – campaigns hidden from the American public – kept his job, while Alexander Haig, a key figure in the withholding of the Watergate tapes, was promoted to become head of NATO. To top it all off, Ford formally pardoned Nixon with unseemly haste, allowing him to live out his retirement without controversy in California but probably costing Ford the 1976 election, won by Jimmy Carter. In a bizarre twist, Richard Nixon slowly rehabilitated himself in the eyes of the political establishment and even the press; when he died in 1994 there was a full turnout at his funeral by leaders of all political hues – however, the ceremony took place not in official Washington but in Yorba Linda, California; unlike Ronald Reagan in 2004, Nixon did not lie in state under the Capitol dome or receive official honors at Washington National Cathedral. The final twist in the story came in 2005, when it was revealed that **Mark Felt**, deputy director of the FBI, was in fact Deep Throat, leaking information to Woodward and Bernstein due to loyalty to the integrity of the FBI, revenge over being passed over for a promotion, civic duty, and patriotism, or a combination of all of the above.

The **Grand Foyer** itself is a real sight: 630ft long and 60ft high, it's lit by gargantuan crystal chandeliers and contains an 8ft-high **bronze bust** of JFK in the moon-rock style favored by sculptor Robert Berks. You can also drop by the **Hall of States**, where states' flags are hung in the order they entered the Union, and the **Hall of Nations**, which honors the nations recognized by the US. In addition, each of the theaters and concert halls has its own catalog of artwork, from the **Matisse** tapestries outside the Opera House and the **Barbara Hepworth** sculpture in the Concert Hall to the **Felix de Welden** bronze bust of Eisenhower above the lobby of the Eisenhower Theater. The **Roof Terrace** level has the Performing Arts Library – filled with scripts, information on historical performances, and recordings (Tues–Fri 11am–8.30pm, Sat 10am–6pm) – and places to eat. While you're up here, step out onto the terrace for great views across the Potomac to Theodore Roosevelt Island, and north to Georgetown and Washington National Cathedral.

Old Downtown and the Federal Triangle

A few decades ago the older section of DC's Downtown, above the eastern half of the Mall, was a pretty bleak place, blighted by crime and deserted at night, with little of interest other than the faded architecture of its nineteenth-century Neoclassical buildings and New Deal–era federal government offices. In recent years, however, **Old Downtown** has experienced an upsurge of interest, thanks to a steady flow of urban-renewal dollars; today you'll find a wide range of chic restaurants, niche museums, fancy hotels, and more, a lively combination that has led the tourism authorities to redub part of the area the "**Penn Quarter**," after Pennsylvania Avenue NW, which provides the southern boundary.

Tours of the zone begin with the landmarks along that avenue and include the **Navy Memorial** and majestic old **Willard Hotel**. North of the avenue, many of the grander municipal buildings have been converted into fine museums – for example, the Pension Building is now the stunning **National Building Museum**, and the Old Patent Office is the **National Portrait Gallery** and **American Museum of Art**. Other key sights include **Ford's Theatre** and the **Museum of Women in the Arts**, from which it's only a short stroll to **Chinatown**, where you can lunch cheaply on noodles and dim sum. Less appealing is the ten-square-block area below Pennsylvania Avenue NW known as the **Federal Triangle**, where eight colossal government buildings hog all the space; it has scattered attractions here and there, but is mainly of interest for the historical exhibits and documents of the **National Archives**.

Some history

The land between the Capitol and the White House, north of the Mall, was the only part of nineteenth-century Washington that remotely resembled a city. A downtown developed in the diamond formed by Pennsylvania, New York, Massachusetts, and Indiana avenues, and fashionable stores and restaurants existed alongside printing presses, shoeshine stalls, oyster sellers, and market traders. Entertainment was provided by a series of popular theaters, including Ford's Theatre, where President Lincoln was shot.

By the late nineteenth century, Pennsylvania Avenue marked the southern limits of Washington society; the shops on its north side were as far as the genteel would venture. The downtown area was given a new lease of life in the 1930s,

▲ Union Station

OLD DOWNTOWN AND THE FEDERAL TRIANGLE

CAFÉS & RESTAURANTS

Acadiana	1
Café Atlantico	30
Café Mozart	3
Corner Bakery	24
District Chophouse & Brewery	27
Eat First	10
Ebbitt Express	16
Ella's Pizza	18
Full Kee	13
Haad Thai	2
Harry's	29
Jackey Café	8
Jaleo	28
Kanlaya Thai	12
Matchbox	6
Old Ebbitt Grill	15
Portico Café	19
Proof	11
Sky Terrace	20
Ten Penh	31
Tony Cheng's	9
Tosca	21
Zengo	14
Zola	23

ACCOMMODATION

Courtyard Washington	E
Grand Hyatt	D
Hampton Inn	L
Harrington	C
Henley Park	K
HI-Washington DC	A
JW Marriott	G
Marriott at Metro Center	H
Monaco	B
Morrison-Clark Inn	F
Red Roof Inn	J
Willard InterContinental	I

BARS & CLUBS

Capitol City Brewing Co.	4
D.A.'s RFD Washington	5
ESPN Zone	26
Fado	7
Gordon Biersch Brewery	22
Round Robin	25
UltraBar	17

Map labels:
M McPherson Square · M Metro Center · M Gallery Place-Chinatown · M Judiciary Square · M Archives-Navy Memorial · M Federal Triangle

▲ New Downtown · ▲ White House · ▲ & Convention Center

Streets: H ST NW · NEW YORK AVE NW · MASSACHUSETTS AVE NW · I ST NW · G ST NW · G PLACE · F ST NW · E ST NW · D ST NW · C ST NW · PENNSYLVANIA AVE NW · CONSTITUTION AVE NW · INDIANA AVE NW · 1ST ST NW · 3RD ST NW · 4TH ST NW · 5TH ST NW · 6TH ST NW · 7TH ST NW · 8TH ST NW · 9TH ST NW · 10TH ST NW · 11TH ST NW · 12TH ST NW · 13TH ST NW · 14TH ST NW · 15TH ST NW

Landmarks: Pension Building (National Building Museum) · National Law Enforcement Officers Memorial · Old City Hall · Lincoln Statue · Marshall Statue · Department of Labor · US (Federal) Court House · Marshall Municipal Center · John Marshall Park · Andrew Mellon Fountain · Grand Army of the Republic Monument · Canadian Embassy · Newseum · Sears House · Federal Trade Commission · Koshland Science Museum · Law Enforcement Officers Visitor Center · The Lansburgh (Shakespeare Theatre) · Verizon Center · Surratt House site · CHINATOWN · Arch · Gallery Place-Chinatown · Market Square · US Navy Memorial · Navy Memorial · National Archives · Department of Justice · Smithsonian American Art Museum · National Portrait Gallery · Martin Luther King Jr Memorial Library · International Spy Museum · Riggs Natl. Bank · Ford's Theatre · Petersen House · Federal Bureau of Investigation · FDR Memorial · Internal Revenue Service · Madame Tussauds Wax Museum · Warner Theatre · Evening Star Building · Old Post Office · Federal Triangle · National Museum of Women in the Arts · 1100 New York Ave · New York Ave Presbyterian Church · Metro Center · National Theatre · National Place · Metropolitan Square · Freedom Plaza · Pulaski Statue · DC Visitor Information Center · Ariel Rios Building · EPA · Wilson Building · National Aquarium · Franklin Statue · Pershing Statue · Pershing Park · Washington Hotel · Department of Commerce · National Mall

N

0   500 yds

0

when the stately buildings of the Federal Triangle were built, but by the 1960s it was a shambling, low-rent neighborhood that would be badly damaged by the 1968 riots. As established businesses fled to the developing area north of the White House, the dilapidated region eventually became known as Old Downtown, and was a potent visual symbol of the divide between the "two Americas," the glittering showpieces of the Mall and Capitol Hill set just blocks from some of the worst urban blight in the US.

In the 1980s, however, Old Downtown began to be rescued from years of neglect. Since then, an enormous amount of money has been pumped into renovations, especially in the easternmost area (south of G St, between 3rd and 12th), now being trumpeted as the Penn Quarter. With an agreeable swatch of delis, restaurants, sports bars, galleries, and landscaping being grafted onto the existing historic buildings and cleaned-up streets, it's sure to remain one of the city's most rapidly evolving areas for years to come.

Along Pennsylvania Avenue NW

Defining the border between Old Downtown and the Federal Triangle (forming its hypotenuse), **Pennsylvania Avenue NW** is one of the District's most famous roads, connecting the Capitol with the White House – where it turns pedestrian-only for one long block. In L'Enfant's original design, the avenue was supposed to allow for unimpeded views of both structures, but this changed when Andrew Jackson had the Treasury Building plunked down on the western end – a move some say was specifically meant to keep the White House away from the prying eyes of Congress. Still, the avenue continues as the site of the president's triumphal January **Inaugural Parade**, going from the Capitol (site of the inauguration) to the White House. Thomas Jefferson led the first impromptu parade in 1805, James Madison made the ceremony official, and every president since then, except Ronald Reagan in 1985, has trundled up in some form of conveyance – though Jimmy Carter famously walked the sixteen long blocks to the White House. In addition, the bodies of nine presidents have been taken from the Capitol to the White House, lying in state in both locations – some of them, such as Gerald Ford in 2006, continuing on to Washington National Cathedral for funeral services.

Pennsylvania Avenue was named after the state that was home to the previous capital, Philadelphia, and was meant to be the center of the new capital's commercial life, though its success was hampered by the piecemeal development taking place all around. While fashionable shops operated along its north side, the swamp-ridden reaches to its south (today's Federal Triangle), close to the filthy C&O canal that isolated the city from the Mall, housed a notorious stew of slum housing, bordellos, and cheap liquor joints. Turn-of-the-twentieth-century additions to the avenue – notably the Post Office and the *Willard Hotel* – were part of an early attempt to transform the district's fortunes, but for much of the twentieth century Pennsylvania Avenue was in severe decline. In the 1970s the Pennsylvania Avenue Development Corporation (PADC) formed and enlivened the area with small plazas, memorials framed by newly planted trees, and attractive Victorian flourishes on lampposts and benches. However, it really took the upsurge in downtown development in the past twenty years to establish the route as an engaging must-walk for hale and hearty tourists.

Pershing Park and Hamilton Place

Beginning at Old Downtown's northwestern end of Pennsylvania Avenue, closest to the White House, pleasant **Pershing Park** was named for the commander of the American forces during World War I, John J. Pershing, popularly known as "Black Jack" for his role as a commander of African American cavalry soldiers in the 1890s. Pershing's statue stands alongside a sunken terrace that becomes a **skating rink** in winter (Mon–Thurs 11am–9pm, Fri 11am–11pm, Sat 10am–11pm, Sun 10am–7pm; $6.50 admission, skate rental $2.50; ⓦ www.pershingparkicerink.com). Just to the west, **Hamilton Place** is named after Alexander Hamilton, first US Treasury secretary, but marks the spot where general William Tecumseh Sherman (also honored by a statue) presided over the Grand Review of the Union Armies in May 1865; six weeks after Lee's surrender, the victorious troops proudly marched up Pennsylvania Avenue in one of the most stirring military parades ever seen in the capital. It was a show of Union strength tinged with sadness, as President Lincoln had been assassinated only a few weeks earlier, his funeral cortege also following the line of Pennsylvania Avenue.

Willard Hotel

1401 Pennsylvania Ave NW ⓣ 202/628-9100, ⓦ www.washington.intercontinental.com; Metro Center or Federal Triangle Metro.

Looming over the north side of Pershing Park at 14th Street is one of the grand old ladies among Washington hotels, the **Willard** – a Washington landmark for over 150 years. Although a hotel has existed on the site for nearly 200 years, it was after 1850, when Henry Willard gave his name to the place, that it became a haunt of statesmen, politicians, top brass, and presidents – including Abraham Lincoln, who was smuggled in here before his first inauguration (during which snipers were placed on the roof). The *Willard*'s opulent public rooms attracted favor-seekers anxious to press their demands on political leaders; it's even believed that the hotel gave rise to the word "lobbyist" for all the deal making that took place in that hotel entryway. A story also tells that Julia Ward Howe wrote "The Battle Hymn of the Republic" while closeted here during the Civil War – supposedly inspired by Union soldiers marching under her window belting out their favorite song, "John Brown's Body" – and, as an appropriate bookend, that Dr Martin Luther King Jr wrote the iconic cadences of the "I Have a Dream" speech while in his hotel room shortly before the 1963 March on Washington.

In 1901 the *Willard* was renovated and became the splendid Beaux-Arts building that you'll find today. It went out of business after the riots of 1968, but a thorough restoration in 1986 and another a decade later recaptured its early style. Drop by the galleried lobby and tread the main corridor's plush carpets to get a feel for where DC's swells and well-heeled still hang out. After spending some time here, you might want to look at the 1917 *Washington Hotel*, on the corner of 15th and F streets, whose rooftop bar provides excellent views across to the White House grounds, though the site is undergoing a major renovation beginning in 2008.

Freedom Plaza and around

The large open space known as **Freedom Plaza** lies where Pennsylvania Avenue kinks into E Street (at 13th) and is the site of numerous festivals, protests, and open-air concerts. Lined in marble, the square is inlaid with a large-scale representation of Pierre L'Enfant's city plan, crafted in bronze and colored stone, and etched with various laudatory inscriptions. From here the view down Pennsylvania Avenue to the Capitol is splendid, but this is a sweltering place to hang around in summer, the only shade provided by the statue of **General Casimir Pulaski**, a Polish hero of the Revolutionary War, at the eastern end.

On the plaza's south side, the Beaux-Arts **Wilson Building**, no. 1350, with its mighty caryatids, Corinthian columns, and bold corner shield emblems, predates all other Federal Triangle edifices. Erected in 1908 to house city council offices, when it was known as the District Building, it escaped demolition in the 1920s and 1930s and now houses the mayor's office and city council chambers. The building also holds the recently opened **City Hall Art Collection** (Mon–Fri 9am–5pm; free), which arrays the work of 175 city sculptors, painters, photographers, and mixed-media artists on all six of the building's floors. You probably won't have heard of any of the artists, but some of the work is still quite good, ranging from pastel abstractions to historic photos of the town to unclassifiable installations and glassworks.

Across the street, at no. 1321, the **National Theatre** – on this site since 1835, though the current building dates from 1922 and was recently restored – has hosted numerous presidents in the audience for its theatrical works, which lately include a lot of off-Broadway toe-tappers (see p.314 for more information). The theater forms part of the **National Place** complex, whose drab exterior hides a three-level shopping mall, **The Shops at National Place**. At the northeastern corner of the plaza, the elegant **Warner Theatre** (at 13th and E) is a classic 1920s movie house that has been reborn as a performing-arts center.

Old Post Office

1100 Pennsylvania Ave NW ☎ 202/289-4224, ⊛ www.oldpostofficedc.com; Federal Triangle Metro. Mon–Sat 10am–7pm, Sun noon–6pm, March–Aug closes an hour later.

Two blocks east of Freedom Plaza is the steel-framed Romanesque Revival **Old Post Office**, which owes its survival more to the depressed real-estate market of the early twentieth century than it does to civic planners' yen for historic preservation. A longtime candidate for demolition, the former post office (1899–1914) has managed to survive through the decades intact, with its towering granite walls, seven-story atrium, restored iron support beams, and burnished wood paneling. Now known as the **Pavilion**, the site mainly provides a grand, out-of-proportion home to rather middling ethnic restaurants and shops, but it does feature a post office counter from the turn of the twentieth century (Mon–Fri 9am–5pm), still in use at the Pennsylvania Avenue entrance.

The stunning **clock tower** is the centerpiece of the building, making it resemble an Old World church, and is worth a look (daily Mon–Fri 9am–4.45pm, Sat & Sun 10am–5.45pm, summer Mon–Fri until 7.45pm; free; ☎ 202/606-8691, ⊛ www.nps.gov/opot); from here park rangers oversee short, free tours up to the **observation deck**, 270ft above Pennsylvania Avenue. The glass-elevator ride allows you to see the building in all its glory, and the viewing platform (three flights of stairs beyond the elevator) offers a stunning city panorama and information about the building's checkered history – including the inauspicious death of the local postmaster, who, during the opening celebration, fatally plummeted down an elevator shaft. More safely ensconced, on the way back down to the elevator you can see the **Congress Bells**, replicas of those in Westminster Abbey. A Bicentennial gift from London, they were installed here in 1983.

Back outside on the avenue, **Benjamin Franklin** – "Philosopher, Printer, Philanthropist, Patriot," as his statue has it – gives a cheery little wave. You can park yourself on a bench and look across to the Beaux-Arts facade of the 1898 **Evening Star Building**, no. 1101, with its attractive balconies, pediments, and carvings.

Federal Bureau of Investigation

9th St and Pennsylvania Ave NW ℡ 202/324-3447, 🌐 www.fbi.gov; Archives–Navy Memorial Metro.

Even if you had somehow never heard of the **FBI**, the presence of countless DC tourists wearing T-shirts emblazoned with that acronym would doubtless get your attention. The bureau's giant, Brutalist home at Pennsylvania Avenue and 9th Street is a clunky modern office that pales by comparison to the Neoclassical-style Department of Justice across the street. This used to be a favorite spot for visitors who fancied themselves as potential lawmen in training, but since 9/11 tours have been canceled and the building's ongoing renovation has kept it off limits to nosy interlopers, T-shirts or not.

From the outside there's not much to look at: the building itself is a 1970s monstrosity named for the organization's notorious Red-baiting, cross-dressing chief, **J. Edgar Hoover**. Established in 1908 with the motto "Fidelity, Bravery, Integrity," the FBI owed its early investigative techniques to those of Scottish immigrant Allan Pinkerton's successful nineteenth-century Pinkerton Detective Agency, and made its reputation in the 1920s and 1930s by battling gangsters and attempting to enforce Prohibition. Today, ten thousand special agents are employed to fight organized and white-collar crime, political corruption, drug traffickers, and terrorists, and to lurk in the shadowy world of counter-intelligence.

Market Square and around

In 1801 the city's biggest outdoor market opened for business at the foot of 7th Street. It backed onto the canal dividing the Mall from downtown, where goods barges could be unloaded; out front, top-heavy carts and drays spilled across Pennsylvania Avenue and up 7th Street on the way out of the city. It was a notoriously noxious spot, and there was little clamor when it was demolished in 1870 to make way for the grand Victorian **Center Market**, a colossus holding seven hundred vendors of meats, fruits and vegetables, and other farm commodities, to be distributed locally and nationwide. By the Depression the market had outlived its usefulness and the **National Archives** (see p.172) was erected on the site in 1935. The concave, colonnaded buildings of the development opposite, known as **Market Square**, are given over to café-restaurants and outdoor seating, while upper-floor apartments have sweeping views over the revitalized Penn Quarter.

US Navy Memorial

701 Pennsylvania Ave NW ℡ 202/737-2300, 🌐 www.lonesailor.org; Archives–Navy Memorial Metro.
Heritage Center open Tues–Sat 9.30am–5pm, also Mon in summer.

Market Square's 100ft-diameter circular plaza is covered by an etched representation of the world, circled by low tiered granite walls lapped by running water. These elements are part of the US **Navy Memorial**, which also includes a statue of a lone sailor, kit bag by his side, and inscribed quotations from the likes of Themistocles, architect of the Greek naval victory during the Persian Wars, and naval aviator Neil Armstrong. Especially worth a look are the 26 bronze relief panels on the walls, which illustrate different aspects of the Navy's mission in various wars. The imagery and captions can be off-kilter – "LSTs: Fondly Known as Large, Slow Targets" – but you do get a sense of the Navy's focus and spirit. In summer, the **Navy Band** holds regular concerts at the memorial.

Directly behind the memorial, in the easternmost Market Square building at 701 Pennsylvania Ave NW, the **Naval Heritage Center** can tell you more

▲ US Navy Memorial

about the service with its changing exhibits. Several films, presented in the Burke Theater, show the glories of sea and air battles, and assorted kiosks give you access to information on current and former US sailors. Portraits honor the US presidents who have served in the US Navy: JFK famously commanded a motor torpedo boat and was awarded the Navy and Marine Corps Medal for heroism, and Johnson, Nixon, Ford, and Carter all served with distinction, too. George H.W. Bush, then the Navy's youngest bomber pilot, received the Distinguished Flying Cross and three air medals for his endeavors.

FDR Memorial

Across Pennsylvania Avenue from here, in the green plot in front of the National Archives at 9th Street, a small marble memorial commemorates wartime president **Franklin Delano Roosevelt**. It was FDR's wish that any memorial to him erected after his death be "plain, without any ornamentation," and no larger than an office desk, and that's what he got – at first. Placed here in 1965 on the twentieth anniversary of his death, the monument is inscribed simply "In Memory of Franklin Delano Roosevelt 1882–1945." But despite his request, the much more elaborate FDR Memorial opened on the National Mall in 1997 (see p.61).

East of the memorials

A little farther up on the north side of Pennsylvania Avenue, the turreted, pink-stone **Sears House**, at no. 633, once contained the studio of nineteenth-century photographer Matthew Brady, whose graphic photographs of the slaughter at Antietam in 1862 first brought home the full horror of the Civil War to the American people. A block northeast of the Navy Memorial on Indiana Avenue, small **Indiana Plaza** is taken up by the monument to the victorious Grand Army of the Republic, a triangular obelisk adorned with figures representing Fraternity, Loyalty, and Charity. Back on the south side of Pennsylvania Avenue, the bronze, triple-decker fountain in the corner plot between 6th Street and Constitution Avenue commemorates former Secretary of the Treasury and art maven **Andrew Mellon**, fittingly sited across from the National Gallery of Art, which he funded and filled with paintings. The monument is also known as the "**Zodiac Fountain**" for its twelve relief images of the astrological signs that run around its middle course. Finally, just before 4th Street NW, the chic stone-and-glass **Canadian Embassy** (see p.42 for contact info) is the closest embassy to the US Capitol, and it presents a striking rivalry between Neoclassical and contemporary elements – though with its templelike columns completely enveloped by aggressive modern angles, it's not much of a contest.

Newseum

555 Pennsylvania Ave NW ☎ 1-800/NEWSEUM, ⓦ www.newseum.org; Archives–Navy Memorial Metro. Call for hours and admission price.

Although some have described Washington journalism as being at a low ebb, with serious news traded out for entertainment, reporters paid by the White House to plant stories, and declining reader- and viewership making it all that much worse, you'd never know it by visiting the **Newseum**. This new "edutainment" colossus opens to the public in 2008 and promises to, if not exactly make journalism into the so-called Fourth Estate again, at least provide a flashy look at the greatest hits of the news biz, loaded with pop-up headlines, electronic ticker tape, and refresher courses on the First Amendment.

There's certainly a lot of space to fill for the purpose: with a quarter-million square feet and seven levels, the Newseum is chock-full of splashy graphics, easy-to-read banners, and a simplified approach to history and information, all of which it has in common with the newspaper whose parent company provided the financial impetus to open the place – *USA Today*. On the various levels, you'll see how modern news is gathered and transmitted, witness pivotal moments in journalism through docudrama re-enactment, bone up on freedom of speech and press, and get a look at the history of news as provided by the News Corporation, owner of controversial *FOX News*. There's also a chunk of the Berlin Wall, a refresher on 9/11, and interactive kiosks where you can answer trivia questions and get to play reporter with your own camera-and-mic setup.

The Federal Triangle

The wedge of land formed by 15th Street and Pennsylvania and Constitution avenues, the **Federal Triangle** is the massively scaled zone linking the White House and US Capitol, with grand Neoclassical piles thrusting their imposing facades out toward passers-by. Most of these structures were erected in the 1930s in an attempt to graft instant majesty upon the capital of the Free World. The Triangle's nineteenth-century origins, however, were distinctly humble: it began as a canal-side slum known as Murder Bay. Hoodlums frequented its brothels and taverns, and on hot days the stench from the town market drifted through the ill-fitting windows of the district's cheap boarding houses. Few improvements came until the 1920s, when a shortage of office space forced the federal government's hand. The Triangle was bought and redeveloped in its entirety between 6th and 15th streets, following a classical plan that featured buildings opening onto interior court-yards. Although never fully realized, the plan made for a remarkably uniform area. Different architects worked on various projects, but all the buildings have the same characteristics: granite facades, stone reliefs, huge columns, inhuman scale, and ponderous inscriptions.

The National Aquarium

14th St south of Pennsylvania Ave NW ☎ 202/482-2825, 🌐 www.nationalaquarium.com; Federal Triangle Metro. Daily 9am–5pm. $5.

Built in 1931, the 1000ft-long **Department of Commerce** was one of the first Federal Triangle buildings to be completed, and today it forms the western side of the Triangle, at 14th Street between E and Constitution. Its main points of interest are that it houses the White House Visitor Center (see p.141), on the north side of the building, and the **National Aquarium**, on the east side, at 14th Street. Founded in 1873, this is the oldest aquarium in the country, and even though it's been here since 1932, the Department of Commerce's drab gray corridors still seem like a strange environment for fish. There are some 1700 creatures of 260 species here, but despite its impressive-sounding name and central location, the aquarium is one of the city's more disappointing sights: the fish-tank displays don't seem to have been updated in at least twenty years, and the atmosphere is stagnant and depressing. An ongoing renovation promises to improve matters, but you should really save your time and effort for the National Museum of Natural History, one long block south and east.

Ronald Reagan Building to the FTC

Heading east of the Commerce Department, the **Ronald Reagan Building**, 1300 Pennsylvania Ave, is the country's second-largest federal building after the Pentagon. Inside, along with the International Trade Center and other offices, you'll find an immense, barrel-vaulted atrium containing a food court, restaurant, and exhibition space on the west side, where a colorful, graffiti-covered chunk of the Berlin Wall provides visual contrast to the antiseptic architecture. The main reason you'll possibly want to visit this building, however, is to check out the **DC Visitor Information Center** (spring and summer Mon–Fri 8.30am–5.30pm, Sat 9am–4pm; fall and winter Mon–Fri 9am–4.30pm; ☎1-866/324-7386, ⓦwww.dcvisit.com), which provides maps, tour information, brochures, and the like. Across the courtyard to the east, and impossible to miss if you're heading toward the Federal Triangle Metro, is the gargantuan **Ariel Rios Building**, a Neoclassical, New Deal–era behemoth that houses both the Environmental Protection Agency and the US Customs Service.

East across 12th Street, the 1930 **Internal Revenue Service** (IRS) building was the earliest federal structure to grace the Federal Triangle area. Its Neoclassical design is textbook material, though libertarians may take issue with the inscription on the facade: "Taxes are what we pay for a civilized society." Across 10th Street is the Art Deco–influenced **Department of Justice**, in whose enclosed courtyard stands a bust of former US Attorney General **Robert F. Kennedy** by Robert Berks, who sculpted the 8ft-tall bronze bust of JFK in the Kennedy Center. Across 9th Street, you'll see the National Archives (see below), and across 7th Street sits the fittingly triangular **Federal Trade Commission** (FTC) building. Friezes over the building's doors on Constitution Avenue depict images of agriculture, trade, and the control of trade, symbolized by twin exterior statues (at the rounded 6th Street side) of a muscular man wrestling a wild horse.

National Archives

700 Pennsylvania Ave NW ☎202/501-5000, tours ☎202/501-5205, ⓦwww.archives.gov; Archives–Navy Memorial Metro. Research room daily 9am–5pm, rotunda and exhibit hall daily 10am–5.30pm, spring and summer closes 7pm; last admission 30min before closing.

John Russell Pope's **National Archives** is by default the greatest building in the Triangle, representing high Neoclassicism with bells on, showing off 72 ornate Corinthian columns (each 50ft high), a dome that rises 75ft above floor level, and a sculpted pediment, facing Constitution Avenue, topped by eagles. The Archives is responsible for the country's federal records dating back to the 1700s, meaning it's stuffed with information, not just here but in dozens of satellite offices and warehouses around the country, and it maintains the presidential libraries of commanders in chief dating back to Herbert Hoover. When the department opened in 1935, its holdings were already formidable; today they are almost unfathomable. What everyone comes to see is the Holy Trinity of American historical records – the **Declaration of Independence**, the **US Constitution**, and the **Bill of Rights** – but the National Archives also keeps hundreds of millions of pages of documents, from war treaties to slave-ship manifests; seven million pictures; 125,000 reels of film; 200,000 sound recordings; eleven million maps and charts; and a quarter of a million other artifacts. If you're a researcher, you can apply for an official ID to give you access to the collection; if not, you'll have to wait in line like all the other visitors.

The Declaration of Independence

We hold these truths to be self-evident: that all men are created equal, that they are endowed by their Creator with certain unalienable rights, that among these are life, liberty, and the pursuit of happiness . . .

Declaration of Independence, Second Continental Congress, 1776

Revolutionary fervor was gaining pace in the American colonies in the early months of 1776, whipped up in part by the demagoguery of **Samuel Adams**'s Sons of Liberty and other militant groups and the publication of **Thomas Paine**'s widely read pamphlet *Common Sense*, which castigated monarchical government in general and **George III** of England in particular. In May, the sitting Second Continental Congress in Philadelphia advised the colonies to establish their own governments, whose delegates in turn increasingly harried the Congress to declare independence. The die was cast on June 7 when Richard Henry Lee of Virginia moved that "these United Colonies are, and of right ought to be, Free and Independent States." Four days later, while debate raged among the delegates, Congress authorized a committee to draft a formal declaration.

Five men assembled to begin the task: **Thomas Jefferson**, Benjamin Franklin, John Adams, Roger Sherman, and Robert Livingston. Jefferson, an accomplished writer, was charged by the others to produce a draft, which was ready to be presented to Congress by June 28. Despite the evidence of most history books, though, Jefferson didn't simply rattle off the ringing declaration that empowered a nation. For a start, he lifted phrases and ideas from other writers – the "pursuit of happiness" was a common contemporary rhetorical flourish, while the concept of "unalienable rights" had appeared in George Mason's recent **Declaration of Rights for Virginia** (see p.352), the most direct influence on Jefferson's work. Moreover, his own words were tweaked by the rest of the committee and other changes were ordered after debate in Congress, notably the dropping of a passage condemning the slave trade, in an attempt to keep some of the Southern colonies on board. However, by the end of June, Congress had a document that spelled out exactly why Americans wanted independence, who they blamed for the state of affairs (George III, in 27 separate charges), and what they proposed to do about it. Read today, this product of considerable debate and negotiation is a model of political thought.

At this point, myths start to obfuscate the real chain of events. After a month of argument – not every delegate agreed with the proposed declaration – Congress finally approved Lee's motion on July 2, 1776. Technically, this was the day that America declared independence from Great Britain, though two days later, on **July 4, 1776**, Congress, representing the "thirteen United States of America," also approved Jefferson's document; within a couple of years, celebrations were being held on the anniversary of the fourth. The only man to actually sign the Declaration on July 4 was **John Hancock**, president of the Continental Congress, who appended his name largely and with such flourish so that the poor-sighted king wouldn't miss it – hence the colloquialism "John Hancock" for someone's signature; other signatures weren't added until August 2 and beyond, since many of the delegates had gone home as soon as the Declaration was drawn up. In any case, if the **War of Independence** didn't go well, those signatures were as good as death warrants and would allow the British to prosecute the signatories for treason and other crimes. And Hancock, as one of the richest and most powerful of delegates, had perhaps the most to lose of all. However, the mood of the occasion was best summed up by Ben Franklin, the oldest of the signatories. With his mordant wit, he reminded his compatriots, "Gentlemen, we must now all hang together, or we shall most assuredly all hang separately."

The Charters of Freedom

The Archives' three key documents, called the **Charters of Freedom**, sit in the magnificent marble **rotunda** within state-of-the-art airtight containers filled with argon gas. The pages of these post-Colonial artifacts are written in elegant calligraphy in closely spaced lines – which, given their faded ink, makes them very hard to read under the low light of the display cases.

Perhaps the most popular of these documents is the **Declaration of Independence**. That it's survived at all since 1776 is rather amazing: not only was the document used as a political, social, and educational tool for the first half-century of its existence – visiting one part of the country after another – but an engraving to make copies wasn't even struck until 1823. The following years didn't save the document from further wear and tear, though, as it was still moved around constantly, even within the city itself, until it was finally preserved with limited technology in the 1920s and more modern methods in the early 1950s. The two other documents here are also very important, if not quite as remarkable in their survival. The copy of the **Constitution** is the one signed at the 1787 Constitutional Convention in Philadelphia by twelve of the original thirteen states (Rhode Island signed three years later), while the first ten amendments to the Constitution became the articles of the **Bill of Rights**, and the one on display here is the federal government's official copy. (For more on the Constitution, see "The American system of government," p.402.) Less familiar but still historically significant documents relating to Western US expansion, law, and politics are on view alongside the Charters of Freedom. However, seeing any of these documents can involve a long wait during summer hours – especially as visitors pore over the words, trying to decipher the intricacies of eighteenth-century penmanship – so try to come during non-peak times.

The 1936 **murals** along the rotunda's walls were created by Barry Faulkner and underscore the documents' significance with their harmonious neo-Renaissance balance and colors. Recently restored to their New Deal–era splendor, they show Thomas Jefferson handing the Declaration of Independence to John Hancock, while other founding figures look on with various states of interest, a few with their backs turned; and James Madison presenting the Constitution to Convention chair George Washington, resplendent in a cloak and sword and looking more like a king than a president.

The rest of the collection

Although the Charters are the only documents guaranteed to be on display, other historic documents that you may find on view are the Louisiana Purchase, with Napoleon's signature, the World War II Japanese surrender document, the Strategic Arms Limitation Treaty of 1972, and President Nixon's resignation letter. It's especially worth checking the temporary exhibitions in the surrounding **O'Brien Gallery**, or getting a refresher on the Charters of Freedom in the **McGowan Theater**, which also has regular nightly showings of documentaries. A more recent arrival in the Archives is the **Public Vaults**, which present a selection of about one thousand of the items the institution holds, made accessible through interactive exhibits and kiosks, as well as simple displays – the 1823 first printing plate of the Declaration of Independence and a draft of the Emancipation Proclamation holding pride of place.

To plunge deeper into the Archives' collection, a **shuttle bus** (free; on the hour Mon–Fri 8am–5pm) can take you to the Archives' College Park, Maryland, depository, where you can track down records on military, bureaucratic, presidential, and all kinds of other matters. Finally, it's a good idea to take one of the excellent **guided tours**, which show you more of the Archives' holdings, as well as its **genealogy center**; indeed, the Archives' resources were of great help to Alex Haley, who spent many hours here tracing his ancestry, and led to the writing of his iconic *Roots* saga.

Judiciary Square

Since the city's earliest days, when storehouses served as rank jails for runaway slaves, **Judiciary Square** – east of 5th Street, between E and F streets – has been the central location for DC's local and federal government and judiciary, with the difference being that in the old days, a surrounding residential community existed of police officers, lawyers, and judges, among others. The construction of the I-395 freeway ensured that those old homes were wiped out, and now almost all that remains are bleak, faceless modern towers, the emblems of justice in contemporary Washington.

The 1820 Greek Revival–style **Old City Hall** is on D Street between 4th and 5th, now occupied by the District of Columbia Court of Appeals. In 1881 it saw the murder trial of Charles Guiteau, who shot President James Garfield in the back just four months after his inauguration. The trial site was appropriate, since the outdoor statue of **Abraham Lincoln**, quickly erected in 1868, is said to be the first such honor bestowed after Lincoln's assassination.

Within a few blocks of here stand the US Tax Court, Department of Labor, Municipal Center, and Army Corps of Engineers buildings – all uniformly gloomy and monolithic. The US Federal Courthouse (main entrance on Constitution Ave) sees the most high-profile action, from the trial of various Watergate and Iran-Contra defendants to that of former mayor Marion Barry. Immediately west of the courthouse, off C Street, is **John Marshall Park**, whose eponymous bronze figure sits in a humble 5ft chair and extends his hand outward to the viewer. The sculpture is little noticed by the public, though, a rather sorry tribute to the man who created the modern American judiciary as the Supreme Court's most legendary chief justice.

National Law Enforcement Officers Memorial

Visitor center at 605 E St NW ☎ 202/737-3400 or 1-866/569-4928, ⓦ www.nleomf.com; Judiciary Square Metro. Mon–Fri 9am–5pm, Sat 10am–5pm, Sun noon–5pm.

The impressive **National Law Enforcement Officers Memorial**, dedicated in 1991, is in the center of Judiciary Square. Walls lining the circular pathways around a reflecting pool are inscribed with the names of more than 17,000 police officers killed in the line of duty, beginning with US Marshal Robert Forsyth, shot dead in 1794, his killers never apprehended. More than the officers' names themselves, which are mostly unknown to the general public, the walls read like a who's who of historical miscreants responsible for such murders: gangsters like John Dillinger and Bonnie and Clyde; gunfighters like Billy the Kid; assassins such as Lee Harvey Oswald; and assorted militants and terrorists, including those responsible for 9/11.

Every year in May, new names are added to the memorial, which has space for 29,000; at the current rate (a police officer is killed every other day on average), it will be full by the year 2050. Directories at the site help you locate a particular name, or you can get assistance at the nearby visitor center, two blocks west.

National Building Museum

401 F Street NW ☎ 202/272-2448, ⊛ www.nbm.org; Judiciary Square Metro. Mon–Sat 10am–5pm, Sun 11am–5pm. $5.

Formerly the Pension Building, the imposing red-brick **National Building Museum** was once home to a courthouse and various federal agencies; now it's a stirring architectural museum focusing on topics like urban renewal, high-rise technology, and environmental matters. The permanent exhibition on the second floor, "Washington: Symbol and City," explores the creation of the capital city itself and shows which of the District's planned buildings have come to fruition. Also worth a look are the Pension Commissioner's three-room office suite – with its fireplaces, decorative friezes, and vaulted ceilings – and the winning scale model from the 1910 competition to design the Lincoln Memorial. Free tours (Mon–Wed 12.30pm, Thurs–Sun also 11.30am & 1.30pm) give you access to the otherwise restricted third floor – the best spot to view the towering columns' intricate capitals.

As much as any exhibit, the building is of most interest for its architectural details and storied history. In the late 1860s the number of Civil War casualties put a huge strain on the government's pension system. Additional offices were required in which to process claims and payments to veterans and dependants; subsequently, in the 1880s, what became known as the **Pension Building** was erected between 4th and 5th streets, framing the entire north side of Judiciary Square.

Montgomery C. Meigs was quartermaster general of the Union Army during the Civil War and, with his astounding logistical prowess, had as much as any general to do with winning the conflict. Afterward, he sought to honor veterans of both sides of the war with a stunningly designed building. The exterior of the oversize Renaissance-style palazzo is enhanced by a 3ft-high terracotta frieze that runs around the building (between the first and second floors) and depicts various military images, including charging cavalry, wounded soldiers, and marines rowing in a storm-tossed sea. Inside, Meigs maximized the use of natural light in his majestic **Great Hall**, inspired by the generous proportions of Rome's Palazzo Farnese, and created one of the most striking interior spaces anywhere in the US. The hall's centerpiece fountain is surrounded by eight **Corinthian columns** measuring 8ft across at the base and more than 75ft high; each is made up of 70,000 bricks, plastered and painted to resemble Siena marble. Above the ground-floor Doric arcade, the three open-plan galleried levels, 160ft high, were once aired by vents and clerestory windows – opened each day by a young boy employed to walk around on the roof. In the upper-floor niches Meigs planned to put busts of prominent Americans, though this never happened; today, the 244 busts are a repeated series of eight figures (architect, construction worker, landscape gardener, and so on) representing the building arts. Not surprisingly, this vast, striking space has been in regular demand since its inception. Grover Cleveland held the first of many presidential **inaugural balls** here in 1885 (when there was still no roof on the building); a century later, it hosted President Reagan's second inaugural ball and President Clinton's first; and every year the televised *Christmas in Washington* special is filmed here.

Marian Koshland Science Museum

500 5th St NW ☎ 202/334-1201, ⊛ www.koshland-science-museum.org; Judiciary Square Metro. Wed–Mon 10am–6pm. $5.

One of the newer institutions in the District, the **Marian Koshland Science Museum** is unique in that it doesn't soft-pedal or dumb down its displays in the manner of some science museums; instead it offers an engaging, vigorous presentation of fact, theory, and speculation relating to some of the core scientific and technological issues of the day. Although it's relatively small, this National Academy of Sciences museum aims to provide comprehensive coverage of its limited subjects, delving into the political and cultural debates relating to them.

The Koshland has one **permanent exhibition** on the latest, and typically controversial, ideas relating to the expansion of the universe, dark matter, and string theory, as well as several long-running **temporary exhibits**. The first deals with the nature of DNA, from its nucleic-acid construction to its use in tracking down criminals and providing antidotes for pandemic diseases; the second is a complex and multifaceted look at global warming, showing the chemical components of greenhouse gases (notably carbon dioxide and methane) and the potential dangers they pose; and the third covers the many dangers and challenges posed by infectious disease. All of these exhibits balance their scientific data with hands-on, user-friendly multimedia elements.

The Penn Quarter

Not to be confused with Pennsylvania Avenue itself, which loosely acts as a southern boundary, the **Penn Quarter**, in the heart of Old Downtown, is the city's official designation for a cache of renovated buildings, new museums, stylish cafés and bars, and other sights that have gone up in the last decade between 3rd and 12th streets, roughly south of G Street. The **Verizon Center**, just north, has played an especially big role in the area's revitalization, beginning life as the MCI Center and luring folks to spend money in an area that was once a blighted symbol of urban decay.

DC's downtown area was marred following the **1968 riots**, spurred by the assassination of Dr Martin Luther King Jr. White residents and institutions fled, and urban disinvestment, federal neglect, and suburbanization contributed to the area's steep decline. It took the full development of the Metro system – connecting downtown with the rest of the city – and a new national attitude toward redeveloping urban cores to bring in the masses; now the Penn Quarter is a must-see for all but the most benighted tourists who come only for the Mall and Capitol Hill, a thriving downtown district that calls to mind some of the more frenetic activity of old Washington, though without the grime and chaos. Be sure to check out the area's better restaurants and notable attractions, including excellent **Smithsonian museums**, the **International Spy Museum**, and **Ford's Theatre**, among many other, lesser-known sights.

National Portrait Gallery

8th and F streets NW ℗ 202/633-8300, Ⓦ www.npg.si.edu; Gallery Place–Chinatown Metro. Daily 11.30am–7pm; free.

In July 2006 two of the crown jewels in the Smithsonian's collection of museums, the **National Portrait Gallery** and **American Art Museum**, reopened to great acclaim after undergoing a lengthy renovation. The history of these institutions is a lengthy one: Before the Smithsonian was founded, the federal government had its own art collection, which, together with pieces loaned by prominent Washington citizens, was displayed in the 1840s in the Old Patent Office (see box, p.178). These works were later given over to the Smithsonian, which had yet to find premises for a planned "National Gallery" to house its expanding art collection. Eventually the

The Old Patent Office

5

Three blocks west of the National Building Museum and in the center of the Penn Quarter, the Greek Revival **Old Patent Office**, begun in 1836 by Treasury Building and General Post Office architect **Robert Mills**, is among the oldest buildings in the city, though it wasn't completed for thirty years. It was designed to hold offices of the Interior Department and the Commissioners of Patents, and models of America's patented nineteenth-century inventions were on display – including Eli Whitney's cotton gin, Samuel Colt's pistol, and Robert Fulton's steam engine, as well as items by Thomas Edison, Benjamin Franklin, and Alexander Graham Bell. During the Civil War the building's halls were filled with over two thousand beds and used for emergency hospital services. One of the clerks in the Patent Office, **Clara Barton**, abandoned her duties to work in the hospital and went on to found the American Red Cross in 1881. The poet **Walt Whitman** worked here, too, as an untrained volunteer, dressing wounds and comforting injured soldiers – an experience that led directly to the long series of poems known as *Drum-Taps*, included in the fourth edition (1867) of *Leaves of Grass*. In March 1865, just before the end of the war, Whitman's "noblest of Washington buildings" hosted Lincoln's second inaugural ball, with four thousand people in attendance for a night of dancing and feasting. "Tonight," wrote Whitman later, "beautiful women, perfumes, the violins' sweetness . . . then, the amputation, the blue face, the groan, the glassy eye of the dying."

Despite its heritage, the building was scheduled for demolition in the 1950s, before the Smithsonian stepped into the breach. Today the Old Patent Office building houses two of the city's major art institutions: the **National Portrait Gallery** and the **American Art Museum**. Note also that some items not found in these museums' holdings may be on display in the Renwick Gallery's impressive Grand Salon (see p.149).

Smithsonian resorted to displaying its paintings in the Natural History Museum, while Andrew Mellon's bequest to the nation resulted in the founding of a separate National Gallery of Art. Not until the Patent Office building became available did the Smithsonian finally find a home for its 38,000 paintings, prints, drawings, sculpture, photographs, folk art, and crafts – the seed of the largest collection of American art, colonial to contemporary, in the world.

Portraits of prominent citizens were the foundation of many early American art collections (Congress itself commissioned a series of presidential portraits for the White House in 1857), but the **National Portrait Gallery** itself didn't open until the 1960s, and now occupies one-half of the space in the building. The permanent collection contains more than four thousand images of notables from every walk of life, but perhaps its best-known piece is **Gilbert Stuart**'s celebrated "Lansdowne" portrait of George Washington. In addition to paintings, the gallery contains numerous sculptures and photographs, including more than five thousand plate-glass negatives of the Civil War era by Matthew Brady. One of the most impressive sights, though, is also the newest – the Norman Foster–designed **Kogod Courtyard**, which debuted in late 2007 to widespread acclaim, crowning the building's large internal space with a huge glass and aluminum canopy supported by steel columns. Its dramatic effect is heightened by tasteful ficus and olive trees and the striking Neoclassical lines to make the courtyard one of the District's greatest spaces, and well worth a visit when you need a break from all the art on the walls.

Popular culture images

The most popular area of the gallery's collection comprises portraits of figures from the worlds of **performing arts** and **sports**. Notable works include **Paul**

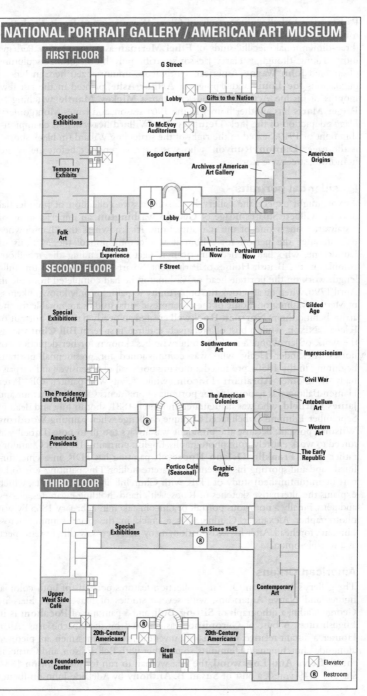

NATIONAL PORTRAIT GALLERY / AMERICAN ART MUSEUM

FIRST FLOOR

G Street

Lobby

Gifts to the Nation

Special Exhibitions

To McEvoy Auditorium

American Origins

Kogod Courtyard

Archives of American Art Gallery

Folk Art

American Experience

Lobby

Americans Now

Portraiture Now

F Street

Temporary Exhibits

SECOND FLOOR

Special Exhibitions

Modernism

Gilded Age

Southwestern Art

Impressionism

Civil War

The Presidency and the Cold War

The American Colonies

Antebellum Art

Western Art

America's Presidents

The Early Republic

Portico Café (Seasonal)

Graphic Arts

THIRD FLOOR

Special Exhibitions

Art Since 1945

Upper West Side Café

Contemporary Art

20th-Century Americans

20th-Century Americans

Luce Foundation Center

Great Hall

⊠ Elevator

Ⓡ Restroom

Robeson as Othello; photographs of **Gloria Swanson** and **Boris Karloff**; a rough-hewn wooden head of **Bob Hope**, with protruding nose; and an almost three-dimensional metallic study of **Ethel Merman** as Annie Oakley. Perhaps most striking, though, is Harry Jackson's terrific polychrome bronze sculpture of an aged **John Wayne**. American sports icons immortalized here include a pugnacious **Joe Louis** and a poignant **Arthur Ashe**, painted in the last few months of his life. Action paintings encompass **Mickey Mantle** watching as **Roger Maris** hits another homer in the 1961 season, and James Montgomery Flagg's depiction of the **Jack Dempsey–Jess Willard** heavyweight championship fight of 1919. Seated to the right of the struggling Willard (in black shorts) is the eager **Damon Runyon**, who was a sports reporter before he wrote humorous, streetwise stories.

Presidential portraits

As you might expect, the gallery has an impressive collection of presidential portraits. Gilbert Stuart's image of **George Washington**, an imperial study of a stalwart man, is one of the star attractions. It's known as the "Lansdowne" portrait after the person for whom it was commissioned: the Marquis of Lansdowne, who had earned American respect by defending the rebellious colonies in the British Houses of Parliament. Stuart (see p.82) based this full-length work on the portrait-head of Washington he had completed from life in April 1796, when he also took the opportunity to paint his only known likeness of Martha Washington. Some of the other presidential studies are notable for the artists behind them: **Norman Rockwell** created an overly flattering portrait of Richard Nixon, while a bust of a relatively carefree, first-term **Bill Clinton** was the work of Jan Wood, a sculptor otherwise best known for her depictions of horses. Alexander Healy, who was commissioned for presidential portraits beginning in the 1850s, produced a moving portrayal of a pensive (and surprisingly handsome) **Abraham Lincoln**, while Civil War painter Ole Peter Hansen Balling was responsible for portraits of presidents Chester A. Arthur and **James Garfield**, who was inaugurated in March 1881, shot in July, and dead in September. Edmund Tarbell faced a unique challenge when painting **Woodrow Wilson**'s portrait; because the president was always too ill to pose, Tarbell was forced to work entirely from photographs. English portraitist Douglas Chandor's rather raffish **Franklin Delano Roosevelt** painting has FDR in a chic, fur-lined cape and sporting his trademark cigarette holder. This painting was to be part of an (unfinished) study of FDR with Churchill and Stalin at Yalta, which explains the alternative sketches of Roosevelt's hands holding cigarettes, glasses, and pens. Finally, a notorious portrait of Lincoln, taken in February 1865 by war photographer Alexander Gardner, has a crack in the plate running across Lincoln's forehead. After his assassination, many observers saw this, in retrospect, as a terrible omen.

American Origins

The gallery's "American Origins" collection features portraits of both colonial figures and Native Americans, with several studies of braves and chiefs by George Catlin, a lithograph of **Sitting Bull**, and a painting of **Pocahontas** in English dress. A bust of **Geronimo** was sculpted by the Apache artist Allan Houser, a distant relative. Industrialists, inventors, and businessmen are pictured alongside churchmen and feminists, so together with Bell, Edison, and Carnegie there's **Belva Ann Lockwood**, the first woman to run for president (in 1884; she got 4149 votes), a bust of **Susan B. Anthony** by Adelaide Johnson (better

▲ National Portrait Gallery

known for her *Suffrage Monument* statue in the Capitol), and a stuffy portrait of feminist **Elizabeth Cady Stanton**.

Literature and the arts

Studies of personalities from literature and the arts include a touching early photograph by Man Ray of **Ernest Hemingway** and his young son, and the extraordinary bulky terracotta figure of **Gertrude Stein**, depicted by Jo Davidson as a tranquil seated Buddha. Fascinating, too, are Edward Biberman's creepy study of **Dashiell Hammett** in a horrible wool coat, and John White Alexander's 1902 depiction of a transfixed Samuel Clemens (better known as **Mark Twain**). In 1889 Alexander painted **Walt Whitman** as a seated sage, with light streaming through his bushy beard. The collection's most prized piece, however, is Edgar Degas's severe portrait (1880–84) of his friend, Impressionist **Mary Cassatt**, hunched over a chair with a sneer on her face. Cassatt hated the image so much that she had it sold with the understanding that it wouldn't be allowed to go to an American collection where her family and friends might see it.

American Art Museum

8th and F streets NW ℗ 202/633-7970, ⓦ americanart.si.edu; Gallery Place–Chinatown Metro. Daily 11.30am–7pm; free.

The **American Art Museum**, or technically, the National Museum of American Art, is the most recent appellation for an institution that has had many names over the years, from the "National Gallery" to the "National Collection of Fine Arts" to simply the "Smithsonian Art Collection." Whatever it's been called, there's always been a good collection of work here, with hundreds of items on display and thousands more on view in the **Luce Foundation Center**. Here, you can spot works arranged cheek by jowl in cozy display cases, shelves, and drawers, with more information on each item in the densely packed collection available on view at computer kiosks around the center. The nearby **Lunder Center** also provides a hint of artistic voyeurism as you watch art conservationists and technicians variously repairing, studying, and fixing artworks from the Portrait Gallery and American Art Museum – a worthwhile endeavor for those fascinated by art preservation.

Western imagery

One of the museum's highlights is its selection of nineteenth-century art of the American West, including almost four hundred paintings by **George Catlin**, who spent six years touring the Great Plains, painting portraits and scenes of Native American life that he later displayed as part of his "Indian Gallery." His paintings were the first contact many white settlers had with the aboriginal peoples of America, and viewers were fascinated by his lush landscapes showing buffalo herds crossing the Missouri, or those featuring tribes at work and play. The contrast between cultures is best seen in Catlin's 1832 painting of a warrior named Pigeon's Egg Head arriving in Washington, DC, in full traditional dress, only to return to his tepee encampment in frock coat and top hat, sporting an umbrella and smoking a cigarette. Catlin is most interesting for recording civilizations and habitats that survived only briefly after the onslaught of the pioneers – soon after he visited and painted the Plains Mandan tribes, they were wiped out by an epidemic of smallpox, brought by white settlers.

Not all of the collection's scenes are of warriors or hunts, however: Catlin also produced many keenly observed domestic studies, like the painting of a woman with a child in an elaborately decorated cradle, while a 1920 **Joseph Henry Sharp** painting shows Blackfoot Indians making medicine by burning feathers over an open fire. One of Catlin's contemporaries, **John Mix Stanley**, primarily depicted Apache warriors, though one of his works captures a graphic *Buffalo Hunt* (1845). There's a remarkable bronze statue, too, called *The Indian Ghost Dancer*, by **Paul Wayland Bartlett** (1888), where the dancer is near total exhaustion after hours of trancelike dancing.

Folk art

The museum's **folk art** collection includes some traditional pieces, notably Native American ceramics, but it's the contemporary works that really stand out. **Malcah Zeldis**'s exuberant *Miss Liberty Celebration* depicts the Statue of Liberty surrounded by a family group comprising Elvis, Einstein, Lincoln, Marilyn, and Chaplin, and was completed to celebrate the artist's recovery from cancer. The most extraordinary piece here is perhaps **James Hampton**'s so-called *Hampton Throne*, a mystic, cryptic cluster of foil- and gilt-covered lightbulbs, boxes, plaques, wings, altars, and furniture capped by the text "Fear Not." Hampton, a solitary figure who referred to himself as "Saint James," worked in a garage on N Street NW between 1950 and his death in 1964. It's believed that *Hampton Throne* is full of obscure religious references and was unfinished at the time of the artist's death. Incidentally, the work's full title is *The Throne of the Third Heaven of the Nations' Millennium General Assembly*.

Early American art

The heavyweights of **nineteenth- and early twentieth-century American art** include significant chunks of work by **Albert Pinkham Ryder**, whose dark, often nightmarish paintings are full of symbolism, twisted landscapes and classical-fiction or mythical allegories rendered in small frames with thick paint. His best pieces here include *Jonah*, a swirling, abstract seascape; *Lord Ullin's*

Daughter, poised amid tumultuous waves and perilous rocks; *King Cophetua and the Beggar Maid*, a dark, surreal encounter in a dreamlike terrain; and *Moonlight* and *With Sloping Mast and Dipping Prow*, both oceanic rides into a sea of gloom. There's more general appeal in those works of **Winslow Homer**, whether it's the rural studies of his *Bean Picker* or *A Country Lad*, or the leisurely antics of female models in his dappled *Sunlight and Shadow* and *Summer Afternoon*, all executed in the same prolific period during the 1870s.

Other works by renowned artists include **Mary Cassatt**'s *Spanish Dancer*, showing little of her later Impressionist flair; accomplished society portraitist **John Singer Sargent**'s study of the beautiful, taffeta-clad *Elizabeth Winthrop Chanler*; and colonial master **John Singleton Copley**'s striking portrait of *Mrs George Watson*. Among the sculpture from this period is Daniel Chester French's *The Spirit of Life*, a winged sprite with laurel wreath fashioned by the man who produced the powerful statue in the Lincoln Memorial. There are also examples from the noted collection of sculptures and models by **Hiram Powers**. The surface of *America*, a plaster model of crowned Liberty, is punctured by the tips of a series of metal rods, inserted to act as a guide for carving the eventual marble version. *Thomas Jefferson* shows the same technique, making it look as if the frock-coated president has a severe case of acne.

Landscapes and portraits

The excellent collection of American **landscapes** includes *Among the Sierra Nevada Mountains*, a superb example of the dramatic power of **Albert Bierstadt**, whose three long trips to the American West between 1858 and 1873 provided him with enough material for the rest of his career. The painting's striking ethereal light illuminates distant ducks in flight, and snowcapped peaks. Likewise, there is no hint of human presence in the enormous **Thomas Moran** landscape *The Chasm of the Colorado*, alive with multifarious reds. Similar, though smaller, expressions of grandeur can be found in scenes of Lake Placid, the Colorado River, and Niagara Falls painted by **Hudson River School** artists such as Jasper Francis Cropsey and John Frederick Kensett, who cast their sensuous eye across what Americans soon came to regard as their own backyard.

Charles Bird King powerfully portrays the original inhabitants of these landscapes in the images of five Pawnee braves wearing red face-paint and ceremonial bead earrings. King studied in London under Benjamin West before moving to Washington, DC, where he earned a comfortable living painting society portraits. The steady flow of Native Americans through the capital in the 1820s – there to sign away their land in a series of worthless treaties – prompted him to divert his attention to recording their likenesses instead. Also extraordinary, though in quite a different fashion, is his contemporaneous portrait of *Mrs John Quincy Adams*, obviously uncomfortable with the artist's suggestion that she sit at a harp in an ill-advised crown of feathers.

Twentieth-century art

The museum's **twentieth-century art** collection is displayed in the spectacular 260ft-long **Lincoln Gallery**, which runs down the east side of the building. It was here, amid the white marble pillars, that Abraham Lincoln and his entourage enjoyed his second inaugural ball. There are notable twentieth-century modern pieces, among them items by Robert Motherwell, Willem de Kooning, Robert Rauschenberg, Clyfford Still, Ed Kienholz, and Jasper Johns, but none is more vibrant than Nam June Paik's jaw-dropping **Electronic**

Superhighway, a huge neon-outlined map of the US with each state represented by TV screens pulsing with hypnotic images. Also look for noteworthy works by less well-known names, like Leon Golub's red, raw *Napalm Head*, which is painted onto a torn canvas sack, and Marisol's comical *Charles de Gaulle*, which depicts the imperious French president as a rectangular wooden box and head atop a small cart. The museum also owns a decent selection of abstract works by the artists of the **Washington Color School** – primarily Gene Davis, Morris Louis, Kenneth Noland, Thomas Downing, Paul Reed, and Howard Mehring – also known as color-field painting. All tended to stain their canvases with acrylic paint to give greater impact to color and form, methods that first came to public attention in 1965 at a groundbreaking exhibition of modern art in DC.

Along 7th and F streets

The downtown transformation is taking place rapidly, with its epicenter around 7th and F streets, where spruced-up buildings that hark back to the post–Civil War era (notably 700–738 F St) form the hub of an arts district studded with boutiques, theaters, and galleries. The Smithsonian museums and the 20,000-seat **Verizon Center**, 601 F St NW (☎202/628-3200, ⓦwww .verizoncenter.com), have had something to do with that transformation as well. Bringing professional sports back to downtown DC from the suburbs – and with it, on game nights, the crowds and the buzz – the Verizon Center is the home of the NBA's mediocre **Wizards**, the WNBA **Mystics**, and the NHL's **Capitals** (see "Sports and outdoor activities," Chapter 18). Elsewhere, with the revival of the neighborhood's fortunes, high-end chain retailers and chic eateries have also migrated here, along with the requisite depositories for all that tourist loot; the most conspicuous such sight is **Madame Tussaud's Wax Museum**, 1025 F St (daily 10am–6pm; $25; ☎1-888/929-4632, ⓦwww .madametussaudsdc.com), which, along with the usual rash of frozen celebrities, provides a selection of political figures done up in wax, among them FDR and Churchill commiserating over World War II, J. Edgar Hoover scheming over the Cold War, and Lincoln getting assassinated for winning the Civil War. However, since there's plenty of real history in Washington, including the actual site where the 16th president died, you might think twice before paying a steep price to see a re-created version of the same.

Elsewhere, **The Lansburgh**, 420 7th St (between D and E), was once a grand department store, its soaring facade now providing a grand frame for the Shakespeare Theatre Company, while at 9th and F streets, the elegant Romanesque Revival **Riggs National Bank Building** has been rescued as a *Courtyard Marriott* hotel (see p.269) and still features its grand 1891 facade, with rough-hewn arches and brick-and-granite cladding. Best of all is the former **General Post Office**, 7th and F streets (☎202/628-7177, ⓦwww.monaco-dc.com), which was inspired by the ancient Roman Temple of Jupiter; the city's first marble building, this Neoclassical masterwork dates back to 1842. Since the post office pulled up stakes later in the nineteenth century, the building has served as site of the US Tariff Commission and, in its present form, the trendy *Hotel Monaco*. With its high-ceilinged offices now remodeled into guest rooms, the luxurious hotel's interiors and public spaces are well worth a look, with wonderfully preserved details and complementary modern touches including vaulted ceilings, marble columns, checkerboard marble floors, spiral stairways, and minimalist contemporary decor.

International Spy Museum

800 F St NW ☎ 202/207-0219, ⓦ www.spymuseum.org; Gallery Place–Chinatown Metro. Hours vary; usually daily 10am–6pm, summer 9am–7pm. $18.

Without question, the **International Spy Museum** is a big part of F Street's revival, residing in five nineteenth-century structures, including the Atlas Building, which, fittingly, was home to the US Communist Party from 1941 to 1948. Experts in the field, ranging from former FBI, CIA, and KGB chiefs to specialists in cryptology, disguise, and clandestine photography, helped create the $40 million museum, whose exhibits aim to illuminate the impact of espionage on various historic events and to showcase dozens of nifty gizmos that would earn Q's grudging respect. Despite the steep entrance fee, the museum is one of DC's most popular sights (call ahead for entry information, as tickets can sell out days in advance during the high season). Its success has even engendered the creation of a theme-park-like interactive game, **Operation Spy**, in which guests have an hour to find a nuclear weapon, a task that sends them scurrying through elevators and corridors and riding on motion simulators using their code- and safe-cracking abilities as well as video and audio surveillance. It's hardly relevant to the alleged educational mission of the museum, but visitors with energetic teenagers in tow and willing to part with an extra $14 per person (12 and above only; $25 combo ticket) might find it worthwhile.

The museum proper is crammed full of the kind of Cold War–era gizmos, weapons, and relics that will make readers of Robert Ludlum and Tom Clancy giddy with delight; it also has items and displays covering thousands of years of spycraft, beginning with a small model of the infamous Trojan Horse and moving on to ancient Rome, imperial China, Elizabethan England, and Civil War–era America. Most of the museum's attention is devoted to the US during the years 1939 to 1991, from the beginning of World War II to the end of the Cold War, with a sizable assortment of multimedia exhibits, walk-through re-creations, dioramas, and video clips.

The presentation begins inauspiciously, in hackneyed, Disney-esque fashion, with a **filmstrip** providing a Hollywood-style view of the spy trade in all its cloak-and-dagger romance. After the film, you're led into a series of interesting galleries that cover topics like celebrities fighting the Nazis through subterfuge (notably Marlene Dietrich) and allow you to view **re-creations** of a cramped East Berlin escape tunnel and a darkened "interrogation room" for captured spies. There's even a **video game** based on the spy-coding Enigma machine.

Among these galleries, the standouts are undoubtedly the **artifacts** from the height of the Cold War in the 1950s and 1960s, presented in glass cases and broken down by theme – "Training," "Surveillance," and so on. Some of the many highlights include tiny pistols disguised as lipstick holders, cigarette cases, pipes, and flashlights; oddments like invisible-ink writing kits and a *Get Smart!–*style shoe phone; a colorful and active model of James Bond's Aston Martin spy car; bugs and radio transmitters hidden in ambassadorial gifts (such as a Great Seal of the US given by Russians); ricin-tipped poison umbrellas used to kill Warsaw Pact dissidents; and a rounded capsule containing a screwdriver, razor, and serrated knife – ominously marked "rectal tool kit." Also highlighted are the many personalities, real and imagined, that make up the colorful world of espionage: Whittaker Chambers and his microfilm-containing pumpkin are here, as are Mata Hari and **celebrity spies** like singer Josephine Baker and, more inexplicably, television superchef Julia Child.

Ford's Theatre and Lincoln Museum

511 10th St NW ℗ 202/347-4833, ⓦ www.fordstheatre.org; Metro Center Metro.

On the west end of the Penn Quarter, the district north of Pennsylvania Avenue has been home to several theaters since the founding of the city, being little more than a stroll from the White House and mansions of Lafayette Square. In 1861, entrepreneur John T. Ford converted a church into an eponymous theater that proved to be popular until April 14, 1865, when, during a performance of *Our American Cousin* (top ticket price, $1), actor and Southern sympathizer John Wilkes Booth shot President Abraham Lincoln. Following Lincoln's assassination, **Ford's Theatre** was draped in black in a show of respect, and it remained closed while the conspirators were pursued, caught, and tried. Ford abandoned attempts to reopen the theater after he received death threats, the government decreed that it could never again be used as a place of public entertainment, and the theater was eventually converted into offices and storage space. It wasn't until the 1960s that it was restored to its former condition – not only using period furnishings but, defying the earlier decree, operating again as a working theater.

All public operations are, however, suspended for the moment while the site is fully renovated in advance of the bicentennial of Lincoln's birth, in February 2009 (more general info at ⓦ www.lincoln200.gov). At that time, a new **Lincoln Campus** will open with the site as its centerpiece, not only recalling the sixteenth president's death in detail but also celebrating his life and considerable achievements. When it does reopen, you'll once again be able to see the damask-furnished presidential box in which Lincoln sat in his rocking chair and, on the lower level, a **Lincoln Museum** (℗ 202/426-6924, ⓦ www.nps.gov/foth) displaying impressive items like the actual murder weapon (a .44 Derringer), a bloodstained piece of Lincoln's overcoat, and Booth's knife, keys, compass, boot, and diary.

Petersen House

516 10th St NW ℗ 202/426-6924, ⓦ www.nps.gov/foth; Metro Center Metro. Daily 9am–5pm.

Having been shot in Ford's Theatre, an unconscious President Lincoln was carried across the street and placed in the back bedroom of a home owned by local tailor William Petersen. Lincoln never regained consciousness and died the next morning. You can walk through the restored **Petersen House**'s gloomy parlor rooms to the small bedroom, where there's a replica of the bed on which Lincoln died (he lay diagonally, since he was too tall to lie straight). Period furniture aside, there's little to see here – the original bloodstained pillow that used to be on the bed has been moved to the theater museum. However, it's interesting to note just how small the room is: Lincoln's immediate family and colleagues were present in the house during his last night, but not all could cram into the room at the same time – something ignored by contemporaneous artists who, in a series of mawkish deathbed scenes popular at the time, often portrayed up to thirty people crowded around the ailing president's bed.

Chinatown and around

DC's version of **Chinatown**, north of the Penn Quarter, stretches no more than a handful of undistinguished city blocks along G and H streets NW, between 6th and 8th. The vibrant triumphal arch over H Street (at 7th), paid for by

Beijing in the 1980s, is hopelessly at odds with the neighborhood itself, since it heralds little more than a dozen restaurants and a few grocery stores. In fact, the city's first Chinese immigrants, in the early nineteenth century, didn't live in today's Chinatown (which began in the early twentieth century) but in the piquant slums of **Swampoodle**, north of the Capitol. At that time, H Street and its environs were home to small businesses and modest rooming houses. In one of these, during the 1860s, Mary Surratt presided over the Lincoln assassination conspirators. A plaque marks the site of the house (then no. 541 H St), now a restaurant at 604 H St NW.

Elsewhere, **Mount Vernon Square**, which blocks the easy diagonal progress of Massachusetts and New York avenues, is the site of the grand, Neoclassical old **Library**, 801 K St NW, now used for researchers only, having been the site of a failed museum about the urban aspects of Washington, DC. Due north, the huge new version of the **Washington Convention Center** (N St, between 7th and 9th, down to Mt Vernon Square; ⑳www.dcconvention.com) hosts big-ticket events as well as political spectacles like the 2005 Bush inaugural gala.

Around Metro Center

Metro Center, the downtown hub of the Metro system, has separate exits along G and 12th streets. From here there are a handful of sights worth a look if you're taking a good walk in the area. To the east is the current main public library, **Martin Luther King Jr Memorial Library**, 901 G St NW (Mon–Thurs 9.30am–9pm, Fri & Sat 9.30am–5.30pm, Sun 1–5pm; ⑦202/727-0321, ⑳www.dclibrary.org), whose sleek lines of black steel and bronze-tinted glass announce it as the work of Mies van der Rohe. Inside, a large mural by Don Miller depicts the life and death of the esteemed civil rights leader. Nearby, the multistory *Grand Hyatt*, 1000 H St NW (see p.269), is worth popping into for its soaring and impressive atrium; **1100 New York Avenue**, a 1939 former bus terminal with a sprightly Art Deco facade, is now preserved within an office complex, its Streamline Moderne lobby open during daylight hours and offering the odd exhibit related to the golden age of bus stations.

West of Metro Center, there are scattered buildings undergoing renovation or being demolished to make way for new retail complexes. The most conspicuous such sight is **Metropolitan Square**, 15th at G St, which established the template in the 1980s when its classically flavored retail block with capacious internal atrium replaced the venerable Rhodes Tavern, which had existed on the site since 1799 and housed British soldiers who watched the White House burn during the War of 1812 – but despite public pleas to the contrary, it was secretively torn down by a developer in the middle of the night.

National Museum of Women in the Arts

1250 New York Ave NW ⑦202/783-5000, ⑳www.nmwa.org; Metro Center Metro. Mon–Sat 10am–5pm, Sun noon–5pm. $10.

Opened in 1987, the **National Museum of Women in the Arts** houses the most important collection of its kind – more than three thousand works by some seven hundred female artists, from the sixteenth century to the present day, as well as silverware, ceramics, photographs, and decorative items. Even the building itself, a former Masonic lodge, is striking for its trapezoidal shape, brick-and-limestone facade, and elegant colonnade. The permanent collection is on the third floor, and rotating selections of contemporary works are displayed in the mezzanine level, with temporary exhibitions on the other floors.

Renaissance to Neoclassical art

The permanent collection runs chronologically, starting with works from the Renaissance, such as those of **Sofonisba Anguissola** (1532–1625), who was considered the most important female artist of her day. From a noble family, Anguissola achieved fame as an accomplished portraitist before becoming court painter to Phillip II of Spain; her evocative *Double Portrait of a Lady and Her Daughter* is on display along with the engaging *Holy Family with St John* by her contemporary **Lavinia Fontana**. A century or so later, Dutch and Flemish women like **Clara Peeters**, **Judith Leyster**, and **Rachel Ruysch** were producing still lifes and genre scenes that were equal to those of their more famous male colleagues – notice the vivacity of Peeters's *Still Life of Fish and Cat*. On occasion, female artists broke out of their limited environment to paint nontraditional subjects: for example, German-born **Maria Sybilla Merian** crafted superb engravings of flora and fauna, inspired by her intrepid explorations in Surinam in 1699. Meanwhile, in France, women like **Elisabeth-Louise Vigée-Lebrun** (1755–1842) held sway as court painters, depicting the royalty fluttering around Marie Antoinette. But as a woman artist, Vigée-Lebrun was marginalized, her paintings denied the respect accorded those of her male contemporaries, and she was kept out of the Académie des Beaux-Arts until the 1780s.

Nineteenth-century art

In the nineteenth century, American women artists began to enter the fray. **Lilly Martin Spencer** was inordinately popular as a producer of genre scenes: *The Artist and Her Family at a Fourth of July Picnic* (1864) is typically vibrant, despite the grim wartime period in which it was painted. As Impressionism widened the parameters of art, painters like **Berthe Morisot** (1841–95) and, particularly, **Mary Cassatt** (1844–1926) produced daring (for the time) scenes of nursing mothers, young girls, and mewling babies. Cassatt, like many of her contemporaries, was intrigued by the forms and colors of Asian art; *The Bath* (1898), an etching of mother and baby created with crisp swatches of pale color, was influenced by an exhibition of Japanese woodblocks she had seen in Paris, where she lived from an early age. **Cecilia Beaux** (1863–1942), also inspired by her stay in Paris, was sought after for her rich, expressive portraits such as that of Ethel Page – so much so that she was honored with a commission to paint Theodore and Mrs Roosevelt in 1903. (One of Beaux's most striking works, *Sita and Sarita*, is on view at the Corcoran Gallery.)

Twentieth-century art

The museum's twentieth-century collection includes classical sculptures by Camille Claudel (1864–1943), paintings by Georgia O'Keeffe and Tamara de Lempicka, linocuts by Hannah Höch, and a cycle of prints depicting the hardships of working-class life by the socialist **Käthe Kollwitz** (1867–1945), part of her powerful *A Weaver's Rebellion* (1893–98). Insightful self-portraits reveal Kollwitz appearing drained by her work in an etching of 1921, and **Frida Kahlo** (1907–54), dressed in a peasant's outfit and clutching a note to Trotsky, dedicating herself to the Revolution. Another, more curious work is Kahlo's *Itzcuintli Dog with Me*, in which she poses next to a truly tiny, strangely adorable mutt. The last gallery reaches into modern times, with striking photographs of

▲ New York Avenue Presbyterian Church

figures from the entertainment and literary worlds by Louise Dahl-Wolfe, and contemporary work by sculptors Dorothy Dehner and Louise Nevelson, minimalist Dorothea Rockburne, and Abstract Expressionists Helen Frankenthaler, Lee Krasner, and Elaine de Kooning, among others. One of the highlights is a series of studies for the *Dinner Party*, by **Judy Chicago**, a groundbreaking feminist work from the 1970s.

New York Avenue Presbyterian Church

1313 New York Ave NW ☎ 202/393-3700, ⓦ www.nyapc.org; Metro Center Metro. Daily 9am–1pm, guided tours Sun after 8.45am & 11am services.

Half a block west of the museum, the red-brick **New York Avenue Presbyterian Church** offers a 1950s facsimile of the mid-nineteenth-century church in which the Lincoln family worshiped. The pastor at that time, Dr Gurley, was at Lincoln's bedside at the Petersen House when he died and conducted the funeral service four days later at the White House. Someone in the church's office (on the New York Avenue side) should be able to point out the president's second-row pew, while downstairs in the "Lincoln Parlor" you can see an early draft of his Emancipation Proclamation and portraits of Lincoln and Dr Gurley.

6

New Downtown and Dupont Circle

Many visitors will have at least passing acquaintance with the part of the city known as **New Downtown**, if only because that's where most of the hotels are. Known by several different names – including West Downtown and Midtown – this is where, in the late Victorian era, businessmen and hoteliers first saw the advantage in being just a few blocks north of the White House. More than anything else, New Downtown is DC's corporate district, defined as the off-center diamond north of Lafayette Square formed by Pennsylvania, New Hampshire, Massachusetts, and New York avenues. Some of its thoroughfares, like 16th Street and Connecticut Avenue, have drawn locals for historic architecture and the odd museum, but the area particularly attracted residents after the panicked flight from Old Downtown following the 1968 riots. These days, the place is primarily ground zero for lobbyists – especially on **K Street** – and offers a smattering of interesting institutions, museums, and some good bars, clubs, and restaurants, though for the most part you'll probably be taking the Metro from your hotel here to the major sights to the south.

Nearby **Dupont Circle** took longer to come into its own but in recent decades has been an essential destination for its hip restaurants and clubs, gay-friendly merchants, charming old buildings, and contemporary-art galleries. As a symbol of gentrification, the neighborhood is often invoked whenever a formerly down-at-the-heel area becomes chic and trendy, with the threat or promise that it's becoming "the next Dupont Circle." Northwest from the Circle itself, turn-of-the-twentieth-century mansions house the denizens of **Embassy Row**, private galleries cluster near the **Phillips Collection**, America's first modern art museum, and townhouse museums are peppered around the elite neighborhood of **Kalorama**.

New Downtown

Much of New Downtown was developed by the time of the Civil War by businessmen and hoteliers with a firm stake in the government's policies toward the private sector, and those forces are still at work: with lobbying as feverish

NEW DOWNTOWN AND DUPONT CIRCLE

CAFÉS & RESTAURANTS	
17th Street Café	21
Afterwords Café	9
Alberto's Pizza	33
Annie's Paramount Steakhouse	11
Asia Nora	48
Bistrot du Coin	5
Bombay Club	63
Café Asia	61
Café Citron	35
Café Luna	26
Café Promenade	54
City Lights of China	4
Dakota Cowgirl	37
DC Coast	59
Firehook Bakery	14
Galileo	52
Gerard Pangaud Bistro	60
Giovanni's Trattu	42
Grillfish	45
Java House	16
Julia's Empanadas	44
Komi	62
Loeb's Deli	10
Luna Grill & Diner	46
Malaysia Kopitiam	10
Marvelous Market	15
McCormick & Schmick's	58
Mio	56
Moby Dick House of Kabob	39
Naan and Beyond	57
The Newsroom	1
Nooshi	51
Nora's	6
The Palm	41
Pizzeria Paradiso	22
Sala Thai	32
Sign of the Whale	46
Skewers	30
SoHo Tea & Coffee	56
Stoney's	25
Sushi Taro	0
Tabard Inn	7
Teaism	23
Urbana	49
Vidalia	46
Zorba's Café	13

ACCOMMODATION	
Beacon	E
Carlyle Suites	H
Doubletree	T
Dupont at the Circle	K
Embassy Circle Guest House	M
Embassy Inn	E
Embassy Row Hilton	R
Hamilton Crowne Plaza	B
Helix	L
Holiday Inn Central	F
Hotel Rouge	S
Madera	N
Mayflower Hotel	S
Palomar	I
St Regis Hotel	U
Swann House	A
Tabard Inn	O
Topaz	P
Westin Embassy Row	G
Westin Washington	Q
William Lewis House	D

BARS & CLUBS	
Andalu	43
Apex	34
Biddy Mulligan's	19
Big Hunt	35
Black Cat	3
Brickskeller	17
Buffalo Billiards	38
Chaos	15
Cobalt	8
Eighteenth Street Lounge	47
FAB Lounge	2
Five	43
Fox and Hounds	20
Gazuza	9
Halo	27
HR-57	18
JR's	12
Logan Tavern	28
Madhatter	40
MCCXXIII	46
New Vegas Lounge	29
Omega	31
Ozio	50
Panache	46
Recessions	53
Sign of the Whale	46
Steve's Bar Room	36

NEW DOWNTOWN AND DUPONT CIRCLE

191

now as it's ever been, it's safe to say as many political and economic decisions are being made in white-collar offices here as in Congress. The area has, however, paid the price for this shotgun arrangement of capital merchants aligned with Capitol legislators: it has little sense of history and virtually no sense of a meaningful neighborhood. In this, of course, New Downtown resembles the anonymous dead zones of other modern American cities – largely white, sterile, and deserted after 6pm. Nonetheless, there are scattered points of interest here that are worth a look, particularly if you want to take a walk near your hotel and expect to see more than just office blocks.

Along K Street

K Street, the spine of New Downtown's business and political lobbying district, is DC's Wall Street in spirit only. When companies first moved in during the 1970s, local zoning ordinances prevented them from aping New York's soaring urban landscape. Restricted to a maximum height of 130ft, the structures are generally production-line boxes of little distinction in which lobbyists, lawyers, brokers, and bankers beaver away from dawn until dark. Between 13th and 20th streets there's barely a building to raise the pulse, though street vendors do their best to inject a bit of life, hustling jewelry, T-shirts, silk ties, hot dogs, and bath salts from the sidewalks.

Franklin, McPherson, and Farragut squares

Although the trio of squares on the south side of K Street are mainly visited for their three outlying Metro stations, there are some interesting sights if you look hard enough. **Franklin Square**, between 13th and 14th streets, is the most inviting, its large, tree-covered expanse broken up by paths, benches, and a central fountain, and overlooked by the Victorian-era, red-brick Franklin School, the place where Alexander Graham Bell sent his first message. A block west, **McPherson Square** is named for James B. McPherson, the Civil War general who saw action with Grant at Vicksburg and later became the highest-ranking Union officer to die in battle, when, commanding the Army of Tennessee, he was killed near Atlanta as his troops marched with Sherman into Georgia. His statue is presented on horseback in the square's center.

Around the square, late nineteenth- and early twentieth-century architects infused their buildings with some flair, like the 1924 Neoclassical-style Investment Building (15th and K), whose limestone Beaux-Arts facade belies a completely redesigned modern lobby and interior, the inspired work of Cesar Pelli; the Renaissance Revival arches of the University Club (900 15th St); and, best of all, the scrupulously carved capitals and lion's head plaques of the terra-cotta Southern Building (805 15th St), dating from 1910. **Farragut Square**, two blocks farther west (at 17th), is the least prepossessing of K Street's open spaces, held beneath the gaze of Admiral David Farragut, whose statue celebrates his reckless heroism during the Civil War battle of Mobile Bay ("Damn the torpedoes. Full speed ahead!") and was cast from the melted-down propeller of his ship.

Connecticut Avenue and around

Along with Pennsylvania Avenue NW, **Connecticut Avenue** NW is one of the two major roads through Washington, leading from New Downtown to Dupont Circle and on to Upper Northwest. Indeed, it's also arguably the most appealing of all the District's thoroughfares, if only because it links so many interesting neighborhoods – from chic and swank to funky and bohemian – and takes you past all sorts of excellent eateries, boutiques, booksellers, bars, clubs, museums, and galleries along the way. While most of these lie beyond the precinct of New Downtown, it's here where the road gets its start.

Mayflower Hotel

The double-bay-fronted **Mayflower Hotel**, 1127 Connecticut Ave NW (⊤202/347-3000; Farragut North Metro; see p.269), has graced its location since 1925, when its first official function was to host President Calvin Coolidge's inaugural ball. Countless other official and unofficial events have taken place here – everything from high-profile diplomatic luncheons to off-the-record journalistic meetings. Designed by the New York architects responsible for Grand Central Terminal, the *Mayflower* is best known for its remarkable 500ft-long **Promenade** – effectively a lobby connecting Connecticut Avenue to 17th Street – which could comfortably accommodate an army division or two. It's rich in rugs, oils, sofas, gilt, and mirrors, as is the hotel's **Grand Ballroom**, in which a dozen incoming presidents have swirled around the dance floor over the years. FDR lived in the *Mayflower* for a while after his inauguration, as did Truman while the White House was being renovated, and J. Edgar Hoover lunched here every day when he ran the FBI. Now part of the Renaissance chain, the renovated hotel is an expensive night's rest, but you don't have to stay here to troop through the marvelous public spaces and watch the swells having lunch in the über-chic *Café Promenade* (see "Eating" chapter, p.288).

National Geographic Society Explorers Hall

1145 17th St NW ⊤202/857-7588, Ⓦ www.nationalgeographic.com/explorer; Farragut North Metro. Mon–Sat 9am–5pm, Sun 10am–5pm.

The National Geographic Society maintains its headquarters near 17th and M streets. Founded in 1888, it began by funding important expeditions to various uncharted territories; its greatest asset, however, was Gilbert Hovey Grosvenor, founding editor of *National Geographic* magazine, who first conceived that geography could be presented in an exciting way, primarily through spectacular illustrations. At the headquarters building, **Explorers Hall** contains excellent rotating exhibits in the tradition of the magazine's globe-trotting coverage, as well as child-friendly geographic displays. Together these cover a range of topics, including global health campaigns, rainforest protection, global warming, endangered creatures, indigenous cultures, and the latest trends in science and technology. The hall also hosts frequent events under the label of "National Geographic Live!," spotlighting explorers, photographers, scientists, and filmmakers through lectures, movies, and multimedia displays, as well as occasional concerts. At the National Geographic **store**, you can choose from a wide selection of maps, globes, videos, photography books, and souvenirs.

Charles Sumner School

1201 17th St NW ⊤202/442-6060; Farragut North Metro. Mon–Sat 10am–5pm; free.

Across M Street from the National Geographic Society, the **Charles Sumner School** honors the nineteenth-century senator nearly clubbed to death in the Old Senate Chamber by pro-slavery Congressman Preston Brooks of South Carolina. Brooks violently objected to a speech Sumner had directed at his uncle, Senator Andrew Brooks, who according to Sumner was in thrall to "a mistress who, though ugly to others, is always lovely to him. . . . I mean the harlot, slavery." It took three years for Sumner to recover from his injuries, but both he and Brooks soon became heroes to their respective sides.

To improve the education offered to black children, this onetime public high school – the first in the country for African American youth – was established in the city in 1870. A harmonious red-brick building with a handsome central clock tower, the school is today largely used for conferences, but a free onsite **museum** has a number of mildly interesting exhibits, which range from temporary shows by black artists to highlights of the life of Frederick Douglass to displays relating to the city's school system.

St Matthew's Cathedral

1725 Rhode Island Ave NW ☎202/347-3215, ⊛www.stmatthewscathedral.org. Mon–Fri & Sun 6.30am–6.30pm, Sat 7.30am–6.30pm.

While not quite on the same level as the National Shrine of the Immaculate Conception, **St Matthew's Cathedral** is still monumental and replete with evocative neo–Gothic character. The centerpiece above the altar is a towering, 35ft **mosaic** of the church's namesake, the patron saint of civil servants; other features include a grand organ with seventy tin pipes, a white-marble altar and pulpit, and four more mosaics depicting the four evangelists (Matthew, Mark, Luke, and John). Beyond its striking appearance, the cathedral is perhaps best known as the place where **JFK**'s funeral mass was held in 1963, and an inlaid plaque honoring the slain president lies in front of the altar (he was buried at Arlington National Cemetery). More surprisingly, in 2005 former Chief Justice William Rehnquist was eulogized here in a Lutheran ceremony, and Protestant presidents as well as just about every notable Catholic politician in Congress have also dropped by. If you want to peer at the bigwig worshipers, church services are open to all.

16th Street and around

Most of the area above K Street was scantily populated until well into the nineteenth century, but post–Civil War expansion changed **16th Street** completely, replacing ramshackle buildings in a predominantly black neighborhood with large mansions, gentlemen's clubs, and patrician hotels, all benefiting from their proximity to the White House. Heading north from the Executive Mansion, the old *Carlton Hotel*, 16th and K streets, has maintained its rich 1920s decor after transforming into the stylish *St Regis* (see p.269), which itself has been recently renovated to restore its historic dash. Farther along on 16th Street, the stately *Jefferson Hotel*, at no. 1220 (see p.268), was built in 1922 and will re-emerge with its classical arches and iron balconies restored by the end of 2008.

About a block east, the **Metropolitan AME Church**, 1518 M St NW (Mon–Sat 10am–6pm, ☎202/331-1426), is a large, neo–Gothic, red-brick structure built and paid for in 1886 by former slaves. It hosted Frederick Douglass's funeral in February 1895, as he had often preached here. On the day of the funeral, crowds swamped the street outside, black schools closed for the day, and flags in the city flew at half-mast. This formidable edifice is one of the District's ecclesiastical high points, with its striking narrow arches and spires and handsome decorative granite trim. Nearby are the offices of the **Washington Post**, 1150 15th St NW, the second most famous daily in America after the *New York Times*, its reputation still based squarely on the investigative coup of its reporters Bob Woodward and Carl Bernstein, who exposed the Watergate scandal that led to the resignation of President Nixon in 1974. One block north of the *Jefferson Hotel*, **Scott Circle**, at Massachusetts and Rhode Island avenues, was once a fashionable nineteenth-century park but is today a traffic roundabout graced with a statue of Union commander General Winfield Scott astride his horse.

North of the circle, architectural highlights on 16th include the **Carnegie Institution**, at P Street, a pleasing Neoclassical monument from 1909, with grand Ionic columns and bronze entry doors that lead to a two-story rotunda; the **Cairo**, at Q Street, an 1894 hodgepodge of Moorish, Romanesque, and early-modern Sullivan-esque designs whose enormous, 164ft height caused the District to impose size restrictions for residential buildings – it's still the tallest in town; the so-called **Green Door**, 1623 16th St, an 1886 Richardsonian Romanesque mansion with stone cladding, red-brick arches, and turrets; and the **Chastleton**, no. 1701, a Gothic Revival apartment complex from the 1920s detailed with arched windows, heraldry, and gargoyles.

Scottish Rite Temple

1733 16th St NW ☏ 202/232-3579, Ⓦ www.srmason-sj.org. Library, museum, and tours Mon–Fri 8am–3.30pm.

John Russell Pope's **Scottish Rite Temple**, halfway between New Downtown and the Shaw district, is one of DC's most eye-catching buildings; indeed, in the 1930s the American Institute of Architects voted it one of the five finest structures in the world. If you're anywhere in the vicinity, you can't possibly miss it, with its towering Ionic columns, ziggurat-like roof, huge base, and ancient-temple design inspired by the Mausoleum at Halicarnassus, one of the Seven Wonders of the Ancient World.

Built in 1915 of limestone and granite, this Masonic temple is predictably loaded with arcane symbolism, striking imagery (notably the two sphinxes guarding the place out front), and inscriptions hailing knowledge, truth, and other values. Unlike many such temples, though, this one has long been accessible to the uninitiated. There's a **museum** that honors the works of selected Masons locally and nationally, among them J. Edgar Hoover, and offers a selection of regalia that includes the ceremonial vestments of each degree of Masonhood (aprons, caps, jewels, rings, and so forth), with each rank getting increasingly elaborate duds. Pride of place, though, goes to the replica of the foundation stone of the US Capitol, laid by George Washington (a Mason) in 1793, a nearly perfect 18in cube. The **public library** also rewards a visit, housing a voluminous collection of works by Scottish Mason and poet Robert Burns, and the temple is open for daily **tours**, though you're not likely to receive any answers if you start asking questions about secret rituals and handshakes.

Logan Circle and 14th Street

In the early twentieth century, an influx of black middle-class residents began to fill the roomy Victorian houses around **Logan Circle**, between New Downtown and Shaw. Fashionable Iowa Circle, as it was then known, became Logan Circle in 1930 in honor of the Civil War general whose impressive equestrian statue lords over the spot. The surrounding Victorians have miraculously survived the neighborhood's slow decline since the 1950s; turrets, terraces, balconies, and pediments in various states of repair signal the fact that this is a protected historic district. The district reached its nadir in the 1980s, but since the mid-1990s there's been a major rebound in housing prices, and the sudden appearance of theatrical companies, trendy bars and restaurants, chic boutiques, and other elements signal the process of gentrification is well under way.

The rise of Mary McLeod Bethune

Mary McLeod Bethune was born on a cotton farm in South Carolina in 1875, one of seventeen children of poor parents, both ex-slaves. A bright, inquiring child, she was sent to a local school and later entertained thoughts of becoming a missionary in Africa (she was turned down because of her race) before moving to Florida in 1904 to found the Daytona Educational and Industrial School for Negro Girls, later **Bethune-Cookman College**. Starting in a rented room and using home-made materials, Bethune persevered with her intention to train teachers who would serve the African American community. In 1935, she was recognized with an award from the NAACP, and soon after President **Franklin Roosevelt** asked her to serve as special adviser on minority affairs. Later, as the director of the Division of Negro Affairs in the National Youth Administration, Bethune became the first African American woman to head a federal office, and was the only woman to work in the ad hoc **"Black Cabinet"** that advised FDR about the implications of his New Deal policies on blacks. In 1945, through the NAACP, Bethune was invited to San Francisco to attend the conference that established the United Nations.

Bethune bought her home on Vermont Avenue in 1942 and lived there for seven years. She also used it as headquarters for the National Council for Negro Women, founded in 1935, which sought to bring various organizations together to fight discrimination more effectively. Her work here formed the basis of her collection of writings called *Legacy*, finished just before her death in 1955, in which she outlined the meaning of her work in a stirring series of messages for those who would follow: "I leave you a thirst for education. I leave you a respect for the use of power. I leave you faith. I leave you racial dignity."

Fourteenth Street, half a block west, had many of its buildings burned in the 1968 riots but has since recovered and become a commercial axis for the neighborhood, with various refurbishment projects regularly taking place. However, keep in mind that Logan Circle is something of an island for redevelopment, and there are plenty of dicey areas further north and east. With the closest Metro access six long blocks away, it's best not to wander the streets alone after dark, especially if you don't know where you're going.

Bethune Council House

1318 Vermont Ave NW ☎202/673-2402, ⓦwww.nps.gov/mamc. Mon–Sat 9am–5pm, last tour 4.30pm.

In one of the restored townhouses just off Logan Circle, the **Bethune Council House** serves as a memorial to one of DC's most prominent African American residents. Administered by the National Park Service, the house serves as a research center and archive, though you're welcome to tour the restored rooms, which contain a few of Mary McLeod Bethune's mementos alongside period photographs and changing exhibitions. The memorial to Bethune in Lincoln Park (see p.121) records more of her legacy. The best way to get here is the fifteen-minute walk up Vermont Avenue from McPherson Square Metro, past Thomas Circle.

Dupont Circle

As a matter of geography, **Dupont Circle** is the great traffic roundabout formed at the intersection of Massachusetts, Connecticut, and New Hampshire avenues with 19th and P streets, making for a two-ringed, ten-spoked wheel that can take forever to drive if you hit it during rush hour. In the streets around the traffic circle, it's a fun, relaxed neighborhood with a good blend of hipsters, yuppies, and old-timers, plus the city's most densely packed choices for lodging, dining, drinking, and clubbing.

Easily accessible on the Metro Red Line, it's also one of the city's best areas for a walk, loaded with gorgeous townhouses and mansions from the nineteenth and early twentieth centuries, as well as a number of museums, bookstores, and galleries. Along with Connecticut Avenue NW, the other major stretches for nighttime entertainment are the gay-oriented P Street west of the Circle and 17th Street east of it. **Embassy Row**, just to the northwest along Massachusetts Avenue, is lined with historic Beaux-Arts mansions now stuffed with diplomats and staffers, with flags of their respective nations flying out front. One of the best times to visit Dupont Circle is the first weekend in June, when a consortium of museums sponsors the Dupont–Kalorama **Museums Walk Weekend** (Ⓦwww .dkmuseums.com), featuring free concerts, historic-house tours, and craft fairs.

Some history

Until the Civil War, Pacific Circle – as Dupont Circle was first known – marked the western edge of the city, beyond which the nation's capital petered out into a series of farms, barns, and slaughterhouses. After the war, however, streets were paved and a bridge was built across Rock Creek to nearby Georgetown. The **British Embassy** was built here in the mid-1870s, and subsequently lawyers and businessmen installed their families in grand Victorian houses. By the turn of the century, Dupont Circle was where all self-respecting industrial barons and high-flying diplomats built their city mansions, often in the favored Beaux-Arts style of the time. Massachusetts Avenue, northwest of the Circle, became so popular with foreign legations that it acquired the tag Embassy Row, while the even more secluded residences north of S Street developed into the exclusive neighborhood of **Kalorama** (see p.204) – named in Greek for the "beautiful view" it afforded of the Rock Creek Valley.

Dupont Circle's golden age of soirées and socialites ended at roughly the same time World War II began. Many of its wealthy residents were hit by the 1929 stock market crash and sold out; other mansions were torn down or, the ultimate ignominy, turned into boarding houses for the postwar influx of federal workers. The Circle became solidly middle-class and, during the 1970s, even vaguely radical, as a younger hippie crowd moved in and gays and lesbians found the tolerant atmosphere to their liking. With the establishment of gay and alternative bars and clubs, the area took on a new energy and identity. For real-estate speculators, though, the Circle was still too close to the perimeter of the 1968 riots near Logan Circle to warrant a significant investment of capital.

This changed beginning in the 1980s, as redevelopment money began to pour in and rampant gentrification took place, driving off the hippies and giving the formerly edgy neighborhood an elite air that appealed to more upscale gays and straights. Near the end of the 2000s, Dupont Circle's course has become appropriately circular, and it's once more an upmarket address, full of designer coffeehouses and swank restaurants – and a slew of new residents barely aware that the district once stood for something beyond attracting tourists and making money.

The traffic circle and around

The large traffic island of Dupont Circle is as much a hub as any roundabout in DC, and centers around a **fountain** whose frolicking nude allegorical figures – representing sea, stars, and wind – were meant to honor the naval exploits of

Civil War admiral Samuel Dupont. Although it's still a little ragged at the edges, the Circle is still far different than it was in the 1970s, when it sported a frenetic scene of "girl-watching businessmen, stoners, cruising homosexuals, short-skirted secretaries, doe-faced chicken hawks eyeing little boys, the whole Dupont stew," according to thriller writer George Pelecanos. On the whole it's an easy-going hang-out with chess players hogging the permanent tables in the center of the Circle – some of the better ones offering ad hoc lessons for $20–50 an hour – and numerous cafés, bookstores, and restaurants close by. There are Metro entrances to the northwest and south.

There are too many notable examples of historic architecture here to mention, but a few buildings stand out. The private Neoclassical **Washington Club**, 15 Dupont Circle NW at Massachusetts Ave, was formerly the Patterson House, built in 1901 by master Beaux-Arts architect Stanford White. In later decades, it was here that the Coolidge family camped out during White House renovations and entertained Charles Lindbergh soon after his solo transatlantic crossing, and the houses' owners, heirs to the Chicago Tribune fortune, influenced city and national politics with their distinctive brand of archconservatism. Another members-only institution, the swanky **Sulgrave Club**, 1801 Massachusetts Ave, has an elegant Beaux-Arts design and terracotta details and was completed a year after the Patterson House, while at 1785 Massachusetts Ave, the **National Trust for Historic Preservation** (☏ 202/588-6000, ⓦ www.nationaltrust.org) occupies the towering edifice once known as the McCormick Apartments. The striking 1922 building has lovely period details, again of a late Beaux-Arts flavor; for a closer look, take one of the Trust's tours, offered by reservation only. The turn-of-the-twentieth century Neoclassical style indeed influences almost every neighborhood building of that vintage, holding up even by 1936, when gas stations like the old **Embassy Gulf**, 2200 P St NW, were built to resemble Classical Revival banks.

Just outside the northwest-side Metro exit, the grand **Blaine Mansion**, at 2000 Massachusetts Ave, is a marvelous red-brick Victorian from 1881 that was once home to three-time presidential candidate James "Slippery Jim" Blaine, whose worst defeat was in 1884, when he became the first Republican nominee to lose the general election since before the Civil War – to Grover Cleveland, who has a DC neighborhood named after him (Cleveland Park).

Heurich House

1307 New Hampshire Ave NW ☏ 202/429-1894, ⓦ www.heurichhouse.org; Dupont Circle Metro. Tours Wed–Sat 11.30am and 1pm, also Sat 2.30pm; $5.

Although most of the grand old mansions are open only to club members, embassy employees, and private owners, one historic residence is regularly open to the public. The wondrous **Heurich House** was built in 1894 for German-born brewing magnate Christian Heurich, and is a stunning, if extreme, example of the Richardsonian Romanesque style popular at the time. With its rough-hewn stone tower and castellations and richly carved wood-and-plaster interior, the mansion – known as "The Brewmaster's Castle" – resembles a miniature medieval fortress. The tours take you through many of the restored rooms and focus on the mansion's lavish decor and the lifestyle of its original occupants. On display are the formal parlor, drawing room, and dining room, a music room with a mahogany musicians' balcony, some of the fifteen opulent marble and onyx fireplaces, and the basement *Bierstube* (beer room), carved with such Teutonic drinking mottos as "He who has never been drunk is not a good man."

Embassy Row

While there are many historic structures housing diplomatic missions in the vicinity of the circle – notably the grand French Revival–style **Wilkins House**, 1700 Massachusetts Ave NW, now the Peruvian chancery – **Embassy Row** starts in earnest a few paces northwest up Massachusetts Avenue. Here, the Indonesian Embassy at no. 2020 occupies the magnificent **Walsh–McLean House**, built in the Second Empire style in 1903 for gold baron Thomas Walsh. It's a superb building – with colonnaded loggia, mansard roof, and intricate, carved windows – that was once one of high society's most fashionable venues. Soirées here were presided over by Walsh's daughter Evalyn, the last private owner of the Hope Diamond (now in the National Museum of Natural History, p.73). Nearby, the **Cosmos Club**, 2121 Massachusetts Ave, is a swank private entity with an agreeable 1901 Beaux-Arts style and has played host to numerous presidents, diplomats, and scientists; the club was founded in 1878 by Western explorer John Wesley Powell.

Along with the historic digs around here, there are a number of **statues**, too. A tall, brooding memorial to Czech president **Tomas Masaryk** stands at 22nd and Q streets; across from the Indian embassy, a skinny **Mahatma Gandhi** with a walking stick presides over a traffic island at Massachusetts, Q, and 21st; and **Winston Churchill** flashes the victory sign outside the residence of the British ambassador, 3100 Massachusetts Ave, supposedly with one foot on DC (American) soil and the other on embassy (British) grounds. The residence itself is a lovely incarnation of an English country manor, designed in 1928 by Edward Lutyens, and in great contrast to the bleakly modern British embassy on the same property.

Although the diplomatic residences in the area are typically closed to the public, occasionally you can take a closer look inside some of them. If you want to know more about a given country's culture (with a heavy PR spin of course), check out Ⓦ www.embassyevents.com for a listing of art shows, lectures, food fairs, films, and displays taking place at selected embassies here and elsewhere in town. Alternatively, you can drop in on the **Goodwill Embassy Tour** ($35; Ⓣ 202/636-4225, Ⓦ www.dcgoodwill.org) on the second Saturday in May, during which five of DC's embassy buildings throw open their doors. For more information on the embassies in the immediate area, check out Ⓦ www.embassy.org.

Anderson House

2118 Massachusetts Ave NW Ⓣ 202/785-2040 ext 427, Ⓦ www.thecincinnati.org; Dupont Circle Metro. Guided tours Tues–Sat 1.15, 2.15 & 3.15pm; free.

The **Anderson House** is a veritable palace, built between 1902 and 1905 as the winter residence of Larz Anderson, who served as ambassador to Belgium and Japan. As a Beaux-Arts residence it has no equal in the city, its gray stone exterior sporting twin arched entrances with heavy wooden doors and a colonnaded portico. Inside, original details – cavernous fireplaces, inlaid marble floors, Flemish tapestries, evocative murals, and a grand ballroom – provide a lavish backdrop for diplomatic receptions. Anderson bequeathed this wonderful house to the **Society of the Cincinnati**, as his great-grandfather was a founding member. Established in 1783, the society – named after Cincinnatus, the legendary Roman general who famously relinquished his command after saving the city from invading hordes – is the oldest patriotic organization in the country and maintains a small museum of Revolutionary War memorabilia here; if you can prove your lineage to an American officer in that conflict, you can apply to become a member. Appropriately enough, **George Washington** was its first president general, and there's a white marble bust of him in the entrance hall by Thomas Crawford, who sculpted the Freedom figure on top of the Capitol. The best time to visit the Anderson House is when it's offering one of its regular **free concerts** (see p.311), typically classical chamber-music recitals.

Sheridan Circle and around

Farther northwest, at **Sheridan Circle**, the 1909 equestrian statue of Union general Phillip H. Sheridan commemorates this controversial figure of modern warfare, who was not only an early proponent of "scorched earth" tactics in the Shenandoah campaign but went on to mercilessly battle native tribes in the Indian Wars of the post–Civil War era and, more surprisingly, advocate the protection of what became Yellowstone National Park. Compared to the 60ft heads of Washington, Jefferson, Lincoln, and Roosevelt that its sculptor, Gutzon Borglum, went on to create at Mount Rushmore, this statue seems positively dainty.

On the south side of the circle, the **Residence of the Turkish Ambassador**, 1606 23rd St, is brimming with Near Eastern motifs; oddly, it wasn't commissioned by the Turks at all but by one Edward Everett, the man who patented the fluted bottle-top. From the circle you can duck down 23rd Street to see **Dumbarton Bridge**, guarded on either side by enormous bronze bison. The bridge provides the quickest route into northern Georgetown, emerging on Q Street by Dumbarton House, about twenty minutes from Dupont Circle.

The Phillips Collection

1600 21st St NW ☎202/387-2151, ⓦwww.phillipscollection.org; Dupont Circle Metro. Tues–Sat 10am–5pm, Sun 11am–6pm, Thurs closes at 8.30pm. Weekday admission free; weekends $10; special exhibitions $12–15.

The **Phillips Collection**'s claim to be "America's first museum of modern art" is based on its having opened eight years before New York's Museum of Modern Art. The oldest part of the Georgian Revival brownstone building was the family home of founder **Duncan Phillips**, who lost his father and brother in little over a year and established a gallery in 1921 in their honor. Financed by the family's steel fortune, Phillips bought nearly 2400 works over the years; during the 1920s, he and his wife, Marjorie, became patrons of young artists like Georgia O'Keeffe and Marsden Hartley. The collection is diverse, though it was initially guided primarily by Phillips's own enthusiasms, which included plenty of French Impressionists and modernists like Mark Rothko and other American Abstract Expressionists, as well as pre-modern artists like Giorgione and El Greco.

From its original building, the museum has expanded considerably, adding the **Goh Annex** on 21st Street in 1989 and a new underground wing, the Sant Building, in 2006 to focus on more contemporary works. There's also a gift shop and the tasty Firehook Café onsite. Introductory tours of the facility take place on Saturdays at 11am and special exhibition tours on Friday at 11am. A full program of **cultural events** includes classical music recitals (Oct–May Sun 4pm; free with admission) and "Artful Evenings" (Thurs 5–8.30pm) that involve live music, lectures (6 and 7pm), and a bar.

European works

The **European** powerhouses of the collection comprise a wistful Blue Period Picasso, *The Blue Room* (1901); Matisse's modernist nude study *Studio, Quai St-Michel* (1916), a Cézanne still life and enigmatic self-portrait, and no fewer than

▲ The Phillips Collection

four Van Goghs, including the powerful *Road Menders* (1889). Pierre Bonnard gets a good showing – you have to stand well back to take in the expansive, post-Impressionist scale of *The Terrace* (1918) and *The Palm* (1926) – just two of his seventeen works in the collection. Top billing generally goes to Renoir's *The Luncheon of the Boating Party* (1891), where straw-boater-wearing dandies linger over a long and bibulous feast. Phillips bought the painting in 1923 for $125,000 as part of a two-year burst of acquisition that also yielded Cézanne's *Mont Saint-Victoire* (1906) and Honoré Daumier's *The Uprising* (1860). There's an impressive selection of **Degas** works, too – from early scenes like *Women Combing Their Hair* (1875) to the late ballet picture *Dancers at the Bar* (c.1900), in which the background and hair of the subjects collide in an orange frenzy.

Other **nineteenth-century works** include pieces by Gustave Courbet and Eugène Delacroix (note his wonderful painting of the violinist Paganini in full fiddle). Phillips's catholic taste comes to the fore with the juxtaposition of two paintings of a repentant St Peter: one, fat and desperate, by Goya, the other a striking, eerie study by El Greco. An odd choice on the face of it, Phillips bought this latter piece for his modern art museum because he considered El Greco "the first impassioned expressionist." A much more familiar sort of modernist is found in the oak-paneled "**Music Room**," where some of the museum's thirteen Cubist works by Georges Braque vie for your attention. Later modernist pieces include Jean Arp's striking *Helmeted Head II* (1957); Mondrian's *Painting no. 9* (1942); and **Paul Klee**'s stick figures embellishing *Arrival of the Jugglers* (1926) and kaleidoscopic maze of rectangles, triangles, and trapezoidal shapes in *The Way to the Citadel* (1937).

American works

Beyond French Impressionism, the collection's strength is **late nineteenth-** and **early twentieth-century American art**, featuring pieces like Winslow Homer's bleak *To the Rescue* (1886); James McNeill Whistler's enigmatic *Miss Lilian Woakes* (1891); and Albert Pinkham Ryder's moody and atmospheric *Macbeth and the Witches* (1895), one of eight works by Ryder owned by the museum. Also worth a look are Charles Sheeler's sleek ode to the modern age, *Skyscrapers* (1922), and a few colorful still lifes by Stuart Davis.

Especially championed by Phillips in the 1920s and 1930s were Milton Avery (who influenced the young Rothko) and Arthur Dove, who despite his obscurity to casual art viewers is represented by some fifty works in the collection. More familiar names include Jacob Lawrence – notably extracts from a powerful 59-piece series called *The Migration of the Negro* (1941) – and **Edward Hopper**, whose works include *Sunday* (1926), featuring a man sitting alone on a bleak, empty street, and the much later *Approaching a City* (1946), viewed from the vantage point of sunken train tracks.

Abstract Expressionist works from the 1950s include a set of paintings by Rothko, such as his *Orange and Red on Red* (1957), set up now in the Rothko Room in the Sant Building. Also on view are Philip Guston's phantasmagoric *The Native's Return* (1957); Helen Frankenthaler's bloody red stain of *Canyon* (1965); Sam Francis's jazzy and vivid *Blue* (1958); Willem de Kooning's swirling and pulsing forms of *Asheville* (1948); and Richard Diebenkorn's California beach abstraction *Ocean Park no. 38* (1971).

Kalorama

North of Sheridan Circle, exclusive **Kalorama**'s quiet streets with manicured lawns stretch out to meet Rock Creek Park, and the diplomatic community thrives behind lace curtains and bulletproof glass in row after row of multimillion-dollar townhouse embassies, private homes, and hibiscus-rich gardens. One of the best such examples, the **Hauge House**, lies on the neighborhood's south end, at 24th and S streets. This sprawling French Renaissance limestone mansion housed the District's first Norwegian embassy in 1907, and today it's home to the Cameroonian embassy.

If you head up 24th Street toward Kalorama Circle, you'll find spectacular views across Rock Creek Park to Georgetown and beyond. Just to the east, the

Residence of the French Ambassador, 2221 Kalorama Rd NW, is the area's most ambitious building; the Tudor Revival country manor was originally built for a mining magnate and sold to the French in 1936 for the then absurdly expensive sum of almost half a million dollars. And unlike the Norwegians, who parted company with their stunning mansion, the French have clung tightly to theirs ever since. Similarly impressive, the **Codman-Davis House**, 2145 Decatur Place NW, is a 1907 Beaux-Arts mansion built by museum founder William Corcoran in smart neo-Georgian style. More surprisingly, the grand Georgian estate known as **The Lindens**, 2401 Kalorama Rd NW, isn't a revival structure at all, but an authentic 1754 Colonial mansion, built in Massachusetts when DC was still swampland, and relocated here as a preservation measure in the 1930s. From the same era, and equally unexpected in this district, is the **Friends Meeting House**, 2411 Florida Ave NW, a Quaker meeting hall and worship center built in the simple fieldstone style of similar structures in rural Pennsylvania.

Woodrow Wilson House

2340 S St NW ☎202/387-4062, ⊛www.woodrowwilsonhouse.org; Dupont Circle Metro. Tues–Sun 10am–4pm; $7.50.

Many commanders in chief lived in Washington, DC, before moving into the White House; all but one of them left the moment they retired from public service. **Woodrow Wilson**, the 28th president, spent the last years of his life in a fine Waddy Butler Wood–designed Georgian Revival house that is now open to the public. It's a comfortable home – light and airy, with high ceilings, wood floors, a wide staircase, and a solarium – which, despite his incapacitating stroke in 1919, Wilson aimed to use as a workplace where he could write political science books and practice law. That his second wife, Edith, a rich jeweler's widow, wanted to stay in DC near her family and friends probably had something to do with the decision to remain; she lived in the house for more than 35 years after Wilson's death. Indeed, Wilson lived here for only three years, and after he passed away was interred in Washington National Cathedral.

Visitors are first ushered into the front parlor, where Wilson liked to receive guests, and then continue on to see other parts of the house including the elevator, installed to help the enfeebled ex-president move between floors, and the bedroom, furnished by Edith as it had been in the White House. The canvas-walled library of the scholarly president (he ran Princeton University before he ran the country) once held eight thousand books, but they were donated to the Library of Congress after his death; the only remaining ones are the 69 volumes of Wilson's own writings. In a separate room is a silent-movie projector and screen that were given to him after his stroke by Douglas Fairbanks Sr. The fully equipped kitchen, straight out of the 1920s, has a blacklead range and provisions stacked in the walk-in pantry.

Textile Museum

2320 S St NW ☎202/667-0441, ⊛www.textilemuseum.org; Dupont Circle Metro. Mon–Sat 10am–5pm; Sun 1–5pm; $5.

Next door to the Woodrow Wilson House, in two equally grand converted residences, the **Textile Museum** presents exhibitions drawn from its 17,000-strong collection of textiles and carpets. The museum had its roots in the collection of George Hewitt Myers, who bought his first Asian rug as a student and opened the museum with three hundred other rugs and textile pieces in

Woodrow Wilson (1856–1924)

He was the perfect prototype of the seventeenth-century Puritan reincarnated.

Alistair Cooke, *America*, 1973

Born **Thomas Woodrow Wilson** in Stanton, Virginia, to a plain-living Presbyterian family, the future president dropped the "Thomas" at a very early age, convinced that the new version of his name would sound better when he was famous. He attended law school and, though he didn't take his final exams, practiced law in Georgia for a year, only to discover that it wasn't for him. Wilson returned to graduate school, earned his doctorate – making him the only American president to have a PhD – and taught law and political economics for twelve years, eventually rising to become a reforming president of **Princeton University**. Known and respected as an academic writer on political science and a stern critic of government corruption, he might have dedicated his life to these pursuits but for the Democratic Party's need for progressive candidates to run against the splintering Republicans. In 1910 Wilson won election as the **governor of New Jersey**, and two years later he received the Democratic nomination for president. The split in the Republican Party – with Theodore Roosevelt running on the Bull Moose Party ticket against the incumbent William Howard Taft, his former Republican protégé turned enemy – gave the Democrats both houses in Congress and let Wilson slip into power.

In his two terms of office, Wilson – a stirring orator (and the last president to write his own speeches) – saw through a batch of reformist legislation that continued Roosevelt's crusade against corporate vice and corruption. The **Federal Reserve** was established to better regulate the banking system, antitrust laws were strengthened, the **19th Amendment** (for women's suffrage) passed, and labor laws were enacted that at least gave a nod to workers' rights. But Wilson also presided over rather darker events – not least the violent breaking of the Colorado coal strike, leaving 66 people dead, and the entrenchment of segregation in the federal system. Indeed, it's misleading to see Wilson as any kind of modern liberal; his reforms made capitalism safe in a period of considerable turmoil and were very much part of the early twentieth-century strengthening of federal power at the expense of individual freedom. It's no coincidence that the **18th Amendment** sanctioning Prohibition was passed during his presidency, and it was Wilson who, upon viewing D.W. Griffith's notoriously racist epic *The Birth of a Nation*, famously remarked that the film was "writing history with lightning."

1925. Based in his family home and designed by no less an architect than John Russell Pope, the museum soon expanded into the house next door; today both buildings and the beautiful gardens are open to the public. Displays might include pre-Columbian Peruvian textiles, Near and Far Eastern exhibits (some dating back to 3000 BC), and rugs and carpets from Spain, South America, and the American Southwest. Other intriguing temporary exhibits cover topics

If Wilson was blind to the concerns of workers and minorities, he had a keen political eye for a broader picture, mixed with a high moral tone that brooked no argument. Inspired by his sound analysis of the mood of the American people, and perhaps also by a gut pacifism, he managed to keep America out of **World War I** until 1917. Within four months of his second inauguration, however, the country was at war, prompted ostensibly by unprovoked German attacks on American shipping, though later critics would claim that the government wanted war orders to stimulate the economy. Abandoning his pacifist stance, Wilson declared a war "for democracy" and devoted his considerable energies to ending it quickly and imposing a new moral order on the world. This manifested in his championing a **League of Nations**, an idea he took to the peace conference in Paris, seeing it as a "matter of life or death for civilization." However, the president was soon outflanked by the wilier leaders of Britain and France, who took the conference as an opportunity to punish Germany for its misdeeds and produced the **Treaty of Versailles**, which led to crushing unemployment, financial collapse, and, eventually, the rise of the Nazi party. Of course, there was no way Wilson could have foreseen such an outcome – indeed, some historians even claim that Wilson had a bout of Spanish influenza, then widespread around the world, when he signed off on some of the European leaders' more draconian measures at the Paris conference.

Returning in June 1919 to sell the League of Nations to the American people and, more important, to the Senate, which has to ratify any treaty by a two-thirds majority, Wilson undertook a draining speaking tour. After a series of blinding headaches, however, he had to cut it short. Shortly after his return to DC, on October 2, 1919, he suffered a huge stroke that half-paralyzed him.

His cherished League was finally rejected by the Senate in March 1920, but by then Wilson was almost completely incapacitated. Few people outside government were informed of this, and in what today looks suspiciously like a cover-up, his wife, Edith – sixteen years his junior – took on many of the day-to-day decisions in the White House, prompting critics to complain of a "petticoat presidency." As inflation rose and the economy slumped, **Warren Harding** was swept into power in the 1920 presidential elections, partly undoing Wilson's legacy through misrule and scandal. Wilson, old and infirm, and his wife left the White House for S Street, where crowds greeted him on the steps. He died in his home three years later, on February 3, 1924.

such as contemporary textile design and the intersection of art, craft, and fashion, with objects designed as much to hang on a wall as on a body. By the end of 2008 a new branch of the museum will be opening in the Penn Quarter, at 421 7th St NW, to accommodate the rotating exhibits and give room to a permanent collection at the Kalorama site.

7

Adams Morgan, Shaw, and Outer Northeast

ew districts represent the gap between tourist-friendly DC and the "real" DC more than **Adams Morgan** and **Shaw**, part of a broad swath of the city that is officially, though less commonly, called Mid-City. Unlike Dupont Circle or Downtown DC to the south, these areas offer little in the way of museums or official attractions, and are rarely visited by folks arriving into town on tour buses. However, for residents of the city, they offer some of the liveliest street culture, best independent shops, and richest blend of races and cultures you're likely to find along the Eastern Seaboard outside of New York. Even better, these are the essential spots for freewheeling dance clubs, rock- and punk-music venues, and cheap bars – notably without the stuffy attitudes found around Dupont Circle. With this authentic edge, however, comes a bit of diciness, and if you're coming at night it's best to take a cab between the popular stretches. Where there are plenty of people around, mainly on the lively commercial stretches of 18th Street and U Street, crime isn't as much of a problem, though you're well advised always to stay alert.

Adams Morgan is one of the few areas in the city with an inexpensive **nightlife scene**, and you should dine out at least once here, since its range of ethnic restaurants is unparalleled in the District. In Shaw, to the east, the spectre of gentrification has loomed large in the last few years. Once *the* thriving black neighborhood, and home to a vibrant music scene in the 1920s and 1930s, the area now boasts scads of new restaurants, bars, and clubs, and developers have begun building condos for the expected next wave of (mostly white) yuppies.

Beyond Adams Morgan and Shaw, the **Outer Northeast** section of DC offers a handful of scattered attractions, like the marvelous **National Arboretum** and the awe-inspiring **National Shrine of the Immaculate Conception**, at some remove from its more crime-ridden areas, and accessible in the daytime with few hassles. Several of the area's other sights are also within easy reach of the Metro system, while others will require a cab or bus ride.

National Shrine and Takoma Park ▲

Georgetown ▼

CAFES & RESTAURANTS	
14U	52
18th and U Duplex Diner	36
Amsterdam Falafelshop	19
Bardia's	27
Ben's Chili Bowl	41
Bukom Café	18
Cashion's Eat Place	14
Coppi's	50
The Diner	10
Dukem	45
El Tamarindo	39
Florida Avenue Grill	33
Grill from Ipanema	9
Harambe Café	37
Henry's Soul Café	38
Jolt 'n Bolt	56
L'Enfant	40
La Fourchette	26
Lauriol Plaza	1
Mama Ayesha's	24
Meskerem	22
Meze	16
Mixtec	54
Mocha Hut	25
Napoleon	20
Pasta Mia	21
Perry's	15
Pizza Mart	6
Saki	17
So's Your Mom	42
Tabaq Bistro	2
Tryst	47
U-topia	

BARS & CLUBS	
2:K9	48
9:30 Club	35
Bedrock Billiards	11
Black Cat	58
Blue Room	31
Bohemian Caverns	43
Bossa	12
The Saloon	44
Solly's	55
Spy Lounge	30
Toledo Lounge	23
Twins Jazz	51
Velvet Lounge	46
Heaven & Hell	29
Latin Alley	49
Madam's Organ	32
Chief Ike's Mambo Room	7
Millie and Al's	34
Polly's Café	53
Rumba Café	13
Bourbon	48
Chi-Cha Lounge	35
Chloe	58
Columbia Station	31
Habana Village	43

ACCOMMODATION	
Adam's Inn	C
Courtyard by Marriott	H
Jurys Normandy Inn	B
Kalorama Guest House	F
Washington Hilton	A
Washington Intl. Student Center	G
Windsor Inn	E
Windsor Park	D

Adams Morgan

Nowhere is gentrification changing the original, ethnic character of a Washington neighborhood faster than in **Adams Morgan**, for the last decade DC's trendiest district. With every passing month new designer restaurants, stylish bars, and hip stores take root here, sharing space with the traditional Hispanic businesses that have thrived here since the 1950s. Spanish signs and notices are still much in evidence, especially along Columbia Road, and the neighborhood certainly celebrates its heritage well at the annual **Calle 12 Festival** (July; ⓦcalle12.org) and **Adams Morgan Day** (Sept) shindigs. Along Adams Morgan's **18th Street** strip are open-to-the-sidewalk bars, restaurants, cafés, and clubs, accommodating such a frenetic and diverse mix of people that overcrowding and the odd fistfight have been known to occur. True to the neighborhood's grungier days, late-night hours for bars and clubs can sometimes see college students battling it out with bouncers, and noisome drunks bothering passers-by. You shouldn't have any troubles, though, if you come for what the district is best known for – its **food**: Adams Morgan is ground zero for new legal and illegal migrants to the US, and as a result has a wide variety of new arrivals owning and patronizing some excellent ethnic restaurants. Ethiopians are responsible for some of the most highly rated eateries, but you can devour anything here from Argentine to Vietnamese cuisine.

Adams Morgan is generally thought of as being bounded by Connecticut and Florida avenues and 16th and Harvard streets, though in practice most visitors see little more than the few blocks on either side of the central **Columbia Road/18th Street intersection**, where most of the bars and restaurants are situated. The eastern boundary of the neighborhood is marked by 16th Street and Meridian Hill Park – at night, don't stray farther east than Ontario Road, beyond which it can get a little dodgy. To the west, the neighborhood boundary is formed by the **National Zoo** and Connecticut Avenue NW, which is where you'll find the nearest **Metro**: from the Woodley Park–Zoo Metro station on Connecticut Avenue, it's a fifteen-minute walk across the striking Neoclassical Duke Ellington Bridge to the Columbia Road/18th Street junction. From the Dupont Circle Metro stop it's a steep twenty-minute hike up 19th Street to Columbia Road. By **bus**, take the #L2 from McPherson Square, which travels up 18th Street to Calvert Street; alternatively, #42 goes via Metro Center (10th and F), H Street, Connecticut Avenue, Dupont Circle, and up to Columbia Road. Note that by the end of 2008, the DC Circulator (see "Basics," p.31) is due to have a new line up and running that will connect this district with Dupont Circle and down to the convention center – not that Adams Morgan ever sees conventioneers.

Some history

The neighborhood's **gentrification** is simply turning Adams Morgan full circle. In the late nineteenth century, its hilly, rural reaches were colonized by wealthy Washingtonians looking for a select address near the power-housing of Dupont Circle. Impressive apartment buildings were erected in the streets off Columbia Road, boasting expansive views and connected to downtown by streetcar. Until World War II some of the city's most prominent politicians and business people lived here, and many of their mansions survive intact. After the war, the city's housing shortage meant that many of the area's signature **row houses** were converted into rooming houses and small apartments; well-to-do families moved farther out into the suburbs and were replaced by a growing blue-collar population, black and white, and, crucially, by increasing numbers of Latin American and Caribbean immigrants in the 1960s. Concerned that the area was becoming too segregated, a local group fashioned a symbolic name from two local elementary schools: one all-white (John Quincy Adams), one all-black (Thomas P. Morgan). The name "Adams-Morgan" served until recent years, when convenience and familiarity led to the dropping of the hyphen.

Today, Adams Morgan is regarded as the most racially mixed neighborhood in the city, and for the most part there's a good-natured atmosphere in the streets, where grocery stores and corner cafés sit alongside arty boutiques and sharp bars. Images of Adams Morgan frequently pop up in movies: *In the Line of Fire*, *Dave*, *A Few Good Men*, and *Enemy of the State* all feature scenes shot in the neighborhood, though the publicity hasn't led to many tourists being aware of the place, unless they're here to seek out a one-of-a-kind ethnic diner or hear the pulsing beat of a rock or dance show. Adams Morgan's Hispanic legacy is at its strongest in the stretch of Columbia Road northeast of 18th Street, a good place to check out the street stalls, jewelry sellers, and thrift stores; the **Saturday market** (May–Dec 8am–1pm; ☎301/587-2248) occupies the southwestern plaza where the two arteries meet.

The Kalorama Triangle

The streets of the eastern side of Adams Morgan provide a generous amount of architectural interest. This is especially true in the **Kalorama Triangle**, between Connecticut Avenue and Columbia Road, which, like its neighbor to the southwest, Kalorama (see p.204), is a well-heeled district that has always been to some degree the province of old money. This area, though, takes the genteel Kalorama look and expands it into high-rise historic-revival blocks, with many fine architectural examples built in the first three decades of the twentieth century. These are almost too numerous to mention, but for a quick glance, check out the Spanish Mission Revival block of the historic **Woodward Apartments**, 2311 Connecticut Ave, or the **neo-Georgian** and **Roman-esque row houses** at the 2300 block of 19th St and 1800 block of Mintwood place, respectively.

At the southern end of the Triangle, the **Wyoming Building**, 2022 Columbia Rd NW, is a classic example of the marvelous apartment houses built in the early twentieth century, its mosaic floor, molded ceilings, and marble reception room with graceful Ionic columns forming one of DC's loveliest interiors. The Eisenhowers lived here between 1927 and 1935, and following an attempt to demolish it in the 1970s, it was converted to condos that now regularly sell for upward of $1 million. Adjacent on the south side, at 1919 Connecticut Ave NW, is the culprit behind the Wyoming's near-demolition, the **Washington Hilton**, a charmless modern block that was eyeing an expansion attempt in those days. A few years later, it became much more famous as the spot where, in the driveway roundabout, John Hinckley Jr fired six shots at Ronald Reagan in a 1981 assassination attempt, leaving the president and three others seriously wounded and his press secretary, James Brady, permanently paralyzed. Across the street, the grand Neoclassi-cism of the 1911 **Lothrop Mansion**, no. 2001, somehow seems fit for the Russian trade delegation now occupying it, while just to the north, the Italian Renaissance–style **Altamont Building**, 1901 Wyoming Ave NW, at 20th St, is visually striking with its rooftop terrace and squat towers, barrel-vaulted and gilded lobby, and an adjoining parlor featuring original, Old English–style furniture.

A bit away from the Triangle, but most glamorous of all the Adams Morgan buildings, is the cupola-topped Beaux-Arts majesty of the **Ontario Building**, up north at 2853 Ontario Rd (at 18th), built between 1903 and 1906. Its roll call of famous former residents includes five-star generals Douglas MacArthur and Chester Nimitz; journalist Janet Cooke, whose Pulitzer Prize-winning story about youth and drugs was later discredited; and *Washington Post* scribe Bob Woodward. Carl Bernstein, Woodward's partner in the Watergate investigation, also lived in Adams Morgan, in the much less grandiose **Biltmore** apartment building, 1940 Biltmore St, off 19th St, just a couple of blocks south.

Along 18th Street

South of Columbia Road, **18th Street** is the center of DC's melting pot, where yuppies from the Kalorama Triangle drop in to sample the funky vibe and snap up streetwear for a song; venturesome gays and hipsters from Dupont Circle come to imbibe at bars and browse in secondhand bookstores; and African Americans from Shaw visit to support independent boutiques and other minority businesses. The broad mix of visitors is equaled by the wide range of restaurants and stores – including pizza joints, ethnic diners, Latin botanicas, junk emporia, bistros, astrologers and palm-readers, antiques sellers, vintage-clothing dealers, book and music shops, coffeehouses, and fringe theaters. The scene is presided over by lines of **Victorian row houses** in various states of disrepair or renovation, with increasing numbers of artists' and yuppies' lofts adding more change and ferment to the neighborhood. The architecture here is more eye-catching than historically unique. To see more classic buildings, venture a few blocks east toward Meridian Hill, preferably in the daytime.

▲ 18th Street, Adams Morgan

Columbia Heights

In some ways, the hilltop precinct of **Columbia Heights**, roughly between Florida Avenue and Columbia Road along 16th Street NW, represents the creeping eastern edge of the gentrification shaping Adams Morgan – though the area is still edgy enough to dissuade you from walking here after dark. In the heart of the neighborhood, at Columbia Road and 16th Street, the Columbia Heights Metro stop is a large reason for the changing demographics of the area, with "urban pioneers" of all races coming in and refurbishing the historic structures into shops, condos, and restaurants. Bold tourists will find this slice of DC's changing social landscape worth a look, especially if they're interested in the finer points of classic Washington **architecture**. Perhaps the most striking is the **Tivoli Theatre**, just northeast of the Metro at 14th Street at Park Road, a 1924 movie palace built in the Italian Renaissance Revival style and still a considerable anchor to the area's street life. Recently restored, it's been reopened as the **GALA Hispanic Theatre** (℡1-800/494-8497, Ⓦwww .galatheatre.org), presenting lively, Latin-themed productions.

Given that most other things worth seeing lie further south on or around **16th Street**, it may be tempting simply to combine a stroll to this neighborhood with one through the northern reaches of New Downtown along the same street. But, again, caution is advised – what looks convenient on a map can involve treks through unexpectedly down-at-the-heel or dangerous pockets. If you're not familiar with the turf under foot, tooling around in a rental car or taking the Metro is probably the safest alternative.

Meridian Hill Park

Although it might be hard to believe these days, the area around **Meridian Hill Park**, between Florida Avenue and Euclid Street, was, in the mid-twentieth century, one of the swankiest areas of DC – its townhouses and condos sought out by the swells of high society. As with so much in the city, though, the riots of 1968 changed everything, and the panicked rush of white flight, brought on by the proximity to burned-out Shaw, emptied the neighborhood of its upper- and upper-middle-class residents and most of its investment capital. There's been a small rebound since then, especially evident in the graceful contours of this fetching greenspace. Although the place has the informal moniker of Malcolm X Park, it gives a broad hint of what things were like in older days: here you'll find nothing less than a twelve-acre French-style **garden**, finished in 1930, with smartly designed greenery and pathways, well-balanced terraces, and a central series of thirteen stepped waterfalls. The park boasts a few other oddments – such as a strange set of **statues**, depicting Joan of Arc, Dante, and one of America's worst presidents, James Buchanan – but the houses surrounding the park are the more eye-popping ornaments.

Around the park

That the streets around the park hold such stunning mansions is largely due to **Mary Henderson**, wife of former senator John Henderson, who felt that either the White House should be relocated to the area or the Lincoln Memorial erected here. Her own marvelous fortress, known as the Henderson Castle, is no longer standing, but its legacy can be seen in some of the homes nearby. One such standout is the so-called **Pink Palace**, on the north side of the park at 2600 16th St, which has been painted many colors but still sports its original Venetian Renaissance windows and overall design. The **Benjamin**

Warder House, across the street, is also hard to miss. This stocky version of a Romanesque castle was designed by H.H. Richardson and has been taken apart, rebuilt, and renovated several times since it first went up in 1888; it's now a luxury apartment building (for a look, call ☎202/332-1717 or visit ⓦwww .wardermansion.com). The former **Embassy of France**, a block south at 2460 16th St, is a stunning 1908 version of a High Baroque palace, while the current Ecuadorian Embassy, 2535 15th St, is done up in smart French Second Empire attire. Further north, a trio of delightful historic-revival churches, from the 1920s and 1930s, cluster around the intersection of 16th Street and Columbia Road; **National Baptist Memorial Church** is the most arresting of the three, with its colonnaded combination of Baroque and Neoclassical elements.

Meridian International Center

1624–1630 Crescent Place NW ☎202/667-6800 or 202/939-5568, ⓦwww.meridian.org; Columbia Heights Metro. Wed–Sun 2–5pm. Free.

The **Meridian International Center** regularly exhibits the work of global artists and has displays on international themes related to science, culture, and education, as well as public lectures and themed concerts by musicians from selected countries (call ☎202/939-5568 for details). However, the interest really lies in the pair of historic-revival mansions that play host to the center and its displays. **Meridian House**, designed by John Russell Pope, was the residence of Irwin Laughlin, a high-powered Spanish ambassador and steel heir who was especially fond of the eighteenth-century French style. The neo-Baroque home features limestone walls, formal European-style gardens, priceless antiques, sculpted Neoclassical busts, and assorted curiosities and treasures gathered from a lifetime's worth of globe-hopping. Next door, the English Georgian–style **White–Meyer House** is where you'll find the center's displays of worthy international art, but the focus here is again the architecture. This is another revivalist work of Pope's for an ambassador (to France), its elegant symmetry and balance and Ionic columns lending it a vaguely Classical feel.

Shaw

East of Adams Morgan and Meridian Hill, the historic district of **Shaw** – roughly between U and M streets and 13th Street and New Jersey Avenue – is one of the oldest residential areas in DC. You can have a festive time in a night out on **U Street** and stroll around some of its historic sights and landmarks. Well-scrubbed chain merchants coexist with storefront churches and businesses that have been around for decades, and the district is racially and ethnically as rich and diverse as any place in the city. Outside the main stretch of U Street, which is mostly safe and engaging, you'll find some strange juxtapositions, as the wider neighborhood is now in the throes of gentrification and is something of a patchwork. Here, hip and lively bars are just blocks from grim pockets of urban poverty, you're as likely to run into a street hustler or homeless person as you are a sightseer, and fancy condos occupying remodeled row-house blocks sit cheek-by-jowl with dilapidated wrecks. It's a strange and fascinating blend, but only those truly interested in the Shaw environment or architecture should go exploring (in the daytime) beyond the tourist zone. A good way to see the neighborhood is to take a **walking tour** or sign up for "**Duke Ellington's Neighborhood**," a summer bus tour that includes visiting several local sites (see p.31).

Some history

First settled by immigrant whites who built shanty housing along 7th Street after the Civil War, the area became majority black by the turn of the century, as thousands of black immigrants from the rural Southern states came here in search of work and to escape the grinding racism of the deeper South. Together with all-black **Howard University** (founded in 1867), Griffith Stadium at 2401 Georgia Ave (now Howard University Hospital) added real vibrancy to this corner of DC in the early twentieth century with its hugely popular black baseball games.

Seventh Street was one of the booming city's main commercial arteries and remained busy during the Depression with pool halls, churches, cafés, theaters,

Duke Ellington (1899–1974)

The brilliant pianist, composer, and bandleader **Edward Kennedy Ellington** was born in Washington, DC (on 22nd St NW), and grew up in Shaw at 1212 T St. A precocious child, nicknamed "**Duke**," at 15 he was playing ragtime in scratch bands at local cafés; he wrote his first composition, *Soda Fountain Rag*, in 1914. Also an accomplished young artist, Ellington turned down a scholarship to New York's Pratt Institute to instead form the Washingtonians, a trio with which he played extensively in DC before making the big move to New York in 1923. By 1927, the trio had expanded to become **the Duke Ellington Orchestra**; a year later, it was a permanent fixture at Harlem's **Cotton Club**, where Ellington made his reputation in five tumultuous years, writing early, atmospheric classics like *Mood Indigo* and *Creole Love Call*. Ellington and his orchestra appeared in their first feature film, *Check and Double Check*, in 1930, and by 1932, they had made more than 200 recordings. Established as one of America's finest jazz composers and bandleaders, Ellington set off on his first European tour in 1933, when he took the continent by storm. The following decade saw the penning of his most celebrated works – from *Sophisticated Lady* and *Take the 'A' Train* to *Don't Get Around Much Anymore*.

The Ellington style was unmistakable: melodious ballads and stomping swing pieces alike employed inventive rhythmic devices and novel key changes to inimitable creative effect. In 1943 Ellington was the first popular musician to perform at Carnegie Hall (where he premiered the ambitious *Black, Brown and Beige*), and despite a decline in **Big Band** popularity after World War II, he managed to keep both his band and personal following largely intact. Ellington spent much of the 1950s and 1960s touring and diversifying his output – recording with younger artists like **Max Roach** and **Charles Mingus**, writing soundtracks for (and appearing in) movies, and composing extended pieces that mixed jazz with classical music. In 1969 he received the **Presidential Medal of Freedom** for his services to music and the arts. By the time of his death in 1974, Duke Ellington had arranged or composed more than six thousand works. Duke married Edna Thompson in 1918 and they had one son, Mercer, though the couple later separated. Mercer went on to play trumpet in his father's band and, after Duke's death, led the Duke Ellington Orchestra. For all these reasons and more, Duke is often regarded as America's greatest composer, of jazz or otherwise.

In DC, the city remembers one of its favorite sons with the **Duke Ellington Birthday Celebration**, a weeklong festival held each year around April 20 in the week leading up to his birthday, April 29. The elegant form of the 1935 Calvert Street Bridge between Woodley Park and Adams Morgan was renamed **Duke Ellington Bridge** in his honor, and the city established the **Duke Ellington School of the Arts** in Georgetown (35th and R sts NW; ☎202/282-0123, ⓦwww.ellingtonschool.org). This public high school offers a four-year course of study for artistically talented youths; free tours are available once a month (except June–Sept) – call for details.

and social clubs; a shopping strip developed on 14th Street; and **U Street** evolved into the "Black Broadway," with theaters like the Lincoln and the Howard putting on splashy vaudeville shows and jazz concerts, among many other kinds of entertainment. For years the neighborhood was known simply as "14th and U," eventually taking the name "Shaw" after **Colonel Robert Gould Shaw**, the (white) commander of the Union Army's first black regiment (the Massachusetts 54th) – the unit featured in the film *Glory*.

Segregation – entrenched in Washington since the late nineteenth century – ironically secured Shaw's prosperity, since black residents stayed within the neighborhood to shop and socialize. However, news of the assassination of Dr Martin Luther King Jr in 1968 sparked three days of arson, rioting, and looting that destroyed businesses and lives along 7th, 14th, and H streets. A dozen people were killed, millions of dollars lost, and the confidence of middle-class blacks jolted so severely that many of them joined middle-class whites in fleeing to the suburbs, leaving behind a fringe of the poor and desperate. Though these weren't the first riots to tear Shaw apart – in the summer of 1919, prompted by the violent antics of vigilante white ex-soldiers, five days of rioting here and in southwest Washington left thirty people dead – it took two decades before Shaw began clawing its way back.

In the first decade of the 21st century, the signs of revival are unmistakable – revitalized U Street has a Metro station and once again figures on the city's nightlife scene, while **14th Street**, continuing south to Logan Circle (see p.195), has blossomed as an alternative theater district, and apartment blocks that once stood abandoned have re-emerged as upscale (black and white) yuppie condos. The main source of friction, as ever in urban America, is between the African American old-timers who saw the neighborhood through its worst days and typically white newcomers who have little knowledge of or interest in the historic character or culture of the place.

U Street and around

The only part of Shaw most visitors see is the thriving section of **U Street** in the blocks near the U Street–Cardozo Metro station, where more trendy bars and clubs move in with every passing year. Between the world wars, U Street ranked second only to New York's Harlem as America's center of black entertainment. Across from the Metro, at the splendid **Lincoln Theatre**, 1215 U St (ⓦ www.thelincolntheatre.org), built in 1921, vaudeville shows and movies were bolstered by appearances of the most celebrated jazz performers of the day: Count Basie, Billie Holiday, Cab Calloway, Ella Fitzgerald, and DC's own Duke Ellington among them. The theater now serves as a

The U Link Shuttle

The DC **Metro** system makes it easy to access the highlights of Adams Morgan and its surrounding areas. Starting at the Woodley Park–Zoo Metro station, the **U Link Shuttle** (line #98; 30min trip) travels along Calvert, 18th, and U streets from Adams Morgan until it reaches the U Street–Cardozo Metro Station. The fare is only 25¢, though you must pay the full $1.25 if you want a transfer to another bus line; hours are Mon–Fri 6pm–3am, Sat 10am–3am, Sun 6pm–midnight. If you don't have a car, this is definitely the best way for clubgoers and imbibers to travel through a dicey area at night – cheaper than a cab, safer than on foot – and it manages to cross a rather wide expanse of the city that lacks subway service.

performing arts center (see p.313). Next door, *Ben's Chili Bowl* (see "Eating" chapter see p.291) is a forty-year-old institution frequented by the likes of Bill Cosby and Denzel Washington.

The dashing **Howard Theatre**, several blocks east of the U Street scene at 624 T St (Ⓦ www.howardtheatre.org), opened in 1910 as the first theater in DC built strictly for black patrons, though that didn't stop hip whites from flocking here to see the shows. An unknown **Ella Fitzgerald** won an open-mike contest here; 1940s big bands filled the auditorium; and later artists such as James Brown, Smokey Robinson, Gladys Knight, and Martha and the Vandellas lined up to appear; in 1962 the **Supremes** played their first headlining gig here. The theater survived the riots in one piece but closed soon after; today it's been renovated as a performing-arts venue, and promises to reopen to the public by the end of 2008.

African American Civil War Memorial and Museum

1200 U St NW Ⓣ 202/667-2667, Ⓦ www.afroamcivilwar.org; U Street–Cardozo Metro. Mon–Fri 10am–5pm, Sat 10am–2pm.

Leave the Metro by the 10th Street exit and you'll emerge near the **African American Civil War Memorial**, one of the country's few monuments honoring African American soldiers who fought for the Union. *The Spirit of Freedom* sculpture stands in the center of a granite-paved plaza, partially encircled by a Wall of Honor, along which you'll find the names of the 209,145 United States Colored Troops (and their 7000 white officers) who served. President Lincoln sanctioned the creation of African American regiments in 1862, and slaves, former slaves, and freedmen joined the fight. The rush to enlist was best summed up by Frederick Douglass, whose words "Who would be free themselves must strike the blow. Better even die free than to live slaves" are inscribed at the site. Sadly, these brave troops were not included in the celebratory Grand Review of the Union Armies along Pennsylvania Avenue after the war's end, an early sign that the battle for equality had only begun.

Three blocks west of the memorial, in the 1903 Italianate **True Reformer Building** – which was designed, built, and financed by African Americans – the associated museum tells the soldiers' largely unknown story as part of its permanent exhibition, "Slavery to Freedom: Civil War to Civil Rights." Composed largely of photographs and documents, the collection begins its African American history with the original bill of sale for an 11-year-old girl. Other features include a "Descendants' Registry," where visitors can look up relatives who may have served with the US Colored Troops, and a "Computer Search For Your Soldier," which employs the Civil War Soldiers and Sailors Names Index to identify troops along with the history of their regiments.

Howard University

2400 6th St NW Ⓣ 202/806-8009 for campus tours, Ⓦ www.howard.edu; Shaw–Howard University Metro.

Prestigious **Howard University** – named for General Otis Howard, commissioner of the Freedmen's Bureau – was established in 1867 by a church missionary society to provide a school for freed blacks after the Civil War. Its first faculties were in law, music, medicine, and theology, though today hundreds of subjects are taken by almost 15,000 students from over a hundred countries. Famous Howard alumni include Pulitzer Prize–winning author Toni Morrison, opera diva Jessye Norman, Supreme Court justice Thurgood Marshall, former mayor of New York City David Dinkins, UN ambassador Andrew Young, activist Stokely Carmichael, and football goalkeeper Shaka Hislop.

Sadly, only one of the original campus buildings remains – **Howard Hall**, 607 Howard Place, a handsome French Second Empire structure built in the 1860s. Many of the other buildings are historic revivals from the 1930s, and few are better than the **Founders Library**, a gigantic edifice modeled after Philadelphia's Independence Hall. The library houses the **Moorland-Spingarn Research Center** (Mon–Thurs 9am–4.45pm, Fri 9am–4.30pm; ☎202/806-4237), which contains the country's largest selection of literature relating to black history and culture, with some 3000 books, articles, and other artifacts. In the library's Wesley Room, the university **museum** (Mon–Fri 9am–4.30pm; ☎202/806-7240) presents rotating exhibits of its holdings, which may include items like African icons and artifacts, memorabilia and antiques from the university's early days, and historic photos and recollections of the Shaw neighborhood and the city in general.

LeDroit Park

Short of money just a decade after its inauguration, the university sold a plot of land (in the rough triangle formed by W Street and Florida and Rhode Island avenues) to developers, who built an exclusive suburb known as **LeDroit Park**. James McGill, in the English country house tradition, created 64 neo-Gothic, French Second Empire, and Victorian homes, of which fifty remain; alongside, row houses still exist in their original brick and terracotta state, and the neighborhood has a whimsical flavor that has withstood decades of decay and indifference to be at least partially refurbished as a fascinating urban village. (It's accessible from a convenient **Metro station**, Shaw–Howard University, three blocks west.)

White university staff were the first to take up residence here, but well-to-do black families moved into the brick row houses built in the 1880s and 1890s. By 1920 LeDroit Park was a fashionable black neighborhood, and it's been declared a historic district. The best-preserved group of original houses is along the 400 block of U Street, though other pockets from the 300 to 500 blocks of T Street also exist. Prominent black citizens continue to be associated with the area – the family of DC's first black mayor, Walter Washington, owned a house here for years, along with Nobel Prize winner Ralph Bunche and Duke Ellington, while Jesse Jackson currently maintains a property here. More curiously, the historically protected landmark of the **Mary Church Terrell House**, 326 T St, named after the activist for racial and gender equality, is a simple Victorian that appears sliced in half by a large blade. Although now shambling, its unusual asymmetrical design is still apparent – probably the result of an unfinished construction project.

Strivers' Section

Not part of Shaw per se, but rather standing as its own independent neighborhood between Dupont Circle, Shaw, and Adams Morgan (bounded by Florida Avenue and 16th and Swann streets), is another historically black area – the **Strivers' Section**. From the 1870s, these Victorian row houses attracted many notable African Americans, including poet **Langston Hughes**, who lived at 1749 S St and worked for the *Washington Sentinel* in the 1920s, and **Frederick Douglass**, who occupied three of the five Second Empire units at 2000 17th Street in the middle part of the 1870s. Although not as architecturally distinguished as the homes of LeDroit Park, those in the section do convey a fetching Victorian-era style in several eye-catching forms, from grand Romanesque (2102 17th St) to Italianate (1700 T St) to Neoclassical (1830 17th St) – with a good number being historically protected and preserved. Some have even been converted to condos and now reach prices of up to $1 million.

Outer Northeast

Conventional wisdom dictates that visitors stick to the central neighborhoods when visiting DC, but a number of unique, fascinating sites make it worth the effort to venture to some farther-flung parts of the city. Spread across the Outer Northeast section of town are the expansive **National Arboretum**, the monumental **National Shrine of the Immaculate Conception**, the quaint and historic **Takoma Park**, and more. For some sights a car will be necessary, for others there's a Metro station within blocks. Keep in mind, though, that none of these spots is very near the others, and in between you may in fact run across some of those down-at-the-heel neighborhoods you've been warned to stay away from – so take heed.

National Shrine of the Immaculate Conception

400 Michigan Ave NE ☏202/526-8300, ⓦwww.nationalshrine.com; Brookland Metro. Daily Nov–March 7am–6pm, April–Oct 7am–7pm.

Two of DC's most interesting spots are easily accessible by Metro heading north from Shaw (with a transfer at the Fort Totten station). The first sight is the largest Catholic church in the US, the **National Shrine of the Immaculate Conception**, which was built in the 1950s. Its grand Byzantine design, looming dome with multicolored mosaics, and towering Roman arch above the entrance would alone make the site an eye-grabber, but added to these features are a sleek bell tower, lovely bas-relief panels, several large buttresses, and a huge circular Celtic *triqnetra*, symbolizing the Trinity – and that's just the exterior. Inside, the church is astoundingly big, with some 75 chapels or alcoves for statues, intricate mosaics showing a fight against a seven-headed serpent (among other scenes), a big pipe organ and even larger baldachin with four great marble columns, and, looming above it all – its eyes seeming to follow you around the church – a jaw-dropping mosaic of Jesus clad in a striking red robe, with jets of flame shooting out from his golden halo. (Guided tours are given Mon–Sat 9am–11am & 1–3pm, Sun 1.30–4pm.)

Adjacent to the Shrine is the **Catholic University** campus, along with the **Pope John Paul II Cultural Center**, 3900 Harewood Rd (Tues & Thurs–Sat 10am–5pm, Sun noon–5pm; $5; ☏202/635-5400, ⓦwww.jp2cc.org), which presents exhibits on art, architecture, culture, and faith, and provides information on the life and works of the head of the Roman Catholic Church from 1978 to 2005, the second longest serving modern pope.

President Lincoln and Soldiers' Home National Monument

3700 N Capitol St ☏202/829-0436, ⓦwww.lincolncottage.org; Brookland Metro. Call or check website for entry details.

Near the National Shrine, just west across North Capitol Street, the awkwardly named **President Lincoln and Soldiers' Home National Monument** is set among 250 acres largely devoted to serving the needs of retired soldiers. For visitors, though, its centerpiece is a recent feat of preservation that opened to the public in February 2008, the Gothic Revival–style **Lincoln Cottage**, which dates from 1843. As much Colonial farmhouse as anything, it initially served to house veterans of the Mexican-American War in 1851. It got its current moniker due to its use by Abraham Lincoln as a presidential retreat: he summered here from 1862 to 1864, at the height of the Civil War, and even wrote a draft of the Emancipation Proclamation on the premises. The story of that famed document occupies pride of place in the second-story Emancipation Room, filled with mementos of the president's career and legacy, including a reproduction of the desk where he wrote the monumental imperative. Elsewhere, you can get more information on the 16th president's role in the war and the history of this and other old soldiers' homes. Sited on one of Washington's highest peaks, the cottage was undoubtedly a source of inspiration for Lincoln, who was perhaps comforted by the irony that his arch-nemesis, Confederate president Jefferson Davis, had, as a US senator, been an ardent proponent of building such retreats in the 1850s and thus inadvertently funded the president's favorite spot during the war.

Takoma Park, MD

Take the northbound Red Line two stops from the Brookland station and you'll come to **Takoma Park**, **Maryland**, America's first planned suburb for urban commuters, as well as the onetime hub of the Seventh Day Adventist Church. Today it is one of the country's most avowedly progressive communities and is still largely intact with its original 1880s buildings and design. Some of the stylish historic homes worth checking out include the **Bliss House**, 7116 Maple Ave, an Italianate charmer made of wood but with a painted brick-and-stone facade; the Victorian bungalows along Willow Avenue north of Tulip Street; the **Zigzag Art Deco structure** at 7000 Carroll Ave, now an antique dealer; and the grand **Cady Lee Mansion**, Chestnut Ave at Eastern, the best of several Queen Anne buildings, rich with gables, gingerbread detailing, a wraparound porch, and slate roof, and which occasionally holds public events (info at ☎202/207-3333, ⓦwww.cadylee.org). The Takoma Metro station is right in the middle of this area (on the border between DC and Maryland), which is an excellent spot for an hour or two of wandering. For neighborhood maps and information, including a free homes tour the first Sunday in May, visit ⓦwww.historictakoma.org.

National Arboretum

3501 New York Ave NE ☎202/245-2726, ⓦwww.usna.usda.gov. Daily 8am–4.30pm, summer Sat & Sun closes 5pm. Free.

Nestled along the Anacostia River roughly two miles northeast of the Capitol building, the sprawling **National Arboretum** is an oasis of green amid an otherwise grim part of the District. The best time to visit is from mid-April to October, when plenty of plants are in bloom and **tram tours** are offered (April–Oct Sat & Sun 10.30am, 11.30am and on the hour 1–4pm; $4); these forty-minute journeys meander along the park's 9.5 miles of roadways past ponds, gardens, and plant collections, taking in everything from colorful bursts of azaleas to the woodlands of Japan. The best way to get to the park is by car or cab; you may also take the bus, though it's a bit of a slog, involving a subway ride to the Stadium-Armory station followed by a transfer to the #B2 line. At the entrance at 24th and R streets (just off the bus line's dropoff on Bladens-burg Road) you'll find the **visitor center**, where you can pick up a visitor's guide, which includes a map, seasonal plant information, and descriptions of the gardens.

Well worth a visit, the surreal gathering of "**Capitol Columns**" stands in a meadow at the heart of the grounds, supporting open sky. Once part of the US Capitol, the sandstone pillars, crafted in the Neoclassical Corinthian style, presided over every presidential inauguration from Jackson to Eisenhower. They were effectively put out to pasture in the 1950s in order to correct a flaw in the

▲ The National Arboretum's "Capitol Columns"

Capitol's design, which caused the columns to appear mismatched relative to the size of the dome. Other arboretum highlights include the **Dogwood Collection**, best seen in bloom on a late spring afternoon; the **National Grove of State Trees**, a thirty-acre site where trees native to each state (plus the District of Columbia) grow on individual plots; and the clumsily named **Dwarf and Slow-Growing Conifer Collection**, basically a set of little pines, spruces, and firs that make for an off-kilter hillside landscape.

Those preferring a short, self-guided walking tour can take in the sights closest to the administration building. Here, in addition to the **National Herb Garden**, the largest of its type in the country, you'll find the arboretum's most popular destination, the renowned **National Bonsai and Penjing Museum** (daily 10am–3.30pm), which celebrates the ancient Chinese and Japanese art form of growing tiny trees, with selections from Asia as well as North America. Even if you have no interest in this sort of thing, the odd, sprightly array of miniature plants is really worth a look, with some of the branches and blooms gnarled and twisted almost to a grotesque degree.

Kenilworth Aquatic Gardens

1550 Anacostia Ave NE ⓣ 202/426-6905, ⓦ www.nps.gov/kepa; Deanwood Metro. Daily 7am–4pm. Free.

Well off the beaten path, **Kenilworth Aquatic Gardens** is a National Park on the eastern fringe of the District, and definitely worth a look if you're interested in horticulture or natural preserves. Set on seven hundred acres of protected marshlands, the twelve-acre gardens are rich with water lilies and lotuses, and you can take an up-close view of them on an elevated **boardwalk** that hovers over the waterline, or get here by way of canoe from the Anacostia River during high tide. Alternatively, there are several good paths for exploring this wet terrain, with its many ponds and pools, as you're able to see a pristine part of the river – hard to imagine in other parts of the District. The lilies are in bloom from May through September, but are at their height in late July, when the park's **Waterlily Festival** provides a very good reason to visit. While the gardens are accessible by the I-295 freeway, you can also reach them by taking the Metro to Deanwood station a few blocks south.

Upper Northwest

I
n the heights above Georgetown, running up to the District's border, the smart neighborhoods of **Upper Northwest** constitute some of the most exclusive territory in Washington. The white upper- and middle-class flight up Connecticut, Wisconsin, and Massachusetts avenues began when a number of nineteenth-century presidents made the cool reaches of rural **Woodley Park** – across Duke Ellington Bridge from Adams Morgan – their summer home; Grover Cleveland later bought a stone cottage farther north in an area that today is called **Cleveland Park**. Few others could afford the time and expense involved in living a four-mile carriage ride from the city center until the arrival in the 1890s of the streetcar; within three decades both Woodley Park and Cleveland Park had become bywords for fashionable, out-of-town living, replete with apartment buildings designed by the era's top architects. The tone is no less swish today, with a series of ritzy suburbs stretching into Maryland – on the DC side of the border, **Tenleytown** and **Friendship Heights** have no proper attractions but offer a few shopping and dining options, notably a number of malls.

Elsewhere in the Upper Northwest you'll find the **National Zoo**, part of the Smithsonian Institution; **Washington National Cathedral**, the sixth-largest cathedral in the world; and the wooded expanse of **Rock Creek Park**, the biggest and most enjoyable of the city's greenspaces. Given the elevation of this area, and the rather strenuous effort you'll need to get around it, you're advised to take the **Metro Red Line**, which runs underneath the area in some of the country's deepest subway channels. Alternative routes are to take **Bus** #L2, which runs up Connecticut Avenue from McPherson Square; #L1, also along Connecticut, connecting the National Mall with Cleveland Park; and buses #30, #32, #34, #35, and #36, which travel up Wisconsin Avenue from Georgetown to Friendship Heights, passing the National Cathedral along the way.

Woodley Park

The first Upper Northwest neighborhood you'll encounter – either north from Georgetown on Wisconsin Avenue or west from Adams Morgan on Calvert Street – is **Woodley Park**, marked at the intersection of Calvert and Connecticut Avenue with a pair of wondrous hotels that give a hint of the serious money that lurks in the surrounding hills. In 1918, architect Harry L. Wardman, who designed many of the apartment buildings and townhouses here, created the massive **Wardman Park Hotel**, Connecticut Ave NW and Woodley Rd (see p.271),

8

UPPER NORTHWEST | Woodley Park

221

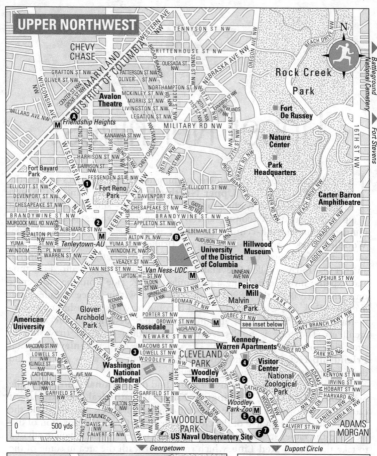

UPPER NORTHWEST

CHEVY CHASE

Rock Creek Park

Avalon Theatre

Friendship Heights

Fort De Russey

MILITARY RD NW

Nature Center

Park Headquarters

Fort Bayard Park

Fort Reno Park

Carter Barron Amphitheatre

Tenleytown-AU

University of the District of Columbia

Hillwood Museum

Van Ness-UDC

Peirce Mill

Malvin Park

Glover Archbold Park

American University

Rosedale

Kennedy-Warren Apartments

see inset below

Washington National Cathedral

CLEVELAND PARK

Visitor Center

Woodley Mansion

National Zoological Park

Woodley Park-Zoo

WOODLEY PARK

US Naval Observatory Site

ADAMS MORGAN

0   500 yds

▼ Georgetown   ▼ Dupont Circle

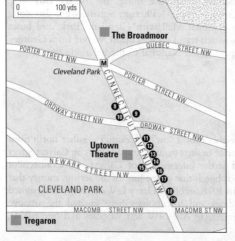

0   100 yds

The Broadmoor

PORTER STREET NW

Cleveland Park

QUEBEC STREET NW

PORTER STREET NW

ORDWAY STREET NW

ORDWAY STREET NW

Uptown Theatre

NEWARK STREET NW

CLEVELAND PARK

Tregaron

MACOMB STREET NW

CAFÉS & RESTAURANTS

Ardeo	19
Cactus Cantina	3
Firehook Bakery	14
Indique	8
Kuma	2
Lebanese Taverna	4
Morty's Delicatessen	1
Nam Viet	12
New Heights	5
Open City	7
Sabores	11
Sala Thai	9
Spices	16
Vace	18
Yanni's Greek Taverna	10

BARS & CLUBS

Aroma	13
Ireland's Four Fields	15
Nanny O'Brien's	17
Zoo Bar	6

ACCOMMODATION

Days Inn	B
Embassy Suites	A
Kalorama Guest House	C
Marriott Wardman Park	E
Omni Shoreham	F
Woodley Park Guest House	D

another gem to add to a collection that would later include the Hay-Adams Hotel and the old British Embassy. This red-brick, vaguely Colonial Revival giant has a tower that still dominates the local skyline and attracts high-profile politicians and social butterflies who entertain guests in the grand public rooms and rent apartments for themselves. Across on Calvert Street, a second landmark, the hybrid Art Deco–style **Shoreham** hotel (now an Omni; see p.271), was built in 1930 for $4 million. Since then it's hosted an inaugural ball or gala for every president from FDR to George W. Bush; here President Truman played poker, JFK courted Jackie, Nixon announced his first Cabinet, and, in the celebrated **Blue Room**, Judy Garland, Marlene Dietrich, Bob Hope, and Frank Sinatra entertained the swells.

To check out where relatively staid nineteenth-century presidents passed their summers, head up Connecticut Avenue to Cathedral Avenue and walk west past 29th Street to the **Woodley Mansion**, now the Maret School. This white stucco Georgian was built in 1800 for Philip Barton Key, whose nephew Francis later penned "The Star-Spangled Banner." Its elevation meant that it was a full ten degrees cooler in the summer than downtown, and presidents Van Buren, Tyler, and Buchanan needed no second invitation to spend their summers here. Its last private inhabitant was Henry Stimson, secretary of War under both FDR and Truman, who assisted in the management of World War II from his study, now part of the school's library.

US Naval Observatory

Massachusetts Ave NW at Observatory Circle ℡ 202/762-1467, ⊛ www.usno.navy.mil; no close Metro. Tours every other Mon night only 8.30–10pm, reserve several months in advance by fax at ℻ 202/762-1489 or on the website. Free.

Half a mile southeast of Woodley Mansion, located where 34th Street reaches Massachusetts Avenue, the **US Naval Observatory** occupies a near-perfect circle of land, inside of which are two noteworthy attractions. The observatory itself is built around a twelve-inch refracting telescope that dates from 1892 and has been recording and studying the position of the planets, comets, stars, and other celestial objects for over a century. Although you can't wander the grounds on your own, you can visit the observatory on one of the site's twice-monthly tours, which take you around the facility and tell you more about the Observatory's overall mission of providing accurate astronomical and navigational information, as well as keeping time with an array of atomic clocks. You can get here from the guard gate at the end of the route Observatory Circle, and by reserving several months in advance. The observatory site also accommodates the official home of the **vice president of the United States**, an 1893 Queen Anne mansion at 1 Observatory Circle that used to be the residence of the observatory superintendent, then chief of naval operations, before Congress decreed in 1974 that it house the nation's second most powerful politician. As Dick Cheney's one disclosed location, he'll be here until January 2009, so you won't get very close to it, but if you want to steal a glance, drive along the northern arc of Massachusetts Avenue and you may be able to take a furtive look through the protective foliage.

Cleveland Park

Back on Connecticut Avenue and heading north past the zoo you'll soon reach **Cleveland Park**, a stylish suburb marked by a few eye-grabbing buildings, including the **Kennedy-Warren Apartments** (no. 3133), a soaring Art Deco evocation of 1930s (and twenty-first-century) wealth; the Art Deco **Uptown Theatre** (no. 3426; see p.315), which has been showing movies since 1933; and the **Broadmoor** (no. 3601), a residential development from 1928 with grand-scale and angular Art Deco versions of Classical motifs, the tallest apartment block in the area. However, it's further west into the hills, around Newark Street and Highland Place, where you'll see the really historic buildings that make this neighborhood unique. These hills hold the area's highest concentration of upper-class residences, dating from its great turn-of-the-twentieth-century expansion: Robert Head, Waddy Butler Wood, and Paul Pelz all built houses here, and it was on Newark Street that Grover Cleveland's (long-demolished) summer house – the one that prompted the whole influx – once stood. Also worth a look are estates like the **Rosedale**, 3501 Newark St NW (ⓦwww .rosedaleconservancy.org), featuring the area's oldest structure – a weathered stone building, which dates from 1740 – amid later Colonial and early American additions; and the **Tregaron**, 3100 Macomb Ave NW (tours by appointment only at ⓣ202/243-1815), a stately Colonial Revival that's now used as the campus for the Washington International School. For more on local highlights, contact the **Cleveland Park Historical Society** (ⓣ202/363-6358, ⓦwww .clevelandparkdc.org), which also provides information on occasional tours ($30) of area homes.

Washington National Cathedral

Massachusetts and Wisconsin aves NW ⓣ202/537-6200 or 364-6616, ⓦwww.cathedral.org/cathedral; Woodley Park–Zoo Metro. Mon–Fri 10am–5.30pm, Sat 10am–4.30pm, Sun 8am–6.30pm. Tours Tues & Thurs–Sat 10–11.30am & 12.45–4pm, Mon & Wed 10–11.30am & 1.15–4pm, Sun 12.45–2.30pm. Donation requested.

Washington National Cathedral is the sixth-largest cathedral in the world, a monumental building so medieval in spirit it should surely rise from a dusty old European town plaza rather than a DC suburb. But the cathedral was intentionally set in this location: on the heights of **Mount St Alban**, unaffected by the city's zoning restrictions, the architects would have free rein to produce their masterpiece. Built from Indiana limestone and modeled on the medieval English Gothic style, it's supported by flying buttresses, bosses, and vaults, and shows off striking stained-glass windows, quirky gargoyles, massive columns, and, as an all-American touch, two rows of state flags hanging below the clerestory level. Continual restoration allows the cathedral always to look stunning to visitors.

The idea of a "national church" in the city was first proposed by George Washington, but it was not until a century later that Congress finally granted a charter for what is officially known as the **Cathedral Church of St Peter and St Paul**. In 1907 the foundation ceremony was held, with President Theodore Roosevelt in attendance, and construction on the building began. **George Bodley**, a noted English church architect, and **Henry Vaughan** designed the cathedral, but they were succeeded after their deaths around World War I by **Philip Hubert Frohman**, who spent the next fifty years on the project. Frohman died in 1972, and the cathedral wasn't finished until 1990 (though parts have been in use since the 1920s).

Although a Protestant church, and the seat of the Episcopal Diocese of Washington, the cathedral hosts services for other denominations as well. Most prominently, it's held memorial services for the victims of 9/11 and a number of presidents: **Woodrow Wilson** was commemorated and interred here upon his death in 1924, which was appropriate since much of the work on the building took place during his presidency; the work fascinated him so much that he used to visit the construction site in his chauffeur-driven limousine. **Gerald Ford** lay in state here most recently in 2007, while three years earlier **Ronald Reagan**, after first lying in state in the Capitol Rotunda, was honored with a memorial service here before his body was flown back to California for burial. **Dwight Eisenhower** received similar honors, though as yet Wilson is the only president to be buried here.

Visiting the cathedral

The center portal in the west facade isn't always open; you may have to enter from the northwest cloister. For a floor plan and information, descend to the **Crypt**, where there's an **information desk** and a huge **gift shop** (daily 9.30am–5pm) that runs nearly the length of the building. **Guided tours** are available regularly, but phone ahead or check the website for schedules of the many **specialty tours**, which feature everything from the cathedral's gardens to its gargoyles to its stained glass. The 57-acre grounds, or **Cathedral Close** (virtually a small fiefdom), hold cathedral offices, three schools, a college, sports fields, and a swimming pool. There is also an **Herb Cottage** that sells dried herbs and teas, a **greenhouse** with various plants for sale, and the **Bishop's Garden**, a walled rose-and-herb garden laid out in medieval style.

It's easiest to reach the cathedral by **bus**, either the #30, #32, #34, #35, or #36 from Pennsylvania Avenue downtown (including Wisconsin Ave via Georgetown), or #N2, #N4, or #N6 from Farragut Square via Dupont Circle and Embassy Row. If you don't mind a twenty-minute walk, you can take the **Metro**. From the Woodley Park–Zoo station, turn left from Connecticut Avenue into Cathedral Avenue and right into Woodley Road to reach the lower-level information center; the west door is around the corner on Wisconsin Avenue. As an alternative, for a longer, downhill walk, go up to the Tenleytown Metro station and head one and a half miles south along Wisconsin Avenue (a route also covered by even-numbered bus lines #30–36 above).

The interior

Place yourself first at the west end of the **nave** to appreciate the immense scale of the building; it's more than a tenth of a mile to the high altar at the other end. Along the south side of the nave, the first bay commemorates **George Washington**, whose marble statue proclaims him to be "First Citizen, Patriot, President, Churchman and Freemason," while five bays down is **Woodrow Wilson**'s sarcophagus. In the adjacent bay, look up to the **Space Window**, whose stained glass incorporating a sliver of moon rock commemorates the flight of *Apollo 11*, while other stained-glass windows cover great

Music in the cathedral

Carillon recitals Sat 12.30–1.15pm, peal bells Sun after service around 12.30pm & Tues 7–9pm.

Adult cathedral choristers, "Cathedral Voices," rehearsals Thurs 7–9.15pm & Sun 8–9am, Eucharist service Sun 9am.

Children's choristers, alternating boys' and girls' performances (rehearsal and evensong) Mon–Thurs 4.45–6.15pm, Sun 9.30–11am & 2.45–4pm.

Organ recitals/demonstrations Mon & Wed 12.30–1pm.

Choral and classical concerts: call for schedule and tickets at ☏202/537-5527 or ⓦwww.cathedralchoralsociety.org; tickets $20–80.

moments in US history from the Lewis and Clark expedition to the landings at Iwo Jima. On the north side, across from Washington, the **Abraham Lincoln Bay** is marked by a bronze statue of Abe, with Lincoln-head pennies set into the floor. The next berth down is for cathedral architect **Philip Hubert Frohman**, a Catholic whose family received special dispensation to have him buried in this Protestant church. The last bay before the North Transept features a small likeness of **Dr Martin Luther King Jr** above the arch, inscribed "I Have A Dream." On Sunday, March 31, 1968, the reverend preached his last sermon here before heading for Memphis, where he was due to lead a march of striking black workers; four days later he was assassinated, with violent repercussions for the poorer sections of the District as well as other parts of America.

From the **High Altar** – adorned with a 6ft-tall gold cross – there's a splendid view back down along the carved vault to the west rose window. The beautifully intricate **reredos** features 110 figures surrounding Christ in Benediction. An elevator from the south porch at the west end of the nave (near the Washington statue) ascends to the **Pilgrim Observation Gallery**, which affords stupendous city views. The 53 copper-and-tin bells of the cathedral's **carillon** ring out 150ft above the nave, and, even higher, its London-made **peal bells** weigh several tons and boom out following weekly services; unlike the carillon, which is played with a modern keyboard, the peal bells are sounded in the medieval fashion, by tugging thick ropes.

National Zoological Park

3001 Connecticut Ave NW ☎ 202/633-4800, ⓦ www.natzoo.si.edu; Cleveland Park or Woodley Park–Zoo Metro. Grounds daily April–Oct 6am–8pm, Nov–March 6am–6pm; buildings daily April–Oct 10am–6pm, Nov–March 10am–4.30pm.

The **National Zoological Park** is part of the Smithsonian Institution and, with its free admission, is always a popular draw for visitors who make it up this far. Sited between Woodley Park and Adams Morgan, the zoo sprawls down the steep sides of Rock Creek, with trails through lush vegetation leading past

▲ Cheetah at National Zoological Park

simulations of more than three thousand creatures' home environments. Although founded in 1889 as a traditional zoo, today it thinks of itself as a "BioPark," combining the usual menagerie of giraffes, elephants, lions, and tigers with botanic gardens, a prairie, natural history displays, aquariums, and a wetlands zone called "Amazonia."

The main entrance on Connecticut Avenue is a ten-minute walk from either **Metro** station, but it's easiest to arrive at the Cleveland Park one; from there the zoo is a level stroll south along Connecticut Avenue; from Woodley Park you'll have to hike uphill. Just inside the gate you'll find the **visitor center**, where you can pick up a map and list of the day's events, including feeding times. From here, three trails loop downhill through the park to Rock Creek: the central **Olmsted Walk**, passing most of the indoor exhibits, the steeper **Valley Trail**, with aquatic exhibits, birds, and "Amazonia," and the **Asia Trail**, which offers a grab bag of leopards, red pandas, and sloth bears. Head down one and back up another, visiting the side exhibits on the way, and you'll walk more than two miles. Allow a minimum of three hours to do the park justice. A café, restaurant, police post, concession stands, paid parking, and restrooms are scattered throughout the park. In summer the zoo hosts "**Sunset Serenades**," popular events that take place on Thursday evenings and involve musical and cultural entertainment.

Olmsted Walk

After beginning your stroll along the **Olmsted Walk**, you'll soon have your first zoo-celebrity sighting: the giant **pandas** Mei Xiang and Tian Tian, who arrived from China in 2000 to fill the absence created by the recent deaths of Ling Ling and Hsing Hsing, the famous pair presented by Beijing during Richard Nixon's 1972 visit. The pandas are on view daily from 9am to 4.30pm and are the constant focus of media interest for their mating activity, which in 2005 produced **Tai Shan**, a precocious little creature who's due to stick around at the zoo until 2009, when he'll be shipped back to China, with his parents following a year later. Continuing on, the zoo's next major addition is **Elephant Trails**, which, when it's completed in stages from 2009 to 2011, will allow the giant pachyderms an opportunity for more freedom from their current confinement, with multiple habitat areas, a socializing center, a greater variety of terrain, and an "Elephant Trek" that allows them to get out on the trail and shake a little trunk.

The path then winds down to the **Small Mammal House**, which showcases some of the zoo's lovable oddballs like golden tamarind monkeys, armadillos, meerkats, and porcupines. Nearby, the **American Indian Heritage Garden** celebrates Native Americans' understanding and use of nature; here you can learn about the healing properties of herbs and plants like the coneflower (used to treat insect bites, venereal disease, and rabies) and the emetic Indian tobacco plant – also known as vomitweed, pokeweed, and gagroot. From here, the orangutans are encouraged to leave the confines of the **Great Ape House** and commute to the "**Think Tank**," where scientists and four-legged primates come together to hone their communications skills and discuss world events as part of the fascinating **Orangutan Language Project**. Between the Ape House and the Think Tank is the **Reptile Discovery Center**, with a full complement of snakes, turtles, crocodiles, alligators, lizards, and frogs. Be sure not to miss the remarkable **komodo dragons**, one of which, Kraken, was the first to be born in captivity outside Indonesia. Since her celebrated birth in 1992, Kraken has grown to a length of 7ft, thanks to a steady diet of rats. The adjacent **Invertebrate Exhibit** covers the lives and loves of everything from ants to coral to tarantula to octopus. Admission to these two popular centers can be restricted at busy times; be sure to first check their status at the visitor center. Beyond here, the moat-surrounded **island** filled with lions and tigers marks the end of the big animals display, but you might want to duck in and out of the thoroughly unpleasant **bat cave** before heading up the Valley Trail.

Valley Trail and Elephant House

The best thing on the **Valley Trail** is undoubtedly the indoor "**Amazonia**" exhibit, which simulates the habitat along the Amazon River Basin. A cleverly constructed undulating aquarium gets you close to the fish – piranhas included – while bombarding you with informative notes. Next you climb up a level into the humid, creeper-clad rainforest thick with monkeys and birds, familiarizing yourself with roots, leaf mold, forest parasites, and birdcalls.

Further along on the trail, seals and sea lions splash in an outdoor pool, and then it's a slow walk uphill to **Beaver Valley**, which not only shows the titular scamp doing his business with massive teeth and paddled tail, but also has gray seals, otters, wolves, and pelicans on view, not to mention a **Bald Eagle Refuge** that showcases a pair of the intense, snowy-domed raptors who arrived here after being rescued from injury in the wild.

The Valley Trail ends a short distance before the current **Elephant House**, back on the Olmsted Trail, which is perhaps most interesting for its selection of hippopotamus and particularly **pygmy hippos**, who all descended from the legendary presidential pet, Billy. This odd, 600-pound choice for a First Animal (for Calvin Coolidge in the 1920s) not only sired around sixty offspring over three decades at the National Zoo but lent his DNA to most of the current array of pygmy hippos now gracing the pens of zoos across America.

Asian Trail and Bird House

After the Elephant House, you can turn onto the new **Asia Trail**, opened in 2006 and displaying eight types of creatures, including the giant pandas that sit between the trail and the Olmsted Walk. Here you can find such curious beasts as the **sloth bear**, whose homely, disheveled appearance seems appropriate for munching on bees and sucking up ants and termites through its prodigious snout; the **fishing cat**, a stocky feline who does his business in the swamps and rivers of South Asia; the giant, somewhat grotesque **Japanese giant salamander**; the curious and furtive **red panda**, which more resembles a raccoon or fox than a giant panda, but is biologically distinct from all of them; and the **clouded leopard**, whose lengthy tail, long fangs, and lean and rangy 40-pound body make it a formidable foe when hunting for monkeys and pigs, or bounding through the trees after birds. Midway along the Asia Trail, a separate path takes you to the **bird exhibits**, a must for fans of any feathered creature, but particularly for the broad selection of cranes. In an outdoor flight cage are egrets, ducks, herons, and the like; also outdoors but uncaged is a majestic flock of flamingos, plus macaws, storks and kookaburras, as well as the curious ibis and king vulture. Finally, in the **Bird House** are owls, magpie, kingfish, and other avian species.

Rock Creek Park and around

Most visitors overlook the city's major natural preserve, **Rock Creek Park** (☎202/895-6000; ⓦwww.nps.gov/rocr), which divides Upper Northwest from Adams Morgan and the north-central part of the District. Established in 1890, its 1800 acres spread out above the National Zoo to form a mile-wide tract of woodland west of 16th Street. The Rock Creek Parkway shadows the creek for much of its length, until it hits the zoo (north of which it's known as Beach Drive). A **car** is the easiest way to get around the park; by public transit, you can take the **Metro** to Cleveland Park, which provides access just north of the zoo via **bus** routes #H2, #H3, and #H4 (or a more lengthy slog on foot), or to Friendship Heights, from which **buses** #E2, #E3, and #E4 run up Western Avenue and McKinley Street before cruising along Military Road into the middle of the park. To reach the east side of the park or the amphitheatre, take bus #S2 or #S4; both run straight up 16th Street from anywhere north of K Street NW. Alternatively, you can hop on a **bike** in Georgetown and ride north along the creek. The park is open during daylight hours. It's not a wise idea to come on foot, on your own, or at night, though cross-street traffic is permitted 24 hours a day.

Park highlights

The park's wooded confines, craggy outcrops, and rambling streams have long been regarded as one of the District's treasures, and it's no surprise that, given its proximity to the Capitol, this was one of the country's first publicly protected parks, dating to 1890. It has fifteen miles of **trails and paths** that run along both sides of the creek and include tracks, workout stations, bridleways (in the wooded northern section), and a cycle route that runs from the Lincoln Memorial north through the park and into Maryland. To the south, Arlington Memorial Bridge links the route to the Mount Vernon Trail in Virginia (see p.252). On weekends (Sat 7am to Sun 7pm) and holidays, Beach Drive between Military and Broad Branch roads is closed to cars, and Rollerbladers, cyclists, runners, and walkers happily make the space their own. The park also has ballparks, thirty picnic areas, and the **Carter Barron Amphitheatre**, 16th St and Colorado Ave NW, which hosts various **summer concerts** (info at ☎202/426-0486; see p.308).

The sights start at the southern end of the park, a mile above the zoo, where the serene **Peirce Barn** (June–Nov Sat & Sun noon–4pm; free) houses the imposing granite **Peirce Mill**, in a beautiful riverside hollow on Tilden Street, near Beach Drive. One of eight nineteenth-century gristmills in the valley, and the last to shut down (in 1897), it used to produce cornmeal and wheat flour for sale to visitors. It's now in the process of being restored.

The **Nature Center**, 5200 Glover Rd, just south of Military Road (Wed–Sun 9am–5pm; ☎202/895-6070), acts as the park **visitor center**, with natural history exhibits and details of weekend **guided walks** and self-guided **nature trails**. There's also an onsite **planetarium** (45min shows Wed 4pm, Sat & Sun 1 & 4pm; free) that presents the sky and its constellations as they will appear that night, and also allows for more in-depth views of longer-term phenomena; ask also about the periodic stargazing sessions that occur monthly from April to November.

Fort Circle Parks

Just on the other side of Military Road from the Rock Creek Nature Center, the remains of Fort De Russey stand as a reminder of the network of defenses that ringed the city during the Civil War, now known as the **Fort Circle Parks** (most daily dawn–dusk; free; ⓦwww.nps.gov/archive/rocr/ftcircle). Guarding against Confederate attack from the north, **Fort De Russey** was one of 68 forts erected around DC. The sites of others have been appropriated as small parks on either side of Rock Creek Park. East on Military Road from the park to 13th Street NW and north of Missouri Avenue, **Fort Stevens** marks the spot at which the city came closest to falling to Confederate troops during the Civil War. An army of 15,000 soldiers crossed the Potomac in July 1864 and got within 150 yards of the fort before the hastily reinforced Union defense drove them back under a barrage of artillery fire. President Lincoln was in the fort during the attack and mounted the parapet for a better look at the Confederate line, drawing a stinging rebuke from a nearby soldier, who shouted, "Get down, you damned fool!" at his commander in chief. Today, you can somewhat imagine the scene, with the earthen mounds, wooden works, and vintage cannons testifying to the site's importance, aided by a podcast that the NPS provides through its website.

Seven blocks farther north, at 6625 Georgia Ave, is **Battleground National Cemetery** (daily dawn–dusk), which holds the remains of the Union soldiers killed in the battle to defend Fort Stevens. Buses #70, #71, and #79 run here, up 7th Street (which becomes Georgia Avenue NW) from the National Mall, but given Georgia Avenue's rather fearsome reputation you're advised to come and go by taxi.

Hillwood Museum and Gardens

4155 Linnean Ave NW ☎202/686-5807, ⓦwww.hillwoodmuseum.org; Van Ness–UDC Metro. Tues–Sat 10am–5pm, closed Jan; by reservation only. $12.

Just west of Rock Creek and a short distance north of Peirce Mill, the 1923 neo-Georgian manor once known as Arbremont was acquired in the 1950s by **Marjorie Merriweather Post**, heir to the cereal-company fortune, and transformed into a showpiece she renamed Hillwood. These days, the red-brick mansion and its lovely grounds – thick with roses and French- and Japanese-style gardens – are part of the **Hillwood Museum**, and while the site is handsome enough, what brings people out here is the cache inside. Through her Russian-ambassador husband, in the 1930s Post managed to collect a treasure trove of Fabergé eggs and boxes, Byzantine and Orthodox icons, eighteenth-century glassworks, and other priceless items that today form the core of the museum's collection. There's also an array of French and English decorative-arts items, including tapestries, gilded commodes, porcelain cameos, parquet-inlaid furniture, and so on, arrayed in cases or on walls almost to the point of nausea. Indeed, many of the lesser works tread a thin line between art and expensive kitsch, crossing it on several occasions.

The easiest way to get here is by **bus** (following the same routes as for the west side of Rock Creek Park) or **Metro** to the Van Ness–UDC station, from which it's a mile walk, first south on Connecticut Avenue and then east along Upton Street. Check the museum's website for details.

Georgetown

C alled by Jan Morris "the most obsessively political residential enclave in the world," **Georgetown** is both a tourist favorite and a bastion of entrenched wealth that sits at some remove from the rest of the District. The Kennedys moved here before JFK made it to the White House and were followed by establishment figures who have adopted Georgetown as their home (or, more usually, one of their homes): crusading scribbler Bob Woodward, *Washington Post* publisher Katharine Graham and her editor Ben Bradlee, art collector and philanthropist Paul (son of industrial titan Andrew) Mellon, first woman secretary of state Madeleine Albright, failed presidential candidate John Kerry, scandal-writer-to-the-stars Kitty Kelley, Elizabeth Taylor (during her marriage to Senator John Warner) – the list goes on and on.

There is, of course, more to Georgetown than its upper-crust inhabitants. The area is at its vibrant best along the spine of **Wisconsin Avenue** and **M Street**, with bars, coffee shops, fashionable restaurants, and boutiques in which Georgetown University students rub shoulders with staid old power brokers. Its history is diverting too, and many of the area's buildings date to the early eighteenth century, making it older than the capital itself. Federal-era and shuttered Victorian townhouses hung with flower baskets stud the streets, while a series of stately mansions and handsome parks, gardens, and cemeteries lies north of Q Street. Down on the **C&O Canal**, below M Street, the odd horse-drawn boat fills the waterway, while the tree-shaded towpaths have been turned over to cyclists and walkers; to the north, upper Georgetown is home to the elite of the elite, and while you won't get to poke around any of the private mansions or Georgian row houses, there are a handful of historic homes that are open to the public.

Georgetown's most annoying feature is that it's not on the **Metro** (Rock Creek and its valley are in the way). And don't even think about driving here: there's nowhere to park. The nearest Metro station is Foggy Bottom–GWU, from which it's a fifteen- to twenty-minute walk up Pennsylvania Avenue and along M Street to the junction with Wisconsin Avenue. Alternatively, approach from Dupont Circle, a similar-length walk west along P Street (or over the Dumbarton Bridge and along Q St; see p.200), which puts you first in the ritzier, upper part of Georgetown – in which case you might want to start your tour with the mansions, parks, and gardens of northern Georgetown. **Buses** #30, #32, #34, #35, and #36 run all the way from Eastern Market up Capitol Hill to the Mall, and on to Pennsylvania Avenue until they reach M Street and Wisconsin Avenue; #D1, #D3, and #D6 go via E St, 13th St, K St, and Dupont Circle to Q St in Georgetown and return via M St; and #G2 runs from Dupont Circle to P and Dumbarton streets. At night you'll find **taxis** relatively easy to come by on the main drags; it's a $10–12 ride to and from most downtown DC

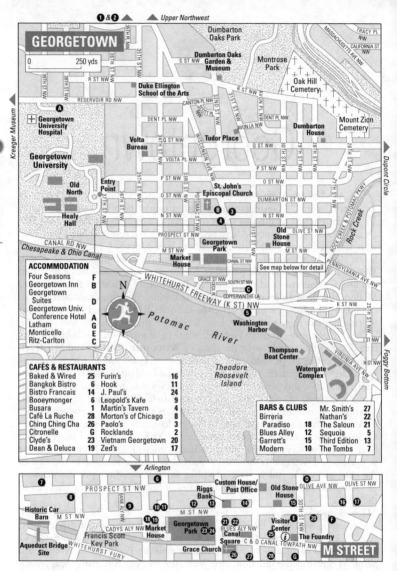

① & **②** ▲ Upper Northwest

GEORGETOWN

0 — 250 yds

Dumbarton
Oaks Park

Dumbarton Oaks
Garden &
Museum

Montrose
Park

Oak Hill
Cemetery

Duke Ellington
School of the Arts

Mount Zion
Cemetery

Ⓐ Georgetown
University
Hospital

Volta
Bureau

Tudor Place

Dumbarton
House

Georgetown
University

St. John's
Episcopal Church

Old
North

Entry
Point

Healy
Hall

Old Stone
House

Georgetown
Park

See map below for detail

ACCOMMODATION

Four Seasons	**F**
Georgetown Inn	**B**
Georgetown Suites	**D**
Georgetown Univ. Conference Hotel	**A**
Latham	**G**
Monticello	**E**
Ritz-Carlton	**C**

Market
House

Chesapeake & Ohio Canal

CANAL RD NW

Kreeger Museum

Dupont Circle

Rock Creek & Potomac Pkwy

Rock Creek

Foggy Bottom

WHITEHURST FREEWAY (K ST) NW

N

Potomac

River

Washington
Harbor

Thompson
Boat Center

Watergate
Complex

Theodore
Roosevelt
Island

CAFÉS & RESTAURANTS

Baked & Wired	25	Furin's	16
Bangkok Bistro	6	Hook	11
Bistro Francais	14	J. Paul's	24
Booeymonger	6	Leopold's Kafe	9
Busara	1	Martin's Tavern	4
Café La Ruche	28	Morton's of Chicago	8
Ching Ching Cha	26	Paolo's	3
Citronelle	G	Rocklands	2
Clyde's	23	Vietnam Georgetown	20
Dean & Deluca	19	Zed's	17

BARS & CLUBS

Birreria		Mr. Smith's	27
Paradiso	18	Nathan's	22
Blues Alley	12	The Saloun	21
Garrett's	15	Sequoia	5
Modern	10	Third Edition	13
		The Tombs	7

▼ Arlington

❼

PROSPECT ST NW

❻

Custom House/
Post Office

Old Stone
House

OLIVE AVE NW   OLIVE ST NW

Ⓓ

Riggs
Bank

❽

Historic Car
Barn

M ST NW

❿ ⓫   **⓬ ⓭**   **⓮**   **⓯**   **⓰ ⓱**

Francis Scott
Key Park

Aqueduct Bridge
Site

WHITEHURST FURY

⓲ ⓳

Market
House

Georgetown
Park

㉓ ㉔

㉑ ㉒
BLUES ALY NW

Canal
Square

Visitor
Center

Ⓔ

㉕

C & O CANAL TOWPATH NW

Ⓕ

⓴

The Foundry

Grace Church

㉖   **㉗**   **㉘**

Ⓖ

M STREET

locations. The best bet might be to take the **DC Circulator** bus (every 10min; daily 7am–9pm; $1; ⓦ www.dccirculator.com), which connects upper Georgetown to the lower part along Wisconsin Avenue and M Street, then heads east to the Foggy Bottom–GWU Metro stop and runs along K Street before its final leg on Massachusetts Avenue to Union Station. There are two other routes in the District for this useful conveyance (see p.31).

Another option is to take the **Georgetown Shuttle** from the Rosslyn Metro station in Arlington, Virginia – a walk is definitely not recommended on the busy Francis Scott Key Bridge from there – which connects to the Dupont

Circle Metro along M and L streets and New Hampshire Avenue; fares are cheap ($1, or 35¢ with subway transfer) and there's a shuttle every ten minutes (Mon–Thurs 7am–midnight, Fri 7am–2am, Sat 8am–2am, Sun 8am–midnight; Ⓦ www.georgetowndc.com/shuttle.php).

Some history

In the early eighteenth century, when this area was part of Maryland, Scottish merchants began to form a permanent settlement around shoreside warehouses on the higher reaches of the Potomac River (or "Patowmack," as it was then known). Here they oversaw a thriving trade, exporting the plentiful **tobacco** from nearby farms and importing foreign materials and luxuries for colonial settlers. In 1751 the Maryland Assembly granted a town charter to the merchants, who named their flourishing port either after their royal protector, George II, or after the town founders, both also named George. Within a decade, "George Towne" was a runaway success, attracting other merchants who built large mansions on estates to the north of the river, and by the 1780s it was America's largest tobacco port.

Once George Washington had selected the Potomac region as the site of the new federal capital, it seemed logical that such a **port** be included in the plans. In 1791, together with Alexandria in Virginia, the town was incorporated within the **federal district** but was still distinct as a township under its own name. And while for many years the new Washington City to the east remained little more than an idea, Georgetown continued to prosper; by 1830 it had a population of nine thousand and was thriving with Georgian and Federal-style brick houses, fashionable stores, well-tended gardens, and even an eponymous university (founded in 1789). By the time of the Civil War, Georgetown was still separate enough from Washington to be considered suspect in Union eyes. Many of the town's early landowners came from the South, but despite their support for the **Confederate** cause, Georgetown's proximity to the capital kept the lid on any overt secessionist feeling, as did the presence of Union troops in the town and Lincoln's suspension of due process (including the writ of habeas corpus) in parts of nearby Maryland.

The war and Georgetown's commercial prospects flickered and died at about the same time. The tobacco trade had recently faltered due to soil exhaustion, while the steady growth of Baltimore and Washington itself badly affected the town's prosperity. The **Chesapeake and Ohio (C&O) Canal**, completed in 1850, represented an attempt to revive trade with the interior, and for a time Georgetown became a regional center for wheat, coal, and timber shipment. But the canal was soon obsolete: the coming of the railroads was swiftly followed by the development of larger steamboats, which couldn't be accommodated by Georgetown's canal or harbor. Relegated to a mere **neighborhood** in the District of Columbia after losing its charter in 1871, Georgetown experienced another blow in 1895 when most of its old street names – some in use for more than 150 years – were abandoned by order of Congress in favor of the numbers and letters of the federal city plan. There was even a suggestion that Georgetown become known as "West Washington."

For much of the late nineteenth and early twentieth centuries, Georgetown was anything but a fashionable place to live. Water-powered foundries and mills provided employment for a growing, predominantly black population based in the neighborhood of Herring Hill, south of P Street and close to Rock Creek. Gardens were lost to speculative row housing, many larger mansions were subdivided, a noisy streetcar system was installed, and **M Street** became a workaday run of cheap stores and saloons owned by immigrant families.

However, a mass influx of white-collar workers to DC during the New Deal era and World War II reversed Georgetown's rather down-at-the-heel image – apartments were turned into houses and mansions renovated. Part of the charm for newcomers was that Georgetown's boundaries – southern river, eastern creek, western university, and northern estates – had prevented indiscriminate development, leaving a collection of picture-perfect houses, stores, and banks still intact from the nineteenth century or earlier.

This character persists and is, of course, zealously preserved by Georgetown residents who, since the 1950s and 1960s, have increasingly included DC's most fashionable and politically well-connected residents. While certain historic houses have been lost to developers, and the 1949 construction of the White-hurst Freeway added a concrete eyesore to line the southern waterfront (helping to bury the trolley system thirteen years later), since 1967 Georgetown has been registered as a **National Historic Landmark**: new buildings and renovations (including house-paint colors) have to be sympathetic to their surroundings, and the canal has been landscaped and preserved as a historic park.

M Street and around

Cutting through the lower town before crossing Rock Creek into Foggy Bottom, **M Street** has been Georgetown's central artery for two centuries, and it still offers a good introduction to the area, providing you with a vibrant glimpse of Washington society amid old-fashioned row buildings packed cheek-by-jowl with scarcely an alley in between. As elsewhere in Georgetown, the street retains many of its original Georgian, Federal, and later Victorian buildings, though the ground floors of the structures have all been converted for retail use. Most new buildings have tended to follow the prevailing red-brick style, none more noticeably than the elegant *Four Seasons Hotel* between 28th and 29th streets (see p.267), which acts as an eastern gateway to the heart of the corridor. A short distance down the street, the **Old Stone House** is one of the District's most venerable structures. The area's **visitor center**, 1057 Thomas Jefferson St (Wed–Fri 9am-4.30pm, Sat & Sun 10am–4pm; ☎202/653-5190, ⓦwww.georgetowndc.com), is stuffed with all kinds of brochures and information on different aspects of the buildings and on the C&O Canal.

Shops, restaurants, and bars proliferate around the main M Street–Wisconsin Avenue junction, where the gold dome of the grand, Neoclassical **Riggs National Bank** stands as a useful landmark; its original owner, financier and later gallery owner William Corcoran, saw the bank become the sole depository of federal funds within Washington and later the dominant player on the local banking scene. Following a string of scandals, the bank is now owned by PNC, which saw fit to cover up the venerable Riggs name above the portico with its own, incongruous corporate logo. Even more historic, though a bit more discreet, is the **City Club Tavern**, nearby at 3206 M St, a sturdy brick Georgian that was put up in 1796 and four years later became the staging ground for President John Adams's final review of the layout for the new capital city. It's managed to survive the centuries well, and now hosts a private, members-only club (for pictures see ⓦwww.citytavernclubdc.org). Just beyond is **Georgetown Park**, 3222 M St, once a parking lot for horse-drawn omnibuses and now a shopping mall (Mon–Sat 10am–9pm, Sun noon–6pm; ⓦwww.shopsatgeorgetownpark.com). A block west, at Potomac

Street, the triple-arched, red-brick **Market House** has hosted a public market since 1795, the current version dating to 1865, though today the butchered carcasses and patent medicines have made way for a Dean & Deluca deli (see p.286).

At the junction with 34th Street, the **Francis Scott Key Bridge** (better known as just "Key Bridge") shoots off across the river to Rosslyn, while a craggy, medieval-looking stone abutment, just west, is the only trace of the structure it replaced, the **Aqueduct Bridge**, dating from 1834 and once part of a canal system that connected Alexandria, Virginia, to the C&O Canal. The Key Bridge's namesake was the author of "The Star-Spangled Banner," who moved to Washington in 1805 and lived in a house here at M Street. His home was later demolished to make way for the **Whitehurst Freeway** – a sacrilege only belatedly atoned for by the establishment of **Francis Scott Key Park**, just off the street. The park contains a bronze bust of Key, a 60ft flagpole flying the Stars and Stripes, a wisteria-covered arbor, and a few benches from which to peer through the break in the buildings to the river. Walk down the steps here and you're standing on the point at which, in September 1781, General Washington and his ally Jean Baptiste Rochambeau, commander in chief of the French army in America, prepared to cross the Potomac en route to Mount Vernon and, ultimately, Yorktown, where a decisive victory against the British the following month effectively secured America's independence during the Revolutionary War.

The Old Stone House

3051 M St NW ☎202/895-6070, ☻www.nps.gov/olst. Wed–Sun noon–5pm; tours by reservation only.

The **Old Stone House** – the only extant pre-Revolutionary house in DC – sits, incongruously, in the center of the M Street action. Built like a small fortress, it was constructed in 1765 by a Pennsylvania carpenter and retains its rugged, rough-hewn appearance. Its 3ft-thick walls are made of craggy blue fieldstone; its wooden beams are massive oak timbers; and its floor is hard with packed earth. The simple kitchen and carpenter's workshop are downstairs, with paneled parlors and bedrooms upstairs. It's certainly quaint enough, but it's unlikely that Pierre L'Enfant used it as a base while designing the federal city, as was suggested when it was slated from demolition in the 1950s; it's of historical value mainly because it was lucky enough to survive the years. Today it's been restored to what it probably looked like in the late eighteenth century, with an attached English garden providing a nice respite from the Georgetown shopping hubbub.

N Street and around

Potomac Street, a few blocks west of the Old Stone House, is a good route to take you north to **N Street**, which contains some of Georgetown's finest Federal-era buildings. None is open to the public, but several particularly attractive facades appear between 29th and 34th streets. Robert Todd Lincoln (President Lincoln's son) lived out the last decade of his life at **no. 3014**; the house was later purchased by *Washington Post* stalwart Ben Bradlee. Four blocks west is **no. 3307**, which JFK and Jackie owned from 1957 to 1961; Jackie also lived briefly in **no. 3017** after JFK's assassination. There's a cluster of other historic houses on **Prospect Street**, one block south, where late eighteenth-century merchants built mansions like those at **nos. 3425** and **3508**; as the street name suggests, they once possessed splendid views down to the river from which they derived their wealth. Appropriately, in this vicinity sits the original **Custom House and Post Office**, 1221 31st St, which occupies a stately 1858 structure that once housed Treasury Department facilities for managing customs for the busy international trade along Georgetown's waterfront. That function is long gone, but a federal post office still occupies the ground floor.

Georgetown University

Before you leave lower Georgetown it's worth swinging by **Georgetown University** (☎ 202/687-3600, ⓦ www.georgetown.edu), located on the heights above the river; the **main gate** is at 37th and O streets. Founded in 1789 as the Jesuit Georgetown College, it's the oldest Catholic university in the country and the spawning grounds for numerous diplomats, Supreme Court justices and politicians – Bill Clinton foremost among them. Today, the university and its six thousand students give the neighborhood much of its buzz. The architecture is a bit of a hybrid, ranging from the graceful porch entry and plain Georgian facade of the **Old North** building, which dates from 1795, to the spooky Romanesque details of **Healy Hall**, finished ninety years later, to a handful of modern buildings.

Just south of the university at 3600 M Street, the Romanesque Revival **Historic Car Barn** is a massive, four-story brick structure with rooftop pavilion that represented the apex of mass transit when constructed in 1897 as the Capital Traction Company's "Union Station" for the many trolley lines serving the city. Rich with black-iron decor, granite floors, and paneled ceilings, the interior of the Waddy Wood–designed colossus no doubt impressed many a commuter. However, the huge spaces were never filled to capacity and the building was an outsize emblem of the decline of mass transit, in the 1950s becoming little more than a decaying eyesore. Amazingly, it was preserved instead of demolished, and now serves as office space for Georgetown University. (Contact the university for information about touring this and other historic college sites.) Still, for all its impressive size and design, the car barn is mainly known to tourists for its 97 vertiginous "**Exorcist Steps**," which connect M and Prospect streets here and send shudders through the spines of moviegoers who remember the two violent deaths that took place in that horror flick. Appropriately, before that 1973 film came out, the perilous flight was known as the "Hitchcock Steps" for their eerie character, though the Master of Suspense never shot a movie here.

The Kreeger Museum

2401 Foxhall Rd NW ☎ 202/338-3552, ⓦ www.kreegermuseum.org. Tours by reservation only Tues–Fri 10.30am & 1.30pm, Sat without reservation 10am–4pm; $8.

As one of Washington's most obscure cultural attractions, the **Kreeger Museum** is little known mainly because of its location in the hills northwest of Georgetown University (in the sub-district of Foxhall), though it well rewards a visit for its splendid array of twentieth-century modernist art. Housed in an ultra-modern white-walled home designed by Philip Johnson, the museum has open hours on Saturday and shows its collection on ninety-minute, reservation-only tours on other days of the week. However you see it, you'll be taking in the works of various major artists – including Impressionists like Monet and Renoir, post-Impressionists like Van Gogh and Cézanne, early moderns such as Picasso, and Abstract Expressionists like Mark Rothko

Georgetown crops up in many movies that are only incidentally set in Washington, DC. Although the house in **The Exorcist** was a stage set, the "Exorcist Steps" were a real location (see p.236); author-screenwriter William Peter Blatty knew them well since he lived nearby. Other movies were filmed on campus at Georgetown University, including the 1980s brat-pack movie **St Elmo's Fire**, in which Rob Lowe, Demi Moore, Emilio Estevez, Judd Nelson, Ally Sheedy, and Andrew McCarthy primp, preen, and throw tantrums all over town as they come to terms with life and love after college. Lawyer-turned-fugitive Will Smith gets a swanky Upper Georgetown pad in **Enemy of the State** (though not much time to enjoy it, as he's arbitrarily pursued from Adams Morgan to Baltimore). The pseudo-Victorian elegance of the Georgetown Park Mall on M Street has turned up in key scenes in Jean-Claude van Damme's goofy **Timecop** and Arnold Schwarzenegger's double-barreled **True Lies**, while Tom Cruise was chased around the area in Steven Spielberg's sci-fi flick **Minority Report**. Top Georgetown thriller honors go to Kevin Costner's underrated **No Way Out**. Largely set in the Pentagon, the film has Costner jogging along the C&O Canal and later chased along the Whitehurst Freeway before escaping into the "Georgetown Metro" station – there is, of course, no such thing – leading to a finale with one of the more unexpected twists in mainstream Hollywood cinema.

and Clyfford Still. Also worth a look are the jagged steel monoliths of David Smith; the lean metallic sculptures of Brancusi; James Rosenquist's huge Pop Art diptychs and triptychs; and Edvard Munch's disturbing Scandinavian brand of Expressionism. It's sometimes hard to predict exactly what will be on view at any one time, but the collection is large enough to ensure most modern art fans won't go away disappointed. Additionally, the museum has a number of works by Indian and African artists, and items from the pre-Columbian world.

Wisconsin Avenue

Georgetown's most bustling area is where M Street meets **Wisconsin Avenue**, the neighborhood's cultural and commercial epicenter. Whereas M Street's offerings tend to be more mainstream chain stores and tourist-friendly boutiques, Wisconsin Avenue caters more to locals and those with a flair for independent shopping. It's not that the shops along Wisconsin (which is at its most enticing from M to Q streets) are necessarily cheap or obscure, but they do have a more creative aspect and irreverent spirit – anything from upstart DC designers and hometown coffeehouses to modernist galleries and engaging bars. The architecture in the vicinity has some highlights too, like **St John's Episcopal Church**, just off Wisconsin at O and Potomac (⒲www.stjohnsgeorgetown.org), a quaint Federal structure built in 1806 by US Capitol architect William Thornton to house DC's oldest Episcopal congregation (dating to 1776). The blocky, Neoclassical **Volta Bureau**, three blocks west of Wisconsin at 1537 35th St, was built in 1893 as an institute for the deaf; the building was funded by Alexander Graham Bell with money he was awarded by the French government's Volta Prize after inventing the telephone (contact ⒯202/337-5220 or ⒲www .agbell.org if you'd like to take a look around). Finally, the **Duke Ellington School of the Arts** (⒲www.ellingtonschool.org; see p.213), at 35th and R streets, is a grand Greek Revival high school founded by the jazz great to serve as a magnet for artistically inspired DC youth.

Along the C&O Canal

On a clear summer's day there's no better spot to be in Georgetown than along the **Chesapeake and Ohio (C&O) Canal**, whose eastern extremity feeds into Rock Creek at 28th Street NW. The canal is overlooked on both sides by restored red-brick warehouses, spanned by small bridges, lined with trees, and punctuated by occasional pastel-colored towpath houses. The prettiest central stretch starts at **30th Street**, where the adjacent locks once opened to allow boatloads of coal, iron, timber, and corn from the upriver Maryland estates to pass through.

Some history

The Potomac River had been used by traders since the earliest days of settlement in the region, but a series of rapids and waterfalls – like those at Great Falls, just fourteen miles from Georgetown – made large-scale commercial navigation all but impossible. A canal was proposed (George Washington was one of the shareholders) that would follow the line of the river and open up trade as far as the Ohio Valley, but when construction finally finished in 1850, the **C&O** reached only as far as Cumberland in Maryland, 184 miles and 74 locks away. Confederate raiding parties found the barges and locks easy targets during the Civil War, and much of the traffic dried up for the duration – doubtless to the satisfaction of the Union troops stationed in Georgetown, who used to swim naked in the canal, offending local sensibilities. Even after the war the canal never attracted sufficient trade, mainly because of competition from the railroads; the last mule-drawn cargo boat was pulled through in the 1920s, after which severe flooding from the Potomac destroyed much of the canal infrastructure. Although the stretch was under threat of being turned into yet another highway in the 1950s, the C&O's historical importance was recognized in 1971 when its entire length was declared a **National Historic Park**, and today scores of visitors hike, cycle, and ride horses along the restored towpaths; canoeing and boating are allowed in certain sections, too, and the National Park Service offers passenger canal boat services (see box opposite).

Along the canal

One of the most appealing stretches of the canal is the short section between **Thomas Jefferson Street** and **31st Street**, where artisan houses dating from the building boom of the mid-nineteenth century have been handsomely restored as shops, offices, and, occasionally, private homes. Thomas Jefferson Street itself is lined with attractive brick houses, some in the Federal style, featuring rustic stone lintels, arched doorways with fanlights, and narrow top-floor dormers. On the south side of the canal, **The Foundry**, 1050 30th St, is just one of the many brick warehouses that line the canal. It was originally built as a machine shop and later served as a veterinary hospital to care for the mules that worked the boats; today it contains office and academic space. Other warehouses have received similar treatment, and frame either side of the waterway as far up as Francis Scott Key Bridge, five blocks west. One good example is **Canal Square**, at 1054 31st St, which began as a sturdy warehouse for barge cargo along the canal, then evolved into a site for "tabulating machines" using punch cards in a primitive form of a computer, circa 1886. This ultimately led the industrial operation to merge with two others to form a technology pioneer, IBM, in the 1920s. The building's now filled with shops and offices.

It's 184 miles from Georgetown to the canal terminus at Cumberland, Maryland. Along the way, the canal wends its way through highly varied scenery: past waterfalls, through forests, and beside the ridges and valleys of the Appalachian Mountains.

Canal boats

To sign up for trips on the 90ft, mule-drawn **canal boats** – accompanied by park rangers in nineteenth-century costume who work the locks – stop in at the **C&O Canal Visitor Center**, 1057 Thomas Jefferson Street NW (Wed–Fri 9am–4.30pm, Sat & Sun 10am–4pm; ☏202/653-5190, ⓦwww.nps.gov/choh). Tickets cost $7, and there are usually 3 or 4 departures per day Wednesday through Sunday mid-June to early September, with reduced service from April to mid-June and mid-September to late October.

Along the canal

A number of outlets **along the canal** rent boats, canoes, and bikes, including several in the first twenty-mile stretch from Georgetown (see p.33). For a day-trip by **bicycle**, Great Falls (see below) – an easy, flat fourteen miles away – is a reasonable destination. You'll need to observe a 15mph speed limit on the towpath, wear a helmet, and give way to all pedestrians and horses. It takes most people a couple of hours to bike to Great Falls from Georgetown, and the only slightly tricky part is just before Lock 15, where you'll have to carry the bike for a couple hundred yards. **Canoes** and **boats** are limited to specific areas (visitor centers and rental outlets can advise) and you shouldn't venture onto the Potomac River, which can be very dangerous, or swim in the canal itself. You can **picnic** anywhere you like, but light fires only in authorized fireplaces. First-come, first-served basic **campsites** are dotted along the entire length of the canal; the one closest to the city is at Swains Lock, twenty miles from Georgetown.

Great Falls Park

Great Falls Park, fourteen miles from Georgetown, is marked by the thrilling and majestic torrent of the Potomac falling 76ft over the course of a mile, through gorges and over rocky precipices, the entire spectacle encouraging death-defying kayakers to risk their necks taking it on. The **Great Falls Tavern Visitor Center**, 11710 MacArthur Blvd, Potomac, MD (daily 9am–4.45pm; ☏301/767-3714, ⓦwww.nps .gov/grfa), has a museum covering the history of the canal, built to get around the perils of the falls. This is the starting point for guided local tours, walks, and canal boat trips (same prices and schedules as in Georgetown). Nearby, a boardwalk offers terrific views of the falls themselves. By car, take MacArthur Boulevard, signposted from Georgetown, or Exit 41W off the Beltway; outside rush hour, it's a 20min drive. There's also a **visitor center** on the Virginia side of the falls (☏703/285-2965) – though no access to the other side of the river – with information on more tours and trails, but no boat trips. Get there by following Route 193 West, also known as Georgetown Pike (Exit 44 off the Beltway); turn right on Old Dominion Drive, from where it's a mile to the entrance station. Parking is $5 for three days of use.

Wisconsin Avenue, south of the canal, anchors the oldest part of Georgetown. This was the first road built from the river into Maryland during colonial times, and was a major route for farmers and traders who used the slope of the hill to roll their barrels down to riverside warehouses. Later, canal boatmen would be lured into the Gothic Revival **Grace Church** on South Street, just off Wisconsin Avenue, by promises of salvation from the earthbound drudgery of hauling heavy goods from barge to warehouse; it now serves part of DC's considerable homeless population. Others sought solace in nearby **Suter's**

Tavern, where, it's claimed, George Washington met Maryland landowners to discuss the purchase of property so that work could start on the federal city. The tavern was knocked down long ago, but there's a plaque marking its approximate site at 31st and K streets.

The waterfront

South of the C&O Canal, **K Street** was once known as Water Street for the very good reason that it fronted the Potomac River, though land reclamation has now pushed the water a hundred yards or so farther south. K Street's most noticeable feature is what's above it, namely the looming **Whitehurst Freeway** – the elevated road built in 1949 to relieve traffic congestion on M Street, one of the earliest such freeways in the country, though now out of place among Georgetown's more genteel surroundings. Cross the road under the freeway and you reach the riverside development of **Washington Harbor** (east of 31st), its interlocking towers set around a circular, terraced plaza with spurting fountains. The waterfront on either side is now being landscaped as part of a new

▲ Grace Church

Georgetown Waterfront Park, planned to have a whole slew of attractions such as shade trees and arbors, river stairs down to the waterfront, paths and gardens, an interactive fountain, and a small labyrinth (info at ⓦwww .georgetownwaterfrontpark.org). There are views upriver to the Francis Scott Key Bridge and downriver to Theodore Roosevelt Island and Bridge, as well as across the river to the backs of the Watergate Complex and Kennedy Center. The restaurants and bars in the Harbor complex are all fairly expensive, but there's nothing more relaxing than a summer evening on the terrace, sipping drinks, and watching the boats sculling by. If you'd like to go for a cruise yourself, several boat-rental shops offer the means to explore the calmer waters around the Key Bridge and Roosevelt Island. Good choices include Fletcher's Boat House, 4940 Canal Rd NW (ⓣ202/244-0461, ⓦwww.fletchers boathouse.com), which rents rowboats and canoes, and Thompson Boat Center, 2900 Virginia Ave NW (ⓣ202/333-9543, ⓦwww.thompsonboatcenter.com), with its single and double kayaks, canoes, and rowing shells.

Northern Georgetown

Set on "The Heights" above Q Street, the grand mansions and estates of **northern Georgetown** sat out the upheavals that took place below during the nineteenth and twentieth centuries. Owned by the area's richest merchants, the land here was never exploited for new construction when Georgetown was in the throes of expansion. Today several of the fine homes and beautiful grounds are open to the public.

From the middle of Georgetown, the easiest way to get to the neighborhood is straight up Wisconsin Avenue (Bus #30, #32, #34, #35, or #36 from M St). From New Downtown, just cross Dumbarton Bridge from Massachusetts Avenue NW (Dupont Circle Metro) and you'll be right on Q Street. The DC Circulator is also a handy choice for accessing the upper reaches of Wisconsin Avenue (see p.31).

Tudor Place

1644 31st St NW ⓣ202/965-0400, ⓦwww.tudorplace.org. Tours Tues–Fri 10am–2.30pm, Sat 10am–3pm, Sun noon–3pm; $6.

Two blocks east of Wisconsin Avenue between Q and R streets, stately **Tudor Place** was designed by William Thornton, who was also responsible for the US Capitol and Georgetown's St John's Episcopal Church. Completed in 1816 for Thomas Peter (descendant of one of the area's original Scottish tobacco merchants and son of Georgetown's first mayor) and his wife Martha Custis Peter (granddaughter of Martha Washington), the house displays an incongruity that was rare for the period – Thornton embellished the fundamentally Federal-style structure with a Classical domed portico on the south side. The exterior has remained virtually untouched since and, as the house stayed in the same family for more than 160 years, the interior has been spared the constant "improve-ments" wrought in Georgetown's other period homes by successive owners.

Guided tours show you furnishings lifted from the Washingtons' family seat at Mount Vernon and fill you in on how Martha Peter watched from her bedroom window in the then-unfinished house as British troops burned down the US Capitol in 1814. You're supposed to reserve in advance for the tours, but ringing the bell at the front gate gives you access to the five and a half acres of gardens during the day (Mon–Sat 10am–4pm, Sun noon–4pm; free). Walk up the path and bear to the right where a white box holds detailed maps ($2 donation) of the paths, greens, box hedges, arbors, and fountains. You can also request a guided garden tour (reserve at ℡202/965-0400 ext. 115) to take you around the fetching surroundings.

Dumbarton Oaks

1703 32nd St ℡202/339-6401, ⓦwww.doaks.org. Gardens daily 2–5pm, until 6pm mid-Mar to Oct; $8.

One long block east of Wisconsin Avenue, and just north of Tudor Place, the grand estate of **Dumbarton Oaks** encompasses a marvelous red-brick Georgian mansion surrounded by gardens and woods. In 1703 Scottish pioneer Ninian Beall was granted almost 800 acres of land, stretching from the river to Rock Creek, and proceeded to make himself a fortune in the tobacco trade. Although much of the land was later sold by his descendants, more than enough of the coveted northern reaches remained for newcomer William H. Dorsey to create the house and landscaping in 1800. The estate was added to and renovated over the years before being acquired by diplomat **Robert Woods Bliss** in 1920 to house his significant collection of world art. In 1940 the house was handed on to Harvard University (the current owner), and in 1944 its commodious Music Room hosted a meeting of American, Russian, British, and Chinese delegates, whose deliberations led to the founding of the United Nations the following year.

Unfortunately, much of the mansion is not open to the public, but its ten acres of **formal gardens** (entrance at 3101 R St), with their beech terrace, evergreens, rose garden, brick paths, pools, and fountains, provide one of DC's quietest and most relaxing retreats. The estate's highlight, however, and the one part of the mansion open to the public, is its terrific **museum**, due to reopen by the end of 2008 after undergoing a long and costly renovation.

Sure to be on view when the place again opens its doors, the striking selection of **pre-Columbian** art, one of the statesman's obsessions, comprises countless gold, jade, and polychromatic carvings, sculpture, and pendants of Olmec, Inca, Aztec, and Mayan provenance – among them ceremonial axes, jewelry made from spondylus shells, stone masks of unknown significance, and sharp jade "celts" possibly used for human sacrifice. Bliss was equally fascinated by the **Byzantine Empire**, and his silver Eucharist vessels, ivory boxes, and painted icons are all standouts. Ancient items like a second-century porphyry urn and Syrian mosaic of Narcissus are equally impressive. Perhaps most extraordinary is the miniature fourteenth-century mosaic icon of the Forty Martyrs, which depicts – in cubes of enamel paste and semiprecious stone – forty Roman soldiers left to freeze to death because they refused to recant their Christian beliefs. Finally, you may be able to take a peek in the **Music Room** and see its wondrous paintings and tapestries, walnut chests and credenzas, decorative wooden ceiling, and vintage pianos and harpsichords.

Dumbarton House

2715 Q St NW ℗202/337-2288, Ⓦwww.dumbartonhouse.org. 45min tours at quarter past the hour Tues–Sat 10.15am–1.15pm; $5.

Past 27th Street, **Dumbarton House** is one of the oldest homes in George-town, built between 1799 and 1804. The construction of the bridge over Rock Creek in 1915 necessitated the house's removal, brick by brick, from farther down Q Street to its present position. Known for a century as "Bellevue," the elegant Georgian mansion housed Georgetown's first salon, as political leaders of the day came to call on Joseph Nourse, registrar of the US Treasury, who lived here until 1813. The following year, as the British overran Washington, Dolley Madison watched the White House burning from Bellevue's windows (the house was the first refuge for the fleeing president and first lady). The **National Society of Colonial Dames of America**, now headquartered here, will provide the historical skinny and escort you slowly through period rooms filled with Federal furniture, early prints of Washington, DC, and middling portraits. If you don't have 45 minutes to spare or an insatiable interest in decorative porcelain that once, possibly, adorned the White House, content yourself instead with a seat in the quiet, restful garden.

Mount Zion and Oak Hill cemeteries

Recalling a time when there was still a significant black presence in Georgetown, **Mount Zion Cemetery** is the oldest burial ground in the city, and is hidden away down an offshoot of 27th Street (northern side of Q St) just five minutes from Dumbarton Bridge. The site is actually a pair of graveyards that together are known as Mount Zion. The first, the Old Methodist Burying Ground, dates from 1808 and was designed for the burial of members of the Mount Zion Methodist Church, whose membership was unusual for the time – half-white, half-black, with the blacks split between freedmen and slaves. (Their fine red-brick church still stands at 1334 29th Street, at Dumbarton Street.) The second burial ground, the Female Union Band Society Graveyard, dates from 1842. The cemetery in full has been neglected over the years, with headstones scattered through the tangled undergrowth, but a start has been made in tidying the place up and restoring some of the monumental gravestones. If you want to take a tour, call the Mount Zion Church at ℗202/234-0148.

There's still a long way to go, however, before Mount Zion matches the pristine grounds of the adjacent **Oak Hill Cemetery**, 3001 R St (Mon–Fri 10am–4pm; ℗202/337-2835), whose tiered gravestones you can glimpse through the trees beyond. Endowed by banker and art collector William Corcoran, exclusive Oak Hill began receiving Georgetown's wealthy dead in 1849. Dating from that time is the brick **gatehouse** at 30th and R streets, where you enter the lovingly kept grounds that spill down the hillside to Rock Creek. Within the grounds, the diminutive brick-and-sandstone **Gothic chapel** is the sprightly work of James Renwick (architect of the Smithsonian Castle), while to the west stands a marble plinth with a bust of John Howard Payne – author of the treacly song "Home, Sweet Home." Ask at the gatehouse for directions to the resting homes of the cemetery's other notable names, including Corcoran himself; Edwin Stanton, secretary of war under President Lincoln; and former Secretary of State Dean Acheson.

10

Arlington, VA

For many visitors, **Arlington, Virginia**, is synonymous with its eponymous cemetery, and little else. However, this small city-county across the Potomac from Washington has experienced an influx of urban refugees in the past decade, giving rise to a number of good restaurants, bars, clubs, and theaters – so sticking around for an evening isn't a bad idea at all.

In the first half of the nineteenth century Arlington was part of the District of Columbia. In 1846, though, in order to secure more pro-slavery delegates in their legislature (which then had a sizable component of anti-slavery figures), Virginia officials demanded back the thirty square miles it had contributed to the capital city 55 years earlier. For many years Confederate commander Robert E. Lee lived on the sloping hills at his **Arlington House**, overlooking the Potomac and beyond, but during the Civil War the federal government confiscated his land to bury the Union dead in what would become **Arlington National Cemetery**. As an act of reconciliation, in the 1930s Arlington Memorial Bridge was dedicated, symbolically connecting the Lincoln Memorial with the dead of both sides of the war now buried in the cemetery.

The Arlington Memorial is one of three bridges (the Francis Scott Key and 14th Street the others) that directly link the suburb to the city; in addition, the **Metrorail** provides easy access on its Orange, Blue, and Yellow lines – the latter two routed through DC's domestic airport, Reagan National, which is also in Arlington. The fact that the **Pentagon**, the country's military headquarters, is sited here only bolsters this close relationship to the capital. Across the Potomac to the immediate east is the pleasant and walkable refuge of **Theodore Roosevelt Island**, while the **Mount Vernon Trail** – which runs to Alexandria and down to George Washington's estate – is to the south.

While its southern neighbor, Alexandria (see p.253), is still a bit better for **dining** and **shopping**, Arlington does boast a few major malls in the neighborhoods of Pentagon City and Crystal City (not themselves destinations), and conveniently, much of the **nightlife** scene is found around the Clarendon and Court House districts and their Metro stations.

Arlington National Cemetery

Across Arlington Memorial Bridge Ⓣ 703/607-8000, Ⓦ www.arlingtoncemetery.org; Arlington Cemetery Metro. Daily: April–Sept 8am–7pm; Oct–March 8am–5pm.

Washington's grand monuments sit across the Potomac from a sea of identical white headstones spreading through the hillsides of **Arlington National Cemetery**. The 624-acre site commemorates the deaths of some 300,000 US soldiers and their dependants, as well as John and Robert Kennedy, whose

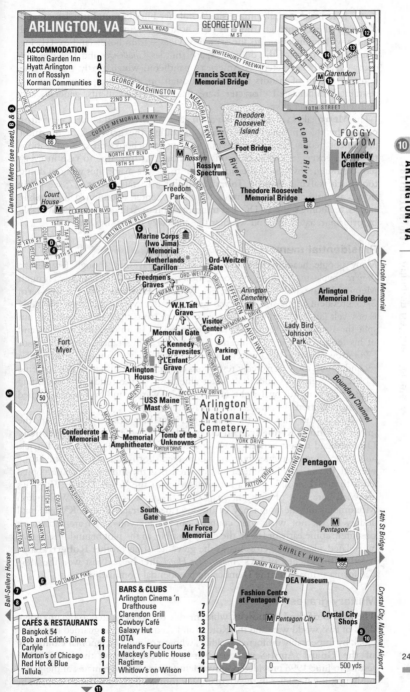

ARLINGTON, VA

GEORGETOWN

M ST

CANAL ROAD

WHITEHURST FREEWAY

Francis Scott Key Memorial Bridge

Theodore Roosevelt Island

FOGGY BOTTOM

Kennedy Center

ACCOMMODATION

Hilton Garden Inn	D
Hyatt Arlington	A
Inn of Rosslyn	C
Korman Communities	B

GEORGE WASHINGTON

22ND ST
21ST ST
UHLE ST
NORTH KEY BLVD
18TH ST
M Rosslyn

CURTIS MEMORIAL PKWY

NORTH NASH ST
N NASH ST
FORT MYER DRIVE
N KENT
MEMORIAL PKWY

Rosslyn Spectrum

Freedom Park

Theodore Roosevelt Memorial Bridge

Little Potomac River

66

Lincoln Memorial

Court House
2 M

CLARENDON BLVD

15TH ST
RHODES ST
PIERCE ST
OAK ST

ARLINGTON BLVD

4 M

14TH ST
13TH ST
SCOTT ST
ROLFE ST
TAFT ST
TROY ST
COURTHOUSE RD
WAYNE ST
VEITCH ST

Marine Corps (Iwo Jima) Memorial
C

Netherlands Carillon

Ord-Weitzel Gate

Freedmen's Graves

ORD-WEITZEL DRIVE

Arlington Cemetery

Arlington Memorial Bridge

W.H. Taft Grave

Visitor Center

Memorial Gate

Lady Bird Johnson Park

Fort Myer

Kennedy Gravesites

L'Enfant Grave

Arlington House

EISENHOWER DRIVE

Parking Lot
P

50

ARLINGTON BLVD

USS Maine Mast

MCCLELLAN DRIVE

Arlington National Cemetery

Boundary Channel

Confederate Memorial

Memorial Amphitheater

Tomb of the Unknowns

PORTER DRIVE

GRANT DRIVE

YORK DRIVE

Pentagon

2ND ST
VEITCH ST
WAYNE ST
ADAMS ST
BARTON ST

WASHINGTON BLVD

South Gate

Air Force Memorial

PATTON DRIVE

WASHINGTON BLVD

M Pentagon

14th St Bridge

Ball-Sellers House

COLUMBIA PIKE

6

7
8

SHIRLEY HWY

ARMY NAVY DRIVE

395

DEA Museum

Crystal City, National Airport

CAFÉS & RESTAURANTS

Bangkok 54	8
Bob and Edith's Diner	6
Carlyle	11
Morton's of Chicago	9
Red Hot & Blue	1
Tallula	5

BARS & CLUBS

Arlington Cinema 'n Drafthouse	7
Clarendon Grill	15
Cowboy Café	3
Galaxy Hut	12
IOTA	13
Ireland's Four Courts	2
Mackey's Public House	10
Ragtime	4
Whitlow's on Wilson	14

Fashion Centre at Pentagon City

M Pentagon City

Crystal City Shops

9
10

N

0   500 yds

Clarendon Metro (see inset; B & 3)

Clarendon inset

KEY BLVD
FANCEY ST
HARTFORD ST
GARFIELD ST
WILSON BLVD
CLARENDON
DANVILLE ST
FRANKLIN RD

12

HERNDON ST
HUDSON ST
IRVING ST

14
13

M Clarendon
15

WASHINGTON

11TH ST

10TH STREET

graves here make it a pilgrimage site. A military burial ground (the largest and oldest in the country), Arlington also holds the remains of other national figures with connections to the armed services – from boxer (and ex-GI) Joe Louis to the crew of the doomed space shuttles *Challenger* and *Columbia*. In many ways the cemetery is America's pantheon, which partly excuses the constant stream of visitors trampling through on sightseeing tours. There's a restrained, understated character here that honors presidents, generals, and enlisted personnel alike.

The **Metro** takes you right to the main gates on Memorial Drive. The **visitor center** by the entrance issues **maps** indicating the gravesites of the most prominent people buried here, while various guidebooks on sale offer more thorough coverage. The cemetery is enormous (far too large to take in every plot on a single visit), so if you simply want to see the major sites without doing too much walking, board a **Tourmobile** for a narrated **tour** ($7; see p.30); tickets are sold at the booth inside the visitor center. (Combined Tourmobile tickets, including sights in DC and transportation to Arlington, are also available by prior purchase.) In good weather the cemetery is busy by 9am.

Presidential memorials

Many people head straight for the Kennedy gravesites, though few realize they're bypassing Arlington's only other presidential occupant. Through Memorial Gate, just to the right, lies **William Howard Taft**, the one-term 27th president (1909–13) who was groomed as a worthy successor to Teddy Roosevelt (and in fact did bust more corporate trusts than his predecessor) but split the Republican Party with his intransigence. In an outburst near the end of his tenure, he said: "The nearer I get to the inauguration of my successor [Woodrow Wilson], the greater the relief I feel." Taft – uniquely – enjoyed a second, much more personally rewarding career as chief justice of the Supreme Court between 1921 and 1930. Later chief justices also reside here, including pioneering constitutional-rights archetype Earl Warren and his less enlightened successors Warren Burger and William Rehnquist.

Farther up the hillside is the marble terrace where simple plaques mark the graves of **John F. Kennedy**, 35th US president, his wife **Jacqueline Kennedy Onassis** (laid to rest here in 1994), and two of their children – a son, Patrick, and an unnamed daughter, both of whom died shortly after birth. Jackie lit the **eternal flame** at JFK's funeral and ordered that the funeral decor be copied from that of Lincoln's, held a century earlier in the White House. When it's crowded here, as it often is, the majesty of the view across to the Washington Monument and the poignancy of the inscribed extracts from JFK's inaugural address ("Ask not what your country can do for you . . .") are sometimes obscured; come early or late in the day if possible. In the plot behind JFK's grave, an isolated, plain white cross marks the gravesite of his brother **Robert**, assassinated in the kitchen of LA's *Ambassador Hotel* after he had just won the 1968 California primary for the Democratic presidential nomination.

Military graves

The **Tomb of the Unknowns**, white marble blocks dedicated to the unknown dead of two world wars and the Korean and Vietnam wars, is guarded round the clock by impeccably uniformed soldiers who carry out a ceremonial **Changing of the Guard** (April–Sept every half-hour, otherwise on the hour). DNA testing in June 1998 provided positive identification of the remains of the previously unknown soldier in the Vietnam War tomb, which now stands empty. The circular, colonnaded **Memorial Amphitheater** behind the tomb is the site of special remembrance services, especially busy during key holidays like Memorial Day and Veterans Day, when the spartan marble columns form an appropriately somber backdrop.

Arlington National Cemetery began as a burial ground for **Union soldiers**, on land taken from Robert E. Lee after he joined the Confederate army at the outset of the Civil War. As a national cemetery, though, it was subsequently deemed politic to honor the dead on both sides of the war; the **Confederate section**, with its own memorial, lies to the west of the Tomb of the Unknowns, while on the very northern edge of the cemetery are buried some 1500 **black troops** who fought for the Union during that war and 3800 **former slaves** who lived in a parcel of land called Freedmen's Village, who were removed from their land during the cemetery's creation. Most of their gravesites are marked without names. Other sections and memorials commemorate America's long list of conflicts, from the Revolutionary War to the current wars in Afghanistan and Iraq, with a few dozen markers for **foreign troops** from Britain, France, Italy, and Canada.

The highest concentration of notable military graves is found in the myriad plots surrounding the Tomb of the Unknowns: with a map, and an eye for knots of camera-toting tourists, you'll find the graves of **Audie Murphy**, the most decorated soldier in World War II, and boxer **Joe Louis** (born, and buried here, as Joe Louis Barrow), world heavyweight champion from 1937 to 1949. Elsewhere are the graves of **Robert Todd Lincoln**, President Lincoln's son; **John J. Pershing**, commander of American forces in World War I (who has a separate park in his honor in the Federal Triangle); Arctic explorer **Robert Peary**; civil rights leader **Medgar Evers**, shot in 1963 by rampaging racists in the Deep South; astronauts **Virgil Grissom** and **Roger Chaffee** of the ill-fated 1967 *Apollo* flight; tough-guy actor **Lee Marvin**; pioneering black lawyer and first African American Supreme Court justice **Thurgood Marshall**, among seven other associate justices; and thriller-writer **Dashiell Hammett**, a World War II sergeant. The latter honoree is perhaps the most unexpected, as the writer was threatened by official Washington throughout much of his later life – denounced as a subversive by self-appointed moral crusaders, investigated and jailed for "un-American" activities during the McCarthyite witch hunts of the 1950s, and finally hounded by the IRS for tax delinquency.

Group memorials

The most photographed of the many group memorials is the one dedicated to those who died aboard the space shuttle **Challenger**; it is located immediately behind the amphitheatre, though a more recent marker commemorates the crew of the similarly doomed **Columbia** mission. Adjacent to the *Challenger* site is the memorial to the **Iran Rescue Mission**, whose failure in snatching American embassy workers from their captors doomed Jimmy Carter at the polls in 1980. Both stand close to the mast of the **USS Maine**, whose mysterious destruction in Havana harbor in 1898 – still debated more than a century later – prompted the rise of "yellow journalism" and the short-lived Spanish–American War; the war itself is commemorated by a memorial and a monument to the **Rough Riders**, a devil-may-care cavalry outfit in which a young Theodore Roosevelt made his reputation.

More controversial is the memorial inscribed with the names of those killed in the 1988 terrorist explosion of **Pan Am flight 103** over Lockerbie, Scotland; some felt its location in a military cemetery was inappropriate. Dedicated in 1997, the **Women in Military Service** memorial, situated at the main gateway, is the country's first national monument to honor American servicewomen, though there's an honorary group statue at the Vietnam Veterans Memorial, while the very recent **Pentagon Memorial** is a five-sided black-granite stone inscribed with the names of Washington's victims of the 9/11 attacks.

Arlington House

Sherman Drive, in Arlington National Cemetery ☏703/235-1530, ⊛www.nps.gov/arho; Arlington Cemetery Metro. Daily 9.30am–4.30pm.

Immediately above the Kennedy gravesites, the imposing **Arlington House** has served as a memorial to Confederate commander Robert E. Lee since 1933. Built in the early nineteenth century by George Washington Parke Custis, the grandson of Martha Washington by her first marriage (the cemetery stands on land that formerly belonged to Custis), the house passed to his daughter, Mary, after his death. Her marriage in 1830 to Lee, a lieutenant in the US Army, was later of enormous consequence: in 1861, Lee was at Arlington House when he heard the news that Virginia had seceded from the Union.

Coming from a proud Virginian family, whose number included two signatories of the Declaration of Independence, the West Point–trained Lee was torn between showing loyalty to his native state and committing himself to the preservation of the Union that he served. His decision was made more difficult when, at Blair House, just a block from the White House itself, President Lincoln offered Lee command of the US Army. But loyalty to his state won out – Lee resigned his commission and left Arlington for Richmond, where he took command of Virginia's military forces. Mary fled Arlington a month later as Union soldiers consolidated their hold on DC, and the federal government eventually confiscated the estate. The two never returned to Arlington, and as early as 1864 a **cemetery** for the Union dead was established on the grounds of the house, with the mansion itself used as an ad hoc **camp** for Union soldiers. A year later, Lee – now general-in-chief of the Confederate armies – surrendered to General Grant at Appomattox Court House. After Lee's death, his family took their case to the US Supreme Court; they argued for the return of the family land and succeeded in getting it back in 1874. However, they ultimately had to sell it back to the government Lee had fought against because, despite their earlier wealth and prominence, the clan had fallen on hard times and needed the money – $150,000.

The house itself is a Greek Revival mansion that features six thick Tuscan columns and a stately Neoclassical style, adding grandeur to its position on the high ground above the Potomac. The interior is being restored in a lengthy process that isn't due to be finished until 2010. Presumably, once the house is reopened, highlights will include the principal bedroom, where Lee wrote his resignation letter from the US Army before the Civil War, and the family parlor, in which he was married; a fair number of the furnishings are original. On the estate's north side is a small **museum** that tells the family saga and recounts Lee's history, though the bent toward the heroic may be too much for visitors lacking ardor for the Confederate "Lost Cause."

From the grounds the views across the river to the Mall are stunning. No less a man than the **Marquis de Lafayette**, a guest at Arlington House in 1824, thought the aspect "the finest view in the world." Fittingly, the grave of Washington DC designer **Pierre Charles L'Enfant** was belatedly sited here in 1909 after the US government forgave his feuding over pay for his services; there is a small memorial to him here as well, though the city itself still lacks a proper monument to his accomplishments.

⑩

Marine Corps Memorial and Netherlands Carillon

Arlington Blvd at Meade St ☎703/289-2500, ⓦwww.nps.gov/gwmp/usmc.htm; Arlington Cemetery Metro. Daily 24hr.

Lying to the north, just outside the cemetery walls, is the hugely impressive 78ft-high bronze **Marine Corps Memorial**. It's about a twenty-minute walk from the cemetery's main visitor center to the **Ord–Weitzel Gate**, though the easiest approach is to take the **Metro** to the **Rosslyn** station, from which it's

▲ Marine Corps Memorial

a ten-minute, signposted walk. The memorial commemorates the Marine dead of all wars – from the first casualties of the Revolutionary War to the fallen in Iraq – but it's more popularly known as the **Iwo Jima Statue**, after the "uncommon valor" shown by US troops in the bloody World War II battle for the small but strategically essential Pacific island where 6800 lives were lost. In a famous image – inspired by a contemporaneous photograph – half a dozen marines raise the Stars and Stripes on Mount Suribachi in February 1945; three of the survivors of the actual flag-raising posed for sculptor Felix W. de Weldon, and the site remains one of the few federal installations that allows Old Glory to fly around the clock, without a ceremonial raising or lowering. In summer (June–Aug), the US Marine Corps presents a **parade** and **concert** at the memorial every Tuesday at 7pm, and the annual **Marine Corps Marathon** starts here each October.

Nearby, to the south, rises the **Netherlands Carillon**, a 130ft-high steel monument dedicated to the Netherlands' liberation from the Nazis in 1945. Given by the Dutch in thanks for American aid, the tower is set in landscaped grounds featuring thousands of **tulips**, which bloom each spring. The fifty copper-and-tin bells of the carillon are rung on Saturdays and holidays (May–Sept), at which times you can climb the tower for superlative city views.

Air Force Memorial

1 Air Force Memorial Dr, Columbia Pike off Washington Blvd ☎703/979-0674, ⓦwww.airforcememorial.org. Daily: April–Sept 8am–11pm, Oct–Mar 8am–9pm.

Lying south of Arlington National Cemetery at Fort Myer is the **Air Force Memorial**, a long-delayed tribute to America's airmen that was originally due to be sited near the Marine Corps Memorial until that service decided it didn't want it anywhere nearby, potentially overshadowing it. In any case, it has become a towering tribute to US pilots, air crews, and support personnel. Dedicated in 2006, the site, which will eventually be on the grounds of the expanding cemetery, is immediately recognizable by its three giant steel arcs, which twist out 270ft into the sky and, by their placement, recall a missing fourth arc – the so-called "missing man" – a familiar maneuver at Air Force flight shows and exhibitions. The image is underlined further by the Contemplation Wall, which shows aircraft in such a display and salutes the dead of the service's twentieth-century wars. Elsewhere, granite entry walls are inscribed with names of the service's Medal of Honor winners and inspirational quotes, and a quartet of 8ft bronze statues recalls an honor guard with crisp, martial form.

The Pentagon

I-395 at Jefferson Davis Hwy ☎703/695-3325, ⓦpentagon.afis.osd.mil; Pentagon Metro. Tours by reservation only.

The locus of modern American war-making, the **Pentagon** is the seat of the **US Department of Defense**, and one of the largest chunks of architecture in the world, with its five 900ft-long sides enclosing 17.5 miles of corridors and a floor area of 6.5 million square feet, all of it now being renovated in a decade-long program.

Terrorists left their mark on this massive structure on 9/11 when they crashed **American Airlines flight 77** into its western flank, tearing open a hole almost 200ft wide – an event that will be remembered when an outdoor **Pentagon Memorial** opens in late 2008, featuring 184 benches that will commemorate each person killed at the site. In the wake of the attack, the military suspended all general Pentagon **tours**, though they've since resumed for veterans and school groups of five or more people. If you're a US citizen, you can also try contacting your senator or representative to gain access; foreign nationals may contact their embassy; check the website for more details. In any case, the tours mainly focus on the prosaic aspects of the building, among them its prodigious size – number of restrooms, pints of milk drunk daily by its 25,000 employees, and so on. What you won't hear about are all the antiwar protests that have taken place near the building over the decades, the most memorable being the 1967 March on the Pentagon in which 35,000 protesters tried to psychically levitate the building 300ft in the air.

Perhaps the most interesting thing about the Pentagon is the structure itself, which was thrown together in just sixteen months during World War II to consolidate seventeen different buildings of what in those days was properly called the **War Department**. Efficiency dictated the five-story, five-sided design: with so many employees, it was imperative to maintain quick contact between separate offices and departments – it takes just seven minutes to walk between any two points in the building. Built on swamp- and wasteland, the building was constructed entirely of **concrete** (fashioned from Potomac sand and gravel) rather than the marble that brightens the rest of Washington; President Roosevelt thus neatly avoided boosting the Axis war effort since Mussolini's Italy was then the world's foremost supplier of marble.

Crossing the Potomac by bridge, the **Metro Yellow Line** affords great views of the Pentagon. The Pentagon Metro station, however, no longer allows you to exit directly into the building lobby. Instead, you'll be let out near the bus stop and have to pass through a new, tightly controlled entry complex. If you're interested in shopping, the next two southbound Metro stations let you off near, or directly in, a pair of massive malls at Crystal City and Pentagon City.

DEA Museum

700 Army Navy Drive ℗202/307-3463, ℗www.deamuseum.org; Pentagon City Metro. Tues–Fri 10am–4pm.

Disappointed perhaps at not being able to tour the Pentagon itself, those still interested in gung-ho military bravado might enjoy a visit to the **Drug Enforcement Agency Museum**, across from the Pentagon City Mall. Here you can ignite your enthusiasm for America's ongoing, and seemingly endless, **War on Drugs** with a cache of exhibits designed to persuade you of the fundamental rectitude of hunting down drug kingpins and sending narcotics users and traffickers to prison for long periods of time. In "**Target America**," the museum goes for broke trying to prove the links between stateless terrorist groups and drug barons, undergirding its presentation with a chunk of actual rubble from the World Trade Center. The most elaborate display, though, is the historical timeline of drugs in the US, which, through photos, documents, and artifacts, traces Americans' fascination with mind-altering substances from the mid-nineteenth-century opium wars to beatnik 1950s hopheads to the rise of cocaine in the 1980s and beyond (conveniently left out is corporate America's role in the development of some of the most dangerous drugs, including OxyContin). But the museum can be strangely captivating, with a score of vintage pipes, rolling papers, posters, and other oddments on view – surely the one and only place in official Washington where this much drug paraphernalia is on public display.

Wolf Trap

About ten miles west of Arlington via Route 7 is what some call the Kennedy Center of folk music. In 1966, Congress declared **Wolf Trap**, 1624 Trap Rd, Vienna, VA (℡703/255-1868 or 255-1900, ⓦ www.wolftrap.org), a "National Park for the Performing Arts," meaning that it would be devoted to American music in all its native forms, like bluegrass, jazz, ragtime, Cajun, zydeco, Native American, and countless others. The space for this music could hardly be better – a pair of remodeled barns from the eighteenth century (moved here from upstate New York), which provide just the right weathered charm and echoey acoustics for instruments such as banjos, guitars, mandolins, gourds, and washboards; in the summer they host local performances of classic operas. The German barn is the larger of the two, giving you a chance to listen to the music on the "threshing floor" or in a hayloft above. Wolf Trap's other venues include the modern, less atmospheric Filene Center and a theatrical stage. Prices can vary widely, so check the website for detailed information. For directions on how to get there by public transportation, call ℡202/637-7000 or visit ⓦ www.wmata.com – Metro shuttle-bus service is available for most performances from the West Falls Church Metro station. The park has concession stands and a restaurant, but in summer it's nicer to bring a picnic and eat on the grass.

The Mount Vernon Trail and Theodore Roosevelt Island

If you've had enough of official government sights and are interested in doing a little hiking or biking, you might consider taking on the 18.5-mile **Mount Vernon Trail**, which runs parallel to the George Washington Memorial Parkway, from Arlington Memorial Bridge south seven miles to Alexandria and on to Mount Vernon in Virginia. The trail sticks close to the Potomac for its entire length and runs past a number of sites of historic or natural interest. For more information, and a free **trail guide**, contact the National Park Service in Washington (℡202/619-7222, ⓦ www.nps.gov). Those looking for a quieter place for a constitutional should head to **Theodore Roosevelt Island** (℡703/289-2500, ⓦ www.nps.gov/this), a nature park with 2.5 miles of trails that meander through marsh, swamp, and forest, presided over by a declamatory statue of the eponymous 26th president himself. Access to the island, which lies at the start of the Mount Vernon Trail, is via a footbridge from the Arlington side of the Potomac, not far from the Rosslyn Metro station.

Ball-Sellers House

5620 S 3rd St ℡703/379-2123, ⓦ www.arlingtonhistoricalsociety.org. April–Oct Sat 1–4pm.

Five miles west of the Potomac, just off Arlington Boulevard, the surprisingly well-preserved **Ball–Sellers House** is one of the oldest homes in the area, and offers a nice counterpart to Georgetown's Old Stone House. Both were crafted from rough-hewn oak logs and built largely by their owners in the mid-1700s, with the Ball-Sellers' beams joined together with notches, its roof made of clapboard panels, and the cracks in its walls sealed with mud. What remains, then, is an eye-opening and heartening image of what it took to survive in the north Virginia country before the nascent city of Washington swallowed up the surrounding land (which it would later relinquish). Although it isn't open very often and is convenient only for those going on a driving tour of the area, the house, listed on the National Register of Historic Places, is worth a visit to see how common folk lived before the advent of the grand capital city a half-century later.

11

Alexandria, VA

S ix miles south of Washington, DC, across the Potomac, **Alexandria, Virginia** – a historic gem thick with restored Georgian manors, revolutionary-era taverns and churches, and other hallmarks of the region's rich past – predates the capital considerably. The area is so rich and alive with history in part because Virginia was the first and biggest British colony on the continent; it generated the bulk of its wealth through a tobacco industry that relied on thousands of imported slaves. Also, the state had a habit of producing national leaders, including the likes of George Washington, Thomas Jefferson, and Robert E. Lee. But following the Civil War, it began a long decline that kept it out of the limelight for many decades; a good thing, too, for this benign neglect also helped it retain many of its historic structures, which otherwise would have been lost to gung-ho 1960s urban renewal, as happened in many other places in DC.

Alexandria's well-preserved city center gives a good idea of what eighteenth-century life was like for the wealthy **tobacco farmers** who lived here. First settled by Scotsman John Alexander in 1699, Alexandria was granted town status fifty years later – a 17-year-old George Washington assisted in the preliminary survey (a claim bolstered by the existence of a contemporaneous parchment map with his name on it in the Library of Congress). By the time of the Revolution, Alexandria was a booming port and trading center, exporting wheat and flour to the West Indies, with a thriving social and political scene. With the establishment of the new capital in 1791, the town was incorporated into the District of Columbia very much against the wishes of its estate- and slave-owning Southern planters, and few were sorry when, in 1846, Virginia demanded its land back from the federal government. Alexandria's Confederate sympathies led to its being occupied by Union troops during the Civil War, which, in turn, led to the town's decline: the railroad tracks built to move troops and supplies throughout northern Virginia were later employed to carry freight, destroying Alexandria's shipping business in one blow.

What's now known as **Old Town Alexandria** – the compact downtown grid by the Potomac – was left to rot in the later nineteenth century. Many of the warehouses and wharves were abandoned, while other buildings became munitions factories during both world wars. Today, after decades of spirited renovation, the Colonial-era streets and converted warehouses are hugely popular attractions, making the town a charming relic just across the water from the nation's capital. Nor is it all preserved in theme-park isolation, since Old Town forms part of the booming commuter town of greater Alexandria. It's also prime **shopping** territory, with antiques, crafts, ethnic, folk-art, vintage-clothing, and gift stores on every corner. Good hunting grounds are at the upper end of

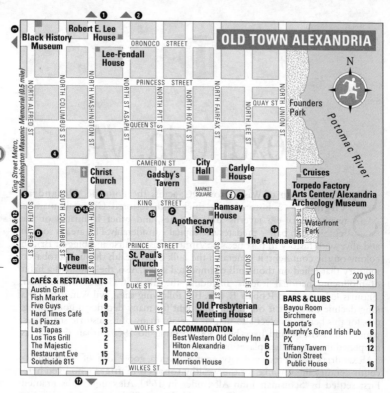

OLD TOWN ALEXANDRIA

N

Black History Museum

Robert E. Lee House

Lee-Fendall House

ORONOCO STREET

NORTH ALFRED ST

NORTH COLUMBUS ST

NORTH WASHINGTON ST

NORTH ST ASAPH ST

PRINCESS STREET

QUEEN ST

NORTH PITT ST

NORTH ROYAL ST

NORTH FAIRFAX ST

QUAY ST

NORTH LEE ST

NORTH UNION ST

Founders Park

Potomac River

King Street Metro, Washington Masonic Memorial (0.5 mile)

CAMERON ST

City Hall

Carlyle House

Cruises

Christ Church

Gadsby's Tavern

MARKET SQUARE

Torpedo Factory Arts Center/ Alexandria Archeology Museum

SOUTH COLUMBUS ST

SOUTH WASHINGTON ST

KING STREET

Ramsay House

THE STRAND

Waterfront Park

SOUTH ALFRED ST

Apothecary Shop

The Athenaeum

PRINCE STREET

SOUTH FAIRFAX ST

SOUTH LEE ST

The Lyceum

St. Paul's Church

DUKE ST

0   200 yds

SOUTH PITT ST

SOUTH ROYAL ST

CAFÉS & RESTAURANTS

Austin Grill	4
Fish Market	8
Five Guys	9
Hard Times Café	10
La Piazza	3
Las Tapas	13
Los Tios Grill	2
The Majestic	5
Restaurant Eve	15
Southside 815	17

WOLFE ST

Old Presbyterian Meeting House

ACCOMMODATION

Best Western Old Colony Inn	A
Hilton Alexandria	B
Monaco	C
Morrison House	D

BARS & CLUBS

Bayou Room	7
Birchmere	1
Laporta's	11
Murphy's Grand Irish Pub	6
PX	14
Tiffany Tavern	12
Union Street Public House	16

WILKES ST

King Street (toward the Metro station), along Cameron Street (behind City Hall), and at the Torpedo Factory Arts Center (on the waterfront).

Although the main drags – particularly King Street – are heavy with traffic, it's not hard to find pockets of peace and quiet here. Cobbled, tree-lined streets with herringbone brick sidewalks are lined with pastel-washed houses featuring boot-scrapers and horse-mounting blocks outside the front door, and cast-iron drainpipes stamped "Alexandria, DC."

Old Town practicalities

The **Metro** station for Old Town Alexandria is King Street (Yellow and Blue lines; twenty-five from downtown DC), a mile or so from most of the sights. Outside King Street station, pick up the local **DASH** bus ($1; for timetable information call ☎703/370-3274, ⓦ www.dashbus.com), which runs down King Street, and get off at Fairfax Street; if you prefer, you can take the twenty-minute walk from the station instead. **Drivers** should follow the George Washington Memorial Parkway south from Arlington and take the East King Street exit. Metered parking in the Old Town is hard to come by, though a free 24-hour parking pass is available by taking ID and car registration to the visitor center (see below). Cyclists or walkers can get here using the **Mount Vernon Trail**; in Old Town Alexandria, Big Wheel Bikes, 2 Prince St (☎703/739-2300, ⓦ www.bigwheelbikes.com; see also p.33), can rent you a bike to ride to and from Mount Vernon, ten miles away.

Old Town is laid out on a grid, and most of the sights lie within a ten-block area. Guided walks, ghost tours, and river cruises (see p.259) operate during the high season. Note that many sights are closed on Monday, and that opening hours are limited on Sunday.

Ramsay House

The town's **visitor center**, in the **Ramsay House**, 221 King St (daily 9am–5pm; ☎703/838-5005, ⓦwww.funside.com), provides pamphlets and information on countless historic sites and curiosities. The house itself is the oldest in town, built (though not originally on this site) in 1724 for **William Ramsay**, one of Alexandria's founding merchants and later its first mayor. Ramsay had the house transported upriver from Dumfries, Virginia, and placed facing the river, where his ships loaded up with tobacco. The water is now three blocks away: the bluff that the town was built on was excavated after the Revolutionary War, and the earth was used to extend the harbor into the shallow bay, which is why Ramsay House stands so high above the street, its foundations exposed.

Carlyle House and City Hall

When the town was established, Ramsay's fellow merchant **John Carlyle** bought two of the most expensive land plots and built Alexandria's finest Colonial-era home. In the 1750s, when all the town's other buildings were constructed of wood, the Georgian, white-sandstone **Carlyle House**, 121 N Fairfax St (Tues–Sat 10am–4pm, Sun noon–4pm; $4, or $9 combo admission with Gadsby's Tavern and Apothecary Museum; ☎703/549-2997, ⓦwww .carlylehouse.org), made a powerful statement about its owner's wealth. Accounts of Carlyle's business dealings – he ran three plantations and traded numerous slaves – inform the half-hour **guided tour** of the restored house. Contrast the family's draped beds, expensively painted rooms, and fine furnishings with the bare servants' hall, which has actually been over-restored – in the eighteenth century it would have had an earthen floor and no glass in the

---

Alexandria's festivals

Alexandria has a full calendar of **festivals**, many of them linked either to the Scottish connections of the town's original settlers or to the Washington and Lee families. Call the visitor center (☎703/838-4200) or visit ⓦwww.funside.com for additional information.

January (3rd Sun): music, Lee-Fendall House tours, and other entertainment to celebrate the birthday of Robert E. Lee, at Fort Ward; ⓦwww.fortward.org

February (3rd weekend): a ball at *Gadsby's Tavern*, a parade, and a mock battle at nearby Fort Ward to celebrate George Washington's birthday; ⓦwww.washington birthday.net

March (17): St Patrick's Day parade; ⓦwww.ballyshaners.org

April (mid): special homes and gardens tours in Old Town; ⓦwww.vagardenweek.org

June (mid): waterfront festival with music, fireworks, tours, cruises, and entertainment; ⓦwww.waterfrontfestival.org

September (late): Historic Alexandria Homes tour, a half-day procession through some of the city's most venerable town homes and manors; ⓦwww.thetwig.org

December (1st Sat): Scottish Christmas Walk with more dancing and parades; ⓦwww.scottishchristmaswalk.com. (2nd Sat): candlelight tours of museums and historic houses, accompanied by traditional music, ⓦoha.alexandriava.gov

ALEXANDRIA, VA | Ramsay House • Carlyle House and City Hall

11

255

windows. To their credit, the displays in the mansion don't shy away from presenting the bare, disturbing details of the lives of slaves during the era. Aside from slavery and domestic matters, the tour discusses how the Carlyle House played a role in intercontinental affairs: in August 1755, it was used as **General Braddock**'s headquarters during the planning of the French and Indian War. George Washington was on Braddock's staff, and after the war he frequently visited the house. Less auspiciously, the estate was also the site, a decade later, for Braddock and a handful of British colonial governors to propose the infamous Stamp Act – one of the many actions that propelled the colonists and Britain toward war in the coming years.

Braddock's troops earlier paraded across the way in **Market Square**, off King Street, the heart of Alexandria since its founding. The modern brick terrace around the square sounds one of the few discordant notes in the Old Town. The Georgian Revival **City Hall** facing the square at 301 King St – notable for its quaint steeple – looks rather sprightly for such an old building; not surprisingly, it's a post–Civil War reconstruction of an early nineteenth-century Benjamin Latrobe creation. A weekly **farmers' market** still sets up in the City Hall arcades (Sat 5–11am), as it has for more than two hundred years.

▲ King Street

Gadsby's Tavern Museum and Christ and St Paul's churches

Gadsby's Tavern Museum, 134 N Royal St (April–Oct Tues–Sat 10am–5pm, Sun & Mon 1–5pm; Nov–March Wed–Sat 11am–4pm, Sun 1–4pm; $4; ☎703/838-4242, Ⓦwww.gadsbystavern.org), occupies two Georgian buildings: the City Hotel from 1792 and the tavern itself from 1785. Downstairs, *Gadsby's Tavern* is still a working restaurant, complete with Colonial-style food and costumed staff. In early American society, anyone who was anyone dropped by here for a visit – from the Marquis de Lafayette to Thomas Jefferson. Short **tours** of the complex by a knowledgeable guide lead you through the old tavern and hotel rooms; summer **lantern tours** offer the same perspective, bathed in a nocturnal romantic glow (June–Aug Fri 7–10pm; $5).

Three blocks west up Cameron Street, the English-style **Christ Church**, 118 N Washington St (Mon–Sat 9am–4pm, Sun 2–4pm; Ⓦwww.historic christchurch.org), a working branch of the Episcopal diocese, contains the Washington family pew. Identified by a striking red-and-white bell tower, the Georgian edifice, set in a legendary churchyard, was built of brick and finished just before the Revolution. During the Civil War, Union soldiers worshiped here, as did FDR and Churchill on one occasion eighty years later; periodically, the sitting president may drop in for a visit, often to coincide with Presidents' Day or Washington's birthday. Further south, the sedate 1808 **St Paul's Church**, 228 S Pitt St (☎703/549-3312, Ⓦwww.stpaulsepis.com), is an altogether more somber affair, its simple facade graced by three gentle arches and its interior a pleasant mix of Gothic arches and classical columns. Its skillful designer was none other than Benjamin Latrobe, architect of the US Capitol.

Lee-Fendall House and Alexandria Black History Museum

The Washingtons weren't the only notable family with ties to Alexandria. A descendant of the Lees of Virginia, Phillip Fendall built his splendid clapboard mansion, the **Lee-Fendall House**, 614 Oronoco St (Tues & Thurs–Sat 10am–4pm, Wed & Sun 1–4pm; $4; ☎703/548-1789, Ⓦwww.leefendallhouse .org), in 1785. Much of the furnishing dates from the antebellum era, and the house has been remodeled in the Greek Revival style you see today. Distinguished Revolutionary War general Henry "Light Horse Harry" Lee composed Washington's funeral oration here (in which, memorably, he declared him "first in war, first in peace, and first in the hearts of his countrymen"), and the home has had other famous residents in the years since. The most notable of these was powerful labor leader John L. Lewis, who moved in during 1937 as the head of the United Mine Workers, soon created the Congress of Industrial Organizations as a rival to the American Federation of Labor, and helped merge both groups in the 1940s. Lewis lived here until his death in 1969.

Just before the War of 1812 Henry Lee bought his own house on the same block and installed his wife and five children there. This, the boyhood **home of Robert E. Lee**, 607 Oronoco St, is a red-brick, Federal-era building first owned by a Virginia tobacco planter who occasionally entertained George Washington at dinner. Although it was open for more than three decades as a house museum, today it's a private home; an online look inside can be found at Ⓦleeboyhoodhome.com.

A distinctly different view of town history is on view three blocks west at the **Alexandria Black History Museum**, 902 Wythe St (Tues–Sat 10am–4pm; free; ☎703/838-4356, ⓦwww.alexblackhistory.org), which principally details some two hundred years of slavery in the city in a once-segregated library building. Using household tools, implements, documents, and photos, the museum traces local African American history back to the early eighteenth century, when Alexandria was a stopover for tens of thousands of African slaves on their way to the plantations of the New World, examines the presence of slaves in the company and houses of prominent figures such as Lee, Carlyle, and Washington, and recalls the black soldiers, freedmen and activists who shaped the Civil War era. More in-depth analysis can be found in the museum's **Watson Reading Room** (Tues–Sat 10am–4pm), which provides a scholarly angle on local history with thousands of noncirculating books, articles, and other materials.

Lyceum and Athenaeum

South of King Street, the **Lyceum**, 201 S Washington St (Mon–Sat 10am–5pm, Sun 1–5pm; ☎703/838-4994, ⓦwww.alexandriahistory.org), houses the town's history museum in a magisterial, 1839 Greek Revival building that was designed to be a centerpiece for the town's cultural pretensions – the evocative name harkening back to classical hubs for learning, discussion, and public oration. Although the place doesn't quite have the same role today, its changing displays, film shows, and associated art gallery can put some flesh on the town's history; varied exhibits range from old photographs and Civil War documents to locally produced furniture and silverware (the latter an Alexandrian specialty in the nineteenth century).

Five blocks east along Prince Street, the **Athenaeum** (Wed–Fri 11am–3pm, Sat & Sun noon–4pm; ☎703/548-0035, ⓦwww.nvfaa.org), another Classical-style edifice, with its mighty Doric columns and high pediment, was built as a bank in 1852, which happened to hold the money of Robert E. Lee and other notables. After a stint as a talcum-powder factory and a church, it's now an art center, where you can check out the latest modern art in a series of galleries, take in music, dance, and theater performances, or listen in on one of the periodic lectures devoted to the arts.

Old Presbyterian Meeting House and Stabler-Leadbeater Apothecary Shop

The tomb of prominent Alexandria merchant John Carlyle lies in the quiet graveyard of the **Old Presbyterian Meeting House**, 321 S Fairfax St (Mon–Fri 9am–4pm; ☎703/549-6670, ⓦwww.opmh.org). From 1772, the Scottish town founders met here regularly – most prominently in December 1799 for George Washington's memorial service. Despite its historic pedigree and religious importance, the site closed for sixty years beginning in 1889, and was allowed to deteriorate until finally being restored in the 1950s. Nearby a similarly venerable property can be found at 105 S Fairfax St, where patent medicines for Washington were concocted behind the tiny yellow windows of the **Stabler-Leadbeater Apothecary Shop** (April–Oct Sun & Mon 1–5pm, Tues–Sat 10am–5pm; Nov–March Wed–Sat 11am–4pm, Sun 1–4pm; $4; ☎703/838-3852, ⓦwww.apothecarymuseum.org), which was founded in 1792 and remained in business until the 1930s; it still displays its original furnishings, herbs, potions, and medical paraphernalia – some eight thousand items in all and well worth a look.

The waterfront

Eighteenth-century Alexandria wouldn't recognize its twentieth-century **waterfront** beyond North Union Street, not the least because the riverbank is several blocks farther east, following centuries of landfill. Where there were once wooden warehouses and wharves heaving with barrels of tobacco, there's now a smart marina and boardwalk, framed by the green stretches of Founders Park to the north and Waterfront Park to the south.

Before this whole area was cleaned up in recent decades, the US government built a torpedo factory on the river, which operated until the end of World War II. Restyled as the diverting **Torpedo Factory Arts Center** (daily 10am–5pm; ☏703/838-4565, ⑩www.torpedofactory.org), its three floors contain the studios of more than two hundred artists. All the studios are open to the public, displaying sculpture, ceramics, jewelry, glassware, and textiles in regularly changing exhibitions. Look, too, inside the center's **Alexandria Archaeology Museum** (Tues–Fri 10am–3pm, Sat 10am–5pm, Sun 1–5pm; ☏703/838-4399, ⑩www.alexandriaarchaeology.org), where much of the town's restoration work was carried out. You can see ongoing preservation efforts in a laboratory open to the public, its specimens covering 250 years of town history and encompassing digs for relics as diverse as Civil War castoffs, freedmen's gravesites, nautical ruins, and lost coins and household implements.

Forty-minute **sightseeing cruises** (May–Aug Tues–Sun, Mar–April & Sept–Oct Sat & Sun only; $12; ☏703/684-0580, ⑩www.potomacriverboatco.com) are run by the Potomac Riverboat Company and depart in front of the Food Pavilion; longer trips run to DC or Mount Vernon and back. In April 2008 a handy **water taxi** service (call for fees and hours) began running between Georgetown and Old Town Alexandria. One particularly interesting thing you can see on the company's regular cruises is the **Jones Point Lighthouse**, basically a small wooden house with little to distinguish it beyond the fact that it's the oldest American lighthouse not sited directly on the ocean; dating from 1855, it's been dark for more than eighty years. Perhaps more interesting, the lighthouse seawall contains a stone **boundary marker** showing the southernmost point of the District of Columbia, laid in 1794, before Virginia regained its acreage from the capital city in 1846. The lighthouse is located nearly under the Woodrow Wilson Bridge off I-495 on Jones Point Road; the grounds, but not the house itself, are open daylight hours as a park.

George Washington Masonic Memorial

In a town bursting with Washington mementos, none is more striking than the **George Washington Masonic Memorial**, 101 Callahan Drive (daily 9am–5pm; ☏703/683-2007, ⑩www.gwmemorial.org), whose 333ft tower – built on top of a Greek temple – looms behind the King Street Metro station, often disappearing into the low-hanging fog during the winter months. The Virginia Freemasons built the memorial in 1932 to honor a "deserving brother," and the tower was designed to resemble nothing less than the long-destroyed Lighthouse at Alexandria, one of the seven wonders of the ancient world. Inside, the glorious visual ode continues with a 17ft-tall bronze **statue** of the general and president, sundry memorabilia, and dioramas depicting events from his life. To see this, and the superb views from the observation platform, you'll have to take a forty-minute **tour**, which leaves from the building's main hall (daily 10am, 11.30am, 1.30pm, & 3pm). But even from the steps outside, the views across the Potomac to the Washington Monument and Capitol dome in the distance are terrific.

Fort Ward

During the Civil War, the federal occupation of Alexandria brought an urgent need to defend it, and built expressly for this purpose was **Fort Ward**, several miles west of town at 4301 W Braddock Rd (April–Oct Tues–Sat 9am–5pm, Sun noon–5pm; Nov–Mar Tues–Sat 10am–5pm, Sun noon–5pm; free; ☎703/838-4848, ⓦwww.fortward.org), which became one of the largest forts defending the capital region in the 1860s. Mainly staffed by black soldiers and liberated slaves, the fort featured rifle trenches, guard towers, and artillery batteries, making for an impressive display to any would-be invaders. Ultimately, though, the Confederates didn't come near the place, choosing to approach Washington from the west instead of the south. In any case, these days there's enough here to get the idea of what wartime challenges were like, with an earthen berm, bomb shelters, trenches, powder magazine, ammo room, and various cannons setting the stage, and a replica officers' hut and onsite museum full of the usual military relics and memorabilia.

Green Spring Gardens Park

Braddock Rd at Little River Turnpike (Rte 236) ☎703/941-7987, ⓦwww.co.fairfax.va.us/parks/gsgp. Grounds daily dawn–dusk, house Wed–Sun noon–4pm.

Several miles west of the city of Alexandria, and east of Pinecrest Golf Course, the natural expanses of **Green Spring Gardens Park** are a terrific spot for a respite from sightseeing. Set on 27 acres, the park is based around the estate of eighteenth-century farmer John Moss. The 1760 red-brick Georgian manor house is the estate's centerpiece, while the grounds surrounding the mansion host farmers' markets, bonsai displays, and seasonal events in the spring, summer, and winter holiday season. The official purpose of the gardens – which hold native Virginian plants – is to educate people about the best ways to plant and maintain their trees and flowers (an onsite horticultural library helps, too). If you have an interest in this sort of thing, the display gardens can be impressive, and in separate plots hold the likes of roses, herbs, shade plants, fruits and vegetables, mixed borders, and more. Garden **tours** offered several times per month provide a good introduction, but more enjoyable are the periodic Sunday-afternoon tours that include a **tea service** in the manor house ($24; call or see website for schedule and reservations).

Listings

Listings

ACCOMMODATION | Hotels and B&Bs

Accommodation

W ithout a doubt, one of the highlights of staying in Washington, DC, is cozying up in a swank **hotel** in the historic center and having the entire District at your feet, either literally or through the Metro system. Of course, for many this is far from reality, and unless you're willing to drop upward of $300 a night, you'll probably be out of luck. That said, great options abound beyond the big-name hotels: the handful of **bed-and-breakfasts** are certainly viable options, particularly in spots like Dupont Circle; **chain hotels** and motels exist everywhere, with affordable rates unless they're in very popular zones; and **hostels** can be found here and there – not in any real abundance, mind you, but frequently enough to allow you to drop anchor in town for less than $40 a night.

Hotels and B&Bs

Standard DC **room rates** begin around $150 a night, but for savvy travelers there's plenty of room for negotiation. Many hotels dramatically discount their rates on weekends (some by up to fifty percent), while prices are low from late fall to winter, and when Congress isn't in session. Always ask if the rate you've been quoted is the best available; often, discount information has to be ferreted out of desk clerks or cross-checked online. Where places offer particularly good deals, we've said so in the review. Also, since hotels charge by the room, three people can often stay in a double for the same price as two, though sometimes there's a small surcharge. Also, don't forget to check online sites like Priceline .com, in which you can wheedle down the cost of a room to a fraction of the official rates quoted below.

There are hotels in all the main downtown areas, though accommodations near the White House, on Capitol Hill, and in Georgetown tend to be business-oriented and pricey. The occasional **budget option** exists in Foggy Bottom and Adams Morgan, while most of the chain hotels and midrange places are in New Downtown – particularly on the streets around Scott and Thomas circles. Dupont Circle and Upper Northwest are also good spots in which to base

---

Hotel reservation services

Bed & Breakfast Accommodations Ltd ☏1-877/893-3233, ⓦwww .bedandbreakfastdc.com
Capitol Reservations ☏202/452-1270 or 1-800/847-4832, ⓦwww .capitolreservations.com
WDCA Hotels ☏202/289-2220 or 1-800/503-3330, ⓦwww.wdcahotels.com

yourself, with the latter considerably more expensive and with fewer options. We've also listed a few options in Arlington and Alexandria, VA, though these towns are easy to see during a day-trip from the capital. A number of B&B agencies (see box, p.263) offer rooms in small inns, private homes, or apartments, starting from around $80 per night; a luxury B&B, though, can be every bit as pricey as a hotel, with rates reaching as high as $200–300 a night.

If you're bringing along a car, you're more likely to find free **parking** in the outer neighborhoods; garage parking is available at most downtown hotels, but you'll be charged $25–30 a night for the privilege. Very occasionally, an inn or hotel we list is on the edge of a dicey neighborhood; where safety is an issue, we've said so, and you're advised to take taxis back to your hotel at night in these areas.

In the off-season you'll often be paying less than what's indicated in our reviews. Groups and families should consider the city's suite hotels, where you'll get a kitchen and possibly a separate living room, too. One other thing to keep in mind: in summer, DC is hot and humid, and air-conditioning is essential for getting a good night's rest.

Adams Morgan

Adam's Inn 1744 Lanier Place NW ☎ 202/745-3600 or 1-800/578-6807, ⊛ www.adamsinn.com; Woodley Park–Zoo Metro. Simple B&B rooms in three adjoining Victorian townhouses on a quiet residential street (just north of Calvert St). No TVs, but free Net access, breakfast, coffee all day, garden patio, and laundry facilities. Decent weekly rates, too. Private bath adds $30, otherwise $109

Courtyard by Marriott 1900 Connecticut Ave NW ☎ 202/332-9300 or 1-800/321-3211, ⊛ www.courtyard.com/wasnw; Dupont Circle or Woodley Park–Zoo Metro. Located at the southern tip of the Kalorama Triangle, the top-floor rooms of this hillside hotel have splendid views, at cheaper rates than the nearby Hilton. Free Internet access, gym, outdoor pool, and location a short walk from the heart of both Dupont Circle and Adams Morgan. $329 weekdays, $169 weekends

Jurys Normandy Inn 2118 Wyoming Ave NW ☎ 202/483-1350 or 1-800/424-3729, ⊛ www.jurys.com; Dupont Circle or Woodley Park–Zoo Metro. Quiet hotel in upscale neighborhood, with comfortable rooms (each with fridge and coffeemaker) and free high-speed Internet access in the lobby. Coffee and cookies are served daily, and there's a weekly wine and cheese reception. $249

Kalorama Guest House at Kalorama Park 1854 Mintwood Place NW ☎ 202/667-6369, ⊛ www.kaloramaguesthouse.com; Woodley Park–Zoo Metro. Smart Victorian townhouses near Adams Morgan restaurants. Spacious rooms (and some suites, for $30 more) in four spotless houses filled with period objets and handsome furniture (no TVs). Free breakfast, papers, coffee, and evening sherry. Booking is essential – single rooms are as cheap as $70, doubles with bath $100, though prices increase at the top of the high season.

Washington Hilton 1919 Connecticut Ave NW ☎ 202/483-3000 or 1-800/445-8667, ⊛ www.hilton.com; Dupont Circle Metro. Massive 1960s convention hotel midway between Dupont Circle and Adams Morgan, a few blocks north of the Metro. More than 1100 smallish rooms geared toward business types, but most have very good views. Facilities include pool, health club, tennis courts, and bike rental. $259

Windsor Inn 1842 16th St NW ☎ 202/667-0300 or 1-800/423-9111, ⊛ www.windsor-inn-dc.com. One of the area's better deals, not too far from the Dupont Circle Metro, with units in twin brick 1920s houses and spacious suites. Some rooms have fridges; ground-floor rooms look onto a terrace. Free WI-FI access and continental breakfast served in the attractive lobby. No onsite parking. $99

Windsor Park 2116 Kalorama Rd NW ☎ 202/483-7700 or 1-800/247-3064, ⊛ www.windsorparkhotel.com; Dupont Circle or Woodley Park–Zoo Metro. Simple rooms with fridges and cable TV, just off Connecticut Avenue. Good value for the area, though don't expect much from the basic units. Eight suites available. Continental breakfast included. $169, though off-season rates can drop by $40

Alexandria, VA

Best Western Old Colony Inn 1101 N Washington St ☎703/739-2222, ⓦ www.bestwestern.com; **Braddock Road Metro.** Less than a mile from the Metro station on the north side of Old Town, this moderately priced choice with standard amenities (plus free breakfast and high-speed Internet access) is one of the better chain options for the historic center. $199

Hilton Alexandria 1767 King St ☎703/837-0440; **King Street Metro.** There are dozens of cookie-cutter chain hotels throughout Alexandria, but this corporate entity stands out: it's close to the Metro, with clean and modern rooms, high-speed Internet access ($10), pool, gym, and business center. $229 weekends, $369 weekdays

Hotel Monaco 480 King St ☎703/549-6080, ⓦ www.monaco-alexandria.com; **King Street Metro.** Remodeled Holiday Inn that's now been turned into one of the city's best properties, with ultra-chic rooms with designer decor, free WI-FI, evening wine tastings, and rooms and suites that variously offer jetted tubs, flat-screen TVs, wet bars, and other swank amenities. $339, but rates drop by $100 on weekends

Morrison House 116 S Alfred St, Old Town ☎703/838-8000, ⓦ www.morrisonhouse .com; **King Street Metro.** Faux Federal-era townhouse (built in 1985) complete with ersatz "authentic" decor like parquet floors, marble bathrooms, and crystal chandeliers, yet with modern comforts like high-speed Internet connections and designer linens. There's also an acclaimed restaurant, The Grille. $399 weekdays, $289 weekends

Arlington, VA

Hilton Garden Inn 1333 N Court House Rd ☎1-800/528-4444, ⓦ hiltongardeninn1.hilton .com; **Court House Metro.** One of many agreeable chain business hotels in the area, a block from the Metro with a business center and gym. Suites have fridges, microwaves, and high-speed Net access. Save $150 by coming on a weekend; otherwise $259

Hyatt Arlington 1325 Wilson Blvd ☎703/525-1234, ⓦ www.arlington.hyatt.com; **Rosslyn Metro.** Modern corporate property in a prime spot near a Metro station, as well as Georgetown and Arlington National Cemetery, with standard chain features plus gym and Internet access. Huge rate drops on weekends, down to $139 or less; otherwise $339

Inn of Rosslyn 1601 Arlington Blvd ☎703/524-3400; **Rosslyn Metro.** Located near the northern edge of the cemetery and the Marine Corps Memorial, this is a basic but clean motel that's one of the few reasonably priced places in town beyond the chain hotels. Rooms are nothing special, but rates are among the area's lowest. $129

Korman Communities 3409 Wilson Blvd ☎1-866/567-6864, ⓦ www.kormancommunities .com; **Virginia Square–GMU Metro.** Rentable furnished one- to three-bedroom apartments with ultra-modern decor and upscale touches like hardwood floors, granite counters and balconies, plus onsite gym, garden, and business center. Expensive, but worth it for a splurge, and with close Metro access. $395

Capitol Hill

Capitol Hill Suites 200 C St SE ☎202/543-6000, ⓦ www.capitolhillsuites.com; **Capitol South Metro.** Converted apartments whose renovated units are equipped with kitchenettes or proper kitchens. Continental breakfast, plus Internet access. Busy when Congress is in session; on weekends and in August the price drops $50–70; otherwise $210

Holiday Inn on the Hill 415 New Jersey Ave NW ☎202/638-1616 or 1-800/638-1116, ⓦ www .hionthehilldc.com; **Union Station Metro.** Recent addition of boutique decor enlivens some of these chain rooms, and there's also a pool, exercise room, WI-FI access, and sports bar and grill. Weekend rates here can be a bargain, starting at $160; otherwise $325

Hotel George 15 E St NW ☎202/347-4200 or 1-800/576-8331, ⓦ www.hotelgeorge.com; **Union Station Metro.** Postmodern design and modern convenience meets 1928 Art Deco architecture, resulting in sleek lines, marble bathrooms, Net access, boutique room furnishings with copious Washington imagery, in-room CD players, and a trendy bar-bistro. $169 on weekends, $319 weekdays

Hyatt Regency Washington on Capitol Hill 400 New Jersey Ave NW ☎202/737-1234 or 1-800/233-1234, ⓦ www.washingtonregency .hyatt.com; **Union Station Metro.** Two blocks from the train station, this 800-room luxury hotel features a multistory atrium, pool, and gym – and a few rooms with views of the Capitol. $239, but rate jumps $100 on weekdays

Maison Orleans 414 5th St SE ☎202/544-3694; Capitol South Metro. Historic 1902 row house that's now a pleasant B&B with wireless Net access and continental breakfast, plus a trio of functional rooms, patio with fountains, and small garden, and within easy reach of the Capitol. $140

Phoenix Park 520 N Capitol St NW ☎202/638-6900 or 1-800/824-5419, ⓦwww.phoenixparkhotel.com; Union Station Metro. Stylish renovation has snazzed up the rooms of this Irish-themed hotel near Union Station with arch-chic decor, designer furnishings, and flat-screen TVs. It's popular with politicos, who frequent its *Dubliner* pub (see "Bars and clubs" chapter). There's a good restaurant, too, serving hearty breakfasts. $209 weekends, $419 weekdays

Dupont Circle

Brickskeller Inn 1523 22nd St NW ☎202/293-1885, ⓦwww.lovethebeer.com; Dupont Circle Metro. Converted apartment house with a stately facade and simple rooms, most of which have sinks; some have a bath and TV. Funky, ultra-basic lodging is mainly useful if you need a crash pad after partying, since it's located above one of the Circle's oldest and best bars (see p.297). Top-floor rooms have a view of Rock Creek Park. $129

Carlyle Suites 1731 New Hampshire Ave NW ☎202/234-3200 or 1-866/468-3532, ⓦwww.carlylesuites.com; Dupont Circle Metro. An Art Deco–style structure with pricey rooms that are more functional than fancy. Offers high-speed Internet hookups, kitchenettes with fridges and microwaves, and an onsite café and laundry. $319

Dupont at the Circle 1604 19th St NW ☎202/332-5251 or 1-888/412-0100, ⓦwww.dupontatthecircle.com; Dupont Circle Metro. Nine handsome units – high ceilings, kitchenettes, marble bathrooms – in a Victorian townhouse near the Circle (at Q St). Continental breakfast included. Offers higher-priced packages (for $100–400 over room rate) with quirky names like the "Metrosexual Special" that include manicures, pedicures, and facials. $150–215 by season

Embassy Circle Guest House 2224 R St NW ☎202/232-7744 or 1-877/232-7744, ⓦwww.embassycircle.com; Dupont Circle Metro. Great B&B choice for Kalorama, set in a recently restored 1902 Georgian mansion with ten elegant rooms that include tasteful, reserved decor, with a hint of the antique, and high-speed Net access. Few better deals for quality and location anywhere in the District. $225

Embassy Inn 1627 16th St NW ☎202/234-7800 or 1-800/423-9111; Dupont Circle Metro. Welcoming bed-and-breakfast on a residential street in northeastern Dupont Circle, well placed for bars and restaurants. Free continental breakfast, WI-FI access, coffee, and papers, plus an early-evening sherry to speed you on your way. $169

Embassy Row Hilton 2015 Massachusetts Ave NW ☎202/265-1600 or 1-800/774-1500, ⓦwww.hilton.com; Dupont Circle Metro. Corporate-flavored Embassy Row standard, with marble bathrooms, cable TV, lobby bar, health center, and seasonal rooftop pool. Rates can plummet up to $100 in low season. $240

Madera 1310 New Hampshire Ave NW ☎202/296-7600, ⓦwww.hotelmadera.com; Dupont Circle Metro. Another terrific property in the Kimpton line of boutique hotels, this one with nice designer decor and amenities, high-speed Net access, CD players, and plenty of space in the rooms. Other options include rooms with gym equipment, computers, or DVD players. $239–389 by season

Palomar 2121 P St NW, Dupont Circle ☎202/293-3100, ⓦwww.hotelpalomar-dc.com. Among the newest and greatest examples of boutique accommodation in DC, offering flat-screen TVs and CD players, onsite pool, fitness center, and stylish lounge, along with an evening "wine hour" for schmoozing with other guests. Plenty of arty touches, too, in the lobby and rooms. $219 weekends, $329 weekdays

Rouge 1315 16th St NW ☎202/232-8000, ⓦwww.rougehotel.com; Dupont Circle Metro. Dupont Circle's hippest hotel (though it's actually on nearby Thomas Circle), where the 137 sleek rooms are outfitted with crimson velvet drapes, red leatherette headboards, and postmodern art. The ground-floor bar-lounge is a definite highlight, where you can indulge in a complimentary cold pizza and Bloody Mary – for breakfast. A quick walk from Dupont Circle's prime haunts. $399

Swann House 1808 New Hampshire Ave NW ☎202/265-4414, ⓦwww.swannhouse.com; Dupont Circle Metro. Elegant B&B in an 1883 Romanesque Revival mansion with striking red-brick arches, gables, and turrets, a 10min walk from both Dupont Circle and Adams Morgan. There are twelve individually decorated rooms – some with fireplaces, DVD players, and whirlpool tubs – as well as porches and decks for reclining, and a private garden with fountain. Free continental breakfast, afternoon refreshments, and an early-evening sherry to round out the day. $175–225 by season

Westin Embassy Row 2100 Massachusetts Ave NW ☏ 202/293-2100 or 1-800/WESTIN-1, ⓦ www.starwood.com/westin; Dupont Circle Metro. Recently renovated business property caters to clubby politicos, media types, and corporate types. Anglo-French country-house chic, with onsite gym and nice rooms with high-speed Internet access. Weekend rates can drop to $350; otherwise $475

Foggy Bottom

Allen Lee 2224 F St NW ☏ 202/331-1224 or 1-800/462-0186, ⓦ www.theallenleehotel.com; Foggy Bottom–GWU Metro. Misleadingly attractive exterior hides musty rooms (with and without private bath) with clunky air-conditioning – inspect a couple before checking in. The place has been spruced up a bit in recent days, though, and is in a convenient location. Ultra-cheap for DC, with shared-bath doubles for as low as $79.

Fairmont 2401 M St NW ☏ 202/429-2400, ⓦ www.fairmont.com; Foggy Bottom–GWU Metro. Classy West End oasis with comfortable rooms, pool, health club, whirlpool, and garden courtyard. Just north of Washington Circle, midway between Foggy Bottom and Georgetown. Save $50 by booking on a weekend; otherwise $279

Hay-Adams 800 16th St NW ☏ 202/638-6600 or 1-800/424-5054, ⓦ www.hayadams.com; Farragut West or McPherson Square Metro. One of DC's finest hotels, from the gold-leaf and walnut lobby to the modern rooms with designer decor, to the suites (which can cost thousands per night) with fireplaces and original cornices, marble bathrooms, balconies, and high ceilings. Upper floors have great views of the White House across the square. Breakfast is served in the Lafayette Room, one of the District's better spots for early-morning power dining. See also p.148. $515

Lombardy 2019 Pennsylvania Ave NW ☏ 202/828-2600 or 1-800/424-5486, ⓦ www.hotellombardy.com; Foggy Bottom–GWU or

Farragut West Metro. Red-brick apartment-style hotel, renovated with modern furnishings, in good location, close to two Metro stations. Spacious rooms, most with kitchenettes and Net access; the café has outdoor seating and serves breakfast. High season can bring a three-night weekday minimum. $179 weekends, $233 weekdays

Ritz-Carlton 1150 22nd St ☏ 202/835-0500, ⓦ www.ritzcarlton.com; Foggy Bottom Metro. Among four Ritz-Carltons in the area, this is the most convenient to central DC, with numerous top-of-the-line suites, business center, and upscale rooms with designer decor, DVD players, and Net access. Weekend rates are reasonable, at $209 or $50 more for a suite, but weekday rates can triple that.

River Inn 924 25th St NW ☏ 202/337-7600, ⓦ www.theriverinn.com; Foggy Bottom Metro. One of the area's best deals, offering decent weekend rates for clean and comfortable suites that have microwaves and kitchenettes, with some designer amenities, and fine onsite *DISH* restaurant (see p.285). $129 weekends, $259 weekdays

State Plaza 2117 E St NW ☏ 202/861-8200 or 1-800/424-2859, ⓦ www.stateplaza.com; Foggy Bottom-GWU Metro. Commodious, stylish suites with Net access, fully equipped kitchens and dining area, plus a rooftop sundeck, health club, spa, business center, and good café. There's often room here when other places are full. $149 weekends, $249 weekdays (sometimes with three-night minimum)

Georgetown

Four Seasons 2800 Pennsylvania Ave NW ☏ 202/342-0444 or 1-800/332-3442, ⓦ www.fourseasons.com. This modern red-brick pile at the eastern end of Georgetown is one of DC's most luxurious hotels. Stars, royalty, and high-rollers hanker for the lavish rooms and suites with views of Rock Creek Park or the C&O Canal. Service is superb, and there's a pool, fitness center, and full-service spa. Weekends $395, weekdays $595

Georgetown Inn 1310 Wisconsin Ave NW ☏ 1-888/587-2388, ⓦ georgetowncollection.com/georgetown_inn. Stylish, red-brick hotel in the heart of Georgetown offering 96 tastefully appointed rooms and suites (those off the avenue tend to be quieter) with marble bathrooms, plush decor, and high-speed

Internet hookups. Excellent deal for the area. Weekdays $269, weekends $149

Georgetown Suites 1111 30th St NW ☎202/298-7800 or 1-800/348-7203, ⓦwww.georgetownsuites.com. Impeccable choice for affordable luxury in a central location. All-suite hotel offers tasteful modern decor, continental breakfast, and rooms with kitchens and Net access, plus gym and laundry. Hotel has two similarly priced facilities on the same block, the other at 1000 29th St NW. $255

Georgetown University Conference Hotel 3800 Reservoir Rd NW ☎202/687-3200, ⓦwww.marriott.com. The drab name belies one of Georgetown's best deals, a simple chain offering that's just north of the major sights and has clean and basic rooms. $149 weekends, $199 weekdays, though you may be able to find half-price rates online

Latham 3000 M St NW ☎202/726-5000 or 1-800/368-5922, ⓦgeorgetowncollection.com /Latham_Hotel. Well-sited hotel with rooftop pool, sundeck, and one of the city's finest dining experiences, *Citronelle* (see "Eating" chapter). Some rooms have canal and river views, but the rooms are on the drab side and the aging facility could use a renovation. Weekends $169, weekdays $249 (off-season rates about $50–70 less)

Monticello 1075 Thomas Jefferson St NW ☎202/337-0900 or 1-800/388-2410, ⓦwww.hotelmonticello.com. Another local big name that could use refurbishment, this one an all-suite hotel located off M Street, in a good spot near the historic C&O Canal; all units have a wet bar, microwave, and fridge. Free Internet access in the business center. Summers see a small discount in price, as do some weekends. $249

Ritz-Carlton Georgetown 3100 South St NW ☎202/912-4100, ⓦwww.ritzcarlton.com. One of the city's more curious hotels: a disused old incinerator now dramatically remodeled into an ultra-chic luxury item rich with decorous rooms and suites. Offers all the designer amenities you expect, plus spa, sauna, fitness room, and onsite movie theater. Weekends $499, weekdays $729

New Downtown

Beacon 1615 Rhode Island Ave NW ☎202/296-2100 or 1-800/821-4367, ⓦwww.capitalhotelswdc.com; Dupont Circle or Farragut North Metro. Although the exterior is unpromising, it offers a relaxed atmosphere inside with decent-size rooms, some with sofa beds and kitchenettes, plus flat-screen TVs and WI-FI. There's a popular bar and grill and a pool, too. $249

Chester Arthur House B&B 13th and P sts NW ☎413/582-9888 or 1/877-893-3233, ⓦwww.chesterarthurhouse.com; no close Metro. Lovely 1883 townhouse right on Logan Circle, with elegant parlors, high ceilings, crystal chandeliers, and numerous fireplaces. Two Victorian rooms and one suite come with antiques and fireplaces, and the suite also with a kitchenette. $115–175 by season

Doubletree 1515 Rhode Island Ave NW ☎202/232-7000, ⓦwww.doubletree.com; Dupont Circle or Farragut North Metro. Comfortable rooms, standard corporate-modern decor, marble bathrooms, and outdoor terrace for summer dining. Not too far from the Dupont Circle nightlife scene or the White House. $399

Hamilton Crowne Plaza 14th and K St NW ☎202/682-0111 or 1-800/227-6963, ⓦwww.hamiltonhoteldc.com; McPherson Square Metro. Resurrected 1920s Beaux-Arts-style hotel with swanky decor in the suites, high-speed Internet access, fine city views, and a central, sought-after Franklin Square location. Lobby espresso bar, health club, and sauna add to the plush atmosphere. $230 weekends, $390 weekdays

Helix 1430 Rhode Island Ave NW, near Logan Circle ☎202/462-9001, ⓦwww.hotelhelix.com; Dupont Circle or Farragut North Metro. A prime choice if you're into a young, convivial atmosphere and bright, festive decor that includes multicolored furniture, boomerang shapes, and other eye-popping detail. Luxury rooms come in three flavors – the chill-out "Zone" suite, food-oriented "Eats," and kid-friendly "Bunk." $399

Holiday Inn Central 1501 Rhode Island Ave NW ☎202/483-2000 or 1-800/248-0016, ⓦwww.inn-dc.com or www.holidayinn.com; Dupont Circle or Farragut North Metro. One of downtown's better midrange options, located at Scott Circle, with basic, modern rooms, a rooftop pool, a bar, and free breakfast. Don't let the grim, corporate-modern exterior keep you away. $259

Jefferson 1200 16th St NW ☎202/347-2200, ⓦwww.thejeffersonhotel.com; Farragut North Metro. Patrician landmark on 16th Street. A bit away from the main action, but still a favorite since the 1920s for its antique-strewn interior with busts, oils, and porcelain at every turn, plus fine restaurant and stylish guest rooms. With extensive restoration and renovation – finished by fall 2008 – expect to pay in the range of $400–500.

Mayflower 1127 Connecticut Ave NW ⊕202/347-3000 or 1-800/228-7697, ⓦwww.renaissancehotels.com/wassh; **Farragut North Metro.** Beautiful and sumptuous Washington classic, with a promenade – a vast, imperial hall – that, from the lobby, appears to be endless. Smart rooms have subtle, tasteful furnishings, and the terrific *Café Promenade* restaurant (see "Eating" chapter) is much in demand with power diners. If there's one spot in DC where the national and international political elite come to roost, this is it. $499 weekends, $665 weekdays

St Regis Washington 923 16th St NW ⊕202/638-2626 or 1-800/562-5661, ⓦwww .starwood.com/stregis; **McPherson Square Metro.** The lobby of this 1920s Italian Renaissance classic just a few blocks north of the White House looks right out of a European palace with antiques, chandeliers, and carved wooden ceiling; President Calvin Coolidge cut the ribbon when it opened. One of DC's cozier luxury hotels, it features elegant rooms with stylish appointments, newly restored to show off the glories of the old style. $450 weekends, $695 weekdays

Tabard Inn 1739 N St NW ⊕202/ 785-1277, ⓦwww.tabardinn.com; **Dupont Circle Metro.** Three converted Victorian townhouses, two blocks from Dupont Circle, with forty unique, antique-stocked rooms with an odd mix of modern and old-fashioned decor – more snuggly than swanky, but an excellent deal for the area. Laid-back staff, comfortable lounges with romantic fireplaces, a courtyard, and an excellent restaurant. Rates include breakfast and a pass to the nearby YMCA. $152, or $107 with shared bath

Topaz 1733 N St NW ⊕202/393-3000, ⓦwww .topazhotel.com; **Dupont Circle Metro.** Boutique hotel whose vibrant rooms have padded headboards with polka dots, striped wallpaper, and funky furniture, plus CD players and high-speed Net access. Several units have space for yoga – complete with workout gear and videos – or treadmills, stationary bikes, and elliptical machines. Weekends $263, weekdays $399

Westin Washington 1400 M St NW ⊕202/ 429-1700, ⓦwww.starwoodhotels.com/westin; **McPherson Square Metro.** Contemporary comfort near Thomas Circle, with rooms offering Net access and chic chain comfort, plus soaring atrium, a coffee shop, fitness club, and bars. Formerly the notorious *Washington Vista*, where ex-mayor Marion Barry was arrested in a drug sting. $229

William Lewis House 1309 R St NW ⊕202/ 462-7574 or 1-800/465-7574, ⓦwww .wlewishous.com; **McPherson Square Metro.** Elegantly decorated, gay-friendly B&B set in two century-old townhouses north of Logan Circle, within blocks of the Shaw neighborhood. All ten antique-filled rooms have shared bath and Net access. Out back there's a roomy porch and a hot tub set in a garden. Rates include continental breakfast on weekdays and a full American breakfast on weekends. Given the price, reservations are essential. $89

Old Downtown

Courtyard Washington 900 F St NW ⊕202/ 638-4600, ⓦwww.marriott.com; **Gallery Place-Chinatown Metro.** Stunning 1891 Romanesque Revival bank that has been converted into a truly original hotel. The lobby overflows with marble columns, elegant bronzework, and grand archways, while the spacious rooms (formerly offices) have varying layouts, and some sport big windows and sweeping views. Also worth a look are the old-fashioned conference rooms – one is housed in the bank's former vault. $329 weekdays, $159 weekends

Grand Hyatt 1000 H St NW ⊕202/582-1234 or 1-800/233-1234, ⓦwww.grandwashington .hyatt.com; **Metro Center Metro.** Nearly 900-room hotel has attractive twelve-story atrium with lagoon, waterfalls, and glass elevators, and sleekly modern rooms. Includes an onsite deli-café, a restaurant, sauna, spa, pool, gym, and bar. Save $100 on weekends; otherwise $499

Hampton Inn 901 6th St ⊕202/842-2500, ⓦwww.hamptoninn.com; **Gallery Place–Chinatown Metro.** Slightly north of the main attractions, but worth it to save (a little) money. No surprises, just clean and modern chain rooms spread over 13 modern stories, with gym, pool, and Jacuzzi. Complimentary breakfast and high-speed Net access. Location is two blocks from the convention center. $289

Harrington 1100 E St NW ☎ 202/628-8140 or 1-800/424-8532, ⊛ www.hotel-harrington.com; Metro Center Metro. One of the old, classic, and basic downtown hotels, of which few remain these days. Has a prime location near Pennsylvania Avenue. Air-con rooms (singles to quads) have TV, though they're quite small and a bit worn around the edges. Still, the prices are tough to beat for the area. $109

Henley Park 926 Massachusetts Ave NW ☎ 202/638-5200 or 1-800/222-8474, ⊛ www.henleypark.com; Mount Vernon Square–UDC Metro. Smart and stylish hotel, formerly an apartment building, is rather at odds with the borderline neighborhood. Though you should be wary at night, it's just a few blocks north of the happening Penn Quarter and right by the convention center. $259, though rates can drop to $199 on off-season weekends

JW Marriott 1331 Pennsylvania Ave NW ☎ 202/393-2000 or 1-800/228-9290, ⊛ www.marriott.com; Metro Center or Federal Triangle Metro. Flagship Marriott property in one of the best locations in the city; part of the National Place development and overlooking Freedom Plaza (ask for a room facing the avenue). Rooms are on the upper end of the corporate standard, with Net access and HDTVs, plus there are good restaurants, a sports bar, and a health club with indoor pool. $479

Marriott at Metro Center 775 12th St NW ☎ 202/737-2200 or 1-800/228-9290, ⊛ www.marriott.com; Metro Center Metro. Upscale hotel west of the Penn Quarter with smart, sizable rooms and a popular bar and grill, as well as pool and health club. The main draw here is the central location a few blocks south of the convention center, which if you have business there makes the expense-account price justifiable. $499

Monaco 700 F St NW ☎ 202/628-7177, ⊛ www.monaco-dc.com; Gallery Place–Chinatown Metro. Perhaps the most architecturally significant hotel in the area. Once a grand Neoclassical post office designed by Robert Mills, nowadays ultra-chic accommodation complete with sophisticated modern rooms (with busts of Jefferson above the armoires), minimalist contemporary decor, and public spaces with marble floors and columns, plus grand spiral stairways. $369, but weekend rates can drop to $190

Morrison-Clark Inn 1015 L St NW ☎ 202/898-1200 or 1-800/332-7898, ⊛ www.morrisonclark.com; Mount Vernon Square–UDC Metro. Antique-and-lace accommodation in a historic mansion complete with veranda. Located one block from the convention center and two blocks from the Metro. Fifty-odd rooms in Victorian and other old-fashioned styles, balconies overlooking a courtyard, a comfortable lounge, and a solid restaurant. Although the area can get dicey at night, this is still one of Old Downtown's better deals. $259

Red Roof Inn 500 H St NW ☎ 202/289-5959 or 1-877/733-7244, ⊛ www.redroof.com; Gallery Place–Chinatown Metro. One of the less expensive chain offerings around here – though hardly cheap – with a central location in the Penn Quarter, and Chinatown and the Verizon Center on the doorstep. The café serves a buffet breakfast (not included in the room rate), and there's an exercise room with sauna, plus the engaging Irish Channel Pub. $289

Willard InterContinental 1401 Pennsylvania Ave NW ☎ 202/628-9100 or 1-800/327-0200, ⊛ www.washington.interconti.com; Metro Center Metro. A signature, iconic Washington hotel that dominates Pershing Park near the Treasury Building. In business on and off since the 1850s, it's a Beaux-

▲ The Willard InterContinental

Arts marvel with acres of marble, mosaics, and glass; a stunning lobby and promenade; finely furnished rooms; and top-drawer clientele thick with politicos, lobbyists, and other honchos. More info on p.166. $679

Upper Northwest

Days Inn 4400 Connecticut Ave NW ☎ 202/244-5600 or 1-800/329-7466, ⓦ www.daysinn .com; Van Ness UDC–Metro. Near the university and a Metro stop, and within reach of Rock Creek Park, it has a colorless, bunkerlike exterior but offers clean, if smallish, rooms with all the usual chain-hotel conveniences, plus free high-speed Net access. $195

Embassy Suites at Chevy Chase Pavilion 4300 Military Rd NW ☎ 202/362-9300, ⓦ www .embassysuites.com; Friendship Heights Metro. Right on the Metro line, it's a good choice if you can't afford the Woodley Park big names, with nice two-room suites, free breakfast, high-speed Net access, HDTVs, plus spa, gym, and pool. Also in the vicinity are several malls. $199 weekends, $329 weekdays

Kalorama Guest House at Woodley Park 2700 Cathedral Ave NW ☎ 202/328-0860, ⓦ www .kaloramaguesthouse.com; Woodley Park–Zoo Metro. Victorian charm not far from the Metro in Woodley Park. Two houses (19 rooms, 12 en-suite) offering comfortable brass beds plus free continental breakfast, aperitifs, papers, and coffee. Book well in advance. Rooms with shared bathrooms go for $75; add another $20 for ones with private baths and $30 on top of that for suites.

🏊 **Marriott Wardman Park** 2660 Woodley Rd NW ☎ 202/328-2000 or 1-800/228-9290, ⓦ www.marriott.com; Woodley Park–Zoo Metro. Woodley Park's historic, celebrity-filled monument that manages to be the largest hotel in DC (and frequent site of political fund-raisers), with two pools, a health club, and restaurants bristling with crackling staff. Convention business keeps rooms full most weekdays of the year. Weekends $329, weekdays $399; add $50 for rooms in the tower

Omni Shoreham 2500 Calvert St NW ☎ 202/234-0700 or 1-800/843-6664, ⓦ www .omnihotels.com; Woodley Park–Zoo Metro. Plush, grand Washington institution bursting with history (see p.223) and overlooking the south chasm of Rock Creek Park. Features swank, comfortable rooms, many with a

view of the park, plus fitness center ($10 per day), pool, tennis courts, sauna, and the Marquee Bar for drinks. $445

Woodley Park Guest House 2647 Woodley Rd NW ☎ 202/667-0218 or 1-866/667-0218, ⓦ www.woodleyparkguesthouse.com; Woodley Park–Zoo Metro. Pleasant guesthouse on a residential Woodley Park side street (opposite the *Marriott*) offers a quiet refuge with 18 rooms and free continental breakfast. Well located near the Metro, the zoo, and a swath of good restaurants along Connecticut Avenue. Two-night minimum stay. Room with shared bath (single occupancy) $115, room with private bath (double occupancy) $166

Waterfront and around

Channel Inn 650 Water St SW ☎ 202/554-2400 or 1-800/368-5668, ⓦ www.channelinn.com; Waterfront Metro. Conveniently sited right on the Waterfront, with some of the spacious rooms looking across to East Potomac Park and having private balconies. There's free parking, an outdoor pool, a lounge, and a sundeck, and a number of seafood restaurants nearby. $169

Holiday Inn Capitol 550 C St SW ☎ 202/479-4000 or 1-800/465-4329, ⓦ www.holidayinncapitol .com; L'Enfant Plaza or Federal Center SW Metro. Within close walking distance of the Capitol and Smithsonian museums, the Holiday Inn Capitol includes a bar, restaurant, deli, and rooftop pool, though rooms are pretty basic. As with all of this chain's hotels in DC, weekend rates are attractive – around $180 – though they double on weekdays.

L'Enfant Plaza 480 L'Enfant Plaza SW ☎ 202/484-1000 or 1-800/635-5065, ⓦ www .lenfantplazahotel.com; L'Enfant Plaza Metro. Faded modern hotel a couple of blocks south of the Mall (and north of the Waterfront itself), with easy access to the Metro. Spacious rooms have river or city views, plus there's a health club and rooftop pool. $219

🏃 **Mandarin Oriental** 1330 Maryland Ave SW ☎ 202/554-8588, ⓦ www.mandarinoriental .com; L'Enfant Plaza Metro. Much-needed dash of upscale color to enliven the Waterfront's drab hotel scene, with exquisite decor and nice views of the riverfront and Tidal Basin, plus in-room designer furnishings, indulgent spa facilities, whirlpool and sauna, and fine restaurant, *CityZen* (see p.293), as well as tasteful garden and lounge. $690

Hostels

Washington, DC, is hardly prime **hostel** territory, though there are a few cheapies – either actual or de facto hostels – scattered around if you know where to look. Except for the HI–Washington, DC, these are all pretty far afield, though not necessarily in the middle of nowhere. For rock–bottom alternatives, students can try contacting a **university** such as Georgetown (☎202/687–4560, ⓦhousing.georgetown.edu); George Washington, in Foggy Bottom (☎202/994–2552, ⓦgwired.gwu.edu/gwhousing); Catholic, near the National Shrine (☎202/319–5277); and American, in Upper Northwest (☎202/885–3370). All offer a variety of dorms, doubles, and apartments at budget rates in summer (June–Aug). Arrangements must be made well in advance, and you may find there's a minimum stay requirement (usually one to three weeks).

Capitol City Hostel 2411 Benning Rd NE ☎202/387-1328; no Metro. If saving money is your paramount concern, consider this basic option located 25 blocks east of the Capitol in a grim neighborhood – to which you'll absolutely have to take a cab. Has computer rooms with high-speed Net access and functional amenities including a kitchen. Foreign guests must bring passport. $20 for singles or $30 for double in dorms

HI–Washington, DC 1009 11th St NW, Old Downtown ☎202/737-2333, ⓦwww .hiwashingtondc.org; Metro Center Metro. Large (270 beds), clean, and very central hostel near the convention center. Offers free continental breakfast, Internet access, dorm rooms (male and female), and shared bathrooms, plus kitchen, lounge, laundry, and organized activities. Also offers internships and volunteer opportunities. Open 24hr, but take care at night around here. Members save $3 on daily room rate. $29

Hilltop Hostel 300 Carroll Street NW, Takoma Park, MD ☎202/291-9591, ⓦwww.hosteldc.com; Takoma Park Metro. Right across from the Metro station, this is a great option for visitors on a budget. Hostel is a converted Victorian that offers wireless Internet access

and computer use, a game room with pool and foosball tables, backyard Ping-Pong and horseshoes, laundry, kitchen, and BBQ space. Convivial atmosphere adds to the fun. Six-to-nine-bed dorms $22, or private doubles $60

Washington International Student Center 2451 18th St NW, Adams Morgan ☎202/667-7681 or 1-800/567-4150, ⓦwww.washingtondchostel .com; Dupont Circle or Woodley Park–Zoo Metro. Backpackers' accommodation in plain, multibedded dorm rooms. Offers Internet access, lockers for personal belongings, cable TV, and free pickup from bus and train stations. Book at least two weeks in advance. $23

William Penn House 515 E Capitol St SE ☎202/543-5560, ⓦwww.williampennhouse.org; Capitol South or Eastern Market Metro. One of the least expensive spots in town, in a prime location just blocks from the Capitol, this Quaker-run hostel doesn't require religious observance but does prefer that guests be active in progressive causes. Rooms hold four to ten people, and breakfast is included. There's no curfew, but also no drugs or booze allowed. Morning services available if you're interested. $40

13

Eating

n many ways, the Washington **dining** scene is an outlet of its power politics: fancy eateries are constantly in demand by politicians, lobbyists, and corporate heavyweights, and there's almost as much business conducted there – quietly, with a wink and a nod over prime rib – as there is in the dull office corridors of K Street or Capitol Hill. That said, the tight competition between DC restaurants ensures that many new contenders on the culinary scene fall by the wayside, regardless of the quality of their food or service. Of course, the old-line stalwarts endure decade after decade, and some of them – most prominently the *Old Ebbitt Grill* – actually serve tempting entrees; others, though, get by for a while on their deal-making atmosphere and leave the food as an afterthought. Our listings below naturally focus on the best places to have an enjoyable meal, and leave the trendy, fly-by-night joints to the pages of tourist brochures and corporate publicity campaigns.

Although it's generally a few steps behind New York, LA, and San Francisco, the District keeps up with the times fairly well, and you're apt to find all manner of stylish Asian-fusion and New American restaurants, just as you would in any other major city. Moreover, talented chefs and restaurateurs are not above cloning their successes, so you can expect new offshoots of DC's most popular eating houses, both in the city and in the suburbs.

As for specific **cuisines**, good Southern and American food isn't hard to find, while Georgetown, in particular, has a rash of renowned New York–style saloon-restaurants serving everything from oysters to strip steaks. Continental restaurants tend to be pricey, but there are some good bistros around, while Cajun, German, Greek, and Spanish restaurants are thinner on the ground. Altogether, the Chinese restaurants in Chinatown pale in comparison to Thai or Vietnamese eateries. There are also a comparatively large number of Ethiopian restaurants, especially in Adams Morgan, and fans will be able to track down places serving food from countries as diverse as Argentina, Malaysia, and El Salvador.

Finally, for a break from the high-pressure dining scene, DC's **cafés** are good spots to knock back a latte while reading the *Post* or surfing the Internet. For a light meal or snack, they're also hard to beat, and of course can be found almost everywhere.

Neighborhoods

Certain **neighborhoods** tend to attract particular kinds of restaurants: homey trattorias are as scarce downtown as power-dining spots are in Adams Morgan. Unfortunately, the areas in which visitors spend much of their time – the Mall and around the White House – have few good-value cafés and restaurants outside the museums and galleries themselves, though there are plenty of street vendors selling bland hot dogs and ice cream.

Happily, the excellent Metro system and abundance of taxis mean that nowhere is really off-limits when it comes to choosing a restaurant. In Old Downtown, Chinatown is the only central ethnic enclave with its own swath of restaurants, though Penn Quarter has emerged as a serviceable dining center. But it's only really in the outer neighborhoods that you can saunter up and down, checking out the options. There are also lots of opportunities to sit outside when the weather's agreeable – patios, sidewalk tables, and open-front windows are all standard in DC.

Georgetown has the most varied selection of dining places – rowdy saloons, diners, ethnic restaurants, and some rather sniffy establishments – most of them in the few blocks on either side of the M Street/Wisconsin Avenue intersection. Dupont Circle (chiefly P St and Connecticut Ave) rivals Georgetown for its selection, with humble coffeehouses cheek-by-jowl with trendy New American, Asian, and Middle Eastern eateries. DC's most down-to-earth area for dining out is Adams Morgan, which also has the city's best bargains. Though prices are moving up slowly, 18th Street at Columbia Road is lined with scores of ethnic restaurants, all of which are still pretty good value. There are also pockets of worthwhile eateries east of Capitol Hill, along Connecticut Avenue in Upper Northwest, in Old Town Alexandria, and in scattered patches in northern Virginia.

The **listings** in this chapter are arranged geographically and alphabetically, and correspond to the neighborhoods in the guide. Neighborhood sections are in turn split into two divisions: "Cafés, snacks, and light meals," detailing spots good for a quick burger, pizza, or coffee, and "Restaurants." These two categories are not mutually exclusive; you can, of course, eat lunch or dinner at many of the diners, cafés, and coffee shops we've listed, and also perhaps get a light meal at many of the restaurants. At some spots it's essential to reserve a table, and you'll need to book well in advance to eat at the most renowned restaurants.

For listings by cuisine, turn to the box on pp.276–277. For restaurants popular with a gay and lesbian clientele, see Chapter 16, "Gay DC." In terms of **price**, entrees will cost less than $12 at inexpensive restaurants, $12–20 at midpriced ones, and more than $20 at expensive spots, with truly elite places charging much more. These are only a guideline, however: most people will be hard pressed to get through three courses in many restaurants, and often you'll be able to eat for less than we suggest; on the other hand, don't forget you have to add the price of drinks to your bill and, in most places, at least fifteen percent for service. To keep the price of meals at a minimum, look for set lunches (from as little as $5) and early-bird dinners (usually served before 7pm); these are not just a feature of inexpensive restaurants, as many fancier establishments maintain sensible prices in the face of a volatile market.

Adams Morgan

All the places listed in Adams Morgan are within a few blocks of the junction of 18th Street and Columbia Road; the nearest Metro stops (noted below) are a good 15min walk away.

Cafés, snacks, and light meals

18th and U Duplex Diner 2004 18th St NW
T 202/234-7828; Dupont Circle Metro.

Long-standing favorite for classic comfort foods such as mac and cheese and meatloaf, which go toe-to-toe with spruced-up favorites like pasta penne and blackened tuna. Sun & Mon 6–11pm, Tues & Wed 6pm–12.30am, Thurs 6pm–1am, Fri & Sat 6pm–1.30am.

Amsterdam Falafelshop 2425 18th St NW
T 202/234-1969; Woodley Park–Zoo Metro.
Nothing but fries, brownies, and (tasty) falafel – the latter served in a pita with your choice of toppings – at this small but

popular stand that's good for a late-night bite. Sun & Mon 11am–midnight, Tues & Wed 11am–2.30am, Thurs 11am–3am, Fri & Sat 11am–4am.

The Diner 2453 18th St NW ☎202/232-8800; **Dupont Circle or Woodley Park–Zoo Metro.** The high ceiling, chrome-and-red-leather stools, and weathered tile floor make this Adams Morgan oasis more stylish café than down-at-the-heel diner. Still, you can't go wrong with old favorites like omelettes, pancakes, and bacon. Daily 24hr.

Pizza Mart 2445 18th St NW ☎202/234-9700; **Woodley Park–Zoo Metro.** Clubgoers mop up an evening's worth of drinks with the hefty slices at this hole-in-the-wall pizzeria, one of several decent choices on this major Adams Morgan strip. Daily 11am–4am.

So's Your Mom 1831 Columbia Rd NW ☎202/462-2666; **Woodley Park–Zoo Metro.** More than fifty types of sandwiches and heaping helpings of tuna salad, bagels, chicken livers, and pastrami make this little Jewish deli a hub of foodie activity, not least for its manageable prices. Mon–Fri 7am–8pm, Sat 8am–7pm, Sun 8am–3pm.

Tryst 2459 18th St NW ☎202/232-5500; **Dupont Circle or Woodley Park–Zoo Metro.** Signature Adams Morgan hang-out where you can enjoy decent pastries, sandwiches, and gourmet coffee drinks but also slurp down wine, beer, and even morning cocktails. Arty and relaxed, with the added bonus of free WI-FI Internet access. Mon–Thurs 6.30am–2am, Fri & Sat 6.30am–3am, Sun 7am–2am.

Restaurants

Bardia's 2412 18th St NW ☎202/234-0420; **Woodley Park–Zoo Metro.** Unassuming little spot that has some of the District's best Creole fare, including beignets, seafood omelettes, po' boy sandwiches, and other Delta faves – all for cheap prices. Tues–Fri 11am–9.30pm, Sat & Sun 10am–10pm.

Bukom Café 2442 18th St NW ☎202/265-4600; **Dupont Circle or Woodley Park–Zoo Metro.** Laid-back restaurant-bar serving delicious West African dishes like oxtail or okra soup; egusi, a broth of goat meat with ground melon seeds and spinach; and chicken yassa, baked with onions and spices, for around $10. All washed down with African beers and music (live Tues–Sat). Daily 4pm–2am.

Cashion's Eat Place 1819 Columbia Rd NW ☎202/797-1819; **Dupont Circle or Woodley Park–Zoo Metro.** New Southern cuisine:

old-time casseroles, tarts, corn cakes, grits, sweet potatoes, and fruit pies are transformed into taste-bud-altering delights, with more traditional favorites like leg of lamb, duck breast, and red snapper for $22–32. Also a solid Sunday brunch (11.30am–2.30pm). Sun & Tues 5.30–10pm, Wed–Sat 5.30–11pm.

El Tamarindo 1785 Florida Ave NW ☎202/328-3660; **Dupont Circle Metro.** A fine spot for supping on Salvadoran-inspired rellenos, burritos, pupusas and other favorites, with a sizable menu that includes breakfast offerings, though many locals find themselves here enjoying a late-night Latin-food blowout. Sun–Thurs 11am–3am, Fri & Sat 11am–5am.

Grill from Ipanema 1858 Columbia Rd NW ☎202/986-0757; **Woodley Park–Zoo Metro.** Midpriced Brazilian staples made with flair, highlighted by the *feijoada* (Brazilian meat stew), shrimp dishes, stuffed avocados, and scrumptious weekend brunch (noon–4pm). Try the baked clams to start, and watch your *caipirinha* (sugar-cane rum cocktail) intake. Mon–Thurs 5–10.30pm, Fri 5–11pm, Sat noon–11pm, Sun noon–10pm.

Harambe Café 1771 U St NW, at Florida Ave and 18th ☎202/332-6435; **Dupont Circle Metro.** Simple, family-run African dining room with some of the cheapest food in town – filling chicken, beef, and lamb wot (spicy stew) served on *injera* bread, plus vegetarian platters and even a few pasta dishes – all accompanied by some great music. Sun–Thurs noon–1am, Fri & Sat noon–2am.

La Fourchette 2429 18th St NW ☎202/332-3077; **Dupont Circle or Woodley Park–Zoo Metro.** The brasserie's been here forever, and the food – affordable French classics including duck, steak, and crepes served at closely packed tables – is good and reliable, if not particularly surprising. Main bonus is the sidewalk patio. Mon–Fri 11.30am–10.30pm, Sat 4–11pm, Sun 4–10pm.

Lauriol Plaza 1835 18th St NW ☎202/387-0035; **Dupont Circle Metro.** Serves scrumptious Tex Mex staples and grilled meats, shrimp and fajitas, plus Cuban steak and roasted chicken. The place frequently gets mobbed with tourists and revelers, and the service can be spotty in such a cramped and busy atmosphere. Sun–Thurs 11.30am–11pm, Fri & Sat 11.30am–midnight.

Mama Ayesha's 1967 Calvert St NW ☎202/232-5431; **Woodley Park–Zoo Metro.** Middle

Eastern favorites like kibbeh, kabobs, grape leaves, and the rest, with a lamb shank you can really sink your teeth into, plus spicy garlic lamb and chicken staples. Come for dinner, and be prepared to bust a gut without busting your wallet. Daily 11.30am–11pm.

Meskerem 2434 18th St NW ☏ 202/462-4100; Dupont Circle or Woodley Park–Zoo Metro. One of the District's favorite Ethiopian hang-outs, with funky decor, decent prices and agreeable staff. Eat with your hands, scooping food up with the *injera* bread. There are lots of lamb, vegetarian, and seafood choices, and the

messob platter gives you a taste of everything. Daily 11.30am–11pm.

Meze 2437 18th St NW ☏ 202/797-0017; Dupont Circle or Woodley Park–Zoo Metro. A wide array of delicious Turkish meze (the Middle East's answer to tapas), both hot and cold, for cheap prices. Kebabs, grape leaves, a sausage-and-pastrami omelette, and the Istanbul burger are among the highlights. Mon–Thurs 5.30pm–1.30am, Fri 4pm–2.30am, Sat 11am–2.30am, Sun 11am–1.30am.

Mixtec 1792 Columbia Rd NW ☏ 202/332-1011; Woodley Park–Zoo Metro. Drab setting, but solid, low-priced Mexican food including

Late-night eats

At the following eateries you'll be able to order a meal at or after midnight on at least one night of the week (usually Fri and/or Sat).

14U, Shaw, p.291
18th and U Duplex Diner, Adams Morgan, p.274
Afterwords Café (24hr Sat & Sun), Dupont Circle, p.282
Alberto's Pizza, Dupont Circle, p.282
Amsterdam Falafelshop, Adams Morgan, p.274
Au Bon Pain, Union Station, p.280
Austin Grill, Alexandria, p.279
Ben's Chili Bowl, Shaw, p.291
Bistrot du Coin, Dupont Circle, p.283
Bistro Français, Georgetown, p.286
Bob and Edith's Diner, Arlington, p.280
Booeymonger, Georgetown, p.285
Bukom Café, Adams Morgan, p.275
Café Asia, New Downtown, p.288
Café Citron, Dupont Circle, p.283
Café La Ruche, Georgetown, p.286
Café Luna, Dupont Circle, p.283
Clyde's, Georgetown, p.286
Coppi's, Shaw, p.291
The Diner (24hr), Adams Morgan, p.275
Dukem, Shaw, p.291
Eat First, Chinatown, p.282
El Tamarindo, Adams Morgan, p.275
Fish Market, Alexandria, p.279
Full Kee, Chinatown, p.282
Giovanni's Trattu, New Downtown, p.288
Harambe Café, Adams Morgan, p.275

Harry's, Old Downtown, p.289
Hook, Georgetown, p.286
J. Paul's, Georgetown, p.287
Jackey Cafe, Chinatown, p.282
Jaleo, Old Downtown, p.290
Las Tapas, Alexandria, p.279
Leopold's Kafe, Georgetown, p.287
Luna Grill, Dupont Circle, p.284
Martin's Tavern, Georgetown, p.287
Mark's Duck House, Arlington, p.280
Matchbox, Chinatown, p.282
Meze, Adams Morgan, p.278
The Monocle, Capitol Hill, p.281
Mr Henry's, Capitol Hill, p.281
Naan and Beyond, New Downtown, p.287
Napoleon, Adams Morgan, p.299
Old Ebbitt Grill, Old Downtown, p.290
Open City, Upper Northwest, p.292
Paolo's, Georgetown, p.287
Pizza Boli's, Capitol Hill, p.281
Pizza Mart, Adams Morgan, p.275
Proof, Old Downtown, p.290
Sabores, Upper Northwest, p.293
Saki, Adams Morgan, p.279
Sign of the Whale, New Downtown, p.289
Stoney's, New Downtown, p.289
Tabaq Bistro, Shaw, p.291
Tryst, Adams Morgan, p.275
U-topia, Shaw, p.291

some very fine tacos, plus roasted chicken, mussels steamed with chilis, and dozens of tequila varieties on offer. You're unlikely to linger, but it's still worth a visit. Sun–Thurs 10am–10pm, Fri & Sat 10am–11pm.

Napoleon 1847 Columbia Rd NW ☏202/ 299-9630; Woodley Park–Zoo Metro. Pleasantly affordable French cuisine that covers such bases as lamb or veal stew; ham, mushroom, beef, and other fine savory crepes; and rack of lamb, duck confit, and other traditional items. Worth a try if you like Gallic fare without galling prices. Mon–Wed 5pm–midnight, Thurs 5pm–2am, Fri 5pm–3am, Sat 10am–3am, Sun 10am–midnight.

Pasta Mia 1790 Columbia Rd NW ☏202/ 328-9114; Woodley Park–Zoo Metro. Expect long lines at this no-frills, family-run pasteria, an authentic Italian eatery whose tasty selections of pasta, sausage, beef, and fish are offered at prices so low it's worth the delay. Daily 6.30–10.30pm.

Perry's 1811 Columbia Rd NW ☏202/234-6218; Woodley Park–Zoo Metro. In-crowd restaurant serving a mid- to high-priced grab bag of savory sushi, lamb chops, mussels, mac and cheese, and grilled salmon. Rooftop tables are always at a premium, and the drag-queen brunch (Sun 10.30am–2.30pm) is a blast. Sun–Thurs 5.30–10.30pm, Fri & Sat 5.30–11.30pm.

Saki 2477 18th St NW ☏202/232-5005; Woodley Park–Zoo Metro. Cheap happy-hour sushi and sashimi are the big draw here, along with other affordable Japanese selections. Downstairs is a festive club room. Sun–Thurs 11.30am–1am, Fri & Sat 11.30am–2.30am.

Alexandria, VA

Cafés, snacks, and light meals

Five Guys 107 N Fayette St ☏703/549-7991; King Street Metro. This branch of a regional chain is an Old Town greasy spoon that cooks its juicy hamburgers to order and piles on the fixin's. And don't forget the fries – the fresh, hand-cut, boardwalk-style chips boast their own loyal following. Daily 11am–10pm.

La Piazza 535 E Braddock Rd ☏703/519-7711; Braddock Road Metro. Straightforward Italian fare, and an especially good choice if a hoagie's what you crave, with the cheesesteak, sausage parmigiana, and veal-and-peppers among the favorites. Mon–Sat 11.30am–3pm & 5–10pm.

Restaurants

Austin Grill 801 King St ☏703/684-8969; King Street Metro. Quality, mid-level Tex-Mex fare packs lively crowds into this Old Town institution. The Cadillac-size fajitas, stacked nachos, steak Laredo, chorizo-and-eggs, and zesty margaritas make the long waits worthwhile. One of seven in a local chain. Sun 9am–10pm, Mon–Thurs 11.30am–11pm, Fri 11.30am–midnight, Sat 9am–midnight.

Fish Market 105 King St ☏703/836-5676; King Street Metro. Midpriced, brick-walled restaurant with terrace a block from the water, serving oysters and chowder at the bar and fried-fish platters, stews, pastas, and fish entrees, not to mention a mean spicy shrimp meal. Daily 11.30am–11pm, weekends until midnight.

Hard Times Café 1404 King St ☏703/837-0050; King Street Metro. Four styles of cheap and fiery chilli, from classic Texas to Greek-style Cincinnati to spicy-as-hell Terlingua, plus a veggie option. Good wings, rings, and fries, too, and savory microbrews – it all adds up to one of Alexandria's better Tex-Mex/American restaurants. One of many in a local chain. Sun–Thurs 11am–11pm, Fri & Sat 11am–midnight.

🏃 **Las Tapas** 710 King St ☏703/836-4000; King Street Metro. Best of the local tapas bars, with a wide selection of authentic small plates – including ceviche, Serrano ham, octopus, and chorizo – plus rich paella, tasty sangria, Spanish guitar music, and free flamenco sessions (Tues & Thurs 7–10pm). Sun–Wed 11.30am–10pm, Thurs 11.30am–11pm, Fri & Sat 11.30am–1am.

Los Tios Grill 2615 Mount Vernon Ave ☏703/299-9290; Braddock Metro. Friendly and upbeat Latin American cuisine, with a bent toward Salvadoran, with the pork morsels, Veracruz chicken, tortilla soup, fried yucca, and especially the fajitas among the inexpensive favorites. A mile and a half north of Old Town. Daily 11am–10pm, weekends 'til 11pm.

The Majestic 911 King St ☏703/837-9117; King Street Metro. Down-home American favorites in this classic upscale diner, with the seafood stew, rib chops, meatloaf, and liver among the more piquant offerings, and fried green tomatoes, crab cakes, and oyster po' boy driving the point home. Also an excellent Sunday dinner (fixed $68). Tues–Fri 11.30am–2.30pm & 5.30–10pm, Sat 5.30–10.30pm, Sun 1–9pm.

Restaurant Eve 110 S Pitt St ☎703/706-0450; King Street Metro. The buzz attached to this warm and homey nouveau American bistro is fairly spot-on. Choices include five- and nine-course meals drawn from a rotating menu of seafood, game, cheese, and desserts for $95 or $125, or expensive bistro fare such as pork belly, sweetbreads, oxtail ravioli, and the like. Mon–Fri 11.30am–2.30pm & 5.30–9.30pm, Sat 5.30–10pm.

Southside 815 815 S Washington St ☎703/836-6222; King Street Metro. Moderately priced Southern cooking just the way you like it, with good old-fashioned favorites like biscuits with ham gravy, thick and buttery cornbread, succotash, BBQ shrimp, ribs, crab fritters, and straight-up crawdads and catfish. Sun–Thurs 11.30am–10.30pm, Fri & Sat 11.30am–11pm.

Arlington and around

Restaurants

Bangkok 54 2919 Columbia Pike ☎703/521-4070. Upscale Thai food you won't forget – among DC's best – with a broad selection of crispy pork, drunken noodles, green papaya or beef salad, spicy calamari, and a fine roasted-duck noodle soup. Daily 11am–10pm, weekends 'til 11pm.

Bob and Edith's Diner 2310 Columbia Pike ☎703/920-6103. Thumbs up to the tasty, gut-busting diner fare at this cheap and alluring breakfast joint. It's open round the clock, so you can get your fill of country ham, eggs, scrapple, omelettes, and home fries whenever you're hungry. Also at 4707 Columbia Pike (☎703/920-4700).

Carlyle 4000 S 28th St ☎703/931-0777. Mid-level steak and seafood with a nouveau twist, mixing in other, more exotic flavors to end up with tasty lobster pot stickers, jambalaya, grits, fondue, and crab fritters. Mon–Thurs 11am–11pm, Fri & Sat 11.30am–midnight, Sun 9.30am–11pm.

Four Sisters 6769 Wilson Blvd, Falls Church, VA ☎703/538-6717; East Falls Church Metro. It's worth venturing out to this affordable, popular spot for delicious squid, crispy

shrimp, lemongrass beef, pho, lotus salad, spicy frog legs, and other Vietnamese favorites. Sun–Thurs 10.30am–10pm, Fri & Sat 10.30am–11pm.

Mark's Duck House 6184 Arlington Blvd, Falls Church, VA ☎703/532-2125; East Falls Church Metro. More top-notch Asian fare in the 'burbs – this midpriced one, located in a mini mall, offers primo Chinese food, such as a mean roasted duck, salty shrimp, and lunchtime dim sum. Not to be missed if you're in the area. Sun–Thurs 10am–10pm, Fri & Sat 10am–midnight.

Morton's of Chicago 1631 Crystal Square Ave ☎703/418-1444; Crystal City Metro. Local branch of the chic steakhouse chain, with the standard array of delicious cuts of beef, veal, and lobster, most for $30 and up, plus a clubby atmosphere good for smoking and boozing. Mon–Sat 5.30–11pm, Sun 5.30–10pm.

Red Hot & Blue 1600 Wilson Blvd ☎703/276-7427; Court House Metro. Also 3014 Wilson Blvd, at Highland ☎703/243-1510; Clarendon Metro. Memphis barbecue joint that spawned a chain, serving the best ribs in the area. A rack, with coleslaw and beans, costs just ten bucks. Many other suburban branches. Sun–Thurs 11am–10pm, Fri & Sat 11am–11pm.

Tacqueria Poblano 2503 N Harrison St ☎703/237-8250. Not close to anything interesting, but rewards a short drive west to sample some of the area's best Mexican food, including shrimp tacos and seafood quesadillas, duck carnitas and other savory, filling offerings for fair prices. Mon 5.30–10pm, Tues–Sat 11.30am–10pm, Sun 10.30am–9pm.

Tallula 2761 Washington Blvd ☎703/778-5051. Chic modern American restaurant six blocks west of the cemetery that serves up expensive Amish chicken, tuna tartare, and New York strip steak, as well as affordable small plates of crab pot stickers and risotto fritters and a chorizo corn dog. Mon–Thurs 5.30–10pm, Fri 5.30–11pm, Sat 11am–2.30pm & 5.30–11pm, Sun 11am–2.30pm & 5.30–10pm.

Capitol Hill

Cafés, snacks, and light meals

Au Bon Pain 50 Massachusetts Ave NE ☎202/898-0299; Union Station Metro. Although there are many better cafés than this chain in town, this is by far the most convenient spot to chow down on sandwiches, soups, pastries, and salads while waiting for your train at Union Station – at any time of the day. 24hr.

Bread and Chocolate 666 Pennsylvania Ave SE ☎202/547-2875; Eastern Market Metro. Popular bakery and coffeehouse with solid sandwiches and street-view seating, located in this strip's main people-watching zone. It can get pretty crowded, so be prepared to wait for service. Mon–Sat 7am–7pm, Sun 8am–6pm.

Le Bon Café 210 2nd St SE ☎202/547–7200; Capitol South Metro. Good for a wholesome lunch of soup, quiche, or a sandwich, or breakfast with pastries and waffles, and close to the Library of Congress. Mon–Fri 7.30am–5pm, Sat & Sun 8.30am–3.30pm.

Market Lunch Eastern Market, 7th Ave SE ☎202/547-8444; Eastern Market Metro. Excellent spot for munch-and-go, market hall-counter meals, known for its pancakes, crab cakes and French toast, but also with fine sandwiches and fries, and assorted fish platters – served to a loyal band of shoppers and suit-and-tie congressional staffers. Tues–Sat 7.30am–3pm, Sun 11am–3pm.

Murky Coffee 660 Pennsylvania Ave SE ☎202/546-5228; Eastern Market Metro. Inspired by Italian brew making, espresso drinks here pack an authentic punch, and are straight-up black – not murky. Also sells pastries and coffee by the pound. One of four area locations. Mon–Sat 7am–9pm, Sun 8am–8pm.

Restaurants

Bistro Bis 15 E St NW ☎202/661-2700; Union Station Metro. Tasty French restaurant connected to a chic boutique hotel (the *George*; see p.265), with the requisite upmarket continental fare – soups, sweetbreads, seafood, grilled meats – featuring the occasional twist. Daily 7–10am, 11.30am–2.30pm & 5.30–10.30pm.

Café Berlin 322 Massachusetts Ave NE ☎202/543-7656; Union Station Metro. The perfect spot to fill up on your favorite gut-busting German food – from pork Jaegerschnitzel to potato pancakes to spiced herring with onions and apples. Sandwiches $6–9, entrees $15–20. Mon–Thurs 11.30am–10pm, Fri & Sat 11.30am–11pm, Sun 4–10pm.

Johnny's Half Shell 400 N Capitol St NW ☎202/737-0400; Union Station Metro. Swank seafood eatery where you can sample local specialties like crab cakes, fried oysters, and seafood stew – go for the gumbo or, in summer, the soft-shell crabs. Also has a good breakfast, lunch, and happy hour. Mon–Fri 7–9.30am, 11.30am–2.30pm & 5–10pm, Sat 5–10pm.

Las Placitas 517 8th St SE ☎202/543-3700; Eastern Market Metro. Great-value Mexican standards like burritos and quesadillas and Salvadoran specials pack the tables nightly at this fine and fun eatery. Mon–Fri 11.30am–3pm & 5–10pm, Sat 4–10pm, Sun 4–11pm.

Montmartre 327 7th St SE ☎202/544-1244, Eastern Market Metro. A handy and comfortable place to sample French bistro fare such as pâté, quiche, seafood, and traditional soups, with most entrees $12–20. Daily 11.30am–2.30pm & 5–9pm, Sun closes 8pm.

The Monocle 107 D St NE ☎202/546-4488; Union Station Metro. If you want to get a glimpse of political powerbrokers stuffing their maws with delicious crab cakes, steaks, pasta, and trout, and sample a little of the fancy fare yourself (entrees $17–35), this is the place to go. Mon–Fri 11.30am–midnight.

Mr Henry's 601 Pennsylvania Ave SE ☎202/546-8412; Eastern Market Metro. Saloon and restaurant with outside patio, grill, and mixed gay and straight crowd. Except for the steak and seafood platters, most entrees – including some good burgers – are less than $10. Sun–Thurs 11am–midnight, Fri & Sat 11am–1am.

Pizza Boli's 417 8th St SE ☎202/546-2900; Eastern Market Metro. For a quick snarf on the way to the Hill, this is a great choice for its cheap, hot pizzas, including some solid specials and white pizzas, right off the Metro. Daily 11am–1am, weekends until 2am.

Two Quail 320 Massachusetts Ave NE ☎202/543-8030; Union Station Metro. Atmospheric bistro (spread over a trio of townhouses) serving changing menus of expensive California cuisine–style food, including dinner entrees such as peach-glazed pork loin and the titular birds in whiskey cider sauce. Lunches are a deal at $10–15. Reservations recommended. Mon–Fri 11.30am–2.30pm & 5–10pm, Sat 5–10pm & Sun 5–11pm.

Zack's Taverna 305 Pennsylvania Ave SE
ⓣ202/547-8360; Capitol South Metro. Order
something from the all-meat grill at this
serviceable, affordable Greek joint and you
won't need appetizers, or choose from the
pricier fish specialties. A carryout section is
in the basement. Mon–Sat 11am–11pm.

Chinatown

Restaurants

Eat First 609 H St NW ⓣ202/289-1703; Gallery
Place–Chinatown Metro. You should scour the
menu first at this wide-ranging, somewhat
divey Cantonese diner, which has an array
of cheap Asian selections such as shrimp
dumplings, roast duck, squid, pan-fried
noodles, and on and on. Daily 11am–2am.
Full Kee 509 H St NW ⓣ202/371-2233; Gallery
Place–Chinatown Metro. Known for its shrimp
and other kinds of dumplings, hot and spicy
soups, roasted meats, pan-fried seafood,
and congee, this is a genuine Cantonese
favorite with a genuine following. Most
dishes are $5–10, though the drab atmos-
phere doesn't exactly inspire. Sun–Thurs
11am–10pm, Fri & Sat 11am–1am.
Jackey Cafe 611 H St ⓣ202/408-8115; Gallery
Place–Chinatown Metro. A recent arrival on
the Chinatown scene, offering a broad,
midpriced menu of Cantonese items like
dumplings, pan-fried noodles, seafood, and
even fried pigeon. Something of a
happening late-night scene, too. Daily
11am–3am.
Kanlaya Thai 740 6th St NW ⓣ202/393-0088;
Gallery Place–Chinatown Metro. A nice, cheap
break from the Chinese fare around (not all
of it good), with delicious Thai soups like
tom kha gai, various curries and stir-fried
noodles, a mean wild-pork dish, and
steamed curry chicken – here called "Rama
in Jacuzzi." Daily 11.30am–10pm.
Matchbox 713 H St NW ⓣ202/289-4441;
Gallery Place–Chinatown Metro. A good
spot if, for some reason, you find yourself in
Chinatown without a hankering for Chinese
food. The gourmet pizzas are the undeni-
able high point, but the seafood and
smallish hamburgers are savory as well. A
range of prices depending on the entree,
usually $10–25. Mon–Thurs 11am–11pm,
Fri & Sat 11am–1am.
Tony Cheng's 619 H St NW ⓣ202/
842-8669 (Mongolian), ⓣ202/371-8669
(seafood); Gallery Place–Chinatown Metro.

Although upstairs is a somewhat pricey
Cantonese seafood restaurant that's been
visited by lots of celebrities, the real highlight
of this place is downstairs, where the cheap
Mongolian barbecue is a fun, do-it-yourself,
all-you-can-eat experience. Mon–Thurs &
Sun 11am–11.30pm, Fri & Sat
11am–midnight.

Dupont Circle

Cafés, snacks, and light meals

17th Street Café 1513 17th St NW ⓣ202/
234-2470; Dupont Circle Metro. Omelettes,
sandwiches, soups, and a dash of Mexican
fare provide the culinary setting at this
casual but pleasant spot, with seating inside
the arty townhouse or out front on the
sidewalk patio. Mon 5–11pm, Tues–Thurs
noon–midnight, Fri noon–2am, Sat
9am–2am, Sun 9am–10.30pm.
Afterwords Café 1517 Connecticut Ave NW
ⓣ202/387-1462; Dupont Circle Metro. This
spot in the back of Kramerbooks serves
breakfast and brunch, great cappuccino,
and full meals – salad, pastas, grills, and
sandwiches, with plenty of vegetarian
choices. Live blues and jazz Wed through
Sat. Sun–Thurs 7.30am–1am, Fri & Sat
24hr.
Alberto's Pizza 2010 P St NW ⓣ202/986-2121;
Dupont Circle Metro. Little more than a
basement-level takeout stand, Alberto's
nevertheless draws major lines on weekend
nights for its excellent deals on thin-crust
pizza: a "slice" is one-quarter of an entire
pie, and starts at just $3. Mon–Tues 11am–
11.30pm, Wed & Sun 11am–12.30am,
Thurs–Sat 11am–4am.
Firehook Bakery & Coffeehouse 1909 Q
St NW ⓣ202/588-9296; Dupont Circle
Metro. Renowned bakery-café serving up
sandwich specials and a huge range of
breads (also pies, desserts, and cookies),
plus good coffee at reasonable prices.
Plenty of other branches citywide, too.
Mon–Fri 6.30am–9pm, Sat 7am–9pm,
Sun 7am–7pm. One nearby branch is at
the Phillips Collection, 1600 21st St NW
(see p.200); Tues–Sat 10am–4pm, Sun
11am–4pm.
Java House 1645 Q St NW ⓣ202/387-6622;
Dupont Circle Metro. A local favorite, arguably
serving the neighborhood's best coffee –
grab a cup to go or scramble for a sunny
seat on the packed patio. A good spot to

read a book, have an afternoon chat, or fire up the laptop for WI-FI access. Desserts, bagels, salads, and sandwiches are on offer throughout the day. Daily 7am–11pm.

Marvelous Market 1511 Connecticut Ave NW ☏202/332-3690; Dupont Circle Metro. Superb carryout deli with ready-made sandwiches, cheeses and olives, fresh produce, and very good brownies and bread. Mon–Sat 8am–8pm, Sun 8am–6pm.

Newsroom 1803 Connecticut Ave NW ☏202/332-1489; Dupont Circle Metro. Coffee, snacks, and pastries are served at this newsstand, which carries one of DC's best selections of hipster magazines, British and French imports, and hard-to-find newspapers. There's Internet access upstairs. Daily 7am–9pm, weekends 'til 10pm.

Teaism 2009 R St NW ☏202/667-3827; Dupont Circle Metro. Serene Dupont Circle teahouse serving Japanese bento boxes, Thai curries, scones, and, of course, lots of good tea, and a fine brunch. If you're looking to stock up on tea leaves, you'll find three dozen types on offer, as well as teapots and mugs. One of three citywide locations. Mon–Thurs 8am–10pm, Fri 8am–11pm, Sat 9am–11pm, Sun 9am–10pm.

Restaurants

Asia Nora 2213 M St NW ☏202/797-4860; Dupont Circle or Foggy Bottom–GWU Metro. Connected in spirit to the equally appetizing Nora's (see p.284), this is signature pan-Asian cuisine prepared organically, with expensive dishes like pan-seared steelhead, coriander lamb sirloin, and ginger pork loin among the many highlights. Mon–Sat 5.30–10.30pm.

Bistrot du Coin 1738 Connecticut Ave NW ☏202/234-6969; Dupont Circle Metro. Classic bistro with a superb bar, boisterous atmosphere, and genuine French food that actually tastes like continental cuisine – goat cheese salad, steamed mussels, pâté and rabbit stew, and other choice offerings – all at prices that won't cost you your Armani shirt. Mon–Wed & Sun 11.30am–11pm, Thurs–Sat 11.30am–1am.

Café Citron 1343 Connecticut Ave NW ☏202/530-8844; Dupont Circle Metro. Trendy restaurant serving tasty Caribbean-influenced Latin food running $10–15 for dishes; try the *ceviche* or fajitas. By ten, the dining crowd gives way to meat-marketing partiers who come to grind to tunes provided by DJs or live Brazilian or salsa/merengue bands – and to fuel up on some of the best *mojitos* in town. Mon–Thurs 11.30am–2am, Fri 11.30am–3am, Sat 4pm–3am.

Café Luna 1633 P St NW ☏202/387-4005; Dupont Circle Metro. One of Dupont Circle's best spots for tasty but cheap food. Soups, salads, sandwiches, pasta, pizza, and Italian coffee are served inside this laid-back hangout or at a handful of sidewalk tables. Also open for breakfast and weekend brunches. Sun–Thurs 10am–11pm, Fri & Sat 10am–midnight.

City Lights of China 1731 Connecticut Ave NW ☏202/265-6688; Dupont Circle Metro. Midpriced Chinese fare such as spicy Szechuan and Hunan specialties and a strong emphasis on seafood, including items like crabmeat asparagus soup. One of the

⑬

EATING | Neighborhoods

Great places for brunch

Weekend **brunch** – especially Sunday brunch – is a Washington institution. The city's most prestigious hotels offer the best spreads and provide visitors and locals with a relatively inexpensive way to experience their dining rooms. But many non-hotel restaurants also pride themselves on their brunches. The places listed below may not offer the swanky surroundings and free champagne refills of the hotels but are still, in their own way, excellent.

Acadiana p.290	Cashion's Eat Place p.275	Perry's p.279
Afterwords Café p.282	Clyde's p.286	Sabores p.293
Ardeo p.292	Grill from Ipanema p.275	Tabard Inn p.289
Café des Artistes p.284	Hook p.286	Teaism p.288 & p.283
Café La Ruche p.286	Kinkead's p.285	U-topia p.291
Café Luna p.283	Martin's Tavern p.287	

few Chinese spots that does vegetarian food right – standouts include the steamed dumplings and garlic eggplant. Mon–Fri 11.30am–11pm, Sat noon–11pm, Sun noon–10.30pm.

Komi 1509 17th St NW ℗202/332-9200, Dupont Circle Metro. High-profile eatery that offers a handful of delicious, fixed-price selections of risotto, pasta, game, seafood, and steak in the neighborhood of $80–100 per person. Worth it for a special occasion. Tues–Sat 5.30–10.30pm.

Luna Grill & Diner 1301 Connecticut Ave NW ℗202/835-2280; Dupont Circle Metro. Inexpensive diner with bright decor, planetary murals and mosaics, and wholesome blue-plate specials, "green plate" (vegetarian) dishes, and organic coffees and teas. The crab cake sandwich, meatball sub, and sirloin and veggie burgers are all worth a taste. An outdoor patio adds to the allure. Mon–Thurs 8am–10.30pm, Fri 8am–midnight, Sat 10am–midnight, Sun 10am–10pm.

🏃 **Nora's** 2132 Florida Ave NW ℗202/462-5143; Dupont Circle Metro. One of DC's best eateries (with prices to match), set in a converted store with folk-art designs and all-organic fare that includes delicious items like wild mushroom risotto, Amish pork roast, braised short ribs, and a French Brie tart. Mon–Sat 5.30–10.30pm.

🏃 **Pizzeria Paradiso** 2029 P St NW ℗202/223-1245; Dupont Circle Metro. Arguably DC's best pizzeria, with lines forming nightly on the steps outside for favorites such as the gut-busting Siciliana, potato-and-pesto Genovese, and ultra-peppery and spicy Atomica. If you've simply got to have a slice but can't bear the wait and the crowd, cross the street to *Alberto's* (see p.282) for quick relief. Mon–Thurs 11.30am–11pm, Fri & Sat 11.30am–midnight, Sun noon–10pm.

Sala Thai 2016 P St NW ℗202/234-5698; Dupont Circle Metro. Prominent and inexpensive Thai restaurant with stylish decor and a range of staples – the usual soups and pad thai – as well as surprises like soft-shell crab and calamari. One of seven District locations. Mon–Thurs 11.30am–10.30pm, Fri & Sat noon–11pm, Sun noon–10.30pm.

Skewers 1633 P St NW ℗202/387-7400; Dupont Circle Metro. It has Dupont Circle's funkiest interior, but the food doesn't take a backseat to the decor. The midpriced restaurant (above *Café Luna*) is tops for kebabs, eggplant, seafood, and oddball items like ravioli and angel-hair pancakes – not to mention belly dancing. Mon–Thurs 11.30am–11pm, Fri 11.30am–midnight, Sat noon–midnight, Sun noon–11pm.

Sushi Taro 1503 17th St NW ℗202/462-8999; Dupont Circle Metro. One of DC's best Japanese restaurants, with plenty of fine sushi, sashimi, tempura and teriyaki, for moderate to expensive prices. If raw fish isn't your thing, choose from the selection of steak and pork cutlets. When the cherry blossoms start to bloom, keep an eye out for the annual all-you-can-eat sushi-fest. Mon–Fri 11.30am–2pm & 5.30–10pm, Sat 5.30–10.30pm.

Urbana in the Palomar Hotel, 2121 P St NW ℗202/956-6650; Dupont Circle Metro. Splashy hotel restaurant that offers continental cuisine along with fine designer pizzas, and also good for its pasta, seafood and osso buco. Not as expensive as you might think, with pizzas $10–15 and entrees $15–30. Mon–Fri 7am–3pm & 5–10pm, Sat 8am–3pm & 5–11pm, Sun 8am–3pm & 5–10pm.

Zorba's Café 1612 20th St NW ℗202/387-8555; Dupont Circle Metro. Filling and cheap Greek combo platters, kebabs, pizzas, and pita-bread sandwiches, as well as daily specials and traditional dishes like bean casserole and spinach pie. Wash down one of the very good gyro sandwiches with pitchers of draft beer. Hard-to-get sidewalk seating in summer. Mon–Sat 11am–11.30pm, Sun noon–10.30pm.

Foggy Bottom

Cafés, snacks, and light meals

🏃 **The Breadline** 1751 Pennsylvania Ave NW ℗202/822-8900; Farragut West Metro. DC's best sandwiches made with DC's best bread, stuffed with spicy chicken, pork sausage, wild boar, and other savory fillings. This superb open bakery (with seats inside and out) also offers pizza, empanadas, flatbreads, salads, smoothies, coffee, and tea, using organic ingredients if possible. Mon–Fri 7.30am–3.30pm.

Café des Artistes 500 17th St NW ℗202/639-1700; Farragut West or Farragut North Metro. Excellent Corcoran Gallery café serving agreeable lunches. Go for a designer pizza, applewood bacon sandwich, or roasted chicken salad. The brunch buffet on Sun also makes a good choice. Mon & Wed–Sun 11.30am–2pm, Thurs also 5–8pm.

Capitol Grounds 1010 17th St NW ☎202/887-8231; **Farragut North or Farragut West Metro.** A lively spot known for gourmet sandwiches and breakfast staples, plus good coffee and a convivial atmosphere. Also at 2100 Pennsylvania Ave NW (☎202/293-2057). Mon–Fri 7am–6pm, Sat 9am–4pm, Sun 9am–3pm.

Cosi 1700 Pennsylvania Ave NW ☎202/638-6366; **Farragut West Metro.** Just a short hop from both the White House and Corcoran, this chain restaurant is good for a quick bite while on the tour circuit – though the other branches can be hit-or-miss. An assortment of tasty, if pricey, sandwiches on freshly baked flatbread. Mon–Fri 7am–7pm, Sat & Sun 9am–5pm.

Lawson's Deli 1776 I St NW ☎202/296-3200; **Farragut West Metro.** Primo bagels, sandwiches, and panini make Lawson's a local favorite; it's also good for salads and pastries. Mon–Fri 8am–8pm, Sat & Sun 10am–6pm.

Restaurants

Art Gallery Bar & Grille 1712 I St NW ☎202/536-3380; **Farragut West Metro.** Play the Wurlitzer jukebox or sit on the outdoor patio as you tuck into an eclectic, affordable array of seafood, salads, burgers, sandwiches, omelettes, or pizza. There are Mexican and Middle Eastern offerings as well. Mon–Fri 6.30am–10pm.

🏃 **Blue Duck Tavern in the Park Hyatt Hotel, 1201 24th St NW** ☎202/419-6755; **Foggy Bottom–GWU Metro.** Designer-decorated finery provides the backdrop for this chic and trendy eatery, offering steak, prawns, softshell crab, and delicious desserts to a crowd of business and diplomatic diners. Entrees from $15–25. Daily 11.30am–2.30pm & 5.30–10.30pm.

DISH in the *River Inn*, 924 25th St NW, ☎202/337-7600; **Foggy Bottom–GWU Metro.** Tasty American fare – from rockfish, pork chops, and lamb shank for expensive dinners to sandwiches, pasta, and wraps for inexpensive lunches – served in posh surroundings. Given the restaurant's popularity with the chattering classes, its name is as much a verb as a noun. Mon–Fri 7am–10am & 11.30am–2.30pm & 5–10pm,

Sat 8–10am & 5–11pm, Sun 8–10am & 5–10pm.

🏃 **Kinkead's 2000 Pennsylvania Ave NW** ☎202/296-7700; **Foggy Bottom–GWU Metro.** One of DC's favorite, and priciest, restaurants, with a contemporary menu specializing in fish and seafood, from salmon and monkfish (entrees $25–32), and a raw bar with oysters, lobsters, crab, and mussels. Since it's plenty popular, you'll need to book ahead. Daily 11.30am–2.30pm & 5.30–10pm (raw bar until 11pm).

Notti Bianche in the *GW University Inn*, 824 New Hampshire Ave NW ☎1-800/426-4455; **Foggy Bottom–GWU Metro.** Quality hotel restaurant serving up mid- to upper-end pasta, risotto, and seafood – including the likes of grilled squid, braised monkfish, and venison carpaccio. Not as expensive as other fine restaurants in the area. Also with pasta and seafood for lunch, and omelettes and frittatas for breakfast. Mon–Fri 7–10am, 11.30am–2.30pm & 5–10pm, Sat 8–10am & 5–10pm, Sun 8–10am & 5–11pm.

Primi Piatti 2013 I St NW ☎202/223-3600; **Farragut West or Foggy Bottom–GWU Metro.** Fine Italian restaurant with a knack for creating savory, affordable gourmet pizzas – with ingredients such as goat cheese and prosciutto – that at $10–15 are much cheaper than the meat and pasta dishes. Mon–Fri 11.30am–2.30pm & 5.30–10.30pm, Sat 5.30–10.30pm.

Thai Coast 2514 L St NW ☎202/333-2460; **Foggy Bottom–GWU Metro.** Neighborhood Southeast Asian eatery with a convivial atmosphere that boasts the usual rolls, satays, and curries, then throws in oddball items like crabmeat sausages and softshell crab. Cheap, filling, and worth it. Daily 11.30am–10.30pm, weekends 'til 11pm.

Georgetown

Cafés, snacks, and light meals

🏃 **Baked & Wired 1052 Thomas Jefferson St NW** ☎202/333-2500. Among the city's finest bakeries, where you can sample great pies – from apple crumb to peach cream – delicious coffee cakes, brownies, cookies, and especially cupcakes. There's a nice selection of coffee and tea, too. Mon–Fri 7am–6pm.

Booeymonger 3265 Prospect St NW ☎202/333-4810. Crowded deli/coffee shop at the corner of Prospect and Potomac streets. Excellent for its signature sandwiches like the Gatsby Arrow (roast beef and Brie) and the Patty Hearst (turkey and bacon with Russian dressing), plus solid breakfast selections. Daily 8am–midnight.

Ching Ching Cha 1063 Wisconsin Ave NW ☏202/333-8288. Bright and pleasant tearoom transports teetotalers to Old Asia with black teas and herbal infusions, delicious hot or iced, a menu of savory items like rolls, tea eggs, and dumplings, and an array of snazzy collectibles for sale. Daily 11.30am–9pm.

Dean & Deluca 3276 M St NW ☏202/342-2500. Superior self-service café in one of M Street's most handsome and historic red-brick buildings, the Market House. Croissants and cappuccino, designer salads, pasta, and sandwiches, with a Southern bent evident in the buttermilk fried chicken, corn pudding, and barbecued ribs. Daily 8am–9pm.

Furin's 2805 M St NW ☏202/965-1000. Georgetown's best bet for a home-cooked eggs-and-hotcakes breakfast, blue-plate deli sandwiches, potato or chicken salads, and tasty desserts like French pastries, fruit tarts and pies, and iced cookies. Mon–Fri 7.30am–7pm, Sat 8am–5pm.

Restaurants

Bangkok Bistro 3251 Prospect St NW ☏202/337-2424. In a stylish, often crowded dining room, this midpriced gem has old favorites (tom yum, pad thai, shrimp cakes, and satay) offered alongside coconut shrimp, duck noodles, spicy beef curries, and chili prawns. Sun–Thurs 11.30am–10.30pm, Fri & Sat 11.30am–11.30pm.

Bistro Français 3128 M St NW ☏202/338-3830. Renowned for its (moderately priced) French cooking, from simple steak frites, baked mussels, and beef tenderloin to lamb steak and liver mousse. Early-bird (5–7pm) and late-night (10.30pm–1am) set dinners for $20. Sun–Thurs 11am–3am, Fri & Sat 11am–4am.

Busara 2340 Wisconsin Ave NW ☏202/337-2340. Designer Thai eatery with super-sleek decor and yuppie clientele. The food is a mix of authentic and inventive, including items like lamb curry, tiger shrimp, and seafood talay running $8–17. Sun–Thurs 11.30am–10.30pm, Fri & Sat 11.30am–11.30pm.

Café la Ruche 1039 31st St NW ☏202/965-2684. Relaxing, inexpensive bistro with patio seating ideal for dining alone or in twos in warmer weather. Sample the onion soup, quiches, and croque monsieur and other fine sandwiches, or drop by for pastries and espresso. Also has a good weekend brunch. Mon–Thurs 11.30am–11.30pm, Fri 11.30am–1am, Sat 10am–1am, Sun 10am–10.30pm.

Citronelle in the Latham Hotel, 3000 M St ☏202/625-2150. Huge player on the DC dining scene, serving up French-inspired cuisine with a California flair, and set-price food and wine pairings starting at $235. Reserve in advance, dress chic, and bring plenty of attitude. Daily 7am–10.30am, Mon–Fri noon–2pm, Sun–Thurs 6.30–10pm, Fri & Sat 6.30–10.30pm.

▲ Citronelle

Clyde's 3236 M St NW ☏202/333-9180. Classic New York–style saloon-restaurant featuring clubby wood interior, plus a menu of crab cakes, steak, burgers, pasta and paella. One of a dozen in a midpriced local chain. Book ahead for the good Sunday brunch. Mon–Thurs 11.30am–midnight, Fri 11.30am–1am, Sat 10am–1am, Sun 9am–10.30pm.

Hook 3241 M St NW ☏202/625-4488. Hard to do better for the catch of the day than this centrally located seafood favorite, which serves up a mean blackfin tuna, sunburst trout, and King salmon for $25 and up. Also affordable lunch specials and a marvelous weekend brunch. Mon 5–10pm, Tues–Thurs 11.30am–2.30pm & 5–11pm, Fri 11.30am–2.30pm & 5pm–midnight, Sat 10.30am–2.30pm & 5pm–midnight, Sun 10.30am–2.30pm & 5–10pm.

J. Paul's 3218 M St NW ☎202/333-3450. A "dining saloon" that offers the standard grill/barbecue menu, with some crab cakes and a good raw bar, plus microbrews. Good enough to stuff your gut, if not to write home about. Mon–Thurs 11.30am–11.30pm, Fri & Sat 11.30am–midnight, Sun 10.30am–11.30pm.

Leopold's Kafe 3315 M St NW ☎202/965-6005. European-chic café that caters to a refined crowd with its mid- to high-priced continental fare like onion tarts, veal schnitzel, bratwurst, smoked fish, and delicious desserts and pastries. Breakfast can be particularly good here. Sun–Tues 8am–10pm, Wed 8am–11pm, Thurs–Sat 8am–midnight.

Martin's Tavern 1264 Wisconsin Ave NW ☎202/333-7370. Four generations have run this place and counted politicos from JFK to Dubya among their regulars. The old-fashioned, clubby saloon serves up steaks and chops, great burgers, linguine with clam sauce, and oyster platters, most for around $12–25. It's also known for its popular brunch (Sun 10am–3pm). Mon–Thurs 10am–1.30am, Fri 10am–2.30am, Sat 8am–2.30am, Sun 8am–1.30am.

Morton's of Chicago 3251 Prospect St NW ☎202/342-6258. The premium steak-house chain's Georgetown branch serves a fabulous porterhouse. Pick your cut – and make sure you've come with a huge appetite – or go for entrees ($25 and up) that range from chicken to swordfish. One of several local branches, including one in Arlington (see p.280). Mon–Sat 5.30–11pm, Sun 5–10pm.

Paolo's 1303 Wisconsin Ave NW ☎202/333-7353. Mid-level Italian dining with a few coveted tables open to the sidewalk. Gourmet pizzas ($10) and even better pastas ($10–15) are specialties, though the entrees cost twice that. Sun 10am–11.30pm, Mon–Thurs 11am–11.30pm, Fri 11am–12.30am, Sat 10am–12.30am.

Rocklands 2418 Wisconsin Ave NW ☎202/333-2558. A bit north of the

main action, almost in Upper Northwest, but still worth the trek to enjoy some of DC's best pork sandwiches, ribs, beans, sausage, and other staples of the Southern barbecue scene, all for cheap prices and good tummy vibes. Two other area locations. Mon–Sat 11am–10pm, Sun 11am–9pm.

Vietnam Georgetown 2934 M St NW ☎202/337-4536. Tourist-friendly, affordable Vietnamese restaurant with decent food and solid specials that include grilled lemon chicken, curry beef, stuffed crepes, seafood platters, and fish fillets. Mon–Thurs 11am–11pm, Fri & Sat 11am–11.30pm, Sun noon–11pm.

Zed's 1201 28 St NW ☎202/333-4710. The spot for Ethiopian food in Georgetown, and an intimate one at that. The set lunch is cheap but so are the dinner entrees. The *doro wot* (chicken stew in a red pepper sauce) is a good, spicy choice, as are the tenderloin beef cubes. There are also plenty of veggie options. Sun–Thurs 11am–10pm, Fri & Sat 11am–11pm.

New Downtown

Cafés, snacks, and light meals

Julia's Empanadas 1221 Connecticut Ave NW ☎202/861-8828; Dupont Circle Metro. Savory Mexican turnovers stuffed with the likes of Jamaican beef, cilantro-turkey, and spicy sausage, and so cheap you'll barely notice the money leaving your wallet. One of five area locations. Mon–Wed 11am–2am, Thurs–Sat 11am–3am, Sun 11am–7pm.

Loeb's Deli 832 15th St NW ☎202/371-1150; McPherson Square Metro. Classic New York–style delicatessen, operating locally since 1959 and at this site since 1979. One of the better places in the District to get a decent pastrami or corned-beef sandwich, plus all the usual blintzes, pastrami, and bagel-and-lox staples. Mon–Fri 6am–4pm.

Naan and Beyond 1710 L St NW ☎202/466-6404; Farragut North Metro. Cheap and tasty Indian dishes highlighted by baked naan sandwiches filled with the likes of tandoori chicken and lamb, all for under $7 – handy alternatives to traditional sandwiches for the Farragut lunch crowd and Friday-night clubgoers. Vegan options available. Mon–Fri 11am–9pm, Sat 11am–5am.

Nooshi 1120 19th St NW ☎ 202/293-3138; **Farragut North Metro.** Lovers of "noodles and sushi" looking for a cheap and hearty meal should sample the serviceable offerings at this lunch favorite, with solid sushi, dumplings, fried noodles, and spicy soups. Mon–Sat 11.30am–11pm, Sun 5–10pm.

Teaism 800 Connecticut Ave NW ☎ 202/835-2233; **Farragut West or Farragut North Metro.** Pleasant spot for a pick-me-up chai or a dose of Pan-Asian cuisine after a White House tour. The light fare includes salads, sandwiches, and bento boxes; afternoon tea service as well. Mon–Fri 7.30am–5.30pm. Also in the Penn Quarter at 400 8th St NW (☎ 202/638-6010), Mon–Fri 7.30am–10pm, Sat & Sun 9.30am–9pm.

Restaurants

Bombay Club 815 Connecticut Ave NW ☎ 202/659-3727; **Farragut North or Farragut West Metro.** Sleek but affordable Indian restaurant a block from the White House, with Raj-style surroundings, piano accompaniment, and dishes that are a little out of the ordinary, like tandoori scallops and mulligatawny soup. Mon–Fri 11.30am–2.30pm & 6–10.30pm, Sat 6–11pm, Sun 5.30–9pm.

Café Asia 1720 I St NW ☎ 202/659-2696; **Farragut West Metro.** Breezy pan-Asian restaurant that's an excellent midpriced choice for sushi and sashimi, or try the lemongrass-grilled chicken soup, satay, or Thai noodles. Altogether, something of a grab bag, though well worth a try. Mon–Thurs 11.30am–10pm, Fri 11.30am–midnight, Sat noon–midnight, Sun noon–9pm.

Café Promenade in the *Mayflower* hotel, 1127 Connecticut Ave NW ☎ 202/347-2233; **Farragut North Metro.** A serenading harpist and pricey but scrumptious Mediterranean menu set the tone in this elegant hotel restaurant, where you can expect to see all types of political heavyweights at nearby tables; the veal chops, swordfish, and lobster are among many other excellent dishes. Delectable breakfasts run $15–20, lunchtime sandwiches about the same, and dinner entrees twice as much. Daily 6.30am–11pm.

DC Coast 1401 K St NW ☎ 202/216-5988; **McPherson Square Metro.** Smart and characterful seafood haunt that presents upscale regional cuisine prepared in a variety of succulent ways: crispy fried oysters, pumpkin soup, crawfish hush puppies, Blue Point oysters, tuna tartare – it's hard to go wrong. Mon–Fri 11.30am–2.30pm & 5.30–10.30pm, Sat 5.30–11pm.

Galileo 1110 21st St NW ☎ 202/293-7191; **Foggy Bottom–GWU or Farragut West Metro.** Superb Northern Italian cuisine has made this upper-crust spot into a favorite for discerning foodies. Risotto makes a regular appearance on the ever-changing menu, and in the exclusive Laboratorio, the top chef presents some of his favorite offerings to a small crowd. Service is snappy, and the wine list impressive. Most dishes $27–40. Book well in advance. Mon–Fri 11.30am–2pm & 5.30–10pm, Sat & Sun 5.30–10.30pm.

Gerard Pangaud Bistro 915 15th St NW ☎ 202/737-4445; **McPherson Square Metro.** Accomplished French cuisine with a mix of classical and modern stylings. The fixed-price dinners are predictably pricey (and delicious) at $87 a head, but your best bet may be to indulge in the $30 lunch. Mon–Fri 11.30am–2pm & 5.30–9pm, Fri closes 9.30pm, Sat 5.30–9.30pm.

Giovanni's Trattu 1823 Jefferson Place NW ☎ 202/452-4960; **Farragut North Metro.** Terrific mid- to high-priced Italian fare that delivers all the essential elements: fresh ingredients, delicate textures and flavors, and Old World staples done very well – veal shank, potato dumplings, sliced octopus, and a full range of pastas among the many fine options, most $16–30. Mon–Fri 11.30am–2.30pm & 5.30–10.30pm, Fri closes midnight, Sat 5.30pm–midnight.

Grillfish 1200 New Hampshire Ave NW ☎ 202/331-7310; **Dupont Circle or Foggy Bottom–GWU Metro.** Industrial-chic eatery offering casual dining and primo grilled seafood. The daily catch options might include sea bass, tuna, monkfish, snapper, trout, mahi-mahi, swordfish, shark, or calamari – grilled, over pasta, or served in a sauté pan. Most dishes under $20. Mon–Thurs noon–10pm, Fri noon–11pm, Sat 5–11pm, Sun 5–10pm.

Malaysia Kopitiam 1827 M St NW ☎ 202/833-6232; **Dupont Circle or Farragut North Metro.** The no-frills decor will hardly draw you in, but if you like eclectic pan-Asian fare, this eatery's extensive selection of Indian, Malaysian, and Chinese dishes will do the trick. Tuck into a bowl of noodles or, for heartier fare, try the spicy beef rendang, chili shrimp, or black pepper lamb. Mon–Thurs 11.30am–10pm, Fri & Sat 11.30am–11pm, Sun noon–10pm.

McCormick & Schmick's 1652 K St NW ⓣ 202/861-2233; McPherson Square Metro. Hugely popular mid- to upscale seafood grill and raw bar, complete with Victorian stained glass and lamps and a buzzing bar. Best food deals are from 10pm until closing, when two drinks gets you access to the tasty happy-hour menu. One of five regional locations. Mon–Thurs 11am–11pm, Fri 11am–midnight, Sat 5–11pm, Sun 5–10pm.

Mio 1100 Vermont Ave NW ⓣ 202/955-0075; McPherson Square Metro. Self-consciously chic eatery that has a wide range of inventive cocktails and desserts, though its fans come for items like rack of lamb, seared monkfish, veal cheeks, venison medallions and other modern mid-Atlantic fare. At around $12–15, the lunch specials are about half the cost of dinner entrees. Mon–Fri 11.30am–2.30pm & 5–10pm, Fri closes 11pm, Sat 5–11pm.

Moby Dick House of Kabob 1300 Connecticut Ave NW ⓣ 202/833-9788; Farragut North Metro. Delicious and cheap Middle Eastern fare that includes spicy and savory gyros, chicken and lamb sandwiches, boneless chicken in pomegranate sauce, braised beef with eggplant, and other delights. Mon–Thurs 11am–10pm, Fri 11am–11pm, Sat noon–11pm.

The Palm 1225 19th St NW ⓣ 202/293-9091; Dupont Circle or Farragut North Metro. This upscale "power meatery" has been newly renovated but is still renowned for its New York strip and lobster – and for the power players and celebrities who wine and dine here both at lunch and dinner. Reservations required for this DC branch of a New York institution. Mon–Fri 11.45am–10pm, Sat 5.30–10pm, Sun 5.30–9.30pm.

Sign of the Whale 1825 M St NW ⓣ 202/785-1110; Dupont Circle or Farragut North Metro. Ever-popular Downtown saloon best known for its supreme burgers grilled to perfection and dozens of beers on tap, though there's also a more uneven selection of jerk chicken, pasta, fish, and crab cakes, most around $10. Mon–Thurs 11.30am–1am, Fri & Sat 11.30am–2am.

Stoney's 1307 L St NW ⓣ 202/347-9163; McPherson Square Metro. Down-to-earth saloon and bar that's more than three decades old, with a menu of burgers, fries, chili, and grilled chicken and grilled cheese sandwiches. Revel in its large, inexpensive portions, but be ready to wait cheek-by-jowl with the other hungry (and thirsty) patrons for the privilege. Sun–Thurs 11am–1am, Fri & Sat 11am–2am.

Tabard Inn 1739 N St NW ⓣ 202/785-1277; Dupont Circle Metro. The restaurant of this mellow Victorian inn rotates its creative and expensive ($25–30 entrees) New American fare – you might find anything from pan-seared salmon to lamb chorizo to braised pork cheek – in dining rooms rich with Old World ambience. Its very pleasant garden is the perfect spot for brunch when the weather's right. Mon–Fri 7–10am, 11.30am–2.30pm & 5.30–10.30pm, Sat & Sun 11am–2pm & 5.30–9.30pm.

Vidalia 1990 M St NW ⓣ 202/659-1990; Dupont Circle or Farragut North Metro. The New American cuisine dished up with a decidedly Southern twang has garnered this pricey eatery a reputation as one of the District's best. Be on the lookout for unique takes on barbecued pork, fried chicken, and the baby octopus stew. Mon–Fri 11.30am–2.30pm, Mon–Thurs 5.30–10pm, Fri & Sat 5.30–10.30pm, Sun 5–9.30pm.

Old Downtown

Cafés, snacks, and light meals

Café Mozart 1331 H St NW ⓣ 202/347-5732; Metro Center Metro. Worth seeking out if you have a yen for rib-stuffing German food. A combo eatery and deli with the requisite schnitzels, bratwursts, roasted meats, and other favorites, plus sweets, cakes, and desserts. Don't miss the weekend accordion music. Mon–Fri 7am–10pm, Sat 9am–10pm, Sun 11am–10pm.

Corner Bakery The Shops at National Place, 529 14th St NW ⓣ 202/662-7400; Metro Center Metro. Popular and busy bakery-café with a nice range of sandwiches, cookies, soups, salads, and breakfast items like French toast and oatmeal – most of it good, though you'll be waiting to chow if you come during rush hour. Mon–Fri 7am–7pm, Sat & Sun 8am–5pm.

Ebbitt Express 675 15th St NW ⓣ 202/347-8881; Metro Center Metro. Carryout eatery adjunct to the much pricier *Old Ebbitt Grill*. Excellent pastas, salads, grilled and cold sandwiches, and snacks to go – altogether affordable and tasty. Mon–Fri 7.30am–5pm.

Harry's in the *Hotel Harrington*, 436 11th St NW ⓣ 202/624-0053; Metro Center Metro. Good old-fashioned American food (burgers, ribs, steak sandwiches, and so forth), with a friendly range of loyalists and decent beers on tap at this relaxed saloon. Sun–Thurs 11am–1am, Fri & Sat 11am–2am.

Portico Cafe 8th at F St NW ☎202/275-1738; **Gallery Place–Chinatown Metro.** A fine spot to take a break from all the art viewing, with nice outdoor views of the Penn Quarter and a reasonable range of wine, espresso, sandwiches, and baked goods, set to the tune of regular jazz and classical combos. April–Oct daily 11.30am–6.30pm.

Restaurants

Acadiana 901 New York Ave NW ☎202/408-8848; **Mount Vernon Square Metro.** Chic Cajun spot near the convention center that serves up midpriced catfish, shrimp po' boys, and crawfish pies for lunch, then saves the big-ticket veal medallions, roasted duck, and grilled swordfish for dinner. Lunch dishes $10–15, dinner twice that. Also a fine Sunday brunch (11.30am–2.30pm). Daily 11.30am–2.30pm & 5.30–10.30pm, closes Sun at 9.30pm.

Café Atlantico 405 8th NW ☎202/393-0812; **Archives–Navy Memorial Metro.** Upscale nuevo Latino treat with spicy spins on traditional cuisine, but really best for its Minibar, a six-seat counter famed for its bizarre "molecular gastronomy" – the likes of beet "tumbleweeds," olive oil bonbons, and lobster injections (into the mouth). Only the adventurous need apply. Reserve at least a month in advance and expect to pay $120 a head. Two, six-person seatings per night, Tues–Sat 6pm & 8.30pm.

District Chophouse & Brewery 509 7th St NW ☎202/347-3434; **Gallery Place–Chinatown Metro.** Classy joint with nice buzzing atmosphere and an enticing grillhouse menu. A bit on the pricey side, but portions are huge. Order a solid burger (with a house salad) or go for steak, lobster or crab cakes. Sun & Mon 11am–10pm, Tues–Sat 11am–11pm.

Ella's Pizza 901 F St NW ☎202/638-3434; **Gallery Place–Chinatown Metro.** There's tasty tapas at this nouveau Italian spot, but most people just come for the designer pizzas: wood-fired, thin-crusted pleasures topped with wild mushrooms, meatballs, prosciutto, shrimp, and artichokes (though not all at once). Mon–Sat 11am–10pm, Sun 4–9pm.

Haad Thai 1100 New York Ave NW, entrance on 11th St ☎202/682-1111; **Metro Center Metro.** Business-oriented Thai restaurant featuring coconut-milk curries, tasty steamed fish and

shrimp, and spicy soups – all good staples, well made, and not too pricey. Mon–Fri 11.30am–2.30pm & 5–10.30pm, Sat noon–10.30pm, Sun 5–10.30pm.

Jaleo 480 7th St NW ☎202/628-7949; **Gallery Place–Chinatown Metro.** Renowned upscale tapas bar-restaurant with flamenco dancing, seafood, and plentiful sangria, plus supreme paella offerings. Limited reservation policy makes for long waits during peak hours. Sun & Mon 11.30am–10pm, Tues–Thurs 11.30am–11.30pm, Fri & Sat 11.30am–midnight.

Old Ebbitt Grill 675 15th St NW ☎202/347-4801; **Metro Center Metro.** One of DC's signature elite eateries, in business in various locations since 1856, this is a plush re-creation of a nineteenth-century tavern featuring a mahogany bar, gas chandeliers, leather booths, and gilt mirrors. Politico clientele indulges in everything from burgers to oysters, breakfasts to late dinners. Mon–Fri 7.30am–1am, Sat & Sun 8.30am–1am, bar open until 2am or 3am.

Proof 775 G St NW ☎202/737-7663; **Gallery Place–Chinatown Metro.** A delicious, upscale grab bag of flavors and styles, with a fine wine selection to boot. Try the charcuterie plates to start, then move on to a huge range of cheeses, sashimi, ceviche, and King salmon or sablefish. Most intriguing to the palate. Mon–Fri 11.30am–2.30pm; Sun–Wed 5.30–10pm, Thurs 5.30–11pm, Fri & Sat 5.30pm–midnight.

Sky Terrace in the *Hotel Washington,* 515 15th St NW ☎202/638-5900 or 1-800/424-9540; **Metro Center Metro.** A romantic spot to enjoy a sweeping view of the city, along with midpriced seafood or sandwiches. The food is nothing special, but it's a bargain considering the outdoor perch above the White House. Daily 11.30am–1am (May–Oct only).

Ten Penh 1001 Pennsylvania Ave NW ☎202/393-4500; **Federal Triangle Metro.** High-profile Asian-fusion restaurant serving up pricey meals like Kobe beef tartar, citrus-glazed salmon, red Thai curry shrimp and the estimable five-spice chili tea-rubbed beef tenderloin. Many dishes are worth the cost (lunch entrees $15–20, dinner $25–30), but head to Chinatown if you want more authentic entrees at cheaper prices. Daily 5.30–10.30pm (Fri & Sat until 11pm), Mon–Fri 11.30am–2.30pm.

Tosca 1112 F St NW ☎202/367-1990; **Metro Center Metro.** Expensive Northern Italian eatery with terrific seafood, lamb, and veal dishes and pasta staples from the Old Country, along with tasty desserts and flavorful juice drinks. Daily 5.30–10.30pm (Fri & Sat until 11pm), Mon–Fri 11.30am–2.30pm.

Zengo 781 7th St NW ☎202/393-2929; **Gallery Place–Chinatown Metro.** Truly eclectic spot for international flavors from Japanese to Indian to Latin American, with delicious $20 bento boxes for lunch (plus cheaper noodles, sushi, and dim sum) and pricey dinners of chili prawns, lamb loin, chicken tandoori, wonton tacos, and Kobe beef. Sun–Thurs 5–10pm, Fri & Sat 5–11.30pm.

Zola 800 F St NW ☎202/654-0999; **Gallery Place–Chinatown Metro.** Don't be deterred by this elite eatery's location in the Spy Museum; instead, enjoy a three-course lunch menu ($25) that lets you pick from items such as lamb sandwiches, ruby trout, and tuna tartar, or a three-course dinner ($30) that may include lobster rolls, skate wing, and poached shrimp. Mon–Fri 11.30am–midnight, Sat 5pm–midnight, Sun 5–10pm.

Shaw

Cafés, snacks, and light meals

14U 1939 14th St NW ☎202/328-1400; **U Street–Cardozo Metro.** Mellow, arty, and friendly café that offers weekend live music, serious gourmet coffee and tea drinks, and serviceable bagels, pastries, and sandwiches. It's also something of a late-night hang-out. Mon–Thurs 7am–11pm, Fri 7am–3am, Sat 8am–3am, Sun 8am–8pm.

Ben's Chili Bowl 1213 U St NW ☎202/667-0909; **U Street–Cardozo Metro.** Venerable U Street hang-out across from the Metro, serving chili dogs, burgers, milkshakes, and cheese fries at booths and counter stools – though at steeper prices than you might expect for fast food. The reason: Hollywood loves this place, as photos on the wall attest. Mon–Thurs 6am–2am, Fri & Sat 6am–4am, Sun 11am–8pm.

Mocha Hut 1301 U St NW ☎202/667-0616; **U Street–Cardozo Metro.** Enticing coffee haunt on the main drag that appeals for its chai and succulent sandwiches, with the Italian-flavored Webster among the highlights, as well as breakfast frittatas, waffles, bagels, and home fries. On Sun come the acoustic troubadours, on Thurs the open mic. Daily 7am–9pm.

Restaurants

Coppi's 1414 U St NW ☎202/319-7773; **U Street–Cardozo Metro.** Very chic and trendy little pizza palace with a brick oven doling out organic pies with a range of fancy ingredients – goat cheese, lamb sausage, and the like – along with spicy calzones. Around $17–24 per pie. Sun–Thurs 6–11pm, Fri & Sat 5pm–midnight.

Dukem 1114 U St NW ☎202/667-8735; **U Street–Cardozo Metro.** One of the many great Ethiopian restaurants in Shaw, offering a fine, inexpensive sampling of traditional fare from the Horn of Africa — gored gored (cubed beef with butter, onion, and jalapeno), doro wat (chicken stew), and minchet abesh (ginger and garlic beef) are among the better options. Daily 11am–2am, weekends 'til 3am.

Florida Avenue Grill 1100 Florida Ave NW ☎202/265-1586; **U Street–Cardozo Metro.** Southern-style diner serving cheap and hearty meals for more than sixty years to locals and stray political celebs. Especially known for its biscuits and gravy, eggs, ham, and grits. Tues–Sat 8am–9pm, Sun 8am–4.30pm.

Henry's Soul Cafe 1704 U St NW ☎202/265-3336; **U Street–Cardozo Metro.** As the name says, one of the District's hot spots for authentic soul food, with the fried chicken wings, fillet of trout, meatloaf, beef liver, and chitterlings giving a savory taste of the Deep South for prices under $10. There's also a signature sweet potato pie or peach cobbler for dessert. Mon–Fri 10.30am–9pm, Sat 7.30am–9pm, Sun 7.30am–8pm.

Tabaq Bistro 1336 U St NW ☎202/265-0965; **U Street–Cardozo Metro.** Mediterranean tapas served with dash and spice, illuminated by the usual lamb shanks and beef kotfe, plus flavorful beef medallions, sauteed octopus, risotto, and marinated chicken "purses." Each plate is $5–15, which can add up if you plan on consuming a lot of them. Mon–Thurs 5–11pm, Fri 5pm–midnight, Sat 11am–midnight, Sun 11am–11pm.

U-topia 1418 U St NW ☎202/483-7669; **U Street–Cardozo Metro.** Arty, romantic bar-restaurant with regular live blues and jazz, art exhibits, good veggie dishes, and affordable prices. Eclectic entrees include Norwegian salmon, blackened shrimp, veggie couscous curry, and plenty of pasta. Also a fine Sunday brunch. Sun–Wed

11am–11.30pm, Thurs 11am–midnight, Fri 11am–1am, Sat 5pm–1am.

Upper Northwest

Cafés, snacks, and light meals

Firehook Bakery & Coffeehouse 3411 Connecticut Ave NW ☎202/362-2253; Cleveland Park Metro. Breads, cakes, pies, cookies, and very good coffee are all on offer at this DC institution's Upper Northwest outpost; seating in the wonderful garden completes the experience. One of eleven local branches. Mon–Fri 6.30am–8pm, Sat & Sun 8am–8pm.

Morty's Delicatessen 4620 Wisconsin Ave NW ☎202/686-1989; Tenleytown Metro. Jewish deli-diner that's a long way from anywhere, but devotees consider the trek worth it for the true tastes of hot corned beef, lox and bagels, whitefish and sablefish platters, stuffed cabbage, pastrami, chicken or matzo-ball soup, and the rest. Daily 8am–9pm.

🏃 **Vace** 3315 Connecticut Ave NW ☎202/363-1999; Cleveland Park Metro. Grab a slice of the excellent designer or traditional pizzas – some of DC's best – and tasty sub sandwiches, focaccia, or pasta, or pack a picnic from the selection of sausages, salads, and olives, then head to the zoo. Mon–Fri 9am–9pm, Sat 9am–8pm, Sun 10.30am–5pm.

Restaurants

Ardeo 3311 Connecticut Ave NW ☎202/244-6750; Cleveland Park Metro. Ultra-trendy but not too expensive spot where you can get your fill of a well-prepared selection of lamb loin, scallops, mussels, pan-roasted shrimp with sweetbreads, and other mid-Atlantic specialties. Has a delicious, affordable brunch that shouldn't be missed either, with Belgian waffles, tuna steak, trout ceviche, and gnocchi. Mon–Thurs 5.30–10.30pm, Fri & Sat 5.30–11.30pm, Sun 11am–2.30pm& 5–10pm.

Cactus Cantina 3300 Wisconsin Ave NW ☎202/686-7222; no nearby Metro. A cheap and festive Tex-Mex treat for Cathedral-goers, with a great veranda and fine eats like fajitas, seafood enchiladas, spicy chips and salsa, and other staples, and new twists on old favorites. Mon–Thurs 11am–11pm, Fri & Sat 11am–midnight, Sun 10.30am–11pm.

Indique 3512 Connecticut Ave NW ☎202/244-6600; Cleveland Park Metro. As the name would suggest, this is chic and stylish Indian cuisine that will either make your mouth dance (the shrimp curry or tikka makhani) or attack it with vigor (the piquant lamb vindaloo). Ask for a towel to wipe away the sweat. Prices $12–20 per dish. Daily noon–3pm & 5.30–10.30pm.

🏃 **Kuma** 4441 Wisconsin Ave NW ☎202/537-3717; Tenleytown Metro. Though Tenleytown is hardly a draw for anyone but nearby students, it does have a Metro stop, a fine deli (Morty's, above), and this supreme, midpriced Korean restaurant – rare for DC – where you can sample the likes of rice with beef and bean sprouts, short-ribs barbecue, and vermicelli noodles with beef. There's also serviceable sushi on offer. Daily 11.30am–10pm.

Lebanese Taverna 2641 Connecticut Ave NW ☎202/265-8681; Woodley Park–Zoo Metro. Delicious, midpriced Middle Eastern joint with soothingly dark, authentic decor inside. Sample something from the assortment of kebobs and grilled-meat platters, or go straight for the leg of lamb. Five other area locations. Mon–Fri 11.30am–2.30pm & 5.30–10.30pm, Sat noon–3pm & 5.30–11pm, Sun 4.30–9.30pm.

Nam Viet 3419 Connecticut Ave NW ☎202/237-1015; Cleveland Park Metro. Cheap and no-frills Vietnamese eatery in the heart of the Cleveland Park dining scene. The soups, including the pho, are good, as are the grilled chicken and fish, the caramel pork, and the marinated or barbecued shrimp. Mon–Thurs 11am–3pm & 5–10pm, Fri & Sat 11am–11pm, Sun 11am–10pm.

New Heights 2317 Calvert St NW ☎202/234-4110; Woodley Park–Zoo Metro. Fashionable, new-wave American restaurant serving an inventive seasonal menu that is likely to include anything from Georgia quail to wild boar chops to trout salad, with predictably steep prices (entrees $19–32). Sun–Thurs 5.30–10pm, Fri & Sat 5.30–10.30pm.

Open City 2331 Calvert St NW ☎202/332-2331; Woodley Park–Zoo Metro. Centrally located, zoo-accessible spot where you can enjoy a good breakfast of omelettes and scrambles, as well as sandwiches, burgers, and seafood at lunch or dinner, plus a nice set of cocktails and dessert treats. Plenty of vegetarian offerings, too. Daily 6am–midnight, weekends 'til 1am.

Sabores 3435 Connecticut Ave T 202/244-7196; Cleveland Park Metro. Smart and elegant tapas restaurant that will enliven your palate with its crab-stuffed avocado, Serrano ham, white-bean stew, crispy potatoes, and churrasco, not to mention a mean ropa vieja (shredded beef). Desserts are also quite fine, and the place offers a savory brunch, too. It's all affordable if you're not too hungry. Mon–Thurs 6pm–1am, Fri 6pm–2am, Sat 10am–2pm & 6pm–2am, Sun 10am–2pm & 6pm–1am.

Sala Thai 3507 Connecticut Ave NW T 202/237-2777; Cleveland Park Metro. Upper Northwest branch of a fine Southeast Asian eatery, with good, fairly traditional, affordable Thai noodle dishes and soups – though some are jazzed up with unexpected, trendy items like seared salmon and soft-shell crab. Mon–Thurs 11.30am–10.30pm, Fri 11.30am–11pm, Sat noon–11pm, Sun noon–10.30pm.

Spices 3333 Connecticut Ave NW T 202/686-3833; Cleveland Park Metro. Stylish pan-Asian place serving creative, cheap to midpriced tangerine-peel beef, crab-claw wontons, ginger salad, and ultra-spicy "suicide curry" in a spacious, high-ceilinged dining room, complete with sushi bar. Mon–Fri 11.30am–3pm & 5–11pm, Sat noon–11pm, Sun 5–10.30pm.

Yanni's Greek Taverna 3500 Connecticut Ave NW T 202/362-8871; Cleveland Park Metro. Popular pit stop before hitting the Cleveland Park bars. Offers bargain grilled-meat platters, a tasty tzatsiki (yogurt garlic dip), and pricier house specials like squid and octopus, plus the usual Greek favorites like gyros, souvlaki, and baklava. Daily 11.30am–11pm.

Waterfront

Cafés, snacks, and light meals

Captain White's Seafood City 1100 Maine Ave SW T 202/484-2722; L'Enfant Plaza Metro. The kind of place that makes the Fish Wharf the city's best spot for fresh seafood, in this case a floating vendor hawking catfish, oysters, crab, and other delicious choices, which you can get fresh to go or fried up in a tasty platter or sandwich. Daily 11am–7pm, weekends 'til 9pm.

Restaurants

Cantina Marina 600 Water St SW T 202/554-8396; Waterfront Metro. One of the few serviceable restaurants in these parts, where you can get your fill of burgers, crab balls, and catfish fingers for cheap prices, while dining right on the water. Daily 11.30am–10pm.

CityZen 1330 Maryland Ave SW T 202/787-6006; L'Enfant Plaza Metro. Lodged inside the chic *Mandarin Oriental* hotel (see p.271), this is a similarly upscale spot where for $105 you can sample a rotating menu of French and Asian hybrids that may include oddball items like smoked vegetable gelée, crispy lamb belly, quail eggs, and truffle foam. Tues–Thurs 6–9.30pm, Fri & Sat 5.30–9.30pm.

Jenny's Asian Fusion 1000 Water St SW T 202/554-2202; L'Enfant Plaza Metro. Upstairs from a yacht club, a fine spot for sampling Chinese staples like sesame chicken, Szechuan beef, and spicy eggplant, as well as crab cakes, beef Wellington, lobster tail, and pan-seared fish. Most dishes $10–25. Mon–Thurs 11am–10pm, Fri & Sat 11am–11pm, Sun midnight–10pm.

Phillips 900 Water St SW T 202/488-8515; L'Enfant Plaza Metro. Another popular seafood spot on the tour-bus circuit, not as good as Captain White's but worthwhile for those looking to pack away giant, affordable helpings of fish and crab from the lunch, dinner, and weekend brunch buffets. Good location near the Fish Wharf. Sun–Thurs 11am–9pm, Fri & Sat 11am–10pm.

14

Bars and clubs

Nightlife in the District is not always the staid affair you might imagine – crowds of dark-suited lawyers and lobbyists swilling martinis as they circulate for the nightly networking session. Although some of this does occur, typically in the dreary hotel bars and corporate-dominated watering holes around New Downtown, in other areas you're likely to find a much livelier scene, attracting all types of revelers from beer-guzzling coeds and funky hipsters to graying hippies and sprightly club kids. The mix depends largely on the neighborhood. Some of the most notable places to drop in for a drink or a dance include Capitol Hill, near Union Station and along Pennsylvania Avenue SE, buzzing with interns looking to cut loose from the suit-and-tie grind; Old Downtown, around the Penn Quarter, for its mix of tourists and locals; Georgetown, at M Street and Wisconsin Avenue, a college-oriented scene; Dupont Circle, along 17th Street and Connecticut Avenue, a gay-and-straight mashup with the District's broadest range of choices; Shaw, along U Street near the Metro, for its trendy vibe; and Adams Morgan, at 18th Street and Columbia Road, for a hearty blend of beats and brews. Across the river, you can find assorted hang-outs in Arlington, along Wilson and Clarendon boulevards, and in Alexandria, around Old Town. There's also a thriving – if relatively small – gay scene, with most of the action in Dupont Circle, especially on P Street (between 21st and 22nd) and 17th Street (between P and R); for more on these spots, turn to Chapter 16.

Note that while there's plenty of crossover among bars, lounges, clubs, and live-music venues – a well-soaked watering hole may have DJs on some nights, rock bands the next – we've categorized the following selections according to the main strength of each. If you're mostly interested in drinking and need little more than background music (live or canned) for your imbibing, look under "**Bars**"; if DJs and a frenetic social scene are the draw, try "**Clubs**"; and if you really want to groove on live jazz, rock, or anything else and don't care much about what cocktails or DJs are on tap, try "**Live music**." If you have multiple nightlife interests, we've also noted those spots that specialize in a range of after-dark entertainment.

Bars

As in other American cities, Washington, DC has gone smoke-free, with rare exceptions granted for cigar bars (see *Ozio* and *Aroma*, below). Obviously, true dive bars and grim, end-of-the-world black holes may allow all sorts of indulgences to go with their rock-bottom prices for mainline brews, but unless they offer some sort of atmosphere, too, we probably haven't included them here.

Brew horizons

Don't want to settle for just another Bud? **Microbrews** are big business these days, and you'll be able to get a decent selection of beers in many bars. For the best choice, hit one of the city's brewpubs – *Capitol City Brewing Company* (see p.297), *District Chophouse & Brewery* (p.300), or *Shenandoah* (p.296) – or the beer specialists *Brickskeller* (p.297), *Birreria Paradiso* (p.299), *The Saloon* (p.301), or *D.A.'s RFD Washington* (p.300). Elsewhere, keep an eye out for the following local brews: Foggy Bottom Ale from DC, Virginia's Chesapeake Bay or Old Dominion; from Maryland, Clipper City and Wild Goose; and from Delaware, Dogfish Head (with a brewpub in Virginia, p.296).

The selections below offer a spectrum of watering holes aimed at several different types of drinkers, from the chic yuppie palaces, offering brushed steel and glass surfaces and $15 cocktails, to the lower-end hang-outs for casual revelry, where well drinks go for as little as $2 and the atmosphere is convivial, if not particularly inspired.

Most bars are open daily until the legal closing time of 2.30am weekends, 1.30am weekdays.Virtually all have **happy hours** during which drinks are two-for-one or at least heavily discounted; the optimum time for these is weekdays between 4pm and 7pm. Some bars also offer free snacks to happy-hour drinkers – usually the standard pub grub of chicken wings and potato skins – while a few offer gourmet treats as well.

Adams Morgan

Bedrock Billiards 1841 Columbia Rd NW ☏202/667-7665; Dupont Circle or Woodley Park–Zoo Metro. A lively subterranean setting with quality bartenders and quirky art set this funky pool hall apart from Adams Morgan's more frenzied club scene, though you can find cheaper prices (and a grungier scene) at more authentic dive pool halls. Mon–Thurs 4pm–2am, Fri 4pm–3am, Sat 1pm–3am, Sun 1pm–2am.

Blue Room 2321 18th St NW ☏202/332-0800; Dupont Circle or Woodley Park–Zoo Metro. Classier than the typical Adams Morgan fare, but more poseurs, too. This chi-chi bar and lounge enforces a dress code and offers nightly DJ selections from techno and house to acid jazz. Wed & Thurs 8pm–2am, Fri & Sat 8pm–3am.

Bourbon 2321 18th St NW ☏202/332-0801; Woodley Park–Zoo Metro. If you feel like getting blotto in style, you could do a lot worse than this whisky bar that serves sixty varieties of the titular brown elixir – some terrific, pricey small-batch labels among them – and has excellent, affordable steaks, seafood dishes, and sandwiches. Mon–Thurs 5pm–2am, Fri 5pm–3am, Sat 11am–3am, Sun 11am–2am.

Millie and Al's 2440 18th St NW ☏202/387-8131; Woodley Park–Zoo Metro. The dive tavern that locals dig and visitors avoid – plenty of cheap beer, not much attitude, and folksy regulars adept at guzzling. Mon–Thurs 4pm–2am, Fri & Sat 4pm–3am.

Temperance Hall 3634 Georgia Ave NW ☏202/722-7669; Georgia Avenue–Petworth Metro. A fun and lively lounge with tasty burgers, sandwiches, and a fine brunch, and spirits that include nearly twenty varieties of rye whiskey, plus Prohibition-themed cocktails. One drawback: a location in a grim neighborhood north of Columbia Heights. Luckily, there's a Metro stop a block north. Sun–Thurs 5pm–1.30am, Fri & Sat 5pm–2.30am.

Toledo Lounge 2435 18th St NW ☏202/986-5416; Woodley Park–Zoo Metro. Cramped and bare-bones café-bar with attitude, featuring windows looking out on the local street life. The patio seats (best spot for hanging out) are primo in summer. Mon–Thurs 6pm–2am, Fri & Sat 6pm–3am.

Alexandria, VA

Bayou Room 219 King St ☏703/549-1141; King Street Metro. Stone-walled dungeon makes for a low-key local pub, with cheap, simple, and tasty Cajun eats, TVs tuned to sports, classic rock blaring over the sound system, and occasional DJs. Above, in *Two Nineteen*, there's a jazz lounge that serves Creole food in a more stylish setting. Mon–Thurs 11am–10.30pm, Fri & Sat 11am–11pm.

Murphy's Grand Irish Pub 713 King St ☎703/548-1717; King Street Metro. Old Town's nightlife buzzes at this boisterous pub, which pours the city's best pint of Guinness. Local solo acts perform upstairs, while a central fireplace and chow like Irish stew add Emerald-Isle–style atmosphere. Mon–Thurs 11am–12.30am, Fri & Sat 11am–1.30am.

PX 728 King St ☎703/299-8384; King Street Metro. If you want to have a swanky night out for your boozing, visit this "speakeasy," where you knock on the blue-lighted door for entry and proceed into the elegant confines of a 1920s-style lounge. The space is cozy (three dozen people max), the prices are outrageous, but the classic and contemporary cocktails verge on the divine. Wed–Thurs 7pm–midnight, Fri & Sat 7pm–1am.

Shenandoah Brewing Co. 652 S Pickett St ☎703/823-9508; King Street Metro. Fine combo pub and brewing academy, where you can learn how to make your own beer as well as snack on spicy chili and sample brews like Whitewater Wheat, Stony Man Stout, and Old Rag Mountain Ale. Thurs 5–10pm, Fri 1–10pm, Sat 10am–6.30pm.

Union Street Public House 121 S Union St ☎703/548-1785; King Street Metro. It's hard to miss this red-brick building with gas lamps. Good steak-and-seafood joint that's just as nice for drinking as eating, with its own handcrafted and hearty microbrews. Very popular on weekends. Daily 11.30am–1am.

Arlington and Northern Virginia

Arlington Cinema 'n' Drafthouse 2001 Clarendon Blvd ☎703/528-4660. A place to drink in midlevel national comedy acts and second-run movies (most $5–6), as well as get your guzzle on some decent brews and service-able pub grub. Daily 11am–2am.

Clarendon Grill 1101 N Highland St ☎703/524-7455; Clarendon Metro. Solid old favorite for boozing, and something of a pickup joint. Music selections (Thurs–Sat) include earnest acoustic strummers, alternative rockers, and occasional DJs – but the real focus is

drinking and watching the HDTVs. Mon–Fri 11am–2am, Sat 10.30am–2am.

Dogfish Head Alehouse 6363 Seven Corners Center, near Arlington Blvd and Leesburg Pike, Falls Church, VA ☎703/534-3342. Headquartered in Delaware but with a pub west of Arlington in Falls Church, Virginia, this is one of the nation's best microbrewers – with regular live music and delicious favorites like the 90-Minute IPA, spicy Raison d'Etre, and the redoubtable Lawnmower summer ale. Daily 11am–1am, until 2am weekends.

Ireland's Four Courts 2051 Wilson Blvd, at N Courthouse Rd ☎703/525-3600; Court House Metro. One of the nicest of the area's Irish bars, drawing a cheery Arlington crowd for the live music, dozen beers on tap, decent whiskey selection, and filling Irish food. The Metro stop is but a short stagger away. Mon–Sat 11am–2am, Sun 10am–1am.

Mackey's Public House 23rd St and Crystal Drive ☎703/412-1113; Crystal City Metro. A relaxed bar in a prime shopping strip, with hefty Irish food like lamb stew and shepherd's pie, and good old Emerald Isle beers such as Guinness and Harp, plus darts and pool. Mon–Sat 11am–2am, Sun 11am–1am.

Old Dominion Brewing 44633 Guilford Drive, Ashburn, VA ☎703/724-9100. Worth a stop if you've got time to kill around Dulles Airport, and excellent for its twenty microbrewed lagers, ales, and stouts (it's the oldest such brewery in the state). Brewery tours available, too. Mon–Thurs 11am–midnight, Fri & Sat 11am–2am, Sun 10am–midnight.

Whitlow's on Wilson 2854 Wilson Blvd ☎703/276-9693; Clarendon Metro. Neighborhood retro lounge with good happy-hour drinks and food, plus pool and wraparound bar. Also good for its nightly selections of live rock, jazz, acoustic, blues, and reggae. Mon–Fri 11am–2am, Sat & Sun 9am–2am.

Capitol Hill

18th Amendment 613 Pennsylvania Ave SE ☎202/543-3622; Eastern Market Metro. Speakeasy-themed bar with vaguely Art Deco decor and cast of lobbyists and staffers in their best meat-marketing attire. Pricey but good cocktails are modern vodkatinis and the like, not 1920s classics. Mon–Thurs 4pm–2am, Fri 4pm–3am, Sat & Sun 11.30am–3am.

Bullfeathers 410 First St SE ☎202/543-5005; **Capitol South Metro.** Pol watchers may catch sight of a famous face at this old-time Hill institution, a dark and clubby spot with affordable beer and solid burgers and bar food, and named for Teddy Roosevelt's favorite term for bullshit during his White House days. Mon–Sat 11.15am–midnight.

Capitol City Brewing Company 2 Massachusetts Ave NE ☎202/842-2337; **Union Station Metro.** Prime microbrewing turf offering average pub food but solid handcrafted beer, highlighted by the Amber Waves Ale, a rich and succulent beverage, and German-style Capitol Kolsch and Prohibition Porter. Another branch in Old Downtown, 1100 New York Ave NW (see p.300). Sun–Thurs 11am–1am, Fri & Sat 11am–2am.

Capitol Lounge 229 Pennsylvania Ave SE ☎202/547-2098; **Capitol South Metro.** Brick-walled saloon on the Hill known for drinkin' and partyin', with pool tables, inexpensive beer, three bars on two levels, and scads of Congressional staffers looking to get wasted thanks to good happy hours. Mon–Thurs 4pm–2am, Fri 4pm–3am, Sat 9am–3am, Sun 10am–2am.

The Dubliner in the *Phoenix Park Hotel*, 520 N Capitol St NW ☎202/737-3773; **Union Station Metro.** A wooden-vaulted, good-time Irish bar, with draft Guinness, boisterous conversation, rib-stuffing food, and live Irish music catering to the more refined Hill set and visiting business and lobbying types. The patio is a nice summer hang-out. Sun–Thurs 11am–2am, Fri & Sat 11am–3am.

Hawk 'n' Dove 329 Pennsylvania Ave SE ☎202/543-3553; **Capitol South Metro.** Iconic DC pub, a bit tatty at the edges now, hung with football pennants, bottles, and bric-a-brac. The young, loud crowd of Hill staffers comes (depending on the night) for the cheap beer, half-price food, or football on TV. Sun–Thurs 10am–2am, Fri & Sat 10am–3am.

Kelly's Irish Times 14 F St NW ☎202/543-5433; **Union Station Metro.** Colorful folk music sets the stage (Wed–Sun nights) at this boisterous, young-skewing pub, which also features weekend club music on the downstairs dance floor and imperial pints of Guinness. Sun–Thurs 11am–2am, Fri & Sat 11am–3am.

Pour House 319 Pennsylvania Ave SE ☎202/546-1001; **Capitol South Metro.** Hill rats pour into this three-bars-in-one Hill hang-out

for the daily food and drink specials. There are pool tables downstairs, plus an unexpected ode to the glories of Pittsburgh on the first floor, complete with Penn State pennants, sausage sandwiches, and Iron City beer on tap. Mon–Fri 4pm–1.30am, Sat & Sun 11am–2.30am.

Tune Inn 331 Pennsylvania Ave SE ☎202/543-2725; **Capitol South Metro.** Old-line neighborhood dive bar that's been around forever and has a mix of grizzled regulars and wide-eyed newbies. Settle down in a booth, munch on the burgers, and feed the jukebox. Sun–Thurs 8am–2am, Fri & Sat 8am–2.30am.

Dupont Circle

Biddy Mulligan's at Jurys Hotel 1500 New Hampshire Ave NW ☎202/483-6000; **Dupont Circle Metro.** Rollicking Irish pub with brews and spirits from the old country, and a bar and fixtures lifted straight from a pub on the Emerald Isle. The drinkers may not all be local, or even Irish (it's right on the Circle), but for gut-stuffing Irish bar fare and a quaff, there are few better spots in the area. Mon–Thurs 11.30am–2am, Fri & Sat 11.30am–3am.

Big Hunt 1345 Connecticut Ave NW ☎202/785-2333; **Dupont Circle Metro.** As well known for its eccentric decor, which includes a tarantula candelabra, as for its beer, which is fairly cheap for the area. More than 25 brews are on tap, including a fair selection of Belgian ales, and it has a good jukebox and a groovy crowd. Always happy during happy hour. Mon–Thurs 4pm–2am, Fri 4pm–3am, Sat 4pm–3am, Sun 5pm–2am.

Brickskeller 1523 22nd St NW ☎202/293-1885; **Dupont Circle Metro.** Renowned brick-lined basement saloon serving "the world's largest selection of

▲ Brickskeller, Dupont Circle

beer" – up to a thousand types, including dozens from US microbreweries, though only a fraction are typically available. Knowledgeable bar staff can advise, or you can try your luck with the colossal menu. Also features its own inexpensive inn upstairs (see p.266). Sun 6pm–2am, Mon & Tues 5pm–2am, Wed & Thurs 11.30am–2am, Fri 11.30am–3am, Sat 6pm–3am.

Buffalo Billiards 1330 19th St NW ☎202/331-7665; Dupont Circle Metro. Happening basement hang-out with plenty of HDTVs for sports viewing, pool tables, darts, shuffleboard, a good selection of tap beers, and tasty pub grub. There's even a lone snooker table. Mon–Thurs 4pm–2am, Fri 4pm–3am, Sat 1pm–3am, Sun 1pm–1am.

Fox and Hounds 1537 17th St NW ☎202/232-6307; Dupont Circle Metro. Friends of this small and easy-going dive bar smack in the middle of the 17th Street action mostly kick back and enjoy the very stiff (and very cheap) rail drinks. Mon–Thurs 11.30am–2am, Fri 11.30am–3am, Sat 11am–3am, Sun 11am–2am.

Gazuza 1629 Connecticut Ave NW ☎202/667-5500; Dupont Circle Metro. Middle Eastern–flavored hookah joint that also has a fair array of cocktails and an outdoor balcony, whose perch above Connecticut Avenue attracts an eclectic mix for booze, smoke, and music. Sun–Thurs 5pm–2am, Fri & Sat 5pm–3am.

Steve's Bar Room 1337 Connecticut Ave NW ☎202/293-3150; Dupont Circle Metro. Trendy little spot that attracts refugees from area

dance clubs for its chic decor, buzzing social scene, regular DJs and karaoke, and weekly rock performances. Sun–Thurs 9pm–2am, Fri & Sat 9pm–3am.

Foggy Bottom

51st State Tavern 2512 L St NW ☎202/625-2444; Foggy Bottom–GWU Metro. Another neighborhood fave for cheap beer (sixteen labels on tap), decent cocktails and spirits, solid sandwiches and bar fare, and a pool table and pair of jukeboxes. Comfortable, friendly, and well worth stopping by for a draft. Daily 5.30pm–2am.

Froggy Bottom Pub 2142 Pennsylvania Ave NW ☎202/338-3000; Foggy Bottom–GWU Metro. Colorful, three-level bar catering to students at nearby GWU. Worth a visit if you're interested in shooting pool, munching on cheap pub grub, and knocking back a good brew or two (or many more). Mon–Sat 11am–2am, Sat opens noon.

Lindy's Red Lion 2040 I St NW ☎202/285-2766; Foggy Bottom–GWU or Farragut West Metro. No gimmicks, few frills – just a GWU student hang-out doing a roaring trade in cheap burgers, fries, and beer. Get ripped and make a new friend or two on the patio. Sun–Thurs 11am–2am, Fri & Sat 11am–2.30am.

Marshall's 2524 L St NW ☎202/333-1155; Foggy Bottom–GWU Metro. Solid brews like Red Hook and classics like Guinness, plus a decent menu of steak, pasta, and seafood, make this upscale bar-and-grill a good spot. The kitchen serves 'til 1am (2am weekends). Daily 11.30am–2am.

Georgetown

Birreria Paradiso 2029 P St NW ☎ 202/223-1245. Downstairs at a branch of Dupont Circle's famed *Pizzeria Paradiso* (see p.284) is this supreme touchstone for beer lovers — who come not to get wasted but to sample some eighty bottled beers and various US and European brews, among them some excellent Belgian ales, lambics, stouts, and porters. Mon–Thurs 11.30am–11pm, Fri & Sat 11.30am–midnight, Sun noon–11pm.

Garrett's 3003 M St NW ☎ 202/333-1033. Amid its brick-and-wood interior, *Garrett's* features a pumping jukebox that keeps the young crowd in a party mood, aided by nightly drink specials, along with a few microbrews. Mon–Thurs 11.30am–2am, Fri 11.30am–3am, Sat noon–3am, Sun noon–2am.

Mr Smith's 3104 M St NW ☎ 202/333-3104. Cheap pub grub and a splendid garden drinking-and-eating area, sing-along piano bar, and $1.50 rail drinks during weekday happy hour make the regulars here give a slurry cheer. Sun–Thurs 11.30am–2am, Fri & Sat 11.30am–3am.

Nathan's 3150 M Street NW ☎ 202/338-2000. Long-standing Georgetown tradition for its sizable bar with plenty of potent choices, and steak-and-potatoes fare in its back dining room. Upstairs club has its own DJs and a festive atmosphere, with the dancing really getting into high gear around midnight. Sun 10am–11.30pm, Mon–Thurs 11.30am–2am, Fri 11.30am–3am, Sat 10am–3am.

Sequoia 3000 K St NW ☎ 202/944-4200. Popular restaurant-bar with one of the best locations in the area – at the eastern end of Washington Harbor – with fine drinks, burgers, sandwiches, and pricey seafood. Outdoor terrace seating nicely overlooks the river. Arrive early on weekends. Daily 11.30am–12.30am.

The Tombs 1226 36th St NW ☎ 202/337-6668. Busy student haunt adorned with rowing blades. Good for catching college football on Sat afternoons in fall or just soaking up the Georgetown vibe. Occasional live bands and club nights. Mon–Thurs 11.30am–1am,

Fri & Sat 11.30am–2am, Sun 9.30am–1am.

H Street Corridor

Located two miles east of Union Station, the neighborhood's a bit dicey, so take a cab or the free Atlas shuttle (Fri & Sat 10pm & 2.30am; ☎ 301/751-1802). No close Metro.

Argonaut 1433 H St NE ☎ 202/397-1416. Pirate-themed grog house with a fun patio, where you can munch on bar fare like fried green tomatoes and sweet potato fries (or a sandwich or pork chop), while slurping a house-infused rum cocktail, including the fearsome Red Eye, a rum-drenched Bloody Mary. Mon–Fri 5pm–2.30am, Sat & Sun 11am–2.30am.

H Street Martini Lounge 1236 H St NE ☎ 202/397-3333. Typical of the gentrification of the district, a two-story yuppie-friendly venue where you can sample from a menu of some sixty martinis (most $10 or more) in a warm, upscale atmosphere. Live jazz on Thurs. Small cover charged on weekends. Tues–Thurs 5pm–midnight, Fri 4pm–3am, Sat 7pm–3am.

Palace of Wonders 1210 H St NE ☎ 202/398-7469. DC's most eccentric pub and show bar – by far – offering two floors of freakish displays, a vaudeville stage, burlesque, belly dancing and fire-juggling shows, and, among everything else, cheap beer and snacks. Cover $8–10. Daily 7pm–2am, weekends 'til 3am.

The Pug 1234 H St NE ☎ 202/388-8554. Comfortable, boxing-themed neighborhood bar that's not as in-your-face as some of the more frenetic bars and clubs on this strip but still appeals for its inexpensive drinks, pool table and convivial atmosphere. Daily 6pm–2.30am.

New Downtown

Logan Tavern 1423 P St NW ☎ 202/332-3710; **Dupont Circle Metro.** Festive Logan Circle watering hole that actually serves fine food – ginger calamari to crab cakes to grilled salmon, plus tasty desserts – to go with the nice selection of cocktails and spirits. Mon–Fri noon–2am, Sat & Sun 11am–2am.

Madhatter 1831 M St NW ☎ 202/833-1495; **Farragut North or West Metro.** Homely but homey saloon where an after-work crowd that comes for the convivial happy hour

(4–8pm) later gives way to a meat-marketing crowd looking mainly to get loaded and laid. Sun–Thurs 11.30am–2am, Fri & Sat 11am–3am.

Ozio 1813 M St NW ☎202/822-6000; **Farragut North or Dupont Circle Metro.** Ritzy cigar bar, lounge, and club popular with the District's well-polished and -varnished scenesters. A major player on the nightlife scene, and more fun if you love to pose. Mon–Thurs 5pm–2am, Fri 5pm–3am, Sat 6pm–3am.

Panache 1725 DeSales St NW ☎202/293-7760; **Farragut North Metro.** Serving excellent tapas until 10.30pm, this bar and restaurant is almost as good for its food as for its drinks – which aren't bad, either, with piquant cocktails and a full bar. Regular live entertainment and DJs, too. Sun–Thurs 11am–11pm, Fri & Sat 11am–2am.

🏃 **Recessions 1823 L St NW** ☎202/ 296-6686; **Farragut North Metro.** Good old-fashioned drinker's bar, with a serious boozing atmosphere fit for slumming K Streeters and the odd hipster, plus plenty of neighborhood types sampling the pool tables, music acts, and, of course, large and potent mugs of beer and choice cocktails. Mon–Thurs 11am–11pm, Fri & Sat 11am–2am, Sun noon–9pm.

Sign of the Whale 1825 M St NW ☎202/ 785-1110; **Dupont Circle or Farragut North Metro.** Downtown saloon with good burgers (see p.289) and dozens of beers on tap, with the industrial brews often ultra-cheap. Also a good spot to hear DJs spinning. Mon–Thurs 11.30am–1.30am, Fri & Sat 11.30am–2.30am.

Old Downtown

Capitol City Brewing Company 1100 New York Ave NW, entrance at 11th and H ☎202/628-2222; **Metro Center Metro.** Copper vats, pipes, and gantries adorn this microbrewery, serving a changing menu of home-brewed beers like Pale Rider Ale, Capitol Kolsch, and Prohibition Porter. Also a branch at Union Station, 2 Massachusetts Ave NW (☎202/842-BEER). Sun–Thurs 11am–midnight, Fri & Sat 11am–1am.

🏃 **D.A.'s RFD Washington 810 7th St NW** ☎202/289-2030; **Gallery Place–Chinatown Metro.** One of the best DC micro-breweries, with three hundred bottled beers and forty locally crafted and international brews on tap – though the food tends to be mediocre. Centrally located near the Verizon Center, so watch for heavy post-game crowds. Mon–Thurs 11am–1.30am, Fri & Sat 11am–2.30am, Sun noon–12.30am.

District Chophouse & Brewery 509 7th St NW ☎202/347-3434; **Gallery Place–Chinatown Metro.** This stunningly converted Old Downtown bank lends a dash of style to the Penn Quarter. The busy bar serves its own brews and offers solid food (see p.290). Sun & Mon 11am–10pm, Tues–Sat 11am–11pm.

ESPN Zone 555 12th St NW ☎202/783-3776; **Metro Center Metro.** For some drinkers, the one unmissable sports bar, conspicuous in the Penn Quarter and thick with arcade games and HDTVs for viewing games. For others, nothing but greasy food and frat-boy torture. Sun–Thurs 11.30am–11pm, Fri & Sat 11.30am–midnight.

Fadó 808 7th St NW ☎202/789-0066; **Gallery Place–Chinatown Metro.** DC outpost of a national Irish-pub chain – with Victorian and Celtic decor – that's a good spot for a Guinness and a bite to eat, though more authentic haunts can be found on Capitol Hill near Union Station. Mon–Thurs 11.30am–1am, Fri & Sat 11.30am–2am, Sun 11.30am–10pm.

Gordon Biersch Brewery 900 F St NW ☎202/783-5454; **Gallery Place–Chinatown Metro.** Yet another chain bar in the Penn Quarter, but its extravagant setting, in a restored 1891 Romanesque Revival bank that's a historic landmark, merits a visit. Mon–Thurs 11am–midnight, Fri & Sat 11am–1am, Sun 11am–11pm.

Round Robin Bar in the Willard Hotel, 1401 Pennsylvania Ave NW ☎202/628-9100; **Federal Triangle Metro.** If you tire of drunken tourist antics in the Penn Quarter, this chic old-line bar is a nice refresher. Packed with political types in suits, it's worth a try for its expensive but well-made classic cocktails, decent sandwiches and burgers, and historical setting (see p.166). Mon–Sat noon–1am, Sun noon–midnight.

🏃 **Sky Terrace in the Washington Hotel, 515 15th St NW** ☎202/638-5900; **Metro Center Metro.** Superb rooftop vista from the hotel's ninth-floor bar terrace. Hotel and bar will be closed through 2008 for renovation, so make sure to check back in 2009 – the views are splendid. Daily 11am–1am (May–Oct only).

Shaw

Polly's Café 1342 U St NW ⓣ 202/265-8385; U Street–Cardozo Metro. Neat little brick-and-board café-bar with a few outdoor tables; good burgers, salads, and brunch offerings; tap beers; and bottled microbrews. Periodic live music as well. Daily noon–2am.

Red Room Bar 1811 14th St NW ⓣ 202/667-7960; U Street–Cardozo Metro. Independent, no-cover bar attached to the *Black Cat* music club (see p.305) with eponymous décor, plus pool, pinball, draft beers, solid jukebox, and amiable, punky clientele. Sun–Thurs 8pm–2am, Fri & Sat 7pm–3am.

The Saloon 1205 U St NW ⓣ 202/462-2640; U Street–Cardozo Metro. If you want some good Old World beer, this is the spot for you, with scads of Belgian, German, and Austrian brews on offer, and a crowd consisting mostly of beer lovers rather than drunken frat rats or pre-clubbing students. Tues–Thurs 11.30am–11pm, Fri 11am–2am, Sat 1pm–2am.

Solly's 1942 11th St ⓣ 202/232-6590; U Street–Cardozo Metro. Convivial neighborhood bar that offers cheap beer, regular live shows, and soccer and other TV sports, in an area quickly gentrifying with pricier and snootier lounges. Mon–Thurs 4pm–midnight, Fri & Sat 4pm–2am, Sun 7–11pm.

Velvet Lounge 915 U St NW ⓣ 202/462-3213; U Street–Cardozo Metro. Schmooze and booze in this relaxed spot, with nightly live music upstairs (small cover) with performances by some of DC's brashest and thrashiest up-and-comers. Sun 8am–midnight, Mon–Thurs 8am–2am, Fri & Sat 8am–3am.

Upper Northwest

Aroma 3417 Connecticut Ave NW ⓣ 202/244-7995; Cleveland Park Metro. With a smart, mildly smug atmosphere, Cleveland Park's cigar-and-martini bar is stylish and chic, but it still feels like a neighborhood watering hole. Mon–Thurs 6pm–2am, Fri & Sat 6pm–3am.

Ireland's Four Fields 3412 Connecticut Ave NW ⓣ 202/244-0860; Cleveland Park Metro. Rollicking Irish music on Tues–Sat draws a crowd to this otherwise uneventful Irish bar. There are outdoor seats in the summer, the usual stews and pies, around a dozen beers on tap, and twenty-ounce (imperial) pints of Guinness. Sun–Thurs 5pm–2am, Fri & Sat 4pm–3am.

Nanny O'Brien's 3319 Connecticut Ave NW ⓣ 202/686-9189; Cleveland Park Metro. The other Irish tavern in Cleveland Park, this is a smaller, more personable joint, but with the same successful mix of heavy drinking and live music (usually no cover). Monday's jam night is good fun. Sun–Thurs 4.30pm–2am, Fri 4pm–3am, Sat noon–3am.

Zoo Bar 3000 Connecticut Ave NW ⓣ 202/232-4225; Woodley Park–Zoo Metro. Timeless dive saloon across from the zoo, with Guinness and microbrews and weekend performances by blues, jazz, and rock acts. They also serve food, but it's better to stick with the suds. Sun–Thurs 11am–2am, Fri & Sat 11am–3am.

Clubs

DC's **club** scene moves at a frenetic pace, and you can check out the *Washington City Paper*, the *Washington Post*'s "Weekend" section, and the gay-oriented *Metro Weekly* and *Washington Blade* for calendars, reviews, and ads. Although clubs come and go in all neighborhoods, DC's trendiest area is in New Downtown, near the intersection of Connecticut Avenue and 18th Street (just north of M St), in a part known as "Dupont South" due to its proximity to Dupont Circle. At many places the music and clientele can change radically on different nights, so you might want to call to confirm the line-up before heading out.

Plenty of spots have low **cover charges**, generally between $5 and $15 (highest on weekends), and some have none at all. Upscale lounges and clubs are most likely to charge a steeper cover (up to $25), and more often than not they have vague and at times completely arbitrary dress codes; if you avoid athletic gear, sneakers, sandals, and baseball caps, you'll greatly enhance your standing with the guardians of the velvet ropes – though at some places, merely being male may be enough to keep you out on evenings when the club decides to enforce a female-leaning two-to-one ratio, or more.

There's not much point in listing **opening hours**; these vary wildly from night to night, and can change randomly from month to month. Generally, though, most places don't get going until well after 11pm and stay open until at least 2.30am, with some continuing (especially on weekends) until 5am. If you're going to be out this late, have a taxi number with you, since some clubs are in dubious parts of town where walking around in the wee hours invites trouble. Also remember to take photo ID or your passport with you; you won't get into many places without one. Lastly, you must be at least 21 to drink alcohol in DC; if you're younger than that, check the local listings for an all-ages club – they do open occasionally, though usually without much success.

Adams Morgan and Shaw

2:K:9 2009 8th St NW ℡ 202/667-7750; U Street–Cardozo Metro. A flashy multilevel nightclub close to Howard University that draws a diverse crowd of twentysomethings with its hip-hop and house, velvet ropes, and dancers in cages.

Chloe 2473 18th St ℡ 202/265-6592; Woodley Park–Zoo Metro. Fairly trendy for this otherwise casual neighborhood, a spot where the young and dizzy step lively to retro-pop, hip-hop, and electronica beats, in a chic club environment spread over two floors.

Heaven & Hell 2327 18th St NW ℡ 202/667-4355; Woodley Park–Zoo or Dupont Circle Metro. While Hell (downstairs) would have trouble making Dante's hit list, Heaven features techno, dance, and live indie, the whole scene a fairly libidinous, cologne-drenched affair. Occasional cover.

Spy Lounge 2408 18th St NW ℡ 202/483-3549; Woodley Park–Zoo Metro. The type of high-profile juggernaut dance club on the leading edge of local gentrification – high-tech modern style, spy-themed decor, house and retro beats, and plenty of attitude. Connected to *Felix*, a snooty supper club.

Dupont Circle

Chaos 1603 17th St NW ℡ 202/232-4141; Dupont Circle Metro. Fun club at the heart of the Dupont scene, with cheap drinks and a well-stocked bar. Well-known events like Tuesday drag bingo and the Saturday cabaret show serve to make this gay club increasingly straight.

MCCXXIII 1223 Connecticut Ave ℡ 202/822-1800; Dupont Circle or Farragut North Metro. The pinnacle of posing in DC, complete with strict velvet-rope and dress-code policies, throngs of yuppie revelers, swank decor,

steep cover ($15–20), a melange of music from hip-hop to house, and attitude so thick you can cut it with a knife.

Play 1219 Connecticut Ave NW ℡ 202/466-7529; Dupont Circle or Farragut North Metro. Like its neighbor MCCXXIII, another scenester joint south of the Circle where you can expect the requisite poseurs and stiff prices, but also some fun music (retro-pop and hip-hop) and a crowd that isn't quite as cologne-drenched as other meat markets.

Georgetown

Modern 3287 M St NW ℡ 202/338-7027. If you're young and looking for a fun meat market, this upscale lounge and club will do, boasting a stylish bar and fittingly mod decor as well as a mix of hip-hop, house, and other beats.

Third Edition 1218 Wisconsin Ave NW, near M St ℡ 202/333-3700. Gung-ho college scene with second-floor dance club featuring DJs and periodic live music. It's a frenzied under-25 cattle call on weekends, when you'll probably have to wait in line and pay a cover.

New Downtown

18th Street Lounge 1212 18th St NW ℡ 202/466-3922; Dupont Circle Metro. Ultra-cool, multilevel spot housed in Teddy Roosevelt's former mansion. While the attitude can be a bit much at times, the DJ music on the dance-floor level is a big draw, along with weekend live jazz. Dress smart and look for the unmarked door. Come early (before 10pm) to avoid the cover and line.

Andalu 1214 18th St NW ℡ 202/785-2922; Farragut North Metro. Stylish, dress-code-oriented place with a mix of moody deep-house and garage dance beats, and the occasional live musicians dabbling in jazz and electronica. Booze is on the expensive side.

Five 1214-B 18th St NW ☎202/331-7123; **Farragut North Metro.** Another staple on the New Downtown club scene, with several levels of party people dancing to the usual 4/4 beats – disco, house, pop, trance, and plenty of rap. Non-weekend nights sometimes feature jazz, reggae, and other styles.

Old Downtown

UltraBar 911 F St NW ☎202/638-4663; **Gallery Place–Chinatown Metro.** As you might have guessed from the name, this is a tourist-oriented club with DJs spinning on the main room and other floors hosting hip-hop and retro sounds. A decent place to party if you don't want to walk too far from your hotel.

Waterfront

Zanzibar on the Waterfront 700 Water St SW ☎202/554-9100; **Waterfront Metro.** Black-oriented club that also draws an international crowd with live bands and DJs who kick out salsa, R&B, reggae, and jazz. The SkyClub is the swank VIP lounge upstairs, where the cover can reach $30.

Live music

As with bars, the **live music** scene in Washington may surprise outsiders expecting a lackluster selection of piano-bar hacks and patriotic anthems sung by frumpy matrons in dusty concert halls. If you want to see the "official" side of culture in the District, there are plenty of opportunities at spots like the Kennedy Center and Constitution Hall (see the "Performing arts and film" chapter), but if you're really interested in head-banging, slam-dancing, or otherwise shaking your ass with abandon, the city has plenty of good choices. It isn't New York or LA, it's true, but DC is cool enough to have venues run by grunge superstars (like Dave Grohl of the Foo Fighters) and a number of classic joints that have left a historic mark on rock, jazz, and even punk history. Jazz and blues clubs are the most common across the city, while country and folk venues are mainly found across the water in Virginia, rock and pop in the H Street Corridor, Arlington, Adams Morgan and Shaw, and salsa and Latin offerings in the latter two neighborhoods. Check local listings for opening times, cover charges, and ticket prices per show, which can vary widely depending on the night and the act.

Blues, folk, and country

Birchmere 3701 Mount Vernon Ave, Alexandria, VA ☎703/549-7500; no nearby Metro. Excellent, long-standing club with some of the region's (and nation's) best names in current and retro acoustic, folk and country music, as well as some up-and-comers.

Cowboy Café 4792 Lee Hwy, Arlington, VA ☎703/243-8010. All-American restaurant that's also a regional favorite for country &

Irish music

There are regular Irish (acoustic and folk) sessions in the following bars and clubs:

The Dubliner, Capitol Hill, p.297
IOTA, Arlington, p.305
Ireland's Four Courts, Arlington, p.296
Ireland's Four Fields, Cleveland Park, p.301
Kelly's Irish Times, Capitol Hill, p.297
Murphy's Grand Irish Pub, Alexandria, p.296
Nanny O'Brien's, Cleveland Park, p.301

western music, rockabilly, and cowboy blues. Also with occasional hollerin' contests.

J.V. Restaurant 6666 Arlington Blvd, Falls Church, VA ☎703/241-9504. Favorite honky-tonk joint that's a local haunt for its mix of live folk, country, blues, and rock – though located a ways out from DC.

New Vegas Lounge 1415 P St NW, Logan Circle ☎202/483-3971; Dupont Circle Metro. Neighborhood favorite that offers jazz, blues, raunchy Chicago R&B, and other favorites in a decidedly funky setting. Cover can go up to $15 for some acts.

State Theatre 220 N Washington St, Falls Church, VA ☎703/237-0300. Suburban venue in a stylish former moviehouse that rewards a drive out if you like country, folk, or blues. Sometimes it mixes things up with retread rockers and novelty acts as well.

Tiffany Tavern 1116 King St, Alexandria, VA ☎703/836-8844; King Street Metro. This Old Town haunt hosts open-mike nights during the week, but on the weekends it's all about bluegrass and its folk-flavored local and regional performers.

Jazz and blues

Blues Alley 1073 Rear Wisconsin Ave NW, Georgetown ☎202/337-4141. This small, celebrated Georgetown jazz bar has been in business for over forty years and attracts top names in R&B, blues, and mainstream jazz. Shows usually at 8pm and 10pm, plus midnight some weekends; cover can run to $45. Book in advance.

Bohemian Caverns 2003 11th St NW, Shaw ☎202/299-0800. U Street–Cardozo Metro. Legendary DC jazz supper club, reopened after three decades. The jazz happens in a basement grotto, below the stylish ground-level restaurant. Cover runs to $15 or more, with a limited number of reserved tickets for bigger acts.

Bossa 2463 18th St NW, Adams Morgan ☎202/667-0088; Woodley Park–Zoo Metro. A range of terrific nightly jazz, from traditional to modern, is the main draw at this engaging club (which also offers an upstairs lounge where DJs spin hip-hop and electronica tunes), and a menu of serviceable pasta and tapas.

Columbia Station 2325 18th St NW, Adams Morgan ☎202/462-6040; Woodley Park–Zoo or Dupont Circle Metro. One of the better places in the area to listen to live jazz, along with blues, presented nightly in a sophisticated supper-club setting.

HR-57 1610 14th St NW, Logan Circle ☎202/667-3700; Dupont Circle Metro. Small but authentic club where jazz in many of its manifestations – classic, hard bop, free, and cool – is performed by ardent professionals as well as newcomers on their way up. One of the essential cultural spots in this gentrifying neighborhood.

Laporta's 1600 Duke St, Alexandria, VA ☎703/683-6313; King Street Metro. Upscale seafood restaurant with a good range of jazz acts performing nightly, everything from Dixieland and traditional to bebop and scat to fusion and contemporary.

Madam's Organ 2461 18th St NW, Adams Morgan ☎202/667-5370; Woodley Park–Zoo Metro. Self-consciously divey spot that has a fine rep for showcasing a variety of driving live blues, grinding, raw R&B, and the odd bluegrass band, plus some solidly rib-sticking soul food and generous cocktails. Upstairs, there's a pool table and a rooftop bar.

Ragtime 1345 N Courthouse Rd, Arlington, VA ☎703/243-4003; Court House Metro. Relaxed bar-and-grill offering live music several nights a week, often in the blues, soul, and jazz vein.

The Saloun 3239 M St NW, Georgetown ☎202/965-4900. Cozy bar with 75 bottled beers and nightly jazz trios or bands, plus occasional R&B and soul acts. Free admission before 8pm; otherwise small cover charge.

Takoma Station Tavern 6914 4th St NW, Takoma Park, MD ☎202/829-1999; Takoma Metro. Laid-back club with live jazz several nights a week, showcasing mostly local acts. On some evenings reggae acts, comedians, or poetry slams take the spotlight.

Twins Jazz 1344 U St NW, Shaw ☎202/234-0072; U Steet–Cardozo Metro. Celebrated jazz haunt drawing talented musicians Tues through Sat night and for its Sun jam sessions. Also serves decent Ethiopian, American, and Caribbean food. Associated with the equally appealing *Twins Lounge*, 5516 Colorado Ave NW (☎202/882-2523), though Twins is in a dicey area of northwest DC, so take a cab or drive.

African American DC

Making up more than half of Washington's population, African Americans have a long history in the capital region, one that stretches back to the colonial era. But only recently have historians begun to understand how inextricably black history is tied to America's growth from New World backwater to globe-trotting superpower.

Slave quarters at Mount Vernon ▲

Uniform worn by black Union troops ▼

Mary McLeod Bethune Council House ▼

Oppression in the New World

As early as the 1600s, the English colonies around the Chesapeake Bay were developing sizable plantations and agrarian economies using **slave labor** imported from West Africa. Indeed, stylish residences such as Mount Vernon and the Carlyle House were built with and functioned through the aid of slave labor, their elegant facades contrasting to the back-breaking drudgery and oppression experienced their kitchens and fields. Even the US Capitol was built from the toil of African American slaves, indicating just how fundamental they were in the creation and expansion of the capital region and the rest of the burgeoning American republic.

The Antebellum and Civil War eras

While some early **free blacks** such as Benjamin Banneker achieved a place in the history books (see box), with the turn of the nineteenth century the majority of African Americans still were not free, and were consigned to performing the duties laid out by their masters, including many members of Congress. Lasting from 1861 to 1865, the Civil War was fought vigorously by **black troops wearing the Union blue**, who risked death or re-enslavement if taken by Confederate soldiers. Inspired by the sacrifice of these men, national figures such as Frederick Douglass emerged to champion the causes of slavery abolition, racial equality, and economic justice, and were followed by leaders such as educator Mary McLeod Bethune, activist Mary Church Terrell, and journalist William Calvin Chase.

Strivers' sections

After the Civil War, a flood of new migrants escaping the South sought refuge in Washington, many in working-class areas such as **Anacostia**. Although segregation was practiced in many sections of DC, other neighborhoods opened to the black middle class, including **Adams Morgan** and, especially, **Shaw**, where the so-called **Strivers Section** of Edwardian residences filled up with well-heeled African Americans and **U Street** became known as the "Black Broadway". Here would emerge the next group of black leaders, who would have a profound impact regionally as well as nationally. Just a few of the emergent names were jurist Thurgood Marshall, UN diplomat Ralph Bunche, and civil-rights activist A. Philip Randolph, along with trailblazing figures in music and the arts like Langston Hughes, Marian Anderson, and Duke Ellington.

The modern era

Although African Americans in the District have experienced setbacks in recent decades – everything from the devastation of the **1968 riots** to the **gentrification** of historically black neighborhoods – rising incomes and new opportunities have led many residents to integrate once-forbidden white enclaves such as Georgetown and seek opportunity in city and national politics, business, science, and arts. Today, the depth of the African American contribution to the District is can be heard in the **fiery jazz** performances at Bohemian Caverns, seen in the **vivid exhibits** of the Anacostia Museum, and experienced at the many memorials and **historic sites** that honor those who made modern DC the city it is, and what it promises to become.

▲ U Street in Shaw

▼ Duke Ellington

▼ Watching an outdoor performance

The Spirit of Freedom ▲

Bohemian Cavern ▼

Founder's Library, Howard University ▼

Notable black heritage sites

Although the number of important black heritage sites in Washington DC is too numerous to mention here, the following list is a good start.

Frederick Douglass National Historic Site (p.136) – One of the District's most famous residents, Douglass is revered for his fight against slavery and championing of equal rights for all citizens; his house in Cedar Hill provides a look at his storied life and career.

Metropolitan AME Church (p.194) – Dating to 1886, when it was constructed and financed by former slaves, this church is among the country's most prominent houses of worship, with a record of social activism and a few famous funerals, including that of Frederick Douglass.

Howard University (p.215) – A historically black college, founded after the Civil War, that's produced legions of important Americans, from Toni Morrison to Andrew Young to Stokely Carmichael.

Alexandria Black History Museum (see p.257) – Antique photos of early pioneers and neighborhoods and artifacts from the eras of slavery and segregation are among the highlights at this Virginia institution.

African American Civil War Memorial (p.215) – Along with its adjacent museum, this is a great place to learn about the heroic sacrifices and groundbreaking effect of the 150 regiments of "US Colored Troops" during that historic conflict.

Bohemian Caverns (p.304) – Scores of legendary performers have appeared at this jazz supper club, including Duke Ellington, Cab Calloway, Billie Holiday, Sarah Vaughan, and many others.

Lincoln Memorial (p.63) – The Greek temple honoring the sixteenth president is just as identified with Martin Luther King Jr, who gave his famous 1963 "I Have a Dream" speech here, as it is with Abe Lincoln himself.

Live music in restaurants and bars

The following restaurants and bars all feature regular live performances, from jazz to R&B to rock; there's usually no charge other than the price of the meal or drink.

Afterwords Café (jazz/blues), Dupont Circle, p.282

Bukom Café (African), Adams Morgan, p.275

Columbia Station (jazz), Adams Morgan, p.304

Kinkead's (jazz), Foggy Bottom, p.285

Mr Henry's (jazz), Capitol Hill, p.281

Mr Smith's (rock/piano bar), Georgetown, p.299

U-topia (jazz/blues/Brazilian), Shaw, p.291

Whitlow's on Wilson (rock/blues), Arlington, p.296

Zanzibar on the Waterfront (jazz/reggae/salsa), p.303

Rock and pop

9:30 Club 815 V St NW, Shaw ☎202/265-0930; U St–Cardozo Metro. If you have even the slightest interest in seeing an indie rock concert in the District, you'll probably find yourself at this top-shelf venue for national names playing for prices ranging anywhere from $4 to $40. Also a solid upstairs bar.

Black Cat 1811 14th St NW, Shaw ☎202/667-7960; U St–Cardozo Metro. Part-owned by Foo Fighter Dave Grohl, this indie institution provides a showcase for veteran alternative acts and up-and-coming rock, punk, and garage bands alike, plus a sprinkling of world beat and retro-pop performers. Also check out the attached *Red Room Bar* (see p.301).

Chief Ike's Mambo Room 1725 Columbia Rd NW, Adams Morgan ☎202/332-2211; Woodley Park–Zoo or Dupont Circle Metro. Ramshackle mural-clad bar with live bands playing rock, reggae, and R&B, or DJs hosting theme nights. Makes for an unpretentious, fun spot to dance. The upstairs bar has live indie music and a pool table.

Clarendon Grill 1101 N Highland St, Arlington, VA ☎703/524-7455; Clarendon Metro. Old favorite for boozing, and something of a pick-up joint. Musical offerings include earnest acoustic strummers, alternative rockers, and occasional DJs.

Galaxy Hut 2711 Wilson Blvd, Arlington, VA ☎703/525-8646; Clarendon Metro. Regular line-up of interesting local indie rockers takes the stage nightly at this tiny neighborhood hang-out, with a bevy of beers on tap.

IOTA 2832 Wilson Blvd, Arlington, VA ☎703/522-8340; Clarendon Metro. One of the area's best choices for music, this warehouse-style joint has nightly performances by local and national indie, folk, and blues bands. A great bar and attached restaurant, too. Cover usually $10–15.

The Red and the Black 1212 H St NE, east of Capitol Hill ☎202/399-3201; no close Metro. Frenetic rock-and-roll bar with tin ceilings, velvet drapes, and a New Orleans theme (and cuisine like jambalaya), where local bands perform in the intimate, narrow confines in a moody atmosphere. (For getting in and out of the area, see p.125.)

Rock and Roll Hotel 1353 H St NE, east of Capitol Hill ☎202/388-7625; no close Metro. Midsize concert venue that hosts a variety of regional rockers (who can crash in the few overnight rooms), in the up-and-coming but still dicey H Street Corridor (see p.125 for access information). Good for its upstairs lounge, too.

Salsa and Latin American

Chi-Cha Lounge 1624 U St NW, Shaw ☎202/234-8400; U Street–Cardozo Metro. Swank candlelit lounge oozing atmosphere, with live Latin music and regulars toking on fruit-cured tobacco from Middle Eastern–style hookahs. Sink into a sofa and sample the excellent Andean tapas.

Habana Village 1834 Columbia Rd NW, Adams Morgan ☎202/462-6310; Woodley Park–Zoo or Dupont Circle Metro. Intoxicating Latin-dance joint spread over two floors with the eclectic spirit of the Adams Morgan of old. Tango and salsa lessons are available, and a good downstairs lounge/bar serves a fine *mojito*.

Latin Alley 1721 Columbia Rd NW, Adams Morgan ☏ 202/328-6190, Woodley Park–Zoo Metro. Fun and frenetic spot where you can set your groove to the rhythms of salsa, merengue, rumba, or bossa nova, with Latin jazz on weekends and dancing lessons offered at 7.30 nightly.

Rumba Cafe 2443 18th St NW, Adams Morgan ☏ 202/588-5501, Woodley Park–Zoo Metro. A Latin oasis, this sliver of a café-bar, its walls rich with paintings and photographs, is a good bet for a night of sipping *caipirinhas* and grooving to live Brazilian bossa nova and Afro-Cuban rhythms.

Performing arts and film

W ashington's **high culture** is supported by a formidable institutional regime second only to New York's in government funding, prestige, and media exposure. Indeed, the city's cultural beacons – from its concert halls to its award ceremonies – regularly make appearances on public television and radio, giving the impression that after a performer "makes it" in DC, he or she is artistically cast in stone, a living legend on the road to national canonization. This, of course, is all properly uplifting and enriching, but it also has the undesired effect of making the city's cultural scene seem hidebound and ossified, a place where artists long past their prime go to receive medals and ribbons from the president and members of Congress.

The city's most prominent institution is the **John F. Kennedy Center for the Performing Arts** – popularly known as the Kennedy Center – encompassing a concert hall, opera house, three theaters, and other elements. Home to the National Symphony Orchestra, it stages seasonal productions by the city's top opera and ballet companies, and also has a full program of visiting national and international

Performance tickets

Prices vary considerably according to the event or production. You can expect to shell out a lot for the high-profile events at the Kennedy Center, National Theatre, and the like, but many places offer half- or cut-price tickets on the day of the performance if there's space. In all instances it's worth a call to the box office: students (with ID), senior citizens, military personnel, and people with disabilities qualify for discounts in most theaters and concert halls. You can also buy tickets over the phone from various **ticket agencies**, which sell advance-reserved, full-price tickets (plus surcharge). Usually no changes or refunds are allowed.

Tickets.com ☎703/218-6500 or 1-800/955-5566, ⓦ www.tickets.com. Full-price tickets for events, by phone or online, with a service charge.

Ticketmaster ☎202/432-7328 or 1-800/551-7328, ⓦ www.ticketmaster.com. Full-price tickets for events, by phone or online, with a service charge.

TicketPlace, 407 Seventh St NW, Old Downtown ☎202/TICKETS, ⓦ www.ticketplace.org. On-the-day (Sun and Mon tickets sold on Sat), **half-price** (plus ten percent surcharge) cash-only tickets for theater and music performances; not all tickets available online — some are walk-in only. Ticket booth sales Tues–Fri 11am–6pm, Sat 10am–5pm; online Tues–Fri noon–4pm.

artists, companies, and ensembles. The other main artistic promoter in town is the **Washington Performing Arts Society** (WPAS; ℡202/833-9800, ⦿www .wpas.org), which sponsors music, ballet, and dance productions across the city.

A host of **smaller theaters** and **performance spaces** dedicated to contemporary, experimental, ethnic, or offbeat productions offer a good alternative to these establishment venues, as tickets tend to be cheaper (and more available) and the productions often more spontaneous and compelling. **Comedy clubs** have made some headway in the District in recent years, while the city's **moviehouses** present a range of interesting fare – foreign to indie to avant-garde – that you might not find in the blander suburban multiplexes.

To find out **what's going on** in any of these categories, consult the Friday edition of the *Washington Post* (⦿www.washingtonpost.com), the monthly Washingtonian (⦿www.washingtonian.com), or the free weekly City Paper (⦿www.washingtoncitypaper.com). Other sources include flyers and posters in bookstores and cafés.

Major concert venues

The big-name **concert venues** in DC and beyond are scattered all over the place, potentially thwarting your desire to see multiple performances within a limited time frame. If you do plan on squeezing a lot of shows into your itinerary, be sure to factor in ample time for travel and traffic. Prices vary broadly according to the site, the venue, and the nature of the program. For more details, call the box office numbers listed below, or Ticketmaster, Tickets.com, or TicketPlace (see box, p.307).

In the District

Carter Barron Amphitheater 4850 Colorado Ave NW, Upper Northwest ℡202/426-0486, ⦿www.nps.gov/rocr/cbarron. Popular summer amphitheater in Rock Creek Park that offers a mix of free and ticketed events, including Shakespeare plays, rock, pop, and blues concerts, dance, and classical-music performances, and much more.

DAR Constitution Hall 1776 D St NW, Foggy Bottom ℡202/628-4780, ⦿www .dar.org/conthall; Farragut West Metro. Widely known as the best concert hall in the city, before its title was usurped in the 1960s by the Kennedy Center. Now the 4000-seat auditorium hosts uneventful mainstream concerts of pop, country, and jazz acts.

Howard Theatre 624 T St, Shaw ℡202/737-2804, ⦿www.howardtheatre.org; Shaw–Howard Univ Metro. Long-shuttered musical, theatrical, and comedy space, first opened as a vaudeville venue in 1910, that's now on track to reopen by the end of 2008 as a showcase for musical, dance, and multidisciplinary performances.

Kennedy Center 2700 F St NW, Foggy Bottom ℡202/467-4600, ⦿www.kennedy center.org; Foggy Bottom–GWU Metro. The National Symphony Orchestra performs in the 2800-seat Concert Hall, the Washington Opera in the Opera House, and opera and dance troupes in the Eisenhower Theater; there are less expensive chamber recitals in the Terrace Theater. See also p.162.

Lincoln Theatre 1215 U St NW, Shaw ℡202/328-6000, ⦿www.thelincolntheatre .org; U Street–Cardozo Metro. Renovated movie/vaudeville house featuring touring stage shows; pop, jazz, soul, and gospel concerts; and dance, with a focus on multi-cultural productions.

Lisner Auditorium George Washington University, 730 21st St NW, Foggy Bottom ℡202/994/6800, ⦿www.lisner.org; Foggy Bottom–GWU Metro. A 1500-seat auditorium with regular classical and choral concerts on campus; often quite good, sometimes free. Comedy, rock, pop, and indie acts also take the stage.

National Theatre 1321 Pennsylvania Ave NW, Old Downtown ℡202/628-6161, ⦿www.nationaltheatre.org; Metro Centre Metro. One of the country's oldest theaters,

Classical music, opera, and dance

Classical music, **opera**, and **dance** are predictably well represented in the nation's capital, where a less-than-respectable showing would be embarrassing to a city with such worldly pretensions. Symphonic classical music is performed at the Kennedy Center and at other big concert halls, while concerts and ensembles take place in a variety of major venues (see box) in and outside the city.

Tickets for these big-name concerts tend to be pricey ($25–100) and need to be purchased in advance, either direct from the venues or from one of the major ticket agencies (see "Tickets" box). Because costs tend to be all over the map, you're encouraged to visit each site's or company's website to check ticket prices for each event. As a rule, any performances at the major venues will cost $30 or more for anything resembling a decent seat. However, free shows at other DC concert halls – just like exhibitions at DC museums – often tend to be free, and where this is true we've noted it below.

it's been on this site (if not in this building) since 1835. Today, it features flashy new premieres, pre- and post-Broadway productions, and musicals.

RFK Stadium 2400 E Capitol St SE (east of Capitol Hill) ☏202/547-9077, ⊛www .dcsec.com; Stadium-Armory Metro. A 55,000-seat stadium and sports venue, RFK is the occasional site of concerts by big-name pop stars and mainstream rock acts.

Verizon Center 601 F St NW, Old Downtown ☏202/628-3200, ⊛www.verizoncenter .com; Gallery Place–Chinatown Metro. Downtown 20,000-seater hosts big-name rock, pop, and country gigs. For more, see p.177.

Warner Theatre 1299 Pennsylvania Ave NW, Old Downtown ☏202/783-4000, ⊛www.warnertheatre.com; Metro Center Metro. Glorious 1920s movie palace that's been remodeled and is now staging post-Broadway productions, musicals, and major concerts.

Outside the District

FedEx Field 1600 FedEx Way, Landover, MD ☏301/276-6050. The 91,000-seat football stadium hosts the Washington Redskins and occasional summer pop and rock concerts.

Merriweather Post Pavilion 10475 Little Patuxent Parkway, Columbia, MD ☏410/715-5550, ⊛www.merriweathermusic.com. Mid-league and major pop, jazz, country, and middle-of-the-road acts perform in spring and summer only. There's pavilion and open-air seating.

Nissan Pavilion at Stone Ridge 7800 Cellar Door Drive, Bristow, VA ☏1-800/455-8999 or 703/754-6400, ⊛www.nissanpavilion.com. Outdoor summer stadium (25,000 seats) plays host to many of the major summer tours, though a bit removed from DC out near Manassas, VA (see p.353).

Patriot Center George Mason University, Fairfax, VA ☏703/993-3000, ⊛www .patriotcenter.com. A 10,000-seat venue for big concerts and family entertainment.

Strathmore Music Center 10701 Rockville Pike, North Bethesda, MD ☏301/581-5100, ⊛www.strathmore.org; Grosvenor-Strathmore Metro. A striking venue that's the occasional home to the Baltimore Symphony Orchestra and National Philharmonic, as well as performances of musicals and pop, folk, jazz, and world-beat concerts.

Wolf Trap Farm Park Filene Center and The Barns, 1624 Trap Rd, Vienna, VA ☏703/255-1860 (Filene Center), ☏703/938-2404 (Barns), ☏703/218-6500 (tickets), ⊛www.wolftrap.org. US Park Service gem plays host to a variety of jazz, country, folk, zydeco, and pop acts. See p.352 for details.

Classical music

The Concert Hall of the Kennedy Center (see p.162), home of the National Symphony Orchestra, is the most prestigious spot in town for **classical music**, and DAR Constitution Hall (p.153) is another long-standing favorite. Other companies and venues, large to small, are noted below for their respective programs and characteristics.

Major companies

Aside from those **major companies** listed here, there are any number of small and midsize entities performing classical music in DC, from virtuosi-in-training on college campuses, to church members singing in choirs, to chamber musicians giving concerts in museums, cathedrals, mansions, and embassies. Check local listings for more details.

The **armed forces** have their own performing ensembles, which tend to be quite accomplished and more varied in their repertoire than you might expect. All groups play weekly during the summer in front of the US Capitol; the big names (Navy and Marine bands) are listed below, but the Army (☎703/696-3399, ⓦwww .usarmyband.com) and the Air Force (☎202/767-5658, ⓦwww.usafband .af.mil) also have a solid reputation, and perform throughout the region.

Choral Arts Society of Washington 5225 Wisconsin Avenue NW, Suite 603 ☎202/244-3669, ⓦwww.choralarts.org. The District's major choir, performing at the Kennedy Center, Wolf Trap, and other region-wide locations. Usually offers traditional pieces (classical to current) and seasonal favorites, especially at Christmas (Handel's *Messiah*, and so on).

Friday Morning Music Club 2233 Wisconsin Ave NW, Suite 326 ☎202/333-2075, ⓦwww.fmmc .org. Long-standing cultural group (est. 1886) that gives performances of classical, romantic, and (traditional) contemporary pieces by major composers. Performs primarily at the Charles Sumner School (see p.193), as well as at area churches and Dumbarton House (see p.243).

National Symphony Orchestra 2700 F St NW ☎1-800/444-1324, ⓦwww .kennedy-center.org/nso; Foggy Bottom–GWU Metro. Performs in the Kennedy Center, serving up the big names in classical music under the baton of conductor Leonard Slatkin, who's best known for championing American composers. Tickets to performances run from $20 to $80, though the orchestra also performs free outside the Capitol on the West Terrace on Memorial Day, July 4, and Labor Day.

US Marine Band 8th and I St SE, Marine Barracks ☎202/433-4011 or 433-6060, ⓦwww .marineband.usmc.mil; Navy Yard Metro. The oldest professional music organization in the country (dating from 1798) and an accomplished vehicle for a.ll kinds of classical music – John Philip Sousa was a legendary director. Smaller ensembles perform folk and jazz, and there are also fall and winter chamber recitals. All concerts are free.

US Navy Band 617 Warrington Ave, Navy Yard SE ☎202/433-2525, ⓦwww .navyband.navy.mil. Offers free weekly summer concerts at the US Capitol and Navy Memorial (see p.168), with eight different performing groups and seven chamber ensembles. Genres range widely, from sea shanties and drum-corps pieces to jazz, big-band, country, and bluegrass – even rock and R&B. The classical-oriented Concert Band has been going strong for eighty years and regularly receives the most publicity.

Washington Performing Arts Society 2000 L St NW, Suite 510 ☎202/833-9800, tickets ☎202/785-9727, ⓦwww.wpas.org.

▲ Kennedy sculpture by Robert Berks, Kennedy Center for the Performing Arts

Coordinator of high-cultural events that puts together shows at twelve prominent venues and offers ticket packages based on the interests of each audience member. Categories (and prices) range widely from jazz to world beat to dance, and the schedule usually includes at least two to five classical shows per month.

Washington Symphony Orchestra 1225 I St NW, Suite 110 ☎724/223-9796, ⓦwww.washsym .org. Started in the 1930s, an agreeable group presenting five concerts per year, usually in the traditional vein – waltzes, Bach, Mozart, and the like – and occasional free outdoor concerts at Dupont Circle and other District locations.

Smaller venues

There's much worth seeking out at the many **smaller venues** for the performing arts in DC. Events take place at university halls (like Lisner Auditorium), as well as museums (the Corcoran Gallery of Art, p.150), historic houses (Dumbarton House, p.243), churches (Washington National Cathedral, p.224), and embassies (see "Embassy events," p.43). For details about Smithsonian Institution concerts, call ☎202/357-2700, or check ⓦwww.si.edu.

Arts Club of Washington 2017 I St NW, Foggy Bottom ☎202/331-7282, ⓦwww .artsclubofwashington.org; Foggy Bottom–GWU Metro. Based in a historic Federal house where President James Monroe lived briefly in 1817, the club presents free Friday concerts at noon, tending toward chamber music and solo recitals.

Coolidge Auditorium Jefferson Building, Library of Congress, 1st St and Independence Ave SE, Capitol Hill ☎202/707-5502, ⓦwww.loc.gov; Capitol South Metro. Free chamber music concerts in a historic venue (see p.119). Sept–May.

Folger Shakespeare Library 201 E Capitol St SE, Capitol Hill ☎202/544-7077, ⓦwww .folger.edu; Capitol South Metro. Medieval and Renaissance music in the Library's Elizabethan Theatre from the Folger Consort ensemble.

National Academy of Sciences 2101 C St NW, Foggy Bottom ☎202/334-2436, ⓦwww .nationalacademies.org/arts; Foggy Bottom–GWU Metro. Pleasing 700-seat auditorium

with free chamber recitals, often monthly from Oct to April.

National Gallery of Art West Building, West Garden Court, Constitution Ave NW at 7th St ☎202/842-6941, ⓦwww.nga.gov; Archives–Navy Memorial Metro. Free concerts every Sunday at 6.30pm (Oct–June) in the lovely West Garden Court, with seats available on a first-come, first-served basis. Also jazz performances in summer.

Phillips Collection 1600 21st St NW; Dupont Circle ☎202/387-2151, ⓦwww .phillipscollection.org; Dupont Circle Metro. Classical music concerts in the museum's Music Room (Oct–May Sun 4pm); free with museum admission (see p.200). Arrive early.

Society of the Cincinnati at Anderson House 2118 Massachusetts Ave NW, Dupont Circle ☎202/785-2040; Dupont Circle Metro. Free chamber recitals once a month in fine mansion surroundings (see p.199), usually Sat at 1.30pm.

Opera

The District's version of **opera** involves one institutional heavyweight supported by a few small companies and entities. Unlike a lot of other performing arts in DC, opera is not one that can be put on casually at a museum, historic mansion, or institution. The listings below offer a representative selection of the limited operatic possibilities.

Opera Camerata 1819 Shepherd St NW, Suite 100 ☎202/545-0114, ⓦwww.operacamerata .org. Small institution that offers periodic productions of German operetta and historically minor or forgotten works. Rotating venues.

Summer Opera Theater Company Hartke Theater, Catholic University, Michigan Ave and 4th St NE ☎202/319-5433, ⓦwww .summeropera.org; Brookland Metro. Independent company staging two operas each summer, mostly staples from the nineteenth-century canon; located near the National Shrine of the Immaculate Conception (see p.199).

Victorian Lyric Opera Company ☎301/ 879-0220, ⓦwww.vloc.org. If it's operetta you're after, consider this regional troupe that principally highlights the works of Gilbert and Sullivan, as well as the frothier works of Donizetti, Mozart, and other

Summer is a good time to catch a free **open-air concert** in Washington, though certain locations host events all year round. Check the following places and see DC's festival calendar (Chapter 17) for more information.

Freedom Plaza, Pennsylvania Ave NW. Year-round venue for folk events and music festivals.

National Zoological Park, Connecticut Ave NW. "Sunset serenades" in summer, featuring a variety of musical performances.

Netherlands Carillon, Marine Corps (Iwo Jima) War Memorial, Arlington, VA. Carillon concerts every Saturday and on national holidays May–Sept; regular summer concerts at War Memorial by US Marine Band.

Sylvan Theatre, Washington Monument grounds. Army, Air Force, Navy, and Marine Corps bands perform during the summer (including annual *1812 Overture* performance in August). Other musical events throughout the year, too.

US Capitol. Armed forces bands perform in summer on the East Terrace, and the National Symphony Orchestra puts on concerts on the West Terrace on Memorial Day, July 4, and Labor Day.

US Navy Memorial, 701 Pennsylvania Ave NW. Spring and summer concert series featuring Navy, Marine Corps, Coast Guard, and high-school bands.

classical composers. Three to four operettas performed per year, in rotating venues in Rockville, MD.

Washington National Opera ☎202/ 295-2400 or 1-800/876-7372, ⓦwww .dc-opera.org. Tickets for one of the country's finest resident opera companies (general director: Placido Domingo) sell out well in advance, though you may get standing-room tickets at the box office. Performances are mainly Romantic European warhorses, staged in the Opera House and the other Kennedy Center theaters. Sept–June season.

Dance

You can find **dance** from ballet to hip-hop in any number of good Washington venues, from international stylings at the various Smithsonian institutions (check ⓦwww.si.edu under "Events") to avant-garde pieces put on by modern-art galleries and museums. These are generally noted throughout the text and this chapter; the companies below are stricter in their focus on dance, and make it a central concern.

Dance Institute of Washington 3400 14th St NW #300 ☎202/371-9656, ⓦwww.danceinstitute.org.

Presents monthly performances at major venues in DC, Maryland, and Virginia, and offers a range of dance classes.

The Dance Place 3225 8th St NE, Brookland ☎202/269-1600, ⓦwww.danceplace.org; **Brookland Metro**. Contemporary and modern dance productions, mainstream and experimental, with a bent toward African- and African American–themed shows.

EDGEWORKS Dance Theater ☎202/ 483-0606, ⓦwww.hjwedgeworks.org. Pioneering, highly regarded troupe of African American men exploring racial, emotional, social, and sexual topics in rotating venues around town.

Momentum Dance Theatre 651 E St NE, **Capitol Hill East** ☎202/785-0035, ⓦwww .momentumdancetheatre.com. Small troupe presenting inventive spins on the classics (such as a jazz hip-hop *Nutcracker*) and jazz- and modern-oriented productions, often with a satiric twist. Irregular shows take place throughout the year at regional venues.

Washington Ballet 3515 Wisconsin Ave NW ☎202/362-3606 or 467-4600, ⓦwww .washingtonballet.org. Classical and contemporary ballet performed in rep by the city's major ballet company at the Kennedy Center. Every December *The Nutcracker* is performed at the Warner Theatre.

Theater

As with other performing arts, **theater** in the District has proven to be a revitalizing force for many formerly down-at-the-heel neighborhoods, with areas from Adams Morgan to Logan Circle to the Penn Quarter to Arlington, VA, experiencing cultural upticks that at least partially owe to the presence of independent theaters and troupes. Major-league shows also have a presence, with most Broadway productions either previewing or touring in Washington. Either way, there's often something engaging playing on any given night, and usually at a Metro-accessible location. As with other arts, ticket prices and policies vary depending on the event and location; call for details.

Adams Morgan and Shaw

DC Arts Center 2438 18th St NW, Adams Morgan ☎202/462-7833, ⓦ www.dcartscenter.org; Woodley Park–Zoo Metro. Performance art, drama, poetry, dance, and a whole range of multicultural activities are held in this Adams Morgan space.

Lincoln Theatre 1215 U St NW, Shaw ☎202/328-6000, ⓦ www .thelincolntheatre.org; U Street–Cardozo Metro. Renovated movie/vaudeville house features touring stage shows, concerts, and dance, with a focus on multicultural productions.

Arlington, VA

Gunston Arts Center 2700 S Lang St ☎703/228-1850. Featuring two theaters – a proscenium stage and smaller "black box" – this facility hosts a range of drama, novelties, and cultural events from local and regional troupes.

Rosslyn Spectrum 1611 N Kent St ☎703/276-6701; Rosslyn Metro. A good venue for theater, concerts, and cultural events, offering an unpredictable mix of classics, multimedia experiments, and off-kilter new plays.

Signature Theatre 4200 Campbell Ave ☎703/820-9771, ⓦ www.signature-theatre.org. Award-winning theatrical group putting on premieres of new works, as well as straight-forward revivals of classics and musicals, and irreverent adaptations of them.

Capitol Hill and H Street Corridor

Atlas Performing Arts Center 1333 H St NE, H Street Corridor ☎202/399-7993, ⓦ www .atlasarts.org. A fascinating grab bag of theater, dance, music, and cabaret helps this performing-arts venue enliven an up-and-coming, if still seedy, part of town east of Capitol Hill.

Folger Shakespeare Library 201 E Capitol St SE, Capitol Hill ☎202/544-7077, ⓦ www.folger.edu; Capitol South Metro. A program of three or four annual works is presented at the Elizabethan Theatre (Sept–June), not solely Shakespeare, but often including his contemporaries and more modern playwrights as well.

H Street Playhouse 1365 H St NE, H Street Corridor ☎1-866/811-4111, ⓦ www .hstreetplayhouse.com. A stately little gem from 1928 that used to be an auto showroom but has been remodeled to anchor this burgeoning area's cultural scene, with a dramatic mix of topical and contemporary offerings from a variety of troupes.

Logan Circle

Source Theatre 1835 14th St NW ☎202/462-1073, ⓦ sourcetheatre.com; U Street–Cardozo Metro. New and contemporary works and classic reinterpretations by the house Constellation Theatre Company (☎202/280-8101). Promotes the Washington Theater Festival, a showcase for new works, every summer. Take a taxi here at night.

Studio Theatre 1501 14th St NW ☎202/332-3300, ⓦ www.studiotheatre.org. Independent theater with two stages presenting classic and contemporary drama as well as comedy.

Old Downtown

Ford's Theatre 511 10th St NW ☎202/547-1122, ⓦ www.fordstheatre.org; Metro Center Metro. The site of Lincoln's assassination (see p.186), this restored nineteenth-century theater stages mainstream musicals and dramas; currently under renovation.

Gala Hispanic Theatre 3333 14th St NW ☎202/234-7174, ⓦ www.galatheatre.org;

Columbia Heights Metro. Specializes in works by Spanish and Latin American playwrights, performed in Spanish or English, as well as performance art and poetry. Operates out of the classic Tivoli Theatre in Columbia Heights; see p.211.

National Theatre 1321 Pennsylvania Ave NW ☎202/628-6161, ⊛www.nationaltheatre.org; Metro Center Metro. One of the country's oldest theaters, it's been on this site (if not in this building) since 1835. Expect to see premieres, pre- and post-Broadway productions, and musicals.

Shakespeare Theatre in the Lansburgh, 450 7th St NW ☎202/547-1122, ⊛www.shakespearedc.org; Gallery Place–Chinatown Metro. Ten annual plays by Shakespeare and his contemporaries, along with the odd newer work. Each June the company stages free, outdoor performances at the Carter Barron Amphitheatre in Rock Creek Park (see p.229).

Warner Theatre 1299 Pennsylvania Ave NW ☎202/783-4000, ⊛www.warnertheatre.com; Metro Center Metro. Glorious 1920s movie palace that's been remodeled and is now staging post-Broadway plays, musicals, and major concerts.

Woolly Mammoth Theatre 641 D St NW ☎202/289-2443, ⊛www.woollymammoth.net; Archives–Navy Memorial. Metro. Popular theater troupe that stages budget- and mid-priced productions of contemporary and experimental plays.

Arena Stage 1101 6th St SW, Waterfront SW ☎202/488-3300, ⊛www.arenastage.org; Waterfront Metro. One of the most popular and well-respected of DC's major theatrical institutions. With the main waterfront facility being redeveloped into a theatrical juggernaut (reopening fall 2010), performances until then take place at 1800 S Bell St in Crystal City, near Arlington, VA; Crystal City Metro.

Discovery Theater at Ripley Center, 1100 Jefferson Drive SW, National Mall ☎202/633-8700, ⊛www.discoverytheater.org; Smithsonian Metro. Year-round daytime children's theater, offering musicals and puppet shows at budget prices.

Kennedy Center 2700 F St NW, at Virginia and New Hampshire Ave, Foggy Bottom ☎202/467-4600, ⊛www.kennedy-center.org; Foggy Bottom–GWU Metro. Offers three theaters: the Eisenhower (drama and Broadway productions), the Terrace (experimental/contemporary works), and the Theater Lab (almost permanently home to the comedy-whodunit *Shear Madness*, plus children's shows and cabaret). The Opera House also hosts musicals.

Comedy

When it comes to **comedy**, several clubs offer the usual mix of big-name stand-up acts, improv, local or regional circuit appearances, and open-mike nights. Apart from these, there are occasional stand-up nights at spots as diverse as Adams Morgan bars or the Arena Stage, Studio Theatre, and the Kennedy Center. Keep an eye out, too, for comedy troupes that appear in cabaret or improv shows at various venues around town, including major hotels. Capitol Steps is the best-known (and most unavoidable) of these troupes, but there are also regular shows by ensembles like ComedySportz and Gross National Product.

Performances can be expensive, since there's often a drinks-and-food minimum charge on top of the ticket price. A big weekend show can cost as much as $40–50, though tickets for basic stand-up and improv nights are more like $15. Reservations are essential.

Capitol Steps Ronald Reagan Building and International Trade Center, 1300 Pennsylvania Ave NW, Old Downtown ☎202/408-8736 or 397-7328, ⊛www.capsteps.com; Metro Center Metro. Well-established political satire by a group of Capitol Hill staffers on Fri and Sat nights at 7.30pm.

The Comedy Spot 4238 Wilson Blvd, Arlington, VA ☎703/294-5233, ⊛www.comedyindc.com; Ballston Metro. Serves up a range of comedy, from family-friendly high jinks to "blue" adult entertainment, in two theaters, seating 200 and 85 people, respectively. Can be amusing, depending on the troupe performing.

Improv 1140 Connecticut Ave NW ☎ 202/296-7008, ⓦ www.dcimprov.com; Farragut North Metro. DC's main comedy stage, part of a chain of such venues nationwide. Draws both up-and-coming performers and the occasional veteran from the TV humor circuit.

Film

As with most American cities, the great majority of **moviehouses** in Washington are owned by a handful of major corporations, and program the same tired Hollywood schlock and teen sex comedies you can see anywhere. Multiplexes are growing in number and size throughout the DC region, and usually feature raked seating and $10+ tickets. What follows below, by contrast, are those unique theaters that, either by their historic pedigree or inventive programming, offer a good reason to venture beyond the big-box mainstream cinemas.

Although nighttime tickets are increasingly pricey, you can often still get a bargain at afternoon matinees, which come in at a few dollars cheaper – while cheapest of all are the free films showing at museums and galleries; indeed, these programs are often among the best in DC, focusing on a single director, genre, style, movement, or national cinema. Also don't forget the IMAX screens at the National Air and Space Museum (see p.88) and the National Museum of Natural History (see p.74), especially if you've got kids to entertain. If you happen to be here in April, be on the lookout for screenings tied to DC's annual Filmfest (ⓦ www.filmfestdc.org), which premieres national and international movies in theaters across town.

American Film Institute 8633 Colesville Rd, Silver Spring, MD ☎ 301/495-6720, ⓦ www.afi.com/silver; Silver Spring Metro. Institutional film heavyweight whose Silver Theatre offers regular programs of art, foreign, and classic films, usually built around certain directors, countries, and themes, often with associated lectures and seminars. Located two blocks from the Metro stop.

Arlington Cinema 'n' Drafthouse 2903 Columbia Pike, Arlington, VA ☎ 703/528-4660, ⓦ www.arlingtondrafthouse.com. Grab a brew or munch on food while you watch a second-run movie or a midlevel comic at this combination pub-theater, with one screen showing three or four movies during the week.

Avalon Theatre 5612 Connecticut Ave NW, Upper Northwest ☎ 202/966-6000, ⓦ www.theavalon.org; Friendship Heights Metro. Near the Maryland border (a 10–15min walk from the Metro), a marvelously refurbished 1930s movie palace with handsomely redecorated lobby, lovely ceiling mural,

and old-fashioned charm, now showing independent films and Hollywood classics.

E Street Cinema 555 11th St NW, Old Downtown ☎ 202/452-7672, ⓦ www.landmarktheatres.com; Metro Center Metro. Fairly recent arrival on the independent film scene, offering eight screens showing indie, foreign, documentary, and classic movies in a comfortable, stylish setting with stadium seating.

Mary Pickford Theater Madison Building, 3rd Floor, Library of Congress, 1st St and Independence Ave SE, Capitol Hill ☎ 202/707-5677, ⓦ www.loc.gov; Capitol South Metro. Free classic and foreign historic movies from the library's voluminous archives.

Uptown Theater 3426 Connecticut Ave NW, Upper Northwest ☎ 202/966-5400; Cleveland Park Metro. Along with the Avalon, this is the District's other extant 1930s moviehouse, with one large screen, plenty of balcony seating, and a slate of contemporary Hollywood movies. Under threat of closure in 2008; call before making the trek.

Gay DC

F or a smallish East Coast city, Washington, DC's **gay and lesbian scene** is surprisingly vibrant. Though you'll find it a bit more buttoned-down than the ones in New York, LA, and San Francisco, times have certainly changed in the nation's capital since 1975, when gay federal employees risked being fired from their government jobs for engaging in "immoral conduct." Within the past decade, the first openly gay city official has been elected, the alternative weekly *Washington Blade* has grown to more than one hundred pages, and, in April 2000, hundreds of thousands of people descended upon DC to attend the Millennium March on Washington for Equality.

The heart of DC's gay community is **Dupont Circle**, where the greatest concentration of shops, bars, and restaurants catering to a gay clientele can be found. Most of the action takes place along P Street, just west of the Circle between 21st and 22nd streets, and on 17th Street, where gay and gay-friendly establishments form a lively strip between P and R streets. Across town in **Capitol Hill**, a handful of gay-friendly spots are clustered in the vicinity of the Eastern Market Metro station, near the intersection of Pennsylvania Avenue and 8th Street.

To get a reading on the local pulse, grab a copy of the *Washington Blade* (ⓦwww.washblade.com) for news, listings, and classified ads. For an insider's guide to the nightlife, turn to the *Metro Weekly* (ⓦwww.metroweekly .com) for up-to-date listings of dining and partying hot spots – including information on special events, DJs, and happy hours – accompanied by a map. Both publications are free and can be picked up at Lambda Rising, 1625 Connecticut Ave (ⓣ202/462-6969, ⓦwww.lambdarising.com), or at various restaurants and clubs in Dupont Circle and Capitol Hill. A list of other gay resources and organizations in DC appears on p.319.

Accommodation

While only a handful of places in DC bill themselves exclusively as gay **hotels** or B&Bs, gay-friendly

▲ Capital Pride

accommodation is scattered throughout the city. You can count on feeling welcome at most of the hotels in the Dupont Circle area. A few recommended spots are listed below, with page references to their fuller descriptions.

Carlyle Suites 1731 New Hampshire Ave NW, Dupont Circle ☎202/234-3200 or 1-866/468-3532, ⓦwww.carlylesuites.com; see p.266.

Dupont at the Circle 1604 19th St NW, Dupont Circle ☎202/332-5251 or 1-888/412-0100, ⓦwww.dupontatthecircle.com; see p.266.

Embassy Inn 1627 16th St NW, Dupont Circle ☎202/234-7800 or 1-800/423-9111; see p.266.

Kalorama Guest House at Woodley Park 2700 Cathedral Ave NW, Upper Northwest ☎202/328-0860, ⓦwww.kaloramaguesthouse.com; see p.271.

Tabard Inn 1739 N St NW, New Downtown ☎202/785-1277, ⓦwww.tabardinn.com; see p.269.

William Lewis House 1309 R St NW, Logan Circle ☎202/462-7574 or 1-800/465-7574, ⓦwww.wlewishous.com; see p.269.

Restaurants and cafés

While more than a few places reviewed in the main "Eating" chapter (see Chapter 13) have won loyal gay followings – including *Pizzeria Paradiso* and *Afterwords Café* in Dupont Circle, *Two Quail* in Capitol Hill, and *The Diner* and *Perry's* in Adams Morgan – the handful of spots listed below have become fixtures on the capital's gay and lesbian scene.

Annie's Paramount Steakhouse 1609 17th St NW, Dupont Circle ☎202/232-0395; Dupont Circle Metro. A local institution, in business since the 1940s, serving midpriced steaks, good burgers, and brunch – including a midnight brunch on weekends. Sun–Thurs 11am–11pm, Fri & Sat 24hr.

Banana Café & Piano Bar 500 8th St SE, Capitol Hill ☎202/543-5906; Eastern Market Metro. An affordable tropical spot serving basic Tex-Mex staples alongside Caribbean and Cuban standouts such as codfish fritters and plantain soup, the house specialty.

Stop by the upstairs *Piano Bar* on weekdays for happy hour, when the piano man is in the house. Sun–Thurs 11.30am–10.30pm, Fri 11.30am–11.30pm, Sat 4–11.30pm.

Dakota Cowgirl 1337 14th St NW ☎202/232-7010; Dupont Circle Metro. Country-themed diner near Logan Circle with a vaguely Southwestern feel, but a handy enough place to power down solid burgers and fries, including some veggie options, before clubbing. Mon–Thurs 11am–10.30pm, Fri & Sat 11am–11pm, Sun 11am–10pm.

Festivals and events

The District's gay community hosts any number of freewheeling **parties** and **festivals** (as well as more sober-minded fund-raisers) throughout the year, usually packed with throngs of locals, and sometimes with the odd politico dropping in for a peek.

Capital Pride (early June): Weeklong festival still going strong after thirty years that features cultural, political, and community events, including films, pageants, a parade, and a street festival along Pennsylvania Avenue NW. ⓦwww.capitalpride.org

Atlantic Stampede (Sept): The East Coast's largest gay rodeo, sponsored by the Atlantic States Gay Rodeo Association. The weekend-long affair comprises two days of rodeo, plus evening dinner-and-dance events. Rodeo grounds at Gaithersburg, MD. ⓦwww.asgra.org

Reel Affirmations (Oct): One of the nation's largest gay and lesbian film festivals, held at various venues. Inquire also about monthly gay-film screenings and Capital Pride cinema events. ⓦwww.reelaffirmations.org

High-Heel Race (Tues before Halloween): Colorful street festival featuring a carnival-like atmosphere, drag queens in all manner of mind-blowing outfits, and a mad dash down 17th Street in three- to six-inch heels.

Jolt 'N Bolt 1918 18th St NW, Adams Morgan ⊕202/232-0077; Dupont Circle Metro. Townhouse tea- and coffeehouse with side-alley patio tucked away up 18th Street. Wraps and sandwiches, pastries, and fresh juices are served. Sun–Thurs 7.30am–11pm, Fri & Sat 8am–midnight.

L'Enfant 2000 18th St NW, Adams Morgan ⊕202/319-1800; Dupont Circle Metro. A French favorite known for its affordable savory and sweet crepes and offerings like quiche, Brie, pâté, and croque monsieur. On "Wine-and-Wig Wednesdays" there's half-priced vino and plenty of fake hair on show. Mon–Fri 6–11.30pm, Sat & Sun 10am–midnight.

Mr Henry's 601 Pennsylvania Ave SE, Capitol Hill ⊕202/546-8412; Eastern Market Metro. Affordable saloon and restaurant with outside patio, charcoal grill, and loyal gay crowd. See also "Restaurants," p.281. Sun–Thurs 11am–midnight, Fri & Sat 11am–1am.

SoHo Tea & Coffee 2150 P St NW, Dupont Circle ⊕202/463-7646; Dupont Circle Metro. Trendy late-night hang-out for P Street clubbers refueling on coffee, cakes, and sandwiches. Occasional entertainment, plus a computer terminal with WI-FI access ($5 minimum purchase). Tues & Thurs–Sat 7.30am–4am; Sun, Mon, & Wed 7.30am–2am.

Bars and clubs

The focus of gay **bars and clubs** in DC is unquestionably Dupont Circle, though Capitol Hill Southeast has scattered points of interest, too. With the latter area, though, try to take a cab around at night, as some of the backstreets can get rather dodgy.

Capitol Hill

Phase One 525 8th St SE ⊕202/544-6831; Eastern Market Metro. Long-standing neighborhood lesbian bar with relaxed and convivial atmosphere, DJs, dancing, and pool table. Men require a female "escort." Sun & Thurs 7pm–2am, Fri & Sat 7pm–3am.

Remington's 639 Pennsylvania Ave SE ⊕202/543-3113; Eastern Market Metro. Signature gay country & western club with four dance floors and two dance floors; events include cornpone singing competitions, spirited hoedowns, and "cowgirl"-themed drag pageants. Sun–Thurs 4pm–2am, Fri 4pm–3am, Sat 8pm–3am.

Dupont Circle and New Downtown

Apex 1415 22nd St NW ⊕202/296-0505; Dupont Circle Metro. Centrally located dance club with DJs spinning pop, house, tribal, and garage for a party crowd, plus karaoke; the insanity is at its best on Fri and Sat nights. Get here early on weekends to beat the cover charge. Mostly men. Tues & Thurs 9pm–1am, Fri & Sat 9pm–2am.

Chaos 1603 17th St NW ⊕202/232-4141; Dupont Circle Metro. Free-spirited club at the heart of the 17th Street scene, where inexpensive drinks are poured from a finely stocked bar. There are drag-king and-queen shows, a cabaret, and drag bingo – the latter popular with the straight crowd, too. Sun–Thurs 6pm–2am, Fri & Sat 6pm–3am.

Cobalt 1639 R St NW ⊕202/462-6569; Dupont Circle Metro. Another fixture on the local scene. The first floor has an engaging bar, and upstairs there's a more frenetic club with theme nights and all kinds of yuppie types gyrating to house and trance tunes. Sun–Thurs 5pm–2am, Fri & Sat 5pm–3am.

FAB Lounge 1805 Connecticut Ave NW ⊕202/797-1122; Dupont Circle Metro. North of the Circle, a spirited Kalorama club that draws a wide variety of people, including women, who come for the uncommon (for DC) lesbian nights at this relaxed but still dance-oriented club. Daily 5pm–2am.

Green Lantern 1335 Green Court NW ⊕202/347-4533; McPherson Square Metro. Broad selection of regulars at this easygoing bar that's a bit removed from the posier Circle scene to the north; regular karaoke nights and weekend video jockeys as well. Mon–Thurs 4pm–2am, Fri & Sat 4pm–3am, Sun 1pm–2am.

Halo 1435 P St NW ⊕202/797-9730; no close Metro. Self-consciously ultra-chic lounge in Logan Circle that hosts a variety of shades of white (decoratively and ethnically) and is one of the District's pinnacles of gay posing. To buy in to this social challenge, wear a new shirt, look smart, and don't let the pretension get you down. Daily 5pm–2am. **JR's 1519 17th St NW** ☎202/328-0090; **Dupont Circle Metro**. A young, mostly male professional crowd packs into this narrow saloon-bar, which boasts a great location along the 17th Street cruise strip. The place to be seen for cocktails. Mon–Thurs 11am–2am, Fri & Sat 11am–3am, Sun noon–2am.

Omega 2122 P St NW, in the rear alley ☎202/223-4917; **Dupont Circle Metro**. Gay-oriented, techno-swanky spot with four bars, pool tables, and a dark video room upstairs. Stop in for happy hour or for a kickoff drink on the weekends. Mon–Thurs 4pm–2am, Fri 4pm–3am, Sat 8pm–3am, Sun 7pm–2am.

Gay organizations and resources

Human Rights Campaign Store and Action Center 1640 Rhode Island Ave NW, New Downtown ☎202/628-4160, ⓦwww.hrc.org; **Farragut North Metro**. A national organization that educates people on political issues affecting gay, lesbian, bisexual, and transgender people; its store sells Equality Wear merchandise to raise funds for its programs.

Lambda Rising 1625 Connecticut Ave NW, Dupont Circle ☎202/462-6969, ⓦwww.lambdarising.com; **Dupont Circle Metro**. The city's best-known gay and lesbian bookstore, which acts as a clearinghouse for information and events.

Metro Weekly ⓦwww.metroweekly.com. Free magazine that makes an excellent guide to DC's gay nightlife scene, stuffed with ads and listings about the latest spots and specials. Available at Lambda Rising (above) and various Dupont Circle and Capitol Hill venues.

Rainbow History Project 1225 I St NW, Suite 600 ☎202/907-9007, ⓦwww.rainbowhistory.org.

Preserves and promotes community history through exhibits, talks, and archives, and publishes Web-based DC timeline and database of gay and lesbian "places and spaces" from the 1920s to the present. Also offers downloadable walking-tour brochures of neighborhoods such as Capitol Hill and Dupont Circle.

Washington Blade ⓦwww.washblade.com. News, listings, and classified ads are featured in this free weekly paper, available at bookstores, restaurants, and cafés around town.

Whitman-Walker Clinic 1407 S St NW, Shaw ☎202/797-3500, ⓦwww.wwc.org; **U Street–Cardozo Metro**. Nonprofit community health organization for the gay and lesbian community, providing accessible health care and services, including AIDS information. Check website for information on other regional facilities.

Festivals and parades

Washington has a huge variety of annual **festivals and parades**, many of them national in scope: America's Christmas Tree is lit each December on the Ellipse in front of the White House; the grandest Fourth of July Parade in the country takes place along and around the National Mall; and every four years in January the newly inaugurated president rides in a triumphal parade up Pennsylvania Avenue, from the US Capitol to the White House. Many of the national holidays are celebrated with special events and festivities in the city – for a comprehensive list contact the Washington DC Convention and Visitors Association (see p.49) or seek out the events calendar at ⓦ www.washington.org. Dedicated websites, if there are any, are included in the listing of each celebration.

Open days at museums, galleries, and attractions are covered in the relevant parts of the guide; for a list of **national public holidays**, see p.47. For a list of gay-oriented festivals, see p.317.

January

Dr Martin Luther King Jr's Birthday 15th
ⓣ 202/619-7222 Wreath-laying at the Lincoln Memorial, a reading of the "I Have a Dream" speech, concerts, and speeches, plus activities at Martin Luther King Jr Memorial Library downtown (see p.187).
Robert E. Lee's Birthday 19th ⓣ 703/548-1789 Music, food, and exhibits at Arlington House in Arlington Cemetery; special events in Old Town Alexandria, VA, including activities like

Information lines

National Park Service
ⓣ 202/619-7222

Post-Haste (Washington Post)
ⓣ 202/334-9000

Smithsonian ⓣ 202/357-2700

Washington DC Convention and Visitors Association
ⓣ 202/789-7000
For more details on these organizations, see p.49.

Civil War re-enactments at Fort Ward — ironically, a Union garrison.

February

Black History Month Special events, exhibits, and cultural programs. Information from Martin Luther King Jr Memorial Library (ⓣ 202/727-1186) or the Smithsonian or National Park Service (see box).
Chinese New Year varies ⓣ 202/638-1041 Dragon dancers, parades, and fireworks light up H Street NW in Chinatown.
Abraham Lincoln's Birthday 12th ⓣ 202/619-7222 Wreath-laying and reading of the Gettysburg Address at the Lincoln Memorial.
Frederick Douglass's Birthday 14th ⓣ 202/426-5961 Wreath-laying, history exhibits, and music at his home (and now National Historic Site) in Cedar Hill, Anacostia.
George Washington's Birthday Parade 22nd
ⓣ 703/991-4474, ⓦ www.washingtonbirthday .net Spectacular parade and events in Old Town Alexandria, VA. Also, concerts and wreath-laying at Mount Vernon (ⓣ 703/799-5203).

March

St Patrick's Day 17th ☏ 202/637-2474, ⓦ www
.dcstpatsparade.com Big parade down
Constitution Avenue NW on the Sunday
before the 17th (call for grandstand seats)
and another through Old Town Alexandria
on the first Saturday of the month
(☏ 703/237-2199, ⓦ www.ballyshaners.org).
Smithsonian Kite Festival late March/early April
☏ 202/633-3030, ⓦ www.kitefestival.org Kite-
flying competitions on the National Mall,
with assorted games and prizes.

April

National Cherry Blossom Festival early
☏ 202/547-1500, ⓦ www.national
cherryblossomfestival.org The famous cherry
trees around the Tidal Basin bloom in late
March/early April; celebrated by a massive
parade down Constitution Avenue NW, the
crowning of a festival queen, free concerts,
lantern-lighting, dances, and origami.
Blessing of the Fleet second Sat ☏ 202/737-2300
Nautical celebrations and services at US Navy
Memorial, including sailors serving a famous
navy bean soup. Boat-related displays and
races at Southwest Waterfront marina.
Thomas Jefferson's Birthday 13th ☏ 202/619-
7222 Wreath-laying and military ceremonies
at the Jefferson Memorial.
Easter Sunrise Service Easter Sun ☏ 703/695-
3250 or 202/685-2851 Sunrise memorial
service at Arlington National Cemetery.
White House Easter Egg Roll Easter Mon
☏ 202/456-2200, ⓦ www.whitehouse.gov/easter
Entertainment and egg rolling (eggs
provided) on the White House South Lawn.
Special garden tours the weekend after
Easter; reserve well in advance.
Filmfest DC late ☏ 202/628-FILM, ⓦ www
.filmfestdc.org Two-week festival premiering
national and international movies in theaters
and museums across the city.
Smithsonian Craft Show late ☏ 202/633-5006
or 1-888/832-9554, ⓦ www.smithsoniancraft
show.org Fascinating craft exhibitions by
regional artists and artisans at the National
Building Museum (see p.176).
William Shakespeare's Birthday 25th
☏ 202/544-7077 The Bard is praised in song,
word, and food at the Folger Shakespeare
Library (see p.117).
Duke Ellington's Birthday 29th ☏ 202/331-9404,
ⓦ www.smithsonianjazz.org Music and events

at Freedom Plaza on Pennsylvania Avenue
NW. Music and lectures are given at some
Smithsonian museums.

May

Flower Mart first weekend ☏ 202/337-9089
Flowers, puppet shows, a carousel, and
entertainment at Washington National
Cathedral, with floral displays themed
around a given country, sponsored by its
embassy.
Garden Day early ☏ 202/965-1950, ⓦ www
.georgetowngardentour.com Self-guided tours
to see private patches of lush greenery at
Georgetown's houses and mansions.
Tickets go for $30 (or $35 day of tour).
Mount Vernon Wine Festival/Sunset Tour mid
☏ 703/799-5203, ⓦ www.mountvernon.org
George Washington's estate hosts this
celebration of early America's homegrown
wine-making, featuring music, food, and a
trip to the first president's own cellar vaults.
$30.
Malcolm X Day 19th ☏ 202/789-7000
Commemorative concerts, films, and
speeches in Anacostia Park in honor of the
1960s black revolutionary leader.
Memorial Day last Mon Wreath-layings,
services, and speeches at Arlington
Cemetery (☏ 202/685-2851), the Vietnam
Veterans Memorial (☏ 202/619-7222), and
the US Navy Memorial (☏ 202/737-2300).
The National Symphony Orchestra performs
on the Capitol's West Lawn on the Sun
before, and there's a jazz festival in Old
Town Alexandria (☏ 703/883-4686).

June

Dupont-Kalorama Museum Walk first weekend
☏ 202/785-2040 ext 428, ⓦ www.dkmuseums
.com Music, food, and historic displays
provide the backdrop to tours of museums
and private homes and estates in the
Dupont Circle, Embassy Row, and Kalorama
neighborhoods.
Marvin Gaye Jr Appreciation Day early
☏ 301/559-3227 Street events and spirited
music at Galludet Market Place, 6th and
Neal St NE, honoring the R&B great born in
the District in 1939.
Alexandria Red Cross Waterfront Festival mid
☏ 703/549-8300, ⓦ www.waterfrontfestival.org
Major Alexandria, VA, event with music,
food, and kids' events, plus visits from tall
ships along the Potomac River.

FESTIVALS AND PARADES

Dance Africa mid ☏ 202/269-1600, ⊛ www
.danceplace.org Festival of African dance,
open-air market, and concerts at Dance
Place, 3225 8th St NE.

National Capital Barbeque Battle mid
☏ 301/860-0630, ⊛ www.bbqdc.com Get your
fill of of gut-busting, rib-stuffing barbecue at
this celebration of the greasy and the grilled,
which culminates with the awarding of the
National Pork Barbeque Champion. Held
along Pennsylvania Ave NW. $10.

DC Caribbean Carnival mid-to-late ☏ 202/726-
2204, ⊛ www.dccaribbeancarnival.com
Caribbean-style parade spread over
consecutive weekends, with masqueraders
and live music, from Georgia and Missouri
avenues to Banneker Park near Howard
University.

Smithsonian Festival of American Folklife late
June/early July ☏ 202/633-6440, ⊛ www.folklife
.si.edu One of the country's biggest festivals,
loaded with American music, crafts, food,
and folk heritage events on the Mall.

July

National Independence Day Celebration 4th
☏ 202/619-7222 Reading of the Declaration of
Independence at National Archives, parade
along Constitution Avenue NW, free concerts
at the Sylvan Theatre near the Washington
Monument, National Symphony Orchestra
performance on west steps of the Capitol,
finishing with a superb fireworks display. Get
there as early as possible for all events.

Mary McLeod Bethune Celebration varies
☏ 202/673-2402, ⊛ www.nps.gov/mamc
Wreath-laying, gospel choir, and speakers at
the Bethune statue in Lincoln Park; ongoing
exhibits at Bethune Council House.

Virginia Scottish Festival mid ☏ 703/912-1943,
⊛ www.vascottishgames.org Alexandria and
Arlington, VA, are the spots for the wearing
of kilts, playing of bagpipes, and eating of
haggis. Also features Highland dancing and
fiddling.

Capital Fringe Festival mid-to-late ☏ 1-866/811-
4111 ⊛ www.capfringe.org Two weeks full of
classic, modern, offbeat, and avant-garde
theater works, more than a hundred in all,
centered around galleries and theaters in
Old Downtown and Mount Vernon Square.

August

Arlington County Fair early ☏ 703/920-4556,
⊛ www.arlingtoncountyfair.org Traditional fair

with rides, crafts, entertainment, food stalls,
concerts, and "racing pigs" at Thomas
Jefferson Community Center, 3501 2nd St,
Arlington, VA.

DC Blues Festival late Aug or early Sept
☏ 202/962-0112, ⊛ www.dcblues.org Free
music, from folky acoustic blues to Chicago
electric, at Rock Creek Park's Carter Barron
Amphitheatre.

September

Labor Day Weekend Concert Sun before Labor
Day ☏ 202/619-7222 The National Symphony
Orchestra plays on the west lawn of the
Capitol to mark the end of the summer
season.

Adams Morgan Day first Sun after Labor Day
☏ 202/232-1960, ⊛ www.adamsmorganday
.org One of the best neighborhood
festivals, with live music, crafts, and
cuisine along 18th Street NW – always
packed and great fun.

Duke Ellington Jazz Festival early-to-mid
☏ 202/232-3611, ⊛ www.dejazzfest.org Free
musical events around town celebrating
DC's native son and favorite composer,
including more than a hundred jazz-oriented
concerts and programs.

Black Family Reunion second weekend
☏ 202/737-0120, ⊛ www.ncnw.org Weekend
African American festival on the Mall
featuring food, dance performances, and
music.

Constitution Day 17th ☏ 202/501-5215 or
1-866/272-6272, ⊛ www.archives.org The US
Constitution is displayed at the National
Archives to celebrate the anniversary of its
signing; naturalization ceremonies, parade,
and concerts as well.

Oktoberfest late Sept/early Oct ☏ 202/310-
4691, ⊛ www.geocities.com/saengerbund
Plenty of high-spirited beer drinking, song,
and dance at area locations, including
Arlington, VA, and several DC restaurants
and microbreweries.

October

Columbus Day second Mon ☏ 202/371-9441,
⊛ www.unionstationdc.com Wreath-laying,
speeches, and music at the Columbus
Memorial in front of Union Station.

White House Fall Garden Tours mid ☏ 202/208-
1631, ⊛ www.whitehouse.gov Free garden
tours and military band concerts. Reserve
well in advance.

Marine Corps Marathon late ☎1-800/RUN-USMC ⓦ www.marinemarathon.com The city's key distance event, beginning and ending at the Iwo Jima Monument and leading runners (all kinds, not just military members) past Georgetown, Capitol Hill, the National Mall and Pentagon along the way. $75 entry.

Halloween 31st ☎703/549-2997 Unofficial block parties, costumed antics, and fright-nights in Georgetown, Dupont Circle, and other neighborhoods. Alexandria, VA, tours visit places like the "haunted" Carlyle House.

November

Seafaring Celebration varies ☎202/433-4882 The Navy Museum hosts a family-oriented event with maritime activities, food, arts, and children's performances.

Veterans Day 11th Solemn memorial services and wreath-laying at 11am at Arlington Cemetery (usually with the president in attendance), African American Civil War Memorial, Vietnam Veterans Memorial, and US Navy Memorial.

December

Candlelight Tours varies Call well in advance for reservations at these extremely popular evening events, which take place at Mount Vernon (☎703/780-2000) and Old Town Alexandria (☎703/838-4242).

Christmas Tree Lightings early ☎202/619-7222 Separate ceremonies for the lighting of the Capitol (west side) and National (Ellipse) Christmas trees – the latter lit by the president. The entire month on the Ellipse sees Nativity scenes, choral groups, and other seasonal displays.

Pearl Harbor Day 7th ☎202/737-2300 Wreath-laying ceremony at the US Navy Memorial to commemorate the 1941 attack on Pearl Harbor.

Christmas Services all month ☎202/537-6200, ⓦ www.cathedral.org/cathedral Carols, pageants, choral performances, and bell-ringing at Washington National Cathedral. There is also much ceremony and ritual at the National Shrine of the Immaculate Conception (☎202/526-8300, ⓦ www.nationalshrine.com).

Sports and outdoor activities

The nation's capital is one of the greenest cities on the East Coast, with easy access to a multitude of woodsy trails and a major waterway, the Potomac River. Thanks to these natural attributes, DC is a great place for people who like to cycle, sail, hike, paddle, skate, run, or just stroll in the great **outdoors** – all a welcome relief from pounding the pavement between monuments and museums.

The capital also has a lot to offer those who prefer to enjoy their **sports** from the sidelines. Unfortunately, the one team that has had any kind of success in recent years, football's Washington Redskins, has a waiting list for tickets that is at least ten years long – and they don't even play in the District. The situation isn't remedied by the area's other teams, which are typically mediocre (basketball's Wizards) or just plain bad (hockey's Capitals). The more you take spectator sports as casual entertainment instead of a feverish pursuit, the less frustrated you'll be.

In 2008, DC's Washington Nationals baseball squad moved from the old RFK Stadium into the new Nationals Park near the waterfront. The team isn't great,

▲ Rollerblading in Rock Creek Park

but it's already attracted a sizable fan base, so if you want to check them out, you're advised to reserve tickets well ahead of your visit.

Outdoor activities

Those looking to stretch their legs after a day on the Tourmobile – or walk on something other than pavement – will find plenty to keep them busy. The green expanse of **Rock Creek Park** – which stretches from the city's northern edge to the Potomac River (see p.228) – and the network of trails heading out from the capital to Virginia and Maryland together offer miles of routes for biking, walking, and inline skating. Downtown, the **Mall** and the **Ellipse** provide the city with a central playground, particularly in summer when softball season swings into gear, and are good spots to go for a run.

Forming DC's southern boundary, the Potomac offers everything from white-water rapids to guided tours for novice paddlers to sunset sails, making it easy to take in spectacular views of DC from the water.

Bicycling

For a pleasant outdoor excursion, the best option might be to rent a bike for short rides along the **Potomac River** or the **C&O Canal towpath**. Bicycle rentals (vendors listed below) run anywhere from $5/hour for a simple cruiser to $50/day for a flashy mountain bike.

Among DC's cycle paths are one in Rock Creek Park, the 18.5-mile **Mount Vernon Trail** (see p.252), and the 184-mile-long C&O towpath (see p.239). The Washington & Old Dominion Trail (ⓦwww.nvrpa.org/parks/wod) starts a bit further out, in Vienna, VA, but offers 45 miles of pavement following the route of an old-time railway, heading westward into northern Virginia.

The eleven-mile **Capital Crescent Trail**, starting at Thompson Boat Center, branches off the C&O towpath after three miles and follows the course of an old railway line up into Bethesda and on to Silver Spring, both in Maryland. Once in Bethesda, cyclists can turn this trip into a 22-mile loop by returning via Rock Creek Park – follow the signs to the unpaved Georgetown Branch Trail, which cuts across Connecticut Avenue, to find the park. On the southern end, the trail links up with the Mount Vernon Trail (via the Key Bridge) and the Rock Creek Trail (via K St). Be warned that this trail is extremely popular on weekends; for more information, call ⓣ202/234-4874 or check out ⓦwww.cctrail.org.

Many trails and bicycle paths criss-cross the Metrorail system, giving you the option of cutting short a trip or avoiding backtracking. Keep in mind that while bikes are permitted on the Metro at any time during the weekend, they are prohibited during weekday rush hours (7–10am & 4–7pm) and on major holidays.

Rentals

Better Bikes ⓣ202/293-2080, ⓦwww.betterbikesinc.com. Delivers anywhere in DC, and has info on bike trails and events.

Big Wheel Bikes 1034 33rd St NW, Georgetown ⓣ202/337-0254; 2 Prince St, Alexandria, VA ⓣ703/739-2300; 3119 Lee Hwy, Arlington, VA ⓣ703/522-1110; 6917 Arlington Rd, Bethesda, MD ⓣ301/652-0192; ⓦwww.bigwheelbikes.com. Georgetown location (closed Mon) convenient to C&O Canal and Capital Crescent trails; Alexandria location near Mount Vernon Trail.

Fletcher's Boat House 4940 Canal Rd NW, Georgetown ⓣ202/244-0461, ⓦwww.fletchersboathouse.com. Located on the C&O Canal.

Thompson Boat Center 2900 Virginia Ave NW, Georgetown ⓣ202/333-9543, ⓦwww.thompsonboatcenter.com. Good prices for cruisers and other models.

Washington Sailing Marina 1 Marina Drive, George Washington Memorial Parkway, Alexandria, VA ☎703/548-9027, Ⓦwww .washingtonsailingmarina.com. Located along the Mount Vernon Trail (see also p.328).

Tours and resources

Bike the Sites ☎202/842-BIKE, Ⓦwww .bikethesites.com. Two- to four-hour guided bike tours of the city's major sights ($30–40, including bike and helmet), plus tours of Mount Vernon and customized tours of the District. No fixed schedule; also rents bikes for $5–10 per hour or $25–60 per day. Tour reservations required.

Bike Washington Ⓦwww.bikewashington.org. Online recreational bicycling guide loaded with tips on local routes and trails.

Washington Area Bicyclist Association 1803 Connecticut Ave NW, 3rd Floor ☎202/518-0524, Ⓦwww.waba.org. Advocacy group whose website offers info on trails, gear, and local events.

Rollerblading

The Capital Crescent and Mount Vernon trails are both traveled by **Rollerbladers** as well as cyclists, but one of the best spots for inline skaters on the weekends is forested **Beach Drive** in Rock Creek Park, which is closed to vehicular traffic on weekends and holidays from 7am Saturday to 7pm Sunday. Near Parking Lot 6, just north of the intersection of Beach and Military roads and near the Public Golf

Course, a gently hilly six-mile stretch is a popular training and cruising ground for local bladers. Skilled skaters shouldn't have too much trouble getting there from the Van Ness–UDC Metro station, though it's probably easier to drive or catch a cab.

Those accustomed to slicing through urban traffic will find the roads and sidewalks in the vicinity of Old and New Downtown hit-or-miss in terms of pavement quality, though you will feel a bit safer than you would, say, blading down Fifth Avenue in New York. Good areas include the Tidal Basin south of the National Mall, and selected parts of the Waterfront, East and West Potomac parks, and the riverside sections of Georgetown and Alexandria, VA. The **Washington Area Roadskaters** (☎202/466-5005, Ⓦwww.skatedc.org) is a local club that organizes group skates of varying lengths, as well as free weekly inline skate clinics (April–Oct Sat noon) in Rock Creek Park.

Jogging and walking

Of course you can walk or jog on any of the trails described under "Bicycling" or "Rollerblading," though many choose to simply put on their running shoes and hit the Mall, where the imperial buildings and monuments provide an inspiring backdrop for a

---

Health clubs

If you'd prefer to sweat it out indoors, Olympus, Gold's Gym, and Bally's are but a few of the big-name **health clubs** that have made their mark on DC. Several other spots open their doors to nonmembers, although it will cost you $25 or more per visit.

City Sports 1111 19th St NW, New Downtown ☎202/467-4100; 727 7th St NW, Old Downtown ☎202/638-3115, Ⓦwww.citysports.com.

Results, the Gym 1612 U St NW, Shaw ☎202/518-0600; Capitol Hill, 315 G St NE ☎202/543-0999; and Old Downtown, 1101 Connecticut Ave NW ☎202/887-0999, Ⓦwww.resultsthegym.com.

Vida Fitness 601 F St NW, Old Downtown ☎1-866/382-VIDA, Ⓦwww.vidafitness .com.

Washington Sports Club nine area locations, including 1211 Connecticut Ave NW, New Downtown ☎202/296-7733; 214 D St SE, Capitol Hill ☎202/547-2255; 1835 Connecticut Ave NW, Dupont Circle ☎202/332-0100; and 738 7th St NW, Old Downtown ☎202/737-3555, Ⓦwww.mysportsclubs.com.

daily workout. The sand and gravel paths circumscribing the mammoth front lawn of the city center provides a surface easier on the knees than your typical city pavement.

Those looking for a quieter place for a constitutional should head to **Theodore Roosevelt Island** (see p.252), a nature park with 2.5 miles of trails that meander through marsh, swamp, and forest. Access to the island, which lies at the start of the Mount Vernon Trail, is via a footbridge on the Arlington side of the Potomac. Other relaxing spots in the daytime include the **National Arboretum** (see p.218), **Rock Creek Park** (see p.228), and **Arlington National Cemetery** (see p.244). Of course, merely wandering around DC itself from neighborhood to neighborhood provides its own sort of workout, and a combination of foot and Metrorail travel can take you to most places worth visiting in the District.

Water activities

The **Potomac River** provides plenty of chances to get out on the water. North of the city, twenty minute beyond the Beltway, lies the 6300-acre **Seneca Creek State Park** (Ⓦwww .dnr.state.md.us/publiclands), where a flat expanse of river is ideal for canoeing. The current picks up and the crowds emerge a bit farther downstream as the Potomac races through **Great Falls** (Ⓦwww.nps .gov/grfa), where Class VI rapids provide ample challenges for whitewater **kayakers** – though make sure you have plenty of experience, as periodic fatalities illustrate the dangers of the swift current.

Near Georgetown, several boat-rental shops offer the means to explore the calmer waters on either side of the Key Bridge and around Roosevelt Island, a stretch of the river that provides a worthy afternoon retreat. From here, it's easy enough to paddle your way into the **Tidal Basin**, an

outing especially pretty in spring, when the cherry blossoms are in bloom. Landlubbers keen on staying closer to shore can rent a **paddle boat** at the Tidal Basin Boat House, 1501 Maine Ave SW (March–Aug Mon–Fri 10am–6pm, Sat & Sun 10am–7pm; Sept & Oct Wed–Sun only; two-seaters $8/hr, four-seaters $16/hr; Ⓣ202/479-2426, Ⓦwww .tidalbasinpaddleboats.com).

Going south, the river widens as it flows past Alexandria toward the Wilson Bridge, an area popular with sailors, windsurfers, and sea-kayakers. South of the bridge on the Virginia side, you can glide into **Dyke Marsh Wildlife Preserve** (Ⓦwww.nps.gov /gwmp/dyke-marsh.htm), a freshwater wetland home to osprey, blue heron, and many other birds.

Rentals, as you'd expect, vary in price with the size and type of boat, with discounted rates offered for booking an entire day. Kayaks, canoes, and rowboats go for anywhere from $10 per hour to $50 per day. **Sailboats** range from $10 to $20 per hour (though you may find that there's a two-hour minimum rental) to $150 per day. As rental service tends to be seasonal (March–Nov), you'd do well to call in advance in early spring or late fall before heading to the waterfront.

Boat rentals

Fletcher's Boat House 4940 Canal Rd NW, Georgetown Ⓣ202/244-0461, Ⓦwww .fletchersboathouse.com. Rents rowboats, canoes, and bikes and sells bait and tackle to the fishing crowd.

Jack's Boats 3500 K St NW, Georgetown Ⓣ202/337-9642. Located under the Key Bridge. Rents canoes, kayaks, and rowboats April–Oct.

Thompson Boat Center 2900 Virginia Ave NW, Georgetown Ⓣ202/333-9543, Ⓦwww .thompsonboatcenter.com. Single and double kayaks, canoes, and recreational and racing rowing shells, plus bikes.

Canoeing and kayaking

Atlantic Kayak Company Ⓣ301/292-6455 or 1-800/297-0066, Ⓦwww.atlantickayak.com.

Kayak tours along the Potomac, including 2.5-hour sunset tours highlighting Georgetown's bridges and monuments or the Dyke Marsh Wildlife area ($40–55 each). Also moonlight tours, full-day trips, and overnight excursions to wildlife areas. No experience necessary; all equipment included.

Outdoor Excursions Boonsboro, MD ☎ 1-800/775-2925, ⊛ www.outdoorexcursions .com. Located below Great Falls, with rafting ($40–50) and tubing ($34) trips, plus white-water kayaking and sea-kayaking instruction (each $98 per day) – the latter on the Chesapeake Bay, near Annapolis.

Sailing

Mariner Sailing School at Belle Haven Marina off George Washington Parkway, Alexandria, VA ☎ 703/768-0018, ⊛ www.saildc.com. Rentals include canoes, kayaks, and rowboats, plus Flying Scot and Sunfish sailboats. A 34ft C&C sloop is available for charter ($90/hour including captain). Also offers sailing instruction.

Washington Sailing Marina 1 Marina Drive, George Washington Memorial Parkway, Alexandria, VA ☎ 703/548-9027, ⊛ www .washingtonsailingmarina.com. Seasonal sailboat rentals (by reservation only). Also rents bikes. Located along the Mount Vernon Trail.

Spectator sports

Although they're not as rabid as the red-blooded fanatics in New York and Philadelphia, DC's sports-crazed fans still make a good show – the Redskins have sold out their games for years to come and even get politicians begging for tickets. Recent years have brought other new franchises as well: the Nationals (baseball), DC United (soccer), and Mystics (women's basketball) have given the capital something new to cheer – or boo, this being the East Coast.

An outing to a sporting event can be expensive, however, once the cost of tickets, snacks, and beer are tallied. Seats for Capitals and Wizards games – professional hockey and basketball, respectively – can run as high as $100, though admission to soccer matches and WNBA games tends to be much cheaper. Buy your tickets through Ticketmaster (☎ 202/432-SEAT, ⊛ www .ticketmaster.com) or directly through the team's or stadium's box office. If going to the game in person isn't your thing, you can always head to a downtown sports bar and catch your team on television – or in the case of *ESPN Zone* (see p.300), some two hundred of them.

Baseball

The capital was without a **baseball** team after the Washington Senators packed their bags for Texas in 1971. However, local politicians and business leaders clamored for a team for many years, and in 2005 succeeded in acquiring the Montreal Expos – now rechristened the **Washington Nationals** (☎ 202/675-NATS, ⊛ nationals.mlb.com; April–Oct season; tickets $10–90). The team moved into its splashy new stadium, Nationals Park, on the Waterfront in 2008, and tickets may be scarce in the next few years, regardless of whether the squad is any good.

As an alternative, you can head up the road to cheer for the **Baltimore Orioles** (☎ 410/685-9800, ⊛ www .theorioles.com; tickets $8–80), whose downtown Camden Yards offers a chance to catch a baseball game in a prime setting. Built in 1992, the stylish red-brick stadium is a throwback to the classic parks of the early twentieth century, and the design has proved so popular that cities across the country have used it as a template for old-fashioned fields of their own.

Basketball

Now that basketball legend Michael Jordan's days of playing with, and

Camden Yards 333 W Camden St, Baltimore, MD ☏1-888/848-BIRD, ⊛www
.theorioles.com. Baltimore Orioles baseball.

FedEx Field 1600 Raljon Rd, Landover, MD ☏301/276-6050, ⊛www.redskins.com
/fedexfield. Redskins football.

Nationals Park 1st St SE at S Capitol St, Waterfront ☏202/675-NATS, ⊛nationals
.mlb.com; Navy Yard Metro. Nationals baseball.

RFK Stadium 2400 E Capitol St SE, Southeast ☏703/478-6600, ⊛www
.rfkstadium.com; Stadium-Armory Metro. DC United soccer.

Verizon Center 601 F St NW, Old Downtown ☏202/628-3200, ⊛www
.verizoncenter.com; Gallery Place–Chinatown Metro; see p.177. Wizards and
Mystics basketball, Capitals hockey.

partly owning, the **Washington Wizards** (☏202/661-5050, ⊛www.nba.com/wizards; Nov–April season) are over, the capital is left with just another mediocre sports squad. Simply put, the best reason to show up is to catch one of the NBA's powerhouses rolling into the Verizon Center to push the team around. For this you can expect to pay extra; tickets average $10–105, but skew toward the higher end when there's a good (Spurs) team on the hardwood.

In summer, the focus swings to the **Washington Mystics** (☏202/661-5050, ⊛www.wnba.com/mystics; June–Aug season; tickets $10–60), DC's pro women's team. Despite struggling since the inception of the WNBA in 1997, the Mystics draw one of the largest crowds in the league to the Verizon Center.

If you're really interested in seeing a solid b-ball squad take to the floor, you'll have to look beyond the pro ranks to the **Georgetown Hoyas** (☏202/687-HOYA, ⊛www.guhoyas.com; tickets $5–28), the dominant team from the mid-1980s, which has recently had another good run of success. Up the road in College Park, Maryland, just beyond the DC border, the **Maryland Terrapins** (☏301/314-7070, ⊛www.umterps.com; tickets $5–35) put on a fine show for their young student fans and alumni at the **Comcast Center**. They won the

Atlantic Coast Conference in 2004 but haven't done much since.

Football

The **Washington Redskins** (☏301/276-6050, ⊛www.redskins.com; Sept–Dec season; tickets $50–100-plus) are the dominant obsession of the capital's sports fans. One of American football's oldest franchises, the team has also been one of the most successful since arriving in DC in 1937, with a total of five championships under its belt – the most recent in 1992. It made the playoffs in 2008, but an early exit prompted its coach Joe Gibbs to abruptly resign. Redskins games, played at 91,000-seat FedEx Field in Landover, MD, remain among DC's hardest tickets to snag – indeed, tickets are sold by the season only and the waiting list is a decade long. So, unless you're prepared to pay ridiculous prices to scalpers, or know someone in DC with an extra ticket, chances are slim that you'll see the 'Skins in action except on TV.

Hockey

The Verizon Center's other main tenant, hockey's **Washington Capitals** (☏202/397-SEAT, ⊛www.washingtoncapitals.com; Oct–April season; tickets $10–95), has been even more disappointing than basketball's Wizards. The Caps have yet to win the coveted Stanley Cup since they joined the league in the 1970s (though they did reach the championship round in 1998), and it looks as if they'll be among the league's cellar-dwellers for many more years to come.

Soccer

The city's only major-league soccer team, **DC United** (☏202/587-5000; ⓦ www.dcunited.com; March–Nov season; $20–50), is among the most successful in the United States. Since the inaugural MLS season in 1996, the team has won the title four times (last in 2004) and was also the first American club to win the CONCACAF Champions' Cup (1998), the major competition for clubs from North and Central America and the Caribbean. The team has fallen off slightly in recent years, but average home attendance is still around 25,000.

Kids' DC

For **children**, there may be no friendlier or more accommodating major city in the nation, or perhaps the world, than Washington DC. Unlike some cities, such as Orlando, Florida, that offer designated family-friendly attractions such as theme parks but are otherwise hit-or-miss, there are practically no significant areas where **children** are off-limits in DC. Indeed, you can bring a tot to practically any museum, historic mansion, art exhibit, memorial, monument, or institution without the staff batting an eyelash. In fact, the District is ruled by children to such a degree that you might find some of its major sights – especially museums on the National Mall – unbearable because of it. Certain neighborhoods, such as Adams Morgan, Shaw, and Dupont Circle, are notable for their relative lack of rug rats pounding the pavement – "relative" lack because there's no place where tourists and their kids are entirely absent.

Instead of dividing Washington into adult- and kid-oriented zones, it's more useful to consider the breakdown between places catering to mature, thoughtful

Practicalities

Given the broad scope of children's activities in the nation's capital, it's not too surprising that kids are accommodated in various ways when it comes to actually staying in and visiting the city. As for **hotels**, you may find that younger children (12 and under) are sometimes allowed to stay in their parents' room free or at a reduced rate; these and other facilities may even offer special games, entertainment, or diversions aimed at their apple-cheeked guests. The only way to know for sure is by calling or checking websites for each hotel.

Kids are generally accepted in most Washington **restaurants**, though such tolerance may be contingent on their maturity level and the hour of night – immature imps will be accorded little slack at an upscale restaurant or lounge at 10pm. In many cases, though, eateries may offer reduced-rate meals to children, or even a separate menu filled with all kinds of kid-friendly, if not exactly healthful, favorites like peanut butter and jelly sandwiches and macaroni and cheese.

One of the reasons DC is so popular with families and others with kids in tow is because so many sights and attractions are free. The Smithsonian is noted for charging no admission at its facilities, as are places like the US Capitol, government parks, the White House, National Gallery of Art, and countless other museums, galleries, and parks. Where admission is charged, it's usually under $10 (except for the International Spy Museum) and children may even be given a break here, too, with reduced or half-price rates. The same is true when it comes to **transportation** in and around the District, with many operators charging lower rates for kids; to cite but one example, the Metro allows two very young kids (age 4 and under) to ride free with an adult without paying a fare; see ⓦ www.wmata.com for details.

young visitors and those throwing open their gates to all manner of screaming urchins. Even childless adult couples will find no difficulty in frequenting sights attended by the former, while the latter are apt to drive even parents with bountiful families to distraction. What follows, then, is a short overview of the best and most appropriate places to bring kids in DC, keeping in mind the above considerations, as well as the fact that children are welcomed almost everywhere in town – outside of bars and clubs, of course.

Museums

Ground zero for kids in DC is undoubtedly the **National Mall**, and in some stretches school groups, Bible-study clans, huge families, and random toddlers are so thick on the ground you can barely wade through them – especially during the high season. That said, there's a definite delineation between Mall museums aimed at inquisitive young learners and those designed more as giant playpens. In the former category, institutions like the **National Gallery of Art**, the **Hirshhorn Museum**, and the national museums of **Asian Art**, **African Art**, and the **American Indian** are excellent spots to educate the mind and get a sense of American and international art and culture; some even provide pamphlets or guides aimed at young patrons. By contrast, the national museums of **Natural History** , **American History**, and **Air and Space** are chaotic environments where ill-behaved hellions often run amok with interactive exhibits and hands-on displays; it's not always so frenetic, of course, but with few museum staff members or adult chaperones around to stop them, the brattier kids usually hold sway.

Away from the Mall, the other major sight that attracts all kinds of young enthusiasts is the **International Spy Museum,** which entices visitors with its displays of Cold War gizmos and exotic weaponry; unlike the Mall museums, though, this one isn't free, and is among the priciest in town. Also around the Penn Quarter, the splashy new **Madame Tussaud's DC** wax museum and the **Newseum**

may capture some kids' imagination with their celebrity waxworks and acres of TV screens, respectively. Only older kids may be able to sit still for the educational **Koshland Science Museum**, **National Building Museum**, or **National Postal Museum**, however.

At other scattered locations around DC, the museums are aimed at even more mature children, or at least those with an appreciation or sense of history and art. The **Renwick** and **Corcoran** galleries and the **National Portrait** and **American Art** museums will be enjoyed most by kids whose parents or guardians take an active role in guiding them through the displays. Finally, the **National Geographic Society's Explorers' Hall** is off the beaten path a bit from the major attractions (though not from the major hotels), and offers intelligent, kid-friendly exhibits focusing on the environment, medicine, science, and world cultures.

Historic sites

Most **historic sites** – be they mansions, monuments, or memorials – can be appreciated by a young audience, and as with the museums, many of these big names are located on the Mall. Typically, the **presidential memorials** (Jefferson, Lincoln, and FDR) are fairly wide-open, so children's behavior can be less inhibited than it would be inside. However, the war memorials demand a certain sort of quietude and reverence – which can be in irritatingly short supply around some high-traffic sites like the **Vietnam Veterans Memorial**, where chatty schoolkids are routinely told to hush by adults mourning family members listed on the wall. The same is true to an even greater degree at **Arlington National Cemetery,** where the solemn tone is occasionally broken by unsupervised children yelling or running around the grounds – although this type of activity is quickly stopped by rangers when spotted.

There are countless other historic sites in the city where well-behaved kids with a knack for learning can find interest and edification – these include **Dumbarton Oaks**, **Tudor Place**, and the **C&O Canal** in Georgetown; the **Woodrow Wilson** and **Anderson** houses around Dupont Circle; the **US Supreme Court** and **Folger Shakespeare Library** on Capitol Hill; **Ford's Theatre** in Old Downtown; and, further afield, **Gunston Hall**, **Mount Vernon**, and **Old Town Alexandria**. Almost all children and their parents will want to visit the **US Capitol**, with its huge new visitor center, and the **White House** – though at the latter, you're well advised to have a backup plan (preferably including some of the above sights) in the event that tours are canceled due to some unforeseen security threat.

Parks and gardens

Aside from the National Mall itself, the District's assorted **parks and gardens** afford a welcome respite from overdosing on history, art, and culture. Here, beleaguered parents can let their unruly spawn run wild amid forested surroundings, or spread out on flowing lawns and hillsides once they've tired themselves out. The city's urban park squares near the White House – such as Lafayette and Franklin – are not the best places for this sort of activity, so you'll have to venture further out. Good choices for

▲ Kids taking a break at the US Botanic Garden

nature-based activity – which may involve bicycling, hiking, water activities, or even Frisbee-playing, depending on the site – include **West and East Potomac parks**, the **Ellipse**, **Theodore Roosevelt Island**, the **Mount Vernon Trail**, **Georgetown waterfront**, and especially **Rock Creek Park**. Other nature-oriented locations are more contemplative in character, less for burning off energy than taking in the natural splendor; these include the **National Arboretum**, which has the added historical attraction of the Capitol Columns; **Kenilworth Aquatic Gardens**; the **US Botanic Garden**, and **Green Spring Gardens Park**.

Another outdoor spot children will inevitably want to see is the **National Zoological Park**, which has the added benefit of free admission, as with all Smithsonian facilities. The National Aquarium, however, is best avoided – the cramped fish tanks and bureaucratic hallways of the Commerce Building are hardly the best places to show off nature in all its glory.

Shops and galleries

N o one really comes to DC to **shop**, and most visitors content themselves with buying a few trinkets or T-shirts at museum stores or government buildings. For those who really want to spend, though, there are malls in **Friendship Heights**, on the border with Maryland, among other places. Beyond this, the best areas for browsing are Adams Morgan, Dupont Circle, Georgetown, and around **Eastern Market**, where arts-and-crafts shops coexist with specialty book and music stores and student-oriented hang-outs. **Adams Morgan** has a strong ethnic flair, while in **Shaw and Logan Circle** a number of hipster boutiques have begun to crop up amid the funky bars, nightclubs, and fringe theaters. Across the river, you'll find a fair share of retailers in **Alexandria**, with many specializing in antiques and arts and crafts, and in the malls of **Arlington**.

The shopping heart has been ripped out of Old Downtown, however, as almost all the major **department stores** have given up the ghost. This situation is slowly improving with new retail units around the Verizon Center, but for the foreseeable future you're best off at one of the mega-malls on the outskirts of the city, where you'll find Nordstrom, Saks Fifth Avenue, Bloomingdale's, and Macy's. Only Filene's Basement has maintained its bargain-priced main outpost

▲ Hand puppets for sale at the Textile Museum gift shop

in the city, at 1133 Connecticut Ave NW, New Downtown (☎202/872-8430), while having a few other locations in the malls as well.

Usual store hours are Monday through Saturday 10am to 7pm; some have extended Thursday-night hours. In Georgetown, Adams Morgan, and Dupont Circle many stores open on Sunday, too.

Arts, crafts, and antiques

The only indigenous local craft is politics, but specialist **arts-and-crafts** stores in DC let you take home a piece of historic memorabilia or American Victoriana if you wish. The richest pickings are in Dupont Circle; Georgetown, which also has a run of antiques shops; and Old Town Alexandria, loaded with antiques/bric-a-brac places aimed at the weekend visitor market. Another great spot to poke around for arts, crafts, and other funky finds is the weekend flea market held at Eastern Market (see p.120). For works of art, visit the **galleries** of Dupont Circle and those in New and Old Downtown.

Appalachian Spring 1415 Wisconsin Ave NW, Georgetown ☎202/337-5780; **Union Station, 50 Massachusetts Ave NE** ☎202/682-0505; **Union Station Metro.** A colorful array of handmade ceramics, jewelry, rugs, glassware, kitchenware, quilts, toys, and other eclectic examples of American craftwork.

Art & Soul 225 Pennsylvania Ave SE, Capitol Hill ☎202/548-0105; **Capitol South Metro.** Handmade clothes and contemporary ceramics, toys, and crafts by more than two hundred regional artists, but mainly good for its eclectic selection of jewelry.

Artcraft Collection 132 King St, Alexandria, VA ☎703/299-6616; **King Street Metro.** A strange and impressive collection of handcrafted artifacts, like painted furniture, exquisitely detailed jewelry, oddball sculptures, anthropomorphic teapots, and iridescent vases.

Beadazzled 1507 Connecticut Ave NW, Dupont Circle ☎202/265-2323; **Dupont Circle Metro.** New and antique beads from all over the world, for which you'll pay a premium, plus ethnic jewelry, folk art, and related books.

Hoopla 2314 18th St NW, Adams Morgan ☎202/797-0730; **Woodley Park–Zoo Metro.** Handcrafted glassworks, designer attire and purses, offbeat adornments (like a bicycle-chain bracelet), and various novelties are but a few of the things that give this alternative-minded shop its cool cachet.

Indian Craft Shop Department of the Interior, 1849 C St NW, Foggy Bottom ☎202/208-4056; **Farragut West Metro.** One of the city's best gift boutiques in a rather bleak stretch for shopping, selling rugs, crafts, beadwork, jewelry, and pottery by artisans from native tribes in the US.

Old Print Gallery 1220 31st St NW, Georgetown ☎202/965-1818. A favorite local seller of historic landscapes, antique maps, old charts, and prints, plus political cartoons, DC scenes, and early-American artisan work.

Wake Up Little Suzie 3409 Connecticut Ave, Upper Northwest ☎202/244-0700; **Cleveland Park Metro.** Trinket emporium with a broad range of interesting items, including homemade jewelry and ceramics, arty novelty items, curious puppets, and more.

Beauty supplies and services

Blue Mercury 1619 Connecticut Ave NW, Dupont Circle ☎202/462-1300; **Dupont Circle Metro.** If you find yourself desperate for fancy face creams, hair products, scents, and salves, this is your shop. There's also a spa for on-the-spot pampering.

Celadon 1180 F St NW, Old Downtown ☎202/347-3333; **Metro Center Metro.** Swanky downtown salon good for getting your hair cut, styled, or dyed, your brows plucked, or your entire look made over.

Norbert Hair Designers 1050 Connecticut Ave NW, New Downtown ☎202/466-2111; **Farragut West Metro.** Along with hair styling, this upscale salon offers a laundry list of services – from acid peels and body bronzing to lip, bikini, and back waxing, to French manicures and pedicures. Just have a full wallet at the ready.

Sephora 3065 M St NW, Georgetown ☎202/338-5644. French makeup boutique offering fragrances, well-being products, and brand-name cosmetics.

Skin Beauty Lounge 404 8th St SE, east of Capitol Hill ☎202/543-6993; Eastern Market Metro. Affordable beauty services that draw a loyal crowd for the various waxing, facials, manicures and pedicures, and body salves and treatments on offer.

Books

Washington's array of **bookstores** is one of the high points of its shopping scene: you'll find a place to suit you whether you're looking for discounted new novels or political science tomes, superstores with coffee bars or cozy second-hand shops. The weekly *City Paper* and Friday's *Washington Post* list bookstore lectures, concerts, readings, and events. Keep in mind that, as everywhere, the Internet has crippled some independent sellers, leaving behind the larger dealers that can afford to compete on price.

General

Barnes & Noble 3040 M St NW, Georgetown ☎202/965-9880; 555 12th St NW, Old Downtown ☎202/347-0176; Metro Center Metro. Familiar chain-store heavyweight with three floors, offering sizable discounts and one of the better crime/mystery sections in the city. Many other area locations; visit ⓦwww.bn.com for full list.

Books a Million 11 Dupont Circle NW ☎202/319-1374; Dupont Circle Metro. Dupont Circle bookseller with a broad selection of books and magazines that's handy for its central location to the tourist hotels, though it's a chain and the title selection is not very adventurous.

Borders 1800 L St NW, New Downtown ☎202/466-4999; Farragut North Metro. Huge chain bookstore with voluminous selection of magazines, newspapers, and discount books, a full CD and tape selection, plus readings and various events. Other area locations listed at ⓦwww.bordersstores.com.

Bridge Street Books 2814 Pennsylvania Ave NW, Georgetown ☎202/965-5200. Independent seller offering volumes on politics, literature, history, philosophy, and film, with author readings of fiction and poetry.

Chapters Literary Bookstore 455 11th St NW, Old Downtown ☎202/737-5553; Federal Triangle Metro. Downtown spot with a high-quality selection of poetry and fiction titles and a program of readings and events.

Kramerbooks 1517 Connecticut Ave NW, Dupont Circle ☎202/387-1400; Dupont Circle

Metro. Esteemed city institution, as well as a fun place to hang out, with a very good and broad general selection, a great café-restaurant called *Afterwords Café* (see p.282), and long hours (24hr on weekends).

Olsson's Books and Records 1307 19th St NW, Dupont Circle ☎202/785-1133; 2211 Wilson Blvd, Arlington, VA ☎703/525-4227. High-speed Internet access ($6/hr) at 418 7th St NW, Old Downtown ☎202/638-7610; and 106 S Union St, Alexandria, VA ☎703/684-0077. Massive range in one of Washington's oldest independent bookstore chains; it's a great spot to browse. Other pluses include tapes and CDs, DVD rentals at most branches, regular book signings, and a café in the 7th Street branch.

Politics & Prose 5015 Connecticut Ave NW, Upper Northwest ☎202/364-1919; no close Metro. Located in the northern reaches of the District, a good independent bookstore/coffee shop with one of the best programs of author appearances and readings in the city.

Vertigo Books 7346 Baltimore Ave, College Park, MD ☎301/779-9300; College Park Metro. Covers everything from politics and social and cultural studies to modern literature. Regular signings and readings, too.

Secondhand

Bartleby's Books 1132 29th St NW, Georgetown ☎202/298-0486. Focuses on American history, law, and politics, with a strong antiquarian bent, and with a good array of art, literature, poetry, and other books as well.

Bryn Mawr Lantern Bookshop 3241 P St NW, Georgetown ☎202/333-3222. This rare and vintage book dealer has a great general selection of secondhand titles, all donated – though it's open only in the afternoon.
Idle Time Books 2467 18th St NW, Adams Morgan ☎202/232-4774; Woodley Park–Zoo Metro. Local favorite for used and vintage titles, with a bent toward fiction, left-leaning politics, science, and the offbeat. Open until 10pm daily.
Red Sky Books 4318 Fessenden St NW, Upper Northwest ☎202/363-9147; Friendship Heights Metro. A fascinating grab bag of material at this bookseller, which specializes in eclectic

subjects like music and songbooks, art and architecture (especially African art), craft-works, photography, travel, and other topics.
Second Story Books 2000 P St NW, Dupont Circle ☎202/659-8884; Dupont Circle Metro. Large range of used books, antiques, and records; also a good spot to find out what's going on in the city, with bulletin boards crammed with flyers for upcoming events and stacks of local papers and cultural calendars.

Official culture

AIA Bookstore 1735 New York Ave NW, Foggy Bottom ☎202/626-7475; Farragut West Metro.

Malls

The **malls** around downtown DC are all pretty uninspiring; for better ones (and lower local sales taxes) you'll have to head for the suburbs. There's direct Metro access to the stores at Friendship Heights, Crystal City, and Pentagon City that are listed below. Opening hours are usually Monday through Saturday from 10am to 8pm, Sunday from noon to 6pm.

Downtown

Old Post Office Pavilion, 1100 Pennsylvania Ave NW ☎202/289-4224; Federal Triangle Metro; see also p.167.

The Shops at National Place, 1331 Pennsylvania Ave NW ☎202/662-1250; Metro Center Metro.

Union Station Mall, 50 Massachusetts Ave NE ☎202/371-9441; Union Station Metro; see also p.122.

Georgetown

Shops at Georgetown Park, 3222 M St NW ☎202/298-5577; Foggy Bottom–GWU Metro or Georgetown Shuttle (see p.232).

Out of town

Chevy Chase Pavilion, 5345 Wisconsin Ave NW ☎202/686-5335; Friendship Heights Metro.

Crystal City Shops, Crystal Drive at Jefferson Davis Hwy, Arlington, VA ☎703/922-4636; Crystal City Metro.

Fashion Center at Pentagon City, 1100 S Hayes St, Arlington, VA ☎703/415-2400; Pentagon City Metro.

Landmark Mall 5801 Duke St, Alexandria, VA ☎703/354-8405; shuttle via Dash Bus (route #AT7 via King St.); see ⓦwww.dashbus.com.

Mazza Gallerie, 5300 Wisconsin Ave NW ☎202/966-6114; Friendship Heights Metro.

Potomac Mills Outlet Mall, 2700 Potomac Mills Circle, Prince William, VA ☎1-800/826-4557; Prince William Metro shuttle from Franconia-Springfield Metro station; see ⓦwww.prtctransit.org/omniride/schedules.php.

Tysons Corner Center, 1961 Chain Bridge Rd, McLean, VA ☎703/847-7300; Capital Beltway (Hwy 495) exit 47B.

Tysons Galleria, 2001 International Drive, McLean, VA ☎703/827-7700; Capital Beltway (Hwy 495) exit 46A.

White Flint Mall, 11301 Rockville Pike, Bethesda, MD ☎301/468-5777; shuttle from White Flint Metro; see ⓦwww.nbtc.org/related.htm.

Operated by the American Institute of Architects, this is a spot to visit if you're interested in local or national architecture, or to learn the difference between Federal, Georgian, and Colonial Revival building styles.

InfoShop in the World Bank, 1818 H St NW, Foggy Bottom ☎ 202/458-4500; Farragut West Metro. An excellent institutional bookstore with fine volumes on finance, education, international relations, the developing world, and the environment, with many educational videos, too.

Library of Congress Shop 101 Independence Ave SE, Jefferson Bldg ☎ 1-888/682-3557; Capitol South Metro. The esteemed institution's own worthy bookseller, which offers volumes on the nation's art, folklore, history, geography, and culture, as well as glossy books about the presidents.

US Government Bookstore 710 N Capitol St, Old Downtown ☎ 202/512-0132; Union Station Metro. Official tomes and publications loaded with all the facts and figures you could ever want, at the central government printing-office bookstore in the nation.

Washington Law Books 1900 G St NW, Foggy Bottom ☎ 202/223-5543; Farragut West Metro. As the name says, devoted to books on the legal system, as well as economics, political science, trade, and foreign relations. Bring a briefcase to look like you belong here.

ADC Map & Travel Center 1636 I St NW, New Downtown ☎ 202/628-2608; Farragut West Metro. Copious selection of helpful maps, atlases, foreign-language dictionaries, and travel guides.

Big Planet Comics 3145 Dumbarton Ave NW, Georgetown ☎ 202/342-1961. An extensive comic-book store specializing in alternative comics, manga, and graphic novels.

Card and Comic Collectorama 2008 Mount Vernon Ave, Alexandria, VA ☎ 703/548-3466. Worth a trip for its stock of ancient Disney memorabilia, long-forgotten trading cards, and rare comics, and all manner of other curious castoffs.

Lambda Rising 1625 Connecticut Ave NW, Dupont Circle ☎ 202/462-6969; Dupont Circle Metro. Extensively stocked gay and lesbian bookstore; see also p.319.

Reiter's 1990 K St NW, New Downtown ☎ 202/223-3327; Farragut North or Farragut West Metro. Books on business, computing, finance, engineering, and other professional and scientific topics.

Trover Shop 221 Pennsylvania Ave SE ☎ 202/547-BOOK; Capitol South Metro. Politics and current events are the name of the game at this Capitol Hill favorite, where you can browse among pols and staffers to find a good selection of periodicals, tomes, and treatises.

Clothing

The best areas for browsing for **clothing** are in New Downtown, along Connecticut Avenue; Dupont Circle, also along Connecticut; and Georgetown, along M Street and Wisconsin Avenue. Tucked among the ubiquitous Gaps and Banana Republics, you'll find a handful of unique boutiques worth a look. Even gentrifying Adams Morgan has begun to get in on the act, with a growing number of ultra-hip clothing shops appearing along 18th Street, amid the trendy bars and restaurants.

But nearly every serious shopper winds up heading to **Georgetown**, the District's retail epicenter. Here you'll find the greatest concentration of the national retail chains, as well as local boutiques and more exclusive shops. There are a few deals to be had here, though, with vendors setting up shop along the sidewalks to sell knock-off designer handbags and the like.

American in Paris 1225 King St, Alexandria, VA ☎ 703/519-8234; King Street Metro. One of the top spots in town to get your fix of fashionable European wear, as well as unique clothes from local designers, with a vigorous French bent and attitude.

Betsey Johnson 1319 Wisconsin Ave, Georgetown ☎ 202/338-4090. The upscale but whimsical creations of this well-known, rather manic designer of women's fashions call out from behind a colorful facade.

Betsy Fisher 1224 Connecticut Ave, New Downtown ⓣ202/785-1975; Farragut North Metro. Sophisticated women's attire, from conservative to hip, comes with sage advice from the owner herself. Popular with urban professionals on the prowl for chic designer names.

Donna Lewis 309 Cameron St, Alexandria, VA ⓣ703/548-2452; King Street Metro. Hip yet classy women's clothes, and a handful of Italian bags and shoes. Prices are on the upper end.

Kenneth Cole 1100 S Hayes St, Fashion Centre at Pentagon City, Arlington, VA ⓣ703/415-3522; Pentagon City Metro. Big name for upper-end men's and women's shoes, belts, sunglasses, jewelry, and jackets.

Muleh 1831 14th St NW, Shaw ⓣ202/667-3440; U Street–Cardozo Metro. An essential stop for those living the elite DC dream, this clothier has a select range of the latest designer fashions (for predictably stiff prices) as well as smart housewares, lamps, and furniture.

Nuevo Mundo 313 Cameron St, Alexandria, VA ⓣ703/549-0040; King Street Metro. Globetrotting mother-daughter team offers stylish clothes, unique "wearable art" from around the world (jewelry, accessories, etc.), and other mildly exotic apparel.

Pua Naturally 701 Pennsylvania Ave NW, Old Downtown ⓣ202/347-4543; Archives–Navy Memorial Metro. Upmarket boutique brings a splash of Nepalese and Indian flair to downtown DC, with fine handwoven skirts, jackets, and scarves, most of which hail from South Asia.

Saks Jandel 5510 Wisconsin Ave, Chevy Chase, MD ⓣ301/652-2250; Friendship Heights Metro. Women's formal wear and cocktail dresses from noted designer collections.

Sugar 1633 Wisconsin Ave NW, Georgetown ⓣ202/333-5331. As the name suggests, girlish and precocious skirts, tops, jeans, and dresses from a range of big-name and up-and-coming designers.

Funky clothing

Backstage 545 8th St SE, Capitol Hill ⓣ202/544-5744; Eastern Market Metro. Whether you're at a loss on Halloween or looking for an elaborate disguise, this costume shop – teeming with wigs, boas, and cat suits – may be able to help. Also sells makeup, masks, dance shoes, and books on the theater.

Coup de Foudre 1001 Pennsylvania Ave NW, Old Downtown ⓣ202/393-0878; Federal Triangle Metro. Top-shelf lingerie with a French cut and attitude, with European-style bikinis, bridal undergarments, and accessories also on offer.

Imagine Artwear 1124 King St, Alexandria, VA ⓣ703/548-1461; King Street Metro. Eclectic array of fashions bridging the gap between the aesthetic and the functional, including brightly colored and detailed garments that could pass for tapestries, handcrafted jewelry, and more.

Leather Rack 1723 Connecticut Ave NW, Dupont Circle ⓣ202/797-7401; Dupont Circle Metro. A bevy of chaps, vests, and boots, plus fetish items and sexual accessories too bizarre to describe.

Screaming Denim 2409 18th St NW, Adams Morgan ⓣ202/745-0144; Woodley Park–Zoo Metro. A range of fancy jeans – from simple but tasteful cuts to the eponymous loud and flashy variety – that often come with price tags that won't make you gasp.

Men's clothing

Beau Monde 1814 K St NW, New Downtown ⓣ202/466-7070; Farragut North Metro. The place on K Street to help you look like you belong here, amid the high-powered lawyers and lobbyists. Somber suits and ties and a stylish range of upscale accessories will give you a flush and fearsome appearance.

Commonwealth 1781 Florida Ave NW, Adams Morgan ⓣ202/265-1830; Dupont Circle Metro. Smart streetwear that includes some of the region's top brands, with splashy sneakers and hats, leather wallets, and a full range of T-shirts and jeans.

The District Line 1250 Wisconsin Ave NW, Georgetown ⓣ202/558-7014. British-oriented styles that encompass top names like Fred Petty and Oliver Spencer and attire that includes trendy and modern shirts, sweaters, suits, and accessories.

Everett Hall 5301 Wisconsin Ave NW, Upper Northwest ⓣ202/362-0191; Friendship Heights Metro. Big-name designer for men's Italian suits and contemporary sportswear, outfitting countless high rollers, celebrities, and athletes – and you, too, if you have the money.

Reiss 1254 Wisconsin Ave NW, Georgetown ☎202/944-8566. Fashion from England and the Continent for men and women, all of it fairly chic and pricey, with tasteful suits and dresses to help you keep up with the DC in-crowd.

Universal Gear 1529 14th St NW, Logan Circle ☎202/319-0136. Gay men's pit stop for current fashion, with T-shirts, swimwear, casual duds, and a full line of skivvies.

Secondhand and vintage

Annie Creamcheese 3279 M St NW, Georgetown ☎202/298-5555. A fun seller of vintage wear that offers scads of items from countless decades, including grandmotherly frocks, ultra-mod jackets and boots, stylish cocktail dresses, and various retro T-shirts and jewelry.

Meeps Vintage Fashionette 2104 18th St NW, Adams Morgan ☎202/265-6546; Woodley Park–Zoo Metro. A neighborhood favorite that offers a cool and groovy selection of men's and women's vintage attire, some of which dates as far back as the 1940s.

Nana 1528 U St NW, Shaw ☎202/667-6955; U Street–Cardozo Metro. One of numerous upscale retailers that have been crowding into the U Street corridor lately, this one with a pleasing blend of new and vintage dresses, hats, jewelry, and accessories, some of it for affordable prices.

Secondhand Rose 1516 Wisconsin Ave NW, Georgetown ☎202/337-3378. A fine spot to pick up the swanky designer dresses, suits, and sunglasses you've seen the DC political glitterati wearing – only for a fraction of the price they paid when the duds were new.

Secondi 1702 Connecticut Ave NW, Dupont Circle ☎202/667-1122; Dupont Circle Metro. Agreeable selection of high-flying designer names, marked down to a more affordable level.

Shoes and accessories

Commander Salamander 1420 Wisconsin Ave NW, Georgetown ☎202/337-2265. Funky T-shirts, sneakers, sportswear, wigs, gimcrack jewelry, and various eclectic and oddball accessories.

Fleet Feet 1841 Columbia Rd NW, Adams Morgan ☎202/387-3888; Woodley Park–Zoo Metro. Provides the proper shoes for running, walking, playing soccer, or doing aerobics, and lets you test-drive the pair outside. An assortment of sports clothes and accessories is also on hand.

Proper Topper 1350 Connecticut Ave NW, New Downtown ☎202/842-3055; Farragut North Metro. A sleek spot with a hip and stylish assortment of purses, bags, makeup, hats, watches, knickknacks, and jewelry. A second location in Georgetown at 3213 P St NW ☎202/333-6200.

Shake Your Booty 2439 18th St NW, Adams Morgan ☎202/518-8205; Woodley Park–Zoo Metro. Hip shoes, zesty jewelry, and one-of-a-kind accessories add a kick to the District's limp shoe scene.

Museum and gallery stores

Virtually all of DC's museums – in particular the Smithsonians – have well-stocked **gift shops**; see the relevant pages for transport and museum details. Note that every other major attraction – from the US Capitol to the White House – also has its own gift shop, selling enough name-emblazoned souvenirs to satisfy even the most avid collectors.

Arthur M. Sackler Gallery 1050 Independence Ave SW, National Mall ☎202/357-4880; Smithsonian Metro. Jewelry, prints, fabrics, Asian art, ceramics, rugs, beads, and calligraphy.

Bureau of Engraving and Printing 14th and C sts SW, south of the Mall ☎1-800/456-3408; Smithsonian Metro. Just the place for that ideal DC gift: presidential engravings, prints of the city, copies of famous texts, even bags of shredded cash.

International Spy Museum 800 F St NW, Old Downtown ☎1-866/779-6873; Gallery Place–Chinatown Metro. A full array of Cold War–style gadgets and devices to help you play spy, as well as toys, books, games, and trinkets based around the espionage trade, or at least the James Bond version of it.

National Air and Space Museum Independence Ave and 6th SW, National Mall ☎202/357-1387; Archives–Navy Memorial Metro. Fantastic array of air- and space-related goodies, from science-fiction books to ray guns and spaceman "ice cream."

National Gallery of Art Constitution Ave, between 3rd and 7th St NW, National Mall ☎202/842-6002 or 1-800/697-9350; L'Enfant Plaza Metro. Perhaps DC's best art shop, with thousands of books, prints, slides, posters, and postcards featuring famous artists and movements.

National Museum of African Art 950 Independence Ave SW, National Mall ☎202/786-2147; Smithsonian Metro. Rich and splendid displays of African arts and crafts, including fine fabrics, icons, and jewelry.

National Museum of American History 14th St and Constitution Ave NW, National Mall ☎202/633-1000; Federal Triangle Metro. Great souvenirs including music, books, T-shirts, kitchenware, ceramics, posters, toys, crafts, jewelry, and reproductions from the museum.

National Museum of Natural History 10th St NW and Constitution Ave, National Mall ☎202/633-1000; Federal Triangle Metro. Though crawling with kids, worth a visit for its huge selection of tomes relating to science, geology, biology, paleontology, and other related fields.

National Portrait Gallery/American Art Museum 8th St at F St NW, Old Downtown ☎202/633-5450; Gallery Place-Chinatown Metro. A splendid assortment of American images, from portraits of the presidents and archaic maps to art-reproduction notecards and posters to the usual T-shirts and tote bags.

Textile Museum 2320 S St NW, Kalorama ☎202/667-0441; Dupont Circle Metro. Unique T-shirts, ethnic fabrics, textile books, silks, cushion covers, ties, kimonos, and jewelry.

Music

CD Cellar 2614 Wilson Blvd, Arlington, VA ☎703/248-0635; Court House Metro. Thousands of CDs, DVDs, vinyl records, and even VHS tapes in stock, most of them used and affordable, with some rare and unexpected titles. Also at 709 West Broad St, Falls Church, VA ☎703/534-6318.

CD Warehouse 3001 M St NW, Georgetown ☎202/625-7101. Good across-the-board selection of used CDs, with some pretty decent prices and a few hard-to-find items too.

Crooked Beat 2318 18th St NW, Adams Morgan ☎202/483-2328; Woodley Park–Zoo Metro. Fine music dealer that tries to bring back the golden days of record stores, when the staff actually knew something about good indie, alternative, and even mainstream music and

could provide solid recommendations for the best choices in CD and vinyl.

DJ Hut 2010 P St NW, Dupont Circle ☎202/659-2010; Dupont Circle Metro. Caters to turntablists, with a bent toward funk, hip-hop, breakbeat, jungle, and so on.

Kemp Mill Music 1309 F St NW, Old Downtown ☎202/638-7077; Metro Center Metro. Local chain for mainstream and chart releases, as well as jazz, gospel, and dance music, often with good discounts.

Melody Records 1623 Connecticut Ave NW, Dupont Circle ☎202/232-4002; Dupont Circle Metro. Well-selected array of CDs and DVDs, with an accent on classical, jazz, and indie music, several listening stations, and a number of rarities and oddments.

Food and drink

Washington isn't exactly known for its sales emporiums of **food and drink**, though a few good places do stand out. Tasty **coffee**, at least, isn't hard to find – many of the coffee bars listed in the "Eating" chapter can sell you the beans. For quality **tea**, try one of *Teaism*'s branches (p.283 and p.288) or *Ching Ching Cha* (p.286) in Georgetown.

Old-style **markets** are thin on the ground: Eastern Market (p.336) is your best bet, while the Fish Wharf (p.134) has a great selection of Chesapeake Bay seafood. There are weekend farmers' markets in Adams Morgan and Dupont Circle in DC, Takoma Park, MD, and Alexandria and Arlington, VA.

For bread, you can't beat the *Breadline* (p.284) or *Firehook Bakery & Coffeehouse* (p.292). The best general deli is the splendid *Dean & Deluca* (p.286) in Georgetown, although Dupont Circle's homespun *Marvelous Market* (p.283) is a great local find; other solid delis are *Loeb's* (p.287), *Morty's* (p.292), and *Café Mozart* (p.289).

Specialty shops

Ginza 1721 Connecticut Ave NW, Dupont Circle ⓣ 202/332-7000; Dupont Circle Metro. Long-standing neighborhood favorite for all things Japanese, including books, toys, screens, woodblock prints, kimonos, and sandals.

Go Mama Go! 1809 14th St NW, Shaw ⓣ 202/299-0850; U Street–Cardozo Metro. Funky home-furnishings store featuring cool and upscale Asian-style art, wall hangings, glassworks and dinnerware, some of it designed by the store's owner.

Movie Madness 1083 Thomas Jefferson St NW, Georgetown ⓣ 202/337-7064. Thousands of movie posters, old and new, plus vintage advertising, celebrity pics, political bric-a-brac, and other visual oddments.

Music Box Center 1920 I St NW, New Downtown ⓣ 202/783-9399; Farragut West Metro. Nothing but sculptures, boxes, figurines, trinkets, and gizmos that play some variety of music, with hundreds of choices from the classically dainty to the heights of modern kitsch.

Pleasure Place 1710 Connecticut Ave NW, Dupont Circle ⓣ 202/483-3297; Dupont Circle Metro. As the name implies, the place to pick up gifts that (cleanly) revel in the hedonistic, from sex toys and gadgets to cheerfully perverse games and party supplies. Also at 1063 Wisconsin Ave NW, Georgetown ⓣ 202/333-8570.

Political Americana 1331 Pennsylvania Ave NW, Old Downtown ⓣ 202/737-7730; Federal Triangle Metro. A good spot to pick up everything from historic and topical buttons and bumper stickers to gifts, books, and videos from every side of the political scene.

Pulp 1803 14th St NW, Shaw ⓣ 202/462-7857; U Street–Cardozo Metro. Eye-popping, purple-fronted shop thick with trinkets and souvenirs, but best for its wide selection of greeting cards – from the mundane to the freakish – which it allows you to make, too, if you have the zeal for it.

Galleries

Most of the District's commercial art **galleries** host rotating exhibitions of paintings, prints, sculpture, photography, applied art, and folk art that you can view at no charge. The galleries listed below are some of the more notable; call for details of current shows or check the *City Paper* or the *Washington Post*'s "Weekend" section. There's also a monthly guide available in bookstores with comprehensive listings of DC's art galleries called *Galleries* (ⓦ www.artlineplus.com/gallerymagazine).

Downtown, the galleries along 7th Street NW specialize in the works of contemporary regional artists, though the major concentration of galleries is in Dupont Circle, where more than thirty are clustered in the area. Georgetown has a handful of good art galleries as well. Most are closed on Monday and many are also closed on Tuesday.

Downtown and Foggy Bottom

406 7th Street NW Archives–Navy Memorial or Gallery Place–Chinatown Metro. A group of galleries featuring the works of DC-area artists – paintings, sculpture, photographs, mixed-media pieces. One of the better galleries is Touchstone ⓣ 202/347-2787.

Arts Club of Washington 2017 I St NW ⓣ 202/331-7282; Foggy Bottom–GWU or Farragut West Metro. Eclectic exhibits of works by local artists; see also "Performing arts and film" chapter, p.311, for its occasional classical-music concerts.

George Washington University Brady Gallery, 805 21st St NW, 2nd Floor ⓣ 202/994-1525; and Dimock Gallery, Lower Lisner Auditorium, 730 21st St NW ⓣ 202/994-1525; Foggy Bottom–GWU Metro. Regular rotating shows by local, student, national, and international artists.

Guarsico Gallery 1120 22nd St NW ⓣ 202/333-8533; Foggy Bottom–GWU Metro. If you have bags of money to spend, this gallery in the Ritz-Carlton Hotel will help take some of it off your hands, offering minor (but still very expensive) paintings and sculpture from the past two hundred years of European and American art.

Long View Gallery 1302 9th St NW T202/232-4788; Mount Vernon Square–UDC Metro. Tasteful, somewhat austere modern sculpture, painting, and photography, with pieces created mostly by regional names. Zenith Gallery 413 7th St NW ☎202/783-2963; Archives–Navy Memorial or Gallery Place–Chinatown Metro. Prints, paintings, and sculpture (both traditional and more offbeat), many of which are by city-based artists.

Dupont Circle

Aaron Gallery 1717 Connecticut Ave NW ☎202/234-3311; Dupont Circle Metro. Abstract Expressionism is alive and well at this showcase for local artists devoted to using composition, color, and line in a variety of media.
Fondo del Sol Visual Arts Center 2112 R St NW ☎202/483-2777; Dupont Circle Metro. Nonprofit gallery-museum featuring Latino-Caribbean art; also hosts lectures, poetry, and performance art, and sponsors the DC Caribbean Festival (see p.322).
Gallery 10, Ltd. 1519 Connecticut Ave NW ☎202/232-3326; Dupont Circle Metro. The one gallery in the District where you can expect to be surprised, featuring a bevy of unusual and experimental pieces that span all kinds of media, from installations and video art to mixed-media sculptures and collage. Well worth a look.
Jane Haslem Gallery 2025 Hillyer Place ☎202/232-4644; Dupont Circle Metro. One of the brasher contemporary DC galleries, showcasing artists willing to experiment with form, color, and content in eye-opening ways, using a wide variety of media.
Kathleen Ewing Gallery 1767 P St NW ☎202/328-0955; Dupont Circle Metro. Highly regarded gallery featuring nineteenth- and twentieth-century photography, plus some multimedia works.
Marsha Mateyka Gallery 2012 R St NW ☎202/328-0088; Dupont Circle Metro. Contemporary painting and sculpture, leaning toward the abstract, by American and European artists.
Spectrum Gallery 1421 22nd St NW ☎202/833-1616; Dupont Circle Metro. Local artists' co-op with an eclectic selection of prints, photos, sculpture, and mixed media.
Studio Gallery 2108 R St NW ☎202/232-8734; Dupont Circle Metro. Established gallery that

appeals for its landscapes and abstracts (both painting and sculpture) by area artists.
Washington Printmakers' Gallery 1732 Connecticut Ave NW ☎202/332-7757; Dupont Circle Metro. Original prints by contemporary artists, plus monotypes, relief works, and other inventive uses of the print medium.

Georgetown

Addison/Ripley Gallery 1670 Wisconsin Ave NW ☎202/333-5180. Contemporary and tasteful fine art – oil paintings, photography, sculpture, and prints.
Cross Mackenzie Ceramic Arts 1054 31st St NW ☎202/333-7970. Art pottery in all of its forms, from whimsical and gently sardonic, to bizarre and quirky, to austere and abstract, at this must-see gallery for fans of modern ceramics.
Fine Art & Artists 2920 M St NW ☎202/965-0780. Pop and Abstract Expressionist art, with an emphasis on big international names from the 1960s and more contemporary minimalists, metal sculptors, and neo-abstract painters.
Prada Gallery 1030 Wisconsin Ave NW ☎202/342-0067. Contemporary art from local and regional artists working in a variety of media, with a bent toward abstraction, but with most forms and styles represented.

Other locations

Arts Afire 1117 King St, Alexandria, VA ☎703/838-9785; King Street Metro. Major dealer in art glass, with a full complement of work from regional and national designers on display, everything from jewelry and home decor to kaleidoscopes, vases, and trinkets.
Irvine Contemporary Art 1412 14th St NW, Logan Circle ☎202/332-8767. Broad, interesting selection of modern or contemporary paintings, prints, and other visual art.
Torpedo Factory Art Center 105 N Union St, Alexandria, VA ☎703/838-4565, ⓦwww.torpedofactory.org; King Street Metro. The central place for art in the Alexandria area, where three floors of galleries showcase contemporary work by more than eighty regional artists in a variety of media.
Village on Capitol Hill 705 N Carolina Ave SE ☎202/546-3040; Eastern Market Metro. Oddball set of art-related items, from abstract paintings to quirky sculptures made by international artisans to colorful hats and jewelry.

Out of
the City

Out of the City

Northern Virginia

espite its considerable historic allure, **Northern Virginia** is increasingly known for becoming one large suburban enclave housing commuters to Washington, DC, including such chic spots as McLean and Fairfax counties, home to a high proportion of US senators. Further south, the Anglophile heartland of Virginia's landed gentry – often called "Hunt Country" for residents' love of horses and fancy-dress blood sports – holds well-preserved historic estates, cottages, churches, barns, and taverns tucked away along the quiet back roads. It's all very popular with tourists, nowhere more so than **Mount Vernon**, the longtime home of George Washington, and the related estates of **Woodlawn Plantation** and **Gunston Hall**. To the west, **Manassas**, the site of the bloody battles of Bull Run, provides a good jumping-off point for a tour of the many preserved Civil War battlefields in the area, while to the south, **Fredericksburg** is a town full of Civil War legend and lore, with modern boutique amenities.

Mount Vernon

3200 George Washington Memorial Pkwy, Mount Vernon, VA ☎703/780-2000, ⓦ www.mountvernon.org.
Daily: April–Aug 8am–5pm; March & Sept–Oct 9am–5pm; Nov–Feb 9am–4pm. $13.

Set on a shallow bluff overlooking the broad Potomac River, sixteen miles south of Washington, DC, **Mount Vernon** is among the most attractive historic plantations in the country. George Washington lived on his beloved estate for forty years, during which he ran it as a thriving and progressive farm, anticipating the decline in Virginia's tobacco cultivation and planting instead grains and food crops with great success. When he died, it seemed only fitting that he be buried on its grounds, as his will directed; America's first president lies next to his wife, Martha, in the simple family tomb.

The estate is an extremely popular site for a day-trip, and summer weekends, especially, can be very busy. Come early or midweek, if you can, and allow at least two hours to see the house and grounds. You can't eat or drink here, but you're allowed to leave the estate to eat and then return without paying a second admission fee.

To reach Mount Vernon, go first to Huntington Metro (Yellow line) and then take Fairfax Connector Bus #101 (hourly; $1 ☎703/339-7200, ⓦ www .fairfaxcounty.gov/connector). It's an easy enough route, and takes only a half-hour. A cab from the Metro station costs $25 (call White Top Cab at ☎703/644-4500). Drivers can follow the George Washington Parkway from DC; there's free parking at the site. The Mount Vernon Trail (see p.252) ends here, too, after starting in Arlington, 18.5 miles away.

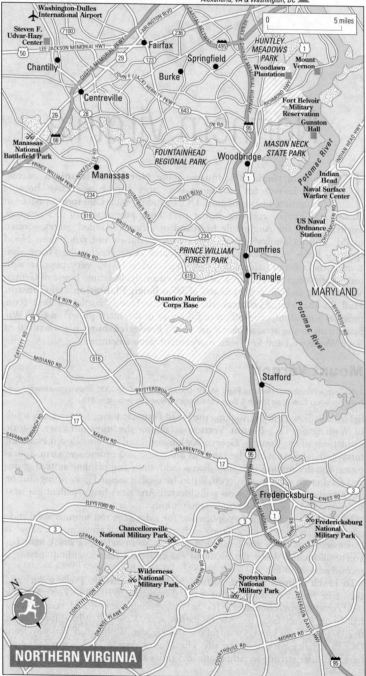

NORTHERN VIRGINIA

Ninety-minute Spirit **cruises** to Mount Vernon depart from Pier 4, 6th and Water streets SW in DC (mid-March to April Thurs–Sun, April–Aug Tues–Sun, Sept & Oct Fri–Sun only; $39 round-trip; reserve at ☎1-866/302-2469, ⓦwww.spiritcitycruises.com), and it's only fifty minutes to Mount Vernon from Old Town Alexandria on cruises offered by the Potomac Riverboat Company (April–Aug Tues–Sun, Sept Fri–Sun, Oct Sat & Sun; $34–36; ☎703/684-0580, ⓦwww.potomacriverboatco.com). The **Tourmobile** bus (mid-June to Aug; $30; ☎202/554-5100, ⓦwww.tourmobile.com) also runs out here from Arlington National Cemetery – a four-hour round-trip that allows you about three hours to appreciate the sight. The prices of both cruise and Tourmobile trips include admission to the house and grounds.

Some history

George Washington's father, **Augustine**, built a house on the Washington estate in 1735. When he died, the house and lands passed to George's elder brother, Lawrence; after Lawrence's death in 1752 and his widow's in 1761, the estate went to George. Not that he had an opportunity to spend any real time here early on, since for much of the 1750s he was away on service with the Virginia militia, and then fighting in the French and Indian War. He married in 1759, and it was during the years before 1775 – when he was next called away on service, as a general in the Continental Army – that Washington came to know his estate. He tripled its size to eight thousand acres, divided it into five separate working farms, and landscaped the grounds; rolling meadows, copses, riverside walks, parks, and even vineyards were all laid out for the family's contemplation and amusement.

Just five hundred acres of the estate remain today, the rest having been split and sold off by the terms of successive wills (including a parcel that became Woodlawn Plantation; see p.351), but there's still more than enough to provide an idea of the former whole. The lifestyle of an eighteenth-century **gentleman farmer** was an agreeable one, in Washington's case supported by the labor of more than two hundred slaves who lived and worked on the outlying farms. The modest house he inherited was enlarged and redecorated with imported materials; formal gardens and a bowling green were added; and the general bred stallions, hunted in his woods, and fished in the river. Daily at dawn he made a personal tour of inspection on horseback, sometimes riding twenty miles around the grounds. He studied scientific works on farming, corresponded with experts, and, introducing new techniques, expanded the farms' output to include the production of flour, textiles, and even whiskey. While he was away fighting the Revolutionary War, Washington was forced to turn over the day-to-day operation

Events at Mount Vernon

Throughout the year, Mount Vernon hosts a range of **festivals** and **special events**. Around the third weekend in February, Washington's **birthday** is celebrated with a wreath-laying ceremony and fife and drum parades; admission to Mount Vernon is free at that time. In mid-May a three-day festival toasts local **winemakers** in a series of evening events, featuring live jazz and visits to the cellar vaults. In December, special **Christmas tours** re-create the Washingtons' yuletide celebrations and allow access to the third floor of the mansion, which is usually closed. On weekend winter evenings (late Nov to mid-Dec Fri–Sun) there are also special "**Mount Vernon by Candlelight**" tours, casting a romantic glow on this historic site. Book ahead for a candlelight visit or for the wine festival; a special admission price applies. For further information, call Mount Vernon or visit its website.

of his estate to others – who were doubtless thrilled to receive his sixteen-page letters from the front directing the latest round of improvements.

Washington spent eight years away from Mount Vernon during the war, and was prevented from retiring there for good at the end of the fighting: in 1787 he headed the Constitutional Convention in Philadelphia, and two years later he was elected to his first term as US president – news he heard first at Mount Vernon from a messenger who had ridden all the way from Philadelphia. He visited his house only another dozen or so times during his presidency, often for just a few days. When he finally moved back in 1797, at the end of his second term in office, he and Martha had just two and a half years together before his death on December 14, 1799. Out on one of his long estate inspections, he got caught in the snow and succumbed to a fever that killed him (for more on Washington's life, see box, pp.390–391).

Slave quarters and museum

The path up to the mansion passes various outbuildings, including a renovated set of former **slave quarters**. Ninety slaves lived and worked on the grounds alone, and though there's evidence that Washington was a kinder master than most – for instance, refusing to sell children away from their parents, allowing slaves to raise their own crops, and providing the services of a doctor when needed – they still lived lives of deprivation and overwork. His overseers were continually enjoined to watch the slaves like hawks and guard against theft and slacking. Washington was quick to realize that the move away from tobacco cultivation to more skilled farming made slavery increasingly unprofitable. He stopped buying slaves in the late 1770s, allowing those he owned to learn occupations such as carpentry, bricklaying, and spinning, and to be kept on and supported once they had reached the end of their working lives. After his death, his will freed all of Mount Vernon's slaves, much to the chagrin of his wife, who wanted to retain as much of the family's "property" as possible.

On the site, the fancy modern **Reynolds Museum** has interactive displays, models of Washington at various points in his life, and assorted short films testifying to the general's character and leadership. It also traces Washington's ancestry and displays porcelain from the house, medals, weapons, silver, and a series of striking miniatures, by Charles Willson Peale and his brother James, of Martha and her two children by her first marriage. The clay bust of Washington was produced by French sculptor Jean-Antoine Houdon, who worked on it at Mount Vernon in 1785 before completing his famous statue for the Richmond capitol.

The house and grounds

Fronting the circular courtyard stands the **mansion** itself, with the bowling green stretching before it. It's a handsome, harmonious wooden structure, reasonably modest, but sporting stunning views from its East Lawn. The wooden exterior was painted white, beveled, and sand-blasted to resemble stone; inside, the Palladian windows and bright rooms follow the fashions of the day, while the contents are based on an inventory prepared after Washington's death. Fourteen rooms are open to the public, including portrait-filled parlors, cramped bedrooms, and the chamber where Washington breathed his last on a four-poster bed still in situ. Curiosities in his study include a wooden reading chair with built-in fan and a globe he ordered from London, while in the central hall hangs a key to the destroyed Bastille, presented to Washington by Thomas Paine in 1790 on behalf of the Marquis de Lafayette.

In addition to the mansion, there's plenty to see on the **grounds**, including the separate kitchen (set apart from the house because of the risk of fire), storehouse, stables, smokehouse, washhouse, overseer's quarters, kitchen garden, and shrubbery. There's also a forest trail nature walk, and you can take a stroll down to the tomb, where two marble **sarcophagi** for George and Martha are set behind iron gates. Washington's will also directed that a new brick vault be erected after his death, since the original family vault on the grounds was in poor shape; the current structure was built in 1831. Nearby lies a slave burial ground, while beyond there's a site where demonstrations of Washington's crop-growing and farming techniques are occasionally held.

The gristmill and distillery

Located three miles west of the estate along Highway 235, George Washington's **gristmill** is much less romantic than anything else on the estate grounds, providing a glimpse into the tedious labor involved with grinding grain to make it usable for other purposes (see also the Peirce Mill in Rock Creek Park, p.229). Guides in period costume go through the rigors of showing how waterpower drove the mill, which in turn produced flour from corn, wheat, and other cereals. A recent reconstruction, the onsite **distillery** features copper stills, a boiler, and mash tubs, sometimes overseen by docents who give you a sense of the labor put into making the potent drink. Upstairs you can look over relics and oddments associated with the antique process, and a short movie explaining what the distillery meant to Washington and the estate. Admission to both sites is $4, or $2 with Mount Vernon admission (April–Oct daily 10am–5pm).

Woodlawn Plantation and Pope-Leighey House

9000 Richmond Hwy (US Rte 1), Alexandria, VA ☎703/780-4000, ⓦ www.woodlawnplantation.org, www.popeleighey1940.org. March–Dec daily 10am–5pm. $7.50 each attraction, $13 combined ticket.

Not far from George Washington's gristmill, near the intersection of highways 1 and 235, lie the sprawling grounds of **Woodlawn Plantation**, which were part of the Mount Vernon estate until, after Washington's death in 1799, two thousand acres were ceded to his nephew, **Major Lawrence Lewis**, and Martha Washington's granddaughter, **Eleanor Custis Lewis**. An impressive red-brick Georgian manor house (finished in 1805) was built on the grounds by no less than US Capitol architect William Thornton, who used Palladian design elements and fashioned its decorative trim from local sandstone. However, much of the substantial labor involved in building the house – all the bricks were fired in a kiln at the site – was provided by slaves. Looking around the estate, you can get a sense of the backbreaking work that was required; this lends an uncomfortable subtext to the graceful design – with its noble marble busts and elegant arched windows and doors – and vividly demonstrates the social extremes that existed in nineteenth-century Virginia.

Perhaps incongruously, Woodlawn Plantation is also the site of a house designed by twentieth-century architect **Frank Lloyd Wright**, whose broad notions of the democratic spirit enabled him to develop "Usonian" (his own coinage, meant as an adjective for "U.S.") homes meant to be affordable for common people. The **Pope-Leighey House** is one such creation, and while the Usonian trend never really caught on – the homes are now collectors' items for the wealthy – it did allow him to experiment with radical concepts within strict limitations of budget, size, and labor. The Pope-Leighey House was not originally built here, but instead moved from another Virginia location when threatened with demolition. Luckily it survived, as this 1200-square-foot residence bears many of

Wright's signature touches: the materials are limited to wood, brick, concrete, and glass; the layout is strongly horizontal, with trellises to control direct sunlight; the clerestory windows employ unique cut-out patterns; the floor plan is open; and the ceilings are low – except for that of the living room, which rises to 13ft and occupies about half the overall space of the house.

Gunston Hall

10709 Gunston Rd, off I-95, Mason Neck, VA ☎ 703/550-9220, ⓦ www.gunstonhall.org. Daily 9.30am–5pm. $8.

A short drive south from Mount Vernon, and designed in a spirit similar to the area's other red-brick Georgian manors, **Gunston Hall** is a Colonial-era plantation once owned by **George Mason**, author of the Virginia Declaration of Rights, upon which the US Bill of Rights was largely based. In both its architecture and decor, Gunston Hall evokes primarily the Federal style, with its striking Neoclassical arches, original boxwood-lined walkway, lovely formal gardens (set on 550 acres that are mostly wooded), and all-around balance and symmetry. This was but one of Mason's many land speculations – the others encompassed some 24,000 acres of property – and like many other planters' estates, Mason's had its slaves; a veritable army of them managed the homestead, carefully trimmed the gardens, grew the crops, and worked in the laundry, smokehouse, and dairy, which have all been reconstructed on the grounds.

What distinguished Gunston Hall from other plantations, though, was less its attractive landscape and elegant manor but rather its owner: unlike George Washington and his elite Virginia associates (who would go on to positions of

▲ Gunston Hall

power under the country's new government), George Mason was a fierce **anti-Federalist** who opposed any establishment of a strong central government, especially an executive branch with broad taxing and military power. As a delegate to the 1787 Constitutional Convention, Mason famously said he "would sooner chop off my right hand than put it to the Constitution as it now stands." After voting against the adoption of the document, and thus pitting himself against Washington and his comrades, Mason then made the dire prediction, in print, that the nation would either "produce a monarchy, or a corrupt, tyrannical aristocracy; it will most probably vibrate some years between the two, and then terminate in the one or the other."

Manassas National Battlefield Park

6511 Sudley Rd, Manassas, VA ☏703/361-1339, 🌐 www.nps.gov/mana. Daily 8.30am–5pm; June–Aug Sat & Sun until 6pm; park admission $3, good for three days.

Manassas National Battlefield Park extends over grassy hills at the western fringes of the Washington, DC suburban belt, just off I-66. Soon after the first shots were fired at Fort Sumter, the first major land battle of the Civil War – known in the North as the **Battle of Bull Run** – was fought here on the morning of July 21, 1861. Anticipating an easy victory, some 35,000 Union troops attacked a similarly sized Confederate detachment – whom they viewed as poorly led irregulars – that controlled a vital railroad link to the Shenandoah Valley, and spectators came in droves to watch what they expected to be a rousing entertainment. The battle was a disaster, though: the rebels proved powerful opponents, and their strength in battle earned their commander, General Thomas Jackson, the famous nickname "Stonewall." He and General Lee also masterminded a second, even more demoralizing Union loss here in late August 1862.

Displays in the small **visitor center** at the entrance describe how the battles took shape and feature old military uniforms, examples of ordnance, tools, and other battlefield necessities. You can go on a guided hike with a ranger over the grassy concourse of the site or wander through the fields yourself, imagining how these pleasant slopes served as a killing ground, not once but twice.

The Steven F. Udvar-Hazy Center

14390 Air and Space Museum Parkway, Chantilly, VA ☏202/633-1000, 🌐 www.nasm.si.edu/museum /udvarhazy. Daily 10.30am–5pm; free admission; parking $12.

Just a few miles northeast of the battlefield, fervent devotees of airplanes and spacecraft can visit the **Steven F. Udvar-Hazy Center**, in the Virginia suburb of Chantilly, not far from Dulles Airport. Everything that's too big to fit into the National Air and Space Museum (see p.88) on the Mall is here, spread across 400 million cubic feet. Among the eighty planes and sixty spacecraft are fighters from America's twentieth-century wars, transport craft, and planes used by the postal service, sports enthusiasts, and commercial airlines. However, the entire experience boils down to checking out four huge items. The first, the SR-71 **Blackbird**, is a legendary spycraft that looks like a sleek black missile. It once tooled around 80,000ft in the atmosphere and, well out of Viet Cong artillery range, provided intelligence to American forces in Vietnam. Elsewhere is the B-29 **Enola Gay**, the plane that dropped the first atomic bomb on Hiroshima – though the exhibit features no discussion about the morality of nuking civilians. Also on display is the colossal Air France **Concorde**, which in 1976 became the only supersonic jet to fly commercially, although now it's no longer in service. Even more eye-opening, the space shuttle **Enterprise**, parked out back, was a prototype for the first space shuttle, though this version has no engine.

Fredericksburg

Only a mile off the I-95 highway, halfway to Richmond from Washington, DC, **FREDERICKSBURG** is one of Virginia's prettiest historic towns, where elegant downtown streets are backed by residential avenues lined with white picket fences. In colonial days, this was an important inland port in which tobacco and other plantation commodities were loaded onto boats that sailed down the Rappahannock River. Dozens of stately early-American buildings along the waterfront now hold antique stores and secondhand bookshops.

In the 1816 town hall, the **Fredericksburg Area Museum**, 907 Princess Anne St (Mon–Sat 10am–4pm, Sun 1–4pm; $7; ℡540/371-3037, Ⓦwww .famcc.org), has a range of displays tracing local history, from Native American settlements to the Civil Rights era, and provides self-guided walking-tour brochures of town highlights. The **Rising Sun Tavern**, 1304 Caroline St, was built as a home in 1760 by George Washington's brother, Charles. As an inn, it became a key meeting place for patriots and a hotbed of sedition. It is now a small **museum** (March–Nov Mon–Sat 9am–5pm, Sun 11am–5pm; Dec–Feb Mon–Sat 10am–4pm, Sun noon–4pm; $5; ℡540-371-1494), where costumed guides take visitors around a collection of pub games and antique pewter. Guides are also on hand to explain eighteenth-century medicine at **Hugh Mercer's Apothecary Shop**, 1020 Caroline St (same hours as tavern museum; $5; ℡540/373-3362), which often involved treating patients with the likes of leeches and crab claws. If you're more interested in George Washington, you can venture out to his family's **Ferry Farm**, 268 Kings Hwy (daily 10am–5pm, except Jan & Feb Sat & Sun only; $5; ℡540/370-0732, Ⓦwww.kenmore.org), where he grew up and which still maintains a bucolic setting and gardens appropriate for the time.

Fredericksburg's strategic location made it vital during the **Civil War**, and the land around the town was heavily contested. More than 100,000 men lost their lives in the major battles of Fredericksburg, Chancellorsville, and Spotsylvania, and in countless bloody skirmishes. Indeed, Stonewall Jackson himself was mistakenly killed by his own troops at Chancellorsville in May 1863. The **visitor center**, 702 Caroline St (daily 9am–5pm, summer 9am–7pm; ℡540/373-1776, Ⓦwww.fredericksburgva.com), has informative exhibits and can provide maps of walking tours and details about discounted tickets to the area's attractions. It will also lead you out to **Fredericksburg and Spotsylvania National Battlefield Park** (dawn–dusk; free; Ⓦwww.nps.gov/frsp), south of town. Contact the visitor center or see the website for information on the other major battlefields in the area, **Wilderness** and **Chancellorsville**, both west of town, as well as the various manors and shrines to be found on or around the killing grounds.

Practicalities

The **Amtrak** station is at 200 Lafayette Blvd and the **Greyhound** station at 1400 Jefferson Davis Hwy. Fredericksburg has many good, old-fashioned **B&Bs**, including the 1812 *Kenmore Inn*, 1200 Princess Anne St (℡540/371-7622, Ⓦwww.kenmoreinn.com; $123), which has stylish rooms with Net access and a cozy pub in the basement that serves traditional fish and ham dishes, occasionally with live music; and the *Richard Johnston Inn*, 711 Caroline St

(☎540/899-7606 or 877-557-0770, ⓦwww.therichardjohnstoninn.com), an elegant, eighteenth-century B&B with plush rooms and a broad range of prices, from $98 to $210. One worthwhile motel to try, for its tasteful rooms stocked with antiques, is the *Inn at the Olde Silk Mill*, 1707 Princess Anne St (☎540/371-5666, ⓦwww.fci1.com; $99). For close access to the four battlefields, try *On Keegan Pond*, 11315 Gordon Rd (☎540/785-4662; $85), in a pleasant rural setting with antique-laden rooms.

Thanks to a lot of weekend tourist activity, the town has several good places to **eat** and **drink**. *Sammy T's*, 801 Caroline St (☎540/371-2008), is a popular bar and diner with substantial sandwiches, salads, and pasta, and a huge range of bottled beers. The *Virginia Deli*, 101 Williams St (☎540/371-2233), doles out hefty sandwiches with names like the Stonewall Jackson (salami and two kinds of ham) and the Blue & Grey (hot chicken, ham, and Swiss); and the *Colonial Tavern*, 406 Lafayette Blvd (☎540/373-1313), is the place to fill up on Irish food, music, and beer.

22

Richmond, VA

RICHMOND, capital of Virginia and bulwark of the old Confederacy, is in many ways still the personification of the upper South, its carefully cultivated gentility, handsome antebellum manors (and manners), and fetching cityscape calling to mind what Southern boosters would have you believe most of the South looks like. However, the city also, like many in the South, has something of a split personality, its memorials to the "Lost Cause" of the Civil War – or "War Between the States," as it's called here – vying with historic monuments to the town's considerable African American history, with the two strands maintaining an uneasy coexistence. For all that, though, the place is also on the edge of the modern South, with financial, light industry, and technology companies all finding a comfortable home here, and various civic and riverfront developments providing contrast to the sometimes-fusty Neoclassical architecture. It may also surprise some to note that Richmond is also fairly liberal, at least by Virginia standards. The mayor is African American (Douglas Wilder, a former governor), and in 2003 a statue was even unveiled at the Tredegar Iron Works of the town's former archenemy **Abraham Lincoln**, to the applause of progressive politicians and the scorn of pro-Confederate groups.

Some history

Founded in 1737 at the farthest navigable point on the James River, Richmond remained a small outpost until just before the end of the colonial era, when Virginians, realizing that their capital at Williamsburg was open to British attack, shifted it fifty miles inland. Ironically, the move ended up preserving Williamsburg for posterity but failed to offer Richmond much protection: the city was raided many times and twice put to the torch, once by troops under the command of Benedict Arnold.

Nonetheless, Richmond subsequently flourished, its population reaching 100,000 by the time of the Civil War. When war broke out it was named the **capital of the Confederacy**, replacing Montgomery, Alabama, when Virginia seceded a few months after the initial seven rebel states. The massive **Tredegar Iron Works**, now a dedicated NPS visitor center (see p.361), became the main engine of the Confederate war machine. For four years the city was the focus of Southern defenses and Union attacks, but despite an almost constant state of siege – General McClellan came within six miles as early as 1862 – it held on almost until the very end. Less than a week after the city's fall, on April 3, 1865, Robert E. Lee surrendered to Ulysses S. Grant at Appomattox, a hundred miles west.

After the war, Richmond was devastated. Much of its downtown was burned, allegedly by fleeing Confederates who wanted to keep its stores of weapons and

RICHMOND, VA

◄ **A** **1** **2** Carytown & Fan District

JACKSON WARD

Maggie Walker House

Black History Museum

Visitor Center

DOWNTOWN

Governor's Mansion

Valentine Richmond History Center

Museum of the Confederacy

RICHMOND-PETERSBURG TURNPIKE

RICHMOND-PETERSBURG TURNPIKE

SHOCKOE BOTTOM

Edgar Allan Poe Museum

CHURCH HILL

St. John's Church

SHOCKOE BOTTOM

Canal Boat Rides

CANAL WALK

DOWNTOWN EXPRESSWAY

DOWNTOWN EXPRESSWAY

American Civil War Center/ Tredegar Iron Works

ROBERT E LEE BRIDGE

Chimborazo Medical Museum

RESTAURANTS & BARS

Border Chophouse	3
Cabo's Corner Bistro	1
Millie's Diner	9
O'Neill's Penny Lane Pub	4
Peking Pavilion	8
Richbrau Brewing Co.	7
Strawberry Street Café	2
Third Street Diner	5
Tobacco Company	6

ACCOMMODATION

The Berkeley	E
Grace Manor Inn	A
The Jefferson	B
Linden Row Inn	C
Richmond Marriott	D
William Catlin House	F

N

0   500 yds

its warehouses full of tobacco out of the victors' hands. Rebuilding, however, was quick, and the city's economy has remained among the strongest in the South. **Tobacco** is still a major industry – machine-rolled cigarettes were invented here in the 1870s, and Marlboro-maker **Philip Morris** runs a huge manufacturing plant just south of downtown.

Arrival, information, and getting around

Two hours by car from Washington DC via I-95, which cuts through the east side of downtown, Richmond is also served by **Amtrak**, which pulls into 1500 East Main Street on its regional route that connects Newport News, VA, with Washington, DC and Boston. Further out of town, the station at 7519 Staples Mill Road covers that route as well as the Silver Service/Palmetto line connecting Miami, Washington, DC, and New York City. **Greyhound**, which stops just off I-64 at 2910 N Boulevard, is also a good distance from the center of town. The **airport**, ten miles east of downtown, is served by major carriers and has a small visitor center (Mon–Fri 9.30am–4.30pm; ☏804/236-3260; ⊛www.flyrichmond.com) in the arrivals terminal. The **main visitor center**, 403 N 3rd St (daily 9am–5pm; ☏804/782-2777 or 1-888/RICHMOND, ⊛www.visit.richmond.com), provides discounts on area hotels and advises on tours. Much of Richmond is compact enough to walk around, but to get to outlying places you can take a GRTC **bus** ($1.25, express routes $1.75; ☏804/358-GRTC, ⊛www.ridegrtc.com).

Accommodation

Finding well-priced **accommodation** in Richmond isn't difficult, with plenty of chain downtown hotels catering to the business and government trade. If you prefer to get a feel for the old city, stay the night in a **B&B** in one of the historic quarters.

The Berkeley 1200 E Cary St ☏804/780-1300 or 1-888/780-4422, ⊛www.berkeleyhotel.com. Elegant small hotel with boutique touches, and suites with private terraces, on the historic Shockoe Slip. $205

Grace Manor Inn 1853 W Grace St ☏804/353-4334, ⊛www.thegracemanorinn.com. Stately B&B housing three tasteful suites rich with antique decor such as chandeliers and stained-glass windows, and some units with fireplaces and claw-foot tubs, in a grand 1910 building. $175

Henry Clay Inn 114 N Railroad Ave, Ashland VA ☏804/798-3100, ⊛www.henryclayinn.com. Excellent B&B eleven miles out of town, built as a replica of an old-time hotel, which has sixteen rooms with antique furnishings, a proper parlor and majestic balcony, and some units with Jacuzzis and fridges. $95

The Jefferson 101 W Franklin St ☏804/788-8000 or 1-800/424-8014, ⊛www.jeffersonhotel.com. Beautifully maintained, five-star grand hotel built like a small castle, with fabulous marble-columned lobby and marble baths, high-speed Net access, and stylish decor in the rooms. $345

Linden Row Inn 100 E Franklin St ☏804/783-7000 or 1-800/348-7424, ⊛www.lindenrowinn.com. A magnificent row of red-brick Georgian terrace houses, now a comfortable modern hotel with antique furnishings, high-speed Net access, and complimentary continental breakfast. $119

Richmond Marriott 500 E Broad St ☏804/643-3400, ⊛www.marriott.com. Corporate-modern chain accommodation that offers high-speed Internet, good downtown location, and nice beds. $159

William Catlin House 2304 E Broad St ☏804/780-3746. B&B dating from 1845 that offers a mix of seven antebellum and Victorian rooms and suites, sited in the Church Hill district, not too far from downtown and the Shockoe Slip. $119

Downtown Richmond

Richmond's **downtown** centers on a few blocks rising up from the James River to either side of Broad Street. Modern office towers front a riverside park, while up the hill in the **Court End District**, dozens of well-preserved antebellum homes provide a suitable backdrop for some important museums and historic sites.

The **Virginia State Capitol**, 910 Capitol St, houses the oldest legislative body still in existence in the US; the site has been in continuous use since 1788 as the state (and, briefly, Confederate) legislature. It's the focal point of the city, visible from all over Richmond and offering a sweeping view from its columned portico. Thomas Jefferson had a hand in the design, based on his favorite building, the Roman Maison Carré in Nîmes, France. The domed central rotunda (not visible from outside) holds the only marble statue of George Washington modeled from life (by sculptor Jean-Antoine Houdon), and busts of Jefferson and the seven other Virginia-born presidents line the walls. Likenesses of famous Virginians, including a solemn bronze of Robert E. Lee, fill the adjacent **Old House Chamber**, where Aaron Burr was tried and acquitted of treason in 1807. Two hundred years later, the capitol has reopened after a lengthy and beautiful restoration (tours Mon–Sat 8.30am–5pm, Sun 1–4pm; free; ☎804/698-1788, ⊛legis.state.va.us).

Also on Capitol Square is the Federal-style **Governor's Mansion**, 901 E Grace St, like the capitol the oldest of its kind in the US, dating to 1813 (for tours call ☎804/371-2642) and renovated many times since then, maintaining its stylish yet tasteful symmetry. Much less reserved, across from Capitol Square is the huge Victorian artifact of **Old City Hall**, 1001 E Broad St, designed in

▲ Virginia State Capitol

1894 in a retro-Gothic style and now housing offices. Thanks to its busy combination of iron, brick, and various shades of granite, the building is so visually busy it makes your head spin, with each of the four corner towers boasting a different design. You can poke around the first floor Mon–Fri 9am–5pm.

Two blocks north of the capitol, and nearly enveloped by a colossal health-care complex, the **Museum of the Confederacy**, 1201 E Clay St (Mon–Sat 10am–5pm, Sun noon–5pm; $8; ☎804/649-1861, ⓦwww.moc.org), covers the history of the Civil War through weapons, uniforms, and the like. Personal effects of Confederate leaders include J.E.B. Stuart's plumed hat, the tools used to amputate Stonewall Jackson's arms at Chancellorsville (he died from friendly fire), and Robert E. Lee's revolver and the pen he used to sign the surrender. Next door and part of the complex, the **White House of the Confederacy** (same hours; $8, or $11 combo ticket) is a Neoclassical mansion dating to 1818 and designed by Robert Mills, where Jefferson Davis later lived as Confederate president, that has been restored to its 1860s appearance. Tours of the house are too reverential but do offer a useful perspective on the man himself, who was indicted for (but not convicted of) treason after the war and lost his US citizenship.

Two blocks west, the 1812 **Wickham House** now forms part of the excellent **Valentine Richmond History Center** at 1015 E Clay St (Tues–Sat 10am–5pm, Sun noon–5pm; $10; ☎804/649-0711, ⓦwww.richmondhistory center.com). This Federal-style monolith houses a small local history museum, focusing on the experience of working-class and black Americans, as well as an extensive array of furniture and pre–Civil War clothing such as whalebone corsets and other *Gone With the Wind*–era apparel.

Jackson Ward

West of the Convention Center on Sixth Street is a neighborhood of early nineteenth-century houses, many fronted by ornate wrought-iron balconies. Known as **Jackson Ward**, and filling a dozen blocks around First and Clay streets, this National Historic Landmark District has been the center of Richmond's African American community since well before the Civil War, when Richmond had the largest free black population in the US. As well as covering local history, the **Maggie L. Walker House**, 110 E Leigh St (Mon–Sat 9am–5pm; free; ☎804/771-2017, ⓦwww.nps.gov/mawa), traces the working life of the physically disabled, black Richmond woman who, during the 1920s, was the first woman in the US to found and run a bank, now the Consolidated Bank and Trust. Nearby, the **Black History Museum**, at 00 Clay St (Tues–Sat 10am–5pm; $5; ☎804/780-9093, ⓦwww.black historymuseum.org), contains displays on Richmond's role as a center of Southern black society and includes a well-presented gallery of artifacts of the Civil Rights movement and textiles from different peoples in Africa and America. It can also provide information on taking historic walking tours of Jackson Ward.

Canal Walk and around

A nice example of urban revitalization is the landscaping of a 1.25-mile stretch of waterfront into **Canal Walk**, which runs between downtown and Shockoe Bottom. **Canal boat rides** depart from around 14th and Virginia streets (April–Nov Fri & Sat noon–7pm, Sun noon–5pm; also June–Aug Wed & Thurs noon–7pm; $5; ☎804/649-2800), providing a leisurely and pleasant half-hour jaunt that recalls the city's considerable nineteenth-century traffic in waterborne

Just 25 miles south of Richmond lies a very unusual sort of battlefield. Although the Civil War did much to modernize (and barbarize) modern conflict with total-war methods like destroying crops and food stores, targeting civilian populations, and introducing ultra-lethal grapeshot cannon fire and strategic mass attrition, **Petersburg** was even more prescient. In many ways, it foreshadowed the **trench warfare** that would come a half century later in World War I.

By June 1864, the Civil War had been raging for three years with no end in sight. General Ulysses S. Grant, recognizing the need to outflank the Confederates to the east and cut off the railroad supply line to their still-functional capital of Richmond, brought his Army of the Potomac south to Petersburg, a city of 18,000. However, the Confederates had in place a twenty-mile stretch of defensive **breastworks** (wooden fortifications) designed to repel the enemy in the classical battlefield style of the time. The "battle" soon became one of attrition, with the armies facing off over a 37-mile front; new works constructed on both sides; and muddy, dreadful trenches dug to secure the troops' positions along **siege lines**. Thus began a nearly 300-day-long series of skirmishes and attacks that helped to bleed both armies white. A decisive moment came when **Col. Henry Pleasants** proposed tunneling under the Confederate lines and exploding a massive charge of 320 gunpowder kegs; the plan worked and several hundred graycoats were killed, but due to Northern political concerns about seasoned black troops being thrown into the breach first, ill-trained white troops rushed into the big hole and were slaughtered. By the time the **Battle of the Crater** was over, the Union lost more than 5,000 troops – five times the Confederate loss.

Despite the debacle, which Grant called "the saddest affair I have witnessed in this war," the ten-month campaign resulted in a tactical draw but a strategic victory for the North: significant long-term losses to the Southern side worsened to the point where Robert E. Lee was finally forced to withdraw in April 1865 and make a final march that ended in surrender. Today, the scars from the battle, including the ragged outline of the crater, are still visible on the landscape, and you can visit **Petersburg National Battlefield** (daily 9am–5pm; $5 for seven-day pass; ☎804/732-3531, ⓦwww.nps.gov/pete), just east of the modern town.

freight. For an interesting insight into the Confederate period, you can start or end your stroll at the **American Civil War Center**, 490 Tredegar St (daily 9am–5pm; $8; ☎804-771-2145, ⓦwww.nps.gov/rich), at the refurbished **Tredegar Iron Works**, a munitions plant whose foundry churned out hundreds of tons of Confederate materiel, including the plating used for the famous *Merrimack* ship. The center has multimedia presentations about Civil War history and three floors of exhibits, including moving personal accounts of the war from ordinary soldiers, and, on the lower level, various guns, artillery, ammunition, and other weapons that remind you why the war was so bloody. Tredegar is also the main visitor center for **Richmond National Battlefield Park**, a collection of dozens of Civil War sites, including one of the bloodiest, Petersburg (see box, above), which can all be accessed on an eighty-mile drive. Four other local visitor centers are also in operation, the most interesting being the **Chimborazo Medical Museum**, a few miles east at 3215 E Broad St (daily 9am–5pm; free; ☎804/226-1981), which has disturbing displays on the medicine and technology available (or not) to help wounded soldiers of the era. Those who weren't so lucky ended up just west of Tredegar at **Hollywood Cemetery**, 412 S Cherry St (daily 8am–5pm; ☎804/648-8501, ⓦwww.hollywoodcemetery.org), where a 90ft-tall granite **pyramid** memorializes the 18,000 Confederate troops killed nearby, and where you can find the graves of US presidents James Monroe, famous for his signature "Doctrine," barring European interference in North and South American affairs, and John Tyler, the first vice president to accede to the top job upon the death of a president (in April 1841, when William Henry Harrison died of pneumonia). Tyler ended his days serving in the Confederate Congress.

Shockoe Bottom, the Poe Museum, and Church Hill

A short walk southeast from the Court End District is a different side of the Richmond story. Split down the middle by the raised I-95 freeway, the gentrified riverfront warehouse district of **Shockoe Bottom** still holds a few reminders of its industrial past among the restaurants and nightclubs on its cobblestoned streets. From **Shockoe Slip**, a fetching old wharf rebuilt in the 1890s after being destroyed in the Civil War, Cary Street runs east along the waterfront, lined by a wall of brick warehouses – now being converted into chic lofts and condos – known as **Tobacco Row**.

Nearby, Richmond's oldest building, an appropriately gloomy 250-year-old stone house, holds the **Edgar Allan Poe Museum**, 1914 E Main St (Tues–Sat 10am–5pm, Sun 11am–5pm; $6; ☏804/648-5523, ⓦwww.poemuseum.org). Poe spent much of his youth in Richmond and considered it his home town; he wrote the *Narrative of Arthur Gordon Pym* while working at the Richmond-based *Southern Literary Messenger*. The museum displays Poe memorabilia and relics, including his walking stick and a lock of his hair, plus a model of Richmond as it was back then, and early copies of his work and etchings and art based on his stories.

Church Hill, a few blocks northeast, is one of Richmond's oldest surviving residential districts, its decorative eighteenth-century houses, adorned with cast-iron porches and rambling magnolia-filled front gardens, looking out over the James River (it's also the site of the Chimborazo Museum; see p.361). Capping the hill at the heart of the neighborhood, **St John's Church**, 2401 E Broad St (tours Mon–Sat 10am–3.30pm, Sun 1–3.30pm, last tour an hour later in summer; $6; ⓦwww.historicstjohnschurch.org), dates back to 1741 and is best known as the place where, during a 1775 debate on whether the Virginia colony should raise a militia against the British, future state governor **Patrick Henry** made the impassioned plea: "Is life so dear, or peace so sweet, to be purchased at the price of chains of slavery? I know not what course others may take, but as for me, give me liberty or give me death." His speech, along with the debate itself, is re-enacted by actors in period dress every summer Sunday at 2pm; it's a popular affair, so get there an hour early to grab a spot on a pew.

The Fan District and Carytown

Surrounding the campus of Virginia Commonwealth University, the **Fan District** is so named because its tree-lined avenues fan out at oblique angles. The district spreads west from the downtown area, beyond Belvidere Street (US-1), and its centerpiece, **Monument Avenue**, is lined with garish Victorian and historic-revival mansions from the turn of the twentieth century. Richmond's most imposing boulevard was laid out by city planners from 1889 onward to commemorate key figures of the Confederacy. Four grand intersections hold statues of J.E.B. Stuart, Robert E. Lee, Stonewall Jackson, and Jefferson Davis. In recent times, the city's black population expressed dissatisfaction with this choice of heroes, and in 1996 a statue was erected of tennis champion **Arthur Ashe**, a native who left the city in 1961 because its tennis courts were segregated. The statue shows Ashe's dedication to education as well as the game of tennis – he's encircled by children and holds books and a racquet aloft.

South of Monument Avenue, at 2800 Grove Ave, stands the **Virginia Museum of Fine Arts** (Wed–Sun 11am–5pm; donation; ℡804/340-1400, ⓦ www.vmfa.museum). An extensive collection of Impressionist and Post-Impressionist paintings is displayed alongside American paintings ranging from Charles Willson Peale's acclaimed portraits to George Catlin's romantic images of Plains Indians to the Pop Art creations of Roy Lichtenstein and Claes Oldenburg. Other galleries contain such items as Frank Lloyd Wright furniture, Lalique jewelry, and Hindu and Buddhist sculpture from the Himalayas; perhaps the most popular part of the museum is a world-class array of over three hundred Carl Fabergé works, including four of his trademark jewel-encrusted Easter eggs crafted in the 1890s for the Russian tsars.

Just beyond the Fan District, **Carytown** is a thriving nine-block area of trendy shops offering Asian art, tarot readings, and holistic medicines alongside restaurants on Cary Street. Here, too, is the **Byrd Theatre**, 2908 W Cary St (℡804/342-9100, ⓦ www.byrdtheatre.com), one of the grandest old movie-houses in the region, dating from 1928 and rich with European marble and crystal chandeliers; it still shows movies and offers Saturday-night performances on its grand Wurlitzer organ.

Eating and drinking

Richmond has a good choice of **eating** options at both ends of the price spectrum, with barbecue and the higher-priced New Southern cuisine being specialties.

Border Chophouse 1501 W Main St, Fan District ℡804/355-2907. Western-style spot that serves up mid-priced pasta, veal, and lamb dishes, but whose specialty is barbecue, be it beef ribs, pork, or chicken. Mon–Fri 11.30am–1am, Sat 11am–2am, Sun 11am–9.30pm.

Cabo's Corner Bistro 2053 W Broad St, Fan District ℡804/355-1144. Swank spot that offers creative steak, seafood, and pasta dishes, as well as taste-bud-tingling desserts and nightly live jazz. Tues–Sat 5–10.30pm.

Millie's Diner 2603 E Main St ℡804/643-5512. Refurbished diner, complete with mini-jukeboxes on each table, a bit out of downtown beyond Shockoe Bottom. The changing menu includes fairly expensive but delicious seafood and steak, plus rack of lamb and duck breast, and there's also a nice range of brews. Tues–Fri 11am–2.30pm & 5.30–10.30pm, Sat 10am–2.30pm & 5.30–10.30pm, Sun 9am–3pm & 5.30–9.30pm.

O'Neill's Penny Lane Pub 421 E Franklin St, Downtown ℡804/780-1682. British-style joint with solid grilled food and other affordable pub grub, including a mean steak-and-Guinness pie, plus a full range of English

and other beers, and European soccer on TV. Mon–Fri 11am–2am, Sat 5pm–2am.

Peking Pavilion 1302 E Cary St ℡804/649-8888. Very good, inexpensive (especially at lunchtime) Chinese restaurant in Shockoe Slip serving Szechuan and Mandarin specialties. One in a local chain. Sun–Thurs 11.30am–2pm & 5–9pm, Fri 11.30am–2pm & 5–10.30pm, Sat 5–10.30pm.

Richbrau Brewing Co 1214 E Cary St, Shockoe Slip ℡804/644-3018. The place to go in town for hearty, handcrafted microbrews, as well as good Southern fare, steak, and fish and chips, along with dancing, pool, and darts. Daily 11.30am–10pm.

Strawberry Street Café 421 N Strawberry St ℡804/353-6860. Casual and comfortable Fan District café offering mainly inexpensive quiches, pasta, and salads, but also jambalaya and crab cakes, and a salad bar nestled in an old bathtub. Mon–Thurs 11am–10.30pm, Fri 11am–11pm, Sat 10am–11pm, Sun 10am–10.30pm.

Third Street Diner 218 E Main St, Downtown ℡804/788-4750. Relaxed 24hr diner with cheap and solid breakfasts and pork chops, omelettes, grits, barbecue, and sausage platters. Draws a stylish student crowd, especially at night when it's also a bar.

The Tobacco Company 1201 E Cary St, Shockoe Slip ℡804/782-9555. Inventive New American food in a stunningly restored three-story tobacco warehouse, complete with antique elevator. Affordable

sandwiches and burgers for lunch; pricier steak and seafood for dinner. Mon–Fri 11.30am–2.30pm & 5.30–10pm, Sat 11.30am–2.30pm & 5.30–10.30pm, Sun 11am–2.30pm & 5.30–9.30pm.

Nightlife

Richmond's main **nightlife** spots are concentrated around the riverside **Shockoe Slip** and **Shockoe Bottom** areas, just east of downtown. A good bet for mainstream **theater** is the Barksdale Theatre, 1601 Willow Lawn Drive (tickets $35–38; ℡804/282-2620, ⓦ www.barksdalerichmond.org), while the Chamberlayne Actors Theatre, 319 N Wilkinson Rd (tickets $15; ℡804/262-9760, ⓦ www.cattheatre.com), offers fringe works that are more daring and contemporary. For details on music and events, check the free *Style Weekly* newspaper or ⓦ www.arts.Richmond.com.

The Historic Triangle

T he **Historic Triangle**, on the thin peninsula that stretches southeast of
Richmond between the James and York rivers, holds the richest concentration of colonial-era sites in the US: **Jamestown**, founded in 1607,
was Virginia's first settlement; **Williamsburg** is a detailed replica of the
colonial capital; and **Yorktown** was the site of the climactic battle in the
Revolutionary War. All are within an hour's drive from Richmond, and
Williamsburg is accessible by Amtrak. If you're in the capital region for a week
or more, these attractions should at least merit consideration for a visit, as they
hold some of the core historic and cultural mileposts of the American nation.

Although I-64 is the quickest way to cover the fifty miles from Richmond to
Williamsburg, it's far more pleasing to drive along US-5, which rolls through
plantation country, where many eighteenth-century mansions, with lovely
grounds, are open to the public. Once you're in the Historic Triangle, the best
way to get around is along the wooded **Colonial Parkway**, which winds west
to Jamestown and east to Yorktown, 23 miles in all. Most of the area's numerous
tourist facilities are to be found around Williamsburg; a few suggestions are
listed under "Historic Triangle practicalities" on p.371.

Jamestown

Jamestown is the place where England first got its feet wet in the New World,
a trade and military outpost whose lore is still being celebrated four hundred
years later, with recent archaeological discoveries adding new insights and
perspectives. If the seventeenth-century expedition was primarily a commercial
enterprise, and a real struggle at first, it established a pattern of settlement and
diplomacy (or lack thereof) to native peoples that would have far-reaching
effects for future endeavors – military, commercial, or otherwise (see box on
p.366). You'll want to visit both the original site and the re-created site; they're
accessible from the scenic Colonial Parkway or highways 5 and 31 from
Williamsburg.

The **Jamestown National Historic Site** (daily 9am–5pm; $10 per car,
includes Yorktown battlefield, see p.370; ☎757/229-1733, ⓦ www.nps.gov
/jame) on Jamestown Island protects the original location of the colony,
though the only structure to survive is the 50ft tower of the first brick church,
built around 1650 (the rest was destroyed by fire in 1698), making it one of
the oldest extant English structures in the US. The site is roughly divided into
two sections: the **New Towne** is where the colonists relocated after the 1620s
to erect businesses, establish permanent residences, build livestock pens, and
so on. Much of what's visible are replicas of the original brick foundations
buried below (to protect from weather damage) and the fenced outlines of

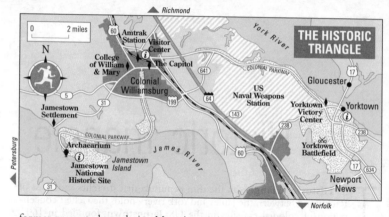

former property boundaries. More interesting is the **Old Towne**, a rich trove for archaeological relics, including ruins from the original, triangular 1607 fort, which are not, as was once believed, mostly underwater. You can watch the several dozen archaeologists and students going about their work or drop in on the **Archaearium**, which displays some of the many treasures discovered here, among them fishhooks, glassware, utensils, and native ceramics, along with the skeleton of a colonist who died a violent death and rusty military armor dug out from a local well, which, though used as a garbage dump, ended up being the perfect repository for artifacts now deemed essential to understanding life in the colony. The very latest finds are on view online at ⓦ historicjamestowne.org.

England comes to the New World

As the first successful English colony in the New World, **Jamestown** was established as a commercial venture, sponsored by King James I but paid for and owned by the **Virginia Company**. On May 13, 1607, the colonists – thirty male aristocrats and seventy-five indentured servants – arrived at the mouth of the Chesapeake Bay after four months at sea, and within two weeks had established a fortified settlement on a low-lying island forty miles up the James River.

Although Jamestown was intended to be self-supporting, not one member of the party had any experience with farming or fishing – their leader, **John Smith**, wrote in 1608 that "though there be Fish in the Sea, and Foules in the ayre, and Beasts in the woods, their bounds are so large, they are so wilde, and we so weake and ignorant, we cannot much trouble them." The company continued to send new recruits, but the loss of life was extreme: of more than seven thousand settlers who came to Jamestown in its first decade, six thousand perished within a year of arriving.

What saved Jamestown, besides the provisions brought by new settlers, was **tobacco**: by 1619 the colony was shipping some twenty tons a year back to England. As it expanded, the colony began to encroach upon the **Powhatan**, an Algonquin-speaking people who controlled most of tidewater Virginia and who until then had been fairly peaceable. In 1622 and again in 1644 provocations caused the Powhatan to attack the colonists, killing around five hundred settlers each time. The most serious damage to Jamestown, however, was caused by the colonists themselves, when they burned the fort to the ground in 1675 in protest at the lack of protection offered them by the Crown. Rather than rebuild the tiny island outpost, by the end of the 1600s they shifted the capital and most commercial activity inland to Williamsburg, and Jamestown slowly disappeared.

At the **visitor center** at the end of the Colonial Parkway (same hours and information as historic site), artists' drawings and audiovisual exhibits endeavor to conjure up the past, and just down the road you can watch artisans making old-fashioned **glassworks** and purchase some of their creations, and see the brick remnants of a seventeenth-century kiln now being excavated.

If looking at dusty artifacts isn't enough for you, head to the adjacent **Jamestown Settlement** (daily 9am–5pm; $13.50, or $19.25 with Yorktown Victory Center, see p.370; ☎757/253-4838, ⓦwww.historyisfun.org), a complex of museums and actual-size replicas that provide details of what went on here. Behind the museum, the reconstructed buildings are staffed by guides in period costume. In **Powhatan Village**, interpreters wearing buckskins engage in weaving, pottery, and other Native American crafts, while in the larger replica of **James Fort**, some fifteen thatched buildings – all built with period tools – include a blacksmith's forge, storehouse and church. Full-size replicas of the three **ships** that carried the first settlers are moored on the James River.

Colonial Williamsburg

Providing vivid details on what the eighteenth-century capital of Virginia may have been like, **Colonial Williamsburg** is an essential tourist experience for anyone with a flair for American history. While you have to buy a pricey ticket to look inside the meticulously restored buildings, the entire historic area, which includes many fine gardens, is open all the time, and you can wander freely down the cobblestone streets and across the lush green commons. Cars are banned, and the area as a whole is a remarkably pleasant – if sometimes crowded – place.

While the interpretive activities and craftspeople – plying around twenty colonial trades, from apothecary to wigmaker – are entertaining enough, as John D. Rockefeller's influence has waned (see box, p.369), Williamsburg has tried to come to grips with the less savory realities of colonial life. Thus people previously referred to as "servants" are now acknowledged as slaves – making up half of Williamsburg's population – and their lives and conditions are covered,

Tickets for Colonial Williamsburg

To set foot inside any of the buildings that have been restored or rebuilt as part of Colonial Williamsburg, you need to buy a ticket, either from the main **visitor center** (daily 9am–5pm; ☎1-800/HISTORY, ⓦwww.history.org), north of the center off the Colonial Parkway, or from a smaller office at the west end of Duke of Gloucester Street. Most buildings in the park are open daily from 9am to 5pm, but about a third of them may have special hours and days they're open; check the website for details, if you're really looking forward to visiting one in particular.

There are several types of **tickets**, which include an introductory guided walk and free parking at the visitor center. The basic **Capital City Pass** ($36, kids $18), valid for one day only, gets you into many of the lesser buildings but excludes the Governor's Palace and the museums; the better-value **Key-to-the-City Pass** ($49, kids $24) includes those buildings and lasts two days; the **Freedom Pass** ($59, kids $29) is the same as the latter but lasts for an entire year; and the less appealing **Independence Pass** ($79, kids $39) is almost the same as the Freedom Pass, but throws in a ticket to the nightly shows as well. Aside from these performances, there are additional charges for the various special programs and events offered by Colonial Williamsburg, such as staged trials in the courthouse, holiday spectacles, and candlelit walking tours.

including those of free blacks who also lived here. On another level, houses and outbuildings formerly repainted every year are now left to age naturally, and once-manicured lawns are now allowed to become a bit overgrown.

From the Wren Building on the William and Mary campus, now separated from Colonial Williamsburg by a mock-historic shopping center, **Duke of Gloucester Street** runs east through the historic area to the old capitol. The first of its eighteenth-century buildings, a hundred yards along, is the Episcopalian **Bruton Parish Church**, where W.A.R. Goodwin preached and all the big names of the revolutionary period were known to visit. It was built in 1715, at a time when all white Virginians were required by law to attend services at least once a month – the names of the old bigwigs are still labeled on their pews. Behind the church, the broad **Palace Green** spreads north to the Governor's Palace. West of the church, the **courthouse** – built in 1771 and still in use when Rockefeller bought it – and the octagonal **powder magazine**, protected by a guardhouse, face each other in the midst of Market Square. Further along, **Chowning's Tavern**, a reconstruction of an alehouse that stood here in 1766, is one of four functioning pubs in the district. As a law student, Thomas Jefferson rented a room in the (no longer used) **Market Square Tavern** across the street. Various other buildings along Duke of Gloucester Street house blacksmiths' shops, printers, and milliners, open only to Colonial Williamsburg ticket-holders. At the east end of the street, a fife-and-drum corps assembles in front of the capitol before its nightly march through town.

The real architectural highlight is the **capitol**, a monumental edifice at the east end of Duke of Gloucester Street. The current building, a 1945 reconstruction of the 1705 original, has an open-air ground-floor **arcade** linking two keyhole-shaped wings. One wing housed the elected legislative body of the colonial government, the **House of Burgesses**, while the other held the chambers of the **General Court** – where alleged felons, including thirteen of Blackbeard's pirates, were tried. The twelve justices of the General Court, all of

▲ Colonial Williamsburg

A year after mosquito-plagued Jamestown burned down in 1676, the colonial capital was moved inland to a small village known as the **Middle Plantation** for its location between the James and York rivers but soon rechristened **Williamsburg** in honor of King William III and made permanent capital (after another Jamestown fire) in 1699. By that time, the second-oldest college in America, **William and Mary**, had been founded (in 1693); its oldest extant academic structure, the grand **Wren Building**, was completed in 1700. To reflect the increasing wealth of the colony, a grand city was laid out and more stately buildings were erected, including the capitol in 1705 and the opulent Governor's Palace in 1720.

By the mid-1700s, tobacco-rich Virginia was the most prosperous American colony, and Williamsburg was its largest city – though with only some two thousand residents, it was not on the scale of Philadelphia, New York, or Boston. Williamsburg remained the seat of colonial government, and William and Mary emerged as one of the leading centers of **revolutionary thought**: George Wythe, Thomas Jefferson, James Monroe, and George Mason argued the finer points of law and democracy, while at the capitol and in the many raucous taverns that surrounded it, firebrand politicians like Patrick Henry held forth on the iniquities of colonialism and organized the first resistance to British rule. When the Revolutionary War broke out, the government moved to the more secure Richmond, and Williamsburg slowly faded from prominence.

Fortunately, lack of commercial or industrial development helped many of the colonial structures survive intact until the 1920s, when oil baron **John D. Rockefeller** answered the pleas of a local priest, **W.A.R. Goodwin**, to support Williamsburg's restoration. Over the ensuing years, Rockefeller, with Goodwin acting as his agent, spent some $90 million buying and restoring the surviving structures to what was believed to be their original condition, in many cases building replicas from scratch, in others knocking down hundreds of attractive Victorian structures because they weren't "historic" enough. In 1934, Colonial Williamsburg opened as the first historic theme park in the US, with costumed guides as interpreters.

Most of the modern town of Williamsburg lies to the west of the historical area and includes some fairly attractive architecture that is over a century old itself. It is dominated by the William and Mary College campus, whose students and staff make up the majority of customers for the modest selection of shops and restaurants, and inhabit the leafy residential streets further west. East of Colonial Williamsburg there's little more than functional motels and drab commercial outlets.

whom were appointed by the king, served as a second legislative body; if the two became deadlocked, they'd meet jointly in a conference chamber bridging the two wings. Every other year, the modern Virginia legislature meets at the capitol for one ceremonial daylong session.

A number of fully stocked gift shops along Duke of Gloucester Street have been done up as eighteenth-century apothecaries, cobblers, and silversmiths. The **Raleigh Tavern** here was where the independence-minded colonial government reconvened after being dissolved by the loyalist governors in 1769 and again in 1774; the original tavern burned down in 1859. Considering that most Virginians of the time, even well-to-do landowners, lived in one- or two-room log cabins, the imposing two-story **Governor's Palace** at the north end of the Palace Green, with its grand ballroom and opulent furnishings, must have served as a telling declaration of royal power – no doubt enforced by the startling display of swords, muskets, and other deadly weaponry interlaced on the walls of the foyer.

The two conventional museums onsite are the **Abby Aldrich Rockefeller Folk Art Center**, with an intriguing collection of household implements, children's toys, and general bric-a-brac, as well as art by primitive or natural artists; and the **DeWitt Wallace Decorative Arts Museum**, featuring clothing, fine furniture, porcelain, and portraits. Admittance to both is included with admission to Colonial Williamsburg, or you can pay for the pair alone with a $9 ticket. They're located near the reconstructed facade of the **Public Hospital**, two blocks south of Bruton Parish Church. The first asylum in North America, the hospital has replicas of the compartments in which patients were kept and compelling exhibits with recorded conversations tracing the treatment of mental illness in the US.

For those in need of further immersion into the re-created past, as well as a heavy dose of theme-park (sur)reality, the park presents "**Revolutionary City**," a two-hour spectacle during the mid-afternoon around the capitol, in which costumed actors on the streets act out the highlights of the 1770s and 1780s, sweeping up tourists in the rebellious fervor of the day with a flurry of angry speeches and shouting matches.

Yorktown

Yorktown, along the York River on the north side of the peninsula, was little more than farmland when, on October 18, 1781, overwhelmed and besieged British (and German mercenary) troops under the command of Charles, Lord Cornwallis surrendered to the joint American and French forces commanded by George Washington in what turned out to be the decisive final major battle of the **Revolutionary War**. (A handy French naval blockade also helped determine the result.) At the heart of the battlefield, a **visitor center** (daily 9am–5pm; $10 per car for seven-day pass, good also for admission to Jamestown National Historic Site, see p.365; ☎757/898-2410, ⒲www.nps.gov/yonb) has interpretive displays including a replica walk-through fighting ship, military artifacts, and a short audiovisual presentation on the war, and provides several tours of the area. A dozen original buildings survive from the era, along the earthworks dug by the troops. The **Siege Line Overlook** at the visitor center has good views of strategic points, while maps and an audio tour are available if you want to explore in greater detail.

The **Moore House** (summer daily guided tours at 1pm & 4.30pm, spring and fall weekends only; free with park admission) is a pleasant Colonial dwelling whose tours provide information on its owners and the details of the "Articles of Capitulation" signed by Cornwallis – offering terms of his army's surrender. The house survived later battles (and eventual use as a barn) before John D. Rockefeller had it restored; it stands along the York River, a mile east of the visitor center.

Though Yorktown survived the battle more or less unscathed – the fighting took place on open fields to the east, and in the waters of the Chesapeake Bay – much of the area was destroyed by fire in 1814 and was further ravaged as a strategic point during the Civil War. However, **the town** itself – within the historic site – has a handful of interesting old structures worth looking at. These include the handsome homes of local gentry, a customhouse, and, best of all, the archaeological remains of the workshop of the **Poor Potter**, who, contrary to his name, was a prosperous merchant and one of the first businessmen in the colonies to produce quality ceramics and glassworks to rival those imported from England.

Note that, as at Jamestown, the state of Virginia and the National Park Service have constructed a mini theme park nearby – this time a re-created Continental Army encampment – as part of the **Yorktown Victory Center** (daily 9am–5pm; $9.25, or $19.25 with Jamestown Settlement, see p.367; ☎757/253-4838,

@www.historyisfun.org), west of the battlefield on US-17. The museum's exhibits cover both British and American perspectives on the Revolutionary War and the events leading up it. Two outdoor installations use docents in historical costume to portray life on a middle-class farm and in a Revolutionary War camp.

Historic Triangle practicalities

Of the three main sites, only Williamsburg is easily reached without a car. Amtrak **trains** and Greyhound **buses** stop at 468 N Boundary St, two blocks from the Governor's Palace. The Colonial Parkway makes an excellent, scenic cycling route to Jamestown (twelve miles away) or Yorktown (fourteen miles), though the road has no lane markings, and can get narrow in some stretches; rent a **bike** for $15–20 a day from Bikes Unlimited at 759 Scotland St in Williamsburg (☎757/229-4620, @www.bikewilliamsburg.com). In Colonial Williamsburg, ticket-holders can use the hop-on, hop-off **shuttle buses** (9am–5.30pm) that leave from the visitor center every ten minutes or so and stop at convenient points in the historic area. You can also pick up the **Historic Triangle Shuttle**, run through the park service, which is free but requires a shuttle pass available at any of the following attractions on the route: the Jamestown National Historic Site, Jamestown Settlement, Yorktown Battlefield, Yorktown Victory Center, and Colonial Williamsburg (Mar–Oct daily every 30min, 9.30am–4pm).

Accommodation

Most **accommodation** in the Historic Triangle is centered around the Williamsburg area, both the Colonial core and the blander modern town surrounding it. The core offers a select number of B&Bs and a narrow range of functional motels within close range of the bus and train stations, while further out, around the modern town, there's plenty of distinctive accommodation – though of course you'll have to drive or take a hotel shuttle (call for availability).

Accommodation in Williamsburg is handled by Colonial Williamsburg (☎1-800/HISTORY), and ranges from crude motels to four-star chain luxury; there are also rooms in some of the restored eighteenth-century homes and inns within the historic part of Williamsburg – reserve well in advance. Good hotel packages with meals, two nights' lodging, and admission are available for $200 per person. To make your search easier, the Williamsburg Hotel/Motel Association (☎757/220-3330 or 1-800/211-7165, @gowilliamsburg.com) can find you a bed at no charge, often for a discounted rate, usually at one of the major chain hotels or motels.

West of the center, US-60 is lined with endless motels, and there are also several cheap options just a few blocks east of the capitol, including the basic *Bassett Motel*, 800 York St (☎757/229-5175, @www.bassettmotel.com; $65), and the clean and conveniently located *Quarterpath Inn*, 620 York St (☎1-800/446-9222, @www.quarterpathinn.com; $62). For a bit more luxury, *Marriott's Manor Club at Ford's Colony*, 101 St Andrews Drive (☎757/258-5705, @www.marriott.com; $206), is four miles outside of town and has expensive villas as well as entry-level units with DVD players, fireplaces, and patios.

Eating and drinking

The various **restaurants** and taverns along Duke of Gloucester Street in Colonial Williamsburg feature good (if overpriced) pub food; some operate on a seasonal basis only (often April–Oct) and all except *Chowning's Tavern* should be reserved in advance (☏1-800/HISTORY). West of the historic area, in the Merchants Square shopping mall, the excellent *Trellis Café* (☏757/229-8610) serves pricey seafood and steak entrees for dinner, but affordable sandwiches and burgers for lunch, and across the street the *Cheese Shop* (☏757/220-0298) has great deli sandwiches, but expect a wait during peak hours. For even fancier fare, try the *Whitehall*, 1325 Jamestown Rd (☏757/229-4677), which offers elegant, upmarket French dining with a heavy accent on seafood and beef. There is also a clutch of solid restaurants near the William and Mary campus, including the *Green Leafe Café*, 765 Scotland St (☏757/220-3405), offering solid chili, burgers, pizza, and pasta and thirty brews on tap.

24

Baltimore

As one of America's classic industrial cities, **Baltimore** has a reputation of not being suited for the new global economy, its glory days of heavy industry along the port now distant, and its grim inner-city horrors evident in vivid detail on TV shows like *The Wire*. And while some of the city is indeed post-industrialized wasteland and shamefully neglected ghetto, Baltimore can also be among the more enjoyable stops on the East Coast, its closely knit neighborhoods and historic quarters providing an engaging backdrop to many diverse attractions, especially those along its celebrated **waterfront**. As the largest city in Maryland, it also boasts top-rated museums, which cover everything from fine arts to black history to urban archaeology. That Baltimore has been home to such diverse figures as writers Edgar Allan Poe and H.L. Mencken, and civil rights icons Frederick Douglass and Thurgood Marshall, goes some way toward explaining its sometimes bizarrely varied character. You won't want to see too much of the bleaker side of town, though, so stick to the sights listed in this chapter and avoid venturing too far afield into uncertain territory.

Some history

Named after Maryland's founder, Lord Baltimore (English politician and colonizer George Calvert), the city of Baltimore was christened in 1729, a half-century after its namesake's death, and was the second-largest city in America up until 1870. Like San Francisco, Baltimore burned to the ground just after the turn of the twentieth century, leaving only its domed 1867 City Hall (100 N Holliday St) standing. Until the last decade, much of the downtown looked burned in a different way, blighted by poverty and decay. Thankfully, many parts of town have undergone a dramatic face-lift, especially in the Inner Harbor, and you won't have to look hard to find a good sporting event to check into, a delicious seafood plate to tuck into, or a convivial bar to duck into – all are good options in this fascinating port city.

Arrival and information

Baltimore is practically a neighbor to Washington, DC, just 25 miles southwest, and **Baltimore–Washington International Airport** (BWI; ☎410/859-7111, ⓦwww.bwiairport.com) sits between them, ten miles south of the Baltimore city center. The cheapest and best way to get into the city from the airport is on the MTA **commuter rail** system, which takes around 25 minutes ($1.60; ☎410/539-5000 or 1-800/RIDE-MTA, ⓦwww.mtamaryland.com) and connects BWI to the restored Pennsylvania Station (also known as Penn Station), half a mile north

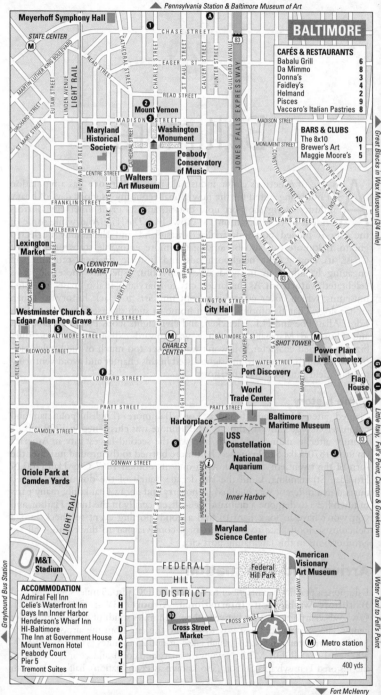

Pennsylvania Station & Baltimore Museum of Art

BALTIMORE

CAFÉS & RESTAURANTS
Babalu Grill	6
Da Mimmo	8
Donna's	3
Faidley's	4
Helmand	2
Pisces	9
Vaccaro's Italian Pastries	8

BARS & CLUBS
The 8x10	10
Brewer's Art	1
Maggie Moore's	5

Meyerhoff Symphony Hall

STATE CENTER

CHASE STREET
EAGER STREET
READ STREET
Mount Vernon
MADISON STREET
Washington Monument
Maryland Historical Society
Peabody Conservatory of Music
Walters Art Museum

FRANKLIN STREET
MULBERRY STREET

Lexington Market
LEXINGTON MARKET
SARATOGA STREET

Westminster Church & Edgar Allan Poe Grave
FAYETTE STREET

BALTIMORE STREET
REDWOOD STREET
LOMBARD STREET
CHARLES CENTER

City Hall
SHOT TOWER
Power Plant Live! complex
Port Discovery
World Trade Center
Flag House

Harborplace
Baltimore Maritime Museum
USS Constellation
National Aquarium
Oriole Park at Camden Yards

CAMDEN STREET
CONWAY STREET

Inner Harbor

Maryland Science Center

M&T Stadium

American Visionary Art Museum

FEDERAL HILL DISTRICT
Federal Hill Park

Cross Street Market
CROSS STREET

Greyhound Bus Station

ACCOMMODATION
Admiral Fell Inn	G
Celie's Waterfront Inn	H
Days Inn Inner Harbor	F
Henderson's Wharf Inn	I
HI-Baltimore	D
The Inn at Government House	A
Mount Vernon Hotel	C
Peabody Court	B
Pier 5	J
Tremont Suites	E

N

(M) Metro station

0   400 yds

Great Blacks in Wax Museum (3/4 mile)

Little Italy, Fell's Point, Canton & Greektown

Water Taxi to Fell's Point

Fort McHenry

24

BALTIMORE

374

of downtown at 1515 N Charles St, which is also the arrival point of Amtrak **trains** (☎1-800/USA-RAIL) from all destinations. Because Penn Station is in a dicey neighborhood, you should either take a cab downtown or get on the **Penn-Camden light-rail shuttle** (Mon–Sat 6am–11pm, Sun 11am–7pm; $1.60 one-way), which stops downtown at Lexington Market, the Convention Center, and Camden Yards. Shuttle **vans** from the airport into Baltimore, including Super Shuttle ($35 one-way; ☎1-800-BLUE VAN, ⓦwww.supershuttle.com), take around twenty minutes to reach downtown. **Taxis** cost around $55. Greyhound **buses** stop south of downtown at 2110 Haines Street, though, as with Penn Station, this is in a grim area and you'll need to take a taxi downtown or bus #27 (weekdays 5am–2am, weekends 6am–1.30am; $1.60 one-way).

Pick up free maps and guides at the **Baltimore Area Convention and Visitors Association**, 401 Light Street, near the Maryland Science Center (April–Oct 9am–6pm, Nov–Mar 9.30am–4.30pm; ☎410/837-7024 or 1-877/BALTIMORE, ⓦwww.baltimore.org), or from its booths at the airport and train station.

Getting around

Because the city is compact – most sights are within a mile or two of the center – you can cover a lot of territory on foot. The **MTA** bus, subway, and light-rail system ($1.60, day pass $3.50; ☎410/539-5000, ⓦwww.mtamaryland.com) covers many locations, including the airport (subway and buses Mon–Fri 5am–midnight, Sat & Sun 6am–midnight; light rail Mon–Sat 6am–11pm, Sun 11am–7pm), though the subway and light rail are limited to one main route each. On buses, have exact change ready. **Taxi** companies include Yellow Cab (☎410/685-1212) and Royal Cab (☎410/327-0330). **Water taxis** link the Inner Harbor and sixteen area attractions, including the National Aquarium, Fell's Point, and Fort McHenry (schedule varies, often summer Mon–Sat 10am–11pm, Sun 10am–9pm, rest of year daily 11am–6pm; usually runs every 15–20min; all-day pass $8; ☎410/563-3901 or 1-800/658-8947, ⓦwww.thewatertaxi.com). Other operators run **cruises** from the Inner Harbor, including Harbor Cruises ($28–50; ☎410/727-3113, ⓦwww.harborcruises.com), which has elaborate dinner outings and special-event cruises.

Accommodation

Baltimore has the usual chain **hotels** available downtown, along with a few unique local institutions that are worth a stay, but the **B&Bs** clustered around the historic waterfront area of Fell's Point are more pleasant. The Convention and Visitors Association (☎410/837-7024 or 1-877/BALTIMORE, ⓦwww.baltimore.org) can help with reservations.

Admiral Fell Inn 888 S Broadway ☎410/522-7377 or 1-866/583-4162, ⓦwww.harbormagic.com. Chic historic hotel spread over seven buildings (some dating back to the 1770s) in the heart of Fell's Point offering rooms with vaulted ceilings, antiques, and fireplaces, and some with Jacuzzis and balconies. $209

Celie's Waterfront Inn 1714 Thames St ☎410/522-2323 or 1-800/432-0184, ⓦwww.Baltimore-Bed-Breakfast.com. Nine exquisite

rooms and suites, all with clean, contemporary design and some with private balconies, and a rooftop deck with superb views of Fell's Point harbor. $169

Days Inn Inner Harbor 100 Hopkins Place ☎410/576-1000, ⓦwww.daysinnerharbor.com. Standard hotel chain with slightly cheaper rates than the rest of the major names, plus pool, gym, and Net access, and centrally located within walking distance to Camden Yards and the Inner Harbor. $180

Henderson's Wharf Inn 1000 Fell St
☏410/522-7087, ⓦwww.hendersonswharf.com.
Prominent waterside presence with modern
rooms boasting fridges, boutique furnishings, and Net access, plus continental
breakfast and onsite gym. $229, though
rates can jump by $70 on weekends

HI-Baltimore 17 W Mulberry St ☏410/576-8880
ⓦwww.baltimorehostel.org. Set in a sturdy
old brownstone from the 1850s, this
centrally located option boasts four dozen
dorm beds in an old-style setting, with
antique furnishings, deck and patio, WI-FI
access, karaoke, and laundry, plus movie
screenings and pasta feeds. $28

The Inn at Government House 1125 N Calvert
St ☏410/539-0566, ⓦwww.baltimorecity.gov
/visitor/inn@gh. Elaborate, restored 1889
Victorian mansion with antique-filled rooms,
grand music and dining rooms, detailed
woodwork, and breakfast and parking
included. $125

Mount Vernon 24 W Franklin St ☏410/727-
2000 or 1-800/245-5256, ⓦwww
.mountvernonbaltimore.com. Formerly a
youth hostel, this large, stately hotel has

comfortable rooms with free high-speed Net
access and complimentary breakfast, plus a
central location. Reserve ahead in summer.
$99

Peabody Court 612 Cathedral St ☏410/727-
7101, ⓦwww.peabodycourthotel.com. Located
in a historic neighborhood, a handsome
1928 apartment building converted into a
luxury hotel, featuring marble bathrooms,
Net access, and upscale decor, and pet-
friendly, too. $209

Pier 5 711 Eastern Ave ☏410/539-2000,
ⓦwww.harbormagic.com. Centrally located,
upscale boutique hotel with plenty of style,
offering smart, modern rooms with CD
players and suites with fridges, microwaves,
and wet bars. $299

Tremont Suites ⓦwww.tremontsuitehotels
.com. A pair of closely sited all-suite hotels
with smart furnishings and central
locations; the Tremont Plaza, 222 St Paul
Place (☏410/727-2222), is an upscale
business property with luxury appointments, while the Tremont Park, 8 E
Pleasant St (☏410/576-1200), offers
modern boutique style. Both are $154–174

Downtown Baltimore

Enlivened by new restaurants and bars, **downtown Baltimore** makes for a pleasant stroll along the brick-lined waterfront and features a bevy of nautical and science-oriented attractions. It's also within walking distance of the two sports stadiums, which makes it a convenient spot for fans to meet for dinner or a drink.

The main cluster of restaurants and cafés is found west of **Charles Street**, in Baltimore's original shopping district, now coming back after a long decline. One Baltimore landmark here, dating from 1782, is the oldest and loudest of the city's covered markets, **Lexington Market**, 400 W Lexington St (Mon–Sat 8.30am–6pm; ☏410/685-6169, ⓦwww.lexingtonmarket.com), with more than a hundred food stalls, including *Faidley's* (see p.382). Safe during the day, the area can become more dicey after dark.

Just south of the market, **Westminster Church**, 519 W Fayette St, was built in 1852 atop the main Baltimore cemetery. Among the prominent figures entombed here is **Edgar Allan Poe**, who lived in town for three years in the 1830s, marrying his 13-year-old cousin and starting a career in journalism before moving on to Richmond, Virginia. In 1849, while passing through Baltimore, Poe was found incoherent near a polling place and died soon after. In 1875 his remains were moved from a pauper's grave and entombed within the stone memorial that stands along Green Street on the north side of the church. Every January 19, a mysterious figure clad in black appears at Poe's grave to offer a toast of cognac and three red roses in honor of his birthday.

Despite the notoriety of the Poe site, most visitors come to visit **Oriole Park at Camden Yards**, five blocks south, the baseball stadium of the Baltimore

Orioles (tickets $8–80; ☎1-888/848-BIRD, ⓦwww.theorioles.com). Open-faced and city-oriented, the park was one of the first to reintroduce a historic flair to stadium design, in contrast to the concrete boxes that had dominated pro sports for a generation. Just next door, looking very much like an alien spaceship that just landed, is the 68,400-seat **M&T Bank Stadium** – built in 1998 and home to the **Baltimore Ravens**, who were named after Edgar Allan Poe's most (in)famous character and won an unexpected Super Bowl victory in 2001 (tickets $50–115; ☎410/547-SEAT, ⓦwww.baltimoreravens.com).

The Inner Harbor

By most estimates, the **Inner Harbor** is a success story of urban revitalization. The rotting wharves and derelict warehouses that stood here through the 1970s have been replaced by the sparkling steel-and-glass **Harborplace** shopping mall (Mon–Sat 10am–9pm, Sun noon–6pm; ☎410/332-4191, ⓦwww.harborplace.com), though the businesses inside aren't too different from what you'll find in any other consumer zone. Sweeping views of the entire city and beyond can be admired from the 27th-story Top of the World observation deck of Baltimore's own **World Trade Center** on the north pier (Oct–April Wed–Sun 10am–6pm; May–Sept 10am–9pm; $5; ☎410/837-VIEW, ⓦwww.viewbaltimore.org). Nothing in the Inner Harbor dates from before its rebuilding, but to lend an air of authenticity, the graceful **USS Constellation** (April–Oct 10am–5.30pm, Nov–Mar 10am–4.30pm; $8.75; ☎410/539-1797, ⓦwww.constellation.org) has been placed here, the only Civil War vessel still afloat and the last all-sail warship built by the US Navy – it was constructed in 1854 and restored in 1999. More ships – a Coast Guard cutter that survived Pearl Harbor, a Chesapeake Bay lightship, and a World War II diesel submarine – and a squat 1856 lighthouse that's been moved here make up the **Baltimore Maritime Museum** (daily 10am–5pm; $6; ☎410/396-3453, ⓦwww.baltomaritimemuseum.org) on the next pier.

Far and away the biggest tourist attraction in Baltimore, the **National Aquarium**, 501 E Pratt St (spring & fall Sat–Thurs 9am–5pm, Fri 9am–8pm, winter opens an hour later, summer daily 9am–8pm; open for 90min after last admission; $22, $26 with dolphin show; ☎410/576-3800, ⓦwww.aqua.org), is an essential sight for anyone with an affection for jellyfish, sharks, rays, sea turtles, and other oceanic creatures, who dart around before visitors in their own enclosed tanks and pools. It is, of course, as much theme park as it is scientific institution, so it's no surprise the aquarium has opened a **Dolphin Amphitheater** in the style of SeaWorld, in which you can see the playful cetaceans cavorting and apparently trying to please the crowd, which is often massive throughout the year.

If this isn't enough for the tykes, try out the gleaming **Port Discovery**, just north of the harbor at 35 Market Place (summer Mon–.Sat 10am–5pm, Sun noon–5pm, rest of year Tues–Fri 9.30am–4.30pm, Sat 10am–5pm, Sun noon–5pm; $10.75; ☎410/727-8120, ⓦwww.portdiscovery.org), a children's museum packed to the ceiling with hands-on exhibits, a media studio where kids can put on their own productions, learning games, interactive toys, and many other amusements.

Federal Hill and around

A short walk south of the Inner Harbor, the **Federal Hill** district is a great place to escape from the crowds. Lined with interesting shops, restaurants, and

▲ USS Constellation

galleries, its main thoroughfare, **Light Street**, leads to the indoor **Cross Street Market**, which opened in 1875 and has two blocks of open-air markets boasting some excellent delis, seafood bars, and fruit stalls. **Federal Hill Park** in the northeast is a quiet public space with fine views over the harbor and the downtown cityscape. In the summer months, it's a popular spot for romance at sunset.

In the northern part of the area, by the harbor at 601 Light St, the sparkling glass, steel, and concrete **Maryland Science Center** (Tues–Thurs 10am–5pm, Fri 10am–8pm, Sat 10am–6pm, Sun 11am–5pm; $16.25, kids $11.75, IMAX show $8; ☎410/685-5225, ⓦwww.mdsci.org) is mainly aimed at kids, with interactive displays on themes ranging from dinosaurs to space travel; an IMAX theater and planetarium provide added interest for youngsters with limited attention spans. More interesting is the **American Visionary Art Museum**, east of Federal Hill Park at 800 Key Hwy (Tues–Sun 10am–6pm; $12; ☎410/244-1900, ⓦwww.avam.org), devoted to the works of untrained or amateur artists, similar to folk art but with a decided edge of off-kilter inspiration ŏr madness. Since the museum holds 4000 pieces by American "visionaries" you're apt to see almost anything on display, crafted from everything from glass and porcelain to toothpicks and tinfoil. Some of the more notable pieces include an obsessively intricate sculpture of the boardwalk of Coney Island, eerie Bosch-like paintings of alien abductions, and all kinds of incarnations of Jesus and the Virgin Mary, formed out of wood, sequins, iron, and many other media.

Mount Vernon

Baltimore's most elegant quarter is just north of downtown on the shallow rise known as **Mount Vernon**. Adorned with eighteenth-century brick townhouses, this district is quite good for strolling and takes its name from the home of George Washington, whose likeness tops the 178ft marble column of the central **Washington Monument** (Wed–Sun 10am–5pm; free), whose 228 steps you can climb for a great view over the city. It's located in a small park next to the spire of the sham-Gothic Mount Vernon Methodist Church at Charles Street and Monument Place.

Across the street, a solemn stone facade of the **Peabody Conservatory of Music** hides one of the city's best interior spaces: the beautiful, skylit atrium of the **Peabody Library**, 17 E Mount Vernon Place (Tues–Fri 9am–5pm, Sat 9am–1pm; ☎410/659-8179), an 1878 Victorian delight rich with cast-iron balconies, soaring columns, and glass skylights. The ground floor features displays of various history books, among them a wonderful illustrated 1555 edition of Boccaccio's *Decameron*, and a 1493 printing of the *Nuremberg Chronicles*. Two blocks west, the **Maryland Historical Society** museum, 201 W Monument St (Wed–Sun 10am–5pm $8; ☎410/685-3750, ⓦwww.mdhs .org), traces the path of local history through portraits of the old Maryland elite and key documents, and its antique-filled chambers give a sense of the maritime wealth created here through nineteenth-century trade. Other items of interest include models of Chesapeake Bay boats, vintage Baltimore hair dryers, a range of decorative arts and furniture from different periods, and the original manuscript of the lyrics to "The Star-Spangled Banner."

A block south of the Washington Monument, the **Walters Art Museum**, 600 N Charles St (Wed–Sun 11am–5pm; $12; ☎410/547-9000, ⓦwww .thewalters.org), is set around a large sculpture court, modeled on an Italian Renaissance palazzo, beyond which modern galleries show off Egyptian jewelry and sarcophagi – including an intact mummy – Greek and Roman antiquities, medieval illuminated manuscripts, Islamic ceramics, and some very fine Byzantine silver. Other floors have pre-Columbian artifacts – among them gold, jade, and shell funerary objects and stone carvings, masks, and sculptures – and French Impressionist works, including Manet's painting of beer-drinking bourgeoisie *At the Café*. Almost everything on display was bought by William Walters, one of the first US collectors of **Chinese** and **Southeast Asian** art. The adjacent restored **Hackerman House** holds some especially beautiful pieces, including a roomful of Chinese jade figurines, a Ming-dynasty hand scroll, some lovely Japanese prints, and a pair of polychrome-and-gilt temple doors carved to look like peacock feathers. The seventh-century lacquered wood statue here of a svelte Buddha is perhaps the oldest such image in the world.

The Flag House and Star-Spangled Banner Museum, and Little Italy

A quarter of a mile east of downtown and the Inner Harbor is the intriguing **Flag House and Star-Spangled Banner Museum**, 844 E Pratt St (Tues–Sat 10am–4pm; last tour at 3.30pm; $7 includes War of 1812 Museum, below; ☎410/837-1793, ⓦwww.flaghouse.org), where in 1813 Mary Pickersgill sewed the 30ft-by-45ft US flag whose presence at the British attack on Baltimore Harbor the following year inspired Francis Scott Key to write "The Star-Spangled Banner." The actual well-worn flag is now in the Museum of American History in Washington, DC (see p.71), but the house is full of other such patriotic tributes, as well as various antiques from the era, and there's a less interesting **War of 1812 Museum** (same hours) that covers that conflict with costumes and military relics.

The densely tangled streets of **Little Italy**, still a strongly Italian neighborhood with dozens of good restaurants and cafés, spread to the east of downtown. The area is built around the 1881 **St Leo the Great** church, 227 S Exeter St, and holds plenty of Baltimore's trademark stone-fronted **row houses**, almost all with highly polished steps quarried from local marble, a rock of such high quality that blocks of it have been used to help construct the stone monuments of Washington, DC.

Fell's Point, Canton, and Greektown

Southeast of Little Italy stands Baltimore's oldest and liveliest quarter, **Fell's Point**, which two hundred years ago hosted many of the region's privateers, leading the British to call Baltimore a "nest of pirates." Projecting into the main harbor, its deepwater frontage made it the heart of the city's extensive shipbuilding industry; the shipyards are long gone, but many old bars and earthy pubs – the highest concentration in the city – have hung on to form one of the better nightlife districts on the East Coast, set in and around handsome nineteenth-century buildings that were luckily spared from the freeway construction that destroyed so many other notable city structures in the twentieth century. Adding to the charm are touches like working tugboats plying the waters and, on the streets, vendors selling produce from horse-drawn carts – they're locally known as "*a*-rabbers." For a more traditional place to pick up a healthy snack, the area's **Broadway Market**, 610 S Broadway (☎410/675-1466), is always a favorite stopping point. The Fell's Point **visitor center**, 808 S Ann St (daily noon–4pm; ☎410/675-6750), provides good self-guided walking-tour maps and tours of the 1765 **Robert Long House**, the oldest surviving urban residence in Baltimore, a handsome Colonial structure dating to 1765.

Other interesting sights include the **Fell's Point Maritime Museum**, 1724 Thames St (Thurs–Mon 10am–5pm; $4; ☎410/732-0278), originally a trolley barn and warehouse, now converted into an exhibition space outlining the area's nautical history as a shipping point for fruit and tobacco, as well as slaves and opium. A different perspective on that history is provided by the new **Frederick Douglass Isaac Myers Maritime Park**, 1417 Thames St (Mon & Wed–Fri 11am–5pm, Sat & Sun noon–5pm; $5; ☎410/685-0295, ⓦwww.douglassmyers.org), a historical museum named after the pioneering black leaders who were active in the area and focusing on their backgrounds and the history of the local port – including the slave trade. It also includes a re-creation of a late nineteenth-century shipyard that employed African Americans.

East of Fell's Point and two miles southeast of downtown, **Canton** is another district full of historic row houses, some of which date back to the Civil War, and is being revitalized with new restaurants and nightlife. North of Canton, the huge and enjoyable **Patterson Park** has jogging paths, duck ponds, and various civic monuments, and is worth a stroll if you're in the area. Along the park's southern edge, one of the city's major arteries, **Eastern Avenue**, makes for a good and fairly safe walk if you want to go back west to Fell's Point and downtown, or a mile east to **Greektown**. Sited between South Haven and Ponca streets, this is still a thriving Hellenic community after almost a century and boasts its share of authentic bakeries, diners, and groceries. The area's centerpiece, and a good place to turn around, is the sturdy brick edifice of **St Nicholas Greek Orthodox Church** at Eastern Avenue and Ponca Street. If your feet give out, you can take the #10 bus from Greektown back to downtown.

Fort McHenry

Linked by water taxi to Fell's Point on the opposite side of the harbor, **Fort McHenry National Monument**, 2400 E Fort Ave (daily 8am–5pm, summer closes 8pm; $7 for seven-day pass; ☎410/962-4290, ⓦwww.nps.gov/fomc), is a star-shaped fort that the British bombed during the War of 1812 to penetrate the harbor to attack Baltimore. The attack failed, and when he saw "the bombs bursting in air," Francis Scott Key was moved to write the poem "The Star-Spangled Banner," first known as "The Defense of Fort McHenry." Over the next century, the fort was used as a prison for Confederate soldiers and pro-Southern political prisoners – with its guns directed *toward* the city – and the country's largest military hospital during World War I. You can tour the fort's old barracks, officers' and enlisted men's quarters, magazine, and guardhouse, and see military hardware and relics of different eras.

Further north

About a mile northeast of the city center, in an old fire station off Broadway at 1601 E North Ave, the **Great Blacks in Wax Museum** (Tues–Sat 9am–6pm, Sun noon–6pm, winter closes an hour earlier; $12; ☎410/563-7809, ⓦwww .ngbiwm.com) uses wax models in posed dioramas to illustrate black history, from Egyptian pharaohs and early Muslims through to Dr Martin Luther King Jr, Marcus Garvey, Rosa Parks, and Malcolm X. The neighborhood is a bit dicey, so drive or take a cab.

Further out on the north side, two miles from downtown, is the Charles Village district, enjoyable for its early twentieth-century row houses and walkable streets. Here, at the top of Charles Street, is the **Baltimore Museum of Art**, 10 Art Museum Drive (Wed–Fri 11am–5pm, Sat & Sun 11am–6pm; free; ☎443/573-1700, ⓦwww.artbma.org). As well as Italian and Dutch works by Botticelli, Raphael, Rembrandt, and Van Dyck, the museum holds Chardin's *A Game of Knucklebones*, played by a smiling scamp, drawings by Dürer and Goya, and photographs from Weston, Stieglitz, and others. One gallery in the West Wing is devoted to Warhol, while the American Wing holds furniture and decorative arts, as well as paintings. The highlight is the **Cone Collection** of works by Delacroix, Degas, Cézanne, and Picasso, as well as over a hundred drawings and paintings by Matisse, among them his signature *Large Reclining Nude* and a *Seated Odalisque*.

Eating

Baltimore's restaurants tend to be unpretentious, family oriented, and reasonably priced (usually under $20 for entrees, and commonly around $10–15), with particularly appealing fresh **seafood** places offering top-notch **steamed crabs** – the city is affectionately known as **Crab City** – as well as the usual range of diners and more than a dozen good family-run restaurants side by side in Little Italy. Fell's Point boasts numerous vegetarian, seafood, and other types of restaurants. Also, search the Web for information on Baltimore's redoubtable monthly tradition of the **Bull & Oyster Roast**, in which a given restaurant is chosen to host a grand feast of pasta, sausage, meatballs, and, of course, oysters on the half shell – all for $35 or so per person, with tickets reserved in advance.

Babalu Grill 332 Market Place, just north of Inner Harbor ☎410/234-9898. A popular restaurant serving well-priced traditional Cuban and Nuevo Latino cuisine in a lively setting – good for its ceviche, ham croquettes, lamb shank, and Cuban sandwich with fried yucca. Tues–Fri 5–10pm, Sat 5–11pm.

Bertha's 734 S Broadway ☎410/327-5795. Casual and inexpensive yet stylish seafood restaurant, tucked away behind a tiny Fell's Point bar, and known for its delicious mussels, crab cakes, high tea, and nightly live blues, Dixieland, and jazz. Sun–Thurs 11.30am–10pm, Fri & Sat 11.30am–11pm.

Black Olive 814 S Bond St, Fell's Point ☎410/276-7141. Expensive but succulent Mediterranean restaurant that has affordable meze (small plates) like grilled octopus salad, calamari, and pan-seared zucchini, as well as pricier, shareable entrees like rack of lamb and lobster tail. Daily noon–2pm & 5–10pm.

Chick 'N Trout 1141 W Baltimore St, Downtown ☎410/528-1339. If you want to try the cheap (under $6) and tasty food locals adore, come to this inner-city eatery (by bus or cab), a mile west of the tourist zone, where the signature "lake trout" – actually a type of whiting – is served fried, piping-hot, and delicious along with other fine soul food. Daily 11am–8pm.

Da Mimmo 217 S High St ☎410/727-6876. Intimate, upscale Little Italy café, with a wide-ranging menu that includes such favorites as clams, saltimbocca, gnocchi, and pasta fagioli, live piano music, and a romantic ambience. Mon–Thurs 11.30am–11pm, Fri & Sat 11.30am–midnight, Sun 11.30am–11pm.

Donna's 800 N Charles St ☎410/385-0180. Delicious sandwiches and burgers for lunch, and savory, midpriced pasta, steak, and seafood for dinner in an elegant Mount Vernon locale. Mon–Thurs 7.30am–10pm, Fri 7.30am–11pm, Sat 9am–11pm, Sun 9am–9pm.

Faidley's 203 N Paca St, Downtown ☎410/727-4898, ⓦ www.faidleyscrabcakes.com. Located in Lexington Market, the best and cheapest of many outlets serving oysters, clams, and other catches from the Chesapeake Bay, including some terrific crab cakes – a business dating back to 1886. Stand-up dining only. Mon–Sat 8.30am–6pm.

Helmand 806 N Charles St ☎410/752-0311. Inexpensive but chic dinner-only Afghan restaurant in Mount Vernon, with plenty of lamb dishes, as well as aushak (leek-filled vegetarian ravioli) and the tasty kaddo borawni (a fried-pumpkin appetizer). Sun–Thurs 5–10pm, Fri & Sat 5–11pm.

Matthew's Pizza 3131 Eastern Ave, west of Greektown ☎410/276-8755. Old-line hole in the wall that looks like it's been around forever and still boasts the city's best slices – rich, tangy, and hot, with a solid crust and traditional ingredients or nuovo toppings like crab.

Obrycki's 1727 E Pratt St, just north of Fell's Point ☎410/732-6399. Baltimore's best and longest-established seafood haunt, with steamed, soft-shell, and broiled crabs at premium prices, among other excellent seafood. Closed in winter. Mon–Thurs 11.30am–10pm, Fri & Sat 11.30am–11pm, Sun 11.30am–9.30pm.

Peter's Inn 504 S Ann St, Fell's Point
☎410/675-7313. Top-notch but casual restaurant with a fine, seasonally rotating menu, where you can get anything from shrimp bisque to seared tuna to a good old New York strip steak, for $14–28 per entree. Tues–Thurs 6.30–10pm, Fri–Sat 6.30–11pm. Also has an enjoyable bar with classic cocktails, open Tues–Sat 5.30pm–1am.

Pisces 300 Light St, Inner Harbor ☎310/528-1234. Swank seafood dining with a view, atop the Hyatt Regency hotel, and fine for its cioppino, lamb chops, and steak at top prices. Also offers a solid Sunday brunch. Tues–Sat 6–10pm, Sun 10am–2pm.

Vaccaro's Italian Pastries 222 Albemarle St, Little Italy ☎410/685-4905. Great spot to load up on cheesecakes, cookies, cannoli, and other sweets, and to indulge in the kind of delicious gelato they make in the Old Country. One of six area locations. Mon–Thurs 11am–7.30pm, Fri–Sat 11am–2am, Sun 11am–4pm.

Ze Mean Bean 1739 Fleet St, Fell's Point ☎410/675-5999. If you're in the mood for rib-stuffing Slavic fare, this is the place to come: get your fill of rich and tasty potato dumplings, crab pierogi, goulash, and even chicken Kiev, most for affordable prices, though the service can be spotty. Mon–Thurs 11am–11pm, Fri 11am–1am, Sat 9.30am–1am, Sun 9am–11pm.

Drinking and nightlife

Baltimore has plenty of places to **drink**, and **Fell's Point** may well have the most. One bar after another lines up along Broadway and the many smaller side streets, and almost all feature some sort of entertainment. The **Power Plant Live!** complex, next to the Inner Harbor at 34 Market Place (☎410-727-LIVE, Ⓦwww.powerplantlive.com), offers a wide selection of dining and mainstream entertainment. In other **music venues**, listen for Baltimore's own club music – with its up-tempo hip-hop, breakbeat, and funk influences – between the standard rock and dance tunes. Meanwhile, the city's highbrow culture is concentrated northwest of the center, in the Mount Royal Avenue area, including the **Meyerhoff Symphony Hall**, 1212 Cathedral St (☎410/783-8000, Ⓦwww.bsomusic.org), and the **Lyric Opera House**, 110 W Mount Royal Ave (☎410/727-6000, Ⓦwww.baltimoreopera.com). For a rundown of what's on, pick up a copy of the excellent free *City Paper* (Ⓦwww.citypaper .com) or check out Ⓦwww.Baltimore.org.

The 8x10 10 E Cross St, Federal Hill ☎410/625-2000. Solid bar and live-music venue that features an eclectic mix of bands, from jazz to indie rock and electronica, often for a cover charge. Hours vary depending on the show.

Brewer's Art 1106 N Charles St, Mount Vernon ☎410/547-9310. The place anyone with a yen for microbrews must visit, a local landmark for beer-making that's tops for its Belgian-style "Ozzy" and dark "Proletary" ales, and good old "Charm City Sour Cherry." Mon–Sat 4pm–2am, Sun 5pm–2am.

Cat's Eye Pub 1730 Thames St, Fell's Point ☎410/276-9085. Cozy, crowded bar, offering a good range of beers and live music nightly, from blues and jazz to bluegrass and folk. Mon–Thurs 3pm–2am, Fri & Sat noon–2am, Sun noon–midnight.

Looney's Pub 2900 O'Donnell St ☎410/675-9235. This animated hang-out, serving up a variety of snacks and beers to the tune of guest DJs, is one of Canton's most popular watering holes. Daily 11.30am–2am, Sun closes midnight.

Lulu's Off Broadway 1703 Aliceanna St, Fell's Point ☎410/537-LULU. Jumping joint where you can sup on BBQ ribs, meatloaf, and lobster sandwiches – as well as vegetarian fare – or knock back a glass of wine or a microbrew while listening to guest DJs on weekend nights. Mon–Fri 5pm–2am, Sat & Sun noon–2am.

Maggie Moore's 21 N Eutaw St, north of Inner Harbor ☎410/837-2100. Smart and appealing Irish pub with handsome decor and nice, dark brews, as well as fare such as a leg-of-lamb sandwich and beef-and-Guinness stew. Daily 11am–2am.

Max's on Broadway 735 S Broadway, Fell's Point ☏410/675-6297. Huge corner venue with a very long bar – doling out some three hundred kinds of beer in bottles, and more than 70 on tap – pool tables, and, upstairs, a clubbier atmosphere in the cigar lounge. Daily 11.30am–2am.

Wharf Rat Bar 801 S Ann St, Fell's Point ☏410/276-9034. This friendly bar, well stocked with English ales and other European imports, as well as regional micro-brews, packs in a trendy and discerning crowd. Also at Camden Yards at 206 W Pratt St (☏410/244-8900). Mon–Sat 11.30am–2am, Sun 11.30am–midnight.

Contexts

Contexts

History

In the two centuries since Washington, DC was founded, it has been at the heart of American government, a showcase city embodying the ideals and aspirations of the United States. Among the mighty monuments and memorials, however, it's often easy to forget it's also a city where people live and work. The **history** below provides a brief exposition of the main themes in the city's development. For more detail on specific matters – from biographies of famous people to histories of buildings – follow the pointers at the end of each section.

Native peoples

The area that is now the nation's capital was, for most of its history of human habitation, populated by native peoples like the **Piscataway**, who spoke an Algonquin dialect and lived on both banks of the Chesapeake Bay. They were content to live a fairly peaceful existence in tepees, hunting and fishing for game, and their dugout canoes and handwoven baskets are evidence of their long-standing culture in the region.

They did, however, have their enemies – the belligerent **Susquehannocks** were perhaps the most fearsome fellow tribe, scheming and attacking their settlements such as Nacotchtant, around present-day Anacostia. The war-mongering of the Susquehannocks, however, could not alone drive the tribe from the region; predictably, it took the presence of **European settlers** to do that. Although Spanish explorer Pedro Menendez cruised around the southern Chesapeake inlets in the sixteenth century, English colonists would later have more interest in the land and prove to be a more formidable foe for the Piscataway than any other they'd encountered.

> National Museum of the American Indian p.87

European settlement

Sponsored by King James I, **English settlers** under Captain John Smith of the Virginia Company in 1608 established the first successful English colony in America at **Jamestown** on the coast to the south. What is now DC was mostly overlooked – though Smith did explore the Potomac River as far as Great Falls, and perhaps beyond. It wasn't until the 1630s that European settlement in the Chesapeake Basin really took off, with the granting to Lord Baltimore of a royal charter establishing a Catholic colony in the region, **Maryland**, that would welcome members of that persecuted denomination from other parts of the British Empire. This grant was timely, since just eight years later, Parliament under Puritan domination would prove openly hostile to any even remotely Catholic enterprises.

Despite early setbacks, the colonists flourished on the back of a thriving **tobacco trade**. In the later seventeenth century both Virginia and Maryland expanded as English, Irish, and Scottish settlers poured into the region, at first allying with the indigenous population of the Piscataway before eventually expelling them from the area. Although Baltimore and other Catholics attempted at first to convert the tribe to Christianity (with little success), much like Protestant colonizers they soon drove the natives further into the wilderness, where they became prey for larger, more dominant tribes. The Europeans also introduced **slaves** from West Africa to work the plantations. Among these slave-holding planters was one Captain John Washington, George's great-grandfather, who in 1656 arrived from Essex in England and immediately set about establishing a plantation on the river. The Potomac remained an important commercial thoroughfare, and vibrant new towns sprang up alongside it: notably **Alexandria** in Virginia (1749) and **Georgetown** in Maryland (1751).

The Revolutionary War and the creation of the capital

Increasing hostilities with England throughout the 1770s led the colonies – now calling themselves states – to draft the Declaration of Independence in 1776. The **American Revolutionary War** (1775–83), however, had already begun, and George Washington was leading troops of volunteer militia, which later formed into something resembling a continental army. The battle that basically guaranteed American independence – Yorktown, in 1781 – was fought just south of DC in Virginia, within 25 miles of the founding colonial site of Jamestown.

After the war, some revolutionary leaders proposed the establishment of a permanent capital city, but conflicting political interests in the new republic made choosing a spot too difficult, so Congress met in several different cities in its early years, including Philadelphia, site of the 1787 **Constitutional Convention**, and New York City, where **George Washington** was inaugurated as the first president of the United States in 1789. The site of present-day DC was chosen for the nation's capital in 1790, largely as a result of **political wrangling**: because the South allowed the federal government to assume the states' Revolutionary War debts (a key Northern demand), the North allowed the new federal capital to be built in the upper South, on the sparsely populated banks of the Potomac River.

With the help of Major **Andrew Ellicott**, a surveyor from Maryland, and the black mathematician and scientist **Benjamin Banneker**, Washington – a mean surveyor himself – suggested a diamond-shaped, hundred-square-mile site at the confluence of the Potomac and Anacostia rivers. Though the land was swampy, it seemed a canny choice: by incorporating the ports of Alexandria in Virginia and Georgetown in Maryland, and building its own port in Anacostia, the city would be ripe for trade, and it was only eighteen miles upriver from Washington's beloved home at Mount Vernon. Maryland ceded roughly seventy square miles of land for its construction, Virginia thirty; and Congress decreed it would be named Washington City, in the Territory (later District) of Columbia, itself a reference to Christopher Columbus. (Thomas Jefferson thought up both monikers.)

L'Enfant's plan

For the job of city planner, Washington recommended **Major Pierre Charles L'Enfant**, a former member of his Continental Army staff and a fellow Freemason who was renowned for his successful redesign of New York's Federal Hall prior to Washington's inauguration. Inspired by the city of Paris and the Palace of Versailles, L'Enfant came up with an ambitious blueprint for the capital, one with both a conventional street grid (Thomas Jefferson's suggestion) and diagonal avenues radiating from ceremonial squares and elegant circles. The avenues were named after the fifteen states that existed in 1791, with those named after Northern states placed north of the Capitol, Southern ones to the south; the most populous states – Virginia, New York, Pennsylvania, and Massachusetts – were represented by the longest roads. A "Grand Avenue" – later known as the National Mall – formed the centerpiece; government buildings were assigned their own plots; a central canal linked the city's ports; and sculptures, fountains, and parks punctuated the design.

Washington was delighted with the scheme, though the existing landowners were less than pleased with the injunction to donate any land needed for public thoroughfares. Moreover, L'Enfant found himself in constant dispute with the District commissioners who had been appointed by Washington to oversee the construction. His obstinacy cost him his job in 1792, and the design of the US Capitol and White House were both later thrown open to public competition.

| The National Mall | p.55 | L'Enfant memorial, Arlington House | p.248 |

Building and rebuilding DC

The first stone of the Executive Mansion – today's **White House** – was laid in 1792, construction of the **US Capitol** followed in 1793, and in 1800 **Congress** and the nation's second president, John Adams, moved from Philadelphia to the nascent city just months before he left office. The following year, **Thomas Jefferson** became the first president to be inaugurated in Washington DC.

The city was scarcely more than a village, however, with only 3500 free residents, largely based around Capitol Hill and the Executive Mansion. And it was far from complete – 3000 slaves, who lived in the swamp-ridden reaches near the river, labored on new buildings, wharves, and streets. Progress was interrupted by the **War of 1812** with England. Although the war was largely fought in far-flung places like Quebec and upstate New York, the British did score a propaganda coup when in 1814 they sailed up the Potomac to burn the

| The Octagon | p.155 | Presidential inaugurations | p.165 |
| US Capitol, history | p.106 | White House, history | p.141 |

C

CONTEXTS | History

The namesake of America's capital city, **George Washington** appropriately shows up everywhere around town – in statues, building names, estates, even on the money you carry. And while it took the general a while to establish himself as a war hero, it was his relative lack of egotism, his political dexterity, and his firm sense of insight that kept his young republic on a course of independence and, ultimately, self-sufficiency.

The Washington family, originally from the north of **England**, emigrated to America in 1656, a decade after the English Civil War (during which they had been fierce loyalists) and the establishment of Oliver Cromwell's military dictatorship. George Washington was born on February 22, 1732, on his wealthy family's plantation in Westmoreland County, Virginia. Although most of what is known about Washington's early life comes from various fawning and fictitious nineteenth-century biographies, it is clear that he received intermittent schooling and excelled in most outdoor pursuits. Because he wasn't his family's first-born son (primogeniture was a big deal in the Cavalier country of north Virginia), he stood to inherit little property other than a small farm on the Rappahannock River. Washington therefore taught himself how to be a **surveyor**, and in 1748 assisted in the surveying of the new port of Alexandria.

At the age of 21 Washington was selected by Virginia's governor to travel into the Ohio Valley to ascertain the strength of the French forces, which had been steadily encroaching on British turf. Soon after, he was appointed **lieutenant colonel** in the Virginia Regiment and, later, aide-de-camp in the French and Indian War, in which he gained his first battle experience, suffering a bad defeat but gaining respect for his leadership qualities. Finishing his service in the war as regimental commander, Washington had few military successes on which to stake his reputation, but he was elected to the **Virginia House of Burgesses** in Williamsburg nonetheless. Giving up his commission, in January 1759, he married the wealthy **Martha Dandridge Custis** – who had two children from a previous marriage – and settled at **Mount Vernon** after his eldest brother died. For a time Washington led the bucolic life of a gentleman plantation owner, a lifestyle buttressed by a large number of slaves. George and Martha never had any children of their own, but they later became guardians to the youngest two of Martha's grandchildren by her first marriage.

Still serving in the House of Burgesses throughout the 1760s, Washington developed a reputation for honesty and good judgment, and was one of the Virginia delegates at the **Continental Congress** in 1774; the following year, when British soldiers clashed with American volunteers at Lexington and Concord, confrontation turned into revolution. At a second meeting of the Continental Congress in June 1775, the 43-year-old Washington was appointed **commander in chief** of the nascent American forces – as much for the fact that he was from Virginia (Congress wanted

White House, the Capitol, and other public buildings to the ground – though they were stopped before they could do the same to Baltimore. President James Madison was forced to relocate to a private DC house, known as the **Octagon**, where the peace treaty ending the war was signed in 1814. Congress met in a hastily assembled Brick Capitol until the original was fully restored in 1819.

The antebellum era

Between the War of 1812 and the Civil War, the new capital struggled to make its mark; it was designed to be America's commercial and industrial showpiece, but was consistently overshadowed by Philadelphia and New York,

to combine the existing New England militia with a general who would also attract Southern volunteers) as for his military experience, which was still fairly modest.

Washington had his limitations as a battlefield tactician; due to early mistakes, his underequipped Continental Army lost more battles than it won. But he did have a knack for imposing order and hierarchy onto the fledgling army and retaining the respect of his forces during trying times. (Throughout the war, Washington shared his soldiers' hardships by spending the winters with them, rather than at Mount Vernon.) He was also a fine judge of talent in his subordinates and promoted such key figures as Friedrich von Steuben and Nathanael Greene, both of whom proved to be excellent tacticians and strategists.

Indeed, Washington proved such an impressive commander that, after the battle at **Yorktown** in 1781 and the establishment of peace two years later, some of his supporters urged him to assume an American "kingship"; instead he resigned his commission and returned to Mount Vernon – a noble act that led many to describe him as a modern **Cincinnatus**, after the Roman general who did much the same thing thousands of years earlier. Four years later, however, he was back in the political arena. After being unanimously elected as the presiding officer at the 1787 **Constitutional Convention** in Philadelphia – where the Constitution was drawn up and ratified – he was unanimously elected by the electoral college in 1789 as the first **President of the United States**.

Washington defined the uncharted role of president while developing the relationship between the executive and other **branches of government**, as well as the relationship between the federal government and those of the states. During his first term, he even negotiated the political minefield that was choosing the site of the new federal capital. The **capital city** was promptly named after him, and the president laid the cornerstone of the US Capitol in 1793 in a ceremony rich with Masonic symbolism (Washington was a committed member). However, he never lived in Washington or the White House – which wasn't finished until 1800 – shuttling instead among New York, Philadelphia, and other Northeastern cities.

Washington was elected to a **second term** in 1793 and would undoubtedly have been granted a third, but in 1797 he was 65 and wanted nothing more than to retire to his farm. Delivering a farewell address to both houses of Congress, he went home to Mount Vernon, where he died two and a half years later on December 14, 1799, from a fever said to have been induced by being caught out in a snowstorm. Congress adjourned for the day, and even the British and French fleets lowered their flags in respect. Martha lived until May 1802, and on her death, Washington's will freed all their slaves. George and Martha are buried together on the grounds of Mount Vernon.

and scarcely had enough residents to make it much of anything except a paper tiger of bureaucracy. **The Mall** – L'Enfant's central thoroughfare – remained a muddy swamp, and construction was slow and piecemeal. Foreign ambassadors collected hardship pay while stationed in this marshy outpost, and criticism was heaped upon the place; early snide detractors included such notable visitors as Charles Dickens (in the 1840s) and Anthony Trollope (1860s).

Despite its critics, however, the capital city was slowly beginning to look the part. **Pennsylvania Avenue** was spruced up as a grand link between the White House and Capitol, monumental buildings like the US Treasury and Patent Office (both by Robert Mills) were added in the 1830s and 1840s, and work started on the **Washington Monument** in 1848. British gentleman scientist and philanthropist James Smithson made a huge bequest in 1829, which led to the founding of the Smithsonian Institution; its first home, the **Smithsonian Institution Building** (or the "Castle"), was completed on the Mall in 1855.

Despite these advancements, Virginia demanded its share of the capital back in 1846, and the District of Columbia lost two of its major components – Arlington and Alexandria. Only Georgetown remained as an independent city in the District outside of Washington.

Though DC's population increased slowly, throughout the first half of the nineteenth century it never reached 60,000. The balance of the steadily rising black population shifted, however, as the number of runaway slaves from Southern plantations and free blacks jumped dramatically. Separate black schools and churches were established as debate intensified between abolitionists and pro-slavery adherents – the so-called **Snow Riots** (1835) saw intimidation and destruction by white mobs intent on maintaining slavery in the capital. Indeed, as it grew, Washington became a microcosm of the divisions searing the country at large – ideologically polarized residents, each eyeing the other with suspicion; political combat so fractious as to make dialogue nearly impossible; and the increasing threat of secession in the air. When the domination of the pro-slavery **Democratic Party** – which had ruled the country for all but eight years since 1800 – came to an end in 1860, so too did the bonds of the nation.

The Civil War

Following the Confederate attack on Fort Sumter in South Carolina, which finally propelled the country into civil war, **Abraham Lincoln**'s call to defend the Union in 1861 brought thousands of volunteer soldiers to Washington, virtually doubling the city's population. Others left to join the Confederate cause, among them **Robert E. Lee**, who abandoned his estate at Arlington and his Union Army post to take command of the Virginia military. Washington, DC, became the epicenter of the Union effort and the North's main supply depot, surrounded by defensive forts (now known as the Fort Circle Parks), its grand Neoclassical buildings turned over to massive makeshift hospitals. Lincoln determined to continue construction in the capital – symbolically, the **Capitol dome** was added in 1863 – despite fear of imminent attack by Southern forces. Though the city was never overrun, several of the bloodiest battles (including Bull Run/Manassas, Antietam, and Gettysburg) were fought within ninety miles of it. Because of these factors, an atmosphere of paranoia developed in the capital, and as reports of spies, saboteurs, and assassins became legion, Lincoln took such drastic measures as suspending certain civil liberties (such as habeas corpus) for residents of nearby Maryland – thought to be a hotbed of rebel intrigue.

As it dragged on, the Civil War became as much about slavery as about preserving the Union, Lincoln's initial goal. Slavery was outlawed in DC in 1862, and in 1863 the **Emancipation Proclamation** freed all slaves in rebel states – though not those of pro-Union slave states like Maryland and Kentucky. Eventually the South was defeated by the North's superior strength and economic muscle, not to mention the striking, yet bloody, strategy of attrition by Union commander **Ulysses S. Grant**, who realized pure, unending carnage – and not elegant battlefield victories of the kind won by Lee – was the way to bring the South to its knees. The war ended in April 1865 with Lee's surrender to Grant at Appomattox Court House in Virginia, not far from the initial battle of the war. Five days later, **Lincoln was assassinated** in Washington while attending a play at Ford's Theatre.

Reconstruction and expansion

The period after the Civil War was an era of tremendous growth in DC, as ex-slaves from the South and returned soldiers settled here; within thirty years, the population stood at 300,000 and distinct neighborhoods had begun to emerge. Black residents now constituted forty percent of the population and enjoyed unprecedented rights and privileges in the aftermath of emancipation. **Suffrage** was extended to all adult men for local DC elections (1866), black public schools were established, the all-black **Howard University** was founded (1867), segregation was prohibited (1870), and ex-slave, orator, and abolitionist **Frederick Douglass** was appointed marshal (and, later, recorder of deeds) of DC (1877).

Just as African Americans were beginning to gain some measure of political rights, the District itself was able to take the first small steps toward the enfranchisement of its citizens, an ongoing process ever since (see box, pp.400–401). At the same time, Washington's cultural profile went from strength to strength, boosted after the 1876 Philadelphia Centennial Exhibition when the Smithsonian Institution built America's first **National Museum** (now the Arts and Industries Building) on the Mall to provide a permanent home for the exhibition's artifacts. The **Renwick** and **Corcoran** galleries – two of the earliest public art museums in the country – both opened during this period. The Washington Monument, first of the city's grand presidential memorials, was finally completed in 1884, as DC began to reshape itself as a national showpiece. As its stock rose, place-seekers and lobbyists (a term first coined during Grant's presidency) flooded into the city, seeking attachment to the administration of the day. One such aspirant, Charles Guiteau, was so incensed at being denied a civil-service post that he assassinated **President James Garfield** in 1881, just four months after his inauguration.

The turn of the century

By the turn of the nineteenth century, Washington had established itself as a thriving, modern capital with civic and federal buildings to match: in a flurry of construction from the 1870s to the 1890s, fine premises for the **Old Post Office**,

The assassination of Abraham Lincoln

In the days after Robert E. Lee surrendered to Ulysses S. Grant on April 9, 1865, officially ending the Civil War, there was a celebratory mood in Washington, DC. On the evening of Good Friday, April 14, 1865, **President and Mrs Lincoln** went to Ford's Theatre to see top actress Laura Keene perform in the comedy *Our American Cousin*, a play about a yokel who travels to England to claim his inheritance. The president's advisers were never very keen on him appearing in public, but Lincoln, as on previous occasions, overrode their objections. The Lincolns were accompanied by their friends Major Henry Rathbone and his fiancée, Clara Harris; the four took their seats upstairs in the presidential box, just after the play had started.

Conspirators had been plotting to kill the president for weeks. **John Wilkes Booth**, a 26-year-old actor with Confederate sympathies and delusions of grandeur, had first conceived of a plan to kidnap Lincoln during the war and use him as a bargaining chip for the release of Southern prisoners. Booth drew others into the conspiracy, notably **John Surratt**, already acting as a low-level courier for the secessionist cause, whose mother owned a rooming house on H Street, where the plot was hatched. **George Atzerodt** from Maryland was recruited because he knew the surrounding countryside and its hiding places, as was **David Herold**, a pharmacist's clerk in DC; **Lewis Powell** (or Paine, as he was sometimes known) was hired as muscle. With Lee's surrender in April, Booth decided to assassinate rather than kidnap the president; Herold, Atzerodt, and Powell were to kill Secretary of State **William Seward** and Vice President **Andrew Johnson**. But these other attacks came to naught: Surratt left the group when the talk turned to murder, Atzerodt chickened out of assassinating Johnson, and while Powell broke into Seward's house and stabbed him in the face and neck, the secretary of state later recovered.

At about 10.15pm, during the third act of the play, when only one actor was on stage and the audience was laughing at a joke, the assassin struck. Lincoln's bodyguard had left the box unattended, and Booth took the opportunity to step inside and shoot Lincoln in the back of the head. Major Rathbone grappled with Booth but was stabbed in the arm with a hunting knife and severely wounded. Booth then jumped the 12ft down onto the stage, catching one of his spurs and fracturing a bone in his left leg as he fell. But he was on his feet immediately – most of the audience thought it was part of the play – and shouted "Sic semper tyrannis!" ("Thus ever to tyrants," the motto of the state of Virginia) before running off backstage and into the alley, where he had a horse waiting.

Pension Building, and **Library of Congress** were erected, while Theodore Roosevelt carried out the first full-scale expansion and renovation of the White House (1901). Meanwhile, LeDroit Park, Adams Morgan, and Cleveland Park became fashionable suburbs, Georgetown was formally merged with DC, and the Smithsonian branched out again with the establishment of the **National Zoo**.

In 1901, a committee under Senator James McMillan proposed the development and extension of the city's park system. Later, the National Commission of Fine Arts was established to coordinate public improvements and new building design: the country's largest train station, **Union Station**, was completed in the prevailing monumental Beaux-Arts style in 1908, and in 1910, height restrictions were

LeDroit Park	p.216	Union Station	p.122
Cleveland Park	p.223	Library of Congress, history	p.118
Foggy Bottom, history	p.154	McMillan Commission	p.64
National Zoo	p.226		

First into the presidential box was **Charles Augustus Leale**, a young army doctor. Lincoln was unconscious and laboring badly, and the decision was made to carry him to the nearest house to care for him better. Once inside the **Petersen House**, Lincoln was placed in the small back bedroom, where Leale and the other doctors strived to save him. Soon the house was bulging at the seams, as Mrs Lincoln, her son Robert, Secretary of War Edwin Stanton, various politicians and army officers, and, eventually, Lincoln's pastor, arrived to do what they could. Lincoln never regained consciousness and died at 7.22am the next morning, April 15; Stanton spoke for all when he declaimed, "Now he belongs to the ages" (or, as some historians assert, to the "angels"). Lincoln's body was taken back to the White House, where it lay in state for three days before the funeral.

Booth, meanwhile, had fled on horseback through Maryland with David Herold, stopping at a certain **Doctor Mudd**'s to have his injured leg treated. The pair hid out for several days, but after crossing into Virginia they were eventually surrounded by Union troops at a farm. Herold surrendered, and on the same day, April 26, Booth was shot dead while holed up inside. All the other alleged conspirators were soon captured and sent for trial on May 10 in a military court at **Fort McNair**. They were kept chained and hooded and, after six weeks of evidence, Herold, Powell, Atzerodt, and Mary Surratt were sentenced to hang, the punishment being carried out on July 7, 1865. A last-minute reprieve for Mary Surratt – who, although she housed the conspirators, probably knew nothing of the conspiracy – was refused, and she became the first woman to be executed by the US government. Dr Mudd received a life sentence, while the stagehand who held Booth's horse at the theater got six years, though both were pardoned in 1869 by Andrew Johnson, Lincoln's successor. John Surratt, who fled America, was recaptured in 1867 and also stood trial, but he was freed when the jury couldn't agree on a verdict.

Much has been written about the effect of the assassination of Lincoln on the country and its future. He was at the start of his second term as president when he died, and many have held that the slavery question and Reconstruction would have been handled with more skill and grace under his leadership. It's impossible to say, though it is interesting to note the personal effect that the close-quarters assassination may have had on the three other occupants of the presidential box that night: ten years later Mary Lincoln – never the most stable of people – was judged insane and committed, and in 1883 Clara Harris (by now Clara Harris Rathbone) was shot by her husband, Henry Rathbone, who died in an asylum in 1911.

imposed on downtown buildings to preserve the cityscape – ensuring that the Capitol remained the tallest and most prominent government edifice. However, after the high hopes of the Reconstruction years, the city's black population suffered from increasing segregation and loss of civil rights. Housing in black neighborhoods like Foggy Bottom and Georgetown was in poor shape, federal jobs became harder to come by, and the black population actually decreased.

World War I and the Depression

The US entered World War I in 1917, despite President **Woodrow Wilson**'s avowed efforts to remain neutral; after the war, Washington's population increased again as soldiers returned home. The postwar years were as troubled for DC as they were for the rest of the US. Under Wilson, **Prohibition** was imposed in a futile attempt to improve the morality of the nation, and a number of strikes were violently broken. **Racial tension** increased in this uneasy climate, which saw segregation become entrenched, with the Ku Klux Klan parading at the Washington Monument and race riots, fanned by demobilized white soldiers, breaking out in the city in 1919. Ironically, segregation also worked to boost the fortunes of DC's black neighborhoods: prevented from socializing elsewhere, African Americans made Shaw's U Street famous as the "Black Broadway," nurturing stars like Duke Ellington – a small bright spot in an otherwise oppressive system of redlining that would exist for another forty years. Elsewhere, the **Phillips Collection**, America's first modern art museum, opened in 1921, while the building of the **Lincoln Memorial** (1922) and the **Freer Gallery** (1923) represented the last cultural gasps of the McMillan Commission.

Washington, with its government agencies and large federal payroll, was not as hard-hit as rural or industrial areas by the **Great Depression**; unemployed "Bonus Marchers" (see p.105) from the rest of the country descended on the Capitol to register their distress in 1931 and 1932, only to be dispersed by the army under the command of Douglas MacArthur. This episode, along with the economic troubles, was another black mark on the record of President Herbert Hoover and led to Franklin Delano Roosevelt's historic victory in the 1932 election.

Roosevelt's **New Deal**, and, specifically, the **Works Progress Administration** (WPA), put thousands of jobless men to work – in DC, building the Federal Triangle and Supreme Court (1935), among other projects. Despite this kind of progressive economic uplift, racial injustice proved a thornier issue. As but one example, in 1939 the **Daughters of the American Revolution** (DAR) infamously banned black contralto Marian Anderson from singing in their Constitution Hall; Anderson subsequently appeared in front of a huge, desegregated crowd at the Lincoln Memorial, in an early hint of the civil-rights battles to come.

▲ Sculpture of 1930s breadline at the FDR Memorial

World War II to the 1968 riots

In 1941 the US entered World War II, and a third great wartime influx boosted the population of Washington, DC. Guards were posted at the White House and Capitol, air defenses were installed in case of Axis attack, and the **Pentagon** was built in 1943 to accommodate the expanding War Department. The war years also saw the opening of the **National Gallery of Art** (1941), one of the nation's finest museums, and the completion of the **Jefferson Memorial** (1943). Following the war, Washington grew as the federal government expanded under presidents Truman and Eisenhower, growing as a result of both the maintenance of New Deal–era programs and fresh military and economic funds to fight the **Cold War**. By 1960, the city's population reached 800,000, the White House was completely overhauled, neighboring Foggy Bottom became the seat of various departments and international organizations, and new housing proliferated in suburban Maryland and Virginia.

The war had gone some way toward changing racial perceptions in America, as black soldiers had again enlisted in droves to fight for freedom, and in the postwar years the **civil rights movement** began to gain strength. Segregation of public facilities was finally declared illegal by the Supreme Court ruling on **Brown v. Board of Education**, and schools in DC were desegregated in 1954. A feeling of progressive hope culminated in the close 1960 election victory of **John F. Kennedy** – the youngest president ever elected, and the only Catholic – and was epitomized by **Dr Martin Luther King Jr**'s famous "I Have a Dream" speech during the **March on Washington for Jobs and Freedom** at the Lincoln Memorial in August 1963. Just three months later, however, JFK was assassinated in Dallas and buried in Arlington Cemetery. In 1964, DC citizens voted in a presidential election for the first time, following the 23rd Amendment of 1961, which gave them new electoral rights. The contest was won in a landslide by Lyndon Johnson, who, as vice president, had become president after Kennedy's death.

By the late 1960s, despite the partial enactment of Johnson's **Great Society agenda**, including new civil-rights and Medicare legislation, the growing **Vietnam War** was taking a huge toll on the president's popularity and national cohesion. Demonstrations in Washington were called against poverty (notably the **Poor People's March**, in 1968) and the war itself, and the assassination of Dr Martin Luther King Jr in Memphis in 1968 led to nationwide **race riots**, including the worst in DC's history: parts of Shaw, Logan Circle, and Old Downtown were devastated. The white flight to the suburbs began in earnest, and DC became a predominantly black city.

Growth and malaise

The 1970s were a time of momentous political upheaval in Washington, DC. In 1970, DC got its first nonvoting delegate to the House of Representatives; three years later, the Home Rule Act paved the way for the city's first elected mayor – **Walter Washington** – in more than a century; and the **Watergate scandal** of 1974 led to the resignation of President Richard Nixon – still the only such occurrence in US history.

Meanwhile, divisions within the city became increasingly stark. Downtown continued to reshape itself – the **Kennedy Center** opened in 1971, the **Hirshhorn Museum** (1974) and East Wing of the **National Gallery of Art** (1979) were added to the Mall, the K Street business and lobbyist district in New Downtown thrived, and artsy **Dupont Circle** became one of the city's trendiest neighborhoods – while Shaw and areas of southeast and northeast Washington slipped further into degradation, with a drug and crime problem that earned DC the enduring tag of "**Murder Capital of America**."

Such contradictions were largely ignored, however, and in 1976, the nation's Bicentennial year, the city celebrated by opening its **Metrorail** system and the **National Air and Space Museum** – still the top museum attraction in America. Jimmy Carter was sworn in as president in 1977 and, after his inauguration, famously walked the distance from the Capitol to the White House, though his tenure was eventually marked by what he called a "malaise," signified by high gas prices, inflation, and unemployment, plus the taking of American hostages in Iran in 1979 – a crisis that Carter failed to resolve, despite a botched rescue attempt. In November 1980 he lost his job to ex-California governor and *Bedtime for Bonzo* co-star Ronald Reagan.

The Reagan era

Under **Ronald Reagan**, the nation's economy boomed and busted as taxes (and welfare and entitlement programs) were slashed and the federal budget deficit soared. In DC, the souped-up economy paved the way for drastic Old Downtown urban-renewal projects, Pennsylvania Avenue and its buildings – eyesores for three decades – were restored, and yuppies began moving into Adams Morgan and Dupont Circle. Reagan survived an assassination attempt at the *Washington Hilton* in 1981, but his reputation (and that of his successor, George Bush) was put in question by the Iran-Contra scandal, involving the sale of illegal arms to the official "enemy," Iran, to finance right-wing Nicaraguan guerrillas. At the same time, as American military spending increased dramatically, major new **memorials** were built to Vietnam veterans (1982) and the US Navy (1987).

Culturally, the city flourished. The Smithsonian expanded its collections on the Mall with the addition of the **Sackler Gallery** and **African Art Museum** (both in 1987), the **National Postal Museum** opened (1986), and Union Station was restored (1988). City politics took a colorful turn with the successive mayoral terms of **Marion Barry** (first elected in 1978), whose initial success in attracting investment soon gave way to conflict with Congress, which was to become the hallmark of the following decade. The city began its slide into insolvency just as Bill Clinton was elected president in 1992 on promises to turn the economy around and restructure welfare.

The Clinton years

To the casual eye, it was business as usual in the 1990s in DC – now one of the most touristed cities in America, with almost twenty million visitors a year – as new attractions continued to open: the **National Law Enforcement Officers Memorial** in 1991, the **US Holocaust Memorial Museum** in 1993, the **Korean War Veterans Memorial** and the **White House Visitor Center** in 1995, and the **FDR Memorial** and **MCI (now Verizon) Center** in 1997. Behind the scenes, though, Washington lurched into crisis in the first half of the 1990s, as the federal budget deficit spiraled. During this period, as the city was grappling with its financial woes, the public exposure of President Clinton's affair with intern **Monica Lewinsky** put DC in the national spotlight in a way not seen since the Watergate hearings of the 1970s. As always, the cover-up seemed worse than the crime, but Clinton, who had scored a political victory in the congressional elections of 1998, survived later impeachment hearings.

The situation was different, though, in 2000, when the Supreme Court for the first time decided a presidential election. The Court, in a still-controversial 5–4 decision, awarded the White House to conservative Texas governor George W. Bush, whose public fight was successfully shepherded by family crony (and former secretary of state) James Baker, while his opponent, Vice President Al Gore, was content to appear before cameras nonchalantly playing touch football with his family.

| US Holocaust Memorial Museum | p.129 | Verizon Center | p.184 |
| Korean War Veterans Memorial | p.62 | Nat'l Law Enforcement Memorial | p.175 |

The new century

On **September 11, 2001**, terrorists hijacked a United Airlines jet and flew it into the Pentagon, killing nearly two hundred people, including those on the plane. A second aircraft, probably headed for the US Capitol, crashed in a Pennsylvania field before reaching its target, while two other hijacked planes destroyed New York City's World Trade Center, killing nearly 3000. Soon after, **anthrax** spores were found in a letter mailed to Senate leader Tom Daschle, heightening tensions in an already shaken DC. The House suspended its session for a week and several federal buildings were closed pending investigation and fumigation. In the aftermath, security was harshly tightened throughout the capital – a lockdown that has slowly loosened in the years since.

Paradoxically, even while the city was on alert its economic fortunes continued to revive. **Anthony Williams**, a former chief financial officer of the council board (who had won election as mayor in 1998) got credit for lower crime rates,

Washington, DC has always had an anomalous place in the Union. It's a **federal district** rather than a state, with no official constitution of its own, and its citizens are denied full representation under the American political system: they have no senator to defend their interests and only a nonvoting representative in the House. This position the capital city shares with American Samoa, Guam, and the Virgin Islands, but unlike those US territories, citizens of the District are responsible for paying federal taxes. And until 1961, when the 23rd Amendment was passed, DC residents weren't permitted to vote in presidential elections.

Although the city has had a mayor and some sort of elected council since 1802, in the early days so many inhabitants were transients – politicians, lobbyists, lawyers, and appointed civil servants – that the local government was denied tax-raising powers; instead, Congress simply appropriated money piecemeal for necessary improvements. In 1871, the District was given **territorial status**. President Grant appointed a governor and city council, and an elected house of delegates and boards of public works and health followed; all adult males (black and white) were eligible to vote. Many of the most significant improvements to the city infrastructure date from this period of limited self-government, with the head of the Board of Public Works, **Alexander "Boss" Shepherd**, instrumental in dredging sewers, paving and lighting streets, and planting thousands of trees. However, Shepherd's improvements and a string of corruption scandals put the city $16 million in debt. Direct control of DC's affairs passed back to Congress in 1874, which later appointed three commissioners to replace the locally elected officials.

And that was how matters stood for a century, until Congress passed the **Home Rule Act** in 1973. Small improvements had already been effected – the first black commissioner (for a city now majority black) was appointed in 1961; later, an elected school board was established. But only in 1974, when the District's first elected mayor in more than a century, **Walter E. Washington**, took office, supported by a fully elected thirteen-member council, did the city wrest back some measure of autonomy. However, Congress still retained a legislative veto over any proposed local laws and kept a close watch on spending limits.

Washington was succeeded as mayor in 1978 by Democrat **Marion S. Barry**, former civil-rights activist and, some would argue, demagogue without compare. At first, he was markedly successful in attracting much-needed investment; he also significantly increased the number of local government workers, which gave him a firm support base among the majority black population. But long-standing whispers about Barry's turbulent private life – charges of drug addiction in particular – exploded in early 1990,

newly paved roads, and a revitalized downtown where restaurants and sports and cultural events began to attract visitors to places once overrun by crime. Areas such as Adams Morgan, Dupont Circle, and especially the **Penn Quarter** attracted new investment and saw their stately, once-decaying old buildings re-emerge as modern showpieces. Perhaps most tellingly, DC's population stabilized at just above half a million after decades of decline, and the city's property values began to soar in places. Still, many parts of the city remained poverty-stricken, and areas of northeast DC – well away from the capital investment zones – sunk even further into economic blight.

The first decade of the twenty-first century saw more openings of new memorials and museums – among them the **National World War II Memorial** and **Newseum** – and visitors returned after some of the terrorist fears ebbed. Washington's **growth** was not without cost, though, as residents priced out of living in the city itself jostled for decent suburban houses near the Metrorail, the thought of doing battle with car commuters on the gridlocked

C

CONTEXTS | History

when he was surreptitiously filmed in an FBI sting operation buying and using crack cocaine. Barry spent six months in prison and was replaced as mayor by Democrat **Sharon Pratt Kelly**, a lawyer who, despite her undoubted expertise, signally failed to improve the city's worsening finances. Nor did she endear herself to the city's employees, and in the mayoral election of 1994, Barry made an astounding comeback after admitting to voters the error of his ways. But a year later, a Republican Congress finally tired of the embarrassment of DC's massive budget deficit and revoked the city's home rule charter. A congressionally appointed financial control board was subsequently given jurisdiction over the city's finances, personnel, and various work departments, stripping away what little responsibility the mayor had left.

Barry didn't stand in the 1998 mayoral election and was succeeded by Democrat **Anthony A. Williams**, a former chief financial officer of the control board, who won a resounding two-thirds share of the vote in his first political foray and, as an avowed technocrat, signaled a shift away from the confrontation of the later Barry years. Washington rebounded under the control board, as deficits became surpluses and city residents could once again afford to be optimistic about their trash being collected. By virtue of its success, the control board put itself out of business in October 2001, and full executive power returned to the mayor and the council ahead of schedule, with Congress (which subsidizes the District) less fearful than before that the federal capital would simply collapse.

But although the District's financial management seems to be improving, a daunting fiscal challenge remains. DC's tax base is too narrow to support the level of services the city requires: two-thirds of the city's workers live (and pay local taxes) in Virginia and Maryland, and roughly forty percent of the land is owned by the government (which excuses itself from taxes). The obvious solution to this problem – a commuter tax – is a nonstarter for political reasons, while past attempts to raise the income tax have only led to more fleeing to the suburbs. Recently elected mayor Adrian Fenty's priorities have been focused more on making the educational system work better than on finding new sources of revenue or restructuring the District's finances.

Whoever DC's leaders may be, many believe that achieving **statehood** would solve the District's financial conundrum (its license plates already decry "Taxation Without Representation"). But the crux of granting statehood to DC lies in the realm of national politics: statehood would likely mean that the District's voters, who are overwhelmingly liberal, would send one Democrat to the House and two to the Senate. Even in the minority, Republicans would almost certainly be able to block such a move with a filibuster.

Beltway just too onerous to imagine. At the same time, places like Shaw and Logan Circle experienced the gentrification that brought new (white) residents even as it drove longer-term (black) residents out.

In November 2006, reform-minded **Adrian Fenty** was elected, becoming at 36 the nation's second-youngest mayor of a major city. Fenty's relaxed and confident style was in contrast to the bombast of some of his predecessors, though his policies were anything but shy and retiring – most prominently, a long-needed overhaul of the ailing city school system. At present, Fenty has more fans than detractors in the city, whose residents also hope for another reform-minded politician to occupy the other major office in town – that of US President – in a pivotal contest due in November 2008.

The American system of government

T he **American system of government** derives squarely from the Constitution of the United States, which was sorted out by the original thirteen states at the Constitutional Convention in Philadelphia and signed on September 17, 1787. Deriving its authority from the essential force of popular sovereignty – "We the People" – the Constitution gave a federal administration certain designated powers so that it could both resist attack from abroad and prevent the fragmentation of the nascent nation. Two centuries and 27 amendments later, its provision of "checks and balances" on the exercise of power still provides the basis for the fundamental stability of a country that has often looked less than united.

The idea was simple enough. The earlier **Articles of Confederation** (adopted during the Revolution) had joined a loose grouping of independent states together in Congress under a weak central legislature with no executive branch, but by the late 1780s it was clear that the system lacked efficiency and coherence. With no separation of powers, Congress had to request permission from the states every step of the way; each state retained the right to refuse consent (whether for money, soldiers, or permission for new laws) and exercised the power in its own interest. What was needed, according to arch-Federalists like Alexander Hamilton, was a strong central government buttressed by a supreme **Constitution**. The anti-Federalists who opposed them (such as fiery orator Patrick Henry, rabble-rouser Sam Adams, and the crafter of Virginia's state bill of rights, George Mason) feared encroachment upon the sovereignty of the states and citizens' liberties, but most were appeased by the promise of the ratification of various amendments (adopted in 1791 in the ten-point **Bill of Rights**) that would encompass many of their demands. What was produced at the Constitutional Convention was nothing less than a triumph: eighty percent of the original text of the Constitution remains unchanged today; only seventeen more amendments have been added in the two centuries following the Bill of Rights; and the United States remains one of the world's most enduring democracies – technically since 1789, but in practice since the abolition of slavery in 1865 and the extension of the right to vote to women in 1920.

As a **federal republic**, the country splits its powers between the government and the fifty individual states, basically protecting the states from unnecessary intrusions from an overbearing central government while allowing federal decisions to be made to benefit (or protect) the whole country, and to manage interstate commerce. Thus the states can police themselves, make local laws and raise taxes, but they can't issue currency, conclude foreign treaties, maintain armed forces, or levy taxes against other states. On the other hand, the Constitution pledges that the federal government shall protect each of the states against invasion or "domestic violence." Moreover, those who framed the Constitution took great pains to emphasize that individual states should retain all powers not specifically "enumerated" by the Constitution; reinforced by the 10th Amendment, this notion remains a fundamental tenet of American democracy, in which local and national powers are stringently defined within the framework of a federal, and not centralized, republic. Thus each state has a significant amount of autonomy, while the states' political structures duplicate the federal system, with their own legislative chambers, state courts, and constitutions.

Finally, over the years constitutional developments have taken place outside the Constitution as **informal changes** have been introduced to the system of government through custom or historical event. The Constitution makes no mention of political parties, primary elections, or congressional committees, for example, though all are now firmly entrenched in the system.

The legislative branch

The **federal government** itself comprises three distinct branches: the **legislative**, **executive**, and **judiciary**. Each operates as a check and balance on the other, and each directly affects individual liberties and not just those of the states.

Article 1 of the Constitution vests all **legislative** powers in a bicameral **Congress** made up of a House of Representatives and a Senate, both of which meet in the US Capitol. When established in the eighteenth century, the House of Representatives was conceived as the body whose directly elected members would represent the people and all their presumably angry, capricious tendencies – essentially the democratic part of the equation. The Senate, or upper house, would not only be a check on the House's power but also a way of balancing the interests of the smaller states against the larger, since each state in the Senate has an equal vote; it was also designed as an elite protector of republican liberty by being a means of controlling the "hot tempers" blowing through the House. Not surprisingly, early senators were sent to Congress by state legislatures – not by direct vote of the people – and were white, property-owning men, largely by design. The separation of roles between House and Senate was institutionalized from the start: representatives and senators are elected at different times, from differently sized constituencies for different terms of office.

The **House of Representatives** (or simply the "House") has 435 members (this number was fixed in 1929), with states allocated a number of representatives based on their population (which is reassessed, or "reapportioned," every ten years; each state is entitled to at least one representative). Members are elected from defined congressional districts (each containing, at present, about 700,000 people, except for the smallest states), serve for two years, and receive $165,200 per annum, rising about three percent annually. The House is still the more representative of the two chambers: more frequent elections mean a closer convergence with the general public's mood, while the House always has a significantly higher percentage of women and ethnic minorities than the Senate (though neither remotely reflects the demographic make-up of the modern US).

Apart from the fifty states thus represented, there are also nonvoting delegates in the House, representing the territories of Samoa, Guam, and the Virgin Islands, and, since 1973, Washington DC itself (see pp.400–401 for more on Washington's peculiar status within the Union). The chief officer of the House is the Speaker – chosen from the ranks of the majority party and paid about $212,100 a year. Each party also elects a leader in the House, known accordingly as the House Majority or House Minority leader, and a House Whip (whose job is to ensure that party members vote the right way).

The **Senate** comprises two senators from each state. In 1913, the 17th Amendment allowed for the direct election of senators by state voters, though the job remains essentially an aristocratic one – this legislative branch is often, and accurately, described as a "millionaires' club." Senators are elected for six years, with one third being elected every two years; like members of the House, they get paid $165,200 a year. The presiding officer in the Senate is the US vice president, but he doesn't have a vote unless it's to break a tie. However, the president pro *tempore* – traditionally the oldest member of the Senate majority party – is by law only two steps below the VP in order of succession to the presidency, with the House Speaker between them.

In Congress, the House and the Senate share certain **responsibilities**, like assessing and collecting taxes, borrowing money, overseeing commerce, minting currency, maintaining the armed forces, declaring war, and, crucially, making "all Laws which shall be necessary and proper for carrying into Execution" of these matters. But each separate chamber also has its own responsibilities: all revenue-raising (tax) bills originate in the House of Representatives, though the Senate can propose changes to such bills; only the Senate can "advise and consent" to the president's foreign treaties, nominations, or appointments. While the House has the sole power of impeachment of the president or other federal officer, the Senate is the body that acts as jury in a political trial, deciding whether or not to remove the office-holder.

The House and Senate have separate chambers in the US Capitol, in which their official debates take place. In practice, however, the **bills** that Congress debates as a prelude to making laws are generally put together and taken apart ("marked up," in the jargon) by more than 250 smaller standing **committees** and **subcommittees** (not to mention ad hoc committees and joint committees) that meet in rooms in the Capitol or in the various relevant House or Senate office buildings. The committees are made up of members from both parties, in rough accordance with their overall strength, and are usually chaired by senior members of the controlling party.

If a bill survives this process (and many don't), it is "reported" to the full House for consideration; at that point **amendments** may be added before the particular bill is voted upon. If it passes, it's sent to the Senate, which can also make amendments before returning it to the House. Any differences are resolved by wrangles in a joint House–Senate **conference committee**, which produces a final bill, acceptable to a majority in Congress. In addition to the standing committees of Congress, on occasion **select committees** are established to deliberate on special congressional investigations or matters of national importance – most famously, perhaps, the unraveling of the Watergate affair (see pp.158–159).

Voting in Congress doesn't always divide up according to party as it usually does in parliamentary democracies. The Speaker and the Rules Committee (which arranges the work of the House) can ensure that the majority party influences the make-up of various committees, the order of debates, and the nature of proposed amendments. In the House, members often vote along state or regional lines on particular issues, while specific matters are increasingly agreed and voted upon by members grouped into caucuses, which can cut across party loyalties.

The executive branch

Once a bill passes Congress, it goes to the **executive** branch of government – whose head is the president, or chief executive – for approval. The **president** can either sign the bill, at which point it becomes law, or veto it, in which case the bill goes back to the chamber where it originated. With two-thirds majority votes in both houses, Congress can override the president to make the bill law. The powers of the president (whose annual salary is currently $400,000, plus expenses; the vice president gets $212,000) are defined in Article 2 of the Constitution.

As well as being chief executive, the president is also **commander in chief** of the armed forces; he or she can make treaties with foreign powers – provided two-thirds of the Senate agrees – and can appoint ambassadors, Supreme Court justices, and other federal officers – with a majority of the Senate approving. Lest the chief executive get too bold, though, the Constitution provides **parameters** for presidential power: under the terms of the 22nd Amendment, ratified in 1951, the president (along with the vice president) is elected to office for four years and may serve only two terms. The amendment was a direct result of the presidency of Franklin Delano Roosevelt, who, determined to preserve his New Deal programs and wary of impending war, was elected for an unprecedented four terms, and served twelve years until his death. Moreover, the president is not above the law and can be removed from office by Congress "on impeachment for, and conviction of, treason, bribery, or other high crimes and misdemeanors."

This, however, is rarely attempted. The **impeachment** of President Clinton in 1999 was only the second such attempt in the country's history (the first was against Andrew Johnson, Lincoln's ill-fated successor; Richard Nixon resigned before he could be impeached), and its failure was due in part to the nebulous nature of the defined standards of impeachment as laid down by the Constitution. "High crimes and misdemeanors" can essentially mean anything the House wants it to – in the eighteenth century, it probably referred to offenses against the state, but thanks to the Clinton impeachment, it now apparently means lying about adulterous affairs with interns as well.

The judicial branch

This entire system is underpinned by the third arm of government, the **judiciary**, whose highest form is manifested in the **Supreme Court**, established by Article 3 of the Constitution. From the outset, the Court was designed as the final protector of the Constitution; its task is to uphold its articles and the laws made under it – in effect, to maintain what the Constitution calls "the supreme law of the land." All members of Congress, and all executive and federal officers, are bound by oath to support and uphold the Constitution since they derive their powers from it. Ultimately, although the Court did not initially have the power to strike down congressional legislation, it gave itself this "judicial review" in the famous case of *Marbury v. Madison* in 1803.

Since then, this notion of judicial supremacy has boiled down to the Constitution's being what the Supreme Court says it is: the country has an "inferior" federal court system, in which legal decisions are made, and states are empowered to pass their own laws, but the appointed justices of the Supreme Court have the absolute right to throw out any legislation or legal argument that, in their opinion alone, violates the Constitution (or for that matter conflicts with the letter of an act passed by Congress). Congress can, however, by the power of the Constitution, bar the Court from ruling on or being involved with certain cases or issues – a right the legislative branch has rarely used, in part because of the murky constitutional implications inherent. The executive branch in the shape of each president is keen to appoint sympathetic justices to the Supreme Court bench. This, fortunately for the system, is not as easy or as predictable as it might appear. For more on the make-up of the Supreme Court itself, see pp.116–117.

Real-world politics

That's the theory of American government. In practice, depending on whom you listen to, the entire structure is in a state somewhere between bare working order and terminal decline, with some even claiming that the framers of the Constitution designed gridlock to be built into the system, so as to slow down the pace of coercive legislation. Political historian David McKay puts his finger on the nub when he says that the "federal system, with its myriad governments and what amounts to fifty-one distinct constitutional structures, is the very essence of fragmentation."

The most obvious drawback of the system of "**checks and balances**" is that it can work both for and against political progress. The Constitution forces the president to work with Congress on policy, and some of the wilder presidential excesses are certainly curtailed by congressional deliberations. But in an entrenched **two-party system** such as exists today, much depends on the prevailing political climate in either House or Senate: stalemate and compromise tend to be the natural outcomes of the checks-and-balances system, though certain legislation brought up in the heat of conflict, such as the Patriot Act in October 2001, can be hurriedly pushed through, its implications to be discovered later.

Real-world congressional politics, as opposed to the theoretical marvel of American democracy, can be an unedifying spectacle, involving the often squalid trading of political favors, known as "**logrolling**." Moreover, the people are increasingly isolated from their elected representatives by the simple fact that candidates now need to be very rich to stand in the first place. Partly in response to the Watergate revelations, the 1974 Federal Election Campaign Act limited party and corporate contributions to a candidate's campaign but failed to place a limit on the candidate's own contributions; unlimited self-financing was upheld by a subsequent Supreme Court decision, and the practice has since become widespread, with millionaires routinely running for House seats that can cost at least $250,000 per campaign, up to ten or twenty times that for a Senate seat, and, in 2008, a quarter-billion for the presidency.

Hardly surprisingly, becoming a member of Congress is now seen as a career move: having invested the time and money, incumbent members are less likely to stand down regardless of their personal or political failings and, statistically, are much more likely to be re-elected than a challenger. At the presidential level, institutional ossification has meant that races for the nation's highest office end up being contests between incumbents of one kind or another – in the past 76 years only one election (1952) has paired two presidential candidates who didn't happen to include one sitting president or vice president (though 2008 promises to be another).

Although Democrats and Republicans are increasingly polarized in liberal and conservative camps, third-party candidates have failed to make any enduring impact. A reasonably high (though ultimately futile) protest vote went to the outspoken Texas billionaire Ross Perot in 1992 and again in 1996. Consumer advocate Ralph Nader nabbed a respectable 2.75 percent share of the popular vote in 2000, but because these votes arguably tipped the election to George

Bush, only one-half of one percent of voters cast their ballots for Nader in 2004. Moreover, voters are becoming less willing to give a president an overwhelming mandate. Since Richard Nixon's landslide in 1972, the presidential victor's share of the popular vote has bobbed under and around fifty percent – the only one to buck the trend was Ronald Reagan, who in 1984 gained almost 59 percent of the vote. In the end, though, the general indifference felt for what happens on Capitol Hill is perhaps best indicated by the fact that only 30 to 55 percent of eligible voters actually cast votes in presidential and House elections – one of the lowest voter turnouts in any democracy in the world.

Presidents of the USA

Name	Party	Date	State of birth	Notable facts
George Washington	–	1789–97	Virginia	Only president unaffiliated by party
John Adams	Federalist	1797–1801	Massachusetts	First to occupy White House; died on July 4
Thomas Jefferson	Democratic-Republican	1801–09	Virginia	Wrote Declaration of Independence; died on July 4
James Madison	Democratic-Republican	1809–17	Virginia	Co-wrote US Constitution; started War of 1812
James Monroe	Democratic-Republican	1817–25	Virginia	Presided over "Era of Good Feelings"; died on July 4
John Quincy Adams	Democratic-Republican	1825–29	Massachusetts	Elected by Congress, not popular majority
Andrew Jackson	Democrat	1829–37	South Carolina	"Old Hickory"; last to have fought in Revolutionary War
Martin Van Buren	Democrat	1837–41	New York	Nickname "Old Kinderhook" may have led to word "OK"
William H. Harrison	Whig	1841	Virginia	"Old Tippecanoe"; died a month after inauguration
John Tyler	Whig	1841–45	Virginia	First unelected president; first to face impeachment attempt
James Polk	Democrat	1845–49	North Carolina	Started Mexican–American War; died 3 months after leaving office
Zachary Taylor	Whig	1849–50	Virginia	"Old Rough and Ready"; died after two years in office
Millard Fillmore	Whig	1850–53	New York	"His Accidency"; not nominated for re-election
Franklin Pierce	Democrat	1853–57	New Hampshire	Friends with Nathaniel Hawthorne; not nominated for re-election
James Buchanan	Democrat	1857–61	Pennsylvania	Only bachelor president; not nominated for re-election
Abraham Lincoln	Republican	1861–65	Kentucky	Preserved Union during the Civil War; first president killed in office
Andrew Johnson	Union	1865–69	North Carolina	Military governor of Tennessee; first president to be impeached
Ulysses S. Grant	Republican	1869–77	Ohio	"Galena Tanner"; Civil War commander of Union forces
Rutherford B. Hayes	Republican	1877–81	Ohio	Elected by Congress, not popular majority
James A. Garfield	Republican	1881	Ohio	Last president born in a log cabin; second killed in office
Chester A. Arthur	Republican	1881–85	Vermont	Diagnosed with fatal kidney disease; not nominated for re-election
Grover Cleveland	Democrat	1885–89	New Jersey	"Uncle Jumbo"; only president married in White House
Benjamin Harrison	Republican	1889–93	Ohio	Elected by Congress, not popular majority
Grover Cleveland	Democrat	1893–97	New Jersey	Only president to serve two non-consecutive terms

William McKinley	Republican	1897–1901	Ohio	First to campaign from front porch; third killed in office
Theodore Roosevelt	Republican	1901–09	New York	Fought at San Juan Hill; Teddy Bear named for him
William H. Taft	Republican	1909–13	Ohio	Got stuck in a White House bathtub; became Chief Justice of Supreme Court
Woodrow Wilson	Democrat	1913–21	Virginia	First directly re-elected Democrat in 84 years; retired and died in DC
Warren G. Harding	Republican	1921–23	Ohio	Known mainly for Teapot Dome scandal and affairs with mistresses; died in office
Calvin Coolidge	Republican	1923–29	Vermont	"Silent Cal"; last Republican not to seek re-election
Herbert Hoover	Republican	1929–33	Iowa	First president born west of Mississippi; second longest-lived
Franklin D. Roosevelt	Democrat	1933–45	New York	Only president to serve more than two terms; died in office
Harry S. Truman	Democrat	1945–53	Missouri	"Give 'em hell Harry"; dropped atomic bomb, fought Cold War
Dwight D. Eisenhower	Republican	1953–61	Texas	Supreme Allied Commander in WWII; last general to be elected
John F. Kennedy	Democrat	1961–63	Massachusetts	Youngest elected president; fourth killed in office
Lyndon B. Johnson	Democrat	1963–69	Texas	"Landslide Lyndon"; last Democrat not to seek re-election
Richard M. Nixon	Republican	1969–74	California	Re-elected with 49 states in 1972; resigned two years later
Gerald Ford	Republican	1974–77	Nebraska	Served as vice president and president; not elected to either position
James (Jimmy) Carter	Democrat	1977–81	Georgia	First Democrat defeated for re-election since Cleveland
Ronald Reagan	Republican	1981–89	Illinois	"The Gipper"; oldest elected president (69 and 73)
George Bush	Republican	1989–93	Massachusetts	First sitting VP to be elected president since Van Buren
William (Bill) Clinton	Democrat	1993–2001	Arkansas	First Democrat to serve two full terms since FDR; first impeached since Andrew Johnson
George W. Bush	Republican	2001–	Connecticut	Chosen by US Supreme Court in 2000; (re-)elected in 2004

Books

T here are plenty of **books** that touch upon the history, politics, and personalities of Washington, DC; the problem is in getting an over-all picture of the city. There's no one single, straightforward, and up-to-date history of the District, and visitors through the ages have tended to include their observations of the capital only as part of wider works about America. However, every book on American history contains at least a few pages about the founding of DC; Civil War treatises highlight the city as Lincoln's headquarters (and place of assassination); and presidential autobiographies and biographies, from those of George Washington onward, necessarily recount the daily experience of political and social life in the District.

Although assembling any selection of books on the US capital can be akin to taking a chip off the tip of an iceberg, what follows are some of the better volumes about Washington, DC, including novels set in the city. Many are available in good bookstores everywhere, and most in stores in DC itself. Every major museum, gallery, and attraction here sells related books, too, and these are a good first stop if you're looking for something arcane or specific. The selection in the National Museum of American History is perhaps the finest, while the Smithsonian Institution publishes a wide range of titles on a variety of city-related topics. Finally, the White House Historical Association (gift shop at 740 Jackson Place, New Downtown ☎202/737-8292, ⊛www.whitehouse history.org) publishes a series of informative accounts of the White House, its architecture and contents, and occupants.

Publishers are listed US first, UK second. Note that titles marked "o/p" are not currently in print, though with sufficient effort on the Web (on sites such as Abebooks.com, Amazon.com, or Bookfinder.com) you may be able to locate them.

Guidebooks

Thomas J. Carrier *Washington DC: Historic Walking Tour* (US, Arcadia). Photographic record of the development of DC, incorporating informed walking tours around downtown areas. Carrier's *Historic Georgetown* is another excellent book in this fine Arcadia series on DC history.

Alzina Stone Dale *Mystery Reader's Walking Guide: DC* (Backinprint. com/iUniverse.com). Eight guided walks around the city in the company of the words of mystery writers, taken from some 200 volumes; one of several city-mystery volumes by this author.

Federal Writers Project *WPA Guide to Washington DC* (o/p). Classic volume detailing a history and survey of then-contemporary

DC, from the view of the 1930s New Deal. Interesting observations penned when many of the Neoclassical structures (such as the Supreme Court and Lincoln Memorial) were relatively new.

Kathryn Allamong Jacob *Testament to Union* (US, Johns Hopkins University Press). Exhaustive record of the District's Civil War monuments and memorials, with more than ninety photographs by Edwin Harlan Remsberg and accompanying historical text.

John J. Protopappas and Alvin R. McNeal *Washington on Foot* (US, Smithsonian). A regularly updated volume providing historic treks around DC, with good maps and diagrams; includes coverage of lesser-known spots like LeDroit Park, Meridian Hill, and Takoma Park, MD.

![icon] **Christopher Weeks, ed.** *AIA guide to the Architecture of Washington, D.C.* (US, Johns Hopkins University Press). A handy resource for exploring the city and deciphering the differences between, say, the Federal and Georgian styles, and for getting the details on all the monuments and memorials.

Travel accounts

Christopher Buckley *Washington Schlepped Here* (Random House/ Crown). Republican's light-hearted view of the capital in a slim, somewhat amusing volume focusing mainly on the Mall and Capitol Hill. The stylings of a poor man's P.J. O'Rourke.

David Cutler *Literary Washington* (o/p). The words and wisdom of celebrated writers, past and present, who have visited, worked in, and lived in DC.

Charles Dickens *American Notes* (US & UK, Penguin Classics). Dickens came here in the early 1840s, when it was still, famously, a "City of Magnificent Intentions." Amusing satirical commentary about the US that's lighter in tone than the author's later, more scabrous *Martin Chuzzlewit*.

Jan Morris *Destinations* (US & UK, Oxford University Press). Typically dry observations of Washington high- and low-life; one of a series of pieces (about international cities) first written in the early 1980s for *Rolling Stone* magazine.

Anthony Trollope *North America* (University of Michigan/Granville). Two-volume account of Trollope's visit to the US in the early 1860s. Picking up where his pioneering mother, Fanny, had left off in her contentious *Domestic Manners of the Americans* (1832; Kessinger/ Penguin), Trollope offers much carping about irredeemably vulgar Yanks.

Art and architecture

Cynthia R. Field, ed. *Paris on the Potomac: The French Influence on the Art and Architecture of Washington, D.C.* (US, Ohio University Press). Compelling account of how the District was developed by Pierre Charles L'Enfant in line with Gallic concepts of what an imperial city should look like, realized much later with the full development of the city and some of the French-inspired art movements that flowered here.

Marjorie Hunt *The Stone Carvers: Master Craftsmen of Washington National Cathedral* (o/p). Eye-opening volume about two Italian American artisans who transformed the look of Washington and other cities with their fluid, detailed stonework. Features many fine photos of their work at the Cathedral.

Luca Molinari *The Italian Legacy in Washington, D.C.: Architecture, Design, Art and Culture* (US & UK, Skira). Although the French usually get credit as being the foremost foreign influence on the city, Washington, DC, also had a considerable Italian presence in its Neoclassical design, Capitol frescoes, and park stylings – as evocatively explored in this photo-heavy tome.

David Ovason *The Secret Architecture of Our Nation's Capital:*

The Masons and the Building of Washington, D.C. (US, Harper). Better researched than it sounds, but still controversial in its thesis that Masons like Washington and Jefferson designed the capital according to the blueprint of Freemasonry.

History

Catherine Allgor *Parlor Politics* (US, University of Virginia Press). As nineteenth-century DC developed from backwater to capital, the arrival of high society in the shape of the First Ladies and their social circles began to have a growing influence on politics – a thesis encapsulated in the book's subtitle: "In which the ladies of Washington build a city and government."

Mark Anderson and Mark Jenkins *Dance of Days: Two Decades of Punk in the Nation's Capital* (US, Akashic). Long-overdue story of DC's impact on subversive culture – in this case, the various forms of punk, as practiced by seminal acts like Bad Brains, Minor Effect, Henry Rollins, and, in more current times, Fugazi.

Tracey Gold Bennett *Washington, D.C. (Black America Series)* (US, Arcadia). Two-volume saga of the prominent African American presence in the city, beginning in the Civil War era and continuing up to the present, and powerfully covering emancipation movements, heroic leaders, race riots, and gentrification along the way.

David Brinkley *Washington Goes to War* (o/p). Acclaimed account of the capital during World War II under FDR, charting its emergence onto the international stage with countless anecdotes and stories of life in the era.

Francine Curro Cary *Washington Odyssey: A Multicultural History of the*

Pamela Scott and Antoinette J. Lee *Buildings of the District of Columbia* (o/p). Though more than a decade old, still the best and most comprehensive guide to the structures in the city, with countless stories and facts behind each, explaining the development of the capital.

Nation's Capital (US, Smithsonian). An interesting account of settlement in the city by all manner of peoples from around the world, as well as of the capital's deeply set racial discrimination.

Alistair Cooke *Alistair Cooke's America* (UK, Weidenfeld & Nicolson). The author's thorough, eloquent overview of American life and customs occasionally touches on DC, as well as US politics. Also worth a look are any of Cooke's other volumes on the American experience.

Jeffrey Meyer *Myths in Stone: Religious Dimensions of Washington DC* (US, University of California Press). Examines the lesser-known spiritual side of the capital, evident in its rituals, culture, and architecture, and places the city in a global religious context.

Anthony S. Pitch *The Burning of Washington: The British Invasion of 1814* (US, Naval Institute Press). Recounting of the dramatic events of the summer of 1814 as the British set fire to the young capital and Francis Scott Key was inspired to write "The Star-Spangled Banner."

Zachary M. Schrag *The Great Society Subway: A History of the Washington Metro* (US, Johns Hopkins University Press). As the title indicates, not just any old subway history, but one that touches on the social and economic challenges that were addressed with the creation of the District's modern mass transit system, which spared the city from being carved up by freeways like other cities of the time.

Paul K. Williams *Greater U Street* (US, Arcadia). Another in an excellent series on DC neighborhoods in the "Images of America" series, this one focusing on the history and culture of Shaw in the days of "Black Broadway," the Lincoln Theatre, and Duke Ellington.

Presidents

See also the *American Presidents* series (Times Books; Arthur Schlesinger, ed.), which cover almost all the presidents, from George Washington to George H.W. Bush, in slim volumes written by noted writers and historians.

Robert Caro *The Years of Lyndon Johnson* (US, Vintage). Essential (and ongoing) history of the champion of the Great Society and purveyor of the Vietnam War. So far the three volumes cover LBJ only to his election as vice president, but these are still rich and revealing volumes about the developing character of this larger-than-life figure – and cumulatively perhaps the best biography of any president.

Robert Dallek *An Unfinished Life: John F. Kennedy, 1917–1963* (Little Brown/Penguin). Detailed and penetrating analysis of JFK's considerable strengths as a leader, as well as his human flaws of philandering and imprudence. The best and most balanced contemporary book on the 35th president.

David Herbert Donald *Lincoln* (US, Simon & Schuster). Hands-down the definitive volume covering the life and legend of the Railsplitter, who guided the Union through its most traumatic period, the Civil War. Lincoln's biography is also covered by authors ranging in the hundreds.

Joseph Ellis *American Sphinx: The Character of Thomas Jefferson* (Vintage/Knopf). Thoughtful volume describing the contradictory aspects of the third president, as a proponent of states' rights who expanded the federal government, and as a champion of liberty who owned slaves. Also outstanding is the author's *His Excellency: George Washington* (Random House/Knopf), providing additional insight on a familiar American icon.

Ulysses S. Grant *Personal Memoirs* (US & UK, Penguin Classics). Indispensable classic written (with the aid of Mark Twain) while the ex-president was dying, covering his life from childhood to the end of the Civil War. A highly readable and illuminating view of war and sacrifice – by far the best book written by, and one of the best written about, any president.

Lloyd Lewis *The Assassination of Lincoln: History and Myth* (UK, Bison). Lyrical, minute-by-minute account of the city's most notorious assassination and the conspiracy's aftermath, first published in 1929 as *Myths After Lincoln*.

David Maraniss *First in His Class: A Biography of Bill Clinton* (US, Simon & Schuster). Fine, balanced look at the strengths and weaknesses of the 42nd president, prescient in some ways in foreseeing his successes and pitfalls. Winner of the Pulitzer Prize.

David McCullough *John Adams* and *Truman* (US & UK, Simon & Schuster). Folksy historian and public-TV personality who's made a career out of resurrecting the reputations of underestimated presidents from the past. The Truman claim to presidential greatness is a lot easier to swallow than that of Adams.

Edmund Morris *The Rise of Theodore Roosevelt* and *Theodore Rex* (Modern Library/Random House). Still the essential accounts of the rise of the New York governor, Spanish-American war hero, corporate trust-buster, namesake of the teddy bear, and "accidental" two-term US president.

Richard Reeves *President Nixon: Alone in the White House* (UK, Simon & Schuster). A scholar's view of the many momentous decisions made in the heady days of the Nixon White House, and how the paranoia and insularity that were the president's flaws eventually consumed him.

Robert V. Remini *Andrew Jackson* (US, Johns Hopkins University). Three thick volumes on the life and times of the seventh president, from his dark side supporting slavers and Indian removal, to his paradoxical role as a fervent democratizer who threw a chaotic inauguration party for the public that nearly ruined the White House.

Jean Edward Smith *FDR* (US & UK, Random House). While there are scores of books on the titanic figure of the 32nd president, this recent one skillfully synthesizes the voluminous information on his lengthy presidency, from the Depression to the New Deal to World War II. Aficionados of the latter conflict will also appreciate Jon Meachem's *Franklin and Winston: An Intimate Portrait of an Epic Friendship* (Random House/Granta).

Henry Wiencek *An Imperfect God: George Washington, His Slaves, and the Creation of America* (US, Farrar, Straus & Giroux). Of the hundreds of volumes dealing with the first president, this is the first to focus, quite incisively, on his actions regarding slavery and thoughts on emancipation.

Bob Woodward and Carl Bernstein *All the President's Men* (US, Pocket); *The Final Days* (US, Simon & Schuster). America's most famous journalistic sleuths tell the gripping story of the unraveling of the Nixon presidency. Although both men have written plenty of investigative books since, none has matched these early classics.

Politics and electioneering

Paul F. Boller *Presidential Anecdotes*; *Presidential Campaigns*; *Presidential Wives*; *Congressional Anecdotes*; *Presidential Inaugurations*; *Presidential Diversions* (all US & UK, Oxford University Press). Amusing, inconsequential political factoids – who did what, where, when, and with whom. Good for a round of trivia while you're waiting in line at the Mall.

George Crile *Charlie Wilson's War* (Grove/Atlantic). Instructive primer on Washington politics, in which a sex-scandalized congressman and a shadowy CIA agent help to secretly funnel millions of dollars to

Afghanistan's Communist-fighting mujahideen – who later became the Taliban. Made into a passable movie.

Doris Kearns Goodwin *Team of Rivals* (US & UK, Simon & Schuster). Acclaimed volume detailing how Abe Lincoln gathered his party adversaries – men he had beaten for the nomination – and used them to fashion the greatest war cabinet, perhaps the greatest cabinet period, in US history.

David Halberstam *The Best and the Brightest* (US, Ballantine). Unforgettable portrait of the proud, swaggering brain trust of secretaries and advisers to JFK and LBJ, who, despite their brilliance and advanced college degrees, led the nation into a disastrous war in Vietnam. A chilling tale with many modern implications.

Richard Hofstadter *The American Political Tradition* (US, Vintage). One of the twentieth century's finest and most insightful volumes on American presidents and politicians and the economic forces behind them. Also essential is the author's *Paranoid Style in American Politics* (US, Harvard University Press), now more relevant than ever.

David McKay *American Politics and Society* (UK, Blackwell). Best introduction to who does what, why, and when in the US government, with diversions into American beliefs and values and coverage of social, economic, and foreign policy, told from a British perspective.

Norman Mailer *The Armies of the Night* (US, Plume). The late author's 1967 Pulitzer Prize–winning description of the March on the Pentagon, protesting the Vietnam War, is still essential reading, full of drama and color – as well as plenty of surly antics by Mailer himself.

P.J. O'Rourke *Parliament of Whores* (Grove/Atlantic). Demented political insights and raving right-wing prejudices, brought together in a scabrous, amusing critique of the American political system as practiced in Washington, DC.

Hunter S. Thompson *Fear and Loathing on the Campaign Trail '72* (Grand Central/HarperPerennial). More than 35 years after its release, still a dark and hilarious look at how campaigns are waged in the media age, with evil, glowering Nixon administering an electoral whipping to George McGovern, in whom the normally cynical Thompson had tragically placed his hopes.

Theodore H. White *The Making of the President 1960* (o/p). Still one of the quintessential books for understanding American politics, using the Kennedy–Nixon race as a case study for the manufactured stagecraft and imagery of contemporary elections. Subsequent, less groundbreaking but still diverting, volumes cover the next three campaigns through 1972.

Biography

Dean Acheson *Present at the Creation: My Years in the State Department* (Simon & Schuster/Norton). One of the best volumes about the Cold War as seen from a political insider, in this case Truman's secretary of state, whose careful use of diplomacy steered US policy (and politics). The author's penetrating self-awareness is refreshing, too.

Ben Bradlee *A Good Life* (US, Simon & Schuster). Autobiography of the executive editor of the *Washington Post*, covering the years between 1968 and 1991, during which Watergate and its fallout made the author America's most famous editor.

Ron Chernow *Alexander Hamilton* (US & UK, Penguin). Standout work that looks at the colorful life, controversial politics, and far-sighted economic policies of America's first Treasury secretary – better known as that wig-wearing fellow on the $10 bill, who happened to be on the losing end of a famous duel.

Frederick Douglass *The Life and Times of Frederick Douglass* (US, Library of America). The third volume (1881) of statesman, orator, and ex-slave Frederick Douglass's autobiography sees him living in DC as US marshal and recorder of deeds.

If Washington has one domestic scandal that still towers above all others, it's **Watergate** (see pp.158–159), whose various aspects have been exhaustively covered since Woodward and Bernstein first set the ball rolling with *All the President's Men*. For the full story, you could consult Fred Emery's *Watergate: The Corruption of American Politics and the Fall of Richard Nixon* (US, Touchstone) or a host of other eyewitness accounts, most of which are out of print but cheap and easily available on the Internet. These include Nixon's own *Memoirs*, Robert Haldeman's *Haldeman Diaries: Inside the Nixon White House*, John Dean's *Blind Ambition* and *Lost Honor*, John Erlichman's *Witness to Power*, and G. Gordon Liddy's *Will: The Autobiography of G. Gordon Liddy* – all first-hand (if not completely reliable) testimony from those who were at the time.

Virtually everyone else involved has written about the affair at some point or other, too, from Watergate burglar James McCord to Judge John Sirica to Mark Felt, whose recent *G-Man's Life: The FBI, Being "Deep Throat" and the Struggle for Honor in Washington* (US, Public Affairs) attempts to explain why this former associate director of the FBI decided to rat Nixon's henchmen out to Woodward and Bernstein. Also interesting, some of the secret tapes recorded by Nixon, betraying his paranoia and prejudices, turn up in Stanley Kutler's *Abuse of Power: The New Nixon Tapes* (Kindle/Pocket).

But the first volume, *Narrative of the Life of Frederick Douglass: An American Slave* (1845), which covers the author's early life (prior to his arrival in DC), is actually more gripping.

Katharine Graham *Personal History* (o/p). Pulitzer Prize–winning autobiography of the *Washington Post* owner and Georgetown society hostess lifts the lid on DC's social and political niceties.

Meg Greenfield *Washington* (US, Public Affairs). Posthumously published memoir by longtime columnist, editorial writer, and, eventually, editor of the *Washington Post*. Greenfield writes perceptively about the cocoon-like qualities of DC life and the range of its beguiling personalities.

Marjorie Williams *The Woman at the Washington Zoo: Writings on Politics, Family and Fate* (US, Public Affairs). Intimate and penetrating profiles of Washington insiders from the Bush and Clinton administrations are leavened with the author's own story of her (ultimately losing) battle with liver cancer, in this poignant and evocative memoir-anthology.

Fiction and literature

Henry Adams *Democracy* (US, Library of America). A story of electioneering and intrigue set in 1870s Gilded Age–era DC, written (anonymously) by the brilliant historian grandson of John Quincy Adams.

Anonymous *Primary Colors* (US, Random House). Published amid great controversy in 1996, a highly readable, barely disguised account of a presidential primary campaign by young, charismatic, calculating, philandering, Southern governor Jack Stanton. Its author was eventually unmasked as Washington insider Joe Klein.

John Barth *The Tidewater Tales* (US, Johns Hopkins University Press). A couple goes sailing in the waters of Chesapeake Bay, only to become immersed in picaresque stories of local history and lore, Eastern legends, and the CIA. Worthwhile for anyone with a taste for postmodern fiction – playing narrative games and turning words and meanings inside out.

William Peter Blatty *The Exorcist* (Buccaneer/Corgi). Seminal horror story about the possession of a teenage girl, written in 1971, set around Georgetown University, and made into one of the scariest films ever produced.

Allen Drury *Advise and Consent* (o/p). Blackmail and slippery Senate politics in Washington's upper echelons in the late 1950s; a cautionary tale that still has an effect a half-century after it was written.

James Ellroy *American Tabloid* (Vintage/Arrow). Scandal-mongering conspiracy tale of biblical proportions, tying the Mafia, JFK, renegade Cubans, and rogue FBI and CIA officers into an infernal web of lies and deception, with all manner of Washington evil at the epicenter.

Sebastian Faulks *On Green Dolphin Street* (US & UK, Vintage). A British diplomat's wife embarks on an affair with an American reporter during the 1960 presidential election. The Cold War politics of the period act as a chilly backdrop to this taut tale of love and deception.

Edward P. Jones *Lost in the City* (o/p). Fourteen moving short stories about residents trying to get by in the depressed under- and working-class world of DC in the 1960s and 1970s, well away from the tourist zones and halls of political power.

Ward Just *Echo House* (UK, Houghton Mifflin). Elegiac, epic novel of a DC political dynasty and its intrigues and impact on national politics, with much to say about the nature of power in the city.

Sinclair Lewis *It Can't Happen Here* (NAL/Signet). Disturbing,

oddly humorous tale of the coming of fascism to the US, brought by a goofy yet conniving politician with a folksy, homespun style – a familiar figure these days.

Robert Littell *The Company* (Overlook/Pan). Thick and impressive tale of postwar subterfuge in which the CIA fights America's secret battles while fictional characters cross paths with real-life Cold Warriors from the time.

H.L. Mencken *The Vintage Mencken* (US & UK, Vintage). Compelling selection of writings by the "Sage of Baltimore," who wryly, sagaciously, and acidly commented on the innovations, intrigues, and idiocies of American life and politics as he saw them in the first half of the twentieth century. Also good is the *American Mercury Reader* (US, Kessinger), excerpting some of the most notable pieces from the literary magazine he founded in 1924.

Gore Vidal *Burr*; *Lincoln*; *1876*; *Empire*; *Hollywood*; *Washington DC*; *The Golden Age* (Vintage/Abacus). DC's – and America's – most potent and cynical chronicler sustains a terrific burst of form in seven hugely enjoyable novels tracing the history of the US from the Revolution to modern times and relying heavily on Washington set-piece scenes. The moving epic *Lincoln* is the best.

Walt Whitman *Leaves of Grass* (US & UK, various). The first edition of this poetic juggernaut appeared in 1855, and Whitman added sections to it for the rest of his life. His war poems, *Drum-Taps* (1865), were directly influenced by his work in DC's Civil War hospitals. *Memories of President Lincoln*, added after the assassination, includes the famous and affecting "O Captain! My Captain!"

Crime and thrillers

Tom Clancy Blockbuster thriller writer who weaves DC scenes into nearly every tale of spook and terrorist intrigue. *Debt of Honor* (US, Random House) has the president, his cabinet, and most of Congress perishing in a terrorist attack on the US Capitol, while *Executive Orders* (Random House/HarperCollins) sees Jack Ryan taking over as president of a shattered US.

John Grisham DC pops up in most of Grisham's work, notably in *The Pelican Brief* (Trafalgar Square/Arrow), a legal whodunit starting with the assassination of two Supreme Court judges and delving into dodgy politics and murky land deals, and in *The Street Lawyer* (Delta/Arrow), an exposé of District homelessness and poverty.

David Ignatius *A Firing Offense* (o/p). *Washington Post* journalist puts his newspaper experience to good use in an intelligent espionage thriller that jumps from DC locations to France and China.

Charles McCarry *Old Boys* (Penguin/Phoenix). Spy yarn by a long-standing espionage stylist that has CIA agents searching for a missing person, with globe-trotting to China, the Middle East, and Europe along the way. His *Shelley's Heart* (o/p) is a page-turning thriller detailing stolen elections, secret societies, and other shenanigans, while *Lucky Bastard* (o/p) details the rise of a (familiar) charismatic, liberal, womanizing presidential hopeful.

Peter Moskos *Cop in the Hood* (US, Princeton University Press). Gripping, true-life story of a sociologist who spent a year in the Baltimore ghetto as a police officer to understand the underpinnings of drug-related violence, and discovered why America's perpetual War on Drugs is destined to fail. A good corollary to *The Wire* (see p.422).

George P. Pelecanos Hip raconteur who writes pointedly about the city in a series of great thrillers, spanning the years and ethnic divide. *A Firing Offense* (his first), *Nick's Trip*, and *Down By the River Where the Dead Men Go* (all US & UK, Serpent's Tail) introduce feisty private eye Nick Stefanos; *King Suckerman* (Dell/Serpent's Tail) is a tour de force of 1970s drugs and racial tension; while *The Sweet Forever* (Dell/Serpent's Tail) updates Suckerman's characters to coke-riddled 1980s DC. Good later novels include the vivid *Hard Revolution* and *The Night Gardener* (both Grand Central/Phoenix).

Phyllis Richman *The Butter Did It* (o/p). The *Washington Post's* longtime restaurant critic tries her hand at mystery, introducing Chas Wheatley, the "*Washington Examiner*" restaurant reviewer-turned-detective.

Elliott Roosevelt *Murder in the . . .* (US & UK, St Martin's Press). White House murder tales (with the dark deed committed in the *Blue Room*, *West Wing*, etc) by FDR's son, with the highly improbable First Lady–turned–sleuth Eleanor riding to the rescue every time.

Margaret Truman *Murder . . .* (US & UK, Ballantine). Harry's daughter churns out murder-mystery potboilers set in various neighborhoods and buildings of DC, from Georgetown to the National Cathedral.

Film

I

t's possible that more **films** have been set in the District of Columbia than any American city outside of LA or New York. However, despite this celluloid familiarity, few movies (aside from a few penetrating documentaries) have ever really examined life in DC, gotten to the core of its politics, or looked beyond Capitol Hill or the White House. Therefore, the list of relevant DC films is much shorter than one might expect, and basically revolves around the decisions, personalities, and antics of fictional presidents; the untrustworthy plotting of politicians on the Hill and generals at the Pentagon; and the lovely historic backdrop of Georgetown. Following the film title are its year of release and director's name – though not all films can be said to have a definite "auteur" style.

Comedies and musicals

1776 (Peter H. Hunt, 1972). Amazingly, this musical view of the American Revolution is one of the very few memorable films on the subject – but if you don't enjoy history set to tub-thumping show tunes, you're out of luck.

Americathon (Neal Israel, 1979). Memorably bad "comedy" (with music) in which a down-on-his-luck presidential sap must rescue the floundering US by holding an oddball telethon; features a cast that somehow includes John Ritter, Meat Loaf, Harvey Korman, Elvis Costello, and Jay Leno.

Being There (Hal Ashby, 1979). Unforgettable comedy about a simple-minded gardener (Peter Sellers) who leaves the Washington estate of his deceased employer and unwittingly becomes a political pawn and, possibly, presidential candidate.

Dr. Strangelove (Stanley Kubrick, 1964). The archetypical satire of the Cold War Pentagon gone berserk, in

which a power-mad general brings the world to the brink of annihilation, fearing a Communist takeover of his "precious bodily fluids."

The President's Analyst (Theodore Flicker, 1967). Political cult film in which James Coburn plays the title character, who gets into all sorts of trouble when various spies and thugs want to find out what he knows. A classic conspiracy-theory satire.

State of the Union (Frank Capra, 1948). Republican bigwig Spencer Tracy asks his estranged wife to return to him to aid his election, putting on a public show for the media and causing all manner of high jinks.

Thank You for Smoking (Jason Reitman 2006). Goofy and amusing story of master lobbyist Aaron Eckhart's shenanigans shilling for tobacco industry while navigating a thicket of corporate and personal politics in the District.

Documentaries

American Hardcore (Paul Rachman, 2005). Riveting tale of how the punk style that involved simple, thrashing rhythms,

slam-dancing and all manner of aggression found its champions across the US, but especially in DC, where Bad Brains, Minor Threat, and Henry Rollins made the capital one of the essential cities, along with LA, for the movement.

Fahrenheit 9/11 (Michael Moore, 2004). The ultimate liberal attack on the controversial policies of George W. Bush, which won the top prize at Cannes and became the most successful documentary in history.

The Fog of War (Errol Morris, 2003). A long dark look at the now-aged former Defense Secretary Robert McNamara, who plunged the US deeper into the Vietnam War despite his own misgivings. Told in the secretary's own paradoxical, ambivalent words.

Milhouse – A White Comedy (Emile de Antonio, 1971). Dark documentary satire about the foibles and trickery of Richard

Nixon, whose own words and deeds are used to indict him. Made three years before his resignation and long before Watergate was a household word.

Point of Order (Emile de Antonio, 1964). Stark black-and-white documentary with images taken from the McCarthy hearings of the 1950s, in which the Wisconsin senator's own ranting paranoia and deceptions are made clear before the cameras.

The Trials of Henry Kissinger (Eugene Jarecki, 2003). Angry polemic about the former secretary of state's alleged misdeeds in toppling the government of Chile, illegally bombing Cambodia, and countless other acts of official wickedness. Based on the book and magazine articles by arch-contrarian Christopher Hitchens.

Horror and sci-fi

The Day the Earth Stood Still (Robert Wise, 1951). Classic sci-fi in which an alien makes the mistake of landing his spaceship in Washington, DC, demanding earthlings give up their warlike ways or else. He is, of course, killed, which sends his trusty robot companion Gort out for vengeance against the town that wronged him.

The Exorcist (William Friedkin, 1973). The lodestar of religious-horror movies, filmed along 36th Street in Georgetown, giving us unforgettable scenes of evil-possessed Linda Blair speaking and retching

with satanic intensity, as well as a famously "head-turning" moment.

Independence Day (Roland Emmerich, 1996). Wildly successful, though crude and ham-fisted, action flick about aliens who greet earth with a barrage of destruction, including blowing up the White House in one of the more famous images of 1990s Hollywood overkill.

Werewolf of Washington (Milton Ginsberg, 1973). Semi-cult film about a White House press secretary who goes lupine and bites the prez and others. More interesting as a period piece than compelling cinema.

Partisan politics

Advise and Consent (Otto Preminger, 1962). Lengthy, close-in view of the tortuous process that secretary of state nominee Henry Fonda must undergo when subjected to the machinations of Congress

– vividly personified in the figure of a drawling Southern pol played with aplomb by Charles Laughton.

Bob Roberts (Tim Robbins, 1992). Dark satire about a right-wing senatorial candidate who uses charm and folksiness to reach the Capitol. Prescient and still amusing, if a bit ponderous in spots.

Citizen Cohn (Frank Pierson, 1992). Incisive look at the closeted gay arch-McCarthyite Red-hunter and right-wing operative Roy Cohn (James Woods), who reviews his life while dying of AIDS.

Mr. Smith Goes to Washington (Frank Capra, 1939). An exercise in earnest, apple-cheeked faith in the body politic, still loved for its image of populist hero Jimmy Stewart fighting wags and charlatans on Capitol Hill and triumphing with his honesty and courage.

Wag the Dog (Barry Levinson, 1997). Political satire that sounds better than it plays – a president desperate to recover from a sex scandal reacts by declaring war and seeing his popularity jump. All well and good, until the movie limps along to the end.

Presidents

🏃 **All the President's Men** (Alan J. Pakula, 1976). Appearing just a few years after the Watergate scandal, one of the few Hollywood films with a premise drawn from real-life politics (crusading journalists exposing a baleful president) that actually made money; shot at many sites across the city.

American President (Rob Reiner, 1995). Dewy-eyed portrait of the life and loves of vaguely Clintonesque president Michael Douglas, who wines and dines tough-gal lobbyist Annette Bening, drawing cheers and tears in equal measure.

Backstairs at the White House (various, 1979). Little-remembered but worthy TV mini-series (available on DVD) that depicted the lives and struggles of the servants in the President's Mansion, bearing witness to monumental events and outsize figures from presidents Taft to Eisenhower.

Dave (Ivan Reitman, 1993). Another strangely affectionate 1990s portrait of a fictional president, this one being Kevin Kline. An earnest Everyman who's also a look-alike for the president subs after the chief exec has a stroke.

Gabriel Over the White House (Gregory La Cava, 1933). Eerie period piece about a corrupt president who sees the eponymous angel and gets inspired to clean up his act, reform the nation, imprison – and execute – his enemies, and force peace upon other countries at the barrel of a gun.

The Man (Joseph Sargent, 1972). James Earl Jones stars as the president *pro tempore* of the Senate who, after a national tragedy, suddenly becomes US president and has to battle racists and thick-headed politicians determined to dethrone him.

Nixon (Oliver Stone, 1995). A grim look into the brooding mind of the only US president to resign. Anthony Hopkins plays Tricky Dick, doing a gallant job of stifling his Welsh accent and looking appropriately sweaty and paranoid.

Primary Colors (Mike Nichols, 1998). John Travolta plays Jack Stanton, a Southern governor seeking the White House with dangerous libidinal tendencies. Mildly amusing and strongly familiar.

The Tall Target (Anthony Mann, 1951). Excellent, nearly forgotten film about an early murder plot against Abraham Lincoln, scheduled to take place on a train headed to his Washington inauguration.

Dick Powell plays the hero – oddly enough named John Kennedy – who must thwart the assassination.

🏃 **Thirteen Days** (Roger Donaldson, 2001). Riveting insider story detailing how the brothers Kennedy and their crony (Kevin Costner) outflanked the Russians in the potentially world-ending nuclear duel of 1962's Cuban Missile Crisis.

Thrillers

Arlington Road (Mark Pellington, 1999). Washington terrorism expert Jeff Bridges sees danger in his well-scrubbed neighbor, Tim Robbins, and thinks he may have stumbled onto an authentic homegrown killer. Complications ensue in this gripping, somewhat uneven thriller.

🏃 **Breach** (Billy Ray, 2007). Absorbing depiction of master spy and FBI agent Robert Hanssen, whose antics spying for the Russians were caught in 2001, but only after he'd caused incalculable damage to US national security. This shifty, contradictory figure is memorably played by Chris Cooper.

Fail Safe (Sidney Lumet, 1964). President Henry Fonda plays a slow, excruciating game of nuclear chicken with the Russians as a US bomber crew is sent on a fatal, erroneous errand to destroy cities in the USSR.

The Good Shepherd (Robert DeNiro 2006). Matt Damon plays a dyed-in-the-wool CIA man whose commitment to the "company" verges on the obsessive, to the point where he endangers his relationships with his family and friends to ferret out Russian moles. Story based on an even stranger historic character, James Jesus Angleton.

In the Line of Fire (Wolfgang Petersen, 1993). Top-notch action-thriller with Secret Service agent Clint Eastwood racing around to protect an undeserving president from the home-made bullets of psycho assassin John Malkovich; filmed around Dupont Circle and Capitol Hill.

No Way Out (Roger Donaldson, 1987). A Pentagon-oriented thriller in which Kevin Costner must investigate a crime whose trail leads squarely back to himself, featuring scenes set in Georgetown and a memorable twist ending. Remake of film-noir classic *The Big Clock*.

🏃 **Seven Days in May** (John Frankenheimer, 1964). Striking conspiracy thriller about thuggish general Burt Lancaster plotting a coup to achieve nefarious right-wing ends; Kirk Douglas fights to stop his evil deeds.

The Wire (various, 2002–08). One of TV's greatest serials shows the side of Baltimore hidden to most tourists, exposing the inner city in its drug dealers, cops, politicians, schoolteachers, and reporters. A brilliant tour de force of television (available on DVD), and better than most movies.

CONTEXTS | Film

Travel
store

ROUGH
GUIDES

NOTES

Small print and

Index

A Rough Guide to Rough Guides

Published in 1982, the first Rough Guide – to Greece – was a student scheme that became a publishing phenomenon. Mark Ellingham, a recent graduate in English from Bristol University, had been travelling in Greece the previous summer and couldn't find the right guidebook. With a small group of friends he wrote his own guide, combining a highly contemporary, journalistic style with a thoroughly practical approach to travellers' needs.

The immediate success of the book spawned a series that rapidly covered dozens of destinations. And, in addition to impecunious backpackers, Rough Guides soon acquired a much broader and older readership that relished the guides' wit and inquisitiveness as much as their enthusiastic, critical approach and value-for-money ethos.

These days, Rough Guides include recommendations from shoestring to luxury and cover more than 200 destinations around the globe, including almost every country in the Americas and Europe, more than half of Africa and most of Asia and Australasia. Our ever-growing team of authors and photographers is spread all over the world, particularly in Europe, the USA and Australia.

In the early 1990s, Rough Guides branched out of travel, with the publication of Rough Guides to World Music, Classical Music and the Internet. All three have become benchmark titles in their fields, spearheading the publication of a wide range of books under the Rough Guide name.

Including the travel series, Rough Guides now number more than 350 titles, covering: phrasebooks, waterproof maps, music guides from Opera to Heavy Metal, reference works as diverse as Conspiracy Theories and Shakespeare, and popular culture books from iPods to Poker. Rough Guides also produce a series of more than 120 World Music CDs in partnership with World Music Network.

Visit www.roughguides.com to see our latest publications.

Rough Guide travel images are available for commercial licensing at www.roughguidespictures.com

Rough Guide credits

Text editor: Shea Dean
Layout: Umesh Aggarwal, Sachin Tanwar
Cartography: Jai Prakash Mishra
Picture editor: Michelle Bhatia
Production: Rebecca Short
Proofreader: Jan McCann
Cover design: Chloë Roberts
Photographer: Paul Whitfield, Angus Oborn
Editorial: **London** Ruth Blackmore, Alison
Murchie, Karoline Thomas, Andy Turner, Keith
Drew, Edward Aves, Alice Park, Lucy White,
Jo Kirby, James Smart, Natasha Foges, Róisín
Cameron, Emma Traynor, Emma Gibbs, James
Rice, Kathryn Lane, Christina Valhouli, Monica
Woods, Mani Ramaswamy, Joe Staines, Peter
Buckley, Matthew Milton, Tracy Hopkins, Ruth
Tidball; **New York** Andrew Rosenberg, Steven
Horak, AnneLise Sorensen, April Isaacs, Ella
Steim, Anna Owens, Sean Mahoney, Paula
Neudorf, Courtney Miller; **Delhi** Madhavi Singh,
Karen D'Souza
Design & Pictures: **London** Scott Stickland,
Dan May, Diana Jarvis, Nicole Newman,
Mark Thomas, Sarah Cummins, Emily Taylor;
Delhi Ajay Verma, Jessica Subramanian,
Ankur Guha, Pradeep Thapliyal, Anita Singh,
Nikhil Agarwal
Production: Vicky Baldwin
Cartography: **London** Maxine Repath, Ed
Wright, Katie Lloyd-Jones; **Delhi** Rajesh
Chhibber, Ashutosh Bharti, Rajesh Mishra,
Animesh Pathak, Jasbir Sandhu, Karobi Gogoi,
Amod Singh, Alakananda Bhattacharya, Swati
Handoo
Online: Narender Kumar, Rakesh Kumar,
Amit Verma, Rahul Kumar, Ganesh Sharma,
Debojit Borah, Saurabh Sati, Ravi Yadav
Marketing & Publicity: **London** Liz Statham,
Niki Hanmer, Louise Maher, Jess Carter, Vanessa
Godden, Vivienne Watton, Anna Paynton, Rachel
Sprackett, Libby Jellie, Jayne McPherson, Holly
Dudley; **New York** Geoff Colquitt, Katy Ball; **Delhi**
Ragini Govind
Manager India: Punita Singh
Reference Director: Andrew Lockett
Operations Manager: Helen Phillips
PA to Publishing Director: Nicola Henderson
Publishing Director: Martin Dunford
Commercial Manager: Gino Magnotta
Managing Director: John Duhigg

Publishing information

This fifth edition published September 2008 by
Rough Guides Ltd,
80 Strand, London WC2R 0RL
345 Hudson St, 4th Floor,
New York, NY 10014, USA
14 Local Shopping Centre, Panchsheel Park,
New Delhi 110017, India
Distributed by the Penguin Group
Penguin Books Ltd,
80 Strand, London WC2R 0RL
Penguin Group (USA)
375 Hudson Street, NY 10014, USA
Penguin Group (Australia)
250 Camberwell Road, Camberwell,
Victoria 3124, Australia
Penguin Books Canada Ltd,
10 Alcorn Avenue, Toronto, Ontario,
Canada M4V 1E4
Penguin Group (NZ)
67 Apollo Drive, Mairangi Bay, Auckland 1310,
New Zealand

Cover concept by Peter Dyer.

Typeset in Bembo and Helvetica to an original
design by Henry Iles.

Printed and bound in China

© Jules Brown and JD Dickey 2008

No part of this book may be reproduced in any
form without permission from the publisher except
for the quotation of brief passages in reviews.

448pp includes index

A catalogue record for this book is available from
the British Library

ISBN: 978-1-85828-053-0

Help us update

We've gone to a lot of effort to ensure that
the fifth edition of **The Rough Guide to
Washington, DC** is accurate and up to
date. However, things change – places get
"discovered", opening hours are notoriously
fickle, restaurants and rooms raise prices or
lower standards. If you feel we've got it wrong or
left something out, we'd like to know, and if you
can remember the address, the price, the hours,
the phone number, so much the better.

Please send your comments with the subject
line "**Rough Guide Washington, DC Update**"
to ®mail@roughguides.com. We'll credit all
contributions and send a copy of the next edition
(or any other Rough Guide if you prefer) for the
very best emails.

Have your questions answered and tell others
about your trip at
®community.roughguides.com

Acknowledgements

J.D. would like to thank his friends and family, as well as his contacts and facilitators including those at the Convention and Visitors Association for the District, including Georgetown, and the Virginia Tourism Corporation. Thanks also to Sarah Crocker and Allison Goldstein for ongoing help with accommodation, and to Zora O'Neill and Peter Moskos for their thoughts and consideration on Baltimore. J.D. would like to offer a hearty huzzah to Andrew Rosenberg and Steven Horak in the Rough Guides' office, and most of all to his editor Shea Dean, who really helped this project realize its full potential and has been an excellent source of insight, analysis, diligence, and vigor. Finally, thanks to Umesh Aggarwal for layout, Michelle Bhatia for photo editing, and Jai Prakash Mishra for cartography.

The editor would like to thank J.D. for another rewarding collaboration. Throughout the process his prodigious talent with words, keen sense of humor, and unflagging professionalism were truly inspiring. Thanks also go out to Umesh Aggarwal for his precision and patience with the layout, to Michelle Bhatia for her dedication to finding just the right images, and to Jai Prakash Mishra and Katie Lloyd-Jones for making the book's maps the best they've ever been. Finally, a big thank you to Jan McCann for careful proofreading and incisive queries, to Ella Steim for indexing, to Steven Horak for keeping on top of it all, and to Andrew Rosenberg for steering the ship.

Photo credits

All photos © Rough Guides except the following:

SMALL PRINT

Front cover
Columns of The Jefferson Memorial
© Photolibrary.com

Back cover
United States Capitol dome shines through spring blossoms © Alamy

Things not to miss
10 Replica Bond car © Courtesy International Spy Museum
13 4th of July fireworks © Olga Bogatyrenko/ iStock
14 Cherry blossoms, Jefferson Memorial © Lance Lehnhof/iStock

African American DC color insert
Martin Luther King, Jr. © Bettmann/Corbis
Mount Vernon: slave quarter's interior © Courtesy Mount Vernon Ladies' Association

Duke Ellington reviewing music © Underwood & Underwood/Corbis
Parents and children watching a show © photolibrary

DC TV color insert
Richard M. Nixon © Bettmann/Corbis
Congress in session © Dennis Brack/drr.net
Pat Buchanan of Meet The Press © Alex Wong/ Getty Images
A reporter behind the camera © Elan Fleisher/ Alamy
Jim Webb © Matthew Cavanaugh/epa/Corbis
Protesters walk down Pennsylvania Ave © Gordon M. Grant/Alamy

Black and whites
Fourth annual gay millennium march © Jamal Wilson/ Reuters/Corbis

Index

Map entries are in color.

M

INDEX

443

INDEX

Map symbols

maps are listed in the full index using colored text

395	Interstate	� Battlefield	
50	US Highway	♥	Museum
	Other road	⊠	Post office
- - - - -	Footpath	⌁	Gardens
⊢ ≡ ≡ ⊣	Tunnel	⏛	Memorial
	Railway	⊙	Statue
	Waterway	⊞	Hospital
— —	Ferry route	ⓡ	Restroom
— — —	Chapter division boundary	⚱	Grave
♦	Point of interest	⬭	Stadium
✈	Airport		Building
Ⓜ	Metro station	⊞	Church
ⓘ	Information office	⁺₊⁺	Cemetery
⏚	Observatory		Park

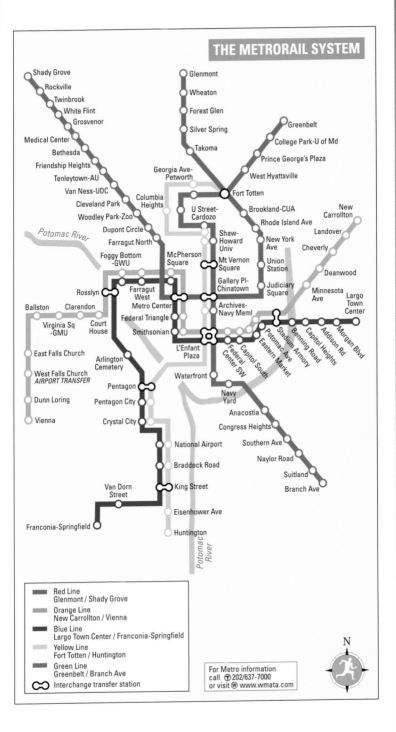

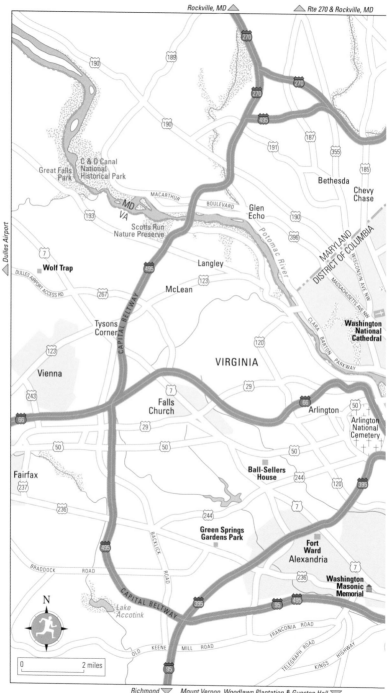

270

189

190

270

270

495

191

187

355

185

C & D Canal
National
Historical Park

Great Falls
Park

MACARTHUR

BOULEVARD

Glen
Echo

Bethesda

Chevy
Chase

MD

VA

193

Scotts Run
Nature Preserve

190

396

MARYLAND

DISTRICT OF COLUMBIA

WISCONSIN AVE NW

7

Wolf Trap

DULLES AIRPORT ACCESS RD

△ Dulles Airport

267

Langley

McLean

123

Potomac River

MASSACHUSETTS AVE NW

Washington
National
Cathedral

Tysons
Corner

CAPITAL BELTWAY

495

CLARA

BARTON

PARKWAY

123

120

Vienna

243

VIRGINIA

66

Falls
Church

7

29

29

Arlington

50

50

Arlington
National
Cemetery

50

50

50

Fairfax

237

236

Ball-Sellers
House

244

120

395

7

244

Green Springs
Gardens Park

Fort
Ward

Alexandria

7

495

BRADDOCK   ROAD

BACKLICK

ROAD

CAPITAL BELTWAY

Lake
Accotink

395

236

Washington
Masonic
Memorial

95

495

N

FRANCONIA   ROAD

0   2 miles

OLD   KEENE   MILL   ROAD

TELEGRAPH ROAD

KINGS   HIGHWAY

95

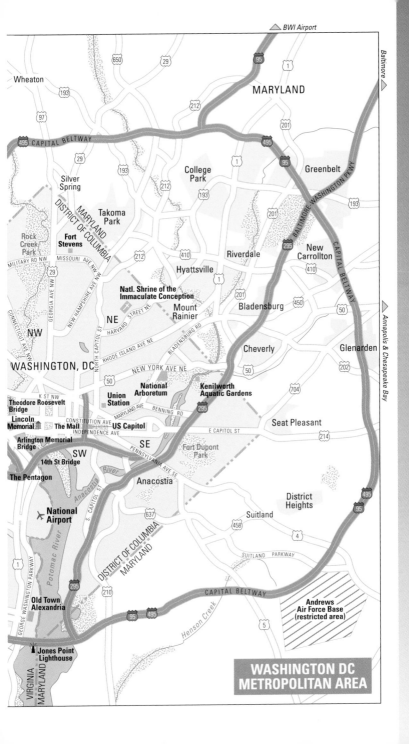

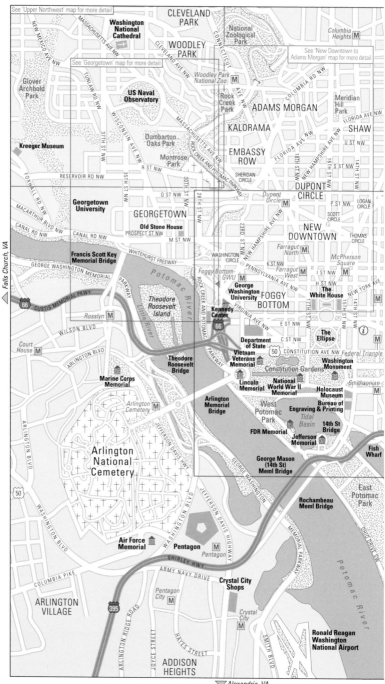

See 'Upper Northwest' map for more detail

CLEVELAND PARK

Washington National Cathedral

WOODLEY PARK

National Zoological Park

Columbia Heights M

See 'New Downtown to Adams Morgan' map for more detail

NEW MEXICO AVE NW

MASSACHUSETTS AVE NW

CLEVELAND AVE NW

CONNECTICUT AVE NW

COLUMBIA RD NW

See 'Georgetown' map for more detail

Woodley Park National Zoo M

Glover Archbold Park

TUNLAW RD NW

US Naval Observatory

Rock Creek Park

ADAMS MORGAN

Meridian Hill Park

FLORIDA AVE NW

SHAW

KALORAMA

MASSACHUSETTS AVE NW

Kreeger Museum

37TH ST NW

Dumbarton Oaks Park

EMBASSY ROW

FLORIDA AVE NW

16TH ST NW

14TH ST NW

U ST NW

S ST NW

Montrose Park

ROCK CREEK AND POTOMAC PARKWAY

SHERIDAN CIRCLE

RESERVOIR RD NW

R ST NW

35TH ST NW

30TH ST NW

Q ST NW

DUPONT CIRCLE

FOXHALL RD NW

MACARTHUR BLVD NW

Georgetown University

GEORGETOWN

Dupont Circle M

P ST NW

LOGAN CIRCLE

28TH ST NW

SCOTT CIRCLE

Old Stone House

PROSPECT ST NW

M ST NW

NEW DOWNTOWN

THOMAS CIRCLE

CANAL RD NW

CANAL RD NW

23RD ST NW

NEW HAMPSHIRE AVE NW

Farragut North M

McPherson Square

Francis Scott Key Memorial Bridge

WHITEHURST FREEWAY

WASHINGTON CIRCLE

K ST NW

Farragut West M

I ST NW M

GEORGE WASHINGTON MEMORIAL

Potomac River

Foggy Bottom-GWU M

PENNSYLVANIA AVE NW

H ST NW

NEW YORK AVE

CUSTIS MEMORIAL PKWY

66

PARKWAY

ROCK CREEK AND POTOMAC

George Washington University

VIRGINIA AVE NW

FOGGY BOTTOM

The White House

14TH ST NW

15TH ST NW

M

Falls Church, VA

Rosslyn M

LITTLE RIVER

Kennedy Center

66

E ST NW

The Ellipse

i

WILSON BLVD

Theodore Roosevelt Island

C ST NW

Federal Triangle

Department of State

50

CONSTITUTION AVE NW

Washington Monument

Court House M

ARLINGTON BLVD

Theodore Roosevelt Bridge

Vietnam Veterans Memorial

Constitution Gardens

National World War II Memorial

Holocaust Museum

Smithsonian M

ARLINGTON BLVD

Marine Corps Memorial

Arlington M *Cemetery*

Lincoln Memorial

Arlington Memorial Bridge

West Potomac Park

Bureau of Engraving & Printing

Tidal Basin

14th St Bridge

JEFFERSON DAVIS HWY

FDR Memorial

Jefferson Memorial

Fish Wharf

ARLINGTON BLVD

Arlington National Cemetery

JEFFERSON DAVIS HWY

GEORGE WASHINGTON

George Mason (14th St) Meml Bridge

East Potomac Park

WASHINGTON BLVD

50

Rochambeau Meml Bridge

MEMORIAL PARKWAY

Potomac River

OHIO DRIVE SW

Air Force Memorial

Pentagon

Pentagon M

SHIRLEY HWY

ARLINGTON BLVD

ARLINGTON RIDGE ROAD

COLUMBIA PIKE

ARMY NAVY DRIVE

395

Crystal City Shops

Pentagon City M

Ronald Reagan Washington National Airport

ARLINGTON VILLAGE

JOYCE STREET

HAYES STREET

Crystal City M

SMITH BLVD

ADDISON HEIGHTS

Alexandria, VA

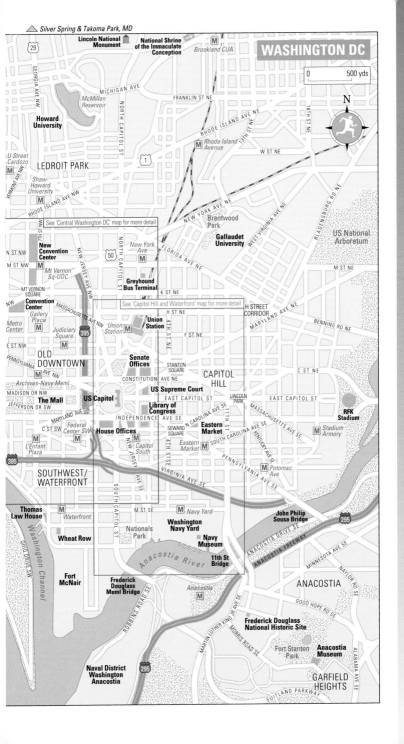

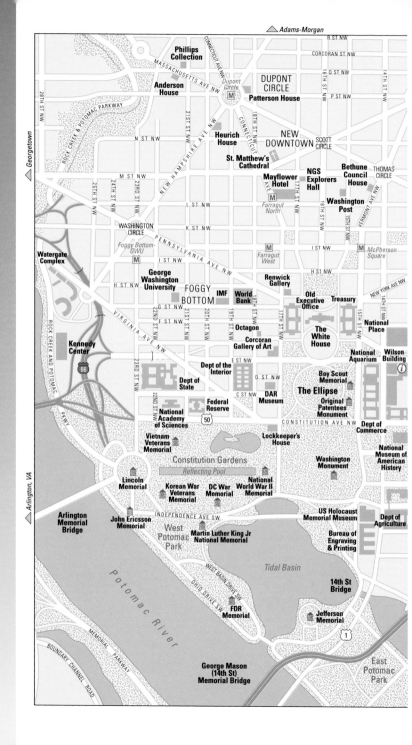

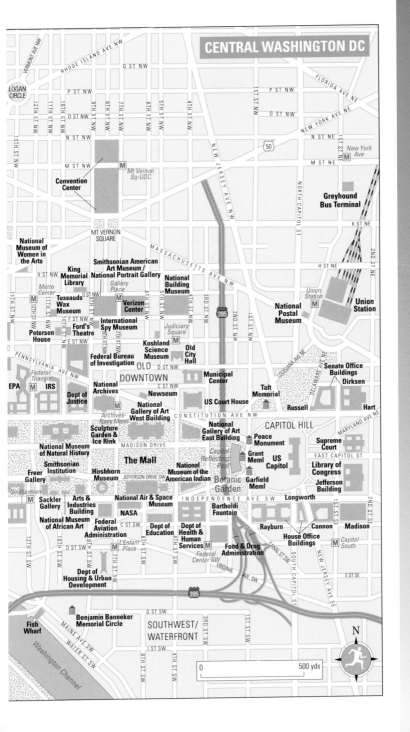

CENTRAL WASHINGTON DC

VERMONT AVE NW
RHODE ISLAND AVE NW
Q ST NW
FLORIDA AVE NE

LOGAN CIRCLE

P ST NW
P ST NW

13TH ST NW
12TH ST NW
11TH ST NW
10TH ST NW
9TH ST NW
8TH ST NW
7TH ST NW
6TH ST NW
5TH ST NW
4TH ST NW
1ST ST NW

O ST NW
O ST NW

N ST NW

NEW YORK AVE NE

N ST NE

M ST NW
Convention Center
Mt Vernon Sq-UDC
50
M ST NE

New York Ave

MT VERNON SQUARE

MASSACHUSETTS AVE NW

Greyhound Bus Terminal

NORTH CAPITOL ST
2ND ST NE

National Museum of Women in the Arts
King Memorial Library
Smithsonian American Art Museum / National Portrait Gallery
National Building Museum

H ST NE

13TH ST NW
Metro Center
Gallery Place
Union Station
Union Station

Tussauds Wax Museum
Verizon Center
International Spy Museum
395
National Postal Museum

Petersen House
Ford's Theatre
Koshland Science Museum
Old City Hall
Judiciary Square

3RD ST NW
2ND ST NW
1ST ST NW

PENNSYLVANIA AVE NW
Federal Bureau of Investigation
OLD D ST NW
Senate Office Buildings
Dirksen

Federal Triangle
DOWNTOWN
C ST NW
Municipal Center
Taft Memorial

EPA IRS
Dept of Justice
National Archives
Newseum
US Court House
Russell
Hart

National Gallery of Art West Building
CONSTITUTION AVE NW
National Gallery of Art East Building
CAPITOL HILL
MARYLAND AVE NE

Sculpture Garden & Ice Rink
MADISON DRIVE
Peace Monument
Supreme Court

National Museum of Natural History
The Mall
Capitol Reflecting Pool
Grant Meml
US Capitol
EAST CAPITOL ST

Smithsonian Institution
Hirshhorn Museum
JEFFERSON DRIVE SW
National Museum of the American Indian
Library of Congress

Freer Gallery
Botanic Garden
Garfield Meml
Jefferson Building

Sackler Gallery
Arts & Industries Building
National Air & Space Museum
INDEPENDENCE AVE SW
Bartholdi Fountain
Longworth

National Museum of African Art
NASA
Federal Aviation Administration
Dept of Education
Dept of Health & Human Services
Food & Drug Administration
Rayburn
Cannon
Madison

12TH ST SW
10TH ST SW
L'Enfant Plaza
C ST SW
Federal Center SW
House Office Buildings
Capitol South

D ST SW
7TH ST SW
6TH ST SW
VIRGINIA AVE SW
E ST SE

Dept of Housing & Urban Development

395

Fish Wharf
MAINE AVE SW
WATER ST SW
Benjamin Banneker Memorial Circle
G ST SW
SOUTHWEST/ WATERFRONT

Washington Channel
I ST SW

6TH ST SW
4TH ST SW
3RD ST SW
1ST ST SW

N

0   500 yds

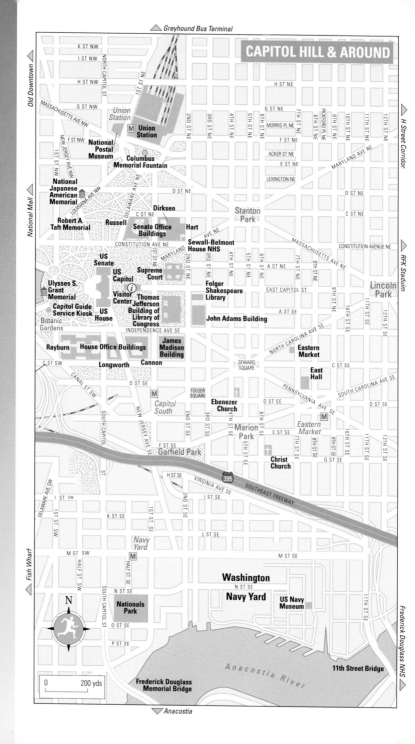

△ Greyhound Bus Terminal

CAPITOL HILL & AROUND

◁ Old Downtown

K ST NW
I ST NW
H ST NW
G ST NW

NORTH CAPITOL ST
1ST ST NW

MASSACHUSETTS AVE NW

NEW JERSEY AVE NW

Union
Station
Ⓜ Union
Station

F ST NW

National
Postal
Museum
Columbus
Memorial Fountain

National
Japanese
American
Memorial

1ST ST NW
LOUISIANA AVE NW

Dirksen

Robert A.
Taft Memorial   Russell   Senate Office
Buildings

DELAWARE AVE NE

H ST NE ▷ H Street Corridor

2ND ST NE
3RD ST NE
4TH ST NE
5TH ST NE
6TH ST NE
7TH ST NE
8TH ST NE
PICKFORD PL NE
9TH ST NE
10TH ST NE
11TH ST NE
12TH ST NE

G ST NE

MORRIS PL NE

F ST NE

ACKER ST NE

E ST NE

LEXINGTON NE

D ST NE

C ST NE

Stanton
Park

MARYLAND AVE NE

D ST NE ▷ RFK Stadium

National Mall ◁

Ulysses S.
Grant
Memorial

Capitol Guide
Service Kiosk

Botanic
Gardens

CONSTITUTION AVENUE NE

US Senate

US
Capitol
ⓘ
Visitor
Center

US
House

Supreme
Court

MARYLAND AVE NE

1ST ST NE
2ND ST NE
3RD ST NE

Hart

Sewall-Belmont
House NHS

A ST NE

EAST CAPITOL ST

A ST SE

Folger
Shakespeare
Library

Thomas
Jefferson
Building of
Library of
Congress

John Adams Building

4TH ST NE
5TH ST NE
6TH ST NE
7TH ST NE
8TH ST NE

MASSACHUSETTS AVE NE

CONSTITUTION AVENUE NE

9TH ST NE
10TH ST NE
11TH ST NE
12TH ST NE

Lincoln
Park

INDEPENDENCE AVE SE

Rayburn   House Office Buildings

Longworth   Cannon

James
Madison
Building

Ⓜ
Capitol
South

FOLGER
SQUARE

Ebenezer
Church

SEWARD
SQUARE

NORTH CAROLINA AVE SE

PENNSYLVANIA AVE SE

Eastern
Market

East
Hall

C ST SE

D ST SE

Eastern
Market Ⓜ

C ST SW
D ST SE

CANAL ST SW

SOUTH CAPITOL ST

NEW JERSEY AVE SE

1ST ST SE
2ND ST SE
3RD ST SE
4TH ST SE
5TH ST SE
6TH ST SE
7TH ST SE
8TH ST SE
9TH ST SE
10TH ST SE
11TH ST SE
12TH ST SE

D ST SE

Marion
Park

E ST SE

Christ
Church

F ST SE
Garfield Park

H ST SE   VIRGINIA AVE SE   395 SOUTHEAST FREEWAY

DELAWARE AVE SW

I ST SW

Fish Wharf ◁

K ST SW

L ST SW

Navy
Yard
Ⓜ

M ST SE

Washington

Navy Yard

US Navy
Museum

11th Street Bridge ▷ Frederick Douglass NHS

1ST ST SE
2ND ST SE

I ST SE

K ST SE

L ST SE

HALF ST SE

M ST SW

N ST SW

SOUTH CAPITOL ST

Nationals
Park

N ST SE

O ST SE

P ST SE

Anacostia River

N

0   200 yds

Frederick Douglass
Memorial Bridge

11th Street Bridge

▽ Anacostia

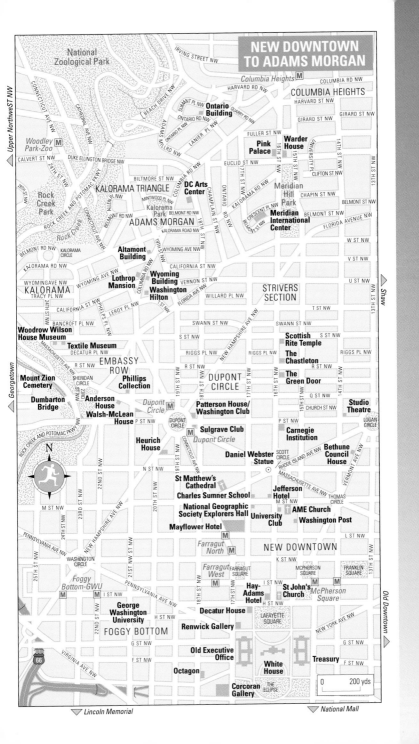

GEORGETOWN

△ Cleveland Park

Washington National Cathedral

Woodley Mansion

CATHEDRAL AVENUE NW

GARFIELD ST NW

FULTON ST NW

MASSACHUSETTS AVE NW

35TH PL NW
36TH PL NW
35TH ST NW
34TH PL NW
34TH ST NW
FULTON ST NW

31ST PL NW
CLEVELAND AVE
GARFIELD TERR NW
28TH ST NW
27TH ST NW
GARFIELD ST NW

EDMUNDS ST NW

WOODLEY RD NW

Marriott Wardman Park

M Woodley Park-Zoo

WISCONSIN AVE NW
36TH ST NW
DAVIS ST NW

31ST ST NW
WOODLAND DR NW
NORMANSTONE TERR NW
29TH ST NW

CALVERT ST NW

OBSERVATORY CIRCLE NW

CALVERT ST NW

Omni Shoreham

28TH ST NW
MCGILL TERR NW

N

39TH ST NW

BEECHER ST NN

Kreeger Museum △

OBSERVATORY PL NW

BENTON ST NW

TUNLAW RD NW
WHITEHAVEN PL NW

WISCONSIN AVE NW
HALL PL NW
W PL NW

W ST NW

US Naval Observatory

OBSERVATORY LANE NW

OBSERVATORY CIRCLE NW

MASSACHUSETTS AVE NW

EDGEVALE TERR NW
TRENTON PL NW
ROCK CREEK DR NW

Rock Creek Park

Woodley Park, National Zoo & Adams Morgan ▷

37TH ST NW

WHITEHAVEN ST NW

ROCK CREEK

ROCK CREEK & POTOMAC PKWY

BELMONT RD NW
KALORAMA RD NW
WYOMING AVE NW
TRACY PL NW

MASSACHUSETTS AVE NW

CALIFORNIA ST NW

Whitehaven Park

WHITEHAVEN PKWY

35TH R NW
35TH ST NW

Dumbarton Oaks Park

Montrose Park

39TH ST NW
38TH ST NW

T ST NW

S ST NW

R ST NW

36TH ST NW
35TH ST NW

S ST NW

Dumbarton Oaks Garden & Museum

32ND ST NW

R ST NW

Oak Hill Cemetery

Dumbarton Bridge/Dupont Circle ▷

Duke Ellington School of the Arts

RESERVOIR RD NW

CANTON PL NW
SCOTT PL NW

31ST ST NW

AVON PL NW

DENT PL NW

AVON LA NW

Dumbarton House

Mount Zion Cemetery

Georgetown University Hospital

DENT PL NW

Tudor Place

34TH ST NW
34TH PL NW

Q ST NW

30TH ST NW
29TH ST NW
28TH ST NW
26TH ST NW

Georgetown University

Volta Bureau

VOLTA PL NW

WISCONSIN AVE

Q ST NW

P ST NW

Old North

37TH ST NW
36TH ST NW
35TH ST NW

P ST NW

33RD ST NW

O ST NW

POTOMAC ST NW

O ST NW

DUMBARTON ST NW

31ST ST NW

OLIVE ST NW

ROCK CREEK & POTOMAC PKWY

Rock Creek

Healy Hall

N ST NW

St. John's Episcopal Church

N ST NW

PROSPECT ST NW

CANAL RD NW

Historic Car Barn

Francis Scott Key Park

Riggs Bank

Old Stone House

Chesapeake & Ohio Canal

Market House

Georgetown Park

ⓘ

Canal Square

Visitor Center ⓘ

Four Seasons Hotel

PENNSYLVANIA AVE NW

CANAL RD NW

GRACE ST NW

Grace Church

SOUTH ST NW

The Foundry

THOMAS JEFFERSON ST NW

25TH ST NW

K ST NW

Washington Circle & Foggy Bottom Metro ▷

WHITEHURST FREEWAY (K ST NW)

COPPERWAITHE LA NW

FRANCIS SCOTT KEY BRIDGE

GEORGE WASHINGTON MEMORIAL PKWY

Potomac River

Washington Harbor

Thompson Boat Center

Watergate Complex

ROCK CREEK & POTOMAC PKWY

VIRGINIA AVE NW

T ST NW

H ST NW

LEE HWY NW
COLONIAL TERR NW
ODE ST NW

NASH ST NW
19TH ST N A N

FORT MYER DRIVE NW

N 1S N A N
MOORE ST NW

66

KEY BLVD NW

M Rosslyn

WILSON BLVD NW

Theodore Roosevelt Island

0 ——————— 500 yds

▽ Rosslyn & Arlington

▽ Kennedy Center

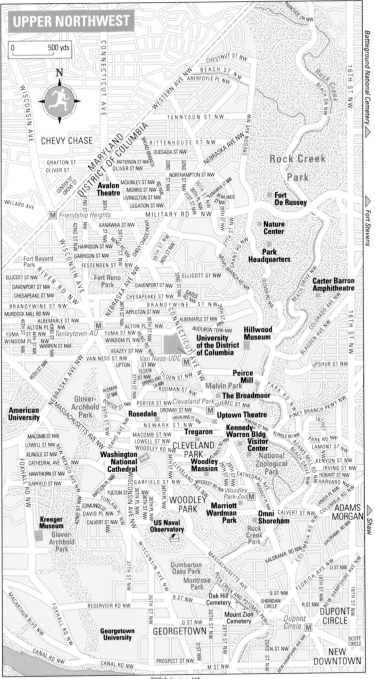

UPPER NORTHWEST

0   500 yds

N

BATTLEGROUND NATIONAL CEMETERY ▷

CHEVY CHASE

WISCONSIN AVE

CONNECTICUT AVE

MARYLAND
DISTRICT OF COLUMBIA

WESTERN AVE NW

PARKSIDE DR NW

CHESTNUT ST NW

BEACH ST NW
ABERFOYLE PL NW

16TH ST NW

BEACH DR NW

Rock Creek

Fort Stevens ▷

TENNYSON ST NW

RITTENHOUSE ST NW

QUESADA ST NW

PATTERSON ST NW
OLIVER ST NW

OLIVER ST NW
GRAFTON ST

CENTER GROVE ST

WILLARD AVE

BROAD BRANCH

33RD

32ND

NORTHAMPTON ST NW

NEBRASKA AVE NW

OREGON AVE NW

Rock Creek
Park

**Avalon
Theatre**

MCKINLEY ST NW
MORRIS ST NW
LIVINGSTON ST NW
LEGATION ST NW

38TH ST

Ⓜ Friendship Heights

MILITARY RD NW

KANAWHA ST NW
RENO RD

KANAWHA ST NW

31ST ST NW

RWLANDS

BROAD BRANCH RD NW

**Fort
De Russey**

**Nature
Center**

HARRISON ST NW
GARRISON ST NW
FESSENDEN ST NW

42ND ST NW

CHEVY CHASE PKWY

NELSIE ST

**Park
Headquarters**

GLOVER RD NW

Fort Bayard
Park

WISCONSIN AVE

RIVER RD

Fort Reno
Park

NEBRASKA AVE NW

ELLICOTT ST NW

**Carter Barron
Amphitheatre**

ELLICOTT ST NW
DAVENPORT ST NW
CHESAPEAKE ST NW
BRANDYWINE ST NW
MURDOCK MILL RD NW
ALBEMARLE ST NW
YUMA ST NW
WINDOM PL NW
WARREN ST NW

45TH ST NW

ALTON PL NW

DAVENPORT ST NW
CHESAPEAKE ST NW
BRANDYWINE ST NW

APPLETON ST NW
ALBEMARLE ST NW

36TH ST NW

GATES
RD NW

AUDUBON TERR NW

29TH ST NW

**Hillwood
Museum**

BEACH DRIVE NW

COLORADO AVE NW

BLAGDEN AVE NW

16TH ST NW

Ⓜ Tenleytown-AU

YUMA ST NW
WINDOM PL NW

ALTON PL NW

**University
of the District
of Columbia**

UPSHUR ST NW

VEAZEY ST NW
VAN NESS ST NW
UPTON

NEBRASKA AVE NW

36TH ST NW
34TH ST NW

CONNECTICUT AVE NW

Ⓜ Van Ness-UDC

ROCK CREEK PARK

American
University

MASSACHUSETTS AVE NW

Glover-
Archbold
Park

RODMAN
ST NW
PORTER ST NW

37TH ST NW

TILDEN
LA NW

SPRINGLAND

RODMAN ST NW

**Peirce
Mill**

Malvin Park

The Broadmoor

PINEY BRANCH PKWY NW

18TH ST

Rosedale

IDAHO AVE NW

PORTER ST NW
Cleveland Park

ORDWAY ST NW

HIGHLAND PL NW

QUEBEC ST NW

Ⓜ **Uptown Theatre**

KLINGLE RD NW

PARK RD NW

MACOMB ST NW
LOWELL ST NW
KLINGLE ST NW
CATHEDRAL AVE NW
HAWTHORN ST NW
GARFIELD ST NW

NEW MEXICO AVE NW

NEWARK ST NW

MACOMB ST NW
LOWELL ST NW
WOODLEY RD NW

Tregaron

34TH ST NW

35TH ST NW

**Kennedy-
Warren Bldg**

**Visitor
Center**

National
Zoological
Park

ADAMS MILL RD NW

LAMONT ST NW
KENYON ST NW
IRVING ST NW
HOBART ST NW
HARVARD NW

**Washington
National
Cathedral**

WISCONSIN AVE NW

GARFIELD ST NW
FULTON ST NW

CLEVELAND AVE NW

**CLEVELAND
PARK**

**Woodley
Mansion**

28TH ST NW

CATHEDRAL AVE NW

Ⓜ Woodley
Park-Zoo

CALVERT ST NW

LANIER PL NW

COLUMBIA RD NW

**ADAMS
MORGAN**

Shaw ▷

FOXHALL RD NW

**Kreeger
Museum**

Glover-
Archbold
Park

MACARTHUR BLVD NW

FOXHALL RD NW

WATSON PL NW
EDMUNDS ST NW
TUNLAW RD NW
DAVIS PL NW
CALVERT ST NW

37TH ST NW

35TH ST NW

**WOODLEY
PARK**

**US Naval
Observatory**

**Marriott
Wardman
Park**

**Omni
Shoreham**

Rock
Creek
Park

CALVERT ST NW

KALORAMA RD NW

KALORAMA RD NW

FLORIDA AVE NW

NEW HAMPSHIRE AVE NW

18TH ST NW

U ST NW

19TH ST NW

RESERVOIR RD NW

35TH ST NW

Dumbarton
Oaks Park

Montrose
Park

MASSACHUSETTS AVE

ROCK CREEK AND POTOMAC PKWY

Oak Hill
Cemetery

S ST NW

SHERIDAN
CIRCLE

R ST NW

T ST NW

**DUPONT
CIRCLE**

16TH ST NW

NEW HAMPSHIRE AVE NW

R ST NW
Mount Zion
Cemetery

Dupont
Circle Ⓜ

23RD ST NW

**Georgetown
University**

CANAL RD NW

37TH ST NW

GEORGETOWN

30TH ST NW

28TH ST NW

Q ST NW

31ST ST NW

25TH ST NW

NEW HAMPSHIRE AVE NW

SCOTT
CIRCLE

**NEW
DOWNTOWN**

CANAL RD NW

PROSPECT ST NW

M ST NW

▽ Arlington, VA

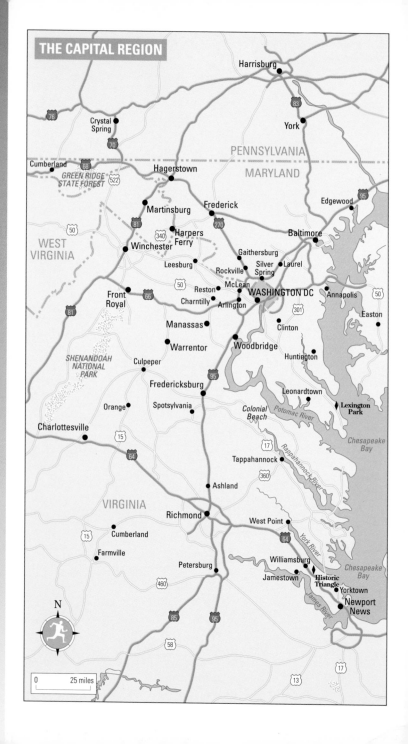